THE CAMBRIDGE

COMM

CW00815793

The second volume of *The Cambridge History of Communism* explores the rise of communist states and movements after World War II. Leading experts analyze archival sources from formerly communist states to reexamine the limits to Moscow's control of its satellites; the de-Stalinization of 1956; communist reform movements; the rise and fall of the Sino-Soviet alliance; the growth of communism in Asia, Africa and Latin America; and the effects of the Sino-Soviet split on world communism. Chapters explore the cultures of communism in the United States, Western Europe and China, and the conflicts engendered by nationalism and the continued need for support from Moscow. With the danger of a new cold war developing between former and current communist states and the West, this account of the roots, development and dissolution of the socialist bloc is essential reading.

NORMAN NAIMARK is Robert and Florence McDonnell Professor of East European Studies and Senior Fellow, Hoover Institution and Freeman-Spogli Institute, Stanford University. He has conducted extensive research abroad in Russia, Poland and Germany on a variety of books, including *The Origins of the "Proletariat"* (1979), *Terrorists and Social Democrats* (2013), *The Russians in Germany* (1995), *Fires of Hatred* (2001), *Stalin's Genocides* (2010) and, most recently, *Genocide: A World History* (2017).

SILVIO PONS is Professor of Contemporary History at the University of Rome "Tor Vergata." He is the president of the Gramsci Foundation in Rome and a member of the Editorial Board of the *Journal of Cold War Studies*. His main publications include *Stalin and the Inevitable War* (2002), *Reinterpreting the End of the Cold War* (2005), *A Dictionary of Twentieth-Century Communism* (2010) and *The Global Revolution: A History of International Communism* (2014).

SOPHIE QUINN-JUDGE is the author of *Ho Chi Minh: The Missing Years* (2003) and *The Third Force in Vietnam: The Elusive Search for Peace* (2017). She was Associate Professor of History and Associate Director of the Center for Vietnamese Philosophy, Culture and Society at Temple University before retiring in 2015.

THE CAMBRIDGE HISTORY OF
COMMUNISM

GENERAL EDITOR

SILVIO PONS, *Università degli Studi di Roma "Tor Vergata"*

The Cambridge History of Communism is an unprecedented global history of communism across the twentieth century. With contributions from a team of leading historians, economists, political scientists and sociologists, the three volumes examine communism in the context of wider political, social, cultural and economic processes, while at the same time revealing how it contributed to shaping them. Volume I deals with the roots, impact and development of communism, analyzing the tumultuous events from the Russian Revolution of 1917 to World War II, and historical personalities such as Lenin, Stalin and Trotsky. Volumes II and III then review the global impact of communism, focusing on the Cold War, the Chinese Revolution, the Vietnam War and the eventual collapse of the Soviet Union. Together the volumes explain why a movement that sought to bring revolution on a world scale, overthrowing capitalism and parliamentary democracy, acquired such force and influence globally.

VOLUME I
World Revolution and Socialism in One Country 1917–1941
EDITED BY SILVIO PONS AND STEPHEN A. SMITH

VOLUME II
The Socialist Camp and World Power 1941–1960s
EDITED BY NORMAN NAIMARK, SILVIO PONS AND SOPHIE QUINN-JUDGE

VOLUME III
Endgames? Late Communism in Global Perspective, 1968 to the Present
EDITED BY JULIANE FÜRST, SILVIO PONS AND MARK SELDEN

THE CAMBRIDGE
HISTORY OF
COMMUNISM

*

VOLUME II

The Socialist Camp and World
Power 1941–1960s

*

Edited by

NORMAN NAIMARK
Stanford University, California

SILVIO PONS
Università degli Studi di Roma "Tor Vergata"

SOPHIE QUINN-JUDGE
Temple University, Philadelphia

CAMBRIDGE
UNIVERSITY PRESS

CAMBRIDGE
UNIVERSITY PRESS

University Printing House, Cambridge CB2 8BS, United Kingdom

One Liberty Plaza, 20th Floor, New York, NY 10006, USA

477 Williamstown Road, Port Melbourne, VIC 3207, Australia

314–321, 3rd Floor, Plot 3, Splendor Forum, Jasola District Centre, New Delhi – 110025, India

79 Anson Road, #06–04/06, Singapore 079906

Cambridge University Press is part of the University of Cambridge.

It furthers the University's mission by disseminating knowledge in the pursuit of education, learning, and research at the highest international levels of excellence.

www.cambridge.org
Information on this title: www.cambridge.org/9781107133549
DOI: 10.1017/9781316459850

© Cambridge University Press 2017

First published 2017
Paperback edition first published 2020

Printed in the United Kingdom by TJ International Ltd. Padstow Cornwall

A catalog record for this publication is available from the British Library.

Three Volume Set ISBN 978-1-316-63458-5 Hardback

Volume I ISBN 978-1-107-09284-6 Hardback
Volume II ISBN 978-1-107-13354-9 Hardback
Volume III ISBN 978-1-107-13564-2 Hardback

Three Volume Set ISBN 978-1-316-63457-8 Paperback

Volume I ISBN 978-1-107-46736-1 Paperback
Volume II ISBN 978-1-107-59001-4 Paperback
Volume III ISBN 978-1-316-50159-7 Paperback

Contents

v

Contents

Contents

Plates are to be found between pp. 336 and 337

Plates

1. A Soviet propaganda poster from the "Great Patriotic War," circa 1942. Galerie Bilderwelt / Contributor / Getty
2. Red Army soldiers preparing to fly a red flag over the Schlisselburg Fortress near Leningrad. Daily Herald Archive / Getty
3. Joseph Stalin and Franklin D. Roosevelt at the first conference of the leaders of the Grand Alliance. Granger Historical Picture Archive / Alamy
4. Writer Ilia Ehrenburg in Vilnius with Jewish partisans who entered the city with the Red Army, July 1944. Sovfoto Universal Images Group / Getty
5. The Yugoslav communist ruling group near the end of World War II, 1944. ullstein bild / Getty
6. Italian partisans, December 1944. Keystone Hulton Archive / Getty
7. Greek National Liberation Front (EAM) poster, 1944. De Agostini Picture Library / Getty
8. Joseph Stalin and Winston Churchill at the second major conference of the leaders of the anti-fascist war coalition held in Yalta, 4–11 February 1945. Photos 12 / Alamy
9. Red Army soldiers reach the Reichstag, Berlin, 1945. Sovfoto Universal Images Group / Getty
10. "Glory to the Red Army!" poster. Hoover Archives Poster Collection
11. Ho Chi Minh meeting Marius Moutet, French minister for overseas affairs, for negotiations in 1946 in Paris. Gamma-Keystone / Getty
12. The Korean communist leader Kim Il Sung at the founding of the North Korean Workers' Party, 1946. Charles Armstrong's personal archive
13. The general secretary of the French Communist Party, Maurice Thorez, speaking at the May Day celebration, Place de la Concorde, Paris, 1 May 1947. INTERFOTO / Alamy
14. Prague 1948: communist demonstration with Soviet flags. CTK / Alamy
15. Strikes in Paris against the Marshall Plan, 1948. Hulton Archive Keystone / Getty
16. The Soviet War Memorial in Treptow, Berlin. John Freeman / Getty
17. Chinese communist troops entering Beijing, 1949. Pictorial Press Ltd / Alamy
18. "Under the Leadership of the Great Stalin – Forward to Communism!" Poster, Gosizdat, 1951. Hoover Archives Poster Collection

Tables

xi

Contributors to Volume II

CHARLES ARMSTRONG is The Korea Foundation Professor of Korean Studies in the Social Sciences in the Department of History at Columbia University. He is the former director of Columbia's Center for Korean Research and former acting director of the Weatherhead East Asian Institute. He is the author, editor or coeditor of five books, including most recently *Tyranny of the Weak: North Korea and the World, 1950–1992* (2013; winner of the John Fairbank Prize of the American Historical Association) and *The Koreas* (2nd edn., 2014).

JÖRG BABEROWSKI is Professor of East European History at Humboldt-University in Berlin, Germany. He is the author of many books and articles on Russian and Soviet history, among others *Scorched Earth: Stalin's Rule of Violence* (2016).

IVO BANAC is Bradford Durfee Emeritus Professor of History at Yale University and Professor of History at the University of Zagreb. His award-winning books are *The National Question in Yugoslavia: Origins, History, Politics* (1984; winner of the Wayne S. Vucinich Prize) and *With Stalin Against Tito: Cominformist Splits in Yugoslav Communism* (1988; winner of the Strossmayer Prize). He is also a corresponding member of the Croatian Academy of Sciences and Arts (HAZU).

THOMAS P. BERNSTEIN is Professor Emeritus of Political Science, Columbia University. Among his publications are *Taxation Without Representation in Contemporary China*, coauthored with Xiaobo Lu (2003) and *Up to the Mountains and Down to the Villages: The Transfer of Youth from Urban to Rural China* (1977), as well as articles on Chinese politics, Soviet and Chinese collectivization and the Soviet and Chinese famines of 1932–33 and 1959–61. More recently, he coedited a book with Hua-yu Li, *China Learns from the Soviet Union, 1949–Present* (2010), for which he wrote the Introduction.

CHEN JIAN is Distinguished Global Network Professor of History at New York University and NYU-Shanghai. He is also Hu Shih Professor of History and China–US Relations and inaugural Michael J. Zak Professor of History for US–China Relations at Cornell University. Among his many publications are *China's Road to the Korean War* (1994) and *Mao's China and the Cold War* (2001). He is now completing a biography of Zhou Enlai.

VICTOR FIGUEROA CLARK is an associate of the Latin America Programme at LSE IDEAS. His work has mainly focused on the Latin American left during the Cold War, in particular analyzing Chilean, Colombian and Nicaraguan revolutionary movements. He is also the author of *Salvador Allende: Revolutionary Democrat* (2013). His research has involved the study of communist parties across the region, and he has worked in former Soviet archives in Moscow.

PHILLIP DEERY is Emeritus Professor of History at Victoria University, Melbourne. Phillip has authored more than 100 scholarly publications in the fields of communism, the labor movement, intelligence and national security, and the Cold War. His most recent publications include *Red Apple: Communism and McCarthyism in Cold War New York* (2014, 2016), *The Age of McCarthyism: A Brief History with Documents*, 3rd edn. (2016), and *Fighting Against War: Peace Activism in the Twentieth Century* (2015, co-editor).

ALLISON DREW is Honorary Professor at the Centre for African Studies, University of Cape Town and Professor Emerita, University of York. Her books include *We Are No Longer in France: Communists in Colonial Algeria* (2014), *Between Empire and Revolution: A Life of Sidney Bunting* (2007), *Discordant Comrades: Identities and Loyalties on the South African Left* (2000) and *South Africa's Radical Tradition: A Documentary History* (1996–97).

JOHAN FRANZÉN is a historian of the modern Middle East, and Senior Lecturer (Associate Professor) at the University of East Anglia, UK. He is the author of *Red Star over Iraq: Iraqi Communism Before Saddam* (2011) and has written extensively on the history of communism, nationalism and anti-imperialist thought in the Arab world.

PIERO GLEIJESES is Professor of American Foreign Policy at the Paul H. Nitze School of Advanced International Studies, Johns Hopkins University. His most recent book is *Visions of Freedom: Havana, Washington, Pretoria and the Struggle for Southern Africa, 1976–1991* (2013), which was awarded the Friedrich Katz Prize from the American Historical Association.

GIOVANNI GOZZINI is full professor of Contemporary History at the University of Siena, Italy (Department of Social, Political and Knowledge Sciences). Among his main publications are: *Firenze francese. Famiglie e mestieri ai primi dell'Ottocento* (1989), *La strada per Auschwitz. Fonti e interpretazioni sullo sterminio nazista* (1996), *Storia del Partito comunista italiano*, vol. VII, *Dall'attentato a Togliatti all'VIII congresso* (1998), *Storia del giornalismo* (2nd edn., 2011), *Migrazioni di ieri e di oggi. Una storia comparata* (2006), *Un'idea di giustizia. Globalizzazione e ineguaglianza dalla rivoluzione industriale ad oggi* (2010) and *La mutazione individualista. Gli italiani e la televisione 1954–2011* (2011).

ANDREAS HILGER specializes in international, Russian and Soviet history of the nineteenth and twentieth centuries. He currently lectures at Hamburg University and manages the German Historical Institute in Moscow's research project on Soviet prisoners of World War II. He has published extensively on Soviet relations with the Third World, on Soviet–German relations and on international history. His professorial dissertation about Soviet–Indian relations after World War II will be published in 2017.

PAVEL KOLÁŘ is Professor of Comparative and Transnational History of 19th–20th Century Europe at the European University Institute, Florence. His latest publications include *Der Poststalinismus. Ideologie und Utopie einer Epoche* (2016) and *What Was Normalization? Essays on Late Socialism* (2016, coauthored with Michal Pullmann; in Czech). He is currently finishing a new book project entitled "The Politics of Capital Punishment in Late State Socialism."

MARK KRAMER is Director of Cold War Studies at Harvard University and a Senior Fellow of Harvard's Davis Center for Russian and Eurasian Studies. Originally trained in mathematics at Stanford University, he went on to study international relations as a Rhodes Scholar at Oxford University and an Academy Scholar at Harvard. In addition to teaching international relations and comparative politics at Harvard, he has been a visiting professor at Yale University, Brown University and Aarhus University in Denmark.

MARC LAZAR is Professor of Political History and Sociology at Sciences Po (Paris) and President of the Advisory Board of this University. He is also professor at Luiss University-Guido Carli (Rome), where he is President of the Advisory Board of the School of Government. At Sciences Po, he is the director of the Centre d'histoire. His more recent books are *Le communisme, une passion française* (2005), *L'Italie à la derive* (2006), *L'Italie des années de plomb* (2010) and, with other authors, *Le Parti socialiste unifié. Histoire et postérité* (2013).

DANIEL LEESE is Professor of modern Chinese history and politics at the University of Freiburg, Germany. He the author of *Mao Cult: Rhetoric and Ritual in China's Cultural Revolution* (2011) and the editor of *Brill's Encyclopedia of China* (2009).

SARA LORENZINI is Associate Professor of International History at the School of International Studies of the University of Trento, Italy. Her latest book is *Una strana guerra fredda* (2017). She is the author of several monographs, including *Due Germanie in Africa. La cooperazione allo sviluppo e la competizione per i mercati di materie prime e tecnologie* (2003). Recent publications include: "Ecologia a parole? L'Italia, l'ambientalismo globale e il rapporto ambiente-sviluppo intorno alla conferenza di Stoccolma," *Contemporanea* (2016), and "Ace in the Hole or Hole in the Pocket? The Italian Mezzogiorno and the Story of a Troubled Transition from Development Model to Development Donor," *Contemporary European History* (2016).

EVAN MAWDSLEY is Honorary Professorial Research Fellow and formerly Professor of International History at the University of Glasgow. His books include *Thunder in the East: The Nazi–Soviet War, 1939–1945* (2001), *World War II: A New History* (2001) and *December 1941: Twelve Days That Began a World War* (2011). He was the general editor of the three-volume *Cambridge History of the Second World War*.

NORMAN NAIMARK is Robert and Florence McDonnell Professor of East European Studies and Senior Fellow, Hoover Institution and Freeman-Spogli Institute, Stanford University. He has conducted extensive research abroad in Russia, Poland and Germany on a variety of books, including *The Origins of the "Proletariat"* (1979), *Terrorists and Social Democrats* (2013), *The Russians in Germany* (1995), *Fires of Hatred* (2001), *Stalin's Genocides* (2010) and, most recently, *Genocide: A World History* (2017).

SILVIO PONS is Professor of Contemporary History at the University of Rome "Tor Vergata." He is the president of the Gramsci Foundation in Rome and a member of the Editorial Board of the *Journal of Cold War Studies*. His main publications include *Stalin and the Inevitable War* (2002), *Reinterpreting the End of the Cold War* (2005), *A Dictionary of Twentieth-Century Communism* (2010) and *The Global Revolution: A History of International Communism* (2014).

SOPHIE QUINN-JUDGE is the author of *Ho Chi Minh: The Missing Years* (2003) and *The Third Force in Vietnam: The Elusive Search for Peace* (2017). She was Associate Professor of History and Associate Director of the Center for Vietnamese Philosophy, Culture and Society at Temple University before retiring in 2015.

SERGEY RADCHENKO is Professor of International Relations at Cardiff University. He is the author of *Two Suns in the Heavens: The Sino-Soviet Struggle for Supremacy, 1962–1967* (2009) and *Unwanted Visionaries: The Soviet Failure in Asia at the End of the Cold War* (2014).

ALFRED J. RIEBER has been teaching and writing about Russian and Soviet history for more than fifty years. For the past twenty years he has taught at the Central European University (CEU) in Budapest, Hungary, where he was also chair of the History Department for four years, and where he now serves as University Professor Emeritus. His most recent scholarly books are *Struggle for the Eurasian Borderlands: From the Rise of Early Empires to the End of the First World War* (2014) and *Stalin and the Struggle for Supremacy in Eurasia* (2015). He is also the author of three historical detective novels, *To Kill a Tsar*, *The Kiev Killings* and *Siberian Secrets*.

FEDERICO ROMERO is Professor of History of Post-War European Cooperation and Integration at the Department of History and Civilization, European University Institute, Florence, where he directs the European Research Council project "Looking West: The European Socialist Regimes Facing Pan-European Cooperation and the European Community." A specialist on twentieth-century international and transnational history, he has worked on various aspects of the Cold War and trans-Atlantic relations, particularly the Marshall Plan and postwar European reconstruction. In 2009 he published *Storia della guerra fredda*.

JOHN ROOSA is the author of *Pretext for Mass Murder: The September 30th Movement and Suharto's Coup d'État in Indonesia* (2006) and numerous articles on the events of 1965–66 in Indonesia. As Associate Professor in the History Department at the University of British Columbia, Vancouver, he specializes in Southeast Asian history. He has also studied South Asia and has written an article on the largest communist revolt in twentieth-century India: "Passive Revolution Meets Peasant Revolution: Indian Nationalism and the Telangana Revolt," *Journal of Peasant Studies* (2001).

HARI VASUDEVAN is Professor at the Department of History, University of Calcutta. He is coeditor of *Indo-Russian Relations, 1917–1947: Select Documents from the Archives of the Russian Federation* (1997) and the author of *Shadows of Substance: Indo-Russian Trade and Military Technical Cooperation Since 1991* (2010).

ANDREW G. WALDER is the Denise O'Leary and Kent Thiry Professor in the School of Humanities and Sciences, and Senior Fellow in the Freeman-Spogli Institute for International Studies, Stanford University. His recent publications include *China Under Mao* (2015) and *Fractured Rebellion: The Beijing Red Guard Movement* (2009).

Introduction to Volume II

NORMAN NAIMARK, SILVIO PONS
AND SOPHIE QUINN-JUDGE

This second volume of *The Cambridge History of Communism* covers the high-water mark of communist power. The victory of the anti-fascist coalition in World War II brought the Soviet Union vastly expanded military reach in Central and Eastern Europe, as well as a period of great prestige as the Red Army defeated Hitler's armies and conquered Berlin. Behind the lines, the military victories of the Soviet Union were matched by the political advances of communist parties throughout Eastern Europe. Moscow oversaw the development of "people's democracies" in the region, while increasing communist control eliminated the possibilities of open and democratic politics and societies. At the same time, anti-fascist resistance highly amplified the role of communists across the continent, particularly in the Balkans and Southern Europe. The robust electoral strength and the sheer size of the French and Italian Communist Parties after the war increased the possibilities of serious Soviet influence in Western Europe. The establishment of the Cominform in September 1947 sanctioned the turn to the division of Europe by gathering all the communist parties in power and the two major Western communist parties in a new international institution – a purported successor to the Comintern.

With the creation of the People's Republic of China in October 1949, the socialist bloc swelled to cover most of Eurasia. In the early days of the Sino-Soviet alliance, this combination of industrial might and a population dwarfing that of Western Europe appeared to threaten the predominance of the West, particularly because of the potential appeal of the Chinese Revolution in the decolonizing Third World. The Soviet Union's successful atomic bomb test in early 1949 contributed to the mood of impending danger that gripped Western capitals, including Washington, DC. By the late 1940s, however, one could no longer speak of monolithic communism, as Tito and the Yugoslavs were able to resist Stalin's pressure to conform after their expulsion from the Cominform in 1948. One decade later, the Sino-Soviet relationship fell apart. The once omnipotent and fatherly image of Joseph Stalin had been dismantled by his successors, and unrest and uprisings in Eastern Europe led to a Soviet invasion of Hungary in October 1956 that disillusioned many believers in the superior virtues of the USSR.

The authors of this volume write at a time when this contest for world power, what we have come to know as the "Cold War," is behind us. Since the fall of the East European communist regimes in 1989 and the end of the Soviet Union in 1991, the bipolar order and world communism itself have disappeared. Marxist-Leninist ideology with its many national variants had long been losing its attraction, as the economic development of noncommunist countries all over the world far outstripped that of their Soviet rivals. Communist China has relaunched the challenge of development in the new century by integrating into the world capitalist economy and building a hybrid form of state capitalism. The history of the post-World War II spread of communist power now has a beginning and a finite end. The passing of a full generation since the Soviet Union imploded has freed historians to write about the socialist bloc dispassionately, as a phenomenon that was far less monolithic than contemporary observers once assumed. The communist world possessed a wide array of internal contradictions and, as we now know, its very successes in the 1950s carried the seeds of its failure.

Access to archival sources in repositories across the communist world has afforded scholars the opportunity to explore the contradictions, problems, failures and achievements of the communist system in its various national contexts. The chapters in this volume demonstrate the extent to which our knowledge has expanded and our questions have become more complex since the fall of communism in Europe and Russia.

Contents

This volume is divided into two parts, with the first, "Expansion and Conflict," covering general multinational issues that have to do with the spread of the communist system after World War II and the global challenges it increasingly represented. This part traces the dynamic proliferation of communist-led governments to Eastern Europe and then to Asia, with revolution in China as the crucial linchpin. But Moscow's attempts to manage this growth and expansion led to serious conflicts both among communist regimes and within individual countries. Complicating matters, Soviet domestic politics, de-Stalinization and post-Stalin succession struggles intersected with political conflicts within the respective communist allies of the Soviet Union. Internal Kremlin politics influenced the extent and resolution of uprisings in Eastern Europe, as well as interactions with Beijing. Soviet hegemony did not overcome the test of de-Stalinization. The breakdown of the Sino-Soviet alliance was of key importance in putting an end to international communism as a unitary actor in world politics.

The second part of the volume, "Becoming Global, Becoming National," deals both with general issues relating to the Third World and with individual communist movements that had a major historical impact in all parts of the world. Most scholars acknowledge that insufficient attention has been paid to the development of communism and the Cold War in Africa, Asia and Latin America, in contrast to the Soviet Union, Europe and the United States. Communists in the Third World were important actors in the conflict between "East" and "West" as they decisively contributed to expanding the conflict into a global arena. At the same time, the Soviet Union established connections and alliances with postcolonial countries such as Egypt, Algeria, Iraq, Syria, India and Indonesia. The encounters between the socialist camp and nationalist elites in the global South had a crucial impact on the Cold War agenda and geopolitics, by enhancing the issues of modernization, state-led development and economic competition on a global scale. These regions also frequently served as tragic surrogates for military competition between the superpowers, suffering death and destruction in wars of insurgency and counterinsurgency. The countries of the developing world continue to suffer from the brutal legacies of the Cold War period.

Communism was a worldwide phenomenon, just as imagined by its purveyors in the Kremlin and among its followers around the world. But it was also an ideological movement deeply tied to national contexts. While this volume makes no claim to covering all the communist parties of the world, it explores in separate chapters a number of the largest and most significant. Moreover, it has chapters on communism in major regions of the world – Latin America, Africa and the Middle East – that follow distinct non-European patterns of development. The purpose of these chapters is to show how communism developed national, international and transnational profiles for decades after World War II, but could never overcome fatal contradictions between state interests, cultural diversity and center–periphery relations.

Common Themes

One of the major themes of this volume is the tension between the center of world communism in Moscow and both the peripheries formed by the states that adopted communist forms of government in the late 1940s and early 1950s and nonruling parties in the West and the Third World. As a world power, the Soviet Union often found its own interests diverging from those of its allies and "friends." In his chapter on "World War II, Soviet Power and International Communism," Evan Mawdsley demonstrates the ways in which the Soviet Union became a world power as a consequence of its great victories in World War II. This marked change in power and status translated into an ability to carry out its will in the territories under the control of the Red Army. Already during the war, communist parties looked to the Soviets to support their ideas of revolution, yet it also became clear that Moscow claimed the prerogatives of a "superpower" early on in its relationship with the East Europeans. However, as Albert Rieber discusses in his "Anti-Fascist Resistance Movements in Europe and Asia During World War II," the communists had experience with leading and fostering resistance against the Nazi occupiers throughout Europe, and also against the Japanese invaders in Asia, affording them a sense of their own claims to political power and legitimacy, social change and even national identity after the war. Though clearly loyal to Moscow, whether in Europe or in Asia, the communist parties nevertheless were able to formulate their own policies within the resistance movements and carry out their own actions in the underground, which was frequently out of touch with the Soviets or their agents. At the same time, as Rieber demonstrates, neither were they able to control the resistance movements nor were they themselves following monolithic policies.

Wary of Western hostility and potential intervention, the Soviets followed a carefully calibrated policy of instituting people's democracies in Eastern Europe and following parliamentary procedures in the West. Norman Naimark, in his chapter on "The Sovietization of East Central Europe 1945–1989," argues that even this policy of flexibility and accommodation was planned from the center and implemented frequently against the wishes of more radical local communists, especially in Yugoslavia. Ivo Banac, in his chapter on "Yugoslav Communism and the Yugoslav State," also emphasizes that the break with Stalin that came in 1948, and the expulsion of the Communist Party of Yugoslavia from the Cominform, came primarily from the radicalism of Tito's programs, not from its reformism.

Though pledging obeisance to Stalin and Moscow, Mao and the Chinese communists pursued the resistance against the Japanese and fought the civil war against the Guomindang according to their own lights. Even after coming to power in 1949, writes Chen Jian, in "The Chinese Communist Revolution and the World," there was an inherent tension between the goals and needs of the Chinese and those of the Soviets. While Mao Zedong expressed warm support for the Soviet Union and gratitude for its aid, he also made it clear that China's experience of revolution would be an important model for other countries in Asia. This implied that "the victory of the Chinese Communist Revolution might result in complications or even tensions between the international communist movement's Moscow-centered structure and the Chinese Revolution's self-claimed and non-Western-oriented 'model.'" And this indeed would be the case, even though much of Mao's thinking on economics came straight from Stalin's writings, as Thomas Bernstein in his chapter on "The Socialist Modernization of China Between Soviet Model and National Specificity 1949–1960s" and other authors note.

Linked to the theme of conflicts between interests of the emerging communist world and Soviet power is the tension between the ideology of "orthodox" communism, as defined by the Moscow leadership, and national variants, especially in the People's Republic of China, which claimed to have created a form of Marxism-Leninism with Chinese characteristics, a form more appropriate for Asian nations than the Moscow variant. Traditionally, analysts have highlighted conflicting views of the peasantry in the Russian and Chinese Revolutions as the heart of these differences. But as the chapters on Chinese communist history demonstrate, the Sino-Soviet split over ideology also grew out of contrasting approaches to communist reforms in the 1950s after Stalin's death, including disagreements on the place of violence in the revolution and "peaceful coexistence" in international relations, as well as the role of class struggle over the long term.

Daniel Leese in his chapter on "Mao Zedong as a Historical Personality" presents the multiple, if personalized, nature of the divergences between Moscow and Beijing. He shows how Mao Zedong's "Sinification" of Marxism-Leninism starting in the late 1930s freed him from having to bow to other sources of authority, so that Mao Zedong Thought could become a "flexible guiding principle." Leese rates the Chinese leader's ability to frame a historical narrative using popular tradition and legend as "among Mao's most outstanding leadership skills," as well as a powerful tool for creating a history that demonstrated the rectitude of his own policies. At the same time, he shows the combined influence of China's tradition and of socialist modernity on Mao's strategies and thinking.

Bernstein also notes that Mao felt more free to pursue his own course after Stalin's death, and even more so after Khrushchev's "Secret Speech" of 1956, condemning the excesses of Stalinism. Yet, ironically, Mao used this freedom to reject Soviet advice that China should advance more slowly toward socialism than had the USSR in the 1930s; in 1953 Mao took Stalin's *History of the CPSU: Short Course* as the guide for China's accelerated socialist transformation, which included forced grain procurement, a high priority on heavy industry and the struggle against societal class enemies. And in 1958, as the Great Leap Forward began, Mao made Stalin's 1952 pamphlet *Economic Problems of Socialism* required reading for cadres.

Andrew Walder pinpoints the moment of ideological no-return as Khrushchev's 1956 Twentieth Party Congress speech. In his chapter on "The Chinese Cultural Revolution," Walder underlines the fact that Mao's rejection of the post-1956 Soviet model was hardened by Khrushchev's criticism of Stalin's cult of personality and his rejection of the need for class struggle. These were aspects of Chinese political life that had blossomed under Mao's leadership. The Cultural Revolution was Mao's response, Walder shows, amounting to a "massive purge" with the explicit purpose of "remov[ing] 'people in authority taking the capitalist road.'" China's public rejection of Soviet policy in 1963 led to the splintering of communist movements in the Third World, as Victor Figueroa Clark shows in his chapter on "Latin American Communism." In Vietnam, as Sophie Quinn-Judge writes in "The History of the Vietnamese Communist Party 1941–1975," the Sino-Soviet split led to the sidelining of leaders who were viewed as "revisionist" or too close to Moscow in the 1960s. Sergey Radchenko, in his chapter entitled "The Rise and Fall of the Sino-Soviet Alliance 1949–1989," sums up the dramatic effects of the split this way:"Just as the rise of the alliance legitimized the global communist project, its demise undermined this project by destroying the political ideological unity of the international communist movement and by setting the socialist camp against itself." According to Radchenko, we can understand such a momentous event in the history of communism only by taking into account an entire set of interactions between ideology and national interests, domestic and international policies, cultural identities and clash of personalities. The consequence was a disruptive competition between the Soviet Union and China, particularly for influence in the Third World.

A third theme is the issue of communist reform and reformers. This relates also to the previous question of ideology, since after the death of Stalin there were movements within the East European parties to pursue their own individual roads to socialism. The ripples from the 1956 Twentieth Party Congress in Moscow affected all parties, those in power and out. Jörg Baberowski's "Nikita Khrushchev and De-Stalinization in the Soviet Union 1953–1964" traces the domestic reforms carried out by Khrushchev as part of his de-Stalinization and demonstrates that the major impetus for the reforms came from Khrushchev's own sense of humiliation under Stalin and determination to do away with the worst of his abuses. Communist parties all over the world were impacted by Khrushchev's reforms – the US communist party, examined by Phillip Deery in his "American Communism" is a case in point – the effects were devastating for the morale of the leadership, which never recovered from the shock of Khrushchev's revelations. In Banac's chapter on Yugoslavia, we see that the Twentieth Party Congress served positive purposes in improving Soviet–Yugoslav relations. However, Tito remained committed to his strategy of developing the "nonaligned" world independent of both Moscow and Washington.

The East European Communist parties, on the other hand, had to find a way to accommodate to the relaxation of Stalinist political domination and ideological conformity. Mark Kramer traces this complex history in his "The Changing Pattern of Soviet–East European Relations 1953–1968." Here the story is of uprisings and interventions, political struggles and shifts in policy emphases. In response to increasing diversity within the bloc, Moscow introduced institutional means of guaranteeing conformity, through the Warsaw Pact, the Council for Mutual Economic Assistance and intensified bilateral relations with individual parties. But, as shown by Kramer and by Pavel Kolar, in his contribution, "Reform Undercurrents and the Prague Spring," this did not prevent the Czechoslovaks from pursuing a renewed, human-centered communism in the Prague Spring. The articulation of the "Brezhnev Doctrine," in response to the Prague Spring, had its origins, in Kramer's view, in Stalin's and Khrushchev's policies toward Eastern Europe, but nevertheless created a new framework for structuring relations with the bloc. Kolar traces the path to the Prague Spring and its implications by showing the interconnections between contrasting national developments, the transnational impact of de-Stalinization toward new forms of socialist legitimacy, and the wider picture of the "global 1968," including the influence of Western-style mass culture. Although the Prague Spring left a legacy of "humanistic socialism" up to Gorbachev's times, its repression decidedly inhibited perspectives of reform in Eastern Europe, producing disillusionment and discrediting any projects inspired by socialism.

The fourth theme in the volume is the frequently misunderstood history of the Soviet relationship with the Third World. In "Communism, De-Colonization and the Third World," Andreas Hilger explores the intricate and sometimes difficult relationship between Moscow, as the "center of world communism," and the decolonization efforts that it supported, especially in the post-Stalin period. The rivalry between nationalist noncommunist movements and communist-led or -inspired ones frequently served as a source of conflict and discord in a "complex trilateral relationship" which could no longer simply rely on shared anti-imperialist assumptions. Sara Lorenzini in her chapter on "The Socialist Camp and the Challenge of Economic Modernization in the Third World" invites taking seriously the powerful attraction of the Soviet model of economic development for countries that viewed the West as the heirs of the colonial world. In her view, the Soviet Union had "huge political capital" that it tried to translate more consistently than we often assume into a genuinely alternative way of organizing trade, commerce and industry for the Third World, while promoting ideas of socialist modernity. However, both Hilger and Lorenzini demonstrate how the relationship between the Second and Third Worlds was a tenuous one, as the supposed anti-imperialist identity of interests eroded and the project to construct independent political economies failed, giving way in the 1970s to the acknowledgement of the interdependence of world trade and commerce.

The chapters on individual Third World parties expand on these themes, while demonstrating the variety of communist experiences that countries in Latin America, Africa, the Middle East and Asia lived through. There are several fascinating aspects of these individual country and regional studies as they illustrate the global reach of communism. From those on "The Cuban Revolution: The First Decade" by Piero Gleijeses and on "Latin American Communism" by Figueroa Clark, one learns not only of the deep influence of communism on the development of the struggle against indigenous ruling classes and US influence in the region, but also of the frequently contradictory impact of communist politics. Gleijeses underlines conflicts and tensions between the Cuban Revolution and the Soviet Union in the aftermath of the missile crisis of 1962. As guerrilla strategies developed in Latin America, they had to face not only US-inspired counterrevolution, but also hostility by Moscow because of détente and the acceptance of spheres of influence. Only in the 1970s, as Cuban internationalism became important in

Africa, was an alliance with the Soviet Union firmly established and combined with economic aid to domestic development. Figueroa shows how Marxist ideas and communist experiences had a long duration in Latin America from the interwar years up to our time, as a result of repeated experiences of violence, repression and illegality. It would be wrong to underestimate the influence of communist ideas, practices and legacies on efforts to undertake social change, promote social movements and trade unions and, at a later stage, democratize the region.

Analyses of communism in Asia take us to scenarios of violence and armed struggle as well, but also of authoritarian power, the impact of personality, local legal experiences and different combinations with nationalism. One of the lessons of Charles Armstrong's "Korean Communism: From Soviet Occupation to Kim Family Regime" is the powerful impact Kim Il Sung had on the Democratic People's Republic of Korea, from the time of its founding in 1948 until the 1960s, when his thinking and political supremacy were transformed into the kind of cult of the supreme leader we see today in North Korea. The North Korean case is characterized by impressive continuity as compared with changes and transformations that emerged in Asian communism and in the wider context of world communism. John Roosa's chapter on "Indonesian Communism: The Perils of the Parliamentary Path" emphasizes the almost European communist-like determination of the members of the Communist Party of Indonesia (PKI) to promote their political program within the structures of the Indonesian political system under Sukarno and its anti-imperialist national ideology. After earlier experiences of failed uprisings, there would be no civil wars or armed struggle as elsewhere in Southeast Asia. On the one hand, this led to the PKI becoming the third-largest communist party in the world, connected to both Moscow and Beijing; on the other hand, the party was vulnerable to the Indonesian military's attack on and elimination of the PKI in 1965–66. Quinn-Judge's contribution on "The History of the Vietnamese Communist Party 1941–1975" shows how closely the development of Vietnamese communism was linked with the anti-colonial struggle. The communists' success clearly was related to their ability to balance communist politics with the language and exigencies of anti-colonialism. Such efforts revealed over time inner conflicts related to the "dual origin" of Vietnamese communism – inspired both by the ideal of national unification and by the model of armed anti-imperialist struggle. The Vietnamese communist experience also reflected the cultural influence of the metropolis in the framework of

the French Empire, while looking at the model of peasant-based movement developed by Chinese communism. Even the outstanding personality of Ho Chi Minh could not prevent divisions in the party and episodic
challenges to his rule. At the same time, Quinn-Judge shows how
Vietnamese communists maintained close connections with Moscow and
with Beijing, which seriously affected party unity, though it did not create
factions that relied entirely on either. Vietnam was the major symbol of
communist anti-imperialism in the war against the United States, but its
internationalist image did not last long after victory in 1975. In Hari
Vasudevan's contribution on "Communism in India," the extraordinary
potential for the growth of the communist party in India, given the
circulation of Marxist revolutionary ideas in the British Empire and, even
more, the inherent attraction of the Soviet model for modernization, was
complicated by the great heterogeneity of the Indian subcontinent.
However, after the political and social turbulence surrounding independence in the late 1940s, the Indian communists established influence in
some regions of the subcontinent by means of legal strategies. In spite of
internal divisions brought about by the Sino-Soviet split, Indian communism maintained a longlasting governmental role in regions such as West
Bengal and Kerala – a unique case in the Third World – though the party
could not compete at the level of national politics.

The experiences of multiple parties and diverse societies are encapsu-
lated in Johan Franzén's chapter on "Communism in the Arab World
and Iran" and Allison Drew's on "Comparing African Experiences of
Communism." Franzén's emphasis is on the duality between the universalist calling of world communism and the Middle Eastern reality, particularly its religious and nationalist character, which had already emerged in
the interwar years. Even if World War II provided new opportunities
to consolidate mass parties, particularly in Iran, such duality was never
reconciled. Nationalist platforms overwhelmed the communists and relegated them to minor roles in the emergence of modern states in the region.
The paradigm of modernization was important to Moscow's influence, but
sometimes worked to the detriment of local communists, who were
repeatedly outlawed and repressed by regimes allied with the Soviet
Union. The African experience, based on the examples of Algeria and
South Africa – where communism could develop more easily because of
European influence and limited industrialization – was different. It was
influenced not only by national constraints and the interests of the Soviet
state, but also by the metropole–colony relationship. Interconnections

between Cold War geopolitics and the collapsing European empires were of particular importance. The Algerian war of liberation opened conflict within the communist world along multiple lines, and not simply between Moscow and local communists. But it was in South Africa that communism found connections with civil society and eventually contributed to its democratic transition. At the same time, the modernization paradigm was appealing in many cases to Africans and led to socialist experiments under Moscow's influence. As Drew points out, however, communism was much more effective as a component of national liberation struggles than as a state-led developmental strategy.

Many contributions in the volume point out from different perspectives the peculiar ethos of communists – their readiness to sacrifice, their internationalist beliefs and their sense of being part of an imagined transnational community. These traits continued to characterize communist militants and cadres engaged in anti-imperialist guerrilla struggles, as well as those living in Western societies up to the 1960s, when they started disappearing. Deery's chapter focuses on American communists and how they achieved influence in a variety of milieus before and during World War II by combining enthusiasm, dedication and rigor, while engaging in the struggles for civil rights and carrying out secret missions for the Soviets. Orthodox policies, Cold War constraints and the "red scare" soon put an end to any relevance of American communism. Things were completely different in Western Europe. It becomes clear in both Marc Lazar's chapter, "The French Communist Party," and Giovanni Gozzini's on "Italian Communism" that the communist movement in Western Europe had a serious effect on the course of European politics and society in the immediate postwar period, when, with Stalin's support, the Italian Communist Party (PCI) and the French Communist Party (PCF) made important electoral headway and shared power with coalition parties up to mid 1947. Both authors show how, in spite of the communists' expulsion from the government sphere because of the Cold War divide, the two parties established strong social bases and intellectual influence that lasted for three decades (and even more in the case of the PCI). Lazar emphasizes the unsolvable tension between the so-called teleological and societal dimensions of French communism, which also had implications for the contradiction between national identity and international loyalty to Moscow. This was obviously true for the PCI too, according to Gozzini's analysis of the party's "double-sided strategy." Despite sometimes going their own way, the PCI and PCF attracted financial and moral support as well as periodic criticism and condemnation from their Moscow sponsors. There were also important differences between the two parties. The PCI alone represented a credible alternative force domestically and maintained hegemony over the Italian left until 1989, which can be explained by its mass following, institutional legitimacy and Gramscian cultural inspiration. However, the destinies of the PCF and PCI remained connected. The peak of their political influence came with the emergence of "Eurocommunism" in the 1970s, which reflected both growing anti-Moscow (though not pro-Washington) sentiments among European leftists and ambitions to build new forms of democratic socialism in Western Europe. But the failure of Eurocommunism led to the quick decline of the French party and a slow crisis in the Italian party. In 1989 the PCF was already an insignificant actor, while the PCI dissolved itself.

As Federico Romero points out in his contribution to this volume, after World War II the PCI and PCF, as well as communist parties throughout Europe and the world, had to face the increasingly determined opposition from and even intervention by anti-communist organizations under the leadership of the United States and its intelligence agencies. His chapter on "Cold War Anti-Communism and the Impact of Communism on the West" provides a focus on Western anti-communism which integrates the volume's perspectives on the role and significance of communism in the Cold War and in global politics. Liberated from the interwar presence of fascism and unified around US liberal capitalism, anti-communism became "a key political language," though hardly a coherent ideology as it implied, at different moments, restrictions on civil rights or emphasis on social inclusion, support to authoritarian regimes in Asia or Latin America or defense of dissidence and freedom under Soviet-type regimes. Even more than in Western Europe, anti-communism had paranoic effects in the United States under the influence of McCarthyism, as Deery shows in his contribution. Ultimately, however, Romero argues, anti-communism helped to promote prosperity and democracy, and proved successful in delegitimizing communism. As a political strategy and a discourse pervading world affairs in the second half of the previous century, Cold War anti-communism indirectly demonstrates the powerful global challenge and the significance of the communist project in the postwar era.

PART I

*

EXPANSION AND CONFLICT

World War II, Soviet Power and International Communism

EVAN MAWDSLEY

It is self-evident that, with the victory of Lenin's October Revolution of 1917, Soviet Russia became the epicenter of international communism. However, despite its sprawling land mass and large population, and despite hopes in the immediate post-1918 period for a European-wide revolution, the new state and its ruling communist party were for the better part of two decades a marginal factor in world affairs. Even at the end of the 1930s the USSR was only one of seven or eight major powers, and it was not generally regarded as among the strongest. The fraternal foreign communist parties were also only on the fringes of political life. Most were illegal; the small minority that could function openly almost never had the chance to take part in government.

A decade later, at the end of the 1940s, the USSR was one of two global superpowers. Three independent Baltic countries had been reannexed. Pro-Soviet, communist-led governments controlled most of the states of East Central Europe, as well as China and half of Korea; this was the global expanse of the "Sino-Soviet bloc." Moreover, the communist parties now had strong electoral support in Western Europe, and communism had become a significant element in the growing anti-colonial movement.

There are detailed chapters within this volume on the communists in the European wartime resistance, on the "Sovietization" of Eastern Europe, on the Cominform and Titoism and on the Chinese Revolution. The intention of the present chapter, however, is to relate these phenomena to World War II, to the ideological framework of Stalin and the Soviet leadership, and to the initiatives they took.

The Sources of Soviet Conduct

The motivation of the communist leaders of the USSR and the formulation of Soviet policy in this crucial period remain the subject of debate. Joseph Stalin was obviously the preeminent figure. Final decisions were made by him, although he took advice, and there were limitations to his power, especially overseas. The unique status of Stalin, as a revolutionary activist, companion of Lenin, civil war leader, theorist, industrializer and wartime commander, was an undoubted asset both at home and abroad – even if his achievements were inflated by propaganda. Nevertheless, I will refer here to policies being from the Soviet government, rather than simply from Stalin. He was not all-knowing, all-powerful or all-correct – although neither can he be dismissed as a "colossal blunderer."[1]

It was aptly observed by Mark von Hagen that the nature of the prolonged Russian Civil War of 1917–20 was to develop something new, a "militarized socialism" which resulted from "an interpenetration of militarist and socialist values." Stalin shared this perspective; he did not create it. Eric van Ree, in a seminal discussion of Stalin's political thought, argued that his main foreign-policy goal was "patriotism, in the sense of the preservation of the Soviet state." David Brandenberger attributed similar ideas to Stalin and his "team," although he saw those ideas not so much as a product of the civil war years as a tool of the 1930s, "a russo-centric form of etatism" which was the "most effective way to promote state-building and popular loyalty to the regime."[2]

I argue here that Stalin, as the ultimate formulator of external policy and leader of the war effort, was neither a pragmatic expansionist nor a revolutionary firebrand. To qualify the well-known "revolutionary-imperial paradigm" of Vladislav Zubok and Constantine Pleshakov, Stalin was neither a simple revolutionary nor a simple imperialist.[3] Basic to the worldview of Stalin and the Stalinist elite, and predating both the stresses of the civil war and the cultural transformation of the 1930s, was an ideologized Leninist conception of the outside world. It was made more complex by an assumption both of the deep hostility of all capitalist states to Soviet Russia and of inherent tension *between* capitalist states.

1 Robert C. Tucker, *Stalin in Power, 1928–1941: The Revolution from Above* (New York: Norton, 1990), 624.
2 Mark von Hagen, *Soldiers in the Proletarian Dictatorship: The Red Army and the Soviet Socialist State, 1917–1930* (Ithaca: Cornell University Press, 1990), 331–36; Erik van Ree, *The Political Thought of Joseph Stalin: A Study in Twentieth-Century Revolutionary Patriotism* (London: RoutledgeCurzon, 2002), 211; David Brandenberger, *National Bolshevism: Stalinist Mass Culture and the Formation of Modern Russian National Identity, 1931–1956* (Cambridge, MA: Harvard University Press, 2002), 2.
3 Vladislav Zubok and Constantine Pleshakov, *Inside the Kremlin's Cold War: From Stalin to Khrushchev* (Cambridge, MA: Harvard University Press, 1996), 4–5, 13–19.

The first strand related to the "two camps" doctrine. This doctrine is often associated with the policy declaration of September 1947, at a Cold War turning point: The Soviet ideologist A. A. Zhdanov, then one of Stalin's closest associates, declared that "the political forces operating in the world arena" had been divided "into two basic camps [*na dva osnovnykh lageria*]," the imperialist and anti-democratic camp on one hand, and the anti-imperialist and democratic camp, on the other. But this was not essentially a post-1945 perspective. It had first been adopted by Stalin – following Lenin – in an article published in *Izvestiia* in February 1919. "The world," Stalin noted then, "has definitely and irrevocably split into two camps: the camp of imperialism and the camp of socialism."[4]

In the 1930s and the first half of the 1940s this polarized worldview was complicated, and muted, by the other "Leninist" conflict, between *rival* imperialist powers or groupings. This latter conflict became more evident with the Japanese annexation of Manchuria in 1931 and the rise to power of the revisionist Hitler government in Germany. In the mid 1930s these developments affected the policy of Stalin's government and the Soviet-dominated Communist International (Comintern). The USSR joined the League of Nations (hitherto despised by Moscow) in September 1934, following a policy of "collective security." It moved toward one of the competing groupings, with measures including the May 1935 Franco-Soviet Pact of Mutual Assistance. The Comintern, meanwhile, endorsed at its Seventh Congress in July–August 1935 the policy of the "popular front," within which a range of parties would work together on an anti-fascist program.

This external rivalry between imperialists represented, in the late 1930s, both threats and opportunities for the leaders of the USSR. A war might spill over into Soviet territory, as had certainly happened in 1917–18. On the other hand, conflict between imperialists had the advantage that it might deflect attention from an anti-communist crusade. Furthermore, its social consequences might lead, as they had in 1917–19, to a revolutionary situation in one or more of the capitalist states.

In any event, as applied concretely to the international situation, the communist line was that by 1937 this conflict between capitalist groupings had degenerated into a "new imperialist war" (the first "imperialist war" being World War I). As the massively circulated Stalinist party history, the

---

4 G. Procacci (ed.), *The Cominform: Minutes of the Three Conferences 1947/1948/1949* (Milan: Feltrinelli, 1994), 226 (25 Sep. 1947); I. V. Stalin, "Dva lageria," in *Sochineniia*, vol. IV (Moscow: OGIZ, 1947), 232 (22 Feb. 1919).

Short Course (*Kratkii kurs*), put it in September 1938, the object of the new imperialist war was "a redivision of the world and of the spheres of influence in favor of the aggressor [*agressivnye*] countries [i.e. Germany, Japan and Italy] and at the expense of the so-called democratic [*demokraticheskie*] states [i.e. Britain, France and the USA]."[5]

The 1919/1947 concept of the "two camps" (socialist vs. imperialist) was not explicitly used in the late 1930s, but the Soviet government was increasingly critical of the apparent lack of resistance by the "nonaggressive" states to the aggressors, especially after the Munich agreement. In the September 1938 *Short Course* it was stated that the democracies, although stronger than the fascists/aggressors, were afraid to confront them (in Manchuria, Abyssinia or Spain), because their governments feared working-class revolution in Europe and colonial rebellion in Asia. Stalin's important Party Congress address in March 1939 attributed more sinister motives to the Western democracies, beyond fear of revolution. The nonaggressive (*neagressivnye*) countries, particularly Britain and France, had moved from a position of collective security to one of nonintervention (*nevmeshatel'stvo*), i.e. neutrality. Their aim, Stalin alleged, was to "entangle" (*vputat'sia*) the "aggressor states" (*gosudarstva-agressory*) and by this means to avoid a direct threat to themselves. Germany would be "entangled" in an East European conflict, "better still" a war with the USSR, and would not attack Britain and France; the Japanese would be "entangled" in the ongoing war in China or with the USSR and would leave the colonies of the West European states alone.[6]

Soviet Communism and the "New Imperialist War"
1939–1941

The signing of the German–Soviet Nonaggression Pact on 23 August 1939 and the abrupt and decisive change of the orientation of the USSR and the Comintern in Europe can at least partly be understood in ideological terms, as the USSR maneuvering between two rival groups of capitalist states. The outbreak of a major European war on 3 September, only a week after the signing of the pact, could perhaps not have been predicted in Moscow, nor could the very rapid destruction of Poland – within five weeks. When the

5 *Istoriia Vsesoiuznoi kommunisticheskoi partii (bol'shevikov): kratkii kurs* (Moscow: Izd. Pravda, 1938), 318.
6 Ibid., 319; *XVIII s"ezd Vsesoiuznoi kommunisticheskoi partii (b): 10–21 marta 1939 g.: stenograficheskii otchet* (Moscow: GIPL, 1939), 13 (10 Mar.).

fighting began, however, Stalin saw the benefits for the USSR and communism in general. Georgi Dimitrov, the Bulgarian general secretary of the Executive Committee of the Comintern (ECCI), noted down Stalin's words in a conversation on 7 September 1939:

> A war is on between two groups of capitalist countries . . . for the redivision of the world, for the domination of the world. We see nothing wrong in their having a good fight and weakening each other. It would be fine if at the hand of Germany the position of the capitalist countries (especially England) were shaken. Hitler, without understanding it or desiring it, is shaking and undermining the capitalist system.

Stalin was now embarked on exactly the same course of action he had accused the "nonaggressive" governments of planning – he was content to "entangle" them in a war with Germany. He also explained to Dimitrov that the USSR had unique opportunities: "We can maneuver, pit one side against the other to set them fighting with each other as fiercely as possible. The non-aggression pact is to a certain degree helping Germany. Next time we'll urge on the other side."[7]

The German–Soviet Pact of August 1939 involved secret agreements to divide up parts of East Central Europe. The eventual result for the Soviets of this agreement, brought to fruition in 1939 and 1940, could be portrayed by them as part of a process of national liberation. The final (secret) terms, after all, gave Moscow freedom of action with respect to the large Belarusian and Ukrainian population of what had been eastern Poland.

Stalin privately justified use of the Red Army for spreading socialism (much as Lenin had in 1920, with relation to Poland). The army was used without full-scale combat to assert Soviet influence in the eastern territories of Poland, and in the Baltic states and Moldova, but real operations – the extremely costly Winter War – were required in 1939–40 to force the Finnish government to make strategic territorial concessions. At the time, Stalin stressed the validity of using the Red Army to extend the "socialist camp." "The Red Army activities," he told Dimitrov in January 1940, "are also a matter of world revolution." In a secret post-mortem, justifying the winter attack on Finland, Stalin made a telling comment about timing and opportunism, which could apply to a range of initiatives then and later. Soviet action, he argued, depended on the "international situation":

---

7 Ivo Banac (ed.), *The Diary of Georgi Dimitrov, 1933–1949* (New Haven: Yale University Press, 2003), 115 (7 Sep. 1939).

There, in the West, the three biggest powers were locked in deadly combat –
this was the most opportune moment [November–December 1939] to settle
the Leningrad problem; it was the time when other countries were busy
elsewhere, so this was the best moment for us to strike ... A delay of
a couple of months would have meant a delay of 20 years, because you
can't predict political developments ... One could not exclude the possibility
of a sudden peace.[8]

The problem with the German–Soviet Nonaggression Pact for the Soviet
leaders was that it did not produce the military "balance" that they had
originally anticipated. The two imperialist groups were not wearing one
another out; instead one group gained a quick victory in June 1940, and
now dominated continental Europe. The wartime spring of 1941 saw
a confused evolution of Soviet policy. Hitler had turned his attention to the
Balkans at the beginning of April, with not only a planned intervention in
Greece on 6 April, but also a hastily arranged attack on Yugoslavia. This
Balkan Blitzkrieg coincided with the visit to Moscow of the Japanese foreign
minister, and the signing (on 13 April) of a Japanese–Soviet five-year
Neutrality Pact. Each signatory agreed to remain neutral should the other
"become the object of military action." The two powers also agreed to
respect the territorial integrity and inviolability of Manchukuo and the
Mongolian People's Republic; the USSR with this accepted the Japanese
1931 annexation of northeastern China, one of the first acts of the "new
imperialist war."

It was at this critical juncture that Stalin suddenly began taking active steps
toward the dissolution of the Comintern. On 20 April 1940, after a rare public
appearance, he intimated this line of thought to Dimitrov and others. Stalin's
motives are not altogether clear. He had never favored a strong independent
Comintern. What he told the ECCI leaders was that the communist movement was important, but that the national parties were seen too much as
subservient sections of the Comintern.[9] The dissolution might also be seen as
an act of appeasement to prevent an attack by Germany and Japan; those two
powers had first been bound together in 1936 as founding members of the
Anti-Comintern Pact.

The next event, and one of the last before the German attack, was a semi-
public series of speeches Stalin made to army leaders and military cadets at

8 Ibid., 124 (21 Jan. 1940); E. N. Kulkov and O. A. Rzheshevskii, *Stalin and the Soviet–Finnish War 1939–1940* (London: Frank Cass, 2002), 264 (17 Apr. 1940). The "Leningrad problem" involved moving the Finnish border away from the city.
9 Banac (ed.), *Diary of Georgi Dimitrov*, 155–56 (20 Apr. 1940).

the Kremlin on 5 May 1941.[10] These speeches are sometimes linked to plans for a preemptive attack on Germany which, had it happened, would have been an extreme case of using military force to achieve Soviet objectives. While I would not interpret the speech as a call for aggressive war, there were a number of important elements in it. First of all, some of Stalin's comments were about the relative strength of rival imperialist groupings. Second, he stated that since September 1939 the German army had changed from a progressive army fighting "under the slogan of the liberation from the yoke of the peace of Versailles" into one fighting "under the slogans of an aggressive war, of conquest." Finally, while at this time he was moving toward the liquidation of the Comintern, Stalin did not forget the role of resistance: "[T]he German army ... has antagonized many countries which have been occupied by it. An army is in serious danger which has to fight having in its rear hostile territory and masses."[11]

Passing the "Examination": The Soviet State Fights and Wins World War II

In many respects the situation was transformed by the German attack on 22 June 1941. The initial military campaign was, for the Soviets, a catastrophe. In political terms, however, it did return the ideology of the USSR to an anti-fascist stance, both at home and abroad. Although apathy and collaboration existed, and the human cost was terribly high, the population rallied around the patriotic/socialist orientation which had been developing since the mid 1930s. This coming together was much furthered by the cruel behavior of the invaders and by the eventual Red Army victories.

Stalin genuinely had a most important role as a military executive during the war. He had had a limited formal position in the prewar armed forces, but became people's commissar of defense and then supreme commander-in-chief. He did make several general comments about military strategy and the course of the war, of which the most important was perhaps his Order of the Day of 23 February 1942 (Red Army Day) in which he stressed long-term material factors ("permanently operating factors") in successful warfare.[12]

---

10 Jürgen Förster and Evan Mawdsley, "Hitler and Stalin in Perspective: Secret Speeches on the Eve of Barbarossa," *War in History* 11, 1 (Jan. 2004), 61–103.
11 Ibid., 97.
12 I. V. Stalin, *O Velikoi otechestvennoi voiny Sovetskogo soiuza* (Moscow: OGIZ, 1946), 37–43.

One feature of Soviet communism in wartime (and in Stalin's later years) was a disregarding of party "norms." There was no congress of the All-Union Communist Party – VKP(b) – between the Eighteenth Congress in March 1939 and the Nineteenth in October 1952 (a party conference met in February 1941). There were very few plenums of the party Central Committee. Stalin relied on patriotism rather than communism in his wartime speeches, especially in the first half of the war. It was not until November 1943 that he referred publicly at length to the "party of Lenin, the party of the Bolsheviks."[13] Nevertheless, party membership grew strikingly, mostly through military party organizations. On 1 July 1941 the communist party had included 2,600,000 full members and 1,210,000 candidates. During the war no fewer than 5,320,000 individuals were admitted as full members, and 3,620,000 as candidates. Remaining in July 1945 were 4,290,000 full members and 1,660,000 candidates; these figures taken together also indicate a high level of loss to enemy action.[14]

This is not the place to discuss in detail military operations or Soviet diplomacy. By December of 1941 the defenders had been driven back to the outskirts of Leningrad and Moscow and beyond Rostov. The successful counterattacks against overextended German armies in front of Moscow and Rostov in early December 1941 were events of great importance. Having failed to achieve an overall victory in a short war of movement, Germany could never defeat the USSR (and its allies) in a prolonged war of attrition. More broadly, the Moscow battle showed, despite previous triumphs, that Hitler's forces were not invincible. The Red Army was, for the moment, the most potent force on the Allied side.

The Soviet leaders expected, after the Battle of Moscow, something along the lines of Napoleon's 1812 defeat. But although the front lines in the north and center, in front of Leningrad and Moscow, were now relatively stable, battles fought in May–June 1942 enabled the Wehrmacht to drive deep into southern Russia, toward the Caucasus and Stalingrad. However, the outcome of Hitler's so-called second campaign was arguably of greater significance even than the Battle of Moscow. The counterattack at Stalingrad, which began in November 1942, was followed at the start of February by the surrender of the entire German Sixth Army, entombed in the city.

13 Ibid., 119 (16 Nov. 1943).
14 "Iz istorii Velikoi otechestvennoi voiny," *Izvestiia TsK* 5 (1991), 213–17.

Entry into World War II, alongside Britain and later the USA, did not change the basic Leninist–Stalinist conception of two rival imperialist blocs, even if the Soviet state was essentially part of one of them. The USSR was now bearing the brunt of the war with Germany and undoubtedly paying the highest cost in human lives. This could be seen as an extreme example of the imperialists "entangling" the USSR in a war with Germany. Stalin and Viacheslav Molotov complained about the failure of the Western Allies to commit to a "second front" in northwestern Europe and at delays in delivery of military supplies under Lend-Lease. An extreme version (possibly intentionally hyperbolic) was Stalin's comment to Ambassador Ivan M. Maiskii in London in October 1942 that he "had the impression that Churchill was aiming for the defeat [*porazhenie*] of the USSR so that he could then come to terms with the Germany of Hitler or [Heinrich] Brüning at the expense of our country":

> Without such an assumption it is hard to explain the conduct of Churchill with respect to the question of the second front in Europe, to the question of the delivery of arms to the USSR, which is becoming progressively smaller and smaller . . . to the question of [Rudolf] Hess, whom Churchill is evidently holding in reserve and, finally, to the question of the [failure to carry out promised] systematic bombing by the British of Berlin.[15]

By the second half of 1943, however, Soviet relations with the Western Allies had improved. The USSR was no longer threatened by military defeat, the British and Americans were winning victories in the Mediterranean (albeit not in a full-scale cross-Channel "second front") and Lend-Lease supplies were arriving on a much larger scale. The Moscow conference of Allied foreign ministers in October–November 1943 had productive discussions regarding the postwar world. At the Tehran conference in November–December 1943 Stalin finally met Churchill and Roosevelt and had a considerable influence on alliance strategy.

The last two years of the war, from June 1943 and the Battle of Kursk, were a time of steady advance by the Red Army. June 1944 was a decisive moment, as both sets of Allies were finally able to deploy massive armies in countries occupied by the Third Reich and forming its outer defenses. The Wehrmacht

15 O. A. Rzheshevskii, *Stalin i Cherchill'. Vstrechi. Besedy. Diskussii* (Moscow: Nauka, 2004), 376 (19 Oct. 1942). Brüning was chancellor of Germany from 1930 to 1932; in 1942 he was living in exile in the USA. Hess, Hitler's deputy, had flown to Britain in mysterious circumstances.

could not hold these areas for more than a few months, and by the end of the 1944 Greater Germany itself was under direct attack. Clutching at straws, the Nazi regime hoped for a breakup of the Grand Alliance. Stalin, however, realized that "entanglement" and the sort of "maneuver" he had described to Dimitrov in September 1939 – pitting "one side against the other" – no longer had any utility.

The Far East was the region where, until the late 1930s, the territorial integrity of the USSR had seemed most threatened. After the signature of the April 1941 Japanese–Soviet Neutrality Pact, Moscow observed a cautious policy for four years. Then, on 9 August 1945, the Red Army entered the war against Japan. This involvement had a limited effect on the outcome of the fighting, but abundant political significance; Soviet forces occupied Manchuria and northern Korea. Considering that Stalin had been a revolutionary who had violently opposed the Russo-Japanese War of 1904–05, his September 1945 broadcast commemorating the Japanese surrender was extraordinary: "For forty years we of the older generation waited for this day, and now this day has arrived."[16]

The USSR and the International Communist Movement During the War Years

The anti-fascist political line of the various communist parties won considerable support in the late 1930s. The Molotov–Ribbentrop Pact of August 1939 abruptly changed this. In September the Comintern instructed members of the French and British Communist Parties not to support the war effort against Nazi Germany, in factories or within the armed forces. The line reversed again with the German invasion of the USSR on 22 June 1941. In the Allied countries there was to be an all-out effort to support the war effort and especially that of the USSR; in the occupied countries and Germany itself everything possible was to be done to bring about defeat.

On the day of the German attack Stalin made his approach clear to Dimitrov: "For now the Comintern is not to take any overt action ... The issue of socialist revolution is not to be raised." The stress was on resistance. In a speech of November 1941 Stalin spoke of the "instability of the European rear of imperial Germany." "[T]he 'new order' in Europe," he

---

16 I. V. Stalin, *Sochineniia* (Stanford: Stanford University Press, 1967), vol. II [XV], 214 (3 Sep. 1945).

declared, "is a volcano which is ready to explode at any time and to bury the Hitlerite adventurers." Three months later, with the Red Army temporarily taking the offensive after the Battle of Moscow, Stalin delivered an overview of the war in which he brought out "stability of the rear" as one of the "permanently operating factors" in modern war, and one which put Germany – with its supposedly unstable rear – at a disadvantage.[17]

However, there was little that the USSR could do in practical terms to set off the "volcano." Even before the war, Soviet territory had been distant from Central Europe, to say nothing of the western or southern parts of the continent. Now the Soviets had retreated 600 miles further east. Available in Europe, however, were the remnants of the prewar communist parties, which in their illegal or semi-legal situation had developed a degree of conspiratorial expertise. Meanwhile, existing governments on the right were increasingly discredited in the eyes of their people by defeat or by military failure. In addition, the resistance of the Red Army and Soviet partisans, followed by the beginning of the expulsion of the German occupiers, was an inspiration to many of those living in Axis-dominated areas in Europe and Asia.

Yugoslavia was, from the first, an active area of resistance and on both sides of the Grand Alliance came to be seen as a model. This success of the communist-led partisan movement in 1941 and 1942 owed as much to ethnic divisions, traditions of insurgency and rugged terrain as it did to the abilities of Tito and his comrades. Nevertheless, unlike all the other countries brought under German control, a numerically significant resistance movement was created, and one with enclaves outside the control of the occupying forces.

Soviet policy at this stage, expressed through the Comintern, endorsed direct action. At several points in 1941 and 1942 the Red Army seemed on the edge of military defeat, and the highest priority was attached to distracting German troops. Unlike the governments-in-exile set up under British control, the Comintern and local communist leaders were not concerned about maintaining the prewar social and political order. Indeed, from this point of view it was an advantage if resistance led to fierce reprisals; a cycle of violence in occupied territories would suck in and tie down more enemy troops.

17 Banac (ed.), *Diary of Georgi Dimitrov*, 167 (22 Jun. 1941); Stalin, *O Velikoi otechestvennoi voiny*, 30 (6 Nov. 1941), 42 (23 Feb. 1942).

However, eleven months later, in May 1943, came the disbandment of the Comintern. As already noted, Stalin had contemplated such action in April 1941, and his motives now were similarly complex. The Soviet leader explained the decision to the Politburo on two related bases: First, it was impractical to direct "the working-class movement" from one center and, second, disbandment strengthened the local communists by demonstrating that communist parties were not "agents of a foreign state."[18] At the same time there must also have been a desire to smooth relations with the leaders of the Western Allies, especially by eliminating an institution which was not central to Stalin's concerns.

The various national communist parties did not become free agents after May 1943. An important role was taken by the secret International Information Department (Otdel mezhdunarodnoi informatsii, OMI) within the VKP(b) Central Committee apparatus. A survey of the wartime activities of the Comintern and its leaders, published in 1998, noted that the OMI helped initiate a (communist-led) partisan staff in Poland in the spring of 1944, sending weapons and communications equipment; the organization, it was noted, "also led [*rukovodil*] the anti-fascist struggle in Yugoslavia, Hungary, Romania, Bulgaria and partly in Finland."[19]

The formal end of the Comintern was indeed followed by the enhanced success of foreign communists. This was not at first *directly* related to Red Army advances, although these certainly enhanced the prestige of the USSR. Most important were the advances of the British and Americans in the West, leading in mid 1943 to control of all North Africa and then the occupation of southern Italy. The changing situation strengthened French resistance forces in occupied France and overseas, and in both areas the French Communist Party (Parti communiste français, PCF) played a role. Then the British–American invasion of Sicily in July 1943 was followed by the overthrow of Mussolini. The new Italian government under Field Marshal Pietro Badoglio agreed to an armistice in early September, as Allied forces landed in Italy. The Wehrmacht was able to keep control of the northern two-thirds of the peninsula, but an armed resistance movement began in which the Italian Communist Party (Partito Comunista Italiano, PCI) took an important role. Allied naval and air bases in southern Italy also allowed greater contact with resistance forces in Yugoslavia and Greece.

---

18 Banac (ed.), *Diary of Georgi Dimitrov*, 275–76 (21 May 1943).
19 N. S. Lebedeva and M. M. Narinskii (eds.), *Komintern i Vtoraia mirovaia voina* (Moscow: Pamiatniki istoricheskoi mysli, 1994–98), vol. II, 74–75. No claims were made for the OMI leading the "anti-fascist struggle" in France, Italy, Yugoslavia, Greece or China.

The communists were instructed by Moscow to take part in liberation governments set up in the West. In October 1943 Britain and the United States recognized the Badoglio government, which was associated with King Vittorio Emanuele III. Dimitrov and PCI leader Palmiro Togliatti (also a prominent figure in the Comintern) opposed supporting this government, which they – correctly – perceived as reactionary, incompetent and unpopular. In March 1944, however, Stalin made it clear in a secret Kremlin meeting with Togliatti that the PCI was to support Badoglio and the king. Stalin's argument was that in-fighting would weaken the anti-German cause; if the king was prepared to fight the Germans there was no point in demanding his abdication.[20] When Togliatti arrived in Italy he made a speech at Salerno (near Naples), in which he endorsed communist participation in the government. The *svolta di Salerno* (Salerno turning point) was a major event in the history of the Italian left.

In the case of France, too, the USSR fostered cooperation with the broader resistance. In the occupied mainland the communist-led Front National worked, at least on paper, under the Gaullist Conseil National de la Résistance (CNR), and communist resistance forces cooperated with other underground fighters. In April 1944 the PCF took posts in de Gaulle's Algiers-based Comité français de Libération nationale (CFLN). It then played a major part in the Provisional Government set up in June 1944 and based in liberated Paris from August. In November 1944 as the French Comintern leader Maurice Thorez prepared to follow Togliatti home from Moscow, Stalin personally urged him to maintain a cautious policy, in particular opposing the maintenance of separate armed detachments by the communists. As Stalin put it,

> The communists are behaving brashly [*braviruiut*] and are continuing to follow the former line at a time when the situation is different ... The Communist Party is not strong enough to bash the government over the head. It must accumulate forces and seek out allies ... If the situation changes for the better, then the forces rallying around the party will be useful to it for the offensive.[21]

Stalin evidently believed that accepting Allied preferences in Italy and France would strengthen the Soviet bargaining position with respect to the countries of Eastern Europe when the Red Army finally arrived there.

20 Banac (ed.), *Diary of Georgi Dimitrov*, 304–05 (5 Mar. 1944).
21 Ibid., 342–43 (19 Nov. 1944); "Anglichane i Amerikantsy khotiat vezde sozdat' reaktsionnye pravitel'stva," *Istochnik* 4 (1995), 155–56 (19 Nov. 1944).

Of course, the eventual advance of the Soviet armed forces, when it came in the second half of 1944, was of even greater importance for the spread of communist power than were developments in Western Europe. For two decades Stalin had looked on the Red Army as an instrument for spreading communist influence. He realized that ultimately physical control could determine the political complexion of neighboring territories. His 1939 comment to Dimitrov that "[t]he Red Army activities are also a matter of world revolution" has already been mentioned. When the British in 1941–42 refused formal recognition of the prewar border of the USSR – with the recently annexed Baltic states, eastern Poland and Bessarabia/Moldova – Stalin reassured Molotov that he need not worry about diplomatic setbacks: "[t]he question of borders . . . in one or other part of our country will be decided by force." Milovan Djilas, one of the leaders of the Yugoslav communists, recalled that in a private conversation in April 1945 Stalin expanded on the connection between military strategy and "revolutionary" politics: "This war is not as in the past; whoever occupies a territory also imposes on it his own social system. Everyone imposes his own system as far as his army has power to do so. It cannot be otherwise."[22]

The Red Army counteroffensive developed more slowly than Stalin and his advisors had originally expected. The Soviet war in Europe lasted some forty-six months, and only in the last eleven (from July 1944) was the Red Army fighting in territory beyond even the August 1939 borders. The details of occupation varied but there were, as we will see, underlying similarities.

Reached first was the belt of territory annexed between September 1939 and July 1940. The Red Army, and "internal" security forces, entered what had been eastern Poland (first western Ukraine and then western Belarus) in the summer of 1944. Most of the territory of the three former Baltic states was reoccupied in the autumn of 1944. Moscow had insisted to the other Allies since 1941 on the reincorporation of these areas into the USSR, despite the provisions of the Atlantic Charter; the British and Americans had accepted at least the Curzon line (in Poland) at the Tehran conference. These regions were rapidly integrated into the Soviet state, regaining their former (short-lived) "union republic" status, or becoming part of expanded versions of the Ukrainian SSR or the Belorussian SSR.

---

22 Banac (ed.), *Diary of Georgi Dimitrov*, 124 (21 Jan. 1940); Rzheshevskii, *Stalin i Cherchill'*, 157 (24 May 1942); Milovan Djilas, *Conversations with Stalin* (Harmondsworth, UK: Penguin, 1962), 90.

The next region to be captured was undeniably "foreign," beyond even the Soviet frontiers of June 1941. The Red Army spearheads approached Warsaw in July 1944 and were met by a Polish national revolt mounted in the name of the government-in-exile in London. There was a contentious pause by the Red Army, which saw the Warsaw Uprising crushed by the Germans, and Poland temporarily split in half at the Vistula. The Soviet military and security organs consolidated their control over the eastern half, in the name of a new government (initially set up at Lublin), which had a leading communist element. Finland left the war in early September but kept a noncommunist government in place (although with some communist ministers). The country was not invaded or occupied – on condition that German forces were ejected. Romania, heretofore a very active German ally in the USSR, changed sides after a palace coup in the late summer. The Red Army quickly occupied the country, en route to the West, but unlike the situation in Poland the Soviets had to deal with a successor government under King Michael; this included a communist as minister of justice. In early March 1945, after a Soviet demonstration of force, a new cabinet was installed, with more pro-Soviet, left-wing ministers. Bulgaria had also been allied to Germany; once the Romanian domino fell, the Red Army occupied the country without meeting resistance in early September 1944. A new coalition government in which the communists played a large part took over in Sofia. Advances further west saw the flank of the advancing Red Army brush against Yugoslavia; Belgrade was captured in late September, but much of the rest of the country was under the control of Tito's communist partisans. As with Finland – but for quite different reasons – there was in Yugoslavia no significant Soviet military or security service presence.

The government of Hungary did not change sides in the autumn of 1944, although the eastern part of the country was occupied by the Red Army, and an Allied-oriented authority, led by a general and with significant communist involvement, was formed there in December. The Red Army was then stalled outside Budapest until the middle of February 1945. The situation in Czechoslovakia was similar; before the last days of the war only the eastern part of pre-1938 territories of the country had been recaptured; a temporary government with a significant communist presence was set up at Košice in Slovakia in April.

In the first months of 1945 the remaining parts of Poland and Hungary (with Warsaw and Budapest) were taken by the Red Army, after fierce battles with the Wehrmacht. The final case, of course, was the conquest of eastern

Germany, which involved fighting for Berlin at the end of April 1945. The Allies by this time had made a number of agreements about Germany, including the marking out of occupation zones; at the Yalta conference of February 1945 they confirmed that Poland would occupy German territory as far west as the Oder–Neisse line and that East Prussia would be divided between Poland and the USSR. The capture of Berlin and Prague by Soviet troops (rather than by American or British ones) in the last days of the war had both military and political implications: The history of the "liberating mission" of the Red Army would be exploited politically by the USSR in the postwar years.

Despite a range of differences, developments in all these regions shared common features. Governments and elites had been compromised by prewar or wartime failures. They had failed to preserve their national independence or they had taken part in a very costly war as subalterns of the Third Reich. Their populations had made very heavy and apparently pointless sacrifices in the war, and they were often physically displaced. And, except for Finland and Yugoslavia, they had been captured or recaptured by invasions mounted by the Red Army.

Stalin's April 1945 remark to Djilas, that "[e]veryone imposes his own system as far as his army has power to do so," was not just about supporting communism with the Red Army; it also indicated the difficulty of installing communist-led governments where Soviet soldiers were *not* present. Churchill flew to Moscow in October 1944, and Stalin accepted his now well-known proposal for spheres of influence – the "percentages" agreement – in the Balkans and the Danubian lands. Britain and its Western Allies would have predominant influence in Greece, and the USSR a comparable position in Romania and Bulgaria; the share of influence in Yugoslavia and Hungary would be about equal. This division reflected military realities. In October 1944 Soviet occupation troops were already the predominant force in Romania and Bulgaria; there was no likelihood of British or American troops arriving. Almost simultaneously – in mid October 1944 – British forces were coming ashore in Greece on the heels of the retreating Wehrmacht.

The Greek communists had played an important part in the resistance, within ELAS (the Greek People's National Army of Liberation). Dimitrov came to sympathize with ELAS, but his request in October 1944 that the USSR openly provide at least moral support was rejected by Molotov. At the start of December, the political wing of ELAS quit the national unity government of Georgios Papandreou over the issue of its guerrilla fighters being disarmed. In mid January 1945, after five weeks of fighting in Athens between ELAS and its political opponents (the latter aided by the British), Stalin reminded Dimitrov of his opposition to the radical actions of the Greek communists: "I advised not starting this fighting in Greece. The ELAS people should not have resigned from the Papandreou government. They've taken on more than they can handle. They were evidently counting on the Red Army's coming down to the Aegean. We cannot do that. We cannot send our troops into Greece, either. The Greeks have acted foolishly."[23]

In Europe the Soviet government did in 1944–45 exercise a high degree of caution (or patience) in spreading communism. Efforts were made to mask the influence of the USSR on foreign communist parties. Stalin was realistic about what could be achieved, and he could see the danger of precipitate political change, not least in his relations with his bourgeois alliance partners. The Red Army was still fighting very costly battles with the Wehrmacht, and a supreme effort might well be required to win the final campaign in Germany. Some areas had a higher military priority than a political one. Poland, Hungary and East Prussia were of central importance for a Red Army drive that was directed toward central Germany; Finland, Yugoslavia and Greece were on the distant flanks. Once victory was achieved in May 1945 the USSR gave high priority to its objectives in Germany; gaining a share in reparations and ensuring the complete suppression of Nazism required temporary cooperation with the British and Americans. At the same time seizure of power by Western communists without the direct presence of the Red Army was unlikely, given the political balance and continued presence of British and American troops.

In terms of the fraternal parties, the Chinese Communist Party (CCP) was a special case. The party had a long and complex history of conflict both with the Chinese central Guomindang (GMD) government and with the Japanese occupiers (after July 1937). From the mid 1930s instructions from Moscow to the CCP emphasized resistance to Japan and – after June 1937 – contribution to the overall Chinese war effort, which was led by the GMD. From Moscow's point of view, the Japanese annexation of Manchuria in 1931 presented a most serious danger to eastern Siberia; joint resistance by the GMD and the CCP would "entangle"

---

23 Banac (ed.), *Diary of Georgi Dimitrov*, 291 (26 Dec. 1943), 352–53 (10 Jan. 1945); Lebedeva and Narinskii (eds.), *Komintern*, vol. II, 78, doc. 188 (21 Oct. 1944), 474.

Japanese forces and reduce the likelihood of a direct Japanese military attack against Soviet territory.

Although the Red Army had in the late 1930s deployed its strongest forces in eastern Siberia, the USSR did not during the Sino-Japanese War send military help to the communists. Nevertheless, under the leadership of Mao Zedong the land-reform programs of the CCP were increasingly popular among the peasantry. Successful guerrilla warfare had given the communists considerable strength in the countryside even of eastern China. And, more important, the authority of the GMD was weakened by the retreat of Chiang Kai-shek's government to Chongqing in 1938 and the continued failure of the GMD army, right through 1944.

The Consequences of World War II

And so, with the formal capitulation of Germany in May 1945 and the Japanese surrender in September, World War II was over. The government of the victorious USSR returned quickly to pre-1941 policies. On 9 February 1946 Stalin made a speech in connection with the Supreme Soviet elections; the war, he argued, had been an "examination" which had been passed with great credit by the Soviet government and the communist party, as well by its leaders. The success of the Red Army, as well as of the social, state and economic systems had been fully verified.

Not only did victory in the war supposedly validate Soviet prewar policies, it also showed the need to continue them. The concentration on heavy industry was to continue: "As to plans for a longer period, our party intends to organize a new powerful upsurge of the economy which will give us the possibility, for instance, to increase the level of our industry threefold as compared with the pre-war level ... Only under such conditions can we regard our country as guaranteed *against any accidents* [emphasis added]. This will require perhaps three new five-year plans if not more."

The need to guarantee against "accidents" was certainly – in part – an entirely rational response to the 1941 invasion by a rapaciously aggressive foreign power and to the devastation that followed. It was also, however, indicative of an unchanging Leninist–Stalinist view of the outside world, one that stressed rival imperialists and inevitable conflict. "It would be wrong," Stalin said in his 1946 speech, "to think that World War II came about accidentally or as a result of mistakes of one statesman or other ... In reality the war came about as the inevitable result of the development

of the world economic and political forces on the basis of modern monopoly capitalism."[24] The Soviet leader had made the same point, more
baldly, at an informal meeting with Yugoslav and Bulgarian communist
leaders in January 1945:

> The crisis of capitalism has manifested itself in the division of the capitalists
> into two factions – one *fascist*, the other *democratic*. The alliance between
> ourselves and the democratic faction of capitalists came about because the
> latter had a stake in preventing Hitler's domination, for that brutal state
> would have driven the workers to extremes and to the overthrow of
> capitalism itself. We are currently allied with one faction against the other,
> but in future we will be against the first [*sic*] faction of capitalists, too.[25]

By 1947, with the defeat and disarmament of Germany and Japan, rivalry
between capitalists was less clear, and the emphasis was, as in 1919, on the
bipolar conflict between imperialism and socialism. The "two camps" speech
by Zhdanov in September 1947 – already mentioned – was the fullest public
elaboration of this theme.

In the postwar years the leaders of the USSR had had to choose a position
on a spectrum of action, all related to the war which had just been fought and
won. They could maintain a positive relationship with Britain and the United
States, their great-power allies. Alternatively, they could strive singlemind-
edly to consolidate their substantial hard-won territorial-strategic gains in
Eastern Europe. Or they could support revolutionary movements on a global
scale. The prospect of nuclear weapons had little impact on Soviet wartime
policy (despite some knowledge – from espionage – of American and British
developments), and Hiroshima did not change the Leninist precept that war
was inevitable. Nevertheless, the Soviets had begun in the autumn of 1945
a rapid and expensive race to develop their own nuclear weapons, and there
was a natural desire to put off a direct confrontation at least until the balance
of nuclear forces was more favorable. The existence of choices did not mean
that Stalin or anyone else had absolute control or was the sole cause of
events. The pace of events in China in 1947–48 was certainly not dictated by
Moscow. Moreover, the USSR did not become a superpower, and the
communist parties did not gain influence, solely because of the personal
decisions and ideology of Stalin; more than forty years of tension between
East and West continued when the Georgian dictator was no longer on the
scene.

---

24 Stalin, *Sochineniia*, vol. III [XVI], 1–28 (9 Feb. 1946).
25 Banac (ed.), *Diary of Georgi Dimitrov*, 357–58 (28 Jan. 1945).

The details of the changes of communist strength after 1945 are dealt with elsewhere in this volume. What might be said here is that it is insufficient to focus solely on Soviet (or Stalinist) manipulation or on imminent terror – although manipulation and terror were certainly evident. There were now strong communist parties in Western Europe, and they had a mass following. In France, in the 1945 legislative election and the first election of 1946, the PCF won 26 percent of the vote; in the second election of 1946 it won 28 percent and had the most seats. The PCI in 1946 won 21 percent of the vote, and in 1948, in coalition with the Partito Socialista Italiano, 31 percent.[26] Another important feature to bear in mind was the great variety of experience. Regional levels of long-term social development differed greatly, but the disparity in *wartime* events between 1937 and 1945 must also be stressed.

In any event the cycle of mistrust with the Western powers turned out to make a halfway house impossible in Eastern Europe. It led eventually to the open declaration of the "two camps," the creation of a watered-down Comintern in the shape of the Communist Information Bureau (Cominform), the Czechoslovak takeover (March 1948) and the Berlin blockade (June 1948).

Postwar events in Yugoslavia and Greece deserve special mention. Neither had fought alongside the Axis, neither had a common border with the USSR and neither ended the war with a significant presence of Soviet troops or security police within its territory. The Yugoslav leadership, despite Tito's prewar service with the Comintern, was unwilling to accept comprehensive Soviet guidance. When civil war flared up in Greece, the Yugoslavs offered more support to the communist insurgents than Moscow was prepared to give; Stalin wished to avoid a direct rupture with Britain and the USA over a secondary issue.

The situation in China and northern Korea was different again. In the immediate aftermath of the Japanese surrender the Soviet government doubted the early success of the CCP. It was impressed by the buildup of the GMD (Nationalist) army and sensitive to American support for Chiang Kai-shek's government. In August 1945 the Soviet Union signed a treaty with the GMD government. The Soviet Army's presence in Manchuria until May 1946 played a part, as the occupiers allowed CCP military forces to take control of the smaller towns in the region and transferred to them

26 Chris Cook and John Paxton, *European Political Facts of the Twentieth Century* (5th edn., Basingstoke: Palgrave, 2001), 227–28, 252.

a quantity of captured Japanese weapons, but Stalin kept the CCP at arm's length. Nevertheless, the success of the CCP in gaining control of most of China north of the Yangzi by the spring of 1949 was followed by the collapse of the GMD forces on the mainland and the creation of the People's Republic.

As a result of all these developments, the fortunes of the USSR and the international communist movement were at their height in about 1950. In April of that year, in the aftermath of the communist victory in China and the unexpectedly early Soviet atomic bomb test, the United States produced a secret assessment, the now well-known NSC-68:

> During the span of one generation, the international distribution of power has been fundamentally altered. For several centuries it had proved impossible for any one nation to gain such preponderant strength that a coalition of other nations could not in time face it with greater strength . . . Two complex sets of factors have now basically altered [the] historical distribution of power. First, the defeat of Germany and Japan and the decline of the British and French Empires have interacted with the development of the United States and the Soviet Union in such a way that power has increasingly gravitated to these two centers. Second, the Soviet Union . . . is animated by a new fanatic faith . . . and seeks to impose its absolute authority over the rest of the world.[27]

Numerous criticisms can be directed against NSC-68, but this outline of the two "sets of factors" is basically correct. The events and consequences of World War II were critical to the history of communism. The USSR had become stronger and – at least as important – its main regional rivals on both the Axis and Allied sides had become weaker or had been destroyed. And, unlike in previous conflicts, ideology played a central role. Moreover, the "fanatic faith" was for the moment, in the 1945–50 period, a global and unified one. There was also, as yet, no overt popular discontent evident in states under communist control.

Looking back from sixty-five years after NSC-68, we can see that the war's outcome would have a negative effect on the USSR and on the international communist movement. First of all, especially for the USSR, there was the huge loss of human life and resources. And then, in the postwar years, came high military expenditure and perpetuation of an unbalanced economy. The momentum of communist gains slowed. The "fanatic faith" shattered:

---

27 Thomas H. Etzold and John Lewis Gaddis (eds.), *Containment: Documents on American Policy and Strategy, 1945–1950* (New York: Columbia University Press, 1978), 385.

Yugoslavia was the first crack, in 1948, and then the alliance with the China could not be sustained, especially after the loss of Stalin's prestige. Control of Eastern Europe perpetuated Soviet conflict with the West and stifled reformers in the USSR; to make matter worse, Stalin's successors and Soviet clients could not in the end manage the region. The Western communist parties, although catapulted by the war into a position of unprecedented electoral strength, were excluded from political power. "Total" defeat of the former Axis states proved a limited event, as the noncommunist ones recovered economically (although not as first-rate military powers). The United States, also because of the war, unexpectedly became a nation of "preponderant strength," committed to Europe and Asia, economically successful on an unprecedented scale and now heavily armed in peacetime and with a head start in nuclear weapons. The victory of communism in 1945–50, gained at a very heavy price, proved unsustainable.

Bibliographical Essay

Collections of documents include I. V. Stalin, *O Velikoi otechestvennoi voiny Sovetskogo soiuza* [On the Great Patriotic War of the Soviet Union] (Moscow: OGIZ, 1946). An English translation is available at www.ibiblio.org/hyper war/UN/USSR/GPW/index.html. G. P. Kynin and J. Laufer (eds.), *SSSR i germanskii vopros, 1941–1949. Die UdSSSR und die deutsche Frage, 1941–1949,* 4 vols. (Moscow: Mezhdunarodnye otnosheniia, 2003–12), includes postwar planning papers from 1944 by M. M. Litvinov and I. M. Maiskii.

A general overview is Geoffrey Roberts, *Stalin's Wars: From World War to Cold War, 1939–1953* (New Haven: Yale University Press, 2006). Relevant articles include Silvio Pons, "The Soviet Union and the International Left," in Richard Bosworth and Joseph Maiolo (eds.), *The Cambridge History of the Second World War* (Cambridge: Cambridge University Press, 2015), vol. II, 68–90, and Vladimir O. Pechatnov, "The Soviet Union and the World, 1944–1953," in Melvyn P. Leffler and Odd Arne Westad (eds.), *The Cambridge History of the Cold War* (Cambridge: Cambridge University Press, 2009), vol. I, 90–111.

Evan Mawdsley, *Thunder in the East: The Nazi–Soviet War 1941–1945* (2nd edn., London: Bloomsbury, 2015), covers operational aspects. Vojtech Mastny, *Russia's Road to the Cold War: Diplomacy, Warfare, and the Politics of Communism, 1941–1945* (New York: Columbia University Press, 1979), is still important; the sequel is Mastny, *The Cold War and Soviet Insecurity: The Stalin*

Years (Oxford: Oxford University Press, 1996). Vladislav Zubok and Constantine Pleshakov, *Inside the Kremlin's Cold War: From Stalin to Khrushchev* (Cambridge, MA: Harvard University Press, 1996), provides an important post-Soviet view.

For the period to June 1941, see Silvio Pons, *Stalin and the Inevitable War, 1936–1941* (Portland, OR: Frank Cass, 2002), and Gabriel Gorodetsky, *Grand Delusion: Stalin and the German Invasion of Russia* (New Haven: Yale University Press, 1999). Also important is Silvio Pons, "In the Aftermath of the Age of Wars: The Impact of World War II on Soviet Security Policy," in Silvio Pons and Andrea Romano (eds.), *Russia in the Age of Wars, 1914–1945* (Milan: Feltrinelli, 2000), 277–307.

Norman Naimark and Leonid Gibianskii (eds.), *The Establishment of Communist Regimes in Eastern Europe, 1944–1948* (Boulder: Westview, 1997), provides a useful collection of articles on the general situation in the region. Of works on Western Europe, Elena Aga-Rossi and Victor Zaslavsky, *Stalin and Togliatti: Italy and the Origins of the Cold War* (Stanford: Stanford University Press, 2011), is valuable for communist policy in the West. On Germany there is Norman M. Naimark, *The Russians in Germany: A History of the Soviet Zone of Occupation, 1945–1949* (Cambridge, MA: Harvard University Press, 1995). Soviet relations with the Chinese communists are covered in detail by Dieter Heinzig, *The Soviet Union and Communist China 1945–1950: The Arduous Road to the Alliance* (Armonk, NY: M. E. Sharpe, 2004).

On Stalin, see Robert C. Tucker, *Stalin in Power, 1928–1941: The Revolution from Above* (New York: Norton, 1990), and Erik van Ree, *The Political Thought of Joseph Stalin: A Study in Twentieth-Century Revolutionary Patriotism* (London: RoutledgeCurzon, 2002). Works on senior comrades include Geoffrey Roberts, *Molotov: Stalin's Cold Warrior* (Washington, DC: Potomac Books, 2012), and Kees Boterbloem, *The Life and Times of Andrei Zhdanov, 1896–1948* (Montreal: McGill-Queen's University Press, 2004).

Among the most important memoirs and diaries are Ivo Banac (ed.), *The Diary of Georgi Dimitrov, 1933–1949* (New Haven: Yale University Press, 2003), and Gabriel Gorodetsky (ed.), *The Maisky Diaries: Red Ambassador to the Court of St. James's, 1932–1943* (New Haven: Yale University Press, 2015). Conversations with the elderly Molotov, written down by Feliks Chuev, are in *Molotov Remembers: Inside Kremlin Politics*, ed. Albert Resis (Chicago: Ivan R. Dee, 1993).

2

Anti-Fascist Resistance Movements in Europe and Asia During World War II

ALFRED J. RIEBER

There are few precedents in modern history for the phenomenon called the resistance during World War II. The French irregulars in the Franco-Prussian War, the Russian peasantry rising against the French in 1812 and the Spanish guerrillas in the Peninsular War are approximate cases. But they do not match the complexities or scale of the resistance movements in Europe and Asia from 1937 to 1945. Churchill's call to the UK's Special Operations Executive (SOE) to "set Europe ablaze," Stalin's summons to all "freedom-loving peoples against fascism" and de Gaulle's appeal to all Frenchmen wherever they were to join him in continuing the fight were in their different ways unprecedented acts by statesmen seeking to engage the civilian population of territories under military occupation by their enemies in armed resistance. They reflected a conviction that they were engaged in a unique conflict. The policies of the aggressors were not merely to conquer territory but to dismember states and radically transform the social and political life of the conquered peoples. Yet, these appeals, dramatic as they were, did not prescribe how this resistance was to be organized or what forms it should take. The Allied powers subsequently developed plans and organized support, reflecting their own national interests. However, the resistance movements also developed spontaneously and acquired a strong local character that influenced their contribution to the war effort and their role in the postwar period. Their war aims did not always correspond to those of London, Moscow and the governments-in-exile.

The resistance was never monolithic or unified. Resistance movements may be roughly divided into two groups, reflecting prewar political polarization of European politics between the socialist–communist left and the nationalist right. Under the pressure of wartime conditions, the more radical elements in both camps gained a preponderant role, laying the groundwork for clashes between them verging on or breaking out into civil war. The polarization was more pronounced in Asia and Eastern Europe where parliamentary forms of government were more weakly rooted than in Western Europe.

Before the Soviet Union entered the war, nationalists monopolized the resistance. In China, Chiang Kai-shek assigned 600,000 men to operate behind the Japanese lines, but they soon reached agreements with the Japanese in order to suppress communist guerrillas. Becoming in effect puppet troops, they anticipated playing an active role after the defeat of Japan in restoring Nationalist rule in the occupied territories. In Europe the earliest nationalist resistance groups emerged in 1939–41 from the defeated armies of Poland, Yugoslavia and Greece. Mainly composed of officers and representatives of the prewar elites who refused to cooperate with the occupation authorities, they formed the core of the Polish Home Army, the Serbian Chetniks, the National Democratic Greek League (EDES) and the National and Social Liberation (EKKA) in Greece. Conservative, nationalistic and anti-communist, their programs were largely restorationist in character. Outside Poland they were not successful in mobilizing large numbers, especially among the peasantry who in Eastern Europe constituted the overwhelming majority of the population, and the small urban working class.

By the eve of the war, the communist parties of Europe and Asia had been outlawed or suppressed, except by the parliamentary governments of Western Europe; however, the Czech party was dismantled only after Munich, and the French party outlawed after the outbreak of war. The war reversed their decline as a political force and in China enabled them to survive the anti-communist campaigns of the Guomindang. The communists, schooled in a highly disciplined and conspiratorial organization, were ideally suited to conduct clandestine activities. At the same time, they broadened their social base by mobilizing peasants, women, left-wing noncommunist intellectuals and especially the youth, breaking out of their narrow appeal to the working class alone. They exhibited considerable skill in shaping an ideology of resistance that combined demands for social reform with invocations of the national spirit. In France the communists claimed to be heirs to the traditions of the French Revolution and named their resistance fighters *Franc-tireurs-et-partisans* after the irregulars who had resisted the Prussian occupation of France in 1870–71. In Italy the appeal was to a new Risorgimento, embodied in the Garibaldi Brigades. In the mountains of Greece, resistance leaders revived the symbols, dress and rhetoric of the guerrillas (*andartes*) led by their legendary *kapetanios* who had fought against the Ottoman Turks. Soviet propaganda restored to a place of honor the partisan war of 1812 against the French. Mao's anti-Japanese political discourse drew heavily on aspects of Chinese traditional culture even as he preached land reform. The Yugoslav communists were exceptional, Tito stressing the multinational character of their resistance, aiming to create a new state with equal rights for all nationalities, except the Germans. As a result of reinventing themselves as the most progressive fighting force dedicated to the liberation and reconstruction of their countries, they rapidly acquired a disproportionately large role in the anti-fascist resistance behind the lines of the conventional war almost everywhere except in Poland.

The ground had been prepared before the war for the nationalizing of the communist parties which had served them so well in mobilizing popular support. By the late 1930s the Comintern was no longer an effective organization to regulate and coordinate the activities of local communist parties. It had been hollowed out by factional fights, denunciations, personal rivalries and above all purges unleashed by Stalin and also generated by local cadres. The trauma of the Nazi–Soviet Pact had further shaken the organization. What remained to guide the local parties through the thicket of wartime occupation was an adherence to a belief in the general principles of Marxism-Leninism-Stalinism and more specifically to the line laid down at the Seventh and last Comintern Congress of 1935 calling for a "popular front" of all democratic parties against fascism. During the war, Stalin revived the line but altered its formulation to a "united front" in order to dampen its revolutionary implications. Stalin had anticipated abolishing the Comintern even before the invasion of the Soviet Union. In April 1941, he dismissed the "parochial interests" of the Comintern executive and spelled out his new approach: "The membership of the Com[munist] parties within the Comintern in current conditions facilitates bourgeois persecution of them and the bourgeois plan to isolate them from the masses of their own countries, while it prevents the communist parties from developing independently and resolving their own problems as *national* parties."[1] During the war, contact with foreign communist parties was maintained almost exclusively by shortwave radio broadcasts dictating *Pravda*. Soviet wartime propaganda echoed the

1 Ivo Banac (ed.), *The Diary of Georgi Dimitrov, 1933–1949* (New Haven: Yale University Press, 2003), 156 (20 Apr. 1941).

theme that anti-fascist resistance took on a distinctive nationalizing colora-tion among the wartime allies. Thus, much room remained for interpreta-tion at the local level, especially in the face of unforeseen practical difficulties, balancing the pressure to take action against the need for survival. To be sure, fence-sitting or *attentism* was condemned, but so was adventurism.

Tactical differences also distinguished the communist from the nation-alist resistance. The communists and their allies on the left were more inclined to engage in violent acts including assassinations and guerrilla warfare. The twin objectives of their militancy were to claim a leading role as the most prominent resisters in the anti-fascist cause and to win adher-ents, even if this meant provoking reprisals, which invariably led to an influx of recruits. The nationalists sought, as a rule, to avoid direct clashes with the occupier, preferring to build their organization in preparation for the moment of liberation by the regular armies of the anti-fascist coalition. In an important exception, the Chinese communist leadership was divided over the question of large-scale attacks on the Japanese. Mao opposed them and, after the first, last and disastrous conventional battle with the Japanese army in the fall of 1940, the so-called One Hundred Regiments Incident, his view prevailed. The communists shifted their priority to securing and building up base areas which they gradually expanded until, by the summer of 1944, the liberated territory under their control was inhabited by 90 million people.

In Europe, resistance movements were slow to develop on a large scale even in the occupied territories of the Soviet Union. Everywhere the initial stimulus to mass participation came principally as a response to the policies of the occupying powers and their collaborators. The brutality and atrocities of the Germans and the Japanese and their exploitation of the conquered peoples through requisition and forced labor were major factors in inciting resistance. In Yugoslavia the dismemberment of the country, the rapid break-down of law and order and the Greater Serbia ideology of the Chetniks as well as their collaboration with the occupying armies, opened the way for the communist party, which had been banned, to organize resistance on a national level. The number of partisans fluctuated in different regions in accordance with the fighting. During the winter of 1942–43, for example, the heavy fighting in western Serbia and Bosnia cut their effectives from 150,000 to fewer than 50,000. But they recovered each time, and by the summer of 1944 their numbers had swelled to 650,000. In France the introduction of the Service du travail obligatoire (STO) in February 1943 – after voluntary recruitment had fallen short drafting Frenchmen of military age for forced labor in Germany – triggered strikes and the flight of thousands of young Frenchmen into the *maquis*. The same month, a massive strike by the Greek trade unions wrecked the German plan to introduce a labor draft, allowing thousands to escape into the mountains where the resistance acquired mass proportions for the first time. Similarly, in northern Italy in November 1943 the attempt of Mussolini's rump Salò government to draft young men into a new fascist army sparked large-scale opposition and flight into the mountains, where both men and women joined small bands of leftist anti-fascists including communists. It is estimated that about 80,000 partisans were operating in northern Italy by the summer of 1944.

In the Soviet Union and China, large-scale resistance followed the rhythm of battle. During the initial defeats, the spontaneous actions scattered, and isolated groups of Red Army men and communist officials caught behind the lines to fight on were quickly destroyed. Stalin was at first suspicious of any Soviet citizens who survived under German occupation, and he had opposed any prewar preparation for guerrilla warfare as a sign of defeatism. It was only after Stalingrad and the announcement of an amnesty for collaborators that the numbers of partisans increased significantly. Estimates vary greatly, but there is general agreement that by the summer of 1944 more than 150,000 partisans were operating in Belarus and another 60,000 in Ukraine. By the end of the war, the overall estimates swell to more than 500,000. In China the communists had steadily built up their armies in the center and north until, in 1941, a tight Nationalist blockade and Japanese attacks reduced the numbers of the Eighth Route Army from 400,000 men to 300,000; recovery was slow but by 1945 the communist army numbered more than a million. The Chinese communists also helped build up the guerrilla forces of the Indochinese Communist Party along their joint border, which swept them to power in the August 1945 insurrection against the Japanese occupation.[2]

Large-scale Jewish resistance to the mass killings and deportation was hampered by the indifference or outright anti-Semitism of most of the peasantry in Poland, Lithuania and Ukraine, as well as the German policy of herding the population into ghettos and extermination camps. In 1943, however, there were several ghetto uprisings, notably in Warsaw and

2 Huynh Kim Khánh, *Vietnamese Communism 1925–1945* (Ithaca: Cornell University Press, 1982), 282, 308–12, 319–29.

Vilnius. The young Jewish resisters received only limited aid from the Polish resistance. In general, the attitude of the Polish Home Army toward the Jews was highly ambiguous. The Polish resistance had been the first to inform the world about the genocidal policy of the Nazis. But the initial sympathy of the leadership inspired by General Władysław Sikorski in London and General Stefan Rowecki in the underground gave way under new leadership in 1943 to a more hostile attitude toward Jews. This was in certain cases a reaction to the anti-Semitism of the population which identified the Jews with Bolshevism. The Home Army (Armia Krajowa, AK) refused to accept Jews in their ranks. In the northeast provinces, local AK commanders denounced small bands of Jewish partisans as bandits or pro-Soviet and attacked them. The advance of the Red Army widened the gap. The Poles anticipated and feared Soviet domination; the Jews greeted the Russians as liberators. Jews fought as individuals in the Warsaw uprising, but often took the precaution of concealing their identity.[3] Meanwhile, the Soviet command discouraged the formation of purely Jewish partisan units, and gradually absorbed them into larger partisan detachments.

The military effectiveness of the resistance movements has been widely disputed. Fulsome praise has come from General Dwight Eisenhower, who estimated that their activity during the liberation of Western Europe was the equivalent of ten divisions, while Field Marshal Sir Harold Alexander declared that the partisans in the Balkans held down six German divisions and prevented them from intervening in the Italian campaign. Such neat evaluations break down completely in China. Many factors have to be considered. There was no liberation from the outside, except in Manchuria, and the Japanese army in mainland China remained undefeated at the end of the war. Moreover, the communists and Nationalists at various times were much more heavily engaged in fighting one another than the Japanese. Throughout the war, the Nationalists maintained large forces blockading the communists in their northern base areas, thus weakening their ability to fight a conventional war against the Japanese. Toward the end of the war, both sides appeared to be more interested in preparing for a postwar struggle than a united military front against Japan. In military terms, the anti-fascist resistance in the Soviet Union was probably the most effective of all. This was due in large part to the creation of Central Partisan

---

3 Joshua D. Zimmerman, *The Polish Underground and the Jews, 1939–1945* (Cambridge: Cambridge University Press, 2015), synthesizes the vast literature.

Command to coordinate the sabotage of German communication lines and diversionary attacks behind the lines in tandem with Red Army offensive operations. But the partisans were also forced to engage in fighting anti-Soviet units, some cooperating with the Wehrmacht, others – such as the Ukrainian Insurgent Army (Ukrains'ka povstans'ka armiia, UPA) – fighting against both Soviet and German armies.[4] In most countries, the resistance movements suffered higher casualties in the armed struggle than the occupation forces, even without taking into account the terrible reprisals inflicted on the civilian population in retaliation for violent acts, ranging from assassinations to diversionary attacks.[5]

The very nature of resistance forced the communists into entanglements with other anti-fascist resistance groups, the general population and the collaborationists. These varied greatly over time from country to country. The most effective cooperation with noncommunist anti-fascists took the form of united front organizations. Among these the most successful were those inaugurated in France, Yugoslavia and Greece. At the same time, the rivalry between the nationalists and communist-dominated fronts in Yugoslavia and Greece sparked outright civil war. The situation in Slovakia was the most complex of all. Although the communists participated in the uprising of October 1944, their failure first to inform and then to coordinate with Moscow aroused suspicions that this was another version of the Warsaw Uprising. Despite subsequent appeals for Soviet help, the rising was abandoned.[6] In Poland deep mistrust virtually precluded any contact between the communists and the Home Army. In China the communist–Nationalist front broke down several times, ending in a hostile standoff.

In Western Europe, antagonism between the two resistance camps was muted. In France the National Council of the Resistance formed with de Gaulle's endorsement in 1943 brought together members of eight resistance organizations, including six prewar parties of the center and left and two trade unions; sympathizers among its members enabled the communists to

4 Leonid D. Grenkevich, *The Soviet Partisan Movement, 1941–1944: A Critical Historiographical Analysis* (London: Frank Cass, 1999).
5 Exact figures are hard to come by, but see the chapters in István Deák, *Europe on Trial: The Story of Collaboration, Resistance, and Retribution During World War II* (Boulder: Westview Press, 2015).
6 Rossiiskii gosudarstvennyi arkhiv sotsial'noi i politicheskoi istorii (RGASPI), f. 17, op. 28, 1–7, 79, 82. To correct the line, Klement Gottwald urged the partisans to adopt the Yugoslav tactics: *ibid.*, 8 and 20.

influence the draft program for postwar France. Resisters loyal to de Gaulle, mainly former officers, formed the Armée secrète which, while maintaining distant contact with the communists, emerged in 1944 to become the core of France's restored regular army together with *Franc-tireurs* militants. In Belgium a small but active group of officers calling itself variously Légion belge and Armée secrète maintained an apolitical stance, loyal to the government-in-exile but separate from the communist armed resistance which was decimated by the Germans in 1943. The return to Italy from Moscow of Palmiro Togliatti with his message of a united resistance against fascism, the so-called Salerno turn, enabled the Italian communists – like the French – to join other anti-fascist groups in fighting a civil war against Mussolini's rump government in the north of the country and liberating several large cities on their own.

Relations with the majority of the occupied population were even more complex. Played out in what has been called a grey or twilight zone, they could change from day to day or day to night. Responsive to the tides of war, many individuals moved from a passive to an active stance as the occupying armies retreated, giving rise to the phenomenon known as resisters of the last moment. The ambiguities of resistance plagued even the communists, especially in France, where they had adopted a form of collaboration during the Nazi–Soviet Pact. In Yugoslavia both the partisans and the Chetniks sought to reach an accommodation with the Germans in order to devote their main efforts to fighting one another; this gamble did not, however, work for the partisans, and the deal collapsed. The problem of authenticating a claim to have resisted became acute after the war, when resistance acquired an almost mythical aura, promoted by the victors to cover the shame of a rapid surrender or the wartime existence of an overly cooperative pro-fascist puppet regime. Similar problems exist in attempting to define who was a collaborator. How to categorize a public official who continued to serve the occupation authorities but claimed to have saved Jews by providing false papers for which there was no record? What did it mean, after all, to resist?

At the most basic level, resistance may be demonstrated by any clandestine, sometimes armed but always hostile reaction to foreign occupation that exposed an individual to arrest, deportation or execution. Clearly, then, there was ample room for a great variety of resistance activities. They ranged from such "small deeds and hidden transcripts" as scrawling graffiti on the walls of public buildings to carrying out sabotage or assassinations, engaging in guerrilla warfare or creating "free zones." They include intelligence gathering, concealing Jews or helping them to escape abroad, rescuing Allied airmen, taking part in strikes, morale-building through writing, publishing and distributing clandestine literature, and promoting social reforms in regions under communist control, especially equal civil rights for women. The scale and form of resistance depended on a number of factors. Partisan warfare could be sustained only in favorable geographical locations: the mountainous regions of the Balkans, the densely wooded areas of Belarus and eastern Poland. But there were disadvantages too. They were thinly populated with limited access to food supplies, restricting the size of bands and their ability to engage in prolonged periods of fighting. With the exception of northern Italy, the communists generally avoided urban insurrections unless a liberating army was within striking distance. In Europe, the communist response to liberation reflected their recognition of geopolitical realities. The leadership of the French Communist Party discouraged a mass uprising to liberate Paris before the arrival of the Allied armies as politically unwise, while the Moscow and the Polish communists condemned the Warsaw Uprising by the Home Army as premature, adventurist and politically motivated. The liberation of Athens by the communist-dominated ELAS (the Greek People's National Army of Liberation) following the German withdrawal was exceptional and not favored by Stalin, but there was no Allied army in the vicinity.

The disintegration of the resistance into civil war in Yugoslavia, Greece, Albania, Ukraine and China each had its unique features but there is good reason here to stress the common elements. In these five countries the resistance movements more profoundly influenced the postwar nature of the state and society than anywhere else in Europe or Asia. To a great degree this was the result of the uncompromising character of the armed struggle. This reflected in turn the long history of social and ethnic conflicts exacerbated by the violence of World War I, its aftermath and the brutality of the occupation. Finally, these were all predominantly peasant societies with long traditions of rural rebellion against exploitation by domestic and foreign landlords.

Resistance in Greece and Yugoslavia: Similarities and Differences

Selecting the Greek and Yugoslav resistance as case studies reveals their common and contrasting features, their links with other movements in southeastern Europe and outcomes at odds with their respective mass support. These two resistance movements (and the Albanian under Yugoslav tutelage) possessed several distinctive characteristics. They were committed to radically remaking their respective nations from within, maintaining only the most tenuous ties with their governments-in-exile which they did not accept as the basis for a postwar regime. They were strongly communist but followed their own path and received little or no aid from the Soviet Union. They fought against the occupying forces and, in a fierce civil war, against the indigenous nationalist resistance which they defeated.

The split in the Greek resistance movement was rooted in deep prewar social fissures. The ordeal of World War I split the country into two hostile camps, beginning "the national schism" that plagued the country throughout the rest of the twentieth century and beyond. One side was devoted to the charismatic leader of the Liberal Party, Eleftherios Venizelos. Committed to the "Megale Idea" of a Greater Greece of "five seas and two continents," he was determined to lead the country into World War I on the Allied side, even though this meant breaking with the pro-German king and plunging the country into a constitutional crisis. His action sparked a virtual civil war between the royalist "State of Athens" and his own rebellious provisional government, the "State of Thessaloniki." Venizelos's attempt to bring the Greek-speaking population of western Anatolia into a Greater Greece led to a disastrous defeat, a massive flight and a population exchange with Turkey that swelled the population of northern Thrace by more than 600,000 immigrants. Their influx diluted the ethnic composition of Thrace and Macedonia, reducing the Slavonic-speakers to a small minority. Initially hostile to the left, these immigrants later became the bulwark of the communist resistance in the region. When the Greek Communist Party reorganized itself in 1930 about half the Central Committee and almost all the members of the Politburo including the secretary general, Nikos Zachariadis, came from the immigrant population of the north.

Emerging in 1928–30 as a real political force, the communists picked up strength from the Venizelists as the depression cut into their constituency of workers and poor peasants. It skillfully exploited the appeals of the popular front, reknitting the divided trade union movement. But it barely survived the coup of General Ioannis Metaxas in 1936. The German invasion probably saved the communists from extinction as it did elsewhere in the Balkans. Their domination of the active resistance movement in Greece was due as much to the political errors of the traditional right as to their own efforts, vigorous as they were. By fleeing the country, King

George II forfeited the loyalty of many of his citizens. The old anti-monarchist sentiment revived with renewed passion.

The split in the Yugoslav resistance had its roots in prewar problems. Assembled in 1918, Yugoslavia was a composite multicultural state. In addition to the three major national groups – Serbs, Croats and Slovenes – there were numerous smaller nationalities including Albanians, Montenegrins, Macedonians, Muslims and Jews. They emerged from different historical experiences: Croatia, Slovenia and Illyria had been part of the Habsburg monarchy; Bosnia and Herzegovina had long languished under Ottoman rule; Serbia and Montenegro struggled throughout the nineteenth century to win independence from the Ottoman Empire. The newly established Kingdom of the Serbs, Croats and Slovenes, later renamed Yugoslavia, although technically a federation, was dominated by the Serbians. Even before the German invasion, the country was racked by internal dissension over the establishment of a legitimate system of representation for all the nationalities. It was only on the eve of the war that the Croatian Peasant Party succeeded in reaching an agreement with Belgrade granting Croatia a modicum of autonomy. Under the shock of defeat and occupation by the Germans, Italians and Bulgarians, Yugoslavia broke up along ethnoterritorial lines. Permitting the existence of puppet governments in a quasi-independent Croatia and a rump Serbia, the occupying powers parceled out the remainder of its fragmented parts. By contrast, the Yugoslav Communist Party, outlawed since 1920, had adopted a new federalist policy on the national question after the Seventh Comintern Congress in 1935, providing the partisans with a strong rallying point by appealing to the idea of the equality of the nationalities. In the resistance, Tito's inner circle was composed of men of different nationalities, Edvard Kardelj, a Slovene, Milovan Djilas, a Montenegrin, Moša Pijade, a Serbian Jew, Aleksandar Ranković, a Serb, and Lola Ribar, a Croat, while Tito was himself half-Croat. The Central Committee was equally balanced. This line-up contrasted sharply with the exclusively Serb leadership of the Chetniks, who also promoted a Greater Serb ideology, and the nationalist composition of the collaborationists in Slovenia, Croatia and Serbia. This characteristic of the Yugoslav partisan resistance contributed to the creation of a genuine federal structure in Yugoslavia after the war.

Early in the occupation of Greece, fighting broke out between armed bands of republican nationalist officers and elements of the left-wing communist-dominated EAM (National Liberation Front)/ELAS over leadership and tactics in the resistance, replicating what was happening in Yugoslavia between the Chetniks and the partisans. It is customary to divide the civil war into three "rounds," from mid October 1943 to March 1944, from December 1944 to the Varkiza Truce Agreement in February 1945, and the fall of 1946 to late summer 1949. The first round was an attempt by the EAM/ELAS to impose unity on the resistance as a prelude to reconstructing the Greek government-in-exile. The second was the result of British intervention in the jockeying for power that followed the liberation; and the third – the most prolonged and bloody phase – featured a direct communist challenge to the right-wing repression that followed the return of the government-in-exile, leading to direct American intervention.

The attempts of ELAS to unify the resistance led to some bizarre twists and turns. In the spring of 1943 it broke up a band headed by General Stefanos Sarafis, a professional soldier, and then recruited him to become its chief military officer/commander-in-chief. The same tactic failed to draft the head of the main nationalist band, Napoleon Zervas of EDES, into its ranks. At the same time, the uncontrollable bandit-revolutionary Aris Velouchiotis, nominally under EAM, wielded a bludgeon to annihilate rival bands. The internecine conflict prompted the British to help negotiate a National Bands Agreement. It committed EAM to cooperating fully with the Allied Mediterranean Command. A Joint Military Headquarters was established in the mountains to coordinate all resistance activity in order to draw off German forces from Italy and facilitate the Allied landings. The fragile truce shortly broke down. In October the British failed to reconcile "mountain Greece" with the government-in-exile in Cairo. Echoing the past, the constitutional conflict proved irreconcilable, "mountain Greece" demanding a plebiscite before the return of the king. Following Italy's surrender, its disintegrating occupation forces turned over massive quantities of arms to EAM, freeing it from dependence on British supplies. Zervas began withdrawing his men from the fighting against the Germans to end the reprisals and avoid annihilation by the reinforced German army in Greece. Although he resisted collaborating with them, ELAS attacked him.

In March 1944 the Greek communists took the lead in creating the Political Committee of National Liberation (Politiki Epitropi Ethikis Apeleftherosis, PEEA), a virtual government modeled on the Anti-Fascist Council of the National Liberation of Yugoslavia (Antifašističko vijeće narodnog oslobođenja Jugoslavije, AVNOJ) formed in November 1943. Like the Yugoslavs, the Greek communists also masked their predominant influence in the underground state and conducted elections in the territory under the control of EAM. By this time, it was clear that the major external influence on the Greek communists was coming from Yugoslavia and the example of Tito, not from the Soviet Union. In Moscow Georgi Dimitrov had already warned Tito the year before about the dangers of turning AVNOJ into a quasi-government.[7] The aims of the Greek communists were, however, more moderate; their intention was to force their government-in-exile into sharing power after the war rather than, as in the case of the Yugoslav communists, taking it.

Tito had already shown signs of using the partisans to expand the influence of the Yugoslav communists outside his borders by influencing the resistance movements in neighboring countries. He exerted a dominant role in shaping the Bulgarian and Albanian resistance. Before the arrival in western (Yugoslav) Macedonia, under Italian and Albanian occupation, of Tito's emissary, Svetozar Vukmanović Tempo, the Bulgarian resistance was small-scale. Tempo organized large partisan detachments which also operated in eastern Macedonia under Bulgarian occupation. Backed by Stalin, the Yugoslav communists took back political control of the Macedonian Communist Party from the Bulgarians. Tito was determined to incorporate all of Macedonia, including the Pirin dis-trict which had been part of Bulgaria. The Yugoslav organization of the resistance helped win him a partial victory when the postwar Bulgarian government recognized the autonomy of Pirin Macedonia. But it was an ephemeral victory doomed by the Soviet–Yugoslav break in 1948.[8] Tito also displayed a vigorous hand in the more active Albanian resistance. In October–November 1941, a Yugoslav emissary, Miladin Popović, had served as midwife to the birth of the Albanian Communist Party by over-coming factional differences. Following the Yugoslav lead, the Albanian communists created a National Liberation Committee together with other resistance bands, although the style, slogans and program bore a greater resemblance to the more moderate PEEA. But the Yugoslavs intervened again when the Albanians sought to reach an accommodation with the nationalist organization, Balli Kombëtar, which had entered into relations

---

7 Yuri S. Girenko, *Stalin–Tito* (Moscow: Izd. politicheskoi literatury, 1992), 146. For the argument that Tito was moving toward the construction of an alternative Comintern to Stalin, see Geoffrey Swain, "The Cominform: Tito's International?," *Historical Journal* 35, 3 (Sep. 1992), esp. 649–51.

8 John D. Bell, *The Bulgarian Communist Party from Blagoev to Zhivkov* (Stanford: Hoover Institution Press, 1986), 64–68, 100–01.

with the Italian occupation authorities. For the Yugoslavs, this was the equivalent of cooperating with the Chetniks.[9] When the Germans began withdrawing from Albania in October 1944, Tito order the arrest of prominent Albanians in Kosovo and collection of arms. This touched off an armed uprising, led by Balli Kombëtar, which took the Yugoslavs more than eight months to repress, leaving behind deep resentments. During the war, Tito's attempt to expand the influence of the partisans into the Austrian provinces annexed by Germany through Slovenia were less successful due in part to the weakness of the Austrian resistance. Following the incursion of the partisans into Austria in 1945, he hoped to absorb part of Carinthia into a Greater Slovenia but met with firm opposition from the Allied Combined Chiefs of Staff.

In his imperialist mood, Tito was also unhappy with the compromises that the Greek communists were making under British pressure. But Tito lacked the resources to impose on the Greeks his version of the resistance as a springboard to power. And the Greek communists lacked the unified leadership of the Yugoslavs, to say nothing of having a Tito at their head; unlike Tito they had to face the full power of a British intervention. By early 1944, the fate of the resistance in southeastern Europe was becoming increasingly dependent on international politics, shaped by military considerations. By the end of 1943 Tito had survived six major Axis offensives. In February 1944, the British and, more reluctantly the Americans, had taken the decision to break off relations with Draža Mihailović because of his collaboration with the Germans. Under British pressure, the Yugoslav government-in-exile agreed to denounce him and reach an agreement for a coalition government with Tito. Although the partisans received an overwhelming quantity of military equipment, clothing and food from Anglo-American air drops, relations with the representatives of the Allied military missions within the country deteriorated toward the end of the war as the Red Army approached the borders of Yugoslavia.

Stalin had stayed his hand until the military-strategic and diplomatic situation shifted in his favor. Throughout the war Stalin and Dimitrov had repeatedly urged Tito to restrain his revolutionary impulses. It was only in February 1944 that Stalin authorized a military mission to Yugoslavia. A year later, he was still warning the Yugoslav communists: "You have

---

9 The following is based mainly on RGASPI, f. 17, op. 128, d. 267, "Albanskaia kommu-nisticheskaia partiia," by the Soviet ambassador in Albania, written in May 1947 before the Soviet–Yugoslav break.

created a situation in which you are at odds with Romania, Hungary and Greece, intending to take on the whole world; don't think of creating such a situation . . . It does not pay to fight with England." The Greek communists had made a mistake, he added, in leaving the coalition.[10] The Yugoslavs reluctantly agreed to Soviet advice to form a coalition with representatives of the royal government-in-exile and reach an accommodation with the Western Allies on their frontiers with Italy and Austria. But there were tense moments when the partisans attempted to occupy Trieste and were faced down by British Commonwealth troops. Building on the mass appeal of the resistance, they rapidly converted the bogus coalition front into a "people's democracy."

The outcome of the entanglement of the resistance with the great powers was dramatically different in Greece. The electoral tactics of PEEA convinced the British and the Greek government-in-exile of the need to seek a compromise with "mountain Greece." Following a mutiny in the Greek Army in Egypt over the constitutional issue, the rival political groups agreed to meet under British auspices and hammered out the Lebanon Charter of 20 May 1944. The communist representatives agreed to enter a coalition government for the first time in Greek history. EAM was promised five cabinet posts out of fifteen. Further negotiations provoked a dual crisis that foreshadowed fiercer struggles ahead. Differences surfaced within the left while the anti-communist moderate republicans moved to the right, once again threatening to polarize Greek politics on the eve of the liberation. In an effort to create a political center, the British threw their weight behind Georgios Papandreou, a staunch anti-communist republican who had been a loyal follower of Venizelos and an associate of Sarafis before he moved over to become military chief of ELAS. His memo, *Pan-Slavist Communism and Anglo-American Liberalism*, had impressed them. He confided to his republican colleagues that once he was installed as premier he intended to break EAM by force.[11]

As early as May 1944 Churchill had come to a verbal agreement with Stalin over their respective interests in Greece and Romania. But Churchill was not convinced. He wrote to Roosevelt on 23 June that the only way to prevent anarchy in Greece was "by persuading the Russians to quit boosting EAM and

10 Galina P. Murashko et al. (eds.), *Vostochnaia Evropa v dokumentakh rossiiskikh arkhivov 1944–1953* (2 vols., Moscow and Novosibirsk: Sibirskii Khronograf, 1998), vol. I, doc. 37, 130–32, conversation between Stalin and Andrija Hebrang.
11 John L. Hondros, *Occupation and Resistance: The Greek Agony, 1941–1944* (New York: Pella Publishing Company, 1983), 215–19.

ramming it forward with all their forces."[12] Contrary to his fears, the Soviet diplomatic representative in Cairo and the head of the first Soviet military mission to Free Greece, Colonel Grigorii Popov, cautioned moderation and made it clear that EAM was on its own. After Churchill won the approval of Roosevelt, Stalin made no objection to the British occupation of Athens as the Germans pulled out, officially recognizing that right on 23 September 1944. The Greek communists then agreed to place their armed guerrillas under the authority of the Papandreou government of national unity and the UK military command of Lt. General Ronald Scobie, who landed with 10,000 men. At about the same time, the Italian and French communist resistance had taken similar action, not without some internal friction. The three countries were within the sphere of Western military operations. Not surprisingly, Stalin expected the noncommunist underground in Poland to follow suit by recognizing the Soviet sphere of military operations and placing itself under Soviet military command. When this did not happen, the Soviet army and secret police moved to arrest the officers and coerce the rank and file of the Home Army into the Polish units of the Red Army.

The political agreement broke down soon after the Papandreou government, with the communist ministers, returned to Athens in the midst of joyous celebrations. There was no indication that EAM/ELAS intended to seize power. Observers at the time and scholars since have differed over the responsibility for the outbreak of violence culminating in Churchill's notorious order to General Scobie to treat Athens as a conquered city and hold it "with bloodshed if necessary." The clash between EAM and the British troops, supported by the security battalions, touched off the second round of the civil war. When neither side could prevail after a month of fighting, a truce was arranged at Varkiza. In the subsequent negotiations it was the turn of the communists to overreach themselves by demanding almost 50 percent of the new cabinet and a plebiscite on the return of the king. The truce broke down. EAM left the coalition, touching off a third round. The external support of the Greek right by Britain and then the United States and the indifference of Stalin were the decisive factors in leading to the defeat and repression of the communists. This brought to an end the entire program of socioeconomic reform which had grown out of the resistance and won over the majority of the Greek population. The different outcomes of the

---

12 US Department of State, *Foreign Relations of the United States, 1944* (Washington, DC: US Government Printing Office, 1944), vol. IV, 126–27.

Greek and Yugoslav resistance movements, similar though they were, fore-shadowed the coming of the Cold War.

Youth and Women in the Resistance

One of the great strengths of the communist resistance was its success in mobilizing youth and women, two supraclass, nontraditional social groups that occupied subordinate, often subservient niches in the patri-archal peasant societies of Eastern Europe and Asia. In the early 1920s, the Comintern had sponsored a youth international which held congresses and fostered the organization of national youth movements along parallel lines with the communist parties. They competed with and attempted to penetrate socialist youth organizations, gaining an advantage on the eve of the war. The international socialist youth organization had opted for the slogan "the struggle for peace," after a fierce internal fight in which the Scandinavian organizations prevailed over the more revolutionary-minded Latin organizations, spearheaded by the Spanish movement which had come under the control of the communists during the Spanish Civil War.[13]

Throughout occupied Europe during the war, the organized participation of youth in social, cultural and political activities assumed unprecedented proportions. Ever since 1789, youth had taken a major role in revolutionary and nationalist movements, inspired by lofty idealism, willing to take risks and strengthened by a sense of solidarity with their classmates and schools. In Yugoslavia, the war opened up new possibilities for the Young Communist League (Savez komunističke omladine Jugoslavije, SKOJ) founded in 1919. Banned two years later, it held clandestine congresses in the 1920s and early 1930s. At the Sixth Congress of the Young Communist International in 1935, Dimitrov had urged the national organizations to form anti-fascist fronts without waiting for agreements between the political parties. On the eve of war, members of SKOJ clashed at the University of Belgrade with the fascist youth organization of the White Eagles. The clandestine regional committees of SKOJ had built up a large following which threw itself into the partisan movement from the beginning. At Bihac in 1942, the communist youth finally succeeded in bringing all local groups into a United League of Anti-Fascist Youth of Yugoslavia, but the SKOJ maintained its own

13 Christine Bouneau, "La jeunesse socialiste et l'action international durant l'entre-deux-guerres," *Le mouvement social* 228, 2 (2008), 41–53.

autonomous organization within the movement. Throughout the war, the anti-fascist youth in Yugoslavia were far more closely controlled by the communists than a similar movement in Greece. And, unlike the Greek youth movement, which was suppressed following the third round of the civil war, SKOJ blossomed after the war into the People's Youth and then the League of Socialist Youth of Yugoslavia, remaining active until its dissolution in 1991.

In Greece in particular, many young people felt keenly the humiliation of defeat, occupation and the political failure of traditional elites, who had fled the country with the king or withdrawn from public activities, leaving the population exposed to the brutality of the occupation and the devastating famine that wracked the country in the fierce winter of 1941–42. Thus, the ground was well prepared for the EAM in February 1943 to unify ten leftist youth organizations under the banner of the United Panhellenic Organization of Youth (EPON). Among its participating organizations were the communist, socialist, peasant and young women's youth movements. They were in the forefront of the urban protests that forced the collaborationist government to discontinue its program of mobilizing young workers for forced labor in Germany. EPON took special pride in sponsoring cultural activities and providing for the education of children. Thousands of young girls defied parental authority and rural conventions to risk their lives as helpers in supplying food for the *andartes*, spreading propaganda and serving as nurses in the mountain redoubts.[14]

In evaluating the impact of the resistance experience on postwar mass politics, the changes in the status and social role of women occupy a prominent place. Varying from country to country, the results were significant everywhere, although not without contradictions and ambiguities, especially when compared to the expectations aroused during the war. In a few countries, such as Yugoslavia and China, the ground had been prepared for change by prewar women's organizations, but the war accelerated the trend toward greater rights for women. Active at all levels of the resistance up to and including combat, women who participated, like men, came from all levels of society, from university students to peasants, and were overwhelmingly young in age. The most striking gender-specific changes were recorded in the patriarchal peasant societies of Yugoslavia, China, Albania, Greece and Vietnam, as the barriers to women's participation

---

14 Mark Mazower, *Inside Hitler's Greece: The Experience of Occupation, 1941–1944* (New Haven: Yale University Press, 1993), 14–15, 279–80.

in political activities broke down. The brutal nature of the occupation authorities, supported by the collaborationists, threatened women's traditional role as nurturers and protectors of the hearth. Gender imbalances as a result of labor drafts, deportations and flight into the forests and mountains to join the partisans forced women to take responsibility for holding communities together under painfully difficult circumstances.

Under clandestine circumstances, women carried out tasks for which they were well suited, such as intelligence gathering and serving as couriers, where they were less likely than men to fall under suspicion. In Italy for example, the *staffetta* (courier) riding her bicycle, transmitting messages and distributing underground newspapers or even arms, became an icon of the resistance. More unusual, the women warrior, the *partizanka*, made a debut, to the consternation of the Italian fascists and Wehrmacht troopers inculcated with the masculine mystique. In Yugoslavia, according to postwar official figures, of 5.7 million participants in the communist resistance, 2 million were women, with 100,000 classified as fighters suffering disproportionate casualties: 25,000 dead and 40,000 wounded. Almost three-quarters of the total were under twenty years of age, the majority from peasant backgrounds. Two thousand women served as officers.

Women were also mobilized into the Anti-Fascist Front of Women (Savez Antifašistička fronta žena, AFZ) with a broad program of promoting the war effort, but also helping to build a power base for the communist party in the postwar era. Women were attracted by the party's promises of equal civil rights for women and, as many memoirs demonstrate, the magnetic personality of Tito. They were also repelled by the hostile attitude toward women's participation in mass movements publicly adopted by the nationalist resistance, the Chetniks of Draža Mihailović. So, too, the positive image of women in early Bolshevik propaganda was more widespread in Yugoslavia than elsewhere in the Balkans, not to speak of Poland. The partisans recruited heavily among women in traditional Muslim communities of west Bosnia and Bosanska Krajina where Ustaše massacres had emptied the villages of males and Chetnik propaganda called all partisan women "whores."[15]

Women's role in the Greek resistance was similar in many ways. But the mobilizing discourse was more populist than communist. In particular, the

---

15 Barbara Jancar-Webster, *Women and Revolution in Yugoslavia, 1941–1945* (Denver: Arden Press, 1990); Marko Attila Hoare, *Genocide and Resistance in Hitler's Bosnia: The Partisans and the Chetniks, 1941–1943* (Oxford: Oxford University Press, 2006), 285–90.

irredentist Megali idea, popular in the nineteenth century, had a greater appeal than the invocations of Stalin and the Communist Party of the Soviet Union. Equal rights for women were strongly articulated in the May 1944 constitution of the Political Committee of National Liberation. Giving women the right to vote for the first time resulted in the election of a number of women's deputies to the government of Free Greece. In response to the terrible famine of 1941, when 3,000 died of starvation, EAM's large-scale organization of soup kitchens was largely managed by women. The mass campaign of EAM to block the deportation of laborers to Germany also elicited a strong response from women. In both these cases, the mobilization of women paradoxically evoked a defense of the traditional moral code and emotional ties deeply imbedded in the sense of family, neighborhood and community violated by foreign occupation. Women fighters were less visible than in Yugoslavia. The leadership of PEEA endorsed the idea and, although official statistics are lacking, a few women rose to prominence in the partisan Officer Training School.[16] Less is known about women in the Albanian resistance. Figures released only in 1984 gave a number of 6,000 participants in the National Liberation Movement, including a few combatants.[17] With the victory of the right in Greece, women's rights suffered a sharp reversal. Even in Yugoslavia the party retreated from its most advanced social positions.

Counterintuitively, women in less culturally developed countries played a proportionately larger role with a greater margin of improvement in their place in postwar societies than in countries such as France. The participation of women in the French resistance was far less significant than in other major countries, amounting to no more than 11 percent of the resisters, none occupying positions of influence or engaged in combat. Women in the Italian resistance occupied a position closer to that in the Balkans. Unlike the latter, however, their participation was not so exclusively controlled by the communist party. Women could be found as well in the partisan units organized by the socialists and radical republicans (Partito d'Azione) despite the widespread chauvinistic attitude of Italian men, extolled by Mussolini, who took a jaundiced view of women in male roles, especially as guerrilla fighters. In the late summer of 1944, there were an estimated 55,000 women

---

16 Janet Hart, *New Voices in the Nation: Women and the Greek Resistance, 1941–1964* (Ithaca: Cornell University Press, 1996).

17 Edwin E. Jacques, *The Albanians: An Ethnic History from Prehistoric Times to the Present* (Jefferson, NC, and London: McFarland & Co., 1995), 418, quoting *Zëri i Populit*, the official publication of the Albanian Communist Party.

out of a total of 200,000 partisans.[18] Women also volunteered for other dangerous work as couriers and radio operators as well as helping to organize strikes, especially in the textile factories.

In China the Nationalist Guomindang limited their organization of women for resistance against the Japanese to promoting conventional gender roles. Even before the war, they relied on women of the urban, educated class, such as the very visible figure of Soong May-ling, "Madame Chiang," to spread their message. After the Japanese invaded, she assumed a public role in promoting social welfare programs, especially the care of orphans of Nationalist soldiers. The communists embraced a far more radical position, but pronounced regional differences and the exceptionally long period of their war make generalizations risky. Overall, communist propaganda and organizational activities emphasized the need to involve women in productive work in order to provide food and clothing for the guerrilla forces and to participate in struggle meetings against the landlords. In rural areas of both occupied and unoccupied China, the communists faced enormous social and cultural obstacles to their campaigns to mobilize women. Patriarchal domination of the family was all but universal, with women being regarded and treated little better than beasts of burden. Foot binding, female infanticide and absence of any legal or civil rights condemned women to a life of unremitting toil and suffering.[19] From its earliest days, the Chinese Communist Party preached against this gendered stranglehold by admitting women into its ranks. But the pace slowed down during the first years of the united front in order to avoid friction with the Nationalists. There was always a discrepancy between Mao's progressive rhetoric and his treatment of women.

With the outbreak of war in 1937 the party stepped up its efforts by creating women's associations. Regional differences showed up, for example, in rural areas of eastern and central China where the party recognized women as citizens and extended them the right to vote for the first time and even approved their membership on election committees. Yet even here, in certain districts of Kiangsi province, the term "citizen" was misrepresented as applying only to males. In central Anhui, one of the poorest provinces, an attempt by party organizations to prohibit the political activities of any family member – that is, women and youth – ran into stiff opposition in the village

18 Jane Slaughter, *Women in the Italian Resistance, 1943–1945* (Denver: Arden Press, 1997), 33.
19 A vivid eyewitness account is Jack Belden, *China Shakes the World* (New York: Monthly Review, 1970 [1st edn. Harper, 1949]), esp. ch. 43.

communities.[20] The advance of women's rights was more rapid in the front-line areas, but even here their roles were largely confined to providing care and moral support to the men. In China, as in most countries, the euphoria of women's liberation dissipated rapidly after the war, with the gradual restoration of the old social order during the Cold War, leaving legal equality and the right to vote as the most significant gains.[21]

The resistance movements did not end in 1945. In France, Belgium, Italy, Yugoslavia, Albania and the Soviet Union, most notably, a fierce postwar *épuration* of collaborators killed thousands and banished many more from public life. Thousands of Spanish exiles from the civil war who had fought in the *maquis* of southwestern France against the Germans launched an ill-fated invasion, organized by the Spanish Communist Party, of Franco Spain. It quickly degenerated into a miasma of betrayal, denunciations and assassinations.[22] Jewish "avengers" (Nokmim) tracked down and killed an unknown number of Nazis. Having wrapped themselves in nationalist colors and promoting social programs, the communists in Belgium, France and Italy became mass parties, achieving legitimacy in parliamentary governments, and registering up to a quarter of the popular vote in the decade or more after the war. The high hopes in some noncommunist resistance groups, especially in France, of creating a great "resistance party" after the war that would unite those who had come together to fight fascism were disappointed. In Western Europe the old parties reasserted their control over politics. Nevertheless, the legacy of the resistance was deeply felt in the greater extension of social rights. In Eastern Europe a parallel disappointment was registered by those, including many communists, who believed that the anti-fascist front organizations would retain their form and function in easing the transition between capitalism and socialism through the creation of "people's democracies." The coming of the Cold War hard on the heels of the liberation doomed these efforts as well. Nevertheless, in Yugoslavia and Czechoslovakia, the communist resistance guaranteed equal rights for the major nationalities in a federal state structure. In Yugoslavia, Albania, China and Vietnam, the

20 Yung-fa Chen, *Making Revolution: The Communist Movement in Eastern and Central China, 1937–1945* (Berkeley: University of California Press, 1986), 233–39. Even greater variation between social activism and passivity existed in northern Henan. See David S. G. Goodman, "Revolutionary Women and Women in the Revolution: The Chinese Communist Party and Women in the War of Resistance to Japan, 1937–1945," *China Quarterly* 164 (Dec. 2000), 915–42.

21 Kay Ann Johnson, *Women, the Family, and Peasant Revolution in China* (Chicago: University of Chicago Press, 2009), esp. 7–10 and ch. 9.

22 Paul Preston, *The Last Stalinist: The Life of Santiago Carrillo* (London: William Collins, 2014), 121–63.

communists harnessed the resistance to ride to power. In all four cases the men who emerged as top leaders could claim to have won their spurs in the resistance movements against the Germans and Japanese: Tito, Enver Hoxha, Mao and Kim Il Sung. By contrast, in Greece the victorious right in the third round of the civil war sought to blacken or efface the memory of the resistance. Any attempt to evaluate the impact of the resistance experience on the social and economic life of postwar Europe and Asia runs into the problem of separating it from both the preparatory period during the Depression in the 1930s and the general postwar shift to the left that took place in parliamentary governments of the West and in one-party regimes in the East. The task is further complicated by the struggle over the historical memory of the resistance as a separate and distinctive phenomenon.

Competing Memories

The celebration or denigration of the resistance through monuments, novels, memoirs and films has acquired an irregular pattern in different countries at different times. Initially, in many countries the resistance was commemorated as part of the liberation or victory day. Up until the 1990s the trend was generally positive. It continues to be so in Italy. There has even been a belated but sustained attempt to endow the conspiracy against Hitler of high-ranking Wehrmacht officers and a few civilian officials with the aura of a German resistance. But discordant voices increased, for example in France where the Gaullist myth of *"France résistante"* to cover the shame of Vichy and the communists' self-ennoblement as the party of 75,000 martyrs (*fusillés*) were debunked. Regime change in Eastern Europe reversed the spin, most radically in the successor states of a disintegrating Soviet Union and Yugoslavia. A powerful countermyth was generated, one of nationalist resistance to communism freed of collaborationism, especially in Estonia, Latvia, Lithuania, Croatia, Slovenia, Bosnia and even Serbia. Throughout all the former republics of Yugoslavia, hundreds of monuments to the resistance, once visited by millions, are now deserted and abandoned. In Russia since 2009 there has been a new series of resistance celebrations, including for the first time a holiday specifically commemorating the anti-fascist partisans. This may be viewed as part of the officially sponsored nationalist revival but also as a reaction to the celebrations of the anti-Soviet resistance in the Baltic republics. In Ukraine memorializing the resistance has undergone the most rapid transformations. After independence but before the outbreak of armed conflict in 2014, the National History Museum created exhibits commemor-ating both the anti-fascist partisans and Ukrainian soldiers in the Red Army on the one hand and on the other hand the members of the UPA, an irregular military formation which at one time or another fought the Wehrmacht, Red Army and Polish Home Army in the name of establishing an independent Ukraine state. The struggle continues to control the historical memory of these complex movements as part of the process to redefine and remake the state and nation.

Bibliographical Essay

There are a number of peculiarities in compiling a bibliography of the anti-fascist resistance. The field still lacks a broad comparative history that covers both Europe and Asia. There is not even an up-to-date synthesis on the resistance in Europe. Tony Judt, *Resistance and Revolution in Mediterranean Europe, 1939–1948* (London: Routledge, 1989), is one of the few comparative studies, stressing both the unity and the diversity of the national movements. Over the past two decades, historians have moved in the opposite direction, toward local studies, especially in France. The country coverage is very uneven. France again is heavily overrepresented, despite the fact that active *résistants* were much less numerous there than in Italy, Poland, Yugoslavia and Greece. The most recent attempt to synthesize a rich literature is Robert Gildea, *Fighters in the Shadows: A New History of the French Resistance* (London: Faber and Faber, 2015). Claudio Pavone, *A Civil War: A History of Italian Resistance*, trans. Peter Levy (New York: Verso, 2013), is a monumental work by a former partisan who identifies three wars: civil, class and for liberation. Charles Delzell, *Mussolini's Enemies: The Italian Anti-Fascist Resistance* (Princeton: Princeton University Press, 1961), is still valuable as a positive evaluation of resistance on the spiritual renewal of democracy in postwar Italy. For Poland, Norman Davies, *Rising '44: The Battle for Warsaw* (London: Macmillan, 2003), is sympathetic but not uncritical. The most comprehensive study of the Home Army is David G. Williamson, *The Polish Underground 1939–1947* (Barnsley: Pen & Sword Books, 2012). But see also Jerzy Borejsza, "La résistance polonaise en débat," *Vingtième Siècle* 67 (Jul.–Sep. 2000), 33–42. For Yugoslavia, Milovan Djilas, *Wartime*, trans. Michael B. Petrovich (London: Seeker and Warburg, 1977), remains indispensable. An outstanding local study is Marko Attila Hoare, *Genocide and Resistance in Hitler's Bosnia: The Partisans and the Chetniks, 1941–1943* (Oxford: British Academy and Oxford University Press, 2006). For Greece, Mark Mazower, *Inside Hitler's Greece: The*

Experience of Occupation, 1941–1944 (New Haven: Yale University Press, 2001), is a masterful and balanced account placing resistance in context of occupation and international politics. For Albania, see Bernd Fischer, *Albania at War, 1939–1945* (West Lafayette, IN: Purdue University Press, 1999). For the Soviet Union, Kenneth Slepyan, *Stalin's Guerrillas: Soviet Partisans in World War II* (Lawrence: University Press of Kansas, 2006), is a social history based on Moscow archives. Valuable materials on the resistance are embedded in studies of its dark twin, collaborationism, such as H. R. Kedward, *Occupied France: Collaboration and Resistance, 1940–1944* (Oxford: Blackwell, 2000), or else may be found in monographs on national communist parties. A full accounting of the resistance would also have to take into account contacts with external agents. For the most active of these, see William MacKenzie, *The Secret History of SOE: Special Operations Executive 1940–1945* (London: St. Ermin's Press, 2000), an in-house survey with full access to the SOE files. Studies on the Chinese resistance have also moved on – from the foundation works of Chalmers Johnson, *Peasant Nationalism and Communist Power* (Stanford: Stanford University Press, 1962), comparing the nationalist motivation with the Yugoslav partisans; Mark Selden, *The Yenan Way in Revolutionary China* (Cambridge, MA: Harvard University Press, 1971), perceiving resistance as a social revolution; and Tetsuya Kataoka, *Resistance and Revolution in China: The Communists and the Second United Front* (Berkeley: University of California Press, 1974), emphasizing party leadership – to provincial and then local studies to further refine geographical differences. More recently the resistance in Europe has become increasingly intertwined with memory studies linked to current political controversies that threaten to shunt aside the historian in favor of the moralists. Too late to be cited is the important work by Jelena Batinić, *Women and Yugoslav Partisans: A History of World War II Resistance* (New York: Cambridge University Press, 2015).

3

The Sovietization of East Central Europe
1945–1989

NORMAN NAIMARK

The history of Sovietization in postwar East Central Europe can be traced back to the initial attempts of the Bolsheviks to spread their revolutionary ideas about organizing society and politics to the vast territory they had conquered. The processes of Sovietization became particularly important in those regions of the former Russian Empire – especially Central Asia, the Caucasus and even Ukraine – that had stood apart from or opposed the October Revolution and were incorporated into the new Soviet polity by a combination of force and persuasion.[1] New state organizations, such as the secret police, the Red Army and Gosplan, became the instruments of Sovietization in the 1920s and 1930s, as did political organizations such as the communist party and the Komsomol (the communist youth organization).

Soviet efforts to shape the policies of the Mongolian Republic in the 1920s and 1930s can be considered the first program of Sovietization carried out abroad. The Bolsheviks directly aided the seizure of power by the Mongolian People's Revolutionary Party; the Comintern assisted in the drafting of the constitution of the Mongolian People's Republic in 1924; and Moscow treated Mongolia as its "first Soviet satellite."[2] The results of Sovietization in Mongolia included the elimination of the "feudal nobility," the attack on Buddhist monasteries and religion, and the collectivization of nomadic herds.[3]

The most important models for the Sovietization of East Central Europe after World War II came from Moscow's domination of the Baltic states, eastern Poland (western Belarus and western Ukraine) and Moldova in the

---

1 E. A. Rees, "The Sovietization of Eastern Europe," in Balázs Apor, Péter Apor and E. A. Rees (eds.), *The Sovietization of Eastern Europe: New Perspectives on the Postwar Period* (Washington, DC: New Academia Publishing, 2008), 3–5.
2 Alfred J. Rieber, *Stalin and the Struggle for Supremacy in Eurasia* (Cambridge: Cambridge University Press, 2015), 143–48.
3 See Adeeb Khalid, "Communism on the Frontier: The Sovietization of Central Asia and Mongolia," *The Cambridge History of Communism*, vol. I, 616–36.

period 1939–41, when Soviet troops marched into the region as a consequence of the Nazi–Soviet Pact of 23 August 1939 and the accompanying secret protocols. The Baltic states and Moldova became constituent republics of the Soviet Union as a result of Soviet political machinations and trumped-up voting procedures. Western Belarus and western Ukraine were absorbed directly into the already existing Belorussian and Ukrainian Soviet Republics. But in all of these cases Moscow employed similar covert and overt tactics to enforce the complete integration of these new territories into the Soviet Union. The Soviet authorities eviscerated former native ruling circles through arrests, executions and deportations carried out by the NKVD (Narodnyi komissariat vnutrennikh del, People's Commissariat for Internal Affairs) while they identified new political allies among the poorer strata of the native populations and among minorities, especially the Jews, and, in former eastern Poland, among Ukrainians and Belarusans, who sometimes felt alienated from the former Polish elite. The Soviets introduced radical land reform as the first stage of the collectivization process to deprive land-owners and nobles of their estates and create alliances between the poorer sections of the peasantry and the newly ascendant communist party. The Soviet occupiers and their domestic allies turned society on its head and attacked preexisting social structures and beliefs, making it easier to impose Soviet-style institutions and values.[4]

The Germans subsequently imposed their own occupation regime in these territories when the Wehrmacht invaded and occupied the region after 22 June 1941. The double occupation, Soviet and then Nazi, experienced by the local population produced deeply fractured societies that succumbed to the race hatred and ethnic enmity evident in the Holocaust, the bloody Polish–Ukrainian conflict in 1943–44 in Volynia and Galicia, and internecine struggles between partisans and local police of various nationalities.[5] The Soviets marched in again at the end of 1944 to reestablish control of territories that they had already begun to incorporate as a result of the Nazi–Soviet Pact and that were now recognized by the Western Allies as justifiable Soviet war claims.[6] The processes of Sovietization started in the 1939–41 period were again forcibly implemented by the same

4 Jan T. Gross, *Revolution from Abroad: The Soviet Conquest of Poland's Western Ukraine and Western Belorussia* (Princeton: Princeton University Press, 1998).
5 Timothy Snyder, *Black Earth: The Holocaust as History and Warning* (New York: Tim Duggan Books, 2015), 116–43.
6 The United States refused to recognize the incorporation of the Baltic states into the Soviet Union.

institutions, most notably the NKVD and the Red Army, and by many of the same officials, such as NKVD generals Ivan Serov and Lavrentii Tsanava.[7] These officials and institutions were also placed in charge of the Sovietization program after World War II in those areas of East Central Europe, such as Poland and eastern Germany, that were occupied by Soviet troops and claimed by Moscow as being within its sphere of influence.

The Sovietization of East Central Europe was not identical to that which occurred in the non-Russian republics of the Soviet Union in the 1920s and 1930s or in territories incorporated directly into the Soviet Union in the periods 1939–41 and 1944–45. In East Central Europe after World War II, Sovietization took place in ostensibly sovereign countries (more so than Mongolia in the interwar period) and in an international context that served as a deterrent, at least initially, to the use of excessive force and illegal tactics. The question remains whether the Soviets intended already before the end of World War II to dominate and Sovietize the countries of East Central Europe that would likely fall under their eventual occupation – to transform them into Soviet-style governments and societies – or whether Moscow's goals were more open-ended and amenable to compromise with Britain and the United States, which sought to establish parliamentary democracies in these newly liberated countries.

In one of the most frequently cited quotes in Cold War historiography, Milovan Djilas recalled Stalin as saying: "This war is not as in the past: whoever occupies a territory also imposes on it his own social system. Everyone imposes his own system as far as his army can reach. It cannot be otherwise."[8] But there is very little evidence that Stalin had a preconceived plan for the erection of a bloc of countries with Soviet-style systems.[9] Certainly his long-term goals were related to the communization of Europe (and the world). But in the short term, he was most concerned that Germany not be rearmed and capable of carrying out another invasion of the Soviet Union through Poland and that the countries of East Central Europe not serve as willing helpmates in such a war. Stalin frequently noted after 1945 that war with Germany was likely in fifteen to twenty years. He also worried about the West's possession of the atomic bomb and the possibility of its use against the Soviet Union militarily, in a direct

---

7 Ivan Serov, *Zapiski iz chemodana. Tainye dnevniki predsedatelia KGB, naidennye cherez 25 let posle ego smerti*, Proekt Aleksandra Khinsteina (Moscow: "Prosveshchenie," 2017), 40–66, 74–80, 214–30.

8 Milovan Djilas, *Conversations with Stalin*, trans. by Michael B. Petrovich (New York: Harcourt Brace Jovanovich, 1962), 114.

9 See my argument in Norman M. Naimark, "Stalin and Europe in the Postwar Period, 1945–1953: Issues and Problems," *Journal of Modern European History* 3, 1 (2004), 28–58.

conflict between Moscow and the West, but also politically as a way to deprive him of his territorial gains in Europe.[10] Stalin's attention to spreading Soviet influence into East Central Europe may well have been related to the idea that increased Soviet "space" would compensate for this postwar asymmetry with the West in nuclear weaponry.[11]

Whether there was intentional Sovietization or not in the last year of the war and the first of the occupation and "liberation" of East Central Europe, Soviet troops brought with them ideas and habits regarding the administrations of the countries that fell in one way or another under their aegis. Poland and Czechoslovakia were formally sovereign countries, but were nevertheless influenced by the actions of the Red Army. Hungary, Romania and Bulgaria were obliged to follow the instructions of their respective Soviet-dominated Allied Control Councils until formal peace treaties were signed in 1947. Eastern Germany and eastern Austria were administered by a Soviet military administration as part of a four-power occupation regime, though Austria had the advantage over Germany of having its own unified civilian government. In all of these cases, the policies of Soviet military and political leaders in East Central Europe reflected "best practices" at home in the USSR about organizing societies, polities and economies. In short, Sovietization came naturally to the Soviet overlords, especially when – as was frequently the case at the outset – Moscow offered few explicit orders about how to build new administrations or how to work with existing civilian authorities in newly liberated territories.[12]

Sovietization and the Making of the Soviet Bloc
1945–1953

There were three distinct stages in the process of the Sovietization of the countries of East Central Europe that culminated in the formation of the Soviet bloc.[13] These stages were determined by a number of factors, including: (1) Moscow's sensitivity to Western views of their actions; (2) the level of opposition to Soviet moves by domestic forces within each country;

10 David Holloway, *Stalin and the Bomb: The Soviet Union and Atomic Energy, 1939–1956* (New Haven: Yale University Press, 1994), 131–33.
11 Jonathan Haslam, *Russia's Cold War: From the October Revolution to the Fall of the Wall* (New Haven: Yale University Press, 2011), 62.
12 See Norman M. Naimark, *The Russians in Germany: A History of the Soviet Zone of Occupation, 1945–1949* (Cambridge, MA: Harvard University Press, 1995), 9–11.
13 A more detailed rendition of the three stages of Sovietization is contained in Norman M. Naimark, "The Sovietization of Eastern Europe, 1944–1953," in Melvyn P. Leffler and Odd Arne Westad (eds.), *The Cambridge History of the Cold War*, vol. I, *Origins* (Cambridge: Cambridge University Press, 2010), 175–97.

(3) the relative strength of the local communist parties; and (4) the gradual emergence of the Cold War. Sovietization did not occur at the same pace in every country of the region nor did its processes penetrate each to the same degree. In some countries, there was more resistance to Sovietization from "domestic" communists, who tended to propound programs that suited their nationalist inclinations. In others, modernizing elites, both communist and noncommunist, supported Soviet programs that emphasized the need for rapid industrial and technological transformations.[14]

The dynamics of "self-Sovietization," whereby rival elites within each country's communist party sought to outdo one another or gain leverage in competition with noncommunist domestic rivals by introducing Soviet-style changes, sometimes drove the process more than did Moscow itself. This was sometimes the case because the Moscow party leadership frequently did not provide the kind of policy guidance that would "fill in the blanks" for the local party chiefs.[15] The complex give-and-take between the Soviet Union and its East European dependencies is sometimes masked by the fundamentally asymmetrical nature of their relationship.[16] Nevertheless, the general homogeneity of the various stages of Sovietization across the region indicates that Moscow both steered and controlled its content, pace and intensity.

The first stage of Sovietization from 1944 to 1947 was unquestionably the most challenging for both Moscow and the East Europeans in that the communists were urged to construct people's democracies, initially defined as a hybrid form of democracy and as a type of transitional politics between bourgeois democracy and Soviet socialism.[17] Here the communist parties were urged to carry through the "anti-fascist democratic revolution" and begin the processes of creating the foundations of socialism by expropriating large landowners and industrialists, but not collectivizing the peasantry or imposing a party dictatorship of the proletariat in place of the parliamentary system. Private property was to be respected and national front programs were to be "impeccably

---

14 Jiri Janac, *European Coasts of Bohemia: Negotiating the Danube-Oder-Elbe Canal in a Troubled Twentieth Century* (Amsterdam: Amsterdam University Press, 2012), 140–41.

15 John Connelly, *Captive University: The Sovietization of East German, Czech, and Polish Higher Education, 1945–1956* (Chapel Hill: University of North Carolina Press, 2000), 45–46, 55.

16 T. V. Volokitina *et al.*, *Narodnaia demokratiia: mif ili realnost'?* (Moscow: Nauka, 1995), 4–6.

17 Norman M. Naimark, "People's Democracy," in Silvio Pons and Robert Service (eds.), *A Dictionary of Twentieth-Century Communism* (Princeton: Princeton University Press, 2010), 607–10.

democratic."[18] Communist party leaders who moved too quickly toward a dictatorship of the proletariat were criticized for "sectarianism," sometimes even severely reprimanded and removed from positions of power. Instead, the party line advocated individual "roads to socialism," which would recognize the socioeconomic and cultural distinctiveness of each of the countries involved. The sheer number of prominent social-democratic, Christian-democratic and peasant party politicians who remained in their respective countries, even when it had become apparent that the communist parties would have Soviet support and be in a position of power, attests to the continuing belief on the part of noncommunist leaders that "people's democracy" would stabilize as a more or less permanent form of a hybrid government with a mixed economy.[19]

The initiation of the second stage of Sovietization in East Central Europe interacted with a series of events during 1947 that, along with more visible acts of Soviet political manipulation itself, can be seen as having initiated the Cold War. On 12 March, President Harry S. Truman announced the American plan to provide aid to counter communist threats to Greece and Turkey, which, in its broader iteration in June, became known as the Truman Doctrine. US secretary of state George Marshall's speech at Harvard graduation in June 1947 announced the offer of financial support by the American government for the recovery of Europe. Initially formulated to include the Soviet Union and the East European countries, the subsequent European Recovery Act, known as the Marshall Plan, was interpreted by Moscow as an effort to undermine Soviet influence in Europe. Not only did Stalin turn down the Marshall Plan for his country, but he insisted that the East Europeans do so as well. Jan Masaryk, Czechoslovak foreign minister, described his visit to Moscow in early July 1947, when Stalin insisted that the Czechoslovaks reverse their stand on the Marshall Plan: "I went to Moscow as Foreign Minister of an independent sovereign state. I returned as a lackey of a foreign country."[20]

In September 1947, Stalin initiated the formation of the Communist Information Bureau, the Cominform, ostensibly to coordinate the responses of European communist parties to the challenges of confrontation with the West. At its first meeting in Szklarska Poręba, a small Polish resort town in

18 Peter Kenez, *Hungary from the Nazis to the Soviets: The Establishment of the Communist Regime in Hungary 1944–1948* (Cambridge: Cambridge University Press, 2006), 27–29.
19 Charles Gati, *Hungary and the Soviet Bloc* (Durham, NC: Duke University Press, 1986), 76–77.
20 Bruce Lockhart, *My Europe* (London: Putnam, 1952), 125.

lower Silesia, Andrei Zhdanov, Stalin's plenipotentiary at the meeting, made it clear that the flexibility and openness of the first stage of Sovietization had come to an end. The world was divided into "two camps," the capitalist and the socialist, Zhdanov underlined; the communist parties would have to assert more leadership and control within their individual countries and among themselves in order to ensure the victory of socialism.[21]

During this second stage, which lasted until 1949–50, Moscow oversaw the process, led by the respective local communist parties, of forcibly incorporating social-democratic parties into their ranks and attacking the center and right wings of the noncommunist parties, termed "salami tactics" by the Hungarians, transforming those parties into compliant allies.[22] The process of the nationalization of major industries, already begun in the first stage, was completed. In many countries, the first serious efforts to collectivize agriculture were now begun. The boundaries of cultural and religious freedom were markedly narrowed. Secret police campaigns against alleged enemies were intensified, frequently overseen by Soviet NKVD "advisors." At the same time, Moscow accelerated "soft power" programs that promulgated Soviet models in culture, science and society.[23]

The increasingly obvious attempts by Soviet officials to control the parties in the region led to tensions between Stalin, on the one hand, and Tito and the Communist Party of Yugoslavia, on the other. One of the dominant methods of the second stage of Sovietization was Moscow's effort to embed Soviet advisors in East European industrial and agricultural enterprises and to plant Soviet agents in local secret police forces and the military. The Cominform itself turned more and more into an institution directed by Moscow to control the actions of East European communist parties, rather than one that could carry on an energetic struggle against the West. The Yugoslav communists, who had come to power predominantly as a consequence of their own efforts, and who were perfectly happy to "self-Sovietize" while paying genuine obeisance to Stalin, resented what they regarded as interference in their domestic affairs and foreign policy. Tito's attempts to foster unity of the party against Soviet inroads and to control the influence of Soviet agents led to Stalin's

---

21 Anna Di Biagio, "The Establishment of the Cominform," in G. Procacci et al. (eds.), *The Cominform: Minutes of the Three Conferences 1947/1948/1949* (Milan: Feltrinelli, 1994), 32–34.
22 On the origins of the term "salami tactics," see Gati, *Hungary and the Soviet Bloc*, 22 n. 12.
23 Patryk Babiracki, *Soviet Soft Power in Poland: Culture and the Making of Stalin's New Empire, 1943–1957* (Chapel Hill: University of North Carolina Press, 2015), 76–93.

censure of him and the Yugoslavs' removal from the Cominform in June 1948.[24] Nikita Khrushchev later famously reported that Stalin had said: "I will wiggle my little finger and Tito will be no more. He will fall."[25] Not only did this not happen, but the Tito–Stalin split also raised Stalin's deep suspicions about the diversity of the individual roads within the bloc, and contributed to the initiation of the third and most virulent stage of Sovietization, which began in 1949–50.

The third stage of Sovietization overlapped with the full-scale Stalinization of East Central Europe as a whole and lasted until after Stalin's death on 5 March 1953; in some countries it came to an end only with Nikita Khrushchev's de-Stalinization speech in 1956. This was the period in which the political leaders of the East European countries – Bolesław Bierut in Poland, Walter Ulbricht in the German Democratic Republic (GDR), Mátyás Rákosi in Hungary, Klement Gottwald in Czechoslovakia, Vulko Chervenkov in Bulgaria, Gheorghe Gheorghiu-Dej in Romania and Enver Hoxha in Albania – modeled their behavior and images on Stalin, becoming in effect "little Stalins."[26] The power of these communist dictators within their countries paralleled that of Stalin within the Soviet Union. Yet they were careful, as the strict hierarchy of Stalinism demanded, to show proper deference to their Moscow boss.

The Stalin cult became a part of daily life in East Central Europe, as children recited poems to "the Great Helmsman," streets and institutions were named after him, and portraits and images of Stalin appeared in schools and factories. The "little Stalins" created their own personality cults and encouraged the kind of hero-worship and unquestioned obeisance in their own countries that Stalin enjoyed in the Soviet Union. The communist parties, themselves modeled increasingly directly on the Soviet party, initiated a variety of programs to mimic the highly touted successes of the Soviet polity. But also just like the Soviet Union during the high Stalinist period, in East Central Europe the role of state (as opposed to party) institutions was increased, and state leaders were given greater responsibility in the polity.

24 Ivo Banac, *With Stalin Against Tito: Cominformist Splits in Yugoslav Communism* (Ithaca: Cornell University Press, 1988), 125–45.
25 Cited in Robert Service, *A History of Modern Russia: From Nicholas II to Vladimir Putin* (Cambridge, MA: Harvard University Press, 2005), 340.
26 Anne Applebaum, *Iron Curtain: The Crushing of Eastern Europe, 1944–1956* (New York: Doubleday, 2012), 43–55.

The allegedly heroic accomplishments of the Stalinist shock worker, Aleksei Stakhanov, were reproduced in factories all over East Central Europe. New factory towns, such as Nowa Huta in Poland and Eisenhüttenstadt in the GDR, became heavily publicized socialist workers' settlements that were modeled on those, such as Magnitogorsk and Norilsk, that had mushroomed in the 1930s under Stalin's leadership in the Soviet Union.[27] New building projects dotted the landscape – bridges, canals, roads and railway lines – as the communist parties emphasized the importance of developing their domestic industrial and commercial infrastructures in the spirit of the Soviet 1930s. Stalinist architectural monuments were similarly mimicked; the Stalinist wedding-cake style spread across the region, Warsaw's Palace of Culture being the most famous example. "To learn from the Soviet Union means to learn how to be victorious" was the ubiquitous slogan of the Socialist Unity Party in Germany, and appeared in various iterations throughout the bloc. "Love of the Soviet Union does not tolerate the slightest reservation," stated *Rude právo* (25 May 1952), in a more ominous tone.[28] Soviet-style socialist realism was also anointed as the supreme form of cultural accomplishment. However, exceptions to the rule of the socialist realist canon occurred more often in the East European people's democracies than in the Soviet Union itself.

Rapid social change accompanied the heightened pace of industrialization and construction that was meant to build the foundations of socialism. Peasants moved in the millions to urban areas, seeking work in factories and construction. Every third worker in Poland by the 1960s, for example, was the child of a peasant, affecting the character of factory and urban culture, not to mention transforming traditional rural life, as many urban workers either continued to live in the villages and commute to work in the cities or returned home to their villages to visit families and engage in part-time agricultural endeavors.[29] More educated workers, often selected by the party for advanced training, sought and found privileged positions in the communist-led bureaucracy, which favored job candidates from the working class. Women became an important part of the labor force, as jobs were opened to them in what had been the exclusively male-dominated

27 Kate Lebow, *Unfinished Utopia: Nowa Huta, Stalinism, and Polish Society, 1949–1956* (Ithaca: Cornell University Press, 2013).
28 Cited in Joseph Rothschild, *Return to Diversity: A Political History of East Central Europe Since World War II*, 2nd edn. (New York: Oxford University Press, 1993), 133.
29 Thomas W. Simons, Jr., *Eastern Europe in the Postwar World* (New York: St. Martin's Press, 1991), 109–10.

construction, steel and coal industries. As a result of rapid industrialization plans, women became "turners, locksmiths, truck and tram drivers, and bricklayers, as well as underground miners."[30]

The Sovietization of East Central Europe in the high Stalinist period of the late 1940s and early 1950s was also defined by the application of methods of terror and coercion to the political process. Prodded by Soviet NKVD officers, who served as advisors in the people's democracies, East European secret police officials concocted conspiracies, arrested alleged traitors within the communist parties and provided trumped-up evidence for a series of purge trials. As in the case of the Soviet Union, innocent citizens were swept up in the arrests and trials and sometimes brutally tortured into confessing their supposed crimes; many were either executed or sent to labor camps constructed on the model of the Soviet Gulag. The East European purge trials, which began with the trial of party leader László Rajk in Hungary (16–24 September 1949), spread throughout the region, as both Soviet and local secret police officials tried to outdo one another in bringing alleged enemies of socialism before judicial tribunals. In some instances, the trials were kept secret, as in the case of Paul Merker in the GDR, who was eventually pardoned. In some cases, the leaders of alleged conspiracies were spared death sentences, as in Poland with Marian Spychalski, who came to trial in 1951, and Władysław Gomułka, who was under house arrest from 1951 to 1954. In some cases, Czechoslovakia most notably, public show trials, such as the Rudolf Slánský trial, were staged and elaborately scripted in the manner of the Soviet show trials of the 1930s. They were also comparable to the Soviet purge trials in their viciousness, scale and number of death sentences.

Unlike the Soviet trials of the 1930s, the East European trials of the late 1940s and early 1950s contained strong elements of anti-Semitism and anti-Zionism. Stalin's growing distrust of the Jews as agents of foreign powers was exemplified by his repression of the Jewish Anti-Fascist Group in 1948 and the Kremlin-directed murder of its leader, Solomon Mikhoels, in January 1948. Anti-Jewish rhetoric and actions on the part of the Soviet government grew ever more extreme after the founding of the state of Israel in May 1948 and the visit of Golda Meir to Moscow in September as Israel's first ambassador, which set off unwelcome demonstrations of the solidarity of Soviet Jews with Israel. Anti-Semitism at the highest level of the Soviet government easily

---

30 Malgorzata Fidelis, *Women, Communism and Industrialization in Postwar Poland* (Cambridge: Cambridge University Press, 2010), 130.

spread to the East European parties. Those communists of a more nationalist bent – usually "home communists," who had spent the war in the underground – saw an opportunity to undermine the relatively large number of Jewish communist leaders and especially secret police agents in their midst, who frequently had spent the war in Moscow.[31] The Rajk and the Slánský trials, especially, contained strong anti-Semitic themes, couched primarily in accusations of a Zionist conspiracy within the Hungarian and Czechoslovak parties.

At the same time, Cold War tensions prompted the East European secret police to search out ties among the accused with the West in general, and the United States in particular. The American communist, Noel Field, who had served in the State Department in the 1930s and carried out anti-fascist activities on the continent during World War II, became a prime suspect of CIA espionage and conspiracy when, fearing arrest if he returned to the United States after the war, he sought to work directly for the Czechoslovak communist authorities in 1948. Field was immediately arrested, interrogated and turned over to the Hungarian authorities, who proceeded to torture him in order to extract confessions about his allegedly nefarious activities.[32] Field became the centerpiece of an elaborate, secret police-concocted conspiracy of the CIA, the Zionists, the Titoists and East European communist traitors, to assassinate loyal communists in the region and wrest it from Soviet control.

The tensions resulting from the Berlin blockade in Europe (1948–49) and the outbreak of the Korean War in Asia (1950–53) prompted Stalin to increase pressure on the East European communists to build up their armies in preparation for a clash with the West.[33] The purge of their parties and the Stalinization of public life would ensure that there would be no opposition in the case of a coming war. But, as in the case of the Soviet purge trials of the 1930s, the costs of the Stalinist repressions in Eastern Europe spread far beyond the party leadership: in Hungary some 750,000 people were convicted

31 Norman M. Naimark, "Gomułka and Stalin: The Antisemitic Factor in Postwar Polish Politics," in Murray Baumgarten et al. (eds.), *Varieties of Antisemitism: History, Ideology, Discourse* (Newark: University of Delaware Press, 2009), 237–51.

32 See the story of Noel Field in his brother's memoirs: Hermann Field and Kate Field, *Trapped in the Cold War: The Ordeal of an American Family* (Stanford: Stanford University Press, 1999).

33 Mark Kramer argues that the militarization of East Central Europe derived in good measure from efforts to prepare for war against Yugoslavia. See Kramer, "Stalin, Yugoslavia and the Efforts to Reassert Control," in Timothy Snyder and Ray Brandon (eds.), *Stalin and Europe: Imitation and Domination, 1928–1953* (New York: Oxford University Press, 2014), 306–07.

between 1948 and 1953; in Romania at least 60,000 were arrested in the same period; in Bulgaria 40,000 were imprisoned and 300,000 placed under police surveillance; in Albania 80,000 were arrested; 90,000 were prosecuted for political crimes in Czechoslovakia, with tens of thousands of others punished economically as a result of their alleged crimes; some 120,000 German civilians were interned in Soviet special camps in the Soviet Zone of Occupation and GDR from 1945 until the early 1950s.[34]

After Stalin

When Stalin succumbed to a cerebral hemorrhage on 5 March 1953, his likely successors viewed one another as rivals for power. Most notably, Lavrentii Beria, Stalin's secret police chief, sought to position himself as the next leader of the Soviet Union. In the power struggle that ensued within the so-called collective leadership, Beria allied himself with Georgii Malenkov. Beria and Malenkov, as leaders of the post-Stalin Politburo, advocated a "New Course" in Soviet domestic and economic policies, reversing the Stalinist emphasis on heavy industry at the cost of consumer industries. They also took the lead in trying to reduce the terror and tension in Soviet society that resulted from Stalin's incessant recourse to violence to defeat his imagined enemies and control his citizenry. The new rulers put out the incendiary fire of the so-called Doctors' Plot, which Stalin had set in late 1952 to stir up another round of repressions, and released the Kremlin doctors, mostly of Jewish origin, who were still held in prison. (Two had been executed already.) The new leadership also let it be known that political prisoners in the Gulag would have their cases reviewed, releasing thousands in the process. The exaggerated claims of the cult of Stalin were gradually, but perceptibly, reduced. Even in the realm of foreign policy, Malenkov and Beria took a "liberal line," suggesting new possibilities of negotiations with the United States.[35] The Korean War was brought to a conclusion on 27 July 1953. Negotiations resumed to conclude the Austrian State Treaty, which was finally signed on 15 May 1955. The new leadership also undertook a series of

34 Kevin McDermott and Matthew Stibbe, "Stalinist Terror in Eastern Europe: Problems, Perspectives, and Interpretations," in Kevin McDermott and Matthew Stibbe (eds.), *Stalinist Terror in Eastern Europe: Elite Purges and Mass Repression* (Manchester: Manchester University Press, 2010), 13; Bettina Greiner, *Verdrängter Terror: Geschichte und Wahrnehmung sowjetischer Speziallager in Deutschland* (Hamburg: Hamburger Edition, 2010), 13.
35 Melvyn P. Leffler, *For the Soul of Mankind: The United States, the Soviet Union, and the Cold War* (New York: Hill & Wang, 2007), 89–91.

initiatives to reestablish relations with the Yugoslavs, which began with an exchange of conciliatory letters between Khrushchev and Tito between 22 June and September 1954, and culminated in Khrushchev's visit to Belgrade in May 1955.[36]

Sovietization did not end in East Central Europe with the death of Stalin on 5 March 1953. Instead, in the fourth stage of Sovietization that lasted until Khrushchev's Secret Speech in 1956, the East Europeans were forced to deal with a variety of signals from Moscow about how they were to approach their political tasks and policy goals. For the supreme leaders in the region, the "little Stalins," these mixed signals were deeply unsettling, since those that reflected forms of liberalization or de-Stalinization threatened their unchallenged rule. Meanwhile, reformist communists within the East European leaderships sought to ally themselves with the new forces aligned with Beria and Malenkov in Moscow and apply the "New Course" in their respective countries. The liberal Hungarian communist, Imre Nagy, became chairman of Hungary's Council of Ministers in 1953. The Bulgarian "little Stalin," Vulko Chervenkov, gave up his party post in favor of Todor Zhivkov, who was more inclined to support a reform program. Transition to a short-lived, more liberal leadership of the Communist Party of Czechoslovakia under Antonín Zápotocký in 1953 was made possible by Klement Gottwald's death in Moscow, shortly after Stalin's death. But this new generation of leaders was forced to coexist, at least for the time being, with the traditionalist Stalinist hierarchs.

The most notable case in this connection was the German Democratic Republic, where Walter Ulbricht, the secretary general of the Socialist Unity Party (Sozialistische Einheitspartei Deutschlands, SED), refused signals from Moscow to relax his program of forced industrialization introduced in 1952. Instead, he dramatically raised industrial targets and work norms in true Stalinist fashion, arousing resentment and anger among workers in East Berlin and throughout the republic. At the same time, Beria let it be known in the Soviet leadership and in the SED that Moscow was ready to negotiate about the unity of Germany, even to the point of giving up the GDR, especially since East Berlin, in Beria's view, had become an unnecessary flashpoint in the center of Europe. Meanwhile, the workers of East Berlin had had enough. On 16 June 1953, they launched a series of strikes and demonstrations that led to a full-scale uprising the following day and then

36 "The Tito–Khrushchev Correspondence, 1954," *Cold War International History Project Bulletin* 12–13 (Fall–Winter 2001), 315–23.

spread throughout the republic. The Soviets felt they had no choice but to crush the uprising with tanks and troops. The costs were severe. Seventy-five East Germans were killed in the events; hundreds were arrested.[37] As the East German playwright Berthold Brecht noted in his bitter poem, "The Solution" ("Die Lösung"):

> After the uprising of the 17th of June
> The Secretary of the Writers Union
> Had leaflets distributed in the Stalinallee
> Stating that the people
> Had forfeited the confidence of the government
> And could win it back only
> By redoubled efforts.
> Would it not be easier
> In that case for the government
> To dissolve the people
> And elect another?[38]

Despite Ulbricht's prominent role in causing the violence, Moscow needed him too much to keep order in the East German party ranks to remove him from power. The bloody denouement of the uprising in the end saved his position. Those who opposed him in the SED, Rudolf Herrnstadt and Wilhelm Zaisser, among others, had allied with Beria in their attempts to reform the SED and forge a new path for German socialism. But Beria himself was in trouble. Inside the Central Committee of the Politburo, Nikita Khrushchev led a coalition of disaffected conservatives, moderates and military leaders, who were unhappy with his German policies and fearful that Beria wanted to seize power himself. Beria was arrested on 26 June 1953, turned over to a secret military tribunal, sentenced to death and executed.

The elimination of Beria did not end the turmoil in the Kremlin's collective leadership. Khrushchev hewed to a middle line between the more "liberal" communists, Beria and Malenkov, and the more conservative clique of long-time Stalinist apparatchiks, led by Viacheslav Molotov and Lazar Kaganovich. His own attempt to secure political power came to a head at the Twentieth Party Congress of the Communist Party in February 1956, where, in a closed session at the end of the proceedings, he delivered his completely unexpected Secret Speech, denouncing the excesses of the cult of Stalin and the routine

37 Applebaum, *Iron Curtain*, 442.
38 Bertolt Brecht, *Poems 1913–1956*, eds. John Willett and Ralph Manheim (London: Methuen, 1976), 440.

violence that was carried out against party members. "It was so quiet in the huge hall you could hear a fly buzzing," Khrushchev wrote in his memoirs, as he detailed the torture and executions that had accompanied Stalin's crimes against party members.[39] Anxious to maintain loyalty to the system, Khrushchev did not provide the same kind of information about the millions of ordinary Soviet citizens who suffered at the hands of Stalin's repressions.

The East European communist leaders who attended the session were clearly shocked by Khrushchev's revelations, as were the vast majority of the attendees. The Polish party chief, Bierut, fell ill and died on 6 March 1956 in Moscow, shortly after the speech. The Albanian party chief, Hoxha, returned to Tirana to denounce Khrushchev as a revisionist. The Albanians exited from the Soviet camp, eventually aligning themselves with Mao's brand of radical Marxism-Leninism-Stalinism. The other party leaders went home in a state of perturbation. Although the full text of the speech was not published until much later, the somewhat sanitized Polish version of it was leaked by the CIA to the *New York Times* and published on 4 June 1956.[40] Word of Khrushchev's message also made its way throughout East European party circles, giving succor to liberal and national communists who sought to wrench power from the Stalinist elites. In this case, then, Sovietization meant reversing the course of Stalinization and introducing reformed communism. But the question of which version of reform should predominate and how much latitude the East Europeans had to define their own future was still to be determined.

Khrushchev's de-Stalinization initiatives met with enthusiastic responses among most East European communists, who were looking for ways to increase their domestic political legitimacy by demonstrating their independence from Moscow. But de-Stalinization also encouraged the local populations to seek increasing freedoms. In July 1956 Polish workers in the western city of Poznań went out on strike, demanding economic concessions from the government, most prominently food price reductions, housing improvements and wage increases. But as the strike proceeded, students and young people joined in and the demands turned increasingly political. There were slogans among the demonstrators of "Long live freedom" and "Down with the USSR." The Polish army and security forces intervened in brutal fashion, shooting into the crowds. Before the strikes and

---

39 *Khrushchev Remembers*, trans. and ed. Strobe Talbott (Boston: Little Brown, 1970), 350.
40 William Taubman, *Khrushchev: The Man and His Era* (New York: W. W. Norton, 2003), 284.

demonstrations were suppressed, some 70 civilians were killed, 300 wounded and another 250 or so were arrested, of them 196 workers.[41] One could argue that the Poznań strike saved Poland from much worse: Because of its violent suppression by the Polish government rather than by the Soviets, it neither spread to the rest of the country in serious ways nor did it bring strong Polish anti-Soviet sentiments to a head.

As a result of the upheaval, Polish party leaders came to the conclusion that the well-known Polish "home communist," Gomułka, should be their leader. Although under house arrest from 1951 to 1954 for his "nationalist" deviations, he was rehabilitated after the Poznań events and made First Secretary of the PZPR (Polska Zjednoczona Partia Robotnicza, Polish United Workers' Party) on 21 October 1956, amidst a wave of demonstrations and intellectual upheaval in Warsaw and around the country that was known as the "Polish October." Gomułka managed to convince the wary Khrushchev and Soviet Central Committee delegation that flew to Warsaw to intimidate the Poles with the threat of Soviet military intervention that the best way forward was to follow a "Polish road to socialism." He assured his interlocutors that the Polish party would maintain control of the country and remain loyal to its Soviet benefactors. There would be no more anti-Soviet slogans, Gomułka promised; at the same time, the most visible symbols of Sovietization in Poland would be curtailed, including the inflammatory appointment of Soviet citizens to Polish political and military positions.

The path of de-Stalinization in Hungary took a particularly dangerous turn in the eyes of its Soviet observers, most importantly Yurii Andropov, the Soviet ambassador in Budapest and Moscow's point man for dealing with the Hungarians. Following the Twentieth Party Congress and the July 1956 forced resignation of the rough-edged Stalinist, Rákosi, from the leadership of the Hungarian party, groups of intellectuals and students agitated for more open and liberal policies.[42] The palpable excitement aroused by the Polish October inspired tens of thousands of Hungarians to take to the streets of Budapest on 23 October, demanding reform. The centrist party leader, Ernő Gerő, could not control the tumult on the streets, as battles erupted between

41 Andrzej Paczkowski, *The Spring Will Be Ours: Poland and the Poles from Occupation to Freedom*, trans. Jane Cave (University Park: Pennsylvania State University Press, 1998), 273.
42 "Report of Anastas Mikoyan on the Situation in the Hungarian Workers' Party, July 14, 1956," in Csaba Bekes, Malcolm Byrne and Janos M. Rainer (eds.), *The 1956 Hungarian Revolution in Documents* (Budapest: Central European University Press, 2002), 144–45.

the Hungarian Ministry of the Interior police units and the demonstrators, whose demands portentously included withdrawal of Hungary from the Soviet bloc. Gerő called on the Soviet garrison to restore order on the night of 23 October. Soviet tanks occupied the central streets of Budapest, while crowds of Hungarians, lightly armed and hoping for Western help in one form or another, engaged in scattered fighting around the city. As the rebellion spread to the rest of the country, the party itself disintegrated. Imre Nagy, who was named prime minister on 24 October, tried to maintain control of the situation by pledging a program of reform and siding with the people on the street. But the crowds were not mollified. On 1 November, Nagy took the fateful step of calling for Hungarian withdrawal from the Warsaw Pact and declaring neutrality. This prompted the second Soviet intervention on 4 November, which made it all too apparent that Moscow would use whatever force was necessary to maintain Hungary's position in the bloc.

Polycentrism

János Kádár emerged out of the political chaos of the Hungarian Revolution of 1956 to forge a compromise with the Soviets, by keeping Hungary in the Warsaw Pact and maintaining strict one-party rule. He also eventually reached a *modus vivendi* with his citizens, by allowing them increased freedom to engage in small business, travel and consumerism, sometimes called "goulash communism," while insisting that they assent to the communist party's monopoly on the political system.

The results of the upheavals of 1956 and the compromises forged by the Polish and Hungarian governments with Moscow led to a period of what was called by Palmiro Togliatti, the Italian communist leader, "polycentrism" – the fifth stage of Sovietization – whereby the former "satellite" communist parties in Eastern Europe gained greater leeway to determine their own paths toward socialism, frequently to the displeasure of the Soviets.[43] Polycentrism developed in East Central Europe in part out of the pressure on the Soviets by the Yugoslav and Chinese parties to pursue their own understanding of communism against Moscow's wishes and in part out of Moscow's unwillingness and inability to impose its viewpoints

---

43 Adam Bromke, "Polycentrism in Eastern Europe," in Adam Bromke and Teresa Rakowska-Harmstone (eds.), *The Communist States in Disarray 1965–1971* (Minneapolis: University of Minnesota Press, 1972), 3–21.

categorically on the East Europeans.[44] After 1956, Marxist-Leninist ideology became less salient to the resolution of every problem facing the states and societies of the region, and, in most countries, the level of personal freedom, the ability to travel abroad and the diversity of economic possibilities were notably increased.

The crushing of the 1968 reform movement of the "Prague Spring" through the Warsaw Pact invasion of Czechoslovakia in August 1968 indicated, however, that the East Europeans could not challenge the domination of Soviet security interests by leaving the Warsaw Pact, nor could they experiment with a genuine multiparty system and free elections. Following the invasion, Moscow articulated the principles of the so-called Brezhnev Doctrine, which demanded that the "achievements" of socialism in East Central Europe could not be seriously threatened or reversed. But, within those strictures, the countries involved could and did introduce a variety of programs that the respective parties decided were in their own national interests. Some countries adhered closely to Soviet models; the German Democratic Republic, Czechoslovakia and Bulgaria were the most willing to adjust their domestic priorities to Soviet ways of doing things. Poland and Hungary were more ready to test the limits of the possible, especially in the spheres of culture, trade and business.

Romania became an outlier, as the government of Nicolae Ceauşescu, which came to power in 1964, increasingly emphasized its national exclusiveness, while forging a harsh dictatorship of the communist party, criticizing Soviet foreign-policy aims, yet remaining within the Warsaw Pact. The idiosyncratic and independent Romanian stance vis-à-vis the Soviet Union and its own participation in the bloc was apparent in 1968, when Ceauşescu criticized and refused to join the invasion of Czechoslovakia by the Warsaw Pact countries.[45] Albania had long since abandoned Soviet leadership as "revisionist " and lined up behind the Chinese, as the Sino-Soviet split, which burst into public view in the early 1960s, offered Hoxha and the Albanian leadership an opportunity to seek the support of Mao and the Chinese, in their view the real Leninists.[46] But, importantly, in every case in East Central Europe, there was a marked growth in the development of nationalism. In the 1960s and 1970s, even the GDR developed its own

44 George F. Kennan, "Polycentrism and Western Policy," *Foreign Affairs* 42, 2 (Jan. 1964), 175–76.
45 Dennis Deletant, "New Evidence on Romania and the Warsaw Pact 1955–1989," *Cold War International History Project*, e-Dossier no. 6 (7 Jul. 2011).
46 Elidor Mëhilli, *Albania and the Socialist World from Stalin to Mao* (Ithaca: Cornell University Press, 2017), 392–404.

nationalist traits of being a better and purer Germany than the Federal Republic with its capital in Bonn.

Despite the evolution of nationally oriented programs within the individual countries of the bloc, programs of Sovietization in some arenas of society and the polity did not cease. Through the Warsaw Pact and CMEA (the Council of Economic Mutual Assistance), Moscow maintained a modicum of Soviet-inspired common policies and coordination, involving economic, military and foreign-policy matters. Regular consultations between government and party leaders organized by the Kremlin ensured that no one strayed too far from the desiderata of Soviet foreign policy and the Soviet model for "real existing socialism." Moscow fostered economic interdependence by supplying the East Europeans with cheap energy imports, which in turn increased the dependence of these countries on Soviet goodwill, especially once the world energy crisis in the early 1970s drove up petroleum prices on the international market.

Even more so than in the earlier stages of Sovietization, East Europeans now routinely studied in the Soviet Union and scientific specialists cooperated with their Soviet counterparts. East European scientists, athletes, cultural figures and media stars frequently visited the Soviet Union. Soviet advisors in various branches of industry, culture and society continued, as they had from the beginning, to visit East European countries. Following Soviet innovations in technology, education and science remained important to the East European research world, though with increasing skepticism toward Soviet "accomplishments" and with growing contacts with the West, fostered by the United States and its allies as a way to undermine Soviet control of the region. Nevertheless, most of the institutions that were set up in East Central Europe in the initial period of Sovietization after World War II – the youth and women's organizations, state and military establishments, party organs, the education system and so on – remained in place and continued to model their activities on Soviet templates. Soviet soft power, despite its many limitations in East Central Europe, remained a powerful aspect of Sovietization processes.

Even after Mikhail Gorbachev came to power in 1985 and articulated his reform program of "new thinking," *perestroika* and *glasnost'* in 1987 and 1988, the East Europeans were urged, even bullied, by their Moscow "big brothers" – and Soviet officials did indeed still assume the pose of "big brothers" – to follow their lead. Moscow's new reform agenda was welcomed for the most part in Poland and in Hungary, but it made the East Germans nervous and unsettled, to the point where the SED banned a Soviet periodical,

Sputnik, in November 1988, setting off an intra-party struggle and societal arguments in the GDR about the perspectives for reform under Erich Honecker. The argument was intensified by a reluctant visit by Gorbachev to East Berlin on 6–7 October 1989, on the fiftieth anniversary of the founding of the GDR. The enthusiasm with which he was met by the East German crowds and the tenor of his speech, scolding the SED's leadership for its conservatism, contributed to the momentum that led to the removal of Honecker as party chief on 17 October.

The Romanians and Albanians wanted nothing to do with Gorbachev and his reforms and sharply criticized them, while the Bulgarian party, under the decades-long leadership of Zhivkov, announced its own platform of changes that fell short of the Soviet ones, in the hope, ultimately futile, of maintaining crucial Soviet economic support and political friendship without undertaking serious reforms.[47]

Perhaps most central to the new phase of "liberal" Sovietization were Gorbachev's pronouncements that for all intents and purposes East European communists were on their own to forge accommodations with their increasingly restless societies. To Sovietize at the end of the 1980s meant that the East Europeans should not only borrow Gorbachev's reform program to modernize their societies, but also that they would have to do it on their own. There would be no military interventions to prop up their political systems and no economic aid in the case that the restructuring failed. This did not mean that Gorbachev did not want the East Europeans to remain in the Soviet camp – on the contrary.[48] But as the period of the revolutions in Eastern Europe started in the early summer of 1989, symbolized by Solidarity's stunning election victory in Poland in June 1989, it became apparent that Gorbachev was in no position to shore up the domestic communist governments, even if he had wanted to. Like a house of cards, one regime after another fell in late 1989 and early 1990, bringing to an end the 45-year history of Sovietization and contributing ultimately to the destruction of the Soviet Union itself.

After 1989, the outward signs of Sovietization in Eastern Europe quickly disappeared. Statues of Lenin and of domestic communists came down – sometimes torn down by angry citizens – and communist heraldry was chiseled off buildings. The communist parties themselves were disbanded and deprived of their legal status, while their resources were confiscated by

47 R. J. Crampton, *Eastern Europe in the Twentieth Century* (London: Routledge, 1994), 353.
48 Gale Stokes, *The Walls Came Tumbling Down: The Collapse of Communism in Eastern Europe* (New York: Oxford University Press, 1993), 68–77.

the state. Along with the parties, the gamut of institutions that had been introduced by the Sovietization program – the youth leagues, the women's organizations, the Academies of Science and the secret police – could no longer function. Postcommunists tended to continue their political involvement in newly established parties, often with social-democratic platforms. Those with influence and positions in industry, agriculture, commerce and banking were sometimes able to make a swift and profitable transition, becoming important economic actors in the postcommunist period.

That the countries of East Central Europe joined both the European Union and NATO also meant that various programs of Sovietization that had been introduced in the 1940s and 1950s were gone forever. One of the most important consequences of joining Europe was the transformation of institutions in East Central Europe to meet West European rather than Soviet standards. But aspects of the social and cultural programs of Sovietization, having to do with day care, social security, right-to-work laws, subsidized arts and many others, if cut back severely by postcommunist governments, remained in high demand by a citizenry that selectively remembered the Sovietized past, even if in sometimes romantic and unrealistic ways. The institutions and visible signs of Sovietization may be gone forever, but the mentality introduced by its programs remains even among some young people born after 1989.

Bibliographical Essay

Three classic studies have defined the contours of Western scholarship on the formation of the Soviet bloc and the Sovietization of East Central Europe: Hugh Seton-Watson's *The East European Revolution* (London: Methuen, 1950); François Fejtő's *History of the People's Democracies: Eastern Europe Since Stalin*, trans. Daniel Weissbort (New York: Praeger, 1971); and Zbigniew Brzezinski's *The Soviet Bloc: Unity and Conflict* (Cambridge, MA: Harvard University Press, 1960). The conclusions of all three books were roughly the same: Moscow designed and executed the communist seizure of power in East Central Europe for the purpose of extending its sphere of influence in Europe and the world. The takeover was performed in stages, though with some variation from country to country. The patterns of Sovietization followed a similar template in each country, and the influence of Soviet models and advisors was both extensive and consequential.

Between the late 1960s and 1989, a period that can be considered the height of Sovietology in Western academic circles, a number of books were published that refined, although they did not fundamentally change, the underlying theses of the earlier works. Some studies were general to the area, like Paul Lendvai's *Eagle in Cobwebs: Nationalism and Communism in the Balkans* (New York: Doubleday, 1969); Thomas W. Simons's *Eastern Europe in the Postwar World* (New York: St. Martin's, 1991); and Joseph Rothschild's *Return to Diversity: A Political History of East Central Europe Since World War II* (New York: Oxford University Press, 1989). The largest number of books focused on individual countries of the region, for example, Paul Shoup, *Communism and the Yugoslav National Question* (New York: Columbia University Press, 1968); Charles Gati, *Hungary and the Soviet Bloc* (Durham, NC: Duke University Press, 1986); Zdenek L. Suda, *Zealots and Rebels: A History of the Communist Party of Czechoslovakia* (Stanford: Hoover Institution Press, 1980); Kenneth Jowitt, *Revolutionary Breakthroughs and National Development: The Case of Romania, 1944–1965* (Berkeley: University of California Press, 1971); and Nissan Oren, *Revolution Administered: Agrarianism and Communism in Bulgaria* (Baltimore: Johns Hopkins University Press, 1973).

The fall of communism in 1989 in Eastern Europe and 1991 in the Soviet Union provided an important impetus to the historiography of Sovietization. A number of Soviet and East European archive collections were opened to historians for scholarly research. Historians and archive administrators collaborated in the publication of crucial document collections. Among them were a series of Russian document collections that bear directly on the history of Sovietization: T. V. Volokitina et al. (eds.), *Vostochnaia Evropa v dokumentakh rossiiskikh arkhivov, 1944–1953*, 2 vols. (Moscow: Sibirskii khronograf, 1997–98); T. V. Volokitina et al. (eds.), *Sovetskii faktor v Vostochnoi Evrope, 1944–1953. Dokumenty*, 2 vols. (Moscow: ROSSPEN, 1999–2002); and Gennadii Bordiugov et al. (eds.), *SSSR–Pol'sha. Mekhanizmy podchineniia, 1944–1949 gg. Sbornik dokumentov* (Moscow: AIRO-XX, 1995). Four volumes of documents on the German question, which illuminate the history of the Sovietization of East Germany and its fellow people's democracies, were published by G. P. Kynin and Jochen Laufer, *SSSR i germanskii vopros, 1941–1949. Die UdSSR und die deutsche Frage, 1941–1949*, 4 vols. (Moscow: Mezhdunarodnye otnosheniia, 2000–12). Document collections published in the individual languages of the East European countries are too numerous to list here. But it is important to mention crucial English-language translations of documents, including Ivo Banac (ed.), *The Diary of Georgi Dimitrov, 1933–1949* (New Haven: Yale University Press, 2003), and Giuliano Procacci et al. (eds.), *The Cominform: Minutes of the Three Conferences, 1947/1948/1949* (Milan:

Feltrinelli, 1994). In addition, the Woodrow Wilson Center's Cold War International History Project (CWIHP) and the National Security Archive, both headquartered in Washington, DC, translated and made available online many documents on Sovietization from East Central Europe, which are readily accessed on their respective webpages.

The availability of new materials has stimulated the publication of a number of valuable collections of articles on the dynamics of Sovietization throughout the region, with country specialists providing contributions on their own areas of interest. Examples of these kinds of collections in English include: Norman Naimark and Leonid Gibianskii (eds.), *The Establishment of Communist Regimes in Eastern Europe, 1944–1949* (Boulder: Westview, 1997); Balazs Apor et al. (eds.), *The Leader Cult in Communist Dictatorships: Stalin and the Eastern Bloc* (London: Palgrave Macmillan, 2004); Balazs Apor et al. (eds.), *The Sovietization of Eastern Europe: New Perspectives on the Postwar Period* (Washington, DC: New Academic Publishing, 2008); Francesca Gori and Silvio Pons (eds.), *The Soviet Union and Europe in the Cold War, 1943–1953* (London: Macmillan, 1996); Vladimir Tismaneanu (ed.), *Stalinism Revisited: The Establishment of Communist Regimes in East-Central Europe* (Budapest: Central European University Press, 2009); Timothy Snyder and Ray Brandon (eds.), *Stalin and Europe: Imitation and Domination, 1928–1953* (New York: Oxford University Press, 2014). For the Russian historiography of Sovietization in the same period, see Norman M. Naimark, "Post-Soviet Russian Historiography on the Emergence of the Soviet Bloc," *Kritika: Explorations in Russian and Eurasian History* 5, 3 (2004), 561–80.

New archival materials have also prompted the publications of a number of monographs on Soviet actions in East Central Europe. Those that relate directly to the Sovietization question include: Norman M. Naimark, *The Russians in Germany: The History of the Soviet Zone of Occupation, 1945–1949* (Cambridge, MA: Harvard University Press, 1995); John Connelly, *Captive University: The Sovietization of East German, Czech, and Polish Higher Education, 1945–1946* (Chapel Hill: University of North Carolina Press, 2000); Peter Kenez, *Hungary from the Nazis to the Soviets: The Establishment of the Hungarian Communist Regime, 1944–1948* (Cambridge: Cambridge University Press, 2009); and Anne Applebaum, *Iron Curtain: The Crushing of Eastern Europe, 1944–1956* (New York: Doubleday, 2012). Among the books that explore the social and cultural dynamics of Sovietization are the recent studies on Poland: Kate Lebow, *Unfinished Utopia: Nowa Huta, Stalinism, and Polish Society, 1949–1956* (Ithaca: Cornell

University Press, 2013); Malgorzata Fidelis, *Women, Communization, and Industrialization in Postwar Poland* (Cambridge: Cambridge University Press, 2010); Patryk Babiracki, *Soviet Soft Power in Poland: Culture and the Making of Stalin's New Empire, 1943–1957* (Chapel Hill: University of North Carolina Press, 2015); and Elidor Mëhilli, *Albania and the Socialist World from Stalin to Mao* (Ithaca: Cornell University Press, 2017).

Of the many noteworthy English-language studies of Soviet relations with East Central Europe in the postwar period, only a few can be mentioned here: Vladislav Zubok and Constantine Pleshakov, *Inside the Kremlin's Cold War: From Stalin to Khrushchev* (Cambridge, MA: Harvard University Press, 1996), and Vojtech Mastny, *The Cold War and Soviet Insecurity: The Stalin Years* (New York: Oxford University Press, 1996). For the Gorbachev period, see Mark Kramer, "The Collapse of East European Communism and the Repercussions Within the Soviet Union," *Journal of Cold War Studies*, part 1: 5, 4 (2003), 178–256; part 2: 6, 4 (2004), 3–64; and part 3: 7, 1 (2005), 3–96; Mary Elise Sarotte, *1989: The Struggle to Create Post-Cold War Europe* (Princeton: Princeton University Press, 2014); and Gale Stokes, *The Walls Came Tumbling Down: Collapse and Rebirth in Eastern Europe* (New York: Oxford University Press, 1993).

4

The Chinese Communist Revolution
and the World

CHEN JIAN

1949 – A Moment of Mixed Meanings
for International Communism

On 30 June 1949, Mao Zedong made his famous "Lean to One Side" statement. He announced that the communist-led "New China" would stand on the side of the Soviet Union and the communist bloc in the ongoing global Cold War. He devoted a substantial part of the statement to describing the Chinese Communist Revolution's relationship with the world proletarian revolution, emphasizing both the huge support that the Chinese Communist Party (CCP) had received from Moscow and revolutionary forces in other parts of the world, and the extraordinary contribution that the CCP had made and would continuously make to the world revolution.[1]

Mao issued the statement at the time that Liu Shaoqi, the CCP's second-in-command, was visiting Moscow and meeting with Soviet leader Joseph Stalin and his top lieutenants. During the visit, Liu and the Soviets reached a "division of labor" agreement: While the Soviet Union would remain "the commander of the world revolution" and play a major role in promoting revolutions in the West, the CCP would play a decisive role in promoting revolutions in the East.[2]

In retrospect, this was a rare yet revealing moment with mixed meanings – both blessings and curses – for the "world proletarian revolution." Mao's China's entry into the Cold War in such a way undoubtedly had greatly strengthened the imagined and actual power and influence of the communist bloc in the world. In the meantime, however, hidden in the "division of labor" deal was also the implication that the victory of the Chinese Communist Revolution might result in complications or even tensions between the

---

1 Mao Zedong, "On the People's Democratic Dictatorship," in *Mao Zedong xuanji* [Selected Works of Mao Zedong] (Beijing: Renmin, 1965), vol. IV, 1477.
2 Shi Zhe, "Liu Shaoqi in Moscow," *Chinese Historians* 6, 1 (Spring 1993), 84–85.

international communist movement's Moscow-centered structure and the Chinese Revolution's self-claimed and non-Western-oriented "model." It was here that history's irony was subtly demonstrated: At the very moment that Mao's statement seemed to have enhanced the "history on our side" conviction on the part of communists and communist sympathizers throughout the world, on a more fundamental level, it might already have opened the path leading up to the decline and demise of the cause of the world proletarian revolution.

In the next two decades, the international communist movement experienced a rise and, then, a decisive decline, as Beijing's relationship with Moscow changed dramatically from close allies to bitter enemies, causing pervasive and deep divisions among communists worldwide. This, to be sure, was a process shaped by many phenomena. What I would like to argue in this chapter is that, if one digs deep into the historical origins of the collapse of the Sino-Soviet alliance, lying there in plain sight were the structural tensions between the legitimacy narratives that the Chinese communists had constructed for their revolution (as epitomized in Mao's "we, the Chinese, have stood up" proclamation) and the logic and rationality, primarily informed by Western experience, underlying the Moscow-dominated international communist movement.

It is not the purpose of this chapter to provide another study on the trajectory of the rise and demise of the Sino-Soviet alliance. Rather, this chapter will concentrate on reconstructing the intricate connections and tensions between the mission statements of the Chinese Communist Revolution and the once Moscow-dictated mainstream discourse of the "world revolution." By doing so, this chapter aims to pursue a deeper understanding of why and how the victory of the Maoism-centered Chinese Revolution, while making the international communist movement a much broader and more diverse global force than if there had not been the Chinese inputs, also nurtured some of the most critical conditions leading up to international communism's eventual collapse as a twentieth-century phenomenon.

Early Development of the Chinese Communist Revolution

In the late 1910s and 1920s, the Chinese Communist Revolution arose in the context of the combined impacts of two trends emerging in China in the wake of the Great War: the profound domestic and international crises that China, as a newly emerged modern state of multiple nationalities, was then facing and, within this context, the introduction and spread of communist ideas in the Chinese intellectual space following the lead of the Russian Bolshevik Revolution.[3] This was a time in which Chinese intellectuals had been exposed to all kinds of Western concepts, such as anarchism, liberalism, democratic reformism and individualism. However, viewing what happened in Russia as a useful example that might provide them with the most rapid and effective way to transform China's status as a weak country, humiliated by its modern experience of imperialism, a group of radical intellectuals established the CCP in 1921.

From the beginning, the young Chinese communists looked upon Moscow as the Mecca of the world revolution, which, as they acknowledged in a series of early CCP documents, should be regarded as a Moscow-centered unified course for oppressed peoples and classes "all under heaven." They announced that the interests of China's own revolution were fundamentally compatible with those of the world revolution, and that the Chinese Revolution was subordinate to and, therefore, should serve the interests of the world revolution.[4]

Yet expression of such a belief did not necessarily prevent the young Chinese communists from identifying some of the specific characteristics of their own revolution as due to China's unique conditions. Particularly noteworthy was that, in the CCP's early representation of the party's missions and tasks, a highlighted theme was the connections between the Chinese revolution as one occurring in a "semi-colonial and semi-feudal" country and the struggles for national liberation by the oppressed peoples in the colonies of Western powers. The Chinese communists thus emphasized that "China's proletarian class must *simultaneously* carry out the national liberation movement and such a complicated struggle as the class movement," and that "our mission is to wage a *national* revolution to liberate the oppressed Chinese nation and, *on the basis of it*, to strive for serving the world revolution and liberation of oppressed nations and classes in the world, so as to liberate the oppressed nations and classes in the whole world."[5]

---

3 In Mao's words, it was "the salvoes of the October Revolution that had brought us Marxism-Leninism."

4 See, for example, "Resolution on the World Situation and the Chinese Communist Party," Jul. 1922; "Resolution on Joining the Third International," Jul. 1922, in *Zhonggong zhongyang wenjian xuanji* [Selected Documents of the CCP Central Committee] (Beijing: Zhonggong zhongyang dangxiao, 1988), vol. I, 59–60, 67.

5 "Draft Constitution of the Chinese Communist Party," Jun. 1923, United Front Department of the CCP (comp.), in *Minzu wenti wenxian huibian* [A Collection of Documents on Nationality Issues] (Beijing: Zhonggong zhongyang dangxiao, 1991), 21–22; "Declaration of the Third Congress of the CCP," Jun. 1923, in *Zhonggong zhongyang wenjian xuanji*, vol. I, 166 (emphasis added).

To a large extent, the above statements reflected the impact of Lenin's ideas of opening new paths for the world revolution through countries such as China and India. In essence, they had also revealed the strong Chinese-nationalist orientation of the conceptual realm of the founding generation of the Chinese communists (including Mao Zedong), and why and how they chose to pursue a communist revolution in China. A majority of them, while radical in their intellectual and political pursuits, had also been deeply influenced by China's ancient history and culture. They were drawn to communist ideas not solely because of Marxism-Leninism's theoretical attractiveness, but also due to their zeal to cope with the profound domestic and international challenges that China was then facing. Indeed, by claiming themselves communists, what they longed for the most was "to save China" while, at the same time, to revive China's lost central position in the world.

These two perceived missions were for the Chinese communist revolutionaries closely interrelated in their outlook on the larger world beyond China, and this, in the final analysis, was profoundly related to their use of the Chinese term "*Tianxia*" ("all under heaven") to define the space in which the revolution should be carried out. This *Tianxia* concept had its historical/cultural origin in the long development of Chinese civilization – implying that the Chinese way of life was the most superior and certainly central in the known universe. Often used in connection with *Tianxia* was the Chinese word "*Geming*," a term that in modern times would be adopted to represent the concept "revolution." The original meaning of *Geming* was that violent means must be used to deprive a ruler of heaven's mandate to rule. By employing *Tianxia* to define the scope of the Chinese Revolution, the Chinese communists, in a China-centered manner, had at once created a unique perspective in defining "world," often confusing it with the Chinese-centered *Tianxia* concept. Consequently, while facing the larger world, what the Chinese communists would take as the lodestar was China-oriented or even China-centered universalism (as the result of confusing *Tianxia* with "world"), rather than genuine internationalism.

The particular use of language by the Chinese communists also suggests that their approach toward the larger world, no matter how revolutionary in its appearance, had a hidden yet profound origin in the age-old Chinese tradition that the communist revolution had promised to transform. This, as this chapter will continuously demonstrate, exposes a fundamental paradox established deep in the settings that had nurtured the Chinese Communist Revolution: The Chinese communists had to find the means needed for transforming the "old" China and world from nowhere else but the very "old" world that was yet to be transformed.

Given that the CCP was still a very small and quite inexperienced political group, it had to wage the revolution by depending upon Moscow's support and following the instructions of the Comintern (Communist International). In 1923–27, under the Comintern's direction, and also with its financial aid and the participation of Soviet advisors, the CCP entered into a "united front" with the Guomindang (Nationalist Party, GMD). The CCP's strategies and policies in forming the united front with the GMD were largely dictated by Moscow, following the Leninist theory of "bourgeois democratic revolution" as preparation for carrying out a genuine socialist revolution in a backward country such as China. Beginning in 1925, with Moscow's support, the CCP and GMD jointly waged an anti-imperialist "Great Revolution," launching the Northern Expedition aimed at establishing a unified, strong and pro-Soviet republic.[6]

This revolutionary episode, however, was short-lived. A critical turning point came in April 1927, when Chiang Kai-shek (Jiang Jieshi), a military strongman who then had seized the GMD's leadership, launched a bloody anti-communist coup. Thousands of CCP members and supporters were ruthlessly murdered or imprisoned. Until a very late stage, the Comintern had instructed the CCP to stick to the strategies of allying with the GMD's "left-wing elements," so as to sustain the united front. The Comintern came up with these "instructions" for the CCP not through a good understanding of China's situation, but, rather, as a way to serve Stalin's need to defeat the "opposition" in Moscow's intra-party struggles. With Chiang's coup, this China strategy, directed by the Comintern, failed miserably.

The Rise of Mao and the Maoist Pattern of Chinese Revolution

In the wake of this disastrous setback to the Chinese communist revolution, the Comintern ordered the Chinese communists to wage armed struggle, with occupying major cities as a main goal. The CCP leadership tried hard to follow Moscow's instructions, but, as the party's strength was too weak in Chinese cities, all of their attempts failed. In the last such attempt, also

---

6 Yang Kuisong, *Zhongjian didai de geming: guoji dabeijing xia zhonggong chenggong zhidao* [Revolution in the Intermediate Zone: The CCP's Path to Victory in Grand International Contexts] (Taiyuan: Shanxi Renmin, 2010), ch. 2. In my opinion, this is one of the best accounts on Mao–Moscow relations published in the past two decades.

perceived as the most important, a military uprising in Guangzhou (Canton), Soviet military advisors and members of the Soviet consulate there even took to the streets and engaged directly in fighting. What followed was the suspension of diplomatic relations between the GMD government and Moscow.

Against this background, a group of CCP members moved to the countryside, where the enemy's control and influence were sporadic, to carry out armed struggle there. Among them was Mao Zedong. By mobilizing the revolutionary peasantry, Mao and his comrades organized the Red Army and created a "Red Zone" in Jiangxi province's mountainous peripheries. Deviating from Marxism-Leninism's orthodox notion, based on Western experience, that a communist revolution had to be carried out by urban proletarians, Mao found it both necessary and possible to create a rural-centered pattern of communist revolution. Supporting Mao's idea were both pragmatism and romanticism. On the one hand, Mao sensed that China, as a country with an overwhelming rural population and insufficient urban and industrial development, precluded an urban-centered communist revolution; on the other, he believed that China's backwardness in development made it easier for a revolution carried out by the peasants, the most oppressed and, therefore, the most revolutionary group in society, to succeed.[7]

Mao's novel revolutionary thesis encountered skepticism from many CCP leaders, almost all of whom were returnees from the Soviet Union, as well as from the Comintern itself. In the meantime, within the Red Zone, Mao's ruthless push for "suppression of reactionaries" (mostly those who disagreed with his policies and strategies) and "dictatorship by the party secretary" (e.g. by himself) had turned many of his comrades into his adversaries, leaving him in an awkward situation of political aloofness and, at times, isolation. Consequently, by late 1932, after the CCP leadership moved from underground Shanghai to the Red Zone, Mao lost his position as the Red Army's general political commissar.

Although Mao was not the Comintern's favorite, as opposed to what CCP official history had long claimed, he was not Moscow's designated dissident or enemy either. Rather, because of his known accomplishments in creating and developing the Red Army and the Red Zone, the Comintern, while discrediting much of his political thought, recognized him as "a popular

7 See, for example, Mao, "Analysis of the Classes in Chinese Society," "Report on the Peasant Movement in Hunan" and "Why Can the Red Political Power Exist in China?," in *Mao Zedong xuanji*, vol. I, 3–11, 13–46, 49–58.

leader" in the Red Zone. After Mao stepped down as the Red Army's actual supreme commander, unlike many of his purged comrades, he retained his position as chairman of the Chinese Soviet Republic, and his life was never in danger.[8] All of this, in retrospect, was of critical importance for Mao's later return to political primacy.

The biggest challenges that the Chinese Communist Revolution encountered were the ones from within. The substantial development of the Red Army and Red Zones up to the early 1930s was to a large extent the result of Chiang Kai-shek's inability to deal effectively with the "red peril," as he had to cope with repeated challenges from other factions within the GMD while at the same time managing Japan's rampant aggression against China. Beginning in 1933, Chiang was finally able to gather momentum and strength to launch massive attacks on the Red Zone. As for the Red Army, while bloody and continuous internal purges had seriously eroded its strength, its capacities to fight a prolonged war against Chiang's government were fundamentally compromised by a series of the Red Zone's own structural problems, especially those between the Zone's limited resources and the Red Army's endless need to fight against Chiang's superior forces. Finally, in the face of the overwhelming and ever-expanding military force that Chiang was able to amass, the Red Army was pushed to the verge of elimination by late 1934. They had no choice but embark upon what would later be called the "Long March."

During the early phase of the Long March, the CCP leadership lost their radio transmitter and, therefore, the means to communicate with Moscow. But this also meant that the CCP leadership could act without Moscow's close scrutiny and intervention. In early 1935, CCP leaders in desperation held an important meeting in Zunyi, in remote southwestern China, at which Mao was called back to the Red Army's commanding circle, opening the door for him to emerge as the party's top leader.[9] At the end of 1935, the remaining units of the Red Army arrived in the caves of northern Shaanxi. By then, after a series of fierce internal struggles, Mao had consolidated his position as a top military commander and political leader of the CCP.

According to the plans of Mao and his comrades, they would take northern Shaanxi as a place for the Red Army to regroup and find reinforcements. Then they would lead the troops to the areas bordering the Soviet Union and

8 Alexander V. Pantsov, with Steven I. Levine, *Mao: The Real Story* (New York: Simon & Schuster, 2012), 262–66.
9 Benjamin Yang, "The Zunyi Conference as One Step in Mao's Rise to Power," *China Quarterly* 106 (Jun. 1986), 235–71.

Outer Mongolia. And, after receiving weapons and ammunition (especially heavy artillery) from the Soviets, they would, with the backing of the Soviet Union, strive for the reconstruction of the Red Army and for the Chinese Communist Revolution.[10]

At this critical juncture, the CCP leadership learned that the Comintern's Seventh Congress, held in July–August 1935, had adopted the new strategy of an anti-fascist international united front. The instructions from the Comintern, combined with the CCP's own need for survival, formed the context in which the CCP leadership turned away from the decade-long strategy of overthrowing Chiang Kai-shek and began to pursue an anti-Japanese united front with the GMD. Thus, the CCP was engaged in negotiations with both Chiang's government and the "Young Marshal," Zhang Xueliang, whose forces were stationed in areas next to the Red Army's new bases. On 12 December 1936, Zhang launched a coup and kidnapped Chiang in Xi'an. Following the Comintern's instructions, the CCP actively participated in the processes that resulted in a peaceful solution of the Xi'an incident. Chiang agreed to stop the war with the CCP, so that the whole country would unite to fight against Japanese aggression.[11]

Despite the long-existing and widely accepted Maoist myth that the Chinese Revolution developed in constant resistance to Stalin's mistaken interference, and that the pre-1949 CCP–Moscow relationship was primarily confrontational, the real picture was much more complicated. In the 1920s and 1930s, the Chinese communists both suffered and greatly benefited from the Comintern's intervention, direction and support.

The Anti-Japanese War, "Rectification" and the CCP's Transformation

In July 1937, China's war of resistance against Japan erupted. The CCP, with the Comintern's full support, quickly entered into an anti-Japanese united front with GMD. In the ensuing eight years, the CCP held high the banner of revolutionary nationalism, thus becoming strikingly successful in creating a powerful public image demonstrating that, no matter to what extent they were loyal to communism, they were also nationalist in their essence. In practice, the party and its military forces made the utmost effort to carry

10 Yang Kuisong, *Zhongjian didai de geming*, 317–20.
11 For an excellent account of the subject, see Yang Kuisong, *Xi'an shibian xintan* [A New Study of the Xi'an Incident] (Taipei: Dongda, 1995).

out Mao's grand strategy of setting as the top priority the expansion of their power, rather than engaging in frontal wars with the Japanese. Consequently, toward the later phase of the war, the CCP, and its military forces in particular, had reached a level of power and influence unprecedented since its establishment.

Viewing Mao's rising power within the CCP leadership, the Comintern endorsed his status as the leader of the Chinese Revolution late in 1938.[12] When the Comintern announced its dissolution in May 1943, Mao and his comrades embraced another major opportunity with a huge impact upon the relationship between their own revolution and that of the world. This was the time that the CCP was engulfed by the Rectification Campaign (*Zhengfeng*), a major endeavor initiated by Mao to reshape the ideological and organizational structure of the Chinese Communist Revolution. Instead of physically eliminating Mao's opponents in intra-party struggles, the Rectification concentrated on transforming party members into "new human beings" through carefully designed and enforced procedures of "criticism and self-criticism." It also strived to achieve "Sinification of Marxism-Leninism" in accordance with China's specific conditions, so as to establish Mao Zedong Thought as the theoretical lodestar of the Chinese revolution. In 1945, the party's constitution formally designated Mao Zedong Thought as its official ideology. As a result, the Mao cult entered the CCP's mainstream discourse, serving as a critical supporting pillar to justify Mao's absolute authority and power within the party leadership.[13]

What, exactly, was Mao Zedong Thought? And, more specifically, how did Mao define the strategies for the Chinese revolution? In Mao's own summary, he highlighted armed struggle, a united front and the party's leadership role as the three keys that would lead the Chinese revolution toward victory. A firm believer in the idea that "political power grows out of the barrel of a gun," Mao invested great energy in developing strategies and tactics for waging revolutionary wars with both domestic and international aims. He particularly emphasized the importance of "making everyone a soldier" in waging a "people's war" against enemies, domestic and foreign. The "united front" strategy was designed to "unite with all of those who can be united" in order to fight against the primary and most dangerous enemy. In the

---

12 *Mao Zedong nianpu 1893–1949* [Chronological Biography of Mao Zedong 1893–1949] (Beijing: Zhongyang wenxian, 1993), vol. II, 90.

13 The best study on the subject is Gao Hua's classic, *Hong taiyang shi zenyang shengqi de* [How Did the Red Sun Rise] (Hong Kong: Zhongwen daxue chubanshe, 2000).

strategy's implementation in international affairs, it was strongly influenced by the traditional Chinese concept of "checking one barbarian by borrowing strength from another." Concerning the importance of the party's leadership role, Mao originally embraced Lenin's "democratic centralism." However, with continuous strengthening of his power and authority in the party's decision-making, he increasingly obscured the distinction between his own leadership role and that of the party. In his later years, Mao openly celebrated the "correct personality cult," making enhancement of the cult of himself a crucial condition for the ongoing revolution.

Mao was certainly a revolutionary romanticist or idealist, and simultaneously he was also a revolutionary pragmatist. In his own words, this duality of his political identity was conceived as a combination of "tiger spirit" and "monkey spirit" (e.g. the spirit to fight and the spirit to compromise).

Although the CCP leadership after the Rectification had been eager to embark upon the path toward constructing new meanings for the Chinese Revolution (which would not necessarily accord with the mainstream discourse of the Moscow-centered world revolution), publicly they continuously claimed loyalty to the international communist movement. Entering 1945, with the Soviet Red Army's rapid advance in Europe, Mao and his fellow CCP leaders believed that the Soviet Union would soon become a central actor in East Asian politics. Early in February 1945, Stalin informed Mao of the convening of the Yalta conference, which convinced Mao that "the possibility of the Soviet Union's voice in determining important Eastern affairs has increased."[14]

It was around this period that Mao and his comrades, in order to strengthen the CCP's position in competing for China's political power, also tried to approach the Americans. Sensing that the American military might be in need of the CCP's assistance in conducting landing operations in China's coastal areas, they took a series of actions in late 1944 to woo Washington. The party thus made every effort to label Chiang Kai-shek and his government as dictatorial, corrupt and incompetent, while presenting itself, nationalists at the core, as a force for "democratic reforms" in China.[15]

---

14 Telegram, Mao Zedong to Zhou Enlai, 3 Feb. 1945, in Zhang Shuguang and Chen Jian (eds.), *Chinese Communist Foreign Policy and the Cold War in Asia: New Documentary Evidence, 1944–1950* (Chicago: Imprint Publications, 1996), 21.
15 Joseph Esherick (ed.), *Lost Chance in China: The World War II Dispatch of John S. Service* (New York: Random House, 1974). Particularly revealing are the records of Service's interview with Mao on 23 August 1944, 295–307.

Great-power politics, however, was much more complicated than the perception of Mao and his comrades. At the Yalta conference, Stalin gained the promise by President Franklin D. Roosevelt of the United States that all former Russian rights and privileges lost to Japan during the 1904 Russo-Japanese War, including those in China's northeast (Manchuria) would be restored; in return, Stalin agreed to enter the war in Asia within two to three months of Germany's defeat. As part of the Yalta deals, Stalin also promised Roosevelt that, in order to fit China into the Yalta system that the Soviets and Americans had worked out, Moscow would recognize Chiang as China's legitimate leader and would not support the CCP in China's internal conflict.[16] As Stalin did not brief his Chinese comrades on such a deal, Mao and the CCP continued to base their strategies for preparing for a showdown with the GMD on the assumption that the Soviet entry into the anti-Japanese war would enhance the CCP's position in China.

War and Revolution in the "Intermediate Zone"

On 15 August 1945, China's war of resistance against Japan ended with Japan's unconditional surrender. Mao and the CCP leadership acted immediately to strive for political dominance in China, and they believed that in this they would receive support from the Soviet Union. On 9 August, the second day after the Soviet Union declared war on Japan, Mao Zedong ordered the communist forces to go all out to "cooperate with the Soviet Red Army" in the final battle to liberate China's lost territory from Japanese occupation.[17]

Chiang, who had also anticipated that a civil war with the CCP would come sooner or later, fully understood that he could ill afford to allow Moscow to stand behind the CCP. One day before Japan's surrender, he authorized the signing of a "Sino-Soviet Treaty of Friendship and Mutual Assistance," in which he accepted the independence of Outer Mongolia, and also acknowledged Soviet privileges in China's northeast. In return, he would get Soviet commitment to treating him as the leader of China's legal government, and not supporting the CCP in a civil war against his government. The same day, Chiang telegraphed Mao to invite him to come to

16 *Zhonghua minguo zhongyao shiliao chubian* [A Preliminary Compilation of Important Historical Materials of the Republic of China] (Taipei: Minguo 70, 1981), series III, vol. II, 542–43, 546–47.
17 Mao Zedong, "The Last Battle Against the Japanese Bandits," in *Mao Zedong xuanji*, vol. III, 1119.

Chongqing to "discuss questions related to reestablishing peace in China."[18]

Stalin then directly pressured his Chinese communist comrades to reach a compromise with Chiang. On 20 and 22 August, he sent two urgent telegrams to the CCP leaders, advising them that, with the surrender of Japan, the CCP should conduct discussions with the GMD about the restoration of peace and the reconstruction of the country. "If a civil war were to break out," warned Stalin, "the Chinese nation would face self-destruction."[19] Mao and his fellow CCP leaders, shocked, found themselves with no choice but to follow Stalin's instructions, as they had to rely heavily upon support from Moscow in their plans to compete for power in China.[20]

This was a bitter yet precious learning experience for Mao and his comrades, which pushed them further toward reevaluating the Chinese Communist Revolution's connections with the Moscow-led world revolution. In practice, however, they still had to count on whatever support Moscow was willing to provide in forming a grand strategy in the civil war against Chiang's government. Stalin was a person who never meant to unconditionally keep his word. Along with the intensification of the Soviet Union's confrontation with the United States in the world, Stalin, first covertly and then overtly, changed Soviet policies toward China in general and the CCP–GMD civil war in the northeast in particular, turning in the direction of supporting the CCP. The logic of the Cold War also made policymakers in Washington feel that they had no other choice but to back Chiang in the civil war. In turn, Stalin also became more willing and, at times, even more eager to back the Chinese communists. Following Stalin's instructions, the Soviet Red Army in the northeast and in Soviet-occupied North Korea offered all kinds of support to the CCP's military operations against the GMD. This transformed the northeast into a strategic and military stronghold for the CCP, creating conditions in which the Chinese communists could finally win the civil war.[21]

18 See Odd Arne Westad, *Cold War and Revolution: Soviet–American Rivalry and the Origins of the Chinese Civil War* (New York: Columbia University Press, 1993), 48–56.
19 Cited from *Mao Zedong nianpu*, vol. III, 13.
20 Chen Jian, *Mao's China and the Cold War* (Chapel Hill: University of North Carolina Press, 2001), 26–29.
21 Westad, *Cold War and Revolution*, esp. chs. 4 and 7; Niu Jun, *From Yan'an to the World: The Origin and Development of Chinese Communist Foreign Policy* (Norwalk, CT: EastBridge, 2005), chs. 10–11.

When the bloody Chinese Civil War was fully unfolding in 1946–47, and Mao and his comrades were formulating the party's grand strategies to fight the civil war for a "New China," they also found the need to come up with their own elaboration of the post-World War II world order and the position of China and the Chinese Revolution in it. Thus came into being what would be known as Mao's "intermediate zone" thesis. In August 1946, in an interview with Anna Louise Strong, a left-wing American journalist, Mao observed that a global confrontation had been emerging between the United States and the Soviet Union, yet between the two big powers existed a vast "intermediate zone" in Asia, Africa and Europe. And until the US imperialists had controlled the "intermediate zone," including China, they could not start a direct attack on the Soviet Union. Mao thus contended that, although the postwar world situation seemed to be characterized by the American–Soviet confrontation, the "principal contradiction in the world" was represented by the struggles between peoples in the "intermediate zone" (including China) and the reactionary US ruling class. It was these struggles, emphasized Mao, that would determine not only the direction of the global confrontation between the two big powers, but also the fate of the entire world.[22] In early 1947, an important article published in the name of Lu Dingyi, the CCP's propaganda chief, further elaborated on Mao's points (Mao personally revised the article):

> After the end of World War II, the principal contradiction in world politics exists not between the capitalist world and the socialist Soviet Union, nor between the Soviet Union and the United States, but between the democratic and anti-democratic forces in the capitalist world. More concretely speaking, the principal contradictions in today's world are those between the American people and American reactionaries, between Britain and the United States, and between China and the United States.[23]

To be sure, the Maoist intermediate-zone notion challenged the United States as a dominant imperialist power, and it also clearly stated that the CCP would stand on the side of the Soviet Union and the revolutionary forces in the world. On a deeper level, though, it also exposed a powerful tendency toward Chinese-centrism in Mao's and his comrades' definition of the Cold War world and China's position in it, indicating they were more than willing to

22 Mao, 'Talks with Anna Louise Strong," in *Mao Zedong xuanji*, vol. IV, 1191–92.
23 Lu Dingyi, "Explanations of Several Basic Problems Concerning the Postwar International Situation," *Jiefang ribao* (4 Jan. 1947); see also Mao's conversation with Liu Shaoqi and Zhou Enlai, 21 Nov. 1946, in *Mao Zedong nianpu*, vol. III, 150–51.

open a new path for the world revolution through promoting a worldwide course of decolonization.

"We, the Chinese, Have Stood Up"

In 1949, the Chinese Civil War ended with a CCP victory, and the People's Republic of China (PRC) – the "New China" – came into being. For Mao Zedong, however, this was not the revolution's conclusion but, rather, the beginning of a "continuous revolution," one that aimed to turn China into a land of universal justice, equality and prosperity while reviving its central position "all under heaven," which had just completed "the first step in a long march." Mao announced to the whole world that "we, the Chinese, have stood up."[24] In retrospect, this was a huge statement of legitimacy that, among its various meanings, linked the Chinese Revolution's previctory endeavors with its postvictory aspirations and strivings. In the ensuing years, Mao's China acted as a radical revolutionary country on the world scene, constantly challenging the legitimacy of the existing international order, which Mao and his comrades viewed as the product of Western domination and thus as inimical to revolutionary China. Accordingly, as mentioned in the opening paragraphs of this chapter, Mao made his "Lean to One Side" statement, and Beijing and Moscow worked out the "division of labor" agreement. In February 1950, the PRC further signed a treaty of strategic alliance with the Soviet Union.

Yet, behind all of this, Mao and his comrades were continuously perceiving the larger world in ways beyond the Cold War's bipolar structure. In November 1949, Liu Shaoqi delivered a widely circulated speech at the opening session of the Trade Union Conference of the Asian–Oceanic Region. By adopting a non-Western-oriented perspective, he emphasized that the CCP's victory served as a successful model for the national liberation movements in all colonial and semi-colonial countries. In particular, he reasoned that, as the Western powers had based their reactionary reigns at home upon the exploitation of the oppressed peoples in other parts of the world, the liberation of the colonies and semi-colonies would not only result in the collapse of the worldwide domination of Western imperialism but also lead to the emancipation of peoples throughout the world.[25] In retrospect,

24 Mao Zedong, 'The Chinese People Have Stood Up," in *Mao Zedong wenji* [A Collection of Mao Zedong's Writings] (Beijing: Renmin, 1995), vol. III, 342–46.
25 *Jianguo yilai Liu Shaoqi wengao* [Liu Shaoqi's Manuscripts Since the PRC's Formation] (Beijing: Zhongyang wenxian, 2005), vol. I, 161–62.

what Liu's approach revealed was, again, a potential challenge to international communism's unified structure with Moscow as the undisputed center.

Against the above background, one year after the PRC's establishment, Mao and the CCP leadership dispatched Chinese troops to Korea, entering into a direct military confrontation with the United States that would last until July 1953. Beijing also provided military and other support to the Vietnamese communists in a war against the French colonialists.[26] In addition to security and geopolitical concerns, by supporting revolutions in Korea (a former colony) and Vietnam (still under France's colonial rule), Mao and his comrades also meant to promote an "Eastern revolution" following the Chinese model, proving that, on a global scale, the victorious Chinese Revolution was indeed playing a central role in bridging the world revolution and the worldwide course of decolonization.[27] Domestically, these developments bolstered Mao's "continuous revolution" plans at home, allowing Mao's regime to occupy a powerful position to penetrate into almost every area of Chinese society through intensive mass mobilization under the banner of revolutionary nationalism.

A turning point came in 1954–55. At the Geneva conference of 1954, PRC premier Zhou Enlai took the initiative to meet with delegates from many noncommunist countries. In late June, Zhou visited India and Burma. Together with India's Prime Minister Jawaharlal Nehru and Burma's Prime Minister U Nu, Zhou introduced the "Five Principles of Peaceful Coexistence." In April 1955, Zhou participated in the Bandung conference of leaders from twenty-nine Asian and African countries. He made extensive efforts to have dialogues with leaders from other non-Western countries, emphasizing the common historical experience between China and them.[28]

Beijing's endorsement of the Five Principles had important normative meanings. Indeed, what Zhou had put forward were meant to form a whole set of new norms and codes in international affairs. They not only negated those by the Western powers but also deviated from those championed by the Soviet Union. For Mao and his comrades, that Beijing was able

---

26 Chen Jian, *Mao's China and the Cold War*, ch. 4; Zhai Qiang, *China and the Vietnam Wars, 1950–1975* (Chapel Hill: University of North Carolina Press, 2000), 1–2.
27 See, for example, Mao Zedong to Stalin, 2 and 13 Oct. 1950, in *Jianguo yilai Mao Zedong wengao* [Mao's Manuscripts Since the PRC's Formation] (Beijing: Zhongyang wenxian, 1987), vol. I, 539–40, 556.
28 *Zhou Enlai waijiao wenxuan* [Selected Diplomatic Papers of Zhou Enlai] (Beijing: Zhongyang wenxian, 1990), 112–34.

to occupy such high political and moral ground would further justify China's central role in transforming all spheres under heaven. Also, by presenting to China's ordinary people a strong case that the PRC's international status had risen, the CCP found itself occupying a more powerful position for promoting the party's – indeed Mao's – "continuous revolution" programs at home.

Not surprisingly, when the Soviet leader Nikita Khrushchev launched the de-Stalinization campaign in February 1956, Mao claimed that Khrushchev, albeit having "exposed problems," had also "made a mess" for the international communist movement.[29] In November 1957, Mao loudly announced at a summit of leaders of communist countries and parties in Moscow that "the east wind is prevailing over the west wind."[30] This was almost a declaration by Mao that Beijing was now ready to claim the leadership role in the world revolution. To demonstrate the fighting spirit of the Chinese communists, Mao even deliberately challenged Khrushchev's emphasis on "peaceful coexistence" with Western imperialist countries.[31]

The PRC's international behavior turned more radical in 1958 when the "Great Leap Forward" swept across China's cities and countryside. Ostensibly, Mao and the CCP leadership claimed that a main goal of the Leap was for China's industrial productivity, and steel production in particular, to surpass Britain's within fifteen years. In essence, Mao's real target was for China to surpass the Soviet Union in the shortest possible time.[32] Mao's main means to achieve such an extraordinarily ambitious goal was excessive mass mobilization. Believing that "a tense international situation can help mobilize the population," Mao ordered the People's Liberation Army to shell the Nationalist-controlled Jinmen islands in late August, as a way to support "the Arabic people's struggles against British–US imperialist intervention in Iraq." Although the Soviet Union was China's ally, Mao did not inform Moscow in advance of his decision to shell Jinmen.[33] This became the actual beginning of the Sino-Soviet split and disintegration of the world proletarian revolution.

---

29 Wu Lengxi, *Shinian lunzhan, 1956–1966: Zhong-Su guanxi huiyi lu* [Ten Years of Debate: Recollections from Sino-Soviet Relations], 2 vols. (Beijing: Zhongyang wenxian, 1999), vol. I, 6.
30 Mao, "Speech at a Meeting of the Representatives of Sixty-Four Communist and Workers' Parties," 18 Nov. 1957, China-Foreign Policy, Wilson Center Digital Archive.
31 Ibid.
32 Mao Zedong's talk during a discussion by group heads at an enlarged conference of the Central Military Commission, 23 Jun. 1958, 101/12/223, Fujian Provincial Archive.
33 Chen Jian, *Mao's China and the Cold War*, ch. 7.

The Great Leap Forward turned out to be a great disaster, causing one of the worst human tragedies in twentieth-century history. It is estimated that 20–30 million people (if not more) starved to death in a nationwide famine during 1959–61. In the wake of the Leap's miserable failure, Mao made a noticeable gesture by temporarily retreating to the "second line" in the Chinese leadership. After 1960–61, his colleagues, such as Liu Shaoqi and Deng Xiaoping, adopted a series of more moderate and flexible domestic policies to pursue economic recovery and social stability. This was accompanied by a softening of the tone of Beijing's international representation as well.

Yet this period was short-lived. Mao was unwilling to give up either his revolutionary programs or his position as China's supreme leader. When the Chinese economy showed signs of recovery from the Great Leap's dark shadow, Mao took action to return to the "first line." In September 1962, at the CCP Eighth Central Committee's Tenth Plenum, Mao called upon the whole party and whole country "never to forget class struggle." Along with continuous championing of anti-US imperialism, he placed "struggles against revisionism" at home and abroad as the party's top priority mission.[34] Lifted was the curtain on the great Sino-Soviet polemical debates. Mao openly criticized Khrushchev's policies of "peaceful coexistence" toward Western imperialist countries. Meanwhile, Mao also contended that Moscow had long carried out a policy of "great-power chauvinism" toward China, characterizing Moscow as a threat to Chinese sovereignty and independence.

This was also the time that Mao introduced a newer version of his "intermediate zone" thesis, arguing that between the United States and the Soviet Union "there existed two intermediate zones." The first was composed of "the vast economically backward countries in Asia, Africa and Latin America," and the second was "imperialist and advanced capitalist countries in Europe." And both the United States and the Soviet Union were being challenged everywhere in the world.[35] Accordingly, Beijing's international discourse increasingly highlighted the central role that China had played and would continuously play in promoting a "world revolution" with an emphasis on countries in the first zone, which, by applying the Chinese Revolution's rural-oriented pattern, were perceived as the "world's countryside."[36]

34 "Mao Zedong's Remarks on the Communiqué of the Tenth Plenary Session of the CCP's Eighth Central Committee," 26 Sep. 1962, *Jianguo yilai Mao Zedong wengao*, vol. X, 195–98.
35 *Mao Zedong on Diplomacy* (Beijing: Foreign Language Press, 1998), 388.
36 Lin Biao, "Long Live Victory of People's War," *Jiefang ribao* (3 Sep. 1965).

In the wake of the Gulf of Tonkin incident of August 1964, Beijing extended comprehensive security commitments and provided all kinds of support to North Vietnam.[37] When Indonesian president Sukarno, with the support of the Indonesian communists, launched the New Emerging Force movement, Beijing supported it enthusiastically. Beijing also endeavored to expand China's influences in Africa, beginning to offer economic, technological and medical support to the African countries that were most friendly to China. When the second Asian-Afro conference was scheduled to be convened in Algeria in June 1965, Beijing firmly opposed Soviet participation in the conference, even as an observer. Beijing also argued that India, which had fought a border war with China in 1962 and had been labeled by Beijing as a "lackey" of Western imperialism, should not play a major role in the conference. In the meantime, "Resisting America and Assisting Vietnam" emerged as a powerful theme that would bring China's domestic mass mobilization to much more intensive levels, serving Mao's efforts to gather popular support for his continuous-revolution programs.[38] What Mao hoped to see was the emergence of "great chaos all under heaven."

Failure of Mao's "Revolution All Under Heaven"

Beginning in summer 1966, Mao's "Great Proletarian Cultural Revolution," as his ultimate effort to instill a new social order into the hearts and minds of the Chinese people was known, engulfed the whole of China. For creating and sustaining the extraordinary momentum deemed necessary for excessive and sustained mass mobilization, Beijing was even more eager to claim the leadership role in the world revolution in 1966–68. Consequently, China's confrontations with the United States and conflicts with the Soviet Union escalated, and the PRC's relations with several friendly neighboring countries, such as Burma and Cambodia, also deteriorated. Within the international communist movement, the CCP had cut off formal relationships with almost all mainstream communist parties, supporting – and being supported by – a handful of pro-Beijing and, in most cases, tiny and little-known "genuine Marxist-Leninist" groups. In the socialist camp, at one point, only Albania gained Beijing's full recognition as a "country of true socialism."

37 Chen Jian, *Mao's China and the Cold War*, ch. 7.
38 For an excellent study on the subject, see Christopher Tang, "Domestic Internationalism, Popular Mobilization, and the Making of China's Cultural Revolution," Ph.D dissertation (Cornell University, Ithaca, 2016).

Still, however, Beijing announced that "the situation all under heaven is excellent," claiming that the Cultural Revolution had achieved "decisive victories." Yet the reality was that, although the Cultural Revolution had succeeded in destroying Mao's opponents and the "old" party-state control system, it was unable to get any closer to creating the new form of state power that he desired so much for building a new social order in China. When, in late 1968, Mao ordered the reestablishment of the party-state control system, he virtually acknowledged that his "continuous revolution" programs, depending so much upon people's "inner support," had failed. By September 1971, when Lin Biao, Mao's designated successor, fled China in mysterious conditions and died in a plane crash in Mongolia, millions and millions of everyday Chinese had lost whatever confidence they might still have had in the ultimate benefits of Mao's "continuous revolution" that had lasted in China for more than two decades.

All of this, combined with an almost desperate external security environment, had created the necessity and the possibility for Mao to improve relations with the United States. In February 1972, during "the week that changed the world," US president Richard Nixon made a historic trip to China and met with Mao in Beijing. In explaining to the Chinese people how the Chinese–American rapprochement happened, CCP organs throughout the country followed Beijing's instructions to emphasize that it was Nixon, head of the strongest imperialist country in the world, who came to Beijing after the total failure of Washington's two-decades-long attempts to isolate the New China in the world. So the Chinese–American opening, boasted of as a "great victory" of Mao's revolutionary foreign-policy lines, once again proved the Maoist proclamation that "we, the Chinese, have stood up" remained relevant and effective. Consequently, Mao's decision on achieving a rapprochement with the United States turned out to be his way to cope with the ever-deepening legitimacy crisis of the Chinese communist state.

The Chinese–American rapprochement dramatically shifted the balance of power between the United States and the Soviet Union and, more importantly, changed the essence of the Cold War. Ever since the Cold War had begun in the mid and late 1940s, it had been characterized by a fundamental confrontation between communism and liberal capitalism. The Sino-Soviet split buried the shared consciousness among communists in the world that communism was the most workable solution to the problems created by the worldwide process of modernization, and the Chinese–American rapprochement obscured the distinctions between socialist and capitalist paths toward modernity.

It was against the above background that Mao introduced his "Three Worlds" theory. On 22 February 1974, Mao told Zambian president Kenneth Kaunda: "The US and the Soviet Union belong to the First World." "The middle elements, such as Japan, Europe, Australia and Canada, belong to the Second World." And the "Third World" was composed of "all Asian countries, except Japan, and all of Africa and also Latin America."[39] Three days later, Mao stated to Algerian leader Houari Boumediene that "China belongs to the Third World, as politically and economically China is not in the same group of the rich and powerful, and thus can only be with those countries that are relatively poor."[40]

There existed striking similarities in perceptions of how the structure of the world should be defined between Mao's Three Worlds notion and his earlier "intermediate zone" and "two intermediate zones" theses that were introduced, respectively, in the late 1940s and early 1960s. In particular, they all envisioned China as a central actor in bringing about changes in the world on the basis of challenging and transforming the existing world order. But there also were significant differences. While the earlier theses were still generally compatible with the concept of "world proletarian revolution," the Three Worlds notion highlighted "development," rather than "revolution," as a question of fundamental importance that China and other Third World countries must encounter. By discarding the discourse of revolution in such a way, Mao's China had made a significant contribution, more than any other actor of the international communist movement was able to do, to the shaping of a noncommunist/postcolonial world.

Not surprisingly, China's external policies in Mao's last years, demonstrating a strong "derevolutionization" tendency, were gradually yet decisively moving away from the previous practices of supporting revolutions in other countries. In the Chinese media, reports about communist-led guerrilla wars in Southeast Asian countries such as Burma, Thailand, Malaysia and the Philippines gradually disappeared, and Beijing dramatically reduced its actual support to communist rebels there. Toward the last stage of the US–Vietnamese talks in Paris, Beijing's leaders urged their comrades in Hanoi to cut a deal with the Americans. After the signing of

39 *Mao Zedong on Diplomacy* (Beijing: Foreign Languages Press, 1993), 454.
40 "Mao Zedong's Conversations with Houari Boumediene," 25 Feb. 1974, CCP Central Committee Document No. 10 (1974), 4, 244-1-106, Fujian Provincial Archive.

the Paris accords, almost immediately Beijing significantly reduced its military and other aid to Hanoi, although the "Vietnamese revolution" was then not yet completed.[41]

In Mao's last years, China was also taking substantial steps to enter the Western/capitalist-dominated world market. Beginning in 1972, Beijing approved and implemented twenty-six major projects to import complete sets of equipment and technologies from Western countries and Japan, with a total budget of more than US$ 4.3 billion.[42] Although Mao himself never totally gave up the use of revolutionary language in describing China's domestic and international policies, the reality was that in his last years China was abandoning the status of a "revolutionary country" on the world scene. The Chinese Communist Revolution that had once aimed to destroy capitalism's global reign was no longer alive.

Epilogue: China's Departure from Revolution

Mao died on 9 September 1976. In less than two years, Deng Xiaoping emerged as China's paramount leader. Almost immediately he launched a grand "reform and opening" project, which, in essence, was also a derevolutionization process. In particular, the CCP leadership under Deng formally abandoned Mao's "continuous revolution" discourse and practice, allowing economic development to take precedence over radical politics. Sensing that the post-Mao Chinese communist state was facing an ever-deepening legitimacy challenge, Deng hoped that the improvement of everyday people's living standards would help bring legitimacy back to the communist state, which, with the unfolding of the reform and opening process, was made anything but "communist."

In the meantime, Beijing adopted a new open approach toward the "world market" dominated by global capitalism, and this was exactly what the "opening" process aimed to embrace. During the Maoist era, markets and the pursuit of profits generally were regarded as values and practices inimical to genuine socialism. In the "reform and opening" era,

41 Chen Jian, "China, the Vietnam War, and the Sino-American Rapprochement, 1968–1973," in Odd Arne Westad and Sophie Quinn-Judge (eds.), *The Third Indochina War: Conflict Between China, Vietnam and Cambodia, 1972–1979* (London: Routledge, 2006), 53–59.

42 Reports on importing technology and whole-set equipment from the United States and other Western countries, Li Xiannian to Zhou Enlai et al., 25 Dec. 1972 and 4 Jan. 1972, in *Jianguo yilai Li Xiannian wengao* [Li Xiannian's Manuscripts Since the PRC's Formation] (Beijing: Zhongyang wenxian, 2011), vol. III, 189, 190.

Deng and his colleagues began to perceive China's path toward modernity in a very different light. For Deng, China's improved relations with the United States remained valuable in the strategic and geopolitical senses. Yet, more importantly, the quasi-strategic partnership between Beijing and Washington was highly compatible with Deng's new vision of looking to the West for models of modernizing China. Reportedly, when Deng was on his way to visit the United States in January 1979, he said that all of those Third World countries on the side of the United States had been successful in their modernization drive, whereas all of those against the United States had not been successful. He said that China should be on the side of the United States.[43] The statement's implication was that China was to change from an "outsider" into an "insider" within the existing international order.

By then, China virtually had withdrawn from the Cold War – although the Cold War would not end until the late 1980s and early 1990s, with the collapse of the Soviet Union and fall of international communism as a twentieth-century phenomenon. At the end of the day, the Chinese Communist Revolution both changed the world and was changed – or, more accurately speaking, "socialized" – by the world. Yet the origins of this development, as revealed by discussion in this chapter, can and must be traced back to the much longer history of the Chinese Communist Revolution's complex relations with the world.

Bibliographical Essay

Early scholarship on the subject, at a time that scholars had only limited access to original documentation, was scarce. Several works had played a pioneering role in establishing the foundation for the field: Allen S. Whiting, *Soviet Policies in China, 1917–1924* (New York: Columbia University Press, 1951); Benjamin Schwarz, *Chinese Communism and Rise of Mao* (Cambridge, MA: Harvard University Press, 1951); Chalmers Johnson, *Peasant Nationalism and Communist Power: The Emergence of Revolutionary China, 1937–1945* (Stanford: Stanford University Press, 1962); and Jerome Chen, *Mao and the Chinese Revolution* (New York: Oxford University Press, 1965). A three-volume collection, *China in Crisis*, edited by Ping-ti Ho and Tang Tsou (Chicago: University of Chicago Press, 1968), presented a systematic effort by a group of leading

---

43 Information gained from an August 2008 interview with a leading Chinese Communist Party historian, and confirmed later through several other sources.

scholars in the field to explore the historical genesis of the Chinese age of crises and revolutions.

From the late 1960s to the 1980s, the field witnessed substantial growth against the background of major changes such as the rise and fall of Mao's Cultural Revolution, China's total split with the Soviet Union and, after twenty years of hostility and confrontation, rapprochement with the United States, and the launch of Deng Xiaoping's "reform and opening" project.

A refined general history of the Chinese Communist Revolution is provided in Lucien Bianco, *Origins of the Chinese Revolution, 1915–1949*, trans. Muriel Bell (Stanford: Stanford University Press, 1971); James P. Harrison, *The Long March to Power: A History of the Chinese Communist Party, 1921–1972* (New York: Praeger, 1972); and John King Fairbank, *The Great Chinese Revolution* (New York: Harper and Row, 1986).

In *Li Tachao and the Origins of Chinese Marxism* (Cambridge, MA: Harvard University Press, 1967), Maurice Meisner offers an insightful account of Marxism's introduction into China and the establishment of the Chinese Communist Party. Martin Wilbur, together with Julie-Lien-ying How, summarized achievements of his four decades of study of the Soviets and the early development of the Chinese Revolution in *Missionaries of Revolution: Soviet Advisers and Nationalist China, 1920–1927* (Cambridge, MA: Harvard University Press, 1989). Also noteworthy is Richard C. Thornton, in *The Comintern and the Chinese Communists, 1928–1931* (Seattle: University of Washington Press, 1969).

The development of the Chinese Communist Revolution and its external policies are covered by Lyman Van Slyke, *Enemies and Friends: The United Front in Chinese Communist History* (Stanford: Stanford University Press, 1967), and John W. Garver, *Chinese–Soviet Relations, 1937–1945: The Diplomacy of Chinese Nationalism* (New York: Oxford University Press, 1988). Mark Selden, in *The Yenan Way in Revolutionary China* (Cambridge, MA: Harvard University Press, 1971), provided a highly positive perspective of the rise of the Maoist pattern of the Chinese Revolution. Joseph Esherick, by editing and publishing *Lost Chance in China: World War II Dispatches of John S. Service* (New York: Random House, 1974), introduced the "lost chance" thesis, arguing that Washington might have lost a "chance" to pursue accommodation with the Chinese communists in the 1940s. The thesis's impact was reflected in James Reardon-Anderson, *Yenan and the Great Powers: The Origins of Chinese Communist Foreign Policy, 1944–1946* (New York: Columbia University Press, 1980), and Dorothy Borg and Waldo H. Heinrichs (eds.), *Uncertain*

Years: Chinese–American Relations, 1947–1950 (New York: Columbia University Press, 1980). Steven Levine, in *Anvil of Victory: The Communist Revolution in Manchuria, 1945–1949* (New York: Columbia University Press, 1987), portrays the CCP's political and social revolutions in the northeast and US responses to them.

Quite useful are several memoirs: *The Rise of the Chinese Communist Party*, 2 vols. (Lawrence: University Press of Kansas, 1972), by Chang Kuo-tao, a founder of the Chinese Communist Party and once a main leader, who later defected from the party; *A Comintern Agent in China, 1932–1939* (Stanford: Stanford University Press, 1982), by Otto Braun, a German military advisor dispatched by the Comintern to work in the innermost decision-making circles of the CCP and the Red Army in the 1930s; and *The Vladimirov Diaries: Yanan, China, 1942–1945* (New York: Doubleday, 1975), by Peter Vladimirov, the Soviet representative in Yan'an who worked closely with Mao and other top CCP leaders.

With the end of the Cold War, and China simultaneously embarking upon the "reform and opening" process, scholars have gained access to previously inaccessible primary sources in China, the former Soviet Union and other communist countries. In the meantime, the end of the Maoist era and China's sharp departure from its revolutionary past also pushed scholars to reconsider how better to understand the Chinese Communist Revolution's complex relations with the world.

Joseph W. Esherick, in "Ten Theses of the Chinese Revolution," *Modern China* 21, 1 (Jan. 1995), 45–76, highlighted the necessity of revisiting a series of widely accepted notions in narrating and interpreting the Chinese Revolution, so as to take the study of China's revolutionary era, including relations between the Chinese Revolution and the world, to deeper levels.

Fresher, more solid and more critical studies on the establishment of the Chinese Communist Party have been offered in Hans J. Van de Ven, *From Friend to Comrade: The Founding of the Chinese Communist Party, 1920–1927* (Berkeley: University of California Press, 1991), and Yoshihiro Ishikawa, *The Formation of the Chinese Communist Party*, trans. Joshua A. Fogel (New York: Columbia University Press, 2012). With the support of newer Russian documentation, Alexander Pantsov wrote *The Bolsheviks and the Chinese Revolution 1919–1927* (Honolulu: University of Hawaii Press, 2005).

The Yan'an years, as a defining period for both the Chinese Communist Revolution and its relationship with the world, have received scholars' fresh attention. Mark Selden revisited his 1971 study and published *China in Revolution: The Yenan Way Revisited* (Armonk, NY: M. E. Sharpe, 1995). The best study on the subject, in my view, is Gao Hua, *Hong Taiyan shi zenyang shengqi de* [How Did the Red Sun Rise?] (Hong Kong: Zhongwen daxue chubanshe, 2000). The book's English translation, after many years of work, is now in press by the Chinese University Press in Hong Kong.

On the making and development of Chinese communist policies, notable studies include: Michael H. Hunt, *Genesis of the Chinese Communist Foreign Policy* (New York: Columbia University Press, 1996); Niu Jun, *From Yan'an to the World: The Origins and Development of Chinese Communist Foreign Policy* (Norwalk, CT: EastBridge, 2005); and Michael M. Sheng, *Battling Western Imperialism: Mao, Stalin and the United States* (Princeton: Princeton University Press, 1997). On the Chinese Civil War of the late 1940s, two books by Odd Arne Westad, *Cold War and Revolution: Soviet–American Rivalry and the Origins of the Chinese Civil War* (New York: Columbia University Press, 1993) and *Decisive Encounters: The Chinese Civil War, 1945–1950* (Stanford: Stanford University Press, 2003), offer narratives both insightful and informative.

Scholars found the need to reconsider the once-prevailing "lost chance" thesis. For a symposium on the subject (organized by Warren I. Cohen, and with the participation of Chen Jian, Michael Sheng, John Garver and Odd Arne Westad), see "Symposium: Rethinking the Lost Chance in China," *Diplomatic History* 21 (Winter 1997), 71–115.

Chen Jian, in *Mao's China and the Cold War* (Chapel Hill: University of North Carolina Press, 2001), discusses China's encounters with the Cold War world. On the CCP and Mao's China's changing relations with Moscow, good studies include: Dieter Heinzig, *The Soviet Union and Communist China 1945–1950: The Arduous Road to the Alliance* (New York: Routledge, 2003); Odd Arne Westad (ed.), *Brothers in Arms: The Rise and Fall of the Sino-Soviet Alliance* (Washington, DC, and Stanford: Wilson Center Press and Stanford University Press, 1998); and Shen Zhihua and Xia Yafeng, *Mao and the Sino-Soviet Partnership, 1945–1959* (Lanham, MD: Lexington Books, 2015).

Mao Zedong and Zhou Enlai were central figures of the Chinese Communist Revolution and Chinese communist foreign policies. A systematic analysis of Mao Zedong Thought was offered in Stuart Schram, *The Thought of Mao Zedong* (Cambridge: Cambridge University Press, 1989). The three most important Mao biographies published in the past twenty years are: Philip Short, *Mao: A Life* (New York: Henry Holt, 1999); Jung Chang and

Jon Halliday, *Mao: The Unknown Story* (New York: Alfred A. Knopf, 2005); and Alexander V. Pantsov, with Steven I. Levine, *Mao: The Real Story* (New York: Simon & Schuster, 2012). These last two were written with insights gained from post-Cold War Russian archives. On Zhou, two biographies are most useful to date: Gao Wenqian, *Zhou Enlai, the Last Perfect Revolutionary: A Biography* (New York: PublicAffairs, 2007); Han Suyin, *Eldest Son: Zhou Enlai and the Making of Modern China, 1898–1976* (New York: Kodansha International, 1994). The author of the former was once head of the Zhou biographical group of the CCP Central Institute of Documentation. Also useful is Chen Jian, "Zhou Enlai and China's 'Prolonged Rise,'" in Ramachandra Guha (ed.), *Makers of Modern Asia* (Cambridge, MA: Harvard University Press, 2014), 147–71.

For reviews of the state of the field, see Michael H. Hunt and Odd Arne Westad, "The Chinese Communist Party and International Affairs: A Field Report of the New Historical Sources and Old Research Problems," *China Quarterly* 122 (Summer 1990), 258–72; see also Michael H. Hunt, "CCP Foreign Relations: A Guide to the Literature," *Cold War International History Project Bulletin* 6–7 (Winter 1995–96), 129, 136–43; and Xia Yafeng, "The Study of Cold War International History in China: A Review of the Last Twenty Years," *Journal of Cold War Studies* 10, 1 (Winter 2008), 81–115.

5

Nikita Khrushchev and De-Stalinization in the Soviet Union 1953–1964

JÖRG BABEROWSKI

Stalin's death caused widespread uncertainty. How could it be that the father of the people was mortal? His subjects had praised and celebrated the despot for years, and now he was dead. Even on the banks of the Kolyma River in the Far East only very few people understood what was happening to them. Yevgenia Ginzburg, who was still in exile in March 1953, recalls the uncertainty that had taken hold of the regime's functionaries upon hearing the news of the leader's illness:

> But his death had a veritable devastating effect upon Kolyma's superiors. No wonder that their blood pressure skyrocketed and bouts of angina pectoris were a daily occurrence. No, despite their realist way of thinking, these people could not come to terms with the vulgar thought that the genius, the leader, father, creator, inspirer, organizer, best friend, the expert and so forth was subject to the same miserable biological laws as any other ordinary prisoner or settler.[1]

Undoubtedly, most people were devastated when they heard of the dictator's death. However, not everyone who learned of his passing felt pain. "What a beautiful day it is today," informers overheard a man saying in Moscow's tram. "Today, we bury Stalin, now we face one villain fewer."[2] Upon hearing of Stalin's death, prisoners in the camps cheered, and joy quietly spread among the victims of the dictatorship. But would the dictator's death usher in the end of repression and terror? In March 1953, no one would have dared to answer this question. The feeling of uncertainty was omnipresent.[3]

1 Jewgenija Ginsburg, *Gratwanderung*, 3rd edn. (Munich: Piper, 1984), 418.
2 Vladimir Kozlov and Sergei Mironenko (eds.), 58–10. *Nadzornye proizvodstva prokuratury SSSR po delam ob antisovetskoi agitatsii i propagande. Annotirovannyi katalog. Mart 1953–1991* (Moscow: MFD, 1999), 13.
3 Yelena Zubkova, *Obshchestvo i reformy 1945–1964* (Moscow: Rossiia molodaia, 1993).

Millions of people, who had never experienced anything but the Stalinist dictatorship, began to ask themselves who would take care of them and what would become of them and their country. Who would succeed the dictator? "We felt helplessness," remembered one female worker from Moscow, "and asked the question: what will we do now?"[4] However, by March 1953 no one could have conceived of what would happen shortly after: Stalin's companions would disengage themselves from their almighty father and end the terror forever.

The new balance of power had already been established while Stalin was on his sickbed. Georgii Malenkov and Lavrentii Beria pledged each other their loyalty and agreed upon a strategy for the succession, even before the members of the Politburo could convene. At least, this is what Nikita Khrushchev would claim afterward.[5] Malenkov was supposed to become the prime minister, Beria would reestablish his total control over the Interior Ministry and the secret police, while Viacheslav Molotov would become foreign minister. Khrushchev himself, who at this point in time was only second in line, was left with the chairmanship of the party, which had lost its importance during the final years of Stalin's life.

Although there was no political pressure to do so, by the spring of 1953 Stalin's heirs had already agreed not only to banish terror and arbitrary violence from the inner circle of power, but also to do away with them as tools of governance in general. They stopped the proceedings against those accused in the Doctors' Plot, the so-called doctor-killers, released all who had been arrested and ended the anti-Semitic campaign that had virtually flooded all aspects of everyday life during the final years of Stalin's rule. They abolished torture and heavily curbed the powers of the security apparatus. When Ginzburg heard the newscaster say that the proceedings against the doctors had been terminated because the security organs had violated the laws, it was as if her world had been turned upside down:

4 Cited in Yurii Aksiutin, *Khrushchevskaia "ottepel'" i obshchestvennye nastroenia v SSSR v 1953–1964 gg.* (Moscow: ROSSPEN, 2004), 26. For additional reports on the mood within society, see Sheila Fitzpatrick (ed.), *Sedition: Everyday Resistance in the Soviet Union Under Khrushchev and Brezhnev* (New Haven: Yale University Press, 2011).
5 "Iz rechi pervogo sekretaria TsK KPSS N. S. Khrushcheva na plenume TsK KP Ukrainy, 18 fevralia 1955," in A. N. Artizov et al. (eds.), *Nikita Sergeevich Khrushchev. Dva tsveta vremeni. Dokumenty iz lichnogo fonda N. S. Khrushcheva* (Moscow: ROSSPEN, 2009), vol. I, 531; N. Kovaleva et al. (eds.), *Molotov, Malenkov, Kaganovich. 1957. Stenogramma iiunskogo plenuma TsK KPSS i drugie dokumenty* (Moscow: Mezhdunarodnyi fond "Demokratiia," 1998), 45.

And now, for the first time since the listeners had been able to think, the voice of power spoke about its own mistakes … These strange words, however, were not spoken very clearly, as if they were forced out of someone's mouth with immense effort. But at least they were spoken at all. For us, this was the beginning of a new era.[6]

But how was it that Khrushchev of all people, the unsophisticated son of a peasant from the village of Kalinovka in Kursk, rose to become the first among equals? Khrushchev struggled to express himself in an appropriate way, he could read and write only with difficulty and he was lost when it came to Marxist terminology. He did not even read any books and only copied what others wrote and said.[7] But still, by 1954, he was no longer simply the First Secretary of the Central Committee but also the undisputed head of the reform party in the Kremlin. Without the communist party, Khrushchev would have remained an official of secondary importance. It was the party that enabled him to climb to the top of the reform movement. Stalin had deprived the communist party of its power. The Central Committee had ceased to convene, and the party had held only one congress in the years between 1939 and 1953, with the sole aim of paying homage to the old dictator. Since the party had stopped being a place for social and political mobilization, all the important decisions were made in the ministries and at Stalin's court.[8] After the dictator's death, the authorities had lost their source of legitimacy. Now, his successors could draw only on the party as a source of legitimacy. They needed the approval of the Central Committee and of the party committees in the provinces. This was Khrushchev's chance: He reactivated the party apparatus because he understood that there would be no change without it. Any authority would be based on belief in its legitimacy. However, this belief could be generated only within the party, because a different kind of public simply did not exist. Without the party's revitalization, de-Stalinization would not have taken place. Khrushchev would have been a reformer without power or backing, and would have been unable to come out on top.[9]

6 Ginsburg, *Gratwanderung*, 423; Wolfgang Ruge, *Gelobtes Land. Meine Jahre in Stalins Sowjetunion*, 2nd edn. (Berlin: Rowohlt, 2012), 421–22.
7 Dmitrii Shepilov, *The Kremlin's Scholar: A Memoir of Soviet Politics Under Stalin and Khrushchev* (New Haven: Yale University Press, 2007), 64–67; William Taubman, *Khrushchev: The Man and His Era* (New York: W. W. Norton, 2003), 18–44, 56–57.
8 Yoram Gorlizki and Oleg Khlevniuk, *Cold Peace: Stalin and the Soviet Ruling Circle, 1945–1953* (Oxford: Oxford University Press, 2004), 17–65.
9 Alexander Titov, "The Central Committee Apparatus Under Khrushchev," in Jeremy Smith and Melanie Ilic (eds.), *Khrushchev in the Kremlin: Policy and Government in the Soviet Union, 1953–1964* (London: Routledge, 2011), 41–60; Yoram Gorlizki, "Party Revivalism and the Death of Stalin," *Slavic Review* 54, 1 (1995), 1–22.

Khrushchev could have simply remained a Stalinist once he had secured power. No one expected him to come to terms with the past in such an uncompromising way. In 1953, not a single Soviet subject or communist would have called for the changes that eventually occurred in 1956. However, de-Stalinization was the project of a humiliated man who had freed himself from his almighty father and could no longer live with his guilt. "I have no doubt," wrote Georgii Arbatov, one of the authors of *perestroika*, "that Stalin's cruelty, perfidy, and despotism were repugnant to Khrushchev, who had been personally humiliated by Stalin more than once."[10] Only a few weeks after the dictator's death, all traces of his presence had been removed, since his former companions did not wish to be reminded of the constant humiliation that they had suffered during his reign. Stalin's books and records – his private belongings – were scattered, his employees and his staff were removed, and even his dacha in Kuntsevo was locked down. By 1955, while the press still mentioned Stalin's birthday, no one within the leadership spoke about the merits of the father and teacher any more.

A new era had undoubtedly begun. In a speech before the Leningrad Party Committee in 1954, Khrushchev broached the issue of the "Leningrad Affair." In 1950, Stalin had called for the execution of both the head of Gosplan, Nikolai Voznesenskii, and Aleksei Kuznetsov, the city's party leader. More than a thousand of their followers also perished along with them. Khrushchev spoke of the crime without naming the criminal. He explained that Beria, rather than Stalin, had been responsible for the murders. It was Beria, the Kremlin's evil spirit, who had duped the old and sick dictator and removed his own rivals, Voznesenskii and Kuznetsov. Nevertheless, for the first time, Khrushchev addressed questions of the perpetrators' responsibility in his speech. According to him, it was impossible to pretend that nothing had happened. "The Central Committee considers itself responsible for restoring the truth and for clearing the name of the Leningrad Party Committee."[11]

Soon after, in June 1955, Khrushchev also confronted the state attorneys with the violence of the previous years. At a procurators' conference, Khrushchev openly spoke about terror and torture, despotism and

---

10 Georgy Arbatov, *The System: An Insider's Life in Soviet Politics* (New York: Random House, 1992), 51.

11 "Rech pervogo sekretaria TsK KPSS N. S. Khrushcheva na soveshchanii apparata leningradskogo oblastnogo i gorodskogo komitetov KPSS," in Artizov et al. (eds.), *Khrushchev*, vol. I, 502; Aksiutin, *Khrushchevskaia "ottepel'*," 113. On the Leningrad Affair, see Jörg Baberowski, *Verbrannte Erde. Stalins Herrschaft der Gewalt* (Munich: C. H. Beck, 2012), 485–87.

lawlessness. People had been shot without receiving a sentence, and public prosecutors had not been able to visit the prisons and question the prisoners. "Why did this happen?" he shouted into the hall, "Why? Because public order had been destroyed. One should not only depend on personal relations, comrades. We need to choose persons, we need to control them, but despite all of this, we have to have strict legality, and legality permits us to control each person."[12]

However, Khrushchev was also a man who knew how to use the power that had landed in his lap. From the very beginning, he used his opportunities as party leader to place his own followers at the center of the apparatus. In September 1953, the First Secretary of the Communist Party of Georgia, Aleksandr Mirtskhulava, was replaced by Khrushchev's follower Vasil Mzhavanadze. The same also occurred in other regions. By March 1954, eighteen members and eleven candidates of the Central Committee had been removed from their offices and replaced by Khrushchev's allies. And by the Twentieth Party Congress in February 1956, forty-five of eighty-four party secretaries within the republic and regional committees had been removed and replaced by Khrushchev's intimates.[13] The distribution of power thus slowly began to shift and, already by 1954, Khrushchev was able to exert pressure upon his adversaries Molotov and Malenkov. Molotov was forced to submit to Khrushchev's new foreign-policy line, while Malenkov lost his post as prime minister in February 1955 because he had, as stated in an explanation by the Politburo, been an accomplice of Beria, and had failed to perform his duties as the head of government. However, Molotov remained in office and Malenkov was merely demoted to the post of deputy prime minister. Both were able to remain members of the Politburo.[14]

Khrushchev himself had experienced what it had meant to live in fear. He had been humiliated by Stalin and had feared the dictator's cruelty. Arbatov recalled that Khrushchev "had suffered the crushing loss of human dignity

---

12 "Iz vystupleniia Khrushcheva N. S. na vsesoiuznom soveshchanii prokurorsko-sledstvennykh rabotnikov," in Artizov et al. (eds.), *Khrushchev*, vol. I, 544.

13 A. A. Fursenko (ed.), *Prezidium TsK KPSS 1954–1964*, vol. II, *Postanovleniia 1954–1958* (Moscow: ROSSPEN, 2006), 35–36; Thomas H. Rigby, "Khrushchev and the Resuscitation of the Central Committee," in Thomas H. Rigby (ed.), *Political Elites in the USSR: Central Leaders and Local Cadres from Lenin to Gorbachev* (Aldershot: Edward Elgar, 1990), 154–60; Thomas H. Rigby, "Khrushchev and the Rules of the Soviet Political Game," in Robert Miller and Ferenc Féhér (eds.), *Khrushchev and the Communist World* (London: Croom Helm, 1984), 55–59.

14 Fursenko (ed.), *Prezidium TsK KPSS 1954–1964*, vol. II, 40–43; Aksiutin, *Khrushchevskaia "ottepel'*," 111–19, 152–75.

that comes from constant fear."[15] But with Khrushchev's ascendance all of this disappeared from the everyday life of the ruling circle, where differences of opinion or a defeat in the vote no longer had to be paid for with one's freedom or even one's life. Not even Stalin's most loyal companions would have longed for a remake of the Stalinist dictatorship. For them, too, Khrushchev's actions came as a relief. In the spring of 1957, Molotov and Malenkov dared to join forces with Lazar Kaganovich and Nikolai Bulganin against Khrushchev in order to oust him from office. Although they were able to prevail in the Politburo, Khrushchev insisted that this question of power be referred to the Central Committee. Because the Central Committee's members had no interest in returning to the old state of affairs, they supported the reformer. Nevertheless, Molotov, Malenkov and Kaganovich were allowed to explain and defend themselves before the Central Committee.[16] Stalin would have undoubtedly forced them to incriminate themselves and would have had them killed had they refused to do so. And this is why Kaganovich, who had been one of the most ruthless and faithful of Stalin's accomplices, initially feared the worst when he was cast out of the inner ruling circle. He was scared and pleaded with Khrushchev for his life. "Comrade Khrushchev, I have known you for several years. I ask you to prevent me from being treated like we treated people under Stalin." "Iron Lazar" served a mild sentence. In 1957, he was ousted from the Politburo and was dismissed to manage an asbestos factory in the Ural Mountains. Even Molotov, who had plotted with Kaganovich against Khrushchev, was dealt no more than a symbolic, humiliating blow. Stalin's foreign minister was sent to Mongolia as an ambassador.[17]

The risks tied to criticism and opposition had become much more predictable, as even the Stalinists neither desired to return to the terror nor believed that it would be possible to do so. When Khrushchev's opponents agreed to overthrow him in the summer of 1964, believing that he presented a security threat to them, they thus took only a slight risk. Khrushchev had been forced to yield to the pressure exerted by the United States during the

15 Arbatov, *The System*, 51.
16 Taubman, *Khrushchev*, 317–24; Oleg Grinevskij, *Tauwetter. Entspannung, Krisen und neue Eiszeit* (Berlin: Sielder, 1996), 58–82; Kovaleva et al. (eds.), *Molotov, Malenkov, Kaganovich*.
17 S. Parfenov, "'Zheleznyi Lazar.' Konets kar'ery," *Rodina* 2 (1990), 74. See also Feliks Chuev, *Tak govoril Kaganovich. Ispoved stalinskogo apostola* (Moscow: Otechestvo, 1992); V. A. Torchinov and A. M. Liontiuk (eds.), *Vokrug Stalina. Istoriko-biograficheskii spravochnik* (St. Petersburg: Filol. Fak. Sankt-Peterburgskogo Gosudarstvennogo Univ., 2000), 237–39.

Cuban Missile Crisis, and his economic policy had failed and had brought the Soviet Union to the brink of a supply crisis in the early 1960s. In 1961, the impulsive and erratic general secretary had wanted to force a new program on the party: Accordingly, public officials were no longer permitted to remain in office for more than three legislative periods. Thereafter, younger communists were to take over their positions. Both ordinary officials and members of the Central Committee felt that the reform threatened their social and political standing. Therefore, they conspired against Khrushchev. Exchanging the cadres would have spelled the end of personal rule. Khrushchev would have destabilized the system and threatened the social privileges and power resources that characterized these powerful personal associations. This was another reason why they conspired and acted against the unpredictable ruler.[18]

Although Khrushchev anticipated what was coming, he offered no resistance and did not even try to shore up support for his political survival. Apparently, he was sure that he would lose neither his freedom nor his life – and he was right on both counts. When his own companions ousted him in 1964, he was neither openly humiliated nor punished. Still, Khrushchev was in pain and broke out in tears in front of the Politburo because he was unable to comprehend why he had been forced out of office. However, he left the Kremlin as a free man and drove home in his government car. Speaking before the Politburo on 13 October 1964, Khrushchev explained that he was glad that the party organs could now control "anyone." On the eve of his removal from power, Khrushchev spoke to Anastas Mikoian about the meaning of that day's events. "Could anyone have even imagined in their dreams," he said, "that we would have told Stalin that we did not like him and that we suggest that he should retire? Nothing would have been left of us [*Ot nas by mokrogo mesto ne ostalos*]. Now, everything has changed. Fear has disappeared and one can talk among equals. And this is my achievement."[19]

18 Alexander Titov, "The 1961 Party Programme and the Fate of Khrushchev's Reforms," in Melanie Ilic and Jeremy Smith (eds.), *Soviet State and Society Under Nikita Khrushchev* (London: Routledge, 2009), 17; Barbara Ann Chotiner, *Khrushchev's Party Reform: Coalition Building and Institutional Innovation* (Westport, CT: Greenwood Press, 1984).

19 Fursenko (ed.), *Prezidium TsK KPSS 1954–1964*, vol. I, *Chernovye protokol'nye zapisi zasedanii stenogrammy* (Moscow: ROSSPEN, 2003), 872; A. N. Artizov (ed.), *Nikita Khrushchev 1964. Stenogrammy plenuma TsK KPSS i drugie dokumenty. Rossiya XX vek. Dokumenty* (Moscow: Materik, 2007); Anastas Mikoian, *Tak bylo. Razmyshleniia o minuvshem* (Moscow: Vagrius, 1999), 614–16; Sergei Chruschtschow, *Nikita Chruschtschow. Marionette des KGB oder Vater der Perestroika* (Munich: Bertelsmann, 1991), 188; William J. Tompson, "The Fall of Nikita Khrushchev," *Soviet Studies* 43, 6 (1991), 1101–21.

Khrushchev had needed only ten years to transform the Soviet Union into a different country. He and his followers in the Politburo could have simply settled for what they had already achieved. They could have swept the past atrocities under the carpet, and no one would have asked them to speak about them. However, Khrushchev was determined to disclose Stalin's crimes out of moral considerations and because he was convinced that the time for truth would come at some point. He wrote in his memoirs:

> For three years we were unable to break with the past, unable to muster the courage and the determination to lift the curtain and see what had been hidden from us about the arrests, the trials, the arbitrary rule, the executions, and everything else that had happened during Stalin's reign. It was as though we were enchained by our own activities under Stalin's leadership and couldn't free ourselves from his control even after he was dead.[20]

Still, Khrushchev found the courage to look the past – even his own – in the eye. "Sooner or later people will be coming out of the prisons and the camps, and they'll return to the cities," he warned the members of the Politburo before the Twentieth Party Congress began in February 1956:

> They will tell their relatives, friends, comrades, and everyone back home what happened. The whole country and the whole Party will find out that people have spent ten to fifteen years in prison – and all for what? For nothing! . . . How can we pretend not to know what happened?[21]

There can be no doubt that Khrushchev also wanted to free himself from the moral burden that rested so heavily upon his shoulders. Khrushchev himself had belonged to the group of Stalin's henchmen, he had also signed off on the death lists and he had issued orders of terror. He had never opposed Stalin and had always followed his orders. However, he had acted out of fear. This is how he justified himself and his peers in his speech at the Twentieth Party Congress. Mikoian, Khrushchev's closest confidant, shared these thoughts. You could be forgiven only if you told the truth, Mikoian believed. Before the Twentieth Party Congress, he told Khrushchev: "If we do it on our own initiative and tell the delegates at the Party Congress the truth, they will forgive us, forgive the responsibility that we hold in one way or another. At least they will recognize that we were honest, that we came clean on our own initiative and that we did not

20 Nikita Khrushchev, *Khrushchev Remembers*, trans. and ed. Strobe Talbott (Boston: Little, Brown and Company, 1970), vol. I, 343.
21 Ibid., 348.

initiate these cruelties. We will defend our honor and if we don't do that we will be deprived of our honor."[22]

Khrushchev's de-Stalinization project was a civilizing achievement that changed the lives of millions of people. The Soviet people's experiences – not the moral and political standards of Western democracies – should serve as the yardstick used to interpret the meaning of de-Stalinization. For people who had lived and survived Stalinism, Khrushchev's rule symbolized a rebirth and an escape from a dark past. The reforms pacified a traumatized society that had been polluted by the terror. And it was the perpetrators themselves who were able to accomplish this without cracking under the weight of their task. After all, Khrushchev and his followers took an unpredictable risk when they spoke about the horrors of the past, which they themselves had been a part of. At the time it was impossible to envision where this liberalization would lead. Would it claim Stalin's companions as its victims? They were certainly aware of these risks, and they spoke openly about the consequences of de-Stalinization. Despite all of this, they opened the gates of the prisons and the camps shortly after the dictator died, although there existed no plan for what to do with the hundreds of thousands of criminals, the traumatized and the uprooted. Where would these people live and work and what would they subsist on? What would happen when victims met perpetrators and informers? No one was able to provide satisfying answers to these questions.

Nevertheless, the reformers stayed true to their course – perhaps also because they had learned in detail of what had happened in the camps and were no longer able to ignore it. The wives and relatives of those who had been imprisoned on Stalin's orders were now able to tell their stories and were the first to speak out: Molotov's wife, Khrushchev's stepdaughter and the wives of the murdered communists. Week after week, Khrushchev and the other Politburo members received letters from communists who had been released from prison and now wanted to bear witness to the arbitrariness and cruelty that they had experienced.[23] After these celebrities had spoken, it was impossible to return to doing business as usual and pretend that nothing had happened.

---

22 Cited in Vladimir Naumov, "Zur Geschichte der Geheimrede N. S. Chruščevs auf dem XX. Parteitag der KPdSU," *Forum für Osteuropäische Ideen- und Zeitgeschichte* 1 (1997), 146.
23 For the relevant documents, see Fursenko (ed.), *Prezidium TsK KPSS 1954–1964*, vol. I, 97; Naumov, "Zur Geschichte der Geheimrede," 144–45.

In 1955, Khrushchev ordered Petr Pospelov, the head of the Secretariat of the Central Committee, to collect material about past crimes. Pospelov and his employees identified perpetrators and victims, and they presented interrogation records, death lists and letters that victims of torture had sent to the dictator and to the Politburo. Khrushchev's secretary, Vladimir Malin, noted that the statements of the abused were read out before the Politburo and that everyone learned of the fate suffered by their former companions. Boris Rodos, Beria's sadistic accomplice, was summoned to the Politburo and questioned. He readily provided information about the fate suffered by prominent communists, who had been tortured and beaten to death on Stalin's orders. Molotov's insistence that Stalin's role as the "great leader" still had to be acknowledged caused a great uproar. Khrushchev and Mikoian objected. After all that had happened, Mikoian said, one could only go insane. And Khrushchev added: "Stalin was committed to the cause of socialism but he did everything with barbaric methods. He destroyed the party. He is not a Marxist. He swept everything holy, everything dear to men, from the earth. He subordinated everything to his moods." Evidently, the members of the Politburo realized that something was happening to them – something they had not expected. "If this is true," shouted Deputy Prime Minister Maksim Saburov at one of the Politburo's sessions, "then what kind of communism do we have? One cannot forgive this."[24] The floodgates had opened. It was impossible to escape from the omnipresence of terror because the outspoken and audible truths could no longer be suppressed. Thus, those who were part of the ruling circle were caught in these dynamic acts against their will. "For months we have been hearing about these horrible things," explained Mikhail Suslov on 1 February 1956 at a Politburo meeting. "This cannot be justified."[25]

At the Twentieth Party Congress in February 1956, Khrushchev spoke openly about Stalin's crimes and about the reasons why he and other members of the political leadership had become the dictator's accomplices. Soon afterward, in August 1956, Khrushchev addressed employees of the Central Committee and admitted that he had joined in the praise for Stalin. However, Khrushchev showed remorse: He himself had suffered from the crimes that he had been involved in and that could never be set right. At the same meeting he explained that his speech at the Party

24 Fursenko (ed.), *Prezidium TsK KPSS 1954–1964*, vol. I, 96.
25 Ibid.; Taubman, *Khrushchev*, 271–74.

Congress had been a purifying ritual. It had allowed the burden of the past to be cast off. "We literally freed ourselves from something heavy; we were relieved."[26]

Khrushchev undoubtedly believed that he had a mission to fulfill: In 1961, when the demand to remove Stalin's body had dropped off, he still ordered that it be removed from the mausoleum on Red Square. At the Twenty-Second Party Congress, taking place in October of the same year, it was not just the victims of the terror who got a chance to speak out. Aleksandr Shelepin, the new head of the KGB (Komitet gosudarstvennyi besopasnosti, Committee for State Security), also addressed the pain still felt by the victims. "Sometimes it makes you wonder," he said about Stalin's helpers in the security apparatus, "how these people walk around and are able to sleep at night. They should be tormented by nightmares, hearing the sobs and the curses of the mothers, wives and children of the innocent comrades, who they murdered." This was the first time that Stalin's heirs had talked about his crimes in such an open way. They admitted that they had been aware of the killings and conceded that the party was capable of making mistakes.[27]

De-Stalinization was not simply a game of words. Words were quickly followed by actions, demonstrating that the leadership was serious this time. By January 1955, the attorney general had already pardoned almost 40,000 people who had been sentenced to long-term prison sentences in 1948 and who had been exiled after having served their sentence – in particular Estonians, Latvians, Lithuanians and Ukrainians, who had stood up to the Red Army's occupation of their homeland after the end of World War II. On Khrushchev's orders, so-called tripartite commissions (*troikas*) were established in 1956 and sent to the camps in order to review the cases of those prisoners who had been sentenced on political grounds. Khrushchev opened the prison gates and millions stepped out into the open. Between April 1953 and January 1956 alone, more than 1.5 million prisoners were released from the camps. Furthermore, rehabilitation commissions were established to dispatch their members throughout the Soviet Union in order to question released prisoners and to receive their applications for

---

26 "Iz vystupleniia Khrushcheva na obshchem partiinom sobranii partorganizatsii apparata TsK KPSS, 6 avgusta 1956g.," in Artizov et al. (eds.), *Khrushchev*, vol. I, 575, 577.

27 *XXII s"ezd Kommunisticheskoi partii Sovetskogo soiuza, 17–21 oktiabria 1961 goda. Stenograficheskii otchet*, vol. II (Moscow: Gosudarstvennoe izdatel'stvo politicheskoii literatury, 1962), 114–20, 404–05; Kathleen Smith, *Remembering Stalin's Victims: Popular Memory and the End of the USSR* (Ithaca: Cornell University Press, 1996), 35.

the restoration of their civil rights. More than 700,000 victims of the Stalinist terror had been rehabilitated by 1960, and several million requests had been processed and answered. After the Secret Speech of 1956, more than 300,000 Chechens and Ingush, who had been deported to Kazakhstan in 1944, returned to their homes. Khrushchev let them go, although they had no permission to leave their place of exile without being ordered to do so. The Chechens' return to their homeland had been possible only because Khrushchev had rejected the strategy of violence, recalled one individual affected by the events.[28]

However, in a society plagued by chronic shortages, only a few people hailed these accomplishments. After all, each released prisoner was an additional rival for resources, and each released criminal posed a security risk. Only some people, therefore, regarded the homecoming of the deported and the release of criminals as blessings. Anyone who had spent several years in prison had a difficult time adapting to ordinary life. Released prisoners had little to expect from those living in freedom, since there was no place for them to reside and no one was willing to employ them.[29] Nevertheless, those released did not remain silent. Communists who had been imprisoned and tortured began asking questions, since they were unable to understand why those with blood on their hands condemned only the supreme leader but not themselves. In the northern Caucasus, bloody skirmishes ensued between Chechen returnees and Russian settlers – skirmishes that could be ended only through military operations. And in Georgia and Azerbaijan students took to the streets in protest because they could not bear the fact that Khrushchev had called the dictator from the Caucasus a criminal.[30]

Throughout the Soviet Union people discussed the Secret Speech, which had been forwarded to all party committees by the spring of 1956. They

28 Miriam Dobson, *Khrushchev's Cold Summer: Gulag Returnees, Crime, and the Fate of Reform after Stalin* (Ithaca: Cornell University Press, 2009), 5, 51; Moshe Gammer, *The Lone Wolf and the Bear: Three Centuries of Chechen Defiance of Russian Rule* (Pittsburgh: University of Pittsburgh Press, 2006), 179; Naumov, "Zur Geschichte der Geheimrede"; Fursenko (ed.), *Prezidium TsK KPSS 1954–1964*, vol. II, 123–26, 194.
29 Nancy Adler, *The Gulag Survivor: Beyond the Soviet System* (New Brunswick, NJ: Transaction Publishers, 2002).
30 Polly Jones, "From the Secret Speech to the Burial of Stalin: Real and Ideal Responses to De-Stalinization," in Polly Jones (ed.), *The Dilemmas of De-Stalinization: Negotiating Cultural and Social Change in the Khrushchev Era* (London: Routledge, 2006), 41–63; Vladimir Kozlov, *Massovye bezporiadki v SSSR pri Khrushcheve i Brezhneve 1953–nachalo 1980-kh gg.* (Novosibirsk: Sibirskii khronograf, 1999), 173–204; Jeronim Perovic, *Der Nordkaukasus unter russischer Herrschaft. Geschichte einer Vielvölkerregion zwischen Rebellion und Anpassung* (Cologne: Boehlau, 2015), 474–77.

listened to what was read to them and asked questions. Stalin had been declared a criminal. But what had his followers done? Why had they praised the dictator only to now drag him through the mud? Had they lied in the past, or were they lying now? Within the intellectual milieu, people asked uncomfortable questions. When the historian Anna Pankratova attempted to explain in front of an audience of party members, artists and teachers in March 1956 why Stalin's crimes had to be condemned, she was confronted by some unpleasant truths. Was Stalin alone to blame for the excesses? Did he not have any helpers? What had his followers, who were now trying to uncover the crimes, done at the time? Why did they cry at Stalin's grave but later turn on him?[31] Apparently, their leaders had been lying for years, and now they were speaking the truth for the first time. This was the only possible interpretation one could arrive at during the discussion of the Secret Speech.

In some places criticism of Stalin evolved into the outright rejection of his image. Workers in Stalingrad tore down a statue of the dictator; Stalin's portraits vanished from offices in the Baltic republics, and the editor of the historical journal *Voprosy istorii* called Stalin a "scoundrel," without anyone protesting against this abuse.[32] As early as 1954, outrageous statements were made in the corridor of the state attorney's offices in Moscow, where victims were waiting for their rehabilitation notices. One woman was offended by Stalin's portrait, which still hung on the wall. "Why is he hanging here? Maybe so that people will not forgot who is responsible for all of this?"[33] And some of the victims, above all persecuted communists, seized the opportunity to speak about their pain and suffering and to incriminate the perpetrators, who had denounced and abused them; they demanded justice for themselves and their families. Ginzburg remembers that the victims were now able to tie together the torn threads of their lives and connect the year 1937 with the year 1956 in a meaningful way.[34] By implicating Stalin, Khrushchev belatedly gave meaning to their suffering. Now, they could frame their ordeal as a service to socialism. Up until this time, Soviet citizens had lived in the wrong kind of socialism. It was impossible to make sense of these changes in any other way.

---

31 Kathleen Smith, *Remembering Stalin's Victims*, 29.
32 Kornei Chukovskii, *Sobranie sochinenii*, vol. XIII, *Dnevnik. 1936–1969* (Moscow: TERRA-Knizhnyi Klub, 2007), 213; Jones, "From the Secret Speech."
33 Ginsburg, *Gratwanderung*, 476.
34 Ibid., 454; Nancy Adler, *Keeping Faith with the Party: Communist Believers Return from the Gulag* (Bloomington: Indiana University Press 2012).

Not everyone was able and willing to speak about the past horrors. But all victims felt that the events had freed them from a heavy burden. Prisoners who had escaped from hell were grateful for Khrushchev's achievements.[35] The musician Aleksandr Konstantinov, who had experienced this new spirit of optimism in Saratov on the Volga, recalled that Stalin had been a "monster." "It was wonderful what Khrushchev did."[36] For the first time, the traumatic experiences of so many people were openly discussed, despite the fact that the perpetrators were hardly ever held accountable.

Power that has to call attention to itself is weak. Only in instances when subjects conform to the regime's demands naturally can power actually be sure of itself. This might have also been a reason for the change that took place within the dictatorship. Chekist (secret police) actions and methods that had become normal in 1953 were completely out of the question by 1957. Khrushchev staffed the security apparatus with his companions and replaced Chekists with technocrats who perfected the technologies of surveillance but did not attempt to master the craft of killing. The KGB's employees were still allowed to monitor, control and intimidate critics and dissidents, but they were no longer allowed to drag them from their houses at night and shoot them. They had lost their authority to punish. Instead, Khrushchev reinstated the judiciary, transferred the monopoly of jurisdiction to the courts and returned law enforcement powers to the state attorney's office.[37]

To be sure, the Soviet Union under Khrushchev was not governed by the rule of law. But people could no longer be imprisoned, terrorized and murdered at random. Khrushchev explained at a KGB assembly as early as June 1954 that the time of arbitrary arrests and torture had ended. One would have to present evidence, and those who could not do so would have to set the accused free and "apologize" to them. No other state official had ever spoken about the tasks of the secret service in this way. "Basically, our security apparatus and our Chekists are honest men devoted to our communist party," shouted Khrushchev. "But comrades, the work of honest and

35 Meinhard Stark, *Die Gezeichneten. Gulag-Häftlinge nach der Entlassung* (Berlin: Metropol, 2010), 129.

36 Donald Raleigh (ed.), *Russia's Sputnik Generation: Soviet Baby Boomers Talk About Their Lives* (Bloomington: Indiana University Press, 2006), 33; Dobson, *Khrushchev's Cold Summer*.

37 George Ginsburgs, "Soviet Court Reform 1956–1958," in Donald D. Barry et al. (eds.), *Soviet Law After Stalin*, vol. I (Leyden: A. W. Sijthoff, 1977), 77–104; H. J. Berman, "Legality Versus Terror: The Post-Stalin Law Reforms," in G. M. Carter and A. F. Westin (eds.), *Politics in Europe 5: Cases in European Government* (New York: Harcourt, Brace & World, 1965), 179–205.

devoted men must also be controlled by the party ... The party has to cement its control over the work of all organs of the Soviet state, but above all it must control an organ as accountable as the Committee for State Security [KGB]."[38]

Regardless of what the future held, the almighty secret service had to find a way to handle these changes. It now acquired a more civilian image. The Chekists exchanged their leather jackets and uniforms for suits and attempted to fill out their new role as custodians of the law. The Lubyanka was no longer to be known as a house of horror, where people were tortured and killed. It now housed public officials, who had to keep the population under surveillance but who were no longer allowed to terrorize it. For Khrushchev, the last true believer, it was important to teach and to instruct dissidents, critics and enemies – but not to kill them. In the Khrushchev era, the terror was replaced by "prophylaxis." The KGB's employees were to monitor, intimidate and "educate" critics and opponents. However, the apparatus would be able to fulfill this task only if it could fall back on educated cadres. The thugs and torturers of 1937 were no longer useful. In 1954, Khrushchev explained in front of KGB employees that "criminals" had worked in the national security apparatus during Stalin's time. They had forced confessions and invented statements. The contemporary Chekist, however, was to be a cultivated official – someone who convinced the people. "An inexperienced person with low culture cannot work on [*razrabatyvat'*] a cultivated person."[39] Khrushchev's ministers for state security – Aleksandr Shelepin and Vladimir Semichastnyi – were representatives of this new era: Both had served as leaders of the Komsomol before being entrusted with the leadership of the KGB. They transformed the security apparatus into a surveillance and education agency, which had to be feared only by those who contradicted the regime's truths. In 1960, when an employee of the KGB spoke about the "glorious Chekist traditions" at a KGB assembly, he was interrupted by Shelepin: "What traditions?! The bloody traditions of the Cheka have been condemned by the party congresses!"[40]

---

38 Artizov et al. (eds.), *Khrushchev*, vol. I, 511–18.
39 "Rech N. S. Khrushcheva na vsesoiuznom soveshchanii rabotnikov komiteta gosudarstvennoi bezopasnosti pri sovete ministrov SSSR, 7 iiunia 1954 g.," in Artizov et al. (eds,), *Khrushchev*, vol. I, 520–22.
40 Cited in Julie Elkner, "The Changing Face of Repression Under Khrushchev," in Ilic and Smith (eds.), *Soviet State and Society Under Khrushchev*, 143.

How were the new rulers of the KGB to deal with the legacy of the security apparatus? Khrushchev found a simple solution. Under Stalin, the new story went, the security apparatus had been involved in serious crimes. However, Feliks Dzerzhinskii, its founder, was a man with an impeccable biography. Dzerzhinskii, who had been entrusted with the care of orphans at the end of the civil war, was now presented as the benefactor of all children. The public was to perceive Dzerzhinsky as an incorruptible and sincere advocate of socialist legality. When Khrushchev ordered that a memorial be erected to the founder of the Cheka in 1958, he sought to evoke the bright rather than the dark sides of the Bolshevik experiment. Now, no one was to know or remember that Dzerzhinskii had been a representative of a ruthless and blood-stained order.[41]

The time of terror had passed, never again to return. Khrushchev let there be no doubt about it, and in the end even the Chekists realized that they too were benefiting from the fact that political life had become much more predictable under Khrushchev. Above all, Khrushchev and his companions had understood that they could not generate trust among the people if they did not reform the way that power was depicted. The Stalinist official had been a fighter, who had conquered every obstacle and mercilessly defeated every enemy. While Stalin's Lenin had been a dark warrior, Khrushchev, on the other hand, gave Lenin a human face. When they were thinking about the revolutionary leader, people's hearts and minds were to warm rather than freeze.[42]

However, it still took years for fear and mistrust to disappear from people's bodies and souls. But by the end of the 1950s, everyone was already seeming to sense that the era of death and arbitrary persecution had finished for good. The pervasive fear of death vanished from everyday life and never returned. The musician Aleksandr Konstantinov from Saratov recalled how his parents had grown up in fear – how they had literally embodied the terror of those days. Their children, however, grew up without constantly fearing for their lives. "We knew that the KGB existed. This didn't concern us at all ... We didn't know real repression."[43] It was much easier to deal with the new situation for those who had not experienced the height of the terror than for the frightened and terrorized people who had suffered through it.

41 Ibid., 142–61; Monica Rüthers, *Moskau bauen von Lenin bis Chrušč̌ev. Öffentliche Räume zwischen Utopie, Terror und Alltag* (Cologne: Böhlau, 2007), 164.
42 Petr Vail and Aleksandr Genis, *60-e. Mir sovetskogo cheloveka* (Moscow: Novoe literaturnoe obozrenie, 1996), 219.
43 Raleigh, *Russia's Sputnik Generation*, 35, 38.

Within a few years of the dictator's death, novels and stories that broached the suffering of the past could be published: Vladimir Dudintsev's *Not by Bread Alone*, Ilia Ehrenburg's novel *The Thaw* (which would give the whole era its name) and later Alexander Solzhenitsyn's story *One Day in the Life of Ivan Denisovich*. Khrushchev himself had decided that Solzhenitsyn's tale about daily life in Stalin's penal colonies could be published in 1962. Aleksandr Tvardovskii's literary magazine *Novyi mir* (New World) became an icon for an entire generation and a window through which one could glimpse freedom. Thousands wrote letters to the magazine's editor and commented on what they had read. Readers experienced being able to write their opinion about what they had read without being held accountable for it.[44] When the writer Anatolii Rybakov heard Khrushchev's Secret Speech, he realized that something enormous had happened. "For the first time in decades we heard humane words, enjoyed the first taste of freedom and turned into different people. Khrushchev had taken the heavy burden of tyranny off our shoulders – now we could walk upright."[45]

However, the regime had to pay a price for their citizens' new posture. De-Stalinization produced criticism and dissent; it gave birth to the Soviet intelligentsia. Around universities discussion groups sprang up, in which students debated the literature of the thaw period and the changes that had occurred in the meantime. After the Secret Speech, a number of spontaneous meetings took place at the University of Moscow, where students not only condemned the Stalinist dictatorship but also demanded a say in politics.[46] For the first time, people dared to assemble openly without any form of permission or authorization. When Anastas Mikoian, a member of the Politburo and one of Stalin's close companions, drove down Gorkii Street toward the Kremlin in the summer of 1955, he was stopped by a group of agitated people. He told his driver to

---

44 Denis Kozlov, "Naming the Social Evil: The Readers of *Novyi Mir* and Vladimir Dudintsev's *Not by Bread Alone*, 1956–1959, and Beyond," in Jones (ed.), *The Dilemmas of De-Stalinization*, 80–98; Denis Kozlov, "'I Have Not Read, But I Will Say': Soviet Literary Audiences and Changing Ideas of Social Membership, 1958–1966," *Kritika* 7, 3 (2006), 557–97; Vladislav Zubok, *Zhivago's Children: The Last Russian Intelligentsia* (Cambridge, MA: Harvard University Press, 2009), 60–87; Stephen V. Bittner, *The Many Lives of Khrushchev's Thaw: Experience and Memory in Moscow's Arbat* (Ithaca: Cornell University Press, 2008).
45 Anatoli Rybakow, *Roman der Erinnerung* (Berlin: Aufbau Verlag, 2001), 224–25.
46 Zubok, *Zhivago's Children*, 68. See also Raissa Orlowa-Kopelew's memoirs: *Eine Vergangenheit, die nicht vergeht. Rückblicke aus fünf Jahrzehnten* (Munich: Albrecht Knaus, 1983), 269–70.

come to a halt and asked the reason for this spontaneous assembly. He was referred to a young man on the sidewalk, reciting poetry. His name was Yevgeny Yevtushenko. People had come together in the middle of the day in Moscow's city center to listen to the words of a poet – to listen to something beautiful rather than political. Two years earlier, Yevtushenko and his listeners would have been arrested, while now not even a member of the Politburo complained about the events. "I saw people," recalled Mikoian, "that stood in line for poetry rather than food. I understood that a new era had begun."[47]

Life became easier, and everyone felt that living conditions had vastly improved since Stalin's death. In Stalin's world, peasants and workers had had to suffer for the glory of the country. Khrushchev, on the other hand, dreamed of flourishing landscapes, of an abundant life, of a communism that could provide running water and well-stocked supermarkets; and he connected his own fate to the fulfillment of these promises. As early as the summer of 1953, the state increased prices for agricultural products and reduced those taxes that had been levied on the produce from private land under Stalin. However, Khrushchev's demand for a regular monthly salary for peasants and their integration into the public pension scheme was realized only after he had been overthrown. Nevertheless, the peasants were no longer second-class citizens who could be harassed and robbed by the state at will.[48] The wages of workers and employees increased because the state subsidized them, and the range of products also improved. In 1956, Khrushchev not only increased pensions for workers and employees but also turned them into a legal right. Millions of people now received pensions that they could actually live on. No other change mobilized more support than the improvement of living conditions.[49]

47 Yevgenii Yevtushenko, *Volchii pasport* (Moscow: Vagrius, 1998), 11; Zubok, *Zhivago's Children*, 59.
48 William J. Tompson, *Khrushchev: A Political Life* (New York: St. Martin's Press, 1995), 127–28; Karl-Eugen Wädekin, *Sozialistische Agrarpolitik in Osteuropa*, vol. I, *Von Marx bis zur Vollkollektivierung* (Berlin: Duncker & Humblot, 1974), 221–36; and Robert F. Miller, *One Hundred Thousand Tractors: The MTS and the Development of Controls in Soviet Agriculture* (Cambridge, MA: Harvard University Press, 1970), 165–87; Karl-Eugen Wädekin, *Die Bezahlung der Arbeit in der sowjetischen Landwirtschaft* (Berlin: Duncker & Humblot, 1972), 131–205.
49 Alastair McAuley, *Economic Welfare in the Soviet Union: Poverty, Living Standards, and Inequality* (Madison: University of Wisconsin Press, 1979); Leonard Joel Kirsch, *Soviet Wages: Changes in Structure and Administration Since 1956* (Cambridge, MA: MIT Press, 1972); Hans-Henning Schröder, "'Lebendige Verbindung mit den Massen.' Sowjetische Gesellschaftspolitik in der Ära Chruščev," *Vierteljahreshefte für Zeitgeschichte* 34, 4 (1986), 529–38.

At the beginning of the 1950s, Khrushchev had decided that it would be the state's responsibility to provide dignified housing for its people. During Stalin's reign, architects were tasked with creating prestigious buildings that would house state officials and be representative of the state's power. An inhabitant of Lviv complained in a letter written to the city's soviet in 1951 that many children had to live like "rats." Even five years after the war had ended, millions of people still lived in ruinous communal apartments, holes in the ground or cellars. Khrushchev regarded the Stalinist architecture of intimidation as a cynical profanity. One could look at the attractive house fronts and the high ceilings, but they were useless, he declared in December 1954 at the Soviet Architectural Congress. Not even during the tsar's reign had the working conditions been as bad as in the Soviet Union. Khrushchev had worked in the mines of Yuzovka but had still been able to move into his own apartment before the revolution. "The apartment had a sitting room, kitchen, bedroom, and dining room. Years later, after the Revolution, it was painful for me to remember that as a worker under capitalism I'd had much better conditions than my fellow workers now living under Soviet power." This had to change.[50]

In 1957, Khrushchev introduced the Soviet Union's largest housing construction project. He promised that the housing shortages of the Soviet Union would be abolished within the next twelve years. Although he would not be able to keep this promise, several million people were able to leave the overcrowded residential homes and ruinous houses in the 1950s and move into modern apartments, which even offered toilets and running water. Leading up to 1962, 9 million new apartments were constructed, changing the lives of 40 million people.[51] The anthropologist Victor Buchli argued that Khrushchev's housing project was a "second cultural revolution" and had changed the lives of millions of people.[52] The apartment was not only the location of a comfortable life. It also turned into a retreat, where everything was possible – even if it would have been otherwise unconceivable outside one's own four walls. The apartments created a form of privacy that most Soviet citizens had never experienced before. The family, rather than the state, became the most important focal point of everyday life.

50 Mark Smith, *Property of Communists: The Urban Housing Program from Stalin to Khrushchev* (DeKalb: Northern Illinois University Press, 2010), 70–73.
51 Ibid., 102; Albrecht Martiny, *Bauen und Wohnen in der Sowjetunion nach dem Zweiten Weltkrieg. Bauarbeiterschaft, Architektur und Wohnverhältnisse im sozialen Wandel* (Berlin: Berlin Verlag, 1983); Timothy Sosnovy, *The Housing Problem in the Soviet Union* (New York: Research Program on the USSR, 1954).
52 Victor Buchli, *An Archeology of Socialism* (Oxford: Berg, 1999), 137.

And within this niche society it was possible to develop and realize needs that were outside the control of the state and its servants. Once the doors closed behind the citizens, the laughter of millions rang out. The state had lost its almighty power.[53]

Khrushchev freed the Soviet Union from its isolation. The Kremlin in Moscow was opened to visitors, while the shopping mall GUM on Red Square and the restaurant Praga, which had been closed on Stalin's orders, were reopened. Khrushchev himself set a good example: He traveled the country, met with citizens and spoke to people in the streets. Kremlin politics were no longer an unfathomable secret. Foreigners were allowed to visit and travel through the Soviet Union. Western artists such as Yves Montand and Benny Goodman performed on Soviet stages, and the American Van Cliburn not only won the Soviet Tchaikovsky Piano Competition in 1958, but also won over the hearts of Russian women, who occupied his hotel and wrote him thousands of love letters. On the occasion of the International Festival of Youth in 1957, more than 30,000 foreign visitors came to Moscow and presented themselves to Soviet citizens with an ease that the country had never witnessed under Stalin.[54] Even for the political elite, this was their first contact with the Western lifestyle.[55]

Khrushchev had opened a window toward the West, through which the dull hate and xenophobia of the Stalin era could evaporate. Scientists, artists and public officials had seen how people lived outside the Soviet borders, and they had stopped demonizing what was no longer a threat. When the pervasive paranoia of the Stalinist dictatorship disappeared, it seemed as if people had woken up from a nightmare. Georgii Arbatov recalled the sense of spiritual liberation that he felt during those years. In 1964, he had watched a movie in one of Moscow's cinemas. The newsreel that had preceded the movie showed Khrushchev inaugurating a canal in Central Asia. The chubby secretary general ran down a hill and, gesticulating vigorously, gave a speech next to the bank of the channel before attempting to climb back up the

53 Vladimir Shlapentokh, *Public and Private Life of the Soviet People: Changing Values in Post-Stalin Russia* (New York and Oxford: Oxford University Press, 1989); Greg Castillo, *Cold War on the Home Front: The Soft Power of Midcentury Design* (Minneapolis: University of Minnesota Press, 2010).
54 Zubok, *Zhivago's Children*, 88–120, in particular 104–05.
55 Ibid., 88–120; Susan E. Reid, "Who Will Beat Whom? Soviet Popular Reception of the American National Exhibition in Moscow, 1959," *Kritika* 9, 4 (2008), 855–904; Anne Gorsuch and Diane Koenker (eds.), *Turizm: The Russian and East European Tourist Under Capitalism and Socialism* (Ithaca: Cornell University Press, 2006); Miriam Dobson, "The Post-Stalin Era: De-Stalinization, Daily Life and Dissent," *Kritika* 12, 4 (2011), 910.

muddy hill with severe difficulty. The entire cinema found the scene hyster-
ical. Who would have dared to laugh at Stalin? The Russian writer Andrei
Bitov, who had seen the same newsreel when he was younger, found the
right words to describe the scene: Khrushchev had taught the Soviet citizens
how to laugh again.[56] Once it had become possible to laugh about the leader
in public, Stalinism was truly dead.

Khrushchev freed Soviet society from mass terror and from the omnipresence of violence. However, the terrors of the past had left a mark on
the minds of the people. In a society still contaminated by mistrust and
violence, it would be extremely difficult to engage in an unsparing examination of the bloody past. After all, the reformers had once been the
perpetrators, and the victims had no choice other than to remain quiescent
vis-à-vis the reformers. Millions of people had died, had lost their homes
and their freedom, and had been traumatized. Victims had turned into
perpetrators and perpetrators had turned into victims, and most people
never found out why they had been arrested and why their relatives had
been killed. It is unlikely that a single family existed in the Soviet Union that
had not experienced violence. And because the terror seemed to have
lashed out arbitrarily and blindly and because it in the end also devoured
its executors, the survivors remembered the events of 1937 as an earthquake
that no one was responsible for. Even in death, perpetrators and victims
were linked to one another. How could one have dealt with the past in
a way that would have done justice to this human catastrophe? Actually,
there was no alternative to the great silence and total absolution because
speaking about the experiences would have driven both perpetrators and
victims mad. We cannot understand the practice of total absolution without taking into account the experience of total violence.

Victims and perpetrators reached an implicit agreement never to speak
about what had happened. In the Soviet Union, any memory of the suffering
of the past was a memory that produced silence: because the victims were
unable to speak about their experiences, because they did not find the
strength to put their terrible experiences into words without damaging
their own souls, because they had to forget so that they would not go insane
and because no one knew whether the regime's violence would one day
return to daily life – whether one could trust the peace. Victims and perpetrators had no choice but to come to terms with the social order. After all, it
was the only one they had.[57] In survivors' memories, the Stalinist mass terror

56 Arbatov, *The System*, 108.   57 Kathleen Smith, *Remembering Stalin's Victims*, 8–11.

merged into one enormous catastrophe with the National Socialist excesses of annihilation that had come over them without its being anyone's fault. Everything that had happened before 1941 paled in comparison with the apocalyptic horrors of the Great Patriotic War. Stalin's successors made peace, and they enabled both victims and perpetrators to find their place within the broader narrative of survivors.

Khrushchev's reforms changed the Soviet Union. However, he failed because he was forced to make promises he could not keep and because his democratic reforms had destabilized the political apparatus and the network of followers upon which he based his power. In the end, he was a reformer without power. The political elite breathed a sigh of relief when the unpredictable and impulsive Khrushchev was ousted in October 1964. Even the intelligentsia held little regard for the simple First Secretary, who was able to read and write only with difficulty, as noted earlier. His primitive ideas about art and literature as well as his erratic insults against modern art – which he characterized as "dog shit" and the work of "gays" when he visited an exhibition in Moscow in 1962 – had won him the reputation of being a simpleton. Boris Pasternak, who had to bow to Khrushchev's pressure and refuse the Nobel Prize for Literature, called him an "idiot and a swine."[58] On the other hand, those such as the poet Anna Akhmatova, who saw their family members freed from camps felt gratitude for Khrushchev's reforms.

But there were two sides to Khrushchev. He did have a conscience; he could not bear the crimes that Stalin had ordered and that he had been a part of; and he did feel compassion for other people. Rybakov remembered how Khrushchev had insulted the poet Margarita Aliger during a reception at his residence. However, Rybakov also heard how Khrushchev apologized to her at the Writers' Congress. In a conversation with the writer Mikhail Shatrov, he deeply regretted what he had done in the past. "My arms are up to the elbows in blood. That is the most terrible thing that lies in my soul."[59] When Khrushchev felt that the end of his life was in sight, he asked the artist Ernst Neizvestnyi, whose sculptures he had described as a "mess," for forgiveness. Neizvestnyi created a bust for Khrushchev's grave. It was

---

58 "Vyskazyvaniia N. S. Khrushcheva pri poseshchenii vystavki proizvedenii moskovs-kikh khudozhnikov 1 dekabria 1962 g.," in Artizov et al. (eds.), *Khrushchev*, vol. II, 522–33; Aksiutin, *Khrushchevskaja "ottepel'*," 368–77; Susan E. Reid, "In the Name of the People: The Manège Affair Revisited," *Kritika* 6, 4 (2005), 673–716; Priscilla Johnson, *Khrushchev and the Arts: The Politics of Soviet Culture, 1962–1964* (Cambridge, MA: MIT Press, 1965), 101–05.

59 Rybakov, *Roman der Erinnerung*, 226; Taubman, *Khrushchev*, 639.

a symbolic portrait: Khrushchev's head, framed by white and black granite. Khrushchev had both a dark and a light side. He would have probably concurred with this description: As Stalin's acolyte, he had become a murderer. But he had also done much that was good. Without him there would have been no de-Stalinization, no rehabilitation and no thaw. The light side had defeated the dark side.

Before Khrushchev, the Soviet Union never experienced such an atmosphere of change and liberation. Khrushchev's fate had been tragic, conceded Rybakov decades later. "But he will go down in Russian history as an honest, conscientious man who sought to destroy evil, as an example of moral courage ... He gave hope to my generation and to the following that we would once more be able to breathe freely, think freely and create freely."[60] Later, in the years of the reaction, Soviet dissidents wistfully recalled the "magic" era of freedom that had ended as quickly as it had begun. The thaw period, wrote human rights activist Liudmila Alekseeva in 1993, had been a "time of awakening" in which she tasted freedom and saw truth. For the first time in her life, she had been allowed to read, write and speak without asking the party and the government for permission. For this, she said, she remained deeply grateful.[61]

There is a tendency in Russia to remember Stalin over the reformer – Nikita Sergeevich Khrushchev – who taught the people how to laugh again. Perhaps one day, Khrushchev's de-Stalinization project will be recognized as one of the most important civilizing achievements of the twentieth century – the work of an uneducated son of a peasant turned reformer, who could not live with his guilt. "Khrushchev," declared Akhmatova, "did the greatest possible thing for me – he gave me back my son."[62]

Bibliographical Essay

The most recent study on Nikita Khrushchev is William Taubman, *Khrushchev: The Man and His Era* (New York: W. W. Norton, 2003). Taubman argues that Khrushchev's politics of de-Stalinization were not only enforced from above but also formed a moral project. Older studies

60 Rybakov, *Roman der Erinnerung*, 227–28.
61 Ludmilla Alexeyeva and Paul Goldberg, *The Thaw Generation: Coming of Age in the Post-Stalin Era* (Pittsburgh: University of Pittsburgh Press, 1993), 4–5; Masha Gessen, *Dead Again: The Russian Intelligentsia After Communism* (London: Verso, 1997), 12; Bittner, *The Many Lives of Khrushchev's Thaw*, 5–7.
62 Quoted in Lidiia Chukovskaia, *Zapiski ob Anne Akhmatovoi*, vol. II, *1952–1962* (Moscow: Soglasie, 1997), 202.

see Khrushchev's reforms also as a product of the power struggle after Stalin's death and of pressures from below. See William J. Tompson, *Khrushchev: A Political Life* (New York: St. Martin's, 1995); Roy Medvedev and Zhores Medvedev, *Khrushchev: The Years in Power* (New York: Columbia University Press, 1976); Roy Medvedev, *Khrushchev* (Garden City, NY: Doubleday/ Anchor, 1983).

The best overviews are William Taubman, Sergei Khrushchev and Abbott Gleason (eds.), *Nikita Khrushchev* (New Haven: Yale University Press, 2000); Martin McCauley (ed.), *Khrushchev and Khrushchevism* (Bloomington: Indiana University Press, 1987); Melanie Ilic and Jeremy Smith (eds.), *Khrushchev in the Kremlin: Policy and Government in the Soviet Union, 1953–1964* (London: Routledge, 2011); Donald Filtzer, *The Khrushchev Era: De-Stalinisation and the Limits of Reform in the USSR, 1953–1964* (London: Macmillan, 1993).

On the effects of Khrushchev's Secret Speech and the de-Stalinization process on Soviet society, see the archive-based studies of Elena Zubkova, *Russia After the War: Hopes, Illusions, and Disappointments, 1945–1957* (Armonk, NY: M. E. Sharpe, 1998); Yurii Aksiutin, *Khrushchevskaia "ottepel'" i obshchest-vennye nastroenia v SSSR v 1953–1964 gg.* (Moscow: ROSSPEN, 2004); and Polly Jones (ed.), *The Dilemmas of De-Stalinization: Negotiating Cultural and Social Change in the Khrushchev Era* (London: Routledge, 2006).

On the end of the Gulag system, the returnees from the camps and the social and cultural consequences of de-Stalinization, see Miriam Dobson, *Khrushchev's Cold Summer: Gulag Returnees, Crime, and the Fate of Reform after Stalin* (Ithaca: Cornell University Press, 2009); Leona Toker, *Return from the Archipelago: Narratives of Gulag Survivors* (Bloomington: Indiana University Press, 2000); Nanci Adler, *The Gulag Survivor: Beyond the Soviet System* (New Brunswick, NJ: Transaction, 2002); Nanci Adler, *Keeping Faith with the Party: Communist Believers Return from the Gulag* (Bloomington: Indiana University Press, 2012); Kathleen Smith, *Remembering Stalin's Victims: Popular Memory and the End of the USSR* (Ithaca: Cornell University Press, 1996).

There are only a few studies on the reform of the judicial system under Khrushchev. See, among others, George Ginsburgs, "Soviet Court Reform 1956–1958," in Donald D. Barry et al. (eds.), *Soviet Law After Stalin*, vol. I (Leyden: A. W. Sijthoff, 1977), 77–104.

The most recent book on the emergence of the intelligentsia, which portrays the thaw as an era of liberty, is Vladislav Zubok, *Zhivago's Children: The Last Russian Intelligentsia* (Cambridge, MA: Harvard University Press, 2009); see also Dina Spechler, *Permitted Dissent in the USSR: "Novyi Mir" and the Soviet Regime* (New York: Praeger, 1982); Edith Rogovin Frankel, *Novj*

Mir: A Case Study in the Politics of Literature, 1952–1958 (New York: Cambridge University Press, 1981); Stephen Bittner, *The Many Lives of Khrushchev's Thaw: Experience and Memory in Moscow's Arbat* (Ithaca: Cornell University Press 2008). On terror and memory, see Polly Jones, *Myth, Memory, Trauma: Rethinking the Stalinist Past in the Soviet Union, 1953–1970* (New Haven: Yale University Press, 2013).

Most books on the economy and social welfare agree that Khrushchev tried to improve living conditions but failed in his agrarian policy. See Alastair McAuley, *Economic Welfare in the Soviet Union: Poverty, Living Standards, and Inequality* (Madison: University of Wisconsin Press, 1979); and Hans-Henning Schröder, "'Lebendige Verbindung mit den Massen.' Sowjetische Gesellschaftspolitik in der Ära Chruščev," *Vierteljahreshefte für Zeitgeschichte* 34, 4 (1986), 523–60.

On Khrushchev's housing policy, see Mark Smith, *Property of Communists: The Urban Housing Program from Stalin to Khrushchev* (DeKalb: Northern Illinois University Press, 2010). The memoirs of Khrushchev, Mikoian and Shepilov tell us about the political debates in the leading circle: Sergei Khrushchev (ed.), *Memoirs of Nikita Khrushchev*, 3 vols. (University Park: Pennsylvania State University Press, 2004–07); Anastas Mikoian, *Tak bylo. Razmyshleniia o minuvshem* [How It Was: Reflections on the Past] (Mosow: Vagirus, 1999); Dmitrii Shepilov, *The Kremlin's Scholar: A Memoir of Soviet Politics Under Stalin and Khrushchev* (New Haven: Yale University Press, 2007).

Memoirs of ordinary citizens and artists on the thaw are included in Donald Raleigh (ed.), *Russia's Sputnik Generation: Soviet Baby Boomers Talk About Their Lives* (Bloomington: Indiana University Press, 2006); Ludmilla Alexeyeva and Paul Goldberg, *The Thaw Generation: Coming of Age in the Post-Stalin Era* (Pittsburgh: University of Pittsburgh Press, 1993).

In recent years, many collections of documents on de-Stalinization have been published, among others: A. N. Artizov et al. (eds.), *Nikita Sergeevich Khrushchev. Dva tsveta vremeni. Dokumenty iz lichnogo fonda N. S. Khrushcheva* [Nikita Sergeevich Khrushchev. Two Colors of Time. Documents from the Private Files of N. S. Khrushchev], 2 vols. (Moscow: ROSSPEN, 2009); N. Kovaleva et al. (eds.), *Molotov, Malenkov, Kaganovich. 1957: Stenogramma iiunskogo plenuma TsK KPSS i drugie dokumenty* [Molotov, Malenkov, Kaganovich. 1957: Report of the June Plenum of the CC CPSU and Other Documents] (Moscow: ROSSPEN, 1998); Andrei Fursenko (ed.), *Prezidium TsK KPSS 1954–1964* [Presidium of the CC CPSU 1954–1964], vol. I, *Chernovye protokol'nye zapisi zasedanii Stenogrammy* [First Draft Notes for the Official

Reports] (Moscow: ROSSPEN, 2003), and vol. II, *Postanovleniia 1954–1958* [Resolutions] (Moscow: ROSSPEN, 2006); A. N. Artizov et al. (eds.), *Nikita Khrushchev 1964. Stenogrammy plenuma TsK KPSS i drugie dokumenty* [Nikita Khrushchev 1964. Report of the CC CPSU Plenum and Other Documents] (Moscow: ROSSPEN, 2007).

6

The Changing Pattern of Soviet–East European Relations 1953–1968

MARK KRAMER

The years 1953 to 1968 were a time of great fluidity in Eastern Europe, marking a shift from Stalinist domination to a looser, albeit ill-defined relationship with the Soviet Union. For a few months in the spring of 1953 the East European countries seemed to have enormous leeway to move away from Stalinist strictures, but this period receded in mid 1953. Even though East–West relations steadily improved over the next two years and gave rise to the "spirit of Geneva," Soviet relations with the East European countries were still shaped by the legacy of Stalinism. But when Nikita Khrushchev made a renewed push for de-Stalinization in early 1956, the potential for momentous change in the Soviet bloc seemed to loom once again. The situation remained fluid as late as October 1956, when crises erupted almost simultaneously in Poland and Hungary. The outcome of those two crises – a peaceful settlement in Poland after a tense confrontation with Moscow and a large-scale Soviet invasion of Hungary to quell revolutionary unrest – defined the future political complexion of Eastern Europe.

For more than a decade after the Soviet invasion of Hungary in late 1956, relative calm prevailed in Soviet–East European relations. From the early 1960s on, the Soviet Union worked closely with the East European countries to consolidate their military ties via the Warsaw Pact and economic ties via the Council for Mutual Economic Assistance (CMEA). The change of political leadership in Moscow in October 1964 had little immediate effect on Soviet–East European relations, which continued to evolve toward greater cohesion and integration. However, in 1968 the USSR's position in Eastern Europe came under a fundamental challenge not from violent unrest as in 1956 but from the "Prague Spring," a wide-ranging effort at political liberalization in Czechoslovakia. After trying in vain for more than half a year to pressure Czechoslovak communist leaders to curtail the far-reaching reform movement, Soviet leaders decided they would have to take military action of their own. The Soviet-led invasion of Czechoslovakia in August 1968, and the enunciation of the "Brezhnev Doctrine" in its wake, reaffirmed Soviet hegemony in Eastern Europe for the remaining decades of the Cold War.

The Early Post-Stalin Period

The death of the long-time ruler of the Soviet Union, Joseph Stalin, in early March 1953, soon led to major changes in the European communist bloc. Within weeks of Stalin's death, his successors encouraged (and, when necessary, ordered) the East European governments to enact wide-ranging "New Courses" of political and economic reforms. The abrupt introduction of these changes, and the sharp rise of public expectations in Eastern Europe, spawned strikes and mass demonstrations in Bulgaria in May 1953, a rebellion in Czechoslovakia in early June and a much larger uprising in the German Democratic Republic (GDR) two weeks later.[1] The Czechoslovak authorities succeeded in putting down a violent revolt in Plzeň (Pilsen) and mass unrest in other Czechoslovak cities on 1–2 June 1953, but in East Germany the government and security forces quickly lost control of the situation on 17 June when hundreds of thousands of people rose up against communist rule in cities and towns throughout the country. Faced with the prospect of "losing" a vital ally, Soviet army troops and security forces in the GDR had to intervene en masse to subdue the revolt and restore a modicum of public order.[2]

The Soviet Union's decisive response to the East German crisis was motivated in part by a concern that destabilizing unrest could spread to other East European countries and even to the USSR itself unless urgent steps were taken. The spate of protests and strikes in Bulgaria, Hungary and Romania in the spring of 1953, and the much larger uprising in Czechoslovakia in early June, had demonstrated the potential for wider turmoil in the wake of Stalin's death. As soon as Soviet diplomats in East

1 For more on this unrest, see Mark Kramer, "The Early Post-Stalin Succession Struggle and Upheavals in East-Central Europe: Internal–External Linkages in Soviet Policy Making (Part 1)," *Journal of Cold War Studies* 1, 1 (Spring 1999), 3–55.
2 Mark Kramer, "Der Aufstand in Ostdeutschland im Juni 1953," in Bernd Greiner, Christian Th. Müller and Dierk Walter (eds.), *Krisen im Kalten Krieg* (Hamburg: Hamburger Edition, 2008), 80–127.

Germany sent urgent cables to Moscow highlighting the scale of the uprising on 17 June, the leaders of the Communist Party of the Soviet Union (CPSU) authorized the use of military force to quell the unrest. In addition, the Soviet minister of internal affairs, Lavrentii Beria, contacted the Soviet foreign intelligence station chiefs in all the other East European countries and warned them that they would "pay with [their] heads if anything like this happens" in their assigned countries.[3] He ordered them to send status reports directly to him every few hours and to work with the local governments to prevent mass unrest and break up any demonstrations in support of the East German protesters.

The use of Soviet military power in East Germany eliminated the immediate problem facing the Soviet Union in Eastern Europe with relatively little bloodshed (only 39 of the 650,000 protesters were killed, including 6 who were executed on the spot), but the suppression of the East German uprising did not impart greater consistency to Soviet policy or eliminate the prospect of further turmoil in the Soviet bloc. Although the sudden downfall of Beria in late June 1953 and the formal appointment of Nikita Khrushchev as CPSU First Secretary in September 1953 helped mitigate the instability in Soviet domestic politics, the leadership struggle in Moscow continued to buffet Soviet–East European relations over the next few years.[4] During the brief tenure of Georgii Malenkov as Soviet prime minister from March 1953 to February 1955, the Soviet government encouraged a significant relaxation of economic and political controls in Eastern Europe, similar to the changes that were being adopted in the USSR itself. Violent mass terror in the region came to an end, and vast numbers of political prisoners were released. The reforms in the Eastern bloc countries after June 1953 were not as far-reaching as those proposed before Beria's ouster, but they still represented a notable departure from Stalinism. In a region like Eastern Europe, which had been so tightly compressed during the Stalin era, the abrupt surge of liberalization greatly magnified the potential for social and political upheaval.[5] Leaders in Moscow, however, were still preoccupied with their

---

3 These emergency directives were recounted by Vitalii Cherniavskii, who in June 1953 was serving as the Soviet intelligence station chief in Bucharest, in a lengthy interview in Moscow in 2005. See also Leonid Mlechin, "Moi pervyi nachal'nik podpolkovnik Cherniavskii," *Nezavisimoe voennoe obozrenie* 26 (15 Jul. 2005), 7.

4 On the general course of the Soviet leadership struggle, see William C. Taubman, *Khrushchev: The Man and His Era* (New York: W. W. Norton, 2003), 264–69.

5 See Yurii Aksiutin, *Khrushchevskaia "ottepel'" i obshchestvennye nastroeniia v SSSR, 1953–1964 gg.* (Moscow: ROSSPEN, 2004), 58–59, 101–03, 112, 147, 178–82, 201–02, 257–63, 311, 319–20. See also Yurii Aksiutin, "Piatyi prem'er, ili pochemu Malenkov ne uderzhal bremia vlasti," *Rodina* 5 (May 1994), 81–88.

own domestic concerns and the ongoing struggle for power, and they failed to appreciate the increasingly volatile conditions in the Eastern bloc. Most of them simply hoped that the uprisings in Czechoslovakia and East Germany in June 1953 were an anomaly and not a portent of more explosive unrest to come.

Vacillation and Change Under Khrushchev

The extent to which Soviet leaders misjudged the situation in Eastern Europe was evidenced by the contradictory policies that Malenkov's chief rival, Nikita Khrushchev, initially adopted. To outflank Malenkov in the leadership struggle in late 1954 and early 1955, Khrushchev had temporarily sided with the hardliners on the ruling CPSU Presidium, and this shift was promptly reflected throughout the Soviet bloc. At Khrushchev's behest, the East European governments slowed or reversed many of the economic and political reforms they had implemented in the first few months after Stalin's death, and in Hungary the reformist prime minister, Imre Nagy, was removed in April 1955 by the neo-Stalinist leader of the Hungarian Workers' Party, Mátyás Rákosi, who had been forced to yield the prime ministerial post to Nagy two years earlier under Soviet pressure. Because the successor to Nagy as prime minister, András Hegedüs, was a much weaker figure overall, Rákosi was able to reacquire a dominant political role in Hungary as party leader and to undo many of the recently enacted political reforms. Khrushchev later acknowledged, in a conversation with Chinese communist leaders, that one of his "most serious mistakes" in 1955 and 1956 was when he started "supporting that idiot Rákosi again."[6]

The sudden dampening of popular expectations in Hungary and other East European countries – expectations that had been raised by the reformist New Courses of the previous two years – fueled strong currents of public discontent. Malenkov had been able to avoid the emergence of widespread political unrest in Eastern Europe after June 1953 by pressing ahead with steps both at home and in the Eastern bloc to improve living

---

6 "Zapis' besedy tovarishcha Khrushcheva N. S. s Predsedatelem TsK KPK Mao Tsze-Dunom, zamestiteliami Predsedatelia TsK KPS Liu Shao-tsi, Chzou En'-Laem, Chzu De, Lin' Biao, chlenami Politbiuro TsK KPK Pyn Chzenem, Chen' I i chlenom Sekretariata Van Tszia-sianom 2 oktiabria 1959 goda," Osobaia papka (Strictly Secret/Special Dossier), 2 Oct. 1959, in Rossiiskii gosudarstvennyi arkhiv sotsial'no-politicheskoi istorii (RGASPI), Moscow, f. 558, op. 1, d. 331, ll. 12–13.

conditions, boost consumer output and provide for greater official respon-
siveness to public concerns on a wide range of matters; but, when
Khrushchev forced Malenkov to the sidelines in early 1955 (replacing him
as prime minister with the more cautious Nikolai Bulganin) and began
scaling back the pace and scope of the post-Stalin reforms, he inadvertently
heightened the potential for mass protest actions and destabilization in
Eastern Europe.

The threat of political instability in Eastern Europe was not as easy to
defuse as it had been during the Stalin era. The Soviet Union no longer had
recourse to classic Stalinist methods of ensuring bloc conformity. Although
economic retrenchment had been possible, a return to pervasive terror was
not, nor would Khrushchev and his colleagues have desired it. Hence,
Khrushchev altered his approach somewhat as he sought to replace the
heavy-handed subjugation of Eastern Europe, which had been possible in
Stalin's time, with economic and ideological cohesion. He advanced the
concept of a "socialist commonwealth" (*sotsialisticheskoe sodruzhestvo*) in
which the East European communist parties would have the right to follow
their "own paths to socialism" – that is, to have somewhat greater leeway on
internal matters – as long as they continued to "base all their activities on the
teachings of Marxism-Leninism."[7] Khrushchev apparently believed that popular support for the East European governments would increase if they were
given greater independence in domestic policymaking, but he wanted to
ensure that the Soviet Union would maintain long-term control of the bloc by
promoting economic and military integration. In keeping with these goals,
Khrushchev attempted to mend relations with Yugoslavia and bring it closer
to the Soviet camp, give greater substance to the CMEA (which had been
formed by Stalin in 1949 but had made little headway during its initial years)
and foster a more concrete Soviet–East European military relationship, most
notably through the establishment of the Warsaw Treaty Organization
in May 1955.

The bid for a rapprochement with Yugoslavia was of particular importance
to Khrushchev, in part because he was able to use the issue as a political
wedge against one of his domestic rivals, Viacheslav Molotov. Stalin and
Molotov had provoked a bitter split with Yugoslavia in 1948 and had subsequently tried to get rid of the Yugoslav leader, Josip Broz Tito. Soviet efforts
to remove Tito ultimately proved futile, but Stalin remained fiercely hostile

---

7 "Zaiavlenie tovarishcha N. S. Khrushcheva na aerodrome v Belgrade," *Pravda* (27 May
   1955), 1.

toward Yugoslavia to the very end and may have been contemplating an invasion in the final two years of his life, when he embarked on a crash military buildup.[8] Within a few months of Stalin's death, however, his successors decided to restore diplomatic relations with Yugoslavia and sent a formal request to the country's leadership about the matter on 16 June 1953, the day before the East German uprising. This gesture marked a striking turnaround in Soviet policy after five years of vehement polemics and recriminations with Yugoslav leaders.

Nevertheless, the significance of the move was limited because it did not yet entail a resumption of formal ties between the two countries' communist parties. Molotov and a few other hardliners in the CPSU remained adamantly opposed to any suggestion of pursuing a full reconciliation with the Yugoslav communists. Whenever the issue of Yugoslavia came up at CPSU Presidium meetings in 1954 and the first few months of 1955, sharp exchanges ensued, as Molotov repeatedly tried to introduce language into Presidium resolutions and other documents that would effectively derail efforts to improve relations with Belgrade and would keep Tito as a pariah.[9]

Khrushchev began laying the groundwork in 1954 for a much fuller rapprochement with Yugoslavia, and he stepped up his efforts in the spring of 1955 to overcome the opposition posed by Molotov. On 26 May 1955, ten days after Khrushchev had returned from Poland for the signing of the Warsaw Pact, he traveled to Belgrade and held an extended series of meetings with Tito and other Yugoslav leaders. The sessions at times were awkward and tense, and Tito was not always receptive to Soviet blandishments, but overall the high-profile visit achieved what Khrushchev was seeking. The communiqué issued by the two sides on 2 June at the end of the discussions – a document that came to be known as the Belgrade Declaration – pledged respect for their "differences in internal complexion, social systems and forms of socialist development."[10] The declaration also committed each side not to interfere in the other's internal affairs "for any reason whatsoever." The visit and the joint declaration were politically valuable for Khrushchev not only in giving him another

---

8 See Mark Kramer, "Stalin, the Split with Yugoslavia, and Soviet–East European Efforts to Reassert Control, 1948–1953," in Svetozar Rajak et al. (eds.), *The Balkans in the Cold War* (London: Palgrave Macmillan, 2016), 29–63.
9 See, for example, "Protokol No. 120: Zasedanie Prezidiuma TsK KPSS, 19 maia 1955 g.," notes from CPSU Presidium meeting (top secret), in Rossiiskii gosudarstvennyi arkhiv noveishei istorii (RGANI), f. 3, op. 8, d. 388, ll. 40–420b.
10 "Deklaratsiia pravitel'stv Soiuza sovetskikh sotsialisticheskikh respublik i Federativnoi narodnoi respubliki Yugoslavii," *Pravda* (3 Jun. 1955), 1–2.

conspicuous foreign-policy accomplishment, but also in allowing him to intensify his political attacks against Molotov. At a CPSU Central Committee plenum in July 1955, which Khrushchev convened shortly after returning from the talks in Belgrade, the delegates praised Khrushchev's meetings with Tito and voiced a torrent of criticism about Molotov's "ridiculous," "deeply misguided," "long-outdated" and "erroneous" approach to Soviet–Yugoslav relations.[11]

The USSR's relationship with Yugoslavia continued to improve over the next several months as a result of Khrushchev's ostensibly "Secret" Speech at the Twentieth CPSU Congress in February 1956 in which he explicitly condemned Stalin's policy toward Yugoslavia, describing it as "arbitrary" and "mistaken."[12] A summary of the Secret Speech, along with highly favorable commentary, was published in the main Yugoslav daily, *Borba*, on 20 March. The following month, Khrushchev agreed to dissolve the Communist Information Bureau (Cominform), the Soviet-dominated organization from which Yugoslavia had been expelled by Stalin in June 1948. Although the Cominform had become mostly a figurehead entity after Yugoslavia's expulsion, the dismantling of it was clearly aimed at alleviating Yugoslav leaders' concerns about "future excommunications."[13] By the time Tito paid a lengthy reciprocating visit to the Soviet Union in June 1956 (a visit that Khrushchev had avidly sought), the reconciliation had proceeded far enough that the two sides could issue a joint communiqué praising the "diversity of forms of socialist development" and affirming the "right of different [communist] countries to pursue different paths of socialist development." The communiqué repudiated the Stalinist legacy by indicating that neither country would "attempt to impose its own views about . . . socialist development on the other side."[14]

Khrushchev proved equally successful in achieving a settlement in Austria, a country that had been a major point of contention between East and West after the end of World War II. Like Germany, Austria had been divided into zones of occupation at the end of the war that were allocated to the Soviet

---

11 "Plenum TsK KPSS – XIX Sozyv, 4–12 iiulia 1955 g.," verbatim transcript (strictly secret), 4–12 Jul. 1955, in RGANI, f. 2, op. 1, dd. 139–180.

12 The text of the speech appeared promptly in the West but was not published in the Soviet Union until 1989. See "O kul'te lichnosti i ego posledstviiakh. Doklad pervogo sekretaria TsK KPSS tov. Khrushcheva N. S. XX S"ezdu Kommunisticheskoi partii Sovetskogo soiuza," *Kommunist vooruzhenykh sil* 11 (Jun. 1989), 63–92.

13 "Informatsionnoe soobshchenie o prekrashchenii deiatel'nosti Informatsionnogo biuro kommunisticheskikh i rabochikh partii," *Pravda* (18 Apr. 1956), 3.

14 "Pust' zhivet i protsvetaet bratskaia sovetsko-yugoslavskaia druzhba!," *Pravda* (22 Jun. 1956), 1.

Union, the United States, Britain and France. Under Stalin, the Soviet Union had consistently linked proposals for an Austrian peace treaty with other issues such as a settlement of the Trieste dispute and a resolution of the German question. The option of neutrality for Austria, which was first floated in the 1940s, was attractive to some officials in Moscow and in most Western capitals as well as in Austria itself.[15] But hardliners in Moscow such as Molotov and Lazar Kaganovich were firmly opposed to the idea if it meant that the Soviet Union would have to pull all its troops out of Austria.[16] Khrushchev, too, initially had been unwilling to accept proposals for Austrian neutrality and a Soviet troop withdrawal, but by early 1955 he had come to view a settlement of the Austrian question as a way of defusing a potential East–West flashpoint, eliminating the US, British and French troop presence in Central Europe, and spurring progress in the long-stalled East–West negotiations on Germany by using Austria as an example of how international guarantees of neutrality could be applied to a united German state.

In closed forums, Molotov and a few other Soviet officials still heatedly opposed the prospective withdrawal of Soviet military forces from Austria, and Molotov sought to quash proposals for an Austrian treaty in early 1955 when the CPSU Presidium discussed the matter.[17] In the end, however, Khrushchev and his supporters were able to face down the hardliners, arguing that the removal of US, British and French troops from Austria would more than compensate for the withdrawal of Soviet forces, not least because the United States geographically was much further from Austria than the Soviet Union was. Khrushchev alleged that Molotov's "insistence on keeping our troops in Austria" must stem from "a desire to start a war."[18] Having overcome the main domestic obstacles, the Soviet leader pursued bilateral talks with the Austrian government in March and April 1955, ironing out what neutrality would mean in practice and how it would affect the rights of outside powers, including the USSR. Those bilateral talks were soon

15 For an analysis of this issue, see Michael Gehler, "From Non-Alignment to Neutrality: Austria's Transformation During the First East–West Détente," *Journal of Cold War Studies* 7, 4 (Fall 2005), 104–36.
16 See, for example, the large volume of documents on this matter in Arkhiv vneshnei politiki Rossiiskoi federatsii (AVPRF), f. 06, op. 14, pap. 9, dd. 107 and 116.
17 "Plenum TsK KPSS – XIX Sozyv. Stenogramma trinadtsatogo zasedaniia 11 iiulia 1955 g. (vechernogo)," 11 Jul. 1955 (strictly secret), in RGANI, f. 2, op. 1, d. 175, l. 178. See also A. M. Aleksandrov-Agentov, *Ot Kollontai do Gorbacheva. Vospominaniia diplomata, sovetnika A. A. Gromyko* (Moscow: Mezhdunarodnye otnosheniia, 1994), 95.
18 "Plenum TsK KPSS – XIX Sozyv. Stenogramma trinadtsatogo zasedaniia 11 iiulia 1955 g. (vechernogo)," l. 178.

followed by a four-power conference and the formal signing of the Austrian State Treaty on 15 May 1955, the day after the USSR and its allies had signed the Warsaw Pact.[19] The settlement marked a triumph for Khrushchev personally as well as for Soviet foreign policy.

Moreover, the establishment of the Warsaw Pact on 14 May 1955 had forestalled any concerns that Khrushchev's domestic opponents might have raised about the implications of the Soviet troop pullout from Austria.[20] Until May 1955 the ostensible justification for Soviet military deployments in both Hungary and Romania had been that they were needed to preserve logistical and communications links with Soviet forces in Austria. The creation of the Warsaw Pact provided a rationale for maintaining the deployments in Hungary and Romania even after all Soviet troops were gone from Austria. The signing of the pact was intended in part as a symbolic counter to the admission of West Germany into NATO in early May 1955, but the legitimacy it conferred on the Soviet troop presence in Hungary and Romania was also a key factor, reflecting Khrushchev's general effort to codify the basic political and military structures of intra-bloc relations. Rather than simply preserving the mechanisms devised by Stalin, who had relied disproportionately on terror and coercion, Khrushchev sought a less domineering approach

19 For an analysis of Soviet policy in the leadup to the treaty (though focusing predominantly on the Stalin period), based in part on declassified Soviet documentation, see Wolfgang Mueller, *Die sowjetische Besatzung in Österreich 1945–1955 und ihre politische Mission* (Vienna: Böhlau, 2005). See also two valuable (and somewhat overlapping) collections of declassified Soviet documents pertaining to Soviet policy vis-à-vis Austria from 1945 to 1955: Stefan Karner and Barbara Stelzl-Marx (eds.), *Die Rote Armee in Österreich. Sowjetische Besatzung 1945–1955* (Graz: Ludwig Boltzmann-Institut für Kriegsfolgen-Forschung, 2005); and Wolfgang Mueller et al. (eds.), *Sowjetische Politik in Österreich 1945–1955. Dokumente aus russischen Archiven* (Vienna: Verlag der Österreichischen Akademie der Wissenschaften, 2005). Unfortunately, the relatively small number of documents in these two volumes from the post-Stalin era shed almost no light on Soviet policymaking and high-level debates. Two recent essays on this topic – Aleksei Filitov, "The Post-Stalin Succession Struggle and the Austrian State Treaty," in Arnold Suppan, Gerald Stourzh and Wolfgang Mueller (eds.), *Der österreichische Staatsvertrag 1955: Internationale Strategie, rechtliche Relevanz, nationale Identität* (Vienna: Böhlau, 2006), 121–43, and Mikhail Prozumenshchikov, "Nach Stalins Tod: Sowjetische Österreich-Politik, 1953–1955," in Karner and Stelzl-Marx (eds.), *Die rote Armee in Österreich*, 729–53 – are intriguing, but a good deal of murkiness remains. For a definitive history of the Austrian State Treaty, along with valuable appendices of documents and an extensive bibliography, see Gerald Stourzh, *Um Einheit und Freiheit. Staatsvertrag, Neutralität und das Ende der Ost-West-Besetzung Österreichs 1945–1955*, 5th edn. (Vienna: Böhlau, 2005).
20 "Podpisanie dogovora o druzhbe, sotrudnichestve i vzaimnoi pomoshchi," *Pravda* (15 May 1955), 1, and the text of the treaty on page 2.

that, he hoped, would foster greater domestic "viability" in Eastern Europe, enabling the Eastern bloc regimes to gain wider public backing.

At the same time, Khrushchev did not want to sacrifice the "cohesion" of the Soviet bloc. He hoped that viability and cohesion would go hand in hand in Eastern Europe, but events in the region increasingly showed that this was not always the case.[21] As the Soviet Union gradually loosened its tight grip on the East European countries after Stalin's death, bolstering the regimes' viability, internal pressures in the region both "from below" and "from above" threatened to erode or even undermine the cohesion of the bloc. The apparent tradeoff between viability and cohesion in Eastern Europe plagued Soviet policymakers over the next year and a half.

Confusion and Turmoil

Despite the successful overtures to Yugoslavia, the conclusion of the Austrian State Treaty and the establishment of the Warsaw Pact, Khrushchev's approach to Eastern Europe as a whole remained erratic. The USSR's vacillations between reform and retrenchment both at home and abroad, far from promoting either "viability" or "cohesion" in the Eastern bloc, directly contributed to a surge of instability in the region, especially in Hungary and Poland. By early 1956, sociopolitical pressures in Eastern Europe were sparking protests and ferment in the region, and the degree of political restiveness increased still further after Khrushchev's Secret Speech at the Twentieth Soviet Party Congress, the content of which quickly became known in Eastern Europe, especially Poland, where the full text of the speech was unofficially on sale at public markets by April.

Although the Secret Speech was geared overwhelmingly toward developments within the Soviet Union, it could not help but undercut the position of many East European leaders who had adhered rigidly to Stalinist principles, as Mátyás Rákosi and Bolesław Bierut had done in Hungary and Poland, respectively.[22] (Rákosi was ousted for good in July 1956 and had to take permanent refuge in the Soviet Union; Bierut might have met the same

---

21 The notion of a potential tradeoff between "viability" and "cohesion" in the Soviet bloc is well presented in James F. Brown, *Relations Between the Soviet Union and Its East European Allies: A Survey*, R-1742-PR (Santa Monica, CA: RAND Corporation, 1975).
22 For the effects on Rákosi's position, see "Shifrtelegramma," encrypted telegram (strictly secret) from Yu. V. Andropov, Soviet ambassador in Hungary, to the CPSU Presidium, 29 Apr. 1956, in RGANI, f. 89, op. 45, d. 1. For the effects in Poland, see the two reports from P. Turpit'ko, counselor at the Soviet embassy in Poland, in AVPRF, f. Referentura po Pol'she, op. 38, por. 42, pa. no. 127, d. 178, ll. 1–11 and 12–24.

fate had he not suddenly died in March 1956 of heart failure and pneumonia.) In East Germany, too, the Stalinist leader Walter Ulbricht, who had nearly been ousted in mid 1953, came under serious challenge once again from his domestic rivals. Khrushchev's speech also emboldened dissenters and critics within the East European regimes, leading to open hints of unrest in communist ranks. In Poland the widespread popularity of one of the victims of the Stalin-era purges, Władysław Gomułka, and in Hungary the continued influence of the erstwhile prime minister, Imre Nagy, merely heightened the instability. Political unrest thus became intertwined with the economic discontent that had followed the restoration of harsh economic policies in 1955.

When the unrest turned violent in the Polish city of Poznań in late June 1956, it ushered in a four-month period of growing turmoil. The Polish army and security forces managed to crush the uprising in Poznań, but the two days of fighting left at least 74 people dead and more than 700 seriously wounded.[23] The two days of armed clashes also caused tens of millions of złotys' worth of damage to buildings, transportation systems and other state property. At least thirty of the Polish army's main battle tanks, ten of its armored personnel carriers and dozens of its military trucks were destroyed or rendered unusable during the operation – an indication of how intense the fighting was. Documents released after 1989 indicate that a few Polish military officers who were sent to Poznań tried to resist the decision to open fire, but their opposition proved futile because the security forces were willing to carry out the orders and because Soviet army commanders (and their Polish allies) still dominated the Polish military establishment and were able to ensure that central orders were carried out.[24]

Having been chastened by the severity of the Poznań crisis, Soviet leaders were hoping that the First Secretary of the Polish United Workers' Party (PZPR), Edward Ochab – or, better yet, a successor – would restore tight political controls in Poland and put an end to the free-ranging discussions in

---

23 Some estimates of the death toll range as high as 120. The most reliable and detailed discussion of the varying estimates is in Edmund Makowski, *Poznański Czerwiec 1956: Pierwszy bunt społeczeństwa w PRL* (Poznań: Wydawnictwo Poznańskie, 2001), 165–71. Estimates of the number of wounded and of the extent of material damage also vary considerably. See ibid., 171–74.

24 See the analysis and valuable collection of declassified documents in Edward Jan Nalepa, *Pacyfikacja zbuntowanego miasta: Wojsko Polskie w Czerwca 1956 r. w Poznaniu w swietle dokumentow wojskowych* (Warsaw: Wydawnictwo Bellona, 1992), 72–74, 111–20.

the Polish press. But the situation in Poland unfolded according to its own logic, regardless of what Soviet leaders wanted.[25] By October a new crisis was brewing in Poland, precipitated by Khrushchev's aversion to Ochab and the ascendance of Gomułka, who was no more willing than Ochab to yield to Soviet pressure. Soviet leaders traveled secretly to Poland in the early morning of 19 October to vent their dismay, and a tense confrontation ensued. For several days, Khrushchev and his colleagues seriously considered whether to use military force in Poland.

Nonetheless, three factors ultimately led to a peaceful outcome of the crisis. First, Gomułka's ability to reassure Moscow about his loyalty to communism and about Poland's commitment to the Soviet bloc was crucial. Even though Soviet leaders had misjudged Gomułka before they arrived in Warsaw on 19 October, they still ultimately trusted him far more by this point than they trusted Ochab. Second, the growing recognition in Moscow of the dangers of large-scale military intervention in Poland ensured that Soviet leaders would not use military force except as a last resort. Khrushchev's contention at an emergency meeting of the CPSU Presidium on 24 October that "finding a reason to go to war now with Poland would be very easy, but finding a way to end such a war would be very difficult" summed up the complications that would have arisen if the Soviet Union had resorted to military options.[26] Third, the outbreak of mass destabilizing unrest in Hungary on 23 October in response to the Polish crisis diverted the CPSU Presidium's attention from Poland and gave the Soviet Union a strong extra incentive to defuse the military standoff with Polish leaders as quickly as possible and at minimal cost.

All three factors were vital in ensuring a peaceful end to the Soviet–Polish confrontation. If Gomułka had not been able to provide his assurances so convincingly to Khrushchev, and if the Hungarian Revolution had not posed such a crucial distraction for the USSR and created the risk of a two-front military contingency for Soviet forces in the heart of Europe, the odds are high that a direct Soviet–Polish military confrontation would have ensued in

25 See Mark Kramer, "Soviet–Polish Relations and the Crises of 1956: Brinkmanship and Intra-Bloc Politics," in Roger Engelmann, Thomas Großbölting and Hermann Wentker (eds.), *Communism in Crisis: The 1956 De-Stalinization and Its Consequences* (Göttingen: Vandenhoeck & Ruprecht, 2008), 61–127; and A. M. Orekhov, *Sovetskii soiuz i Pol'sha v gody "ottepeli": iz istorii sovetsko-pol'skikh otnoshenii* (Moscow: Izdatel'stvo Indrik, 2005).
26 "Zpráva o jednání na ÚV KSSS 24. řijna 1956," handwritten notes compiled by Jan Svoboda from CPSU Presidium meeting, 24 Oct, 1956, in Narodní Archiv České Republiky (NAČR), Archiv Ústředního vyboru Komunistické strany Československa (Arch. ÚV KSČ), f. 07/16, svazek 3.

late October, with grave consequences for both sides as well as for East–West ties and European security.

The peaceful outcome of the Soviet Union's confrontation with Poland enabled Soviet leaders to focus their efforts on the burgeoning revolution in Hungary. A crucial turning point came on the evening of the first day, 23 October, when the CPSU Presidium met in a hastily convened session and adopted a fateful decision, in response to the urging of Soviet ambassador Yurii Andropov and an "appeal" from the Hungarian leader Ernő Gerő (an appeal that had been orchestrated by Andropov), to send Soviet military forces into Budapest to help quell the unrest. This decision was approved by Khrushchev and his colleagues after remarkably little deliberation.[27] (The near-total lack of debate at this stage makes a notable contrast to the extensive and highly charged debate that occurred within the CPSU Presidium several days later about whether to send in a much larger contingent of Soviet troops to crush the revolution once and for all.) At the brief CPSU Presidium meeting on the evening of 23 October only one person, Anastas Mikoian, opposed the decision to resort to military intervention. Mikoian urged his colleagues to "rely on political measures" and to do everything possible to find a "political solution" before dispatching Soviet military forces into Hungary, which he predicted would simply make things worse.[28] Khrushchev and the other CPSU Presidium members brushed aside Mikoian's admonitions and endorsed Khrushchev's proposal to "send troops into Budapest" to "restore order."

By 2:15 a.m. on 24 October 1956, the first Soviet soldiers were moving in from Ukraine.[29] However, the entry of Soviet troops into Budapest not only failed to put an end to the rebellion but actually led to more intense fighting and large-scale bloodshed – precisely the danger that Mikoian had warned about. What had begun as a peaceful revolt against Stalinist hardliners in Hungary was transformed, by the introduction of Soviet military forces, into an armed anti-Soviet uprising and a war of independence, spreading to all major Hungarian cities.

The CPSU Presidium's nearly unanimous decision on 23 October to proceed with military intervention in Hungary did not mean that the much

---

27 "Rabochaia zapis' zasedaniia Prezidiuma TsK KPSS, 23 oktiabria 1956 g.," notes from CPSU Presidium meeting (top secret), 23 Oct. 1956, in RGANI, f. 3, op. 12, d. 1005, ll. 4–40b.

28 Ibid.

29 "TsK KPSS," memorandum no. 6764/p (top secret) from Soviet Deputy Minister of Internal Affairs Semen Perevertkin, 24 Oct. 1956, in Gosudarstvennyi arkhiv Rossiiskoi federatsii (GARF), f. R-9401, op. 2, d. 482, ll. 26–27.

larger Soviet invasion of the country on 4 November was inevitable, but it did mean that the odds of averting a more intense rebellion and a full-scale crackdown by Soviet troops were much lower than they otherwise might have been. If the CPSU Presidium had instead heeded Mikoian's advice on the evening of 23 October to let the Hungarian authorities try to restore order on their own, the Hungarian police and army might have been able to bring the unrest under control without endangering Soviet influence and communist rule in Hungary. The entry of Soviet soldiers into Budapest drastically changed the dynamic of the revolution. In that sense, the USSR's hasty decision to send military forces into Hungary in response to Andropov's urgent appeals markedly narrowed the range of options available to Soviet leaders as the revolution unfolded.

At the CPSU Presidium's sessions over the next week, the tenor of the discussions varied a great deal, depending in part on the latest events in Hungary and in part on political maneuvering in Moscow. Khrushchev and his colleagues were increasingly worried about what they saw as the continued breakdown of law and order in Hungary and even more about the steady evisceration of the major organs of communist rule there. They hoped that János Kádár, who replaced Gerő as general secretary of the reconstituted Hungarian Socialist Workers' Party on 25 October, and Nagy, who returned as prime minister on 28 October, would be able to restore a modicum of stability and forestall the need for further Soviet military intervention, but no one in Moscow was yet fully confident about it. Mikoian and another CPSU Presidium member, Mikhail Suslov, traveled to Hungary as envoys for the CPSU Presidium, and the reports they sent back to their colleagues in Moscow reflected the ambivalence and uncertainty in Soviet decision-making.[30] Mikoian remained relatively confident that a political solution was still feasible, but other members of the CPSU Presidium harshly criticized his position on the matter.[31] Although Mikoian was far from uniformly optimistic about the odds of success, his stance in favor of peacefully defusing the crisis influenced the debate and ensured a thorough review of possible options.

30 The encrypted cables they sent back to Moscow are reproduced in T. M. Islamov et al. (eds.), *Sovetskii soiuz i vengerskii krizis 1956 goda. Dokumenty* (Moscow: ROSSPEN, 1998).
31 "Rabochaia zapis' zasedaniia Prezidiuma TsK KPSS, 28 oktiabria 1956 g.," notes from CPSU Presidium meeting (top secret), 28 Oct. 1956, in RGANI, f. 3, op. 12, d. 1005, ll. 54–63.

On 30 October the CPSU Presidium initially decided to let events proceed in Hungary and to pull all Soviet troops out of the country – steps that, if left unchanged, almost certainly would have brought an end to communist rule in Hungary.[32] This decision, however, was inherently fragile and subject to reversal. When the CPSU Presidium met again on 31 October, the assembled officials rightly described the previous day's decision as a "compromise" or "preliminary" outcome, not a decision they had irrevocably embraced or intended to stick with short of a dramatic turnaround in Hungary.[33] They would have upheld the decision only if the political situation in Hungary had seemed to be distinctly improving and if the Hungarian government and the reconstituted Hungarian Communist Party clearly had been able to regain control of events and "defend socialist gains."

The CPSU Presidium's decision on 31 October to reverse the previous day's position and authorize a large-scale invasion was made under great stress in a highly compressed timeframe on the basis of incomplete and sometimes inaccurate or misleading information. The reversal was spurred by a combination of factors, above all the growing fear in Moscow that Soviet influence in Hungary was disintegrating and that Hungary's communist system was on the verge of total collapse. Soviet leaders were worried that events in Hungary would increasingly spill over into other East European countries (especially Czechoslovakia and Romania) and possibly even into the western areas of the Soviet Union, including the Baltic republics and Belarus as well as Ukraine.

The decision to crush the "counterrevolutionary rebellion" in Hungary through large-scale military force profoundly shaped Soviet–East European relations for the next thirty years, marking a turning point in the NATO–Warsaw Pact standoff.[34] In early November Soviet troops began moving back into Budapest, and on 4 November they undertook a massive crackdown, touching off four days of grueling urban combat that left more than 2,500 Hungarians and 720 Soviet troops dead.[35] The invasion made clear

---

32 "Rabochaia zapis' zasedaniia Prezidiuma TsK KPSS, 30 oktiabria 1956 g.," notes from CPSU Presidium meeting (top secret), 30 Oct. 1956, in RGANI, f. 3, op. 12, d. 1006, ll. 6–14.
33 "Rabochaia zapis' zasedaniia Prezidiuma TsK KPSS, 31 oktiabria 1956 g.," notes from CPSU Presidium meeting (top secret), 31 Oct. 1956, in RGANI, f. 3, op. 12, d. 1006, ll. 15–180b.
34 "Vypiska iz protokola No. 49 zasedaniia Prezidiuma TsK KPSS ot 31 oktiabria 1956 g. O polozhenii v Vengrii," CPSU Presidium Resolution No. P49/VI (strictly secret), 31 Oct. 1956, in RGANI, f. 3, op. 72, d. 484, l. 41.
35 Data on Hungarian and Soviet casualties come, respectively, from Peter Gosztonyi, "Az 1956-os forradalom szamokban," *Népszabadság* (3 Nov. 1990), 3; and "Sobytiia v Vengrii

to all the Warsaw Pact countries the bounds of Soviet restraint and the limits of what could be changed in Eastern Europe.[36] Far more than the uprisings of 1953 in Czechoslovakia and East Germany, the Hungarian Revolution posed a fundamental threat to Soviet hegemony in the region. By reestablishing military control over Hungary and by exposing – more dramatically than in June 1953 – the hollowness of Western governments' rhetoric about "rolling back" Soviet power and "liberating" the communist bloc, the November 1956 invasion stemmed any further loss of Soviet power in Eastern Europe.

Consolidation, Reform and Reaction

By 1968, when the Soviet Union faced its next major challenge in Eastern Europe, relations within the Soviet bloc had undergone several notable changes. Certain developments had facilitated greater Soviet control over Eastern Europe and better cohesion among the Warsaw Pact countries. Other developments, however, gave greater leeway to the East European states and helped to erode rather than tighten Soviet control in the region.

Sources of Cohesion

From the early 1960s on, the Soviet Union sought to invigorate the CMEA, which had been largely dormant after it was created in 1949. Soviet leaders hoped to use the CMEA as a means of formally integrating the Soviet and East European economies.[37] The "Basic Principles of Socialist Economic Integration," announced with much fanfare in 1961, did not yield many results in the end; but the Soviet Union was able to exploit its economic preponderance to promote bilateral integration with each of the CMEA member-states, especially in trade.

1956 g.," in Col.-Gen. G. A. Krivosheev (ed.), *Grif sekretnosti sniat. Poteri vooruzhenykh sil SSSR v voinakh, boevykh deistviiakh i voennykh konfliktakh. Statisticheskoe issledovanie* (Moscow: Voenizdat, 1993), 397.

36 These events are covered in Mark Kramer, "The Soviet Union and the 1956 Crises in Hungary and Poland: Reassessments and New Findings," *Journal of Contemporary History* 33, 2 (Apr. 1998), 163–215.

37 Jozef M. van Brabant, *Socialist Economic Integration: Contemporary Economic Problems in Eastern Europe* (New York: Cambridge University Press, 1980), esp. ch. 1; Alan H. Smith, *The Planned Economies of Eastern Europe* (London: Croom Helm, 1983), 174–202; and Michael Kaser, *Comecon: Integration Problems of the Planned Economies* (Oxford: Oxford University Press, 1967).

The Soviet Union also fostered greater intra-bloc cohesion in the military sphere, a policy reflected in the newly emerging concept of "coalition warfare." This approach called for a rapid, massive offensive against NATO by a combination of Soviet and East European forces using both nuclear and conventional weaponry:[38] Soviet leaders took several steps to improve the capacity of East European troops to perform effectively alongside Soviet forces. With Moscow's backing, all the East European states significantly modernized and expanded their armies in the 1960s; and they made renewed efforts to promote the interoperability and standardization of Warsaw Pact armaments. From October 1961 on, the Soviet and East European armies conducted joint military exercises.[39] As a result, the Warsaw Pact, which had been little more than a paper organization for several years after it was founded, finally started to acquire a few of the trappings of a real alliance.

These efforts to strengthen the Warsaw Pact were initiated by Khrushchev, but they were given even greater emphasis by his successor, Leonid Brezhnev. Unlike Khrushchev, who had sought to cut Soviet conventional forces and to rely predominantly on long-range nuclear missiles, Brezhnev committed the Soviet Union to a full-scale military buildup that expanded both conventional and nuclear weapons. The rapid growth and modernization of Soviet conventional forces during the Brezhnev era facilitated major improvements in Soviet combat units in Eastern Europe, whose role was to serve as the "main strategic echelon" of the Warsaw Pact.[40]

In the political sphere, as with the drive for economic integration and closer military relations, the Soviet Union accorded high priority to the goal of increased Soviet–East European cohesion. That goal was strongly endorsed by East European leaders who had come to be key figures in the 1960s, notably Gomułka and Ulbricht. Soviet backing for Ulbricht during the

---

38 "Razvitie voennogo iskusstva v usloviiakh vedeniia raketno-iadernoi voiny po sovremennym predstavleniiam," Report No. 24762s (top secret) from Col.-Gen. P. Ivashutin, chief of the Soviet General Staff's Main Intelligence Directorate, to Marshal M. V. Zakharov, head of the General Staff Military Academy, 28 Aug. 1964, in Tsentral'nyi arkhiv Ministerstva oborony, Moscow, d. 158, esp. l. 400.

39 V. V. Semin et al., *Voenno-politicheskoe sotrudnichestvo sotsialisticheskikh stran* (Moscow: Nauka, 1988), 72–74, 185–201 and 231–43. Secret accounts of many of these exercises, prepared by officers in the East German National People's Army, can be found in the Militärisches Zwischenarchiv in Potsdam.

40 US Central Intelligence Agency, Foreign Assessment Center, *The Development of Soviet Military Power Trends Since 1965 and Prospects for the 1980s*, SR SI 100353 (top secret/ intelligence sources and methods involved), Apr. 1981 (declassified Mar. 2001), esp. 1–20.

severe crises of the late 1950s and early 1960s was crucial in preserving the contribution of the German Democratic Republic to the Warsaw Pact. In particular, Khrushchev's decision to permit the construction of the Berlin Wall in August 1961 halted the efflux of refugees from the GDR, staved off a further deterioration of the East German economy and allowed the East German communist party (formally known as the Socialist Unity Party of Germany, Sozialistische Einheitspartei Deutschlands or SED) to reestablish its "leading role."[41]

The Soviet Union's position in Eastern Europe was further enhanced by a highly publicized conference in Moscow in November 1960 that brought together officials from eighty-one of the world's communist parties and reaffirmed the "universally recognized vanguard role" of the CPSU in the international communist movement.[42] East European party leaders worked closely with Soviet officials at the conference to ensure that the participants would support Moscow's calls for increased "unity" and "solidarity" in the "stand against imperialism." Much the same was true of a subsequent all-European conference of communist parties, held in Karlovy Vary in April 1967.

Sources of Friction

Despite these signs of greater Soviet–East European cohesion, most developments in the 1960s pointed not toward an increase of Soviet control in Eastern Europe, but toward a loosening of that control. In part, this trend reflected the growing heterogeneity of the East European societies, but it also was spurred on by the Sino-Soviet conflict and the schism it provoked in world communism. An acrimonious split between Moscow and Beijing, stemming from genuine policy and ideological differences as well as from a personal clash between Khrushchev and Mao Zedong, erupted in the late 1950s and flared into intense hostility at the beginning of the 1960s.[43]

---

41 A valuable first-hand Soviet account of this whole episode can be found in the memoir by Yulii Kvitsinskii, a long-time Soviet diplomat and Foreign Ministry expert on Germany, *Vor der Sturm: Erinnerungen eines Diplomaten* (Munich: Siedler Verlag, 1993).

42 See the CPSU Central Committee's own assessment of the gathering in "Plenum TsK KPSS 10–18 ianvaria 1961 g.," marked-up verbatim transcript (strictly secret), Jan. 1961, in RGANI, f. 2, op. 1, d. 495.

43 On the sources of the Beijing–Moscow dispute, see Mark Kramer, "Sino-Soviet Relations on the Eve of the Split," *Cold War International History Project Bulletin* 6–7 (Winter 1995–96), 170–85.

The downfall of Khrushchev and ascendance of Brezhnev in October 1964 failed to ameliorate the situation. Initially, officials on both sides were hopeful that the change of leadership in Moscow would permit the two countries to achieve at least a partial rapprochement, but those hopes proved illusory, and the enmity between the two sides intensified. The spillover from the Sino-Soviet conflict into Eastern Europe was evident almost immediately, as the Soviet Union and China vied with one another for the backing of foreign communist parties. In late 1960 and early 1961 the Albanian leader, Enver Hoxha, broke out of the Soviet sphere in Eastern Europe by openly aligning his country with China, a precedent that caused alarm in Moscow.[44] The "loss" of Albania, though trivial compared to the earlier rift with Yugoslavia and the deepening confrontation with China, marked the second time since 1945 that Soviet hegemony in Eastern Europe had been severely challenged from within.

To make matters worse, Soviet leaders soon discovered that China was secretly attempting to induce other East European countries to follow Albania's lead. At a closed plenum of the CPSU Central Committee in December 1963, Andropov, who by this time was overseeing intra-bloc relations for the CPSU, reported that the Chinese had been focusing their efforts on Poland, Hungary and East Germany:

> The Chinese leaders are carrying out a policy of crude sabotage in relation to Poland, Hungary and the GDR. Characteristic of this is the fact that in September of this year, during conversations with a Hungarian official in China, Politburo member Chu De declared that China would welcome it if the Hungarian comrades diverged from the CPSU's line. But, Chu De threatened, if you remain on the side of the revisionists, we will have to take a stance against you.[45]

44 Valuable documentation on the Soviet–Albanian rift is available in *Albania Challenges Khrushchev Revisionism* (New York: Gamma Publishing, 1976), a compilation put out by the Albanian government which includes full transcripts of meetings between senior Soviet and Albanian officials in 1960 as well as cables and other messages between Hoxha and the Albanian participants in the meetings. A somewhat expanded edition of the collection is available in French: *La grande divergence 1960* (Paris: Nouveau Bureau d'Édition, 1976). Key insights can also be gained by reading the surprisingly compatible accounts in Hoxha's and Khrushchev's memoirs: N. S. Khrushchev, *Vremia, liudi, vlast'* (Moscow: Moskovskie novosti, 1999), vol. II, 138–42; and Enver Hoxha, *The Artful Albanian: The Memoirs of Enver Hoxha*, ed. Jon Holliday (London: Chatto and Windus, 1986), 141–247, esp. 224–47. For an early but still useful overview of the crisis, along with a handy collection of public statements and press articles, see William E. Griffith, *Albania and the Sino-Soviet Rift* (Cambridge, MA: MIT Press, 1963).

45 "Materialy k protokolu No. 6 zasedaniia Plenuma TsK KPSS. O deiatel'nosti Prezidiuma TsK KPSS po ukrepleniiu yedinstva kommunisticheskogo dvizheniia, postanovlenie Sekretariata TsK KPSS ob izdanii tekstov vystuplenii na Plenume TsK

China's overtures to these three countries bore little fruit in the end, but Soviet leaders could not be sure of that at the time. The very fact that China was seeking to foment discord within the bloc was bound to generate alarm in Moscow.

Soviet leaders' unease about the effect of the Sino-Soviet split in Eastern Europe was piqued still further when Romania began to embrace foreign and domestic policies in the 1960s that were at times sharply at odds with Soviet ones.[46] Initially, the Romanian quest for autonomy was inspired by the Soviet Union's attempts in 1961 to mandate a supranational economic integration program for the CMEA, which would have relegated Romania to being little more than a supplier of agricultural goods and raw materials for the more industrialized communist countries. In response, the Romanian government began shifting much of its foreign trade away from CMEA countries. Before long, Romania's defiance extended from economic matters into foreign policy and military activities. Bucharest staked out a conspicuously neutral position in the Sino-Soviet dispute, refusing to endorse Moscow's polemics or to join in other steps aimed at isolating Beijing. In 1967, Romania became the first East European country to establish diplomatic ties with West Germany, a step that infuriated East German leaders. That same year, Romania refused to take part in the Karlovy Vary conference and declined to go along with other Warsaw Pact states when they cut off diplomatic relations with Israel after the June 1967 Arab–Israeli War.

More important, Romania adopted an independent military doctrine and a national military command structure separate from that of the Warsaw Pact.[47] Shortly after coming to power in Bucharest in 1965, Nicolae Ceauşescu prohibited joint Warsaw Pact maneuvers on Romanian territory and stopped sending Romanian army officers to Soviet military academies for training. He also began openly challenging Soviet domination of the Warsaw Pact military command structures. When the Soviet–Romanian treaty of friendship and cooperation came up for renewal in 1967, Ceauşescu insisted that

Ponomareva B. N., Andropova Yu. V. i Il'icheva L. F., rechi sekretarei TsK KPSS Ponomareva, Andropova, Il'icheva, i Khrushcheva N. S.," 9–13 Dec. 1963 (top secret), in RGANI, f. 2, op. 1, d. 665, l. 30.

46 Vladimir Tismaneanu, "Gheorghiu-Dej and the Romanian Workers' Party: From De-Sovietization to the Emergence of National Communism," Cold War International History Project Working Paper No. 37 (Washington, DC: Woodrow Wilson International Center of Scholars, 2002).

47 Denis Deletant, "Taunting the Bear: Romania and the Warsaw Pact, 1963–1989," Cold War History 7, 4 (Nov. 2007), 495–507. For a much older but still useful survey, see Alexander Alexiev, Romania and the Warsaw Pact: The Defense Policy of a Reluctant Ally, P-6270 (Santa Monica, CA: RAND Corporation, Jan. 1979).

provisions be added to ensure that Romanian troops would be used only against "imperialist" countries, not against other socialist states. Soviet leaders strongly resisted Ceaușescu's demands, but ultimately gave in.[48] Although Romania had never been a crucial member of the Warsaw Pact, Ceaușescu's growing recalcitrance on military affairs posed serious complications for the Soviet Union.

Developments outside the bloc also contributed to the erosion of Soviet control in Eastern Europe. The perceived threat of German aggression, which for so long had unified the Warsaw Pact governments, had gradually abated. In the mid 1960s, West Germany had launched its *Ostpolitik* campaign to increase economic and political contacts in Eastern Europe (especially the GDR), a campaign whose potentially disruptive impact on the Soviet bloc was clear. Soviet policy in Eastern Europe was also increasingly constrained by the incipient US–Soviet détente, with its promise of arms control and increased East–West trade. This new relationship gave Moscow an incentive to proceed cautiously in Eastern Europe before taking actions that could antagonize the West and undermine détente.

The Prague Spring and the Soviet Invasion

Against this backdrop, the events of 1968 unfolded in Czechoslovakia, a country that had been under harsh communist rule for twenty years. Sweeping internal liberalization during the "Prague Spring" brought a comprehensive revival of political, economic and cultural life in Czechoslovakia. The reforms earned overwhelming popular support in Czechoslovakia and were also hailed in many foreign countries, where observers across the political spectrum hoped that Czechoslovakia's effort to fashion "socialism with a human face" (*socialismus s lidskou tváří* – a slogan that became identified with the Prague Spring) would succeed. But the process alarmed Czechoslovakia's Warsaw Pact allies, especially the Soviet Union, East Germany and Poland, about the potential ramifications.[49] Both the internal and the external repercussions of the reforms in Czechoslovakia

---

48 The new treaty was finally concluded in July 1970, more than two and a half years later than planned. See "Dogovor o druzhbe, sotrudnichestve i vzaimnoi pomoshchi," *Pravda* (8 Jul. 1970), 2.

49 For a comprehensive overview of the Prague Spring, see H. Gordon Skilling, *Czechoslovakia's Interrupted Revolution* (Princeton: Princeton University Press, 1976). On the Soviet response, see Mark Kramer, "The Kremlin, the Prague Spring, and the Brezhnev Doctrine," in Vladimir Tismaneanu (ed.), *Promises of 1968: Crisis, Illusion, Utopia* (Budapest: Central European University Press, 2010), 285–370.

were regarded by Soviet leaders as a fundamental threat to the USSR's internal security and to their sphere of influence in Eastern Europe. The Prague Spring raised doubts about the cohesion of the Warsaw Pact, and those doubts were bound to multiply if the developments in Czechoslovakia spread to other Eastern bloc countries.

When Czechoslovak leaders declined to rein in the Prague Spring, the irritation in Moscow became palpable. The members of the CPSU Politburo, as Brezhnev noted when they met in early May, were "united in the view that [the reform agenda espoused by the Communist Party of Czechoslovakia's First Secretary Alexander Dubček] is a harmful program, which is paving the way for the restoration of capitalism in Czechoslovakia."[50] Of particular concern to Soviet leaders were the uncensored political discussions in the Czechoslovak media and the continued removal of hardline opponents of the Prague Spring. During a Warsaw Pact meeting in Dresden on 23 March 1968, Brezhnev and Ulbricht had rebuked Dubček for allowing "the press, radio and television to slip away from the party's control" and for dismissing many "loyal and seasoned cadres, who have proven their mettle in years of struggle."[51] Events over the next several weeks greatly reinforced the Soviet and East German concerns.

As the rift between Czechoslovakia and the Soviet Union widened in the spring of 1968, the CPSU Politburo authorized Soviet defense minister Marshal Andrei Grechko to begin preparing Soviet forces in Eastern Europe for a large-scale military contingency.[52] This decision marked the initial step in planning for "Operation Danube," the eventual codename of the August 1968 invasion. Within the Soviet Politburo, however, there was not yet full agreement about the best course to pursue. Brezhnev initially was unwilling to embrace a clear-cut position, and he permitted and indeed encouraged other members of the Politburo to express their own opinions about particular matters and appropriate responses. The transcripts of CPSU Politburo meetings from 1968 reveal that some members, such as Yurii Andropov, Nikolai Podgornyi and Petro Shelest, were consistent proponents

50 "Rabochaya zapis' zasedaniia Politbiuro TsK KPSS ot 6 maia 1968," verbatim transcript (top secret), 6 May 1968, in Arkhiv Prezidenta Rossiiskoi federatsii (APRF), f. 3, op. 45, d. 99, l. 202.
51 "Protokol der Treffen der Ersten Sekretäre der kommunistischen Parteien Bulgariens, der ČSSR, der DDR, Polens, der Sowjetunion und Ungarns," verbatim transcript (top secret), 23 Mar. 1968, in Stiftung Archiv der Parteien und Massenorganisationen der DDR im Bundesarchiv, Berlin (SAPMO), Zentrale Parteiarchiv (ZPA), IV 2/201/778.
52 Directive No. MO/GOU/1/87567 (top secret – eyes only), 5 Apr. 1968, to Col.-Gen. K. I. Provalov, in Magyar Honvédség Központi Irattára (MHKI), Budapest, 5/12/16.

of military intervention, whereas others, particularly Mikhail Suslov, were far more circumspect. Several Politburo members, notably Aleksei Kosygin, fluctuated during the crisis, at times favoring "extreme measures" (i.e. Soviet military action) and at other times advocating a political solution with Dubček.

Nevertheless, even when top-ranking Soviet officials disagreed with one another, their disagreements were mainly over tactics rather than strategic considerations or fundamental goals. All the members of the Soviet Politburo agreed that the reform process in Czechoslovakia was endangering the "gains of socialism" in that country and the "common interests of world socialism." By the late spring of 1968, most of them sensed that drastic action, including the use of violence, would be necessary to curtail the Prague Spring. Although some still hoped that Czechoslovak leaders themselves would be willing to crack down, many had begun to suspect that Dubček was disinclined to pursue harsh measures himself and that external intervention would be necessary.

The concerns in Moscow – political, ideological and military – gradually fused into a widely shared perception that events in Czechoslovakia were spinning out of control. The sense of impending danger – or of "spontaneity" and "unlimited decentralization" as a Soviet Politburo member, Viktor Grishin, put it – eventually colored Soviet views of the whole Prague Spring.[53] The cumulative impact of events, rather than any single development, is what seems to have convinced Brezhnev that internal changes in Czechoslovakia were threatening vital Soviet interests. The necessity of countering that threat was no longer in doubt by mid 1968; the only question remaining for Soviet leaders was whether – and when – external military intervention would be required.

By July and early August 1968, the Soviet Union was applying relentless pressure on the Czechoslovak authorities to reverse the liberalization program. The Soviet campaign was vigorously supported by Poland, the GDR, Bulgaria and anti-reformist members of the Communist Party of Czechoslovakia's ruling Presidium, who secretly conspired with Soviet leaders to end the Prague Spring.[54] Brezhnev used a variety of bilateral channels to urge Dubček and other senior Czechoslovak officials to combat

---

53 "Stenogramma tret'ego zasedaniia 10 aprelia 1968 g., utrennego," marked-up verbatim transcript of CPSU Central Committee Plenum (top secret), 10 Apr. 1968, in RGANI, f. 2, op. 3, d. 97, l. 85.
54 For a detailed discussion, see Kramer, "The Kremlin, the Prague Spring, and the Brezhnev Doctrine."

"anti-socialist" and "counterrevolutionary" elements; and he even
approached a few of Dubček's reformist colleagues surreptitiously in the
hope of finding a suitable replacement who would be willing to implement
a crackdown.[55] These efforts, however, failed to pay off.

Nor did any other attempts by the Soviet Politburo to compel the
Czechoslovak Presidium to change course prove successful. A lengthy
series of conspicuous troop movements, thinly veiled threats and
political and economic coercion failed to curtail the liberalization in
Czechoslovakia. If anything, the Czechoslovak reformers seemed to benefit domestically the stronger the pressure from the Soviet Union and its
hardline allies became.

Brezhnev spoke by phone with Dubček on 9 and 13 August 1968, but he
failed to secure a firm pledge from the Czechoslovak leader to roll back
the reforms and crack down on "hostile" elements in Czechoslovakia (i.e.
the officials who most ardently championed the Prague Spring).
The failure of these last-ditch contacts seems to have been what finally
spurred Brezhnev to conclude that "nothing more can be expected from
the current [Czechoslovak] Presidium" and that a military solution could
no longer be avoided.[56] From then on, the dynamic of the whole situation
rapidly changed, and Soviet leaders reached a firm consensus in favor of
military action.

On 17 August 1968, after a three-day session focusing on the situation in
Czechoslovakia, the CPSU Politburo unanimously approved a resolution
authorizing the use of military force to bring an end to the Prague Spring.[57]
The following day, the CPSU general secretary, Leonid Brezhnev,
informed his East German, Polish, Bulgarian and Hungarian counterparts
of the decision at a hastily convened meeting in Moscow. Unlike in 1956,
when Soviet troops intervened in Hungary unilaterally, Brezhnev was
determined to give the invasion in 1968 a multilateral appearance.

---

55 See the interview with Josef Smrkovský in "Nedokončený rozhovor: Mluví Josef
    Smrkovský," Listy: Časopis československé socialistické opozice 4, 2 (Mar. 1975), 17; and
    the interview with Oldřich Černík in "Bumerang 'Prazhskoi vesnoi,'" Izvestiia (21 Aug.
    1990), 5.
56 Cited in Tibor Huszár, 1968: Prága, Budapest, Moszkva. Kádár János és a csehszlovákiai
    intervenció (Budapest: Szabad Tér, 1998), 180. For a translation into Czech, see
    "Vystoupení J. Kádára na zasedání ÚV MSDS a rady ministrů 23.8.1968 k maďarsko-
    sovětskému jednání v Jaltě, 12.–15.8.1968," in Ústav pro soudobé dějiny, Sbírka Komise
    vlády ČSFR pro analyzu událostí let 1967–1970 (ÚSD-SK), Z/M 19.
57 "K voprosu o polozhenii v Chekhoslovakii: Vypiska iz protokola No. 95 zasedaniia
    Politbiuro TsK ot 17 avgusta 1968 g.," No. P95/1 (top secret), 17 Aug. 1968, in APRF, f. 3,
    op. 496, d. 2, prot. no. 38.

As a result, some 80,000 combat soldiers from Poland, Bulgaria and Hungary and a liaison unit from East Germany ended up taking part alongside Soviet ground and air units. In reality, though, Operation Danube was not truly a "joint" undertaking. Soviet paratroopers and special operations forces spearheaded the invasion, and a total of more than 400,000 Soviet troops eventually moved into Czechoslovakia, roughly five times the number of East European forces. Moreover, even though the Warsaw Pact had overseen most preparations for the invasion in the spring and summer of 1968, the Soviet high command was the body that exercised sole command of the operation in August 1968.

The invasion of Czechoslovakia explicitly introduced what became known in the West as the Brezhnev Doctrine into Soviet–East European relations. In effect, the doctrine linked the fate of each socialist country with the fate of all others, stipulated that every socialist country must abide by the norms of Marxism-Leninism as interpreted in Moscow, and rejected "abstract sovereignty" in favor of the "laws of class struggle." The Brezhnev Doctrine thus laid out even stricter "rules of the game" than in the past for the "socialist commonwealth":

> Without question, the peoples of the socialist countries and the communist parties [that rule them] have and must have freedom to determine their country's path of development. Any decision they make, however, must not be inimical either to socialism in their own country or to the fundamental interests of other socialist countries . . . A socialist state that is in a system of other states composing the socialist commonwealth cannot be free of the common interests of that commonwealth. The sovereignty of individual socialist countries cannot be set against the interests of world socialism and the world revolutionary movement . . . The weakening of any of the links in the world system of socialism directly affects all the socialist countries, and they cannot look indifferently upon this.[58]

The enunciation of the Brezhnev Doctrine codified Soviet attitudes toward Eastern Europe as they had developed over the previous two decades. The doctrine owed as much to Stalin and Khrushchev as to Brezhnev, inasmuch as the policies of these earlier Soviet leaders toward Eastern Europe were merely reaffirmed in the Brezhnev era. Nonetheless, the promulgation of the doctrine was significant both in restoring a firmer tone to

---

58 S. Kovalev, "Suverenitet i internatsional'nye obiazannosti sotsialisticheskikh stran," *Pravda* (26 Sep. 1968), 4.

Soviet–East European relations and in defining the limits of permissible "deviations" from the Soviet model of communism.

Bibliographical Essay

Useful studies published since 1991 that draw on archival materials and memoirs include T. V. Volokitina (ed.), *Moskva i vostochnaya Evropa: Neprostye 60e – ekonomika, politika, kul'tura* [Moscow and Eastern Europe: The Complicated 60s – Economy, Politics, Culture] (Moscow: Institut slavanovedeniia RAN, 2013); F. I. Novik, *V lovushke kholodnoi voiny: Sovetskaia politika v otnoshenii Germanii, 1953–1958 gg.* [In the Cold War Trap: Soviet Policy in Relations with Germany] (Moscow: Institut rossiiskoi istorii, 2014); Kevin McDermott and Matthew Stibbe (eds.), *Revolution and Resistance in Eastern Europe: Challenges to Communist Rule* (Oxford: Berg, 2006); and Laurien Crump, *The Warsaw Pact Reconsidered: International Relations in Eastern Europe, 1955–1969* (New York: Routledge, 2015). Perceptive essays on the Soviet bloc in the larger East–West context during the first few years after Stalin's death can be found in Klaus Larres and Kenneth A. Osgood (eds.), *The Cold War After Stalin's Death: A Missed Opportunity for Peace?* (Lanham, MD: Rowman & Littlefield, 2006).

On the hegemonic relationship between the Soviet Union and Eastern Europe under Khrushchev and Brezhnev, as well as comparisons with other highly unequal relationships, see Jan B. Triska (ed.), *Dominant Powers and Subordinate States: The United States in Latin America and the Soviet Union in Eastern Europe* (Durham, NC: Duke University Press, 1986); Paul Keal, *Unspoken Rules and Superpower Dominance* (London: Macmillan, 1983); Edy Kaufman, *The Superpowers and Their Spheres of Influence: The United States and the Soviet Union in Eastern Europe and Latin America* (London: Croom Helm, 1976); Mark Kramer, "The Soviet Union and Eastern Europe: Spheres of Influence," in Ngaire B. Woods (ed.), *Explaining International Relations Since 1945* (New York: Oxford University Press, 1996), 98–125; Mark Kramer, "The Soviet Bloc and the Cold War in Europe," in Klaus Larres (ed.), *A Companion to Europe Since 1945* (New York: Oxford University Press, 2009), 67–96; William Zimmerman, "Dependency Theory and the Soviet–East European Hierarchical Regional System: Initial Tests," *Slavic Review* 37, 4 (Dec. 1978), 604–23; Cal Clark and Donna Bahry, "Dependent Development: A Socialist Variant," *International Studies Quarterly* 27, 3 (Sep. 1983), 271–93; William M. Reisinger, "The International Regime of Soviet–East European Economic Relations," *Slavic Review* 49, 4 (Winter 1990), 556–67; and James Lee Ray,

"Dependence, Political Compliance, and Economic Performance: Latin America and Eastern Europe," in Charles W. Kegley, Jr., and Patrick McGowan (eds.), *The Political Economy of Foreign Policy Behavior* (Beverly Hills, CA: Sage, 1981), 111–36.

Among many useful works on Soviet–East European economic relations are Alan H. Smith, *The Planned Economies of Eastern Europe* (London: Croom Helm, 1983); Peter Murrell, *The Nature of Socialist Economies: Lessons from Eastern European Foreign Trade* (Princeton: Princeton University Press, 1990); and Franklyn D. Holzman, *The Economics of Soviet Bloc Trade and Finance* (Boulder: Westview Press, 1988). For hundreds of additional sources on Soviet–East European economic relations, see the annotated bibliographic compilation in Jenny Brine, *Comecon: The Rise and Fall of an International Socialist Organization* (New Brunswick, NJ: Transaction Publishers, 1992).

On the crises within the Soviet bloc in 1953, 1956 and 1968, the most useful studies published before documents from communist-era archives became accessible include Arnulf Baring, *Der 17. Juni 1953* (Berlin: Kiepenheuer & Witsch, 1965); Charles Gati, *Hungary and the Soviet Bloc* (Durham, NC: Duke University Press, 1986); Ferenc A. Vali, *Rift and Revolt in Hungary: Nationalism Versus Communism* (Cambridge, MA: Harvard University Press, 1961); Paul Kecskemeti, *The Unexpected Revolution: Social Forces in the Hungarian Uprising* (Stanford: Hoover Institution Press, 1961); Bill Lomax, *Hungary 1956* (London: Allison & Busby, 1976); Paul E. Zinner, *Revolution in Hungary* (New York: Columbia University Press, 1962); Karen Dawisha, *The Kremlin and the Prague Spring* (Berkeley: University of California Press, 1984); and H. Gordon Skilling, *Czechoslovakia's Interrupted Revolution* (Princeton: Princeton University Press, 1976).

The availability of archival materials and memoirs since 1991 has facilitated a wealth of new scholarship on the crises of 1953, 1956 and 1968 and the Soviet responses. With regard to 1953, see Mark Kramer, "The Early Post-Stalin Succession Struggle and Upheavals in East-Central Europe: Internal–External Linkages in Soviet Policymaking," *Journal of Cold War Studies* 1, 1 (Winter 1999), 3–54 (part 1); 1, 2 (Summer 1999), 3–38 (part 2); and 1, 3 (Fall 1999), 3–65 (part 3); Mark Kramer, "Der Aufstand in Ostdeutschland im Juni 1953," in Bernd Greiner, Christian Th. Müller and Dierk Walter (eds.), *Krisen im Kalten Krieg* (Hamburg: Hamburger Edition, 2008), 80–127; Kevin McDermott, "Popular Resistance in Communist Czechoslovakia: The Plzeň Uprising, June 1953," *Contemporary European History* 19, 4 (Nov. 2010), 287–307; and Gary Bruce, *Resistance with the People: Repression and Resistance in Eastern*

0.99

Germany, 1945–1953 (Lanham, MD: Rowman & Littlefield, 2003). For an overview of German literature on the East German uprising, see Peter Bruhn, *17. Juni 1953: Bibliographie* (Berlin: Berliner Wissenschafts-Verlag, 2003), which lists 2,345 items.

On 1956, see Mark Kramer, "The Soviet Union and the 1956 Crises in Hungary and Poland: Reassessments and New Findings," *Journal of Contemporary History* 33, 2 (Apr. 1998), 163–215; Mark Kramer, "New Evidence on Soviet Decision-Making and the 1956 Polish and Hungarian Crises," *Cold War International History Project Bulletin* 8–9 (Winter 1996–97), 358–410; Mark Kramer, "Soviet–Polish Relations and the Crises of 1956: Brinkmanship and Intra-Bloc Politics," in Roger Engelmann, Thomas Großbölting and Hermann Wentker (eds.), *Communism in Crisis: The 1956 De-Stalinization and Its Consequences* (Göttingen: Vandenhoeck & Ruprecht, 2008), 61–127; Edmund Makowski, *Poznański Czerwiec 1956: Pierwszy bunt społeczeństwa w PRL* [The Poznań June of 1956: The First Popular Rebellion in the People's Republic of Poland] (Poznań: Wydawnictwo Poznańskie, 2001); A. M. Orekhov, *Sovetskii soiuz i Pol'sha v gody "ottepeli": iz istorii sovetsko-pol'skikh otnoshenii* [The Soviet Union and Poland in the Years of the Thaw: The History of Soviet–Polish Relations] (Moscow: Izdatel'stvo Indrik, 2005); Charles Gati, *Failed Illusions: Moscow, Washington, Budapest, and the 1956 Hungarian Revolt* (Washington, DC: Woodrow Wilson Center Press, 2006); A. S. Stykalin, *Prervannaia revoliutsiia. Vengerskii krizis 1956 goda i politika Moskvy* [Interrupted Revolution: The 1956 Hungarian Crisis and Moscow's Policies] (Moscow: Novyi khronograf, 2003); Miklós Horváth and Jenő Györkei (eds.), *The Soviet Military Intervention in Hungary, 1956*, trans. Emma Roper Evans (Budapest: Central European University Press, 1999); Miklós Horváth and Vilmos Kovács, *Hadsereg és fegyverek, 1956* [The Army and Weaponry, 1956] (Budapest: Zrínyi, 2011); and Gábor Gyáni and János M. Rainer (eds.), *Ezerkilencszázötvenhat az újabb történeti irodalomban: Tanulmányok* [New Historical Literature on 1956: A Survey] (Budapest: 1956-os Intézet, 2007).

On 1968, see Mark Kramer, "The Kremlin, the Prague Spring, and the Brezhnev Doctrine," in Vladimir Tismaneanu (ed.), *Promises of 1968: Crisis, Illusion, Utopia* (Budapest: Central European University Press, 2010), 276–362; Mark Kramer, "The Czechoslovak Crisis and the Brezhnev Doctrine," in Carole Fink, Philipp Gassert and Detlef Junker (eds.), *1968: The World Transformed* (New York: Cambridge University Press, 1998), 111–75; Günter Bischof, Stefan Karner and Peter Ruggenthaler (eds.), *The Prague Spring and the Warsaw Pact Invasion of Czechoslovakia in*

1968 (Lanham, MD: Rowman & Littlefield, 2011); Kieran Williams, *The Prague Spring and Its Aftermath: Czechoslovak Politics, 1968–1970* (New York: Cambridge University Press, 1997); Mark Kramer, "New Sources on the 1968 Soviet Invasion of Czechoslovakia," *Cold War International History Project Bulletin* 2 (Fall 1992), 1, 4–13; Mark Kramer, "The Prague Spring and the Soviet Invasion of Czechoslovakia: New Interpretations," *Cold War International History Project Bulletin* 3 (Fall 1993), 2–13, 54–55; Mark Kramer, "Ukraine and the Soviet–Czechoslovak Crisis of 1968 (Part 1): Revelations from the Diaries of Petro Shelest," *Cold War International History Project Bulletin* 10 (1998), 353–66; Mark Kramer, "Ukraine and the Soviet–Czechoslovak crisis of 1968 (Part 2): New Evidence from the Ukrainian Archives," *Cold War International History Project Bulletin* 14–15 (Winter 2003–Spring 2004), 273–368; Mikhail V. Latysh, *Prazhskaia vesna 1968 g. i reaktsiia Kremlia* [The 1968 Prague Spring and the Kremlin's Reaction] (Moscow: Obshchestvennyi nauchnyi fond, 1998); Stefan Karner et al. (eds.), *Prager Frühling: das internationale Krisenjahr 1968*, vol. II, *Beiträge* (Vienna: Böhlau Verlag, 2008); Antonín Benčík, *Operace "Dunaj": Vojáci a Pražské jaro 1968* [Operation "Danube": Soldiers and the Prague Spring, 1968] (Prague: Ústav pro soudobé dějiny AV ČR, 1994); and György Homor, *Hívatlan vendégként északi szomszédainknál, 1968* [Uninvited Guests in the Northern Neighbors, 1968] (Pápa: Jókai Mór Városi Könyvtár, 2010).

On the military dimension of Soviet–East European relations, including the formation of the Warsaw Pact in May 1955, useful works produced during the Cold War include A. Ross Johnson, Robert W. Dean and Alexander Alexiev, *East European Military Establishments: The Warsaw Pact Northern Tier* (New York: Crane, Russak, 1982); Iván Völgyes, *The Political Reliability of the Warsaw Pact Armies: The Southern Tier* (Durham, NC: Duke University Press, 1982); David Holloway and Jane M. O. Sharp (eds.), *The Warsaw Pact: Alliance in Transition?* (Ithaca: Cornell University Press, 1984); Alexander Alexiev and A. Ross Johnson, *East European Military Reliability: An Émigré-Based Assessment* (Santa Monica, CA: RAND Corporation, 1986); Arlene Idol Broadhurst (ed.), *The Future of European Alliance Systems: NATO and the Warsaw Pact* (Boulder: Westview Press, 1982); Daniel N. Nelson, *Alliance Behavior in the Warsaw Pact* (Boulder: Westview Press, 1986); Christopher D. Jones, *Soviet Influence in Eastern Europe: Political Autonomy and the Warsaw Pact* (New York: Praeger, 1981); Daniel N. Nelson (ed.), *Soviet Allies: The Warsaw Pact and the Issue of Reliability* (Boulder: Westview Press, 1984); Hugh Faringdon, *Strategic Geography: NATO, the Warsaw Pact, and the Superpowers* (New York: Routledge, 1989); Gerard Holden, *The Warsaw Pact: Soviet Security and Bloc Politics* (Oxford: Blackwell, 1989); and Neil Fodor, *The Warsaw Treaty Organization: A Political and Organizational Analysis* (New York: St. Martin's Press, 1990).

For analyses of Soviet–East European military relations and the Warsaw Pact based on declassified archival documents and memoirs, see Jan Hoffenaar and Dieter Krüger (eds.), *Blueprints for Battle: Planning for War in Central Europe, 1948–1968* (Lexington: University of Kentucky Press, 2012); Vojtech Mastny, Sven G. Holtsmark and Andreas Wenger (eds.), *War Plans and Alliances in the Cold War: Threat Perceptions in the East and West* (London: Routledge, 2006); Mark Kramer, "Warsaw Pact Military Planning in Central Europe: Revelations from the East German Archives," *Cold War International History Project Bulletin* 2 (Fall 1992), 1, 13–19; and Beatrice Heuser, "Warsaw Pact Military Doctrines in the 70s and 80s: Findings in the East German Archives," *Comparative Strategy* 12, 4 (Oct.–Dec. 1993), 437–57. On the role of Czechoslovakia in the Warsaw Pact's war plans, see Petr Luňák, *Plánováni nemyslitelného: Československé válečné plány 1950–1990* [Planning for the Unthinkable: Czechoslovak War Plans, 1950–1990] (Prague: Dokořán, 2007); and Josef Fučík, *Stín jaderné války nad Evropou: ke strategii vojenských bloků, operačním plánům a úloze Československé lidové armády na středoevropském válčišti v letech 1945–1968* [The Shadow of Nuclear War over Europe: On the Strategy of Military Blocs, Operational Plans, and the Role of the Czechoslovak People's Army in the Central European Military Theater in 1945–1948] (Prague: Mladá fronta, 2010).

Many important collections of declassified documents have appeared relating to this phase of Soviet–East European relations, including Christian Ostermann (ed.), *Uprising in East Germany 1953: The Cold War, the German Question, and the First Major Upheaval Behind the Iron Curtain* (Budapest: Central European University Press, 2001); T. M. Islamov et al. (eds.), *Sovetskii soiuz i vengerskii krizis 1956 goda: dokumenty* [The Soviet Union and the Hungarian Crisis of 1956: Documents] (Moscow: ROSSPEN, 1998); Galina P. Murashko, Tat'yana V. Volokitina and Aleksandr S. Stykalin (eds.), *1968 god: "Prazhskaia vesna"–Istoricheskaia retrospektiva* [1968: "The Prague Spring." A Historical Retrospective] (Moscow: ROSSPEN, 2010); Lyudmila A. Velichanskaia et al. (eds.), *Chekhoslovatskii krizis 1967–1969 gg. v dokumentakh TsK KPSS* [The Czechoslovak Crisis of 1967–1969 in CC CPSU Documents] (Moscow: ROSSPEN, 2010); Stefan Karner et al. (eds.), *Prager Frühling: Das internationale Krisenjahr 1968,* vol. I, *Dokumente* (Vienna: Böhlau Verlag, 2008); Natal'ya G. Tomilina, Stefan Karner and Aleksandr Churbar'yan (eds.),

"Prazhskaya vesna" i mezhdunarodnyi krizis 1968 goda, vol. I, *Dokumenty* ["The Prague Spring" and the 1968 International Crisis, vol. I, Documents] (Moscow: Mezhdunarodnyi fond "Demokratiia," 2010); *Prameny k dějinám československé krize v letech 1967–1970* [Sources on the History of the Czechoslovak Crisis in 1967–1970] (Brno: Doplněk, 1993–2009); Komisia vlády SR pre analýzu historických udalostí z rokov 1967–1970, *Slovensko v rokoch 1967–1970: Vyber dokumentov* [Slovakia 1967–1970: Selected Documents] (Bratislava: n.p., 1992); and Vojtech Mastny and Malcolm Byrne (eds.), *A Cardboard Castle? An Inside History of the Warsaw Pact, 1955–1991* (Budapest: Central European University Press, 2005).

7

Post-Stalinist Reformism and the Prague Spring

PAVEL KOLÁŘ

The Czechoslovak attempt in 1968 to reform the Soviet-type system resulted from both the overall liberalization after Stalin's death and national developments. Aiming to combine socialism with civic freedoms, the Prague Spring constituted the peak of post-Stalinist reformism. Its suppression by the Warsaw Pact intervention in August 1968 marked the end of any efforts at radical socialist transformation. After that point, changes were understood exclusively in terms of a gradual improvement of the existing order, as expressed by Leonid Brezhnev's ideology of stabilization.

Some long-term trajectories of European socialism crossed in 1968 in Czechoslovakia. The Prague Spring was a fairground of post-Stalinist ambiguities, in which bold reformist visions blended with anti-utopian skepticism. Democratic socialism collided with bureaucratic dictatorship, free artistic creation with dogmatic schemes, the market with the planned economy, workers' self-rule with managerial control. At the same time, the Czechoslovak project dovetailed with the 1968 global revolution in behavior, habits, leisure and popular culture, as Eric Hobsbawm described it.[1] Yet in every sphere of life, be it politics, culture or economy, Stalinism cast its long shadow, causing uncertainty and contradictions.

The Zeitgeist of Post-Stalinism

After Stalin's death in 1953 the Soviet system in Eastern Europe fell into a deep legitimacy crisis. First were the workers in East Germany and western Bohemia who, as early as June 1953, rebelled against high norms and low wages. Though suppressed, their revolt sent a powerful signal to party

---

1 Eric J. Hobsbawm, *The Age of Extremes: The Short Twentieth Century, 1914–1991* (London: Joseph, 1995), 321–43.

leaders that changes were inevitable. With Nikita Khrushchev's attack on Stalin at the Twentieth Congress of the CPSU (Communist Party of the Soviet Union) in February 1956, the project of accelerated societal change along one single model collapsed, paving the way for "national roads" to socialism. The critique of mass terror and bureaucratic rule spread across the bloc, activating the communists' determination to build a new, genuine socialism.

The forms of de-Stalinization, however, differed considerably between the satellite states. While in Hungary and Poland revolutionary upheavals brought about a change in leadership, with Władysław Gomułka in Poland and János Kádár in Hungary pursuing (from 1960 onward in the latter case) a moderate reform program within the boundaries of Soviet consent, in East Germany, Czechoslovakia and Romania the party top brass dismissed all accusations of "Stalinism" and sought to do business as usual, with some minor adjustments. In the CPC (Komunistická strana Československa, Communist Party of Czechoslovakia), the strong sense of continuity and circumspection originated from the specific tradition of Czechoslovak socialism. Unlike in Poland and Hungary, radical communism was deeply rooted, particularly in Czechia, resulting in what Ágnes Heller called "hyper-Stalinism."[2] It was characterized by fanatic mass campaigns, strong support among intellectuals and the sweeping socialization of the economy. Despite the shock of the Stalinist crimes, the CPC was not shattered enough to introduce a substantial shift in its policy. At the same time, the rather favorable social and economic situation in 1956 watered down criticisms, particularly among the working class. In addition, the skillful propaganda exploitation of the "fascist threat" in Hungary and of West German "revanchism" helped the CPC leadership around Antonín Novotný not only to survive but also to reinforce its conservative move from 1957 onward.

Nevertheless, this ostrich-like rejection could not protect the party leadership from the overall critical Zeitgeist of post-Stalinism that pushed for change. First of all, Khrushchev's secret report on Stalinist crimes to the Twentieth CPSU Congress dealt a serious blow to communist identity, destabilizing the belief in linear progress. From this point on, every attempt at socialist construction was downgraded to "reform." The new socialism could only be a repair. With time, "reform" became the most powerful buzzword that legitimized the new system. Controlled by the experts, reform

2 Ágnes Heller, "Vier Arten des gesellschaftlichen Aufstandes," in Zdeněk Mlynář (ed.), *Der "Prager Frühling": ein wissenschaftliches Symposion* (Cologne: Bund-Verlag, 1983), 82–99, 85.

was to replace the accelerated revolutionary change and mass mobilization. At the same time, the post-Stalinists faced a permanent tension between the new utopian zeal, reinforced by Khrushchev at the Twenty-Second CPSU Congress in 1961, and the burden of the Stalinist past. The credentials of peaceful coexistence abroad and socialist legality at home as well as the green light to "national roads" to socialism paved the way for a variety of possible futures.

In general, we can distinguish four interconnected traits of the post-Stalinist mindset.[3] First, the linear conception of time declined, engendering not only the idea of open-ended history and a fragmented narration of the national past, but also the first signs of cyclicality including nostalgic longing for a pre-Stalinist golden age. Second, the revived "Leninist" party became the main vehicle of historical development, determined to wipe out the cult of personality as the evil force of history. Third, the concept of the nation started to prevail over class. And, fourth, the Stalinist notion of a lethal enemy transformed into a more open and ambivalent concept. All these aspects crucially shaped the Prague Spring.

After 1956 the CPC's leaders retained their mixed strategy of repression and relaxation, Sovietization and the national road. "Deformations" were acknowledged, but the general line was to remain unvaried. Unlike in Poland, the collectivization of agriculture resumed after 1956, so that Czechoslovakia eventually became the most collectivized of the bloc countries. In 1960 a new constitution was adopted that renamed the country a "socialist" republic, expressing the post-Stalinist optimism. However, from the early 1960s, particularly in the shadow of the economic crises, Novotný was compelled to make more concessions. A half-hearted liberalization followed the Twelfth Congress of the CPC in 1962, which included a reduction in the control over culture, the loosening of censorship and the opening of borders to the West.

With advancing liberalization, Novotný gradually dissociated himself from the old Stalinist guard, appointing more reformers to the Politburo. The reform demands made to the party from below increased. A generational change took place in the party concurrently with a "stabilization of cadres." There were no more purges. The later reform leaders, such as Alexander Dubček and Zdeněk Mlynář, were examplars of the new post-Stalinist biographies. They joined the party after the war and studied in Moscow in the 1950s, breathing the air of early de-Stalinization.

3 Pavel Kolář, *Der Poststalinismus. Ideologie und Utopie einer Epoche* (Cologne: Böhlau, 2016).

It was these people who brought the climate of transformation into the party, and at the same time the voice of intellectuals in the party grew stronger, nurtured by the revisionist currents and the critical mood in arts and literature that were spreading across the bloc.

Besides growing economic problems and dissatisfaction about the slow coming to terms with Stalinism, two other factors contributed to the failure of the Novotný regime. While the workers stayed tranquil after 1953, a fresh phenomenon was the critical outlook of the new student generation, born during or after the war, who developed a different attitude toward socialism. The second burning issue was the national question, aiming at correcting Czech–Slovak relations. While Novotný continued the politics of Czech hegemony, officially adhering to the "anti-nationalist" line from the previous period, Slovaks perceived Stalinism as a Czech import, epitomized by the Prague process against the Slovak "bourgeois nationalists" in 1954.

These trends gained momentum in 1967. In June, the critical voices raised at the Czechoslovak Writers' Congress were silenced by the expulsion of some of the most outspoken critics and the closing down of the writers' magazine *Literární noviny*. Opposition, however, could not be contained any more, as repression only disclosed the leadership's lack of legitimacy. In October the police violently suppressed a peaceful march by Prague students who were protesting against poor living conditions in university dormitories. Police violence mobilized further opposition, since unfounded brutality seemed to support the opinions of those who accused the regime of being "neo-Stalinist." Slovak discontent grew, as Novotný rejected further demands for decentralization, having behaved dismissively toward the national aspirations of the Slovaks.

The situation of the party leadership became critical in December 1967. Brezhnev unofficially visited Prague but did not support Novotný, famously declaring that "this is your own affair" (*eto vashe delo*). During the Central Committee meeting that followed Brezhnev's visit, the criticism of Novotný climaxed, led by the reform economist Ota Šik and the Slovaks. It took only one month for the noose around Novotný's neck to be tightened. He was definitively suspended in January 1968, to be replaced by Dubček as the new party leader. This was when the actual reform process started, and at the time the expression "post-January period" was used.

During the following eight months a dense sequence of events ensued, in which the interplay of domestic affairs and outside pressure was strongly present. In February, the government lifted censorship, launching freedom of information unparalleled in the communist realm. In late March, Novotný was replaced as president of the state by general and war hero Ludvík Svoboda. In April the party adopted the main official document of the Prague Spring, its "Action Program," which heralded "socialism with a human face," while a new government headed by Oldřich Černík was appointed, pursuing economic reform as its principal goal. In May and June the situation radicalized with the establishment of various noncommunist organizations, while the manifesto "Two Thousand Words" urged the continuation of reforms. In the meantime, reactions of the "brotherly parties" grew disapproving, as expressed at the meetings of East European communist leaders in Dresden in March and later in Warsaw. The negotiations between the Czechoslovak and Soviet leaders at the Slovak–Ukrainian border in late July gave some hope, which was reinforced by Tito's triumphant visit to Prague on 9–11 August. But Brezhnev had already lost patience with Dubček's evasive tactics, and on 20–21 August the Warsaw Pact armies terminated the Czechoslovak experiment. The "normalization" process began.

Toward a New Model of Socialism

While the revolts of 1956 in Hungary and Poland were largely spontaneous actions followed by reflection, in the case of the Prague Spring the reflection anticipated the revolt. The 1956 CPSU Congress provoked in the national parties of the Eastern bloc countries a process of rethinking how to reform the bureaucratic Stalinist system. A crucial task was to enhance the relationship between the party and the rest of society. The party leadership faced the fundamental dilemma of how to criticize the Stalinist "deformations," while at the same time rescuing the party by disconnecting it from Stalin. This maneuver was carried out by employing the discourse of "personality cult," which operated like a euphemism for crimes and systemic failures. At the same time, the post-Stalinist leaders constructed a temporal separation from Stalinism by delineating a "period that irrevocably belongs to the past," as Gomułka put it in October 1956. At the core of this new narrative stood the calls for a "return to Leninism," to an authentic communism free of Stalinist distortion, demanding a search for the "real roots" of socialist revolution.

This search for authenticity brought about a deep reconsideration of the party's past, a critical scrutiny that should purify it from the ballast of Stalinism. One way was the rehabilitation of those unjustly persecuted;

another was the creation of a new image of the party history, one that would give dignity back to ordinary party militants. The coming to terms with the past became an obsession of the parties throughout the Soviet bloc, which took the form of memory work, stressing the anti-fascist resistance while maintaining the workerist ideal of "true comradeship" before the war. This trend toward the critical treatment of the past gained strength with the second wave of de-Stalinization in 1961, which was later moderated but not completely ended by Brezhnev. The rehabilitations, however inconsequential, formed an important part of this purification. An offshoot of opening the archives was that an unvarnished version of the parties' pasts – not completely favorable – came to light, undermining the political action in the present. Thus, the decade prior to the Prague Spring was characterized by a continuous back-and-forth between reform and retreat, with reform attempts dissolving one after another. The tension continued between the different visions of a communist future (enhanced now by the bold futuristic images of cosmic exploration, technology and science) and the recurrent burden of the Stalinist past.

Given the disintegrating image of socialist revolution, smaller ersatz utopias developed, such as socialist humanism, "apolitical" technocracy, science fetishism, devotion to private life and the idolization of security and efficiency. On an international level the one-model construction of socialism collapsed with the acceptance of national roads to communism, through Palmiro Togliatti's *policentrismo* and through the rise of Mao's China as an alternative center of revolution (indeed an anecdote circulated that the socialist camp was steadily growing, as there were already two of them). A new space opened for revisions of ideological doctrine, as the leaderships temporarily descended into "ideological unclarity" after Stalin's monopoly on interpretation faded. In place of a single exegete, competing ideological centers – the party leaders, ideology departments and the party "clerics" such as Mikhail Suslov in the USSR, Kurt Hager in East Germany (GDR) and Jiří Hendrych in Czechoslovakia – had to assume responsibility for ideology. The previous praxis of merely commenting on Stalin's infallible decisions was replaced by a weary quest for consensus and the maintenance of the party's command. Ideology changed its function from being a means of conquering power into a balancing act of the interplay of interests within the party. An outburst of revisionist critique made necessary a constant effort toward ideological consolidation, a permanent combating of heresy. Nevertheless, this ideological struggle varied from the Stalinist demonization, as the parties preferred to "persuade" heretics back into line and did not opt for outright repression.

The "revisionists" represented the most dangerous challenge to this consensus. They attempted to find authentic Marxism, first in Lenin, but later increasingly in the young Marx and Gramsci. The notion of "truth and authenticity" supported a fondness for "discovering" unknown sources of Marxist wisdom, or for rediscovering and dusting off old theories. The backbone of the revisionist conception was "humanist Marxism," which brought humanity back into the core of philosophical reflection. Yet the concern with anthropology was not a purpose in itself, but rather a vehicle through which to address various societal problems, especially bureaucracy. Drawing on the concept of "alienation," the revisionists critiqued not only capitalism as had the young Marx or Franz Kafka, but also the distortions of the Soviet system. Philosophers such as Karel Kosík and Milan Machovec explored the "meaning of life," making man appear as an autonomous entity, not a mere reflection of big history. Kosík rejected the dualism of subject and object, pleading instead for "concrete totality" shaped by human practice in everyday life. Other philosophers, such as Ivan Sviták, sought to reconcile socialism and freedom, which was seen by many as the main contradiction of the Prague Spring. At the same time, they warned against the tendency within post-Stalinist society to retreat into the private sphere, into the routine of everyday concerns, which runs the risk of apolitical apathy. De-Stalinization, they argued, must be seen not as a return to the past, but as a higher stage of socialism.

The post-Stalinist dilemma between the burden of the past and a radiant future entered also into the CPC Action Program from April 1968. The program stood out among similar party documents for the systematic way in which it was prepared, yet at the same time it reflected the post-Stalinist eclecticism and indecisiveness. Members of the party perceived it as open and transitional. Dubček himself repeatedly stressed its open-endedness.[4] Hopeful and yet skeptical at the same time, the program opened a space for a new future but immediately relativized it by referring to the burden of the past. On all party levels the program met with a rather lukewarm reception. For some it was not radical enough, but above all it appeared too late, at a time when Czechoslovak society had its sights on a new path toward the end of

---

4 H. Gordon Skilling, *Czechoslovakia's Interrupted Revolution* (Princeton: Princeton University Press, 1976), 217.

censorship, the reemergence of noncommunist organizations and the promise of economic reforms.

The most ambivalent part of the program was the reform of the political system drafted by Zdeněk Mlynář, who had directed a research team working on a "new model of socialist democracy." This new model rested on the idea of representation of diverse societal groups, bringing to the fore the notion of "interest" as a foundation of politics. Democratic centralism was to be replaced by the concept of socialist democracy with the National Front, an umbrella organization of parties and mass organizations, being restructured and democratized. These changes expressed the new weight given to society as an entity distinct from the state.

The hardest nut to crack, however, was the leading role of the party. The Action Program left the issue open to debate, and it later became the main source of argument between the CPC and Brezhnev. However, even dedicated reformers such as František Kriegel always dismissed the idea of allowing oppositional parties, while Prague Spring sympathizers such as Tito repeatedly warned the Czechoslovak leadership not to touch the issue. In this sense, the argument that the Prague Spring constituted an attempt to restore pluralist democracy seems misplaced, which is also supported by the absence of broader support for the noncommunist organizations that emerged in 1968. Party leaders saw the only true danger as lying in the restoration of social democracy, which was traditionally strong in Czechia, because many former social democrats, such as Foreign Minister Jiří Hájek, held important positions in the CPC. The myth of social democracy fit well the post-Stalinist nostalgia for the lost past of the real working class – a longing for the return to the intimate world of the Czech skilled worker, of solidarity and real comradeship before Stalinist alienation set in.

This nostalgia for a vanished past was also fostered by the mass, alienating character of the CPC. By 1968 the party had 1.7 million members, which effectively meant that every fifth adult was a party member. Therefore, democratization of the party appeared to be a prerequisite for the democratization of the country. Although the division between party members and nonparty members continued to matter, other dividing lines began to emerge. Different strata of the population engaged in the reform process differently: For instance, the enthusiasm for change among white-collar employees and professionals was stronger than in the working class. Yet, on the whole, 78 percent of the population supported Dubček's reform, according to the opinion polls from July 1968.

Moreover, the party itself was not a monolith. From the mid 1960s onward, the ossified nomenclature loosened, while horizontal communication within the party proliferated, crossing established hierarchies. Informal networks burgeoned, particularly among intellectuals. Political strategies were discussed much more widely, making the production of party texts a rather experimental pursuit. This diversity benefited from the miscellaneous nature of the reformist leaders themselves: Dubček's dynamism and authenticity contrasted with the neo-Stalinist apparatchiks from the Novotný era; Šik combined intellectual vigor with a capacity for explaining complex economic matters in comprehensible language; Josef Smrkovský embodied the traditional character of the *Volkstribun*; while popular media figures such as the television director Jiří Pelikán, the radio director Jiří Hejzlar and the head of the Writers' Union Eduard Goldstücker gained popularity among the youth.

Besides the ambiguous reorganization of the National Front, which was to remain under the party's control, the leadership's limited trust in democracy from below is best documented by the debate on self-government and the nationality question. Originally, the Košice Governmental Program from spring 1945 envisioned self-rule for Slovakia within the common state. During Stalinism, however, any efforts at autonomy in Slovakia were suppressed and treated as "bourgeois nationalism," with its alleged supporters jailed (Gustáv Husák, later the leader of the post-1968 "normalization," spent nine years in prison). Ironically, de-Stalinization did not entail autonomy for Slovaks either: Quite the reverse, the state's unitary character deepened, generating what was called "Pragocentrism." Only in 1968 did the Federation Act, eventually adopted two months after the Warsaw Pact invasion, grant two national administrations.

Alongside the crucial Czech–Slovak arrangement, other nationality issues shaped the reform agenda as, despite war-induced population changes, Czechoslovakia remained a multinational state with hundreds of thousands of Hungarians, Poles, Ruthenians, Germans and Roma. Slovak–Hungarian relations in particular were marked by mutual anxieties, while the confessional-ethnic conflict in eastern Slovakia between the Greek Catholic and Orthodox Churches turned violent in 1968. The post-Stalinist reopening of some historical issues, such as the treatment of minorities after World War II, bolstered these conflicts. The new Constitutional Act of 1968 codified the rights of minorities, securing education and media in minority languages. In general, for Slovaks and some ethnic minorities the period after 1968 was one of emancipation and betterment, a fact overlooked by many Czechs who perceived the post-1968 "normalization" as a process controlled by the Slovaks.

The federalization debate reflected the diverging approaches toward reform in both parts of the country: While the Slovaks associated reformism with national autonomy, seeing greater rights to national administration as a gateway to a more prolific civil society, most Czechs viewed federalization as secondary. The Action Program remained vague on the point, while the manifesto "Two Thousand Words" from June 1968 expressed the tepidness with which Czechs dealt with Slovak demands: "Let us consider federalization as a method of solving the question of nationalities, but let us regard it as only one of several important measures designed to democratize the system ... The problem of government is not solved merely by having separate governments in the Czech Lands and in Slovakia."[5] This Czech reservation created further tensions between the two nations, leading the Slovaks around Husák gradually to abandon the reformist line.

This divergence on national issues shows also the inaccuracy of subsuming the Prague Spring under the rubric of "national communism." For the Czechoslovak reformers, mostly former Stalinists, national communism was not ambitious enough. They saw in Gomułka's, Tito's and Kádár's program only a temporary emergency solution, a detour coerced by external forces but not a project resulting from the authentic traditions of popular democracy. The Czechoslovaks sought to resume Marxist universalism in searching for an authentic socialism aspiring to become a global blueprint. Against the national models, be they Yugoslav self-management or Hungarian goulash communism, they overconfidently aimed at "socialism with a human face," which they put above national, especially Slovak, efforts. Real sovereignty was understood as universal self-government, not as giving rights to individual national communities.

Culture as the Engine of History

It is frequently asserted that the Prague Spring was initiated not by the party from above, but by intelligentsia from below. This reading fits the stereotype of the Czechs as a "nondominant nation," which, unlike Hungary and Poland, lacked a political elite, aristocracy and bourgeoisie. Therefore, the

---

5 "Two Thousand Words," in Jaromír Navrátil (ed.), *The Prague Spring 1968: A National Security Archive Documents Reader* (Budapest: Central European University Press, 1998), 181.

cultural intelligentsia had to substitute for this group – culture stood in for politics. The robust engagement of intellectuals in political debates since the 1960s reinforced the local self-perception of a Czechoslovak *Sonderweg*. Unlike Hungary in 1956, Poland in 1980–81 and *perestroika* in the USSR, the Prague Spring was allegedly set in train by critical intellectuals and artists.

Yet this narrative of creative ideas challenging power must be put into context. Paradoxically, Stalinism substantially heightened the status and material standing of many intellectuals, especially writers, by giving them a privileged position within society. Transforming culture into a "cultural front," the Stalinist regimes pampered leading writers like Vítězslav Nezval, who in turn celebrated the construction of socialism. Artistic creativity to a large extent came to rest on generous support by the communist government that took the form of stipends, autonomous publishing houses, journals, advantageous credits and even "writers' homes" including a resort on the Adriatic coast in Yugoslavia.

The great degree of material autonomy enjoyed by writers made their relationship to the authorities more complex than the cliché of a "transmission belt" suggests. Often, the main umbrella organization, the Writers' Union, enabled the survival of those who fell out of favor with the party authorities by providing them with shelter from attacks. This typically post-Stalinist approach on the one hand took advantage of Stalinist structures, yet on the other did not persecute troublemakers as "enemies of the people," seeking rather to bring "the confused" back into line through discussion. In this intricate situation, no open confrontation emerged before 1967.

Although the importance of other kinds of arts grew, especially of cinema, writers remained the most listened-to interpreters of the world. Take, for example, the unprecedented influence of *Literární listy*, the Czech periodical of the Writers' Union. This highly intellectual weekly reached in 1968 a print run of 300,000 copies in a nation of fewer than 10 million inhabitants (in Slovakia an analogous periodical, *Kultúrny život*, appeared). Ironically, this position of literature owed much to the Stalinist reinforcement of the printed word, as Stalin had communicated his main ideological decisions through books, articles and "readers' letters."[6] Thus, an explosion of interest in books after 1956, as censorship and the separation from the West lifted, was a paradoxical fruit of Stalinism. The hunger

---

6 Jan Mervart, "Fenomén Literárních novin," in Jan Mervart, Petr Dvorský and Martin Kučera, *Inspirace Pražské jaro 1968* (Hradec Králové: Vysoké Mýto-Sumbalon, 2014), 169–90.

for books found its best expression in "book events," important editorial undertakings that received huge public attention. Among such events stands out the Czech publication of Alexander Solzhenitsyn's *One Day in the Life of Ivan Denisovich* in 1963, which became an instant hit. Similar sensations followed the publication of Ladislav Mňačko's novel *Delayed Reportages*, a Slovak adjunct to Solzhenitsyn from the same year, dealing with the 1950s show trials, Jaroslav Pecka's *Fever* (1967), about forced labor in the uranium mines in the 1950s, and Milan Kundera's *The Joke* (1967), which powerfully questioned the supremacy of man as the creator of history.

The demolition of Stalin's monumental statue towering over Prague in November 1962 symbolically marked the second de-Stalinization after the Twenty-Second CPSU Congress. It was at this time that the cultural scene, including the young generation of poets, started to adopt a more radical political agenda. Journals thrived on heavy exposure to Western intellectual and artistic currents. Besides humanist Marxism, existentialism also quickly found followers. Literary events triggered debates and nurtured the readers' interest. Among them the May 1963 conference in Liblice stands out, which opened Franz Kafka's novels to Marxist analysis, followed shortly thereafter by Jean-Paul Sartre's Prague visit in autumn 1963 and György Lukács' ground-breaking interview in the journal *Plamen* in 1964. Space for free artistic activity was steadily renegotiated between authors and the authorities. Now communist leaders did not wish to enslave cultural creativity but rather to present their countries to the West as modern, using the arts as a shop window for socialism.

The opening toward the West and more independence were complemented by a critical retrospective of the past, with culture as the main engine in this quest for truth and authenticity. Writers stood at the forefront, pursuing a conscious shift away from "socialist realism." They demanded less monumentality and a more psychological approach, less schematic heroism and more concern with everyday life. In poetry, new forms developed that came closer to authentic life, reading more like reflections upon reality than a triumphant song. The poetic form turned from metric regularity to a prose-like spoken style and nonrhyming verse. Thematically, poets moved from historical epoch to man, from big history to everyday concerns, from the collective future to the individual past. Death became a key subject, reflecting the post-Stalinist grief and new tendency to honor victims rather than celebrate heroes. Language itself, compromised during Stalinism, ceased to serve as a mere instrument to voice outside meaning. Instead experimental poets such as Jiří Kolář approached language as a self-standing entity, intertwining poetry and visual arts. The hybridization of poetic genres expressed the inquiring Zeitgeist of post-Stalinism, be it the attempts at a synergy between poetry and theater, or the emerging protest singers' effort to fuse lyrical elements with political expression, deriding the mechanical phrases of official ideology through poetical means.[7]

Similar shifts occurred in prose. From the early 1960s, novelists abandoned large synthesis to embrace a more analytical approach that focused on conflict situations in everyday life. In terms of form, the big novel yielded to novellas and short stories. Rather than political struggles, writers dealt with serious moral dilemmas, transferring the social conflict into the hero's inner world. While political commitment gave way to existential issues, heroes became more convoluted and torn inside, no longer mere implementers of big history. Preference was now given to those who were on the downside of the big Hegelian process: outsiders, the underdog and those trampled upon. Victims fit perfectly this role, and we see a rise in Jewish and Roma protagonists. Many writers employed a view from the society's margins to display the complexity of history. The deconstruction of the hero by concentrating on the oppressed was underpinned by a narrative bifurcation and temporal synchronization, as demonstrated in Ladislav Fuchs's novel *Mr. Theodore Mundstock* (1963), which tells the story of a Prague Jew who is in constant fear of deportation. The Jewish theme paved the way for grotesque horror and lyricization of evil, underlining the atmosphere of dread and uncertainty.[8]

The style of storyline fragmentation announced the decline of the grand narrative. Most notably, Bohumil Hrabal organized his novels around dynamic currents of narration while reducing the main plot to a minimum. Whereas Hrabal's technique came across as somewhat disorganized patchworks of small episodes, Milan Kundera's method of "novel as construction" unfolded a backward teleology with a plot development gradually decomposing the notion of universal history. Kundera's novels heralded the end of the traditional epos: Following the modernists Robert Musil and Hermann Broch, Kundera sought to eliminate the novel as a representation of real worlds, changing it into a comment on that world from an ironical distance.

7 Pavel Janoušek (ed.), *Přehledné dějiny české literatury 1945–1989* (Prague: Academia, 2012), 199–232.
8 Aleš Haman, "Česká literatura druhé poloviny šedesátých let," in *Pražské jaro 1968: literatura–film–media* (Prague: Literární akademie, 2009), 17–28.

In *The Joke*, Kundera employs a multiperspective narration, disclosing a paradoxical interplay between intention, action and their consequences. This decline of the progressive vision of history is on display in the novels of Vladimír Páral, which unravel a mechanization of personal life, choked by the uncontrolled expansion of technology. Consistent with the increasingly pessimistic Zeitgeist of post-Stalinism, Páral depicts human history not as progress but as a vicious circle in which new ideologies and conflicts steadily crop up but in which human nature remains the same.

Under Stalinism, the ideological dictates upon theater were more severe than upon literature, given the nature of drama as based on conflict. The thaw brought a shift from schematic contradiction to a lyrical Chekhovian style, aiming at the self-introspection of dramatic heroes. Again, this approach helped disintegrate the central narrative in plays. Inspired by contemporary avant-garde works by the likes of Eugen Ionesco, Sławomir Mrożek and Harold Pinter, playwrights created a specifically Czech absurdist drama, as epitomized by Václav Havel's plays *Garden Party* and *Memorandum*. Havel and others revisited the Kafkaesque account of dull bureaucracy and alienation of the individual, taking up the main lines of contemporary political critique. Theater life in pre-1968 Czechoslovakia was equally shaped by big events where art met with politics, the most significant being the production of Friedrich Dürrenmatt's *Anabaptists* in March 1968. Dürrenmatt was the symbol of the theater thaw in Eastern Europe, and in Czechoslovakia his plays were staged, along with those by Arthur Miller and Tennessee Williams, from the late 1950s. The staging of *Anabaptists* presented a parable of belief and delusion, of political fanaticism and scheming cynicism, and Dürrenmatt himself understood the performance as clearly directed against the Novotný regime. Yet on the other hand, the play, climaxing in Bishop Franz von Waldeck impassionedly asking the audience how to create a more humane world, also displayed the search for a new universal utopia in the Prague Spring, as a second attempt after the Stalinist disaster.[9]

The interest of writers, poets and playwrights in everyday life and the repudiation of Stalinism in 1960s cinema by no means indicates a full dismissal of utopia. Influenced by Italian neorealism, French new wave and other progressive currents, Czechoslovak filmmakers turned away from historical traumas and ideological blueprints toward individual cognisance. The focus

---

9 Ulrich Weber, "Dürrenmatt und der Prager Frühling," in Cornel Dora (ed.), *Prager Frühling 1968* (St. Gallen: Kantonsbibliothek Vadiana, 2008), 13–17.

was on man in terms of his elementary expression, including comical, wretched and nondescript phenomena, free from external purpose. The young directors explored life beyond big structures, as first elaborated in their "manifesto" *Pearls of the Deep* (1966), a series of short films based on Hrabal's writings, which display the genuineness of their observation of life, connecting absurdist, black-humored and tragicomic narration. But like the *Pearls* anthology, the entire new wave came to the fore with no explicit program. Rather, it was driven by the push toward diversity and resistance against any patterns imposed from the outside.

At the same time, like writers, filmmakers enjoyed generous state provision, gaining space for criticism in the liberalization of 1962. Paradoxically, young directors were supported by the very party bureaucracy they mocked in their movies. For instance, directors such as Miloš Forman, Jiří Menzel and Karel Kachyňa received an award named for the Czechoslovak Stalinist leader Klement Gottwald. Nevertheless, their critical view of the Novotný regime intensified in the second half of the 1960s. At this time, film became, next to literature, the key carrier of radical reformism, and indeed the Soviets regarded cinema as an "active center of oppositional, anti-socialist tendencies among the intelligentsia."[10]

There were, however, certain limits in the new wave's popularity, and criticism of this film style by the ideological establishment often fell on fertile ground. Not all new wave movies were easily comprehensible to a broader public, which enabled the authorities to criticize the genre for its apparent lack of clarity. Indeed, some of the movies were not actually box-office hits: Jan Němec's *A Report on the Party and the Guests* (1966), for instance, attracted only 86,000 viewers. It troubled the authorities that, although most of these films did not tell a clear story and did not criticize reality, it was somewhat obvious that they were no mere escapes from the present and that behind the scenes they possessed strong topicality. Miloš Forman's *The Firemen's Ball* (1967) employed this hidden transcript with the greatest bravura: The film tells the story of the decline of collective plans, opposed as they are by anarchic human nature – no matter what kind of authorities are in charge, whether governments or local firemen's committees. In most cases even the best intentions gradually give way to hypocrisy and indifference.[11]

10 Jan Lukeš, "Filmová tvorba (1965–1969)," in *Pražské jaro 1968: literatura–film–media*, 33.
11 Herbert J. Eagle, "East European Cinema," in Sabrina P. Ramet (ed.), *Eastern Europe: Politics, Culture, and Society Since 1939* (Bloomington: Indiana University Press, 1998), 338.

The most visible breakthrough, however, occurred in popular culture, particularly pop music, where Westernization exercised vast influence. The "swinging Sixties" in Czechoslovakia were most importantly shaped by rock and pop, both by imports as well as by domestic production. Open political connotations were rare, but lyrics often took up as a motif the decline of the Stalinist linearity of time, such as the central line of the famous musical *Hop Pickers* (1964) "it would be foolish to seek for life a timetable."[12] The scarcity of Western LPs made their popularity even greater. From the early 1960s, East European leaders understood that popular music could not be contained. They made concessions and even helped domesticize Western music by founding music magazines and record companies producing domestic rock music, or permitting clubs for live music. Overall, the authorities gradually accepted Western-style popular culture as a component of the socialist way of life. The Polish leader Gomułka, for example, succumbing to pressure from his granddaughters who were desperate to see the *Stonesi*, personally authorized a concert by the Rolling Stones in April 1967 in the Stalinist Palace of Culture in Warsaw.

This cultural development formed a mental framework for the Prague Spring, revealing why any new blueprint for socialism was difficult to force through. Whether in literature, film or theater, the erosion of the Stalinist revolution surfaced everywhere. The deconstruction of language in poetry, the decline of big narration in novels and the disintegration of dramatic conflict in theater all helped create a new form of utopia, one that was transferred into everyday life. The ongoing conflict with the bureaucratic system formed the backdrop for reaching a new meaning in literature. Although the artists formed a manifold group, from functionaries loyal to the party and critical Marxists to noncommunists, hardly anyone thought about a return to liberal democracy. A progressive betterment of the existing world remained the principal goal.

Repairing the Base: Economy and Society

The Prague Spring's reform of the socialist planned economy, later celebrated as "marketization," was designed neither to end nor in any way to relativize socialism. Ota Šik, the reform's chief architect, insisted that no one intended any kind of return to capitalism. Rather, the

---

12 Peter Bugge, "Swinging Sixties Made in Czechoslovakia: The Adaptation of Western Impulses in Czechoslovak Youth Culture," in Oldřich Tůma (ed.), *Pražské jaro 1968* (Prague: ÚSD AV ČR, 2011), 143–57.

reformers aimed at reducing the huge degree of bureaucracy and fighting economic backwardness, which surfaced painfully in the 1960s in comparison with the West, particularly as the growing consumption needs of the population could not be met. For the communist economists, often former Stalinists, accepting this bitter reality was a long and painful process. As Šik put it, his own personal de-Stalinization ensued as a transformation from an uncritical believer in the construction of socialism to a "critically thinking scientist."[13]

Initially few could agree in the early 1960s about how much market should be adopted. The belief in planning remained robust, by no means confined to the insulated Novotný leadership. Dismissal of capitalism was deeply rooted in society, most importantly among the proud Czech working class. In Slovakia, the forced Sovietization after 1948 was seen rather positively as a first wave of modernization in the country's history. Fostered by the traumatic experience of the depression of the 1930s, the radical anti-capitalist attitude in Czech and Slovak society continued after 1945. The 1946 sweeping victory of the CPC in a relatively free election displayed the high degree of anti-capitalist consensus across the working class, small-holders and parts of the middle class. It was the idea of social security, buttressed by the experience of the capitalist crisis of the 1930s, with which the CPC gained broad support for its economic policies after 1948, albeit at the cost of civic freedoms.

Nevertheless, the Stalinist transformation of the Czech economic base from high-level light industry to heavy industry caused serious problems, as rapid growth rates intensified the demands on the workforce, while enterprises strained under strict control by the party and security organs. Stalinism limited the autonomy of trade unions and tied social rights to full-time employment. Traditional independent institutions of the working class such as cultural organizations and adult education vanished. Social rights were heartlessly subjected to macroeconomic planning, and in June 1953 workers' protests finally broke out in Plzeň (Pilsen) and other towns as a result of growing dissatisfaction. Deterred by this experience, the government redesigned its policy, enlarging social protections, supporting training schemes and improving the healthcare system. These changes effectively stabilized communist power.

It is often forgotten that de-Stalinization in the USSR had not only to heal the harm created by the repressive system, but also to repair the social misery

---

13 Ota Šik, *Prager Frühlingserwachen: Erinnerungen* (Herford: Busse Seewald, 1988), 11.

Stalinism left behind. Indeed, Georgii Malenkov's "New Course" after 1953 was also a program of social reconstruction. The economy had to be reoriented from heavy toward light industry to meet the growing consumption needs of the population. At the same time, however, Khrushchev's optimism compelled East European leaders to continue some reform experiments, squeezed between new utopian visions and the burdensome economic reality. The party leaderships launched various programs, described mostly as "new," which often had an ephemeral life, like the "New Economic System" in the GDR, which was launched in 1963, but already by 1965 had come under heavy criticism, to be substantially modified in 1967. The overall confusion of reform politics was only underlined by the Kremlin's change of leadership in 1964 as Khrushchev's unsystematic experimenting gave way to a more pragmatic approach. Indeed, Aleksei Kosygin's reforms in 1965 sought to make production more responsive to demand, giving enterprises greater freedom to decide on how to use their profits. But Kosygin's plan also stopped halfway, not allowing enterprises to set their own prices, and finally foundered on the party apparatus's opposition.[14]

Rather than copying foreign models, Šik's Czechoslovak reform in the 1960s resumed some earlier domestic reform attempts, most importantly the "Rozsypal Plan" from 1959. Based on the favourable economic indicators of the post-1956 years, this earlier reform emerged in the overall optimism of the Khrushchev era, being a genuinely post-Stalinist mix that gave enterprises greater independence in the handling of the imposed norms while at the same time retaining authority control over basic economic structures. The cult of the planned economy remained largely untouched. Due to a slowdown in economic growth and steady conflict between economists and planners, the Rozsypal Plan was discarded in 1961. What followed was the triumph of planners resulting in the devastatingly megalomaniac Five-Year Plan for 1961–65. Soon after its takeoff, serious problems surfaced, and criticism of the Novotný leadership grew stronger. For the first time in state socialist Czechoslovakia, production stagnated, and in 1963 labor productivity sank by 2 percent. Disastrous for a highly industrialized economy and until then unparalleled in the Soviet bloc, this economic decline undermined belief in a planned economy just as Khrushchev's critique of the Stalinist crimes had undermined belief in

14 Geoffrey Hosking, *The First Socialist Society: A History of the Soviet Union from Within* (Cambridge, MA: Harvard University Press, 1985), 363.

the Party. The determination to commence yet another "authentically" socialist reform was strong, however, and after heated debate in the Politburo in October 1963 Šik, then head of the Economic Institute of the Academy of Sciences, was charged with directing the reform.[15]

From the outset, Šik faced strong resistance from conservatives, who launched a campaign exploiting the anti-capitalist anxieties of the working class, especially the fear of unemployment. At the same time, many reform communists also had a rather vague sense of the reform, often sticking to the old directive approach. Because of these tensions, the reform had to accept several concessions and was frequently amended. Its main tenets were the relative autonomy of enterprises as well as some changes in the banking system and financial policy, such as the convertibility of the Czechoslovak currency. Despite some Soviet resistance, the reform was started by the Thirteenth Party Congress in June 1966, but modified already in 1967 by reintroducing controls on wages and state restrictions. Only the removal of Novotný and the takeoff of the Prague Spring enabled the realization of a more consequential reform.

The main bone of contention was the term "market." All post-Stalinist reformers did their utmost to avoid the word, but by the late 1950s they began reevaluating market-like relations such as supply and demand, selling and buying, "commodity relations" or "markets" in the plural. Šik did not view nationalization of the means of production as the end goal in the construction of socialism, calling for a further transformation by bringing into the socialist economy more space for supply–demand relations. Firms were given greater autonomy and, instead of having central norms imposed, the hope was that they would operate on the market at a profit. Prices were liberalized, and investment was up to the enterprise and not allocated through the state budget. From now on, national plans represented a general framework rather than an exact blueprint. Although it was intended that most of the economy should remain in collective ownership, a new concept cropped up: mixed "social ownership," which did not necessarily mean state control.

Šik's reform differed from the Rozsypal Plan in that it could not simply be enforced from above but had to be justified through discussion in a more open political context. The most serious challenge came from the industrial working class, whose attitude was ambiguous, as many workers felt insecure because of the increased power of factory managers that was envisaged.

---

15 Zdeněk Jirásek, "Rok 1968 a ekonomická reforma v Československu," in Miroslav Londák and Stanislav Sikora (eds.), *Rok 1968 a jeho miesto v našich dejinách* (Bratislava: Věda, 2009), 120–27.

More than two decades after the war, workers still held a fiercely anti-capitalist stance and had a strong belief in the welfare state, however discredited it had been by Stalinism. Strong egalitarianism manifested itself in comparatively high wages, as skilled workers earned only 20–30 percent less than managers and 15 percent more than white-collar employees. In terms of social and cultural habits, too, differences tended to be small, as directors, shop-floor workers and even cleaners lived in the same apartment blocks. Worried that the reform might result in the dismantling of heavy industry, unemployment and regional unevenness, the workers saw these egalitarian certainties at risk.

Despite all the pitfalls, the reform started to bear fruit soon after its launch in 1966 as wages continued to grow and consumption increased. The attitude of the working class, which had at first been hesitant, was reversed by steady economic growth of 7 percent a year from 1965 onward. In 1968 alone, average workers' wages increased by 10 percent compared to just 2 percent between 1960 and 1965.[16] Yet the introduction of some market elements, especially granting enterprises more autonomy, made unemployment a real danger. The reform therefore also had an eye on the social compensation of risks, above all introducing a new policy of employment, which aimed at emboldening workers through various bonuses and profit shares. Social protection was strengthened, including the extension of maternity leave, an increase in child benefits and pensions, and the shortening of the working week down to five days in 1968. These measures seemed to satisfy a great deal of the working class, and indeed in 1967–68 no larger social protests erupted.

On paper both the economic reform and the democratization, as envisaged by the Action Program of April 1968, aimed to improve the position of trade unions as one of the "interest groups" within the new model of democratic socialism. In the 1968 debates, central to the future self-management system were work councils consisting of the unions. Such councils had been established earlier without a legal basis, most importantly in the Škoda works in Plzeň, which set a model for other big enterprises. A huge wave of setting up work councils followed on the back of a new law which continued even after such councils were prohibited as part of the suppression of the Prague Spring. The workers' insistence on work councils stemmed from the long-term workerist traditions, which outlasted even

16 Lenka Kalinová, "Das Verhalten der tschechischen Arbeiter im Jahre 1968," in Gerd-Rainer Horn and Bernd Gehrke (eds.), *1968 und die Arbeiter: Studien zum "proletarischen Mai" in Europa* (Hamburg: VSA-Verl., 2007), 160–84.

Stalinism. Although the party tried to dominate the unions after 1948, the latter constantly maintained the power to resist by creating informal structures in the factories. After 1953 the authority of the party declined, and enterprises developed into a bastion against centralization. Throughout the entire period of state socialism, the Czech working class held on to a traditional conception of a moral economy, which included an anti-bureaucratic mentality and syndicalist egalitarianism that tried to diminish the disparity between managers and workers.[17]

It was on the last point that workers started to object to the reform, since it soon became obvious that Šik's program, by giving more power to enterprises, would actually reduce workers' autonomy, creating unlimited control by management. The participation in self-rule offered to workers seemed insufficient, being more a compensation for losses than an extension of enterprise democracy. After all, the Action Program gave management a monopoly over enterprise control. The reformists had deliberately not included more workers' participation since it was a component of their attack on "egalitarianism," perceived as a remnant of Stalinism. Paradoxically, the unions equally understood their demands for more participation as a step against Stalinism, but specifically against the Stalinist surveillance policy.

With the post-1968 normalization, Šik's reform was withdrawn and denounced as a "betrayal of socialism." In the 1970s, however, the new government took up some of its elements, but without using the word "reform," which was replaced with various euphemisms (such as the 1980 "packet" of the Lubomir Štrougal government). These new reform attempts evaporated quickly, being corrected or replaced by new ones. Throughout the Prague Spring, the workers maintained their anti-capitalist stance, but also resisted the normalizers' efforts to ban the work councils. In the end, however, the continuation by the post-1968 rulers of some parts of the Prague Spring's social program secured social peace and convinced the working class to get behind the "normalization." The emphasis on social and consumption policy was thus not a strategic innovation by the normalizers to appease society. Rather, they perpetuated the previous development of consumerism set in motion in the post-Stalinist period.

---

17 Peter Heumos, "Betriebsräte, Betriebsausschüsse der Einheitsgesellschaft und Werktätigenräte," in Horn and Gehrke (eds.), *1968 und die Arbeiter*, 131–59.

After 1956, the Czechoslovak leadership attached great importance to presenting itself as a modern country, for example through promoting modern design at Expo 58, introducing to the market the Coke substitute Kofola in 1959, and in 1957 founding the Tuzex shops, in which Western consumer goods could be purchased for hard currency. In doing this Czechoslovakia followed the Khrushchev maxim that communism was a state of consumerist abundance, as consecrated by the Eleventh CPC Congress of 1958.[18] In a post-Stalinist reading of Marx, consumerism formed a new "base" on which to erect a genuinely socialist superstructure, a higher form of human spiritual development. Prominent place in the new policy was given to housing and cars, with the Western middle-class lifestyle increasingly setting the standards. This transfer of capitalist products into the socialist context created a specific form of socialist consumption, characterized by scarcity and the lower quality of substitute goods, but creating more enthusiasm, eagerness to get hold of goods and prestige of owning them than among Western citizens. The outburst of mass popular culture, including advertisements, beauty pageants and striptease shows, stood for the advancement of socialism with a human face, as naked women appeared on newspaper pages next to horrifying reports on Stalinist crimes. In 1968, Westernization reached its peak, embodied by the purchase of a Coca-Cola license in that year. While most of the democratic reforms were withdrawn, Coke production went on throughout the alleged dark years of post-1968 normalization.

On the Threshold of a New Era

As with similar reform movements, the Prague Spring started to disperse from within before a lethal blow was dealt from the outside in August 1968. Conservative positions were regaining power from late June 1968 as the reformers receded vis-à-vis the mounting threat of Soviet intervention. Internationally, the Soviets rightly saw that they had the upper hand, as it was evident that the West would undertake nothing, just as in 1956. For President Lyndon B. Johnson of the United States, the Czechoslovak question was a case of chickenpox, while President Richard Nixon and Secretary of State Henry Kissinger wanted to continue détente at any cost. Although the Prague Spring served as a midwife to Eurocommunism, in the Western

18 Martin Franc, "Coca-cola je zde! Aneb konzumní společnost v Československu?," in Tůma (ed.), *Pražské jaro 1968*, 133–42.

political mainstream the suppression of reform reinforced the skepticism about any third way and, in the long run, bolstered neoliberal politics that began to assert itself from the late 1970s.

In Eastern Europe, many thought Husák would become the Czechoslovak Kádár, a "realist whose bark was worse than his bite," and hoped for later relaxation. [19] Yet being under pressure both from Brezhnev and from the hawks at home, Husák soon abandoned any bolder reformist plans. The main blow was to socialism in general, as the new dissident movement gave up formulating any socialist program, concentrating instead on the legalist struggle for human rights. On the oppositional agenda, civic rights replaced social and economic rights, as overall the pendulum swung away from socialist solutions. The ideas of the Prague Spring disappeared with the passage of time and Gorbachev's *perestroika* deliberately avoided the notion of reform, so as not to evoke any associations with 1968. In 1989 the left-wing visions soon dissipated in the global swing toward the neoliberalist end of history.

In today's European memory, the legacy of the Prague Spring is rather pale. It passed into the irrevocable past shortly after 1989, when any dreams of socialist ways faded. The heroic story of a peaceful fight against a big external power did not rescue socialism with a human face from the condescension of posterity, which classifies the Czechoslovak reform as a great upsurge, but conducted by a small nation. The Paris protests of May 1968 will remain more global than the Prague Spring. Despite its local character, the latter appears above all an intersection at which reform ideas of a global nature crossed, as well as a turning point anticipating the later decline of the left on a world scale, a juncture in which a daring vision of democratic socialism blended with anti-utopian skepticism. As a lesson for the left, the Prague Spring will remain a courageous example of historical experimentalism, exploring the possibilities of the expansion of human freedom. [20]

Bibliographical Essay

A useful introduction to the Prague Spring is the rich memoir literature by the main protagonists. Several of these are available in English and

---

19 Kenneth N. Skoug, *Czechoslovakia's Lost Fight for Freedom, 1967–1969: An American Embassy Perspective* (Westport, CT: Praeger, 1999), xii.
20 Axel Honneth, *Die Idee des Sozialismus: Versuch einer Aktualisierung* (Berlin: Suhrkamp, 2015).

German, including Zdeněk Mlynář, *Nightfrost in Prague: The End of Humane Socialism* (New York: Karz Publishers, 1980); Jiří Pelikán, *Ein Frühling, der nie zu Ende geht* (Frankfurt am Main: S. Fischer, 1976); Ota Šik, *Prager Frühlingserwachen. Erinnerungen* (Herford: Busse Seewald, 1988); Ivan Sviták, *The Czechoslovak Experiment, 1968–1969* (New York: Columbia University Press, 1971); Alexander Dubček, *Hope Dies Last: The Autobiography of Alexander Dubček* (New York: Kodansha International, 1993); Pavel Tigrid, *Why Dubček Fell* (London: Macdonald & Co., 1971); Jiří Hájek, *Begegnungen und Zusammenstösse. Erinnerungen des ehemaligen tschechoslowakischen Aussenministers* (Freiburg im Breisgau: Herder, 1987); and Mikhail Gorbachev and Zdeněk Mlynář, *Conversations with Gorbachev: On Perestroika, the Prague Spring, and the Crossroads of Socialism* (New York: Columbia University Press, 2002). The volume edited by Zdeněk Mlynář, *Der Prager Frühling. Ein wissenschaftliches Symposion* (Cologne: Bund-Verlag, 1983), offers a post-Solidarność perspective on East European exile; and the chapter by Agnes Heller, in particular, is critical of reform socialism.

H. Gordon Skilling's monumental *Czechoslovakia's Interrupted Revolution* (Princeton: Princeton University Press, 1976) remains the most exhaustive overview of events and debates based on published sources. A lucid, well-balanced introduction to the intellectual contexts comes in the form of Vladimir V. Kusin, *The Intellectual Origins of the Prague Spring* (Cambridge: Cambridge University Press, 1971), and his edited volume *The Czechoslovak Reform Movement, 1968* (Santa Barbara, CA: ABC-Clio, 1973). For an overview of 1960s debate in the press, see Frank Kaplan, *Winter into Spring: The Czechoslovak Press and the Reform Movement, 1963–1968* (Boulder: East European Monographs, 1977). From the point of view of political science, see Kieran Williams, *The Prague Spring and Its Aftermath: Czechoslovak Politics 1968–1970* (Cambridge: Cambridge University Press, 1997).

For the international and global context, see Jaromír Navrátil (ed.), *The Prague Spring 1968: A National Security Archive Documents Reader* (Budapest: Central European University Press, 1998), which gives a selection of the most important sources. Kenneth N. Skoug, *Czechoslovakia's Lost Fight for Freedom, 1967–1969: An American Embassy Perspective* (Westport, CT: Praeger, 1999), offers titillating insider insights. *The Prague Spring and the Warsaw Pact Invasion of Czechoslovakia in 1968*, edited by Günter Bischof, Stefan Karner and Peter Ruggenthaler (Lanham, MD: Lexington Books, 2009), and *1968. The World Transformed*, edited by Carole Fink, Philipp Gassert and Detlef Junker (Cambridge: Cambridge University Press,

1999), are collections of essays on international politics and protest movements that cover Western Europe, Eastern Europe and the Third World. A comprehensive overview of protest movements including a contribution on Czechoslovakia by Jan Pauer is provided by *1968 in Europe. A History of Protest and Activism, 1956–1977*, edited by Martin Klimke and Joachim Scharloth (New York: Palgrave Macmillan, 2008). For analysis of the repercussions of the Prague Spring in the French and Italian Communist Parties, see Maud Bracke, *Which Socialism? Whose Détente? West European Communism and the Czechoslovak Crisis, 1968* (Budapest: Central European University Press, 2007).

The Prague Spring is placed within the broader chronological context of state socialism in Kevin McDermott, *Communist Czechoslovakia, 1945–1989: A Political and Social History* (London: Palgrave Macmillan, 2015), 121–51. For economic policy, see the programmatic *Plan and Market Under Socialism* (Prague: Academia, 1967), written by the main protagonist Ota Šik. On the economic reform in state socialism and the plan vs. market dilemma, see Martin Myant, *The Czechoslovak Economy, 1948–1988: The Battle for Economic Reform* (Cambridge: Cambridge University Press, 1989), and Jan Adam, *Planning and Market in Soviet and East European Thought, 1960s–1992* (New York: St. Martin's Press, 1993). Very helpful for understanding the broader East European context are Geoffrey Swain and Nigel Swain, *Eastern Europe Since 1945* (Basingstoke: Palgrave Macmillan, 2003) 114–69; Ivan T. Berend, *Central and Eastern Europe, 1944–1993: Detour from the Periphery to the Periphery* (Cambridge: Cambridge University Press, 1996), 94–221; and Mark Pittaway, *Eastern Europe 1939–2000* (London: Arnold, 2004), 63–86. German and Czech research has been particularly productive on the history of the working class; see the chapters in *Arbeiter im Staatssozialismus. Ideologischer Anspruch und soziale Wirklichkeit*, edited by Peter Hübner, Christoph Klessmann and Klaus Tenfelde (Cologne: Böhlau, 2005); Christiane Brenner and Peter Heumos (eds.), *Sozialgeschichtliche Kommunismusforschung. Tschechoslowakei, Polen, Ungarn und DDR 1948–1968* (Munich: Oldenbourg, 2005); and *1968 und die Arbeiter: Studien zum "proletarischen Mai" in Europa*, edited by Gerd-Rainer Horn and Bernd Gehrke (Hamburg: VSA-Verl., 2007), especially contributions by Peter Heumos and Lenka Kalinová. On youth, see Filip Pospíšil, "Youth Cultures and the Disciplining of Czechoslovak Youth in the 1960s," *Social History* 37, 4 (Nov. 2012), 477–500.

On emerging "normalization," see the classic essay by Milan Šimečka, *The Restoration of Order: The Normalization of Czechoslovakia, 1969–1976* (London: Verso, 1984), and Vladimir V. Kusin, *From Dubček to Charter 77: A Study of*

Normalisation in Czechoslovakia, 1968–1978 (Edinburgh: Q Press, 1978). Paulina Bren, *The Greengrocer and His TV: The Culture of Communism After the 1968 Prague Spring* (Ithaca and London: Cornell University Press, 2010), focuses on the post-1968 "normalization" through popular culture, especially family television series.

8

The Socialist Modernization of China Between Soviet Model and National Specificity 1949–1960s

THOMAS P. BERNSTEIN

Introduction

The creation of the Soviet bloc in the wake of World War II led to the diffusion of the Soviet model of building socialism to Eastern Europe and East Asia, China included. When the Chinese Communist Party (CCP) was about to take power over the Chinese mainland in 1949, Chairman Mao Zedong announced that China would "lean to one side." The Cold War, especially friction with the United States, precluded adoption of a feasible alternative to an alliance with the Soviet Union, all the more so since it provided the model for socialist construction. As Mao Zedong put it: "the Communist Party of the Soviet Union [CPSU], under the leadership of Lenin and Stalin . . . learned not only how to make the revolution but also how to carry on construction. It has built a great and splendid socialist state. The [CPSU] is our best teacher and we must learn from it."[1]

Party leaders eagerly sought Soviet advice and assistance on a wide variety of challenges centering on national state institutions and economic development. China's situation, however, differed from that of the East European satellites which from 1948 on were compelled by Moscow to emulate and copy the Stalinist model for building socialism. China's rural road to power differed from that of the Soviets, causing conflict with Moscow until Stalin accepted Chinese revolutionary strategies.[2] The CCP had come to power with significant Soviet assistance but largely on its own. During the civil war, it had disregarded Stalin's advice not to aim for all-out victory. The Chinese

1 "On the People's Democratic Dictatorship," in *Selected Works of Mao Zedong*, vol. IV (Peking: Foreign Languages Press, 1961), 423.
2 Alexander V. Pantsov with Steven I. Levine, *Mao: The Real Story* (New York: Simon & Schuster, 2012), chs. 17 and 23.

regarded the 1950 Sino-Soviet agreements as unequal. Until China entered the Korean War, Stalin distrusted Mao, worrying that he might turn into a Tito. The CCP accepted the leadership of the Soviet Union and of Stalin but did not complain until the Khrushchev era.

During the years of recovery from wartime devastation and of the take-over campaigns, 1949–52, the People's Republic of China (PRC) defined its rule as a "New Democracy," a mixed economy in which the major industries were state-owned but coexisted with a sizable sector of private manufacturing and trading enterprises, as well as a handicrafts industry. Agriculture, once landlords had been violently dispossessed, was dominated by small-holder peasants. When it came to planning socialist transformation, CCP leaders agreed that private property in the means of production would be abolished but the process would be gradual and take a long time, probably decades.

This approach took its inspiration from the Soviet New Economic Policy (NEP, 1921–27), and specifically from one of Lenin's last articles, "On Cooperation," published in early 1923, several years after the Bolshevik victory in the civil war and the radical pursuit of "war communism."[3] For Lenin, the biggest problem was how to deal with the peasantry, the country's largest group. Peasants distrusted the communist government, remembering forced requisitioning of grain during the civil war. Lenin argued that the socialist transformation of the peasantry would require several decades. During these years the smallholder peasantry should be drawn into the orbit of the socialist urban-industrial sector by means of marketing, consumer and credit cooperatives. While experiencing a rural cultural revolution that would eliminate illiteracy, peasants would gradually become accustomed to socialist ways, paving the way toward eventual collectivization.

During the Soviet industrialization debates of the mid 1920s, Nikolai Bukharin, who was supported by Stalin until 1927, further expounded Lenin's moderate and gradual line.[4] His proposals were known to some Chinese leaders who had studied in the Soviet Union during that time. One of them was Deng Xiaoping, the "paramount leader" of the reform period that began in 1978, two years after Mao's death, during which Chinese communes were dismantled.

---

3 Vladimir I. Lenin, *Alliance of the Working Class and the Peasantry* (Moscow: Foreign Languages Publishing House, 1959), 386–94.
4 See Stephen P. Cohen, *Bukharin and the Bolshevik Revolution: A Political Biography, 1888–1938* (New York: Vintage Books, 1971).

Some Chinese leaders, notably Liu Shaoqi, Mao Zedong's second-in-command, favored the gradual and moderate approach. In agriculture, they wanted to encourage the smallholder economy, including rich peasants, by maintaining the incentives necessary for agricultural growth, until the conditions for the future transition to socialism had been created.[5] Liu believed that the order of priority of the three branches of the economy after the completion of reconstruction should be agriculture first, followed by light and, last, heavy industry. He also believed that agriculture should not be collectivized before industry could supply machinery, i.e. until a change in the agricultural forces of production had taken place.[6]

Stalin recommended to the Chinese that they pursue a long-term, moderate approach to socialist transition, which was in sharp contrast to the policies of radical socialist transformation that he adopted in 1929. Chairman Mao did not overtly question Stalin's cautious recommendations but in fact he wanted to pursue a more radical agenda. His burning ambition was to accelerate the transition to socialism, a quest that characterized his outlook from the late 1940s to the collapse of the Great Leap Forward (GLF, 1958–62).[7] Even before the formal establishment of the state, he had asked Stalin whether he would agree to an accelerated transition, but Stalin discouraged him. Mao formally accepted Stalin's views but sought to circumvent them.[8]

The issue of how to proceed came to the fore in 1951. In "old liberated areas" where land reform had long been carried out, the establishment of small mutual-aid teams was promoted. These were based on private property but used draft animals and large tools in common. In 1951 party leaders in Shanxi province sought to go further by merging small teams into larger, "semi-socialist producers' coops" with a higher level of socialized property. Liu Shaoqi condemned these efforts as "utopian agrarian socialism," since there was no corresponding change in the productive forces. The authors of a two-volume Chinese biography of Mao Zedong published in 2003 commented that "Liu Shaoqi's opinion had a certain representativeness within the party."[9]

5 See Hou Xiaojia, "'Get Organized': The Impact of the Soviet Model on the CCP's Rural Economic Strategy, 1949–1953," in Thomas P. Bernstein and Hua-yu Li (eds.), *China Learns from the Soviet Union, 1949–Present* (Lanham, MD: Lexington Books, 2010), 167–96.
6 Pang Xianzhi and Jin Chongji, *Mao Zedong Zhuan, 1949–1976* [Mao's Biography, 1949–1976] (Beijing: Zhongyang wenxian chubanshe, 2003), 346ff.
7 Bo Yibo, *Ruogan zhongda juece yu shijian de huigu* [Recollections of Certain Major Policy Decisions and Events] (Beijing: Zhongguo dangxiao chubanshe, 1991), vol. I, 211.
8 Hua-yu Li, *Mao and the Economic Stalinization of China, 1948–1953* (Lanham, MD: Rowman & Littlefield, 2006), ch. 2.
9 *Mao Zhuan*, 346.

However, Mao used his unrivaled prestige and authority in the CCP to criticize Liu sharply for failing to recognize the potential of turning mutual-aid teams into larger producers' cooperatives. Liu came around to Mao's view, and a movement to promote "mutual aid and cooperation" was begun in late 1951, which would in the future culminate in full collectivization. Stalin continued to stick to his recommendations for avoiding a premature Chinese socialist transition. In the fall of 1952, Stalin told a delegation to the Nineteenth Congress of the CPSU led by Liu Shaoqi, "Your ideas are correct. After we seized political power, the transition to socialism should have been done with a step-by-step approach [*yinggai caiqu zhubu de banfa*]. Your attitude toward China's capitalists is correct."[10]

The Stalinist Model

After Stalin's death in March 1953, Mao felt freer to push for accelerated socialist transformation. In late 1953 the CCP set down its "General Line for the Transition to Socialism," and continued to draft the PRC's first Five-Year Plan (FYP). Mao reiterated his 1949 call for learning from the Soviet Union:

> In front of us lie very difficult tasks and we do not have enough experience. Therefore, we must seriously study the advanced experiences of the Soviet Union. Whether within or outside the communist party, whether old or new cadres, technicians, intellectuals, worker or peasant masses, all must learn sincerely from the Soviet Union. We must . . . study . . . the advanced science and technology of the Soviet Union. In order to build up our great country, we must launch a nationwide upsurge of studying the Soviet Union.[11]

In order to learn more about the building of Soviet socialism, the CCP with Mao in the lead embarked on intensive study of Stalin's *Short Course* on the history of the CPSU, a book published in 1938 to glorify Stalin. It was translated into Chinese in 1939. The *Short Course* provided an authoritative Stalinist account of the history of the party with strong emphasis on struggle against societal class enemies and elite opponents. Chapters 9–12 on socialist transformation became compulsory reading for Chinese cadres.[12]

---

10 Bo Yibo, *Ruogan zhongda juece yu shijian de huigu*, 221.
11 *Xinhua yuebao* [New China Monthly], 3 (1953), 13.
12 Commission of Central Committee of CPSU(b), *History of the All-Union Communist Party (Bolsheviks): Short Course* (New York: International Publishers, 1939).

The most important of the Soviet Union's "advanced experiences" was the building of a socialist economic system. One indicator of Soviet influence is that more than 10,000 advisors served in China in the 1950s, until Khrushchev abruptly pulled them out in 1960. They served in ministries, the planning apparatus, national defense, higher education, science and technology, and on major industrial projects. The Stalin model prescribed a centrally planned economy and absolute priority to the growth of heavy industry. The Chinese had much to learn about economic planning as well as establishment and management of large-scale enterprises. China transplanted the industrial model virtually in its entirety. One indicator of the intensity of this effort is that, from August 1952 to May 1953, a Chinese delegation of top-level industrial and planning officials, initially led by Premier Zhou Enlai, visited the USSR. Their goal was to learn how the Soviets drew up the components of a five-year plan. Its members listened to authoritative lectures, which then became embodied in successive drafts of China's First FYP. They visited Soviet enterprises to learn the specifics of the operations of large-scale industrial undertakings. Their activities were of vital importance because the core of the Chinese industrialization program of the First FYP relied heavily on Soviet assistance, especially the delivery of 156 turnkey plants.[13] A US analyst, writing in 1975, appraised Soviet technical assistance in these glowing terms: "In the 1950s ... China eagerly accepted ... the most comprehensive technology transfer in modern history ... The Chinese obtained from the Soviet Union the foundation of a modern industrial system ... This was invaluable to China's subsequent development. It would have taken the Chinese decades to evolve such a comprehensive industrial system on their own."[14] Kong Hanbing, a Chinese economist, observed that, to the Chinese, the Soviet model exemplified "the sacred cause of socialism and ... it represented the material embodiment of Marxism."[15] With Soviet help, Chinese industry grew at 17 percent per annum during the period 1952–57, a remarkable success.

Agriculture was a different story. In order to legitimate rapid collectivization, Stalin reinterpreted Lenin's article "On Cooperation" as calling for the immediate establishment of collective farms. The Soviet approach was to

13 Kong Hanbing, "The Transplantation and Entrenchment of the Soviet Economic Model in China," in Bernstein and Li (eds.), *China Learns*, 151–66.
14 Hans Heyman, "Acquisition and Diffusion of Technology in China," in *China: A Reassessment of the Economy* (Washington, DC: US Government Printing Office, 1975), 678, 687.
15 Kong Hanbing, "The Transplantation," 161–62.

exploit agriculture by acquiring a state-defined surplus at state-determined prices. Stalin demanded that peasants pay a "tribute" in support of industrialization.[16] Collective farms provided an organized means to capture this "tribute." Compulsory deliveries of grain and other agricultural produce to the state became the "first commandment" of collective farms. Price scissors operated: The state bought grain at below-market prices and sold industrial goods at high prices. The consequent absence of adequate material incentives necessitated the imposition of tight bureaucratic and repressive controls which robbed farmers of independent initiative. Low productivity and stagnant output resulted. Yet industrialization and urbanization proceeded apace, seemingly independent of the state of agriculture, at least until the 1950s, when agricultural stagnation could no longer be sustained.[17]

China, in contrast, could not rely on extraction of a surplus alone to support rapid industrialization, urbanization and population growth. As of 1952, per capita grain output was 311 kg, significantly lower than the Soviet equivalent in 1928 of 566 kg. The Chinese problem was how to grow an adequate surplus in the first place.[18] As in the Soviet Union, China imposed a state monopoly over the purchase and sale of agricultural commodities in 1953, chiefly grain and cotton, and also used price scissors to exploit agriculture. But China's leaders understood that growth in agriculture was essential for the success of their development project. In 1955, Vice-Premier Li Fuchun noted that China's national economy was more backward than that of the Soviet Union. Accumulating funds for investment would therefore be more difficult than it was in the Soviet Union. "We cannot industrialize our country without an adequate development of agriculture."[19] For his part, Mao Zedong pointed to the contradiction between the low yields of staple crops and the ever-increasing demand for marketable grain and industrial raw materials.[20]

16 J. V. Stalin, "Industrialization and the Grain Problem," 9 Jul. 1928, in J. V. Stalin, *Works*, vol. XI (Moscow: Foreign Publishing House, 1954), 167.
17 See Karl-Eugen Waedekin, *Agrarian Policies in Communist Europe: A Critical Introduction* (The Hague: Allanheld, Osmun and Martinus Nijhoff, 1982), ch. 4.
18 K. C. Yeh, "Soviet and Communist Chinese Industrialization Strategies," in Donald W. Treadgold (ed.), *Soviet and Chinese Communism: Similarities and Differences* (Seattle: University of Washington Press, 1967), 343.
19 Li Fuchun, "Report on the First Five-Year Plan for Development of the National Economy, June 1955," in Center for International Affairs and the East Asian Research Center (eds.), *Communist China 1955–1959: Policy Documents and Analysis* (Cambridge, MA: Harvard University Press, 1962), 65–68.
20 Mao Zedong, "The Question of Agricultural Cooperation," 31 Jul. 1955, in *Policy Documents*, 100–01.

Chinese leaders wanted to have their cake and eat it too by extracting a maximum surplus while also motivating peasants to work hard and carefully so as to increase output. But while the leaders claimed to be attentive to farmers' interests, procurement quotas in some areas had to be increased to offset losses in others due to severe natural disasters. Peasants complained that quotas were too high and prices too low. They periodically erupted in protests when state procurements exceeded levels acceptable to them.

Mao Zedong strongly believed that collectivization of agriculture would lead to major increases in output and hence spur industrialization.[21] China had actually worked out a progressive stage-by-stage formula for reorganizing agriculture that improved on the Soviet approach. As noted, the process began with mutual-aid teams that were to be gradually enlarged, socializing more property and eventually turning into "higher-stage producers' collectives," or full collective farms. The idea was that gradualism would enable cadres to learn to manage larger groups of laborers; villagers would get accustomed to collective production; initial payment for pooled assets such as land would ease the transition; and, as expected, with rising output, peasant incomes would increase, thereby making the new system acceptable. The full stage would not be reached until the 1960s.

Mao Zedong, however, succeeded in launching a national mass movement, the "high tide of cooperativization" in the summer of 1955, which resulted in full collectivization by late 1956, in striking contrast to earlier projections. Mao disingenuously justified plunging ahead even without mechanization, pointing out that in the Soviet Union as of 1932 only 20 percent of Soviet arable land was plowed by tractors.[22] He also argued that collective farms would permit mobilization of surplus labor that would boost output. And he sternly warned that without collectivization class enemies, e.g. rich peasants, would again exploit villagers.

As is well known, Soviet collectivization was extremely costly, destructive, bloody and violent. The *Short Course* criticized serious official abuses, enabling the Chinese to learn something about them.[23] When Mao launched the "high tide," he pointed to the *Short Course* but insisted that "what we should not do is to allow some comrades to cover up their dilatoriness by

---

21 Bo Yibo, *Ruogan zhongda juece yu shijian de huigu*, 364.
22 *A Critique of Soviet Economics by Mao Tse-tung*, trans., annotated and intro. Moss Roberts, Richard Levy and James Peck (New York: Monthly Review Press, 1977), 48.
23 *Short Course*, 307–18.

quoting the experience of the Soviet Union."[24] There were lessons to be learned from the setbacks suffered by the Soviet Union, namely that the Chinese must make great efforts to secure increased output and prevent slaughter of livestock.

The "high tide" predictably caused great difficulties in consolidating the prematurely established large collective farms, but on the whole the CCP did better in accomplishing this feat than its Soviet mentors. CCP history helps explain this success. The party had come to power by mobilizing the countryside. Its land reform created a huge group of beneficiaries. In the process, the CCP not only gained substantial peasant support but also recruited a large cohort of formerly poor peasants who became upwardly mobile village cadres. The party used "mass line" skills to disseminate its ideology and policies. These policies gave the CCP a rural political base, which greatly facilitated socialist transformation. In the Soviet Union, in contrast, the Bolshevik victory in the civil war left a lasting urban–rural cleavage. Peasant resentment and distrust centered on memories of forced requisitioning of grain to feed starving cities. This was one source of Bolshevik difficulty in creating strong, supportive rural organizations.

But Chinese rural organizational capabilities could not substitute for inadequate peasant incentives. Grain output increased but was still below the regime's expectations. Much of the gain was absorbed by population growth and the demands of a rapidly increasing urban populace. Three factors explain the disappointment. First, as noted above, heavy state procurements were a disincentive to faster growth. Second, the haste with which increasingly complex organizational forms were adopted without allowing adequate time for consolidation rendered them less effective than might otherwise have been the case. During the reform era, senior leaders voiced regret that China had prematurely abandoned New Democracy and failed to adhere to a more gradual socialist transformation. Retired Politburo member Bo Yibo observed:

> if we had paid attention to what Lenin said about the social results of the New Economic Policy, and if we had done a political and economic calculation, perhaps we might have maintained a more sober outlook and the entry into the transition and the procedural arrangements might have been done somewhat more carefully and stably.[25]

24 *Policy Documents*, 101.   25 Bo Yibo, *Ruogan zhongda juece yu shijian de huigu*, 218.

Bo also said that after land reform small-scale agriculture should have been allowed to prosper for some time before starting socialist transformation. Deng Xiaoping, China's reform leader, made a similar point.[26] Premature abandonment of the NEP model thus exacted a major price.

Third, a systemic attribute of collective farming made incentives less effective, namely the temporal separation between work done by collective farm members and the harvest, the final result. In the absence of a compelling ideological glue, as was present in the Israeli kibbutz, a complex system of work points for performing a task or laboring for a day was used to measure members' efforts. But the accumulated work points bore little relation to what really mattered, namely the size of the harvest. During the agricultural cycle, whether or not work was performed efficiently would become apparent only at harvest time.[27] This problem could be reduced by allowing small groups whose members could supervise one another to be responsible for specific fields during the entire cycle. The Soviet regime experimented with such a system in the 1960s and 1970s, but despite successes it was not widely adopted. Family farming was most appropriate for motivational purposes. Households were tied together by bonds of solidarity. Each member was expected to labor year-round for the common good of the family. This was especially true of the Chinese family with its culturally ingrained entrepreneurial orientation. After the collapse of the GLF, large portions of rural China switched in 1961–62 to an effective incentive system, household contracting, with continued collective owner-ship, which boosted recovery but ran afoul of Mao's fear that it would lead to capitalist restoration. Eighteen years later, after Mao's death and after the onset of China's reform period, the adoption of the "family responsibility system with reward linked to final output" proved to be much more productive, becoming a powerful factor in China's rapid growth. Chairman Mao thus succeeded in delaying the adoption of an effective method to boost incentives for almost twenty years.

Criticism of the Soviet Model

Doubts about the value of the Soviet model were being voiced already in 1955 but increased in the wake of the Soviet Twentieth Party Congress, held

26 Ibid., 206; *Selected Works of Deng Xiaoping*, vol. II, *1975–1982* (Beijing: Foreign Languages Press, 1984), 315.
27 Michael E. Bradley and M. Gardner Clark, "Supervision and Efficiency in Socialized Agriculture," *Soviet Studies* 23, 3 (Jan. 1972), 465–73.

in February 1956, when Nikita Khrushchev, the First Secretary of the CPSU, castigated Stalin as a murderous tyrant, shocking Chinese leaders. Only a year before he had promised to treat China as an equal – a fervent desire of the Chinese – but now he had failed to consult them before taking so momentous a step. The CCP responded by rejecting wholesale condemnation of Stalin and extolled him as a flawed but great theorist and leader. Their confidence in Khrushchev's judgement was deeply shaken. For Mao, this was another episode – Stalin's death having been the first – that liberated him from Soviet tutelage. On 24 March 1956, he told an enlarged meeting of the Politburo that the speech "was a sudden attack on us," but that it also sent a positive message. Invoking a well-known character from Chinese literature, the monkey Sun Wukong, he said that

> Khrushchev struck some tight fetters [*jingu*] off us. He broke through super-stitions and helped us to examine problems. It is not necessary to build socialism by wholly relying on the Soviet formula. We can begin from the concrete situation in our own country, and set a direction and policy that correspond to the national characteristics of China.[28]

In a major speech, "The Ten Great Relationships," delivered a month later to a closed audience, Mao observed that "it is particularly worthy of attention that certain defects and errors that occurred in the course of their building socialism have lately come to light." One of these was that the Soviets "squeezed the peasants very hard" for industrialization, greatly harming their motivation to produce. "In view of the grave mistakes made by the Soviet Union on this question, we must take greater care and handle the relationship between the state and the peasants well." Mao claimed that China had done better than its elder brother in protecting peasants from exploitation. But he also acknowledged that China had a similar problem by proposing that the ratios of investment between heavy and light industry as well as agriculture should be somewhat adjusted in favor of the latter two, a proposal that was not carried out when Mao launched the GLF in 1958.[29]

28 Wu Lengxi, *Shinian lunzhan, 1956–1966: Zhong-Su guanxi huiyi lu* [Ten Years of Debate: Recollections from Sino-Soviet Relations], 2 vols. (Beijing: Zhongyang wenxian chu-banshe, 1999), vol. I, 14–15. Wu was then head of the New China News Agency and attended top-level meetings. He reports that his book disclosed "what he personally saw and heard" without adding anything but that he also received primary source material from scholars. See vol. II, 940.

29 "On the Ten Great Relationships," in *Selected Works of Mao Tse-tung* (Beijing: People's Publishing House, 1977), vol. V, 284, 286, 291.

Opposition to "Rash Advance" in 1956–1957

Beginning in later 1955 and under the impetus of Mao-generated anti-rightist pressures, China embarked on a small leap forward. Targets were raised – industry was to grow by 22 percent in 1956 – large numbers of peasants were recruited for urban work; collectivization was pushed to its highest pre-Leap level; and the private sectors in industry and commerce were socialized overnight. All this caused economic dislocations and imbalances, overheating and inflationary pressures. Several top leaders, including Premier Zhou, Liu Shaoqi and Chen Yun, a major economic planner, criticized "rash advance" and advocated moderating the pace of growth. The discussions and controversies persisted until the fall of 1957.[30]

Chen Yun proposed some reduction in industrial investment, especially in capital construction, which would reduce inflationary pressures and the need to recruit workers from the countryside. In order to reduce the gap between agricultural and industrial growth, he suggested that peasant incentives be improved by using market forces, reducing state controls and allowing competition between trade channels so as to stimulate the supply of light industrial goods to the countryside. Peasant markets, household handicrafts, other subsidiary activities and private plots, which had been eliminated or curtailed to varying degrees during the anti-rightist high tide, should be restored.[31] These ideas were similar to Bukharin's and, if adopted, might have been a step toward the "market socialism" adopted during the reform era.

Mao Zedong at times agreed with the need for cutbacks and for balanced development, but his overall commitment was to speed up, an attitude that led to the GLF. At conferences in early 1958, Mao severely chastised the opponents of "rash advance," compelling them to make humiliating self-criticisms.[32]

China Turns Left: The Great Leap Forward

Mao's version of balanced growth was to pursue simultaneously breakthroughs in all three sectors of the economy and, above all, to eliminate the agricultural bottleneck. The Leap was an extreme case of voluntarism.

30 Frederick C. Teiwes with Warren Sun, *China's Road to Disaster* (Armonk, NY: M. E. Sharpe, 1999), ch. 1.
31 Nicholas R. Lardy and Kenneth Lieberthal (eds.), *Chen Yun's Strategy for China's Development: A Non-Maoist Alternative* (Armonk, NY: M. E. Sharpe, 1983), xiv–xxi.
32 Teiwes and Sun, *China's Road to Disaster*, Appendix 2, 248–58.

Euphoric expectations were aroused of "three years of hardship and a hundred years of happiness." Faith in willpower to overcome obstacles regardless of objective circumstances was propagated.[33] The Leap relied on coercion and persuasion, but these were two sides of the same coin, since skeptics who doubted the feasibility of this or that project were silenced by repeated anti-rightist campaigns. These began in June 1957 and were aimed at intellectuals who had criticized regime fundamentals during the "Hundred Flowers," a short period of relatively free speech. Perceived attacks on socialism led Mao to greater distrust of intellectuals, including technical experts. Many were purged, and many kept silent for fear of political reprisals. Strident opposition to conservatism was accompanied by whipping up bureaucratic and mass enthusiasm for all-out advance. Territorial party secretaries competed with one another to promise extraordinary, even miraculous achievements in raising steel and grain output.[34]

China's transition to socialism began only in 1953, but in the frenzied atmosphere of summer and fall of 1958 Chairman Mao and his theoreticians gave thought to the possibility of speeding up the transition to the communist stage. This was a challenge to the Soviet Union, whose economic base was far more advanced than China's. Mao's hubris angered the Soviets and was a factor in the growing tensions with Moscow. Soviet planning for entry into communism also began in 1958, culminating in adoption of a program at the Twenty-Second Party Congress in 1961.[35]

In China, new, advanced institutions sprang up. The collective farms established by 1957, most not yet consolidated as fully functioning entities, were thought to be inadequate for the mass mobilization of peasant labor. Mergers of 750,000 collective farms led to the formation of about 25,400 people's communes. Communes were thought of as multifunctional units somewhat analogous to what Marx had imagined for the communist stage. They were to combine agriculture, industry, commerce, education, militias, nurseries, homes for the aged and even sewing groups. Collective consumption in canteens would displace the family as a unit of consumption. Huge gains in grain output would permit partial introduction of free supply ("eating without paying"), meaning distribution according to the communist

33 Chen Boda, "New Society, New People," *Red Flag* (1 Jul. 1958), in *Policy Documents*, 451–56.
34 For an authoritative analysis, see Roderick MacFarquhar, *The Origins of the Cultural Revolution*, vol. II, *The Great Leap Forward, 1958–1960* (New York: Oxford University Press, 1983).
35 William Taubman, *Khrushchev: The Man and His Era* (New York: W. W. Norton, 2003), 507–11.

principle of need rather than labor. The prospect of abundance also justified the confiscation of private plots, which peasants needed for subsistence. The participation of cadres and educated elites in physical labor would overcome the difference between mental and physical labor, and the industrialization of rural China would eliminate the difference between town and country: "In future when transitions have been completed the commune will be the basic mechanism of communist society."[36] It is worth noting that the Soviet *Short Course* condemned attempts to set up Soviet communes as "pigheaded" leftism.[37] During the Leap, Khrushchev and others used their country's own experience with egalitarian communes during "war communism" (1918–20) and in 1929–30 to discredit Chinese communes.[38] Sticking more closely to Soviet experience might thus have prevented the extreme move to communes.

Chairman Mao hoped to turn communes from collective farms into "whole-people's property," i.e. ownership by the state.[39] Achieving this, he asserted, would give a big boost to the productive forces. When collective property is raised to the state level, peasants would turn "into workers under uniform contract to the state for wages."[40] Whole-people's ownership would still be socialist but, after another period of time, it would transition to payment according to need. He added that "if we fail to propose transforming ... subsidiary occupations into public ownership" – a major source of household incomes – "peasants will be peasants forever." The crucial issue was how much time would be needed until production had increased to the point at which commune or state ownership had increased peasants' incomes above previous levels and hence made the change acceptable to them.

The chairman variously spoke of three, five, ten years or longer until communes could be converted into state property. In some parts of China, Mao claimed that this was already happening.[41] A December 1958 party decision insisted that building socialism was still the main task, but left the door open to go further. In the hothouse, anti-rightist atmosphere of the Leap, when Mao issued one of many cautionary injunctions, namely not to disregard objective conditions and to gain mass consent, it was easy for officials, eager to demonstrate their forward-looking commitment and loyalty, to claim that, indeed, conditions were ripe and the masses were ready. The result was a "wind of communism" or extreme leveling. In order

36 *Critique*, 134.   37 *Short Course*, 307.
38 Taubman, *Khrushchev*, 392, and MacFarquhar, *GLF*, 132–35.   39 *Critique*, 133.
40 Ibid., 101.   41 Ibid., 132.

to build factories and large irrigation projects, commune centers freely requisitioned productive assets from their subordinate units, brigades and teams, as well as labor from households, a process known as "equalization and transfer" (*yiping erh diao*). Centralization penalized brigades and teams whose natural endowments yielded higher incomes than less fortunately situated units, inevitably causing resentment.

One concept of the Leap was to "walk on two legs," meaning using both indigenous and modern methods. It meant organizing China's biggest resource, peasant labor, to build irrigation works, local industry and other infrastructure projects. Intrinsically, this was a valuable idea appropriate to China's conditions. Rural industrialization – an idea quite foreign to the Soviet model – could, for instance, promote local processing of farm products and manufacture of farm tools. During the Leap, however, mobilization of labor took on highly irrational proportions. In the fall of 1958, the country embarked on an immense campaign involving 90 million villagers to make rudimentary steel in the countryside.[42] Mao took responsibility for the resulting disaster but insisted that it had been a useful learning experience. This was not the end of mobilization of rural labor for large, often poorly planned projects. A major negative effect was to divert labor from timely performance of agricultural tasks even during the busy seasons. In 1958, for instance, harvests were not fully collected. Rural labor shortages were also caused by the recruitment during the Leap of 25–30 million villagers to work on GLF projects in the urban sector. During the reform period, in contrast, the idea of rural industrialization was pursued in a much more rational way. The rise of township and village industries made a major contribution to the country's rapid development.[43]

Information reached Mao in late fall of 1958 of gross abuses in project implementation, especially excessively long work hours, causing illness and deaths. Mao drew back and until summer 1959 sought to maintain the Leap but eliminate excesses. Mao vehemently criticized leftist errors: "Stalin drained the pond to catch the fish. We now have the same problem," he admitted, referring to excessive local investments that left too little for consumption.[44] He inveighed against the communes for taking team and

---

42 "Speech at the Lushan Conference, July 23, 1959," in Stuart Schram (ed.), *Chairman Mao Talks to the People: Talks and Letters, 1956–1971* (New York: Pantheon Books, 1974), 146.
43 See Jean C. Oi, *Rural China Takes Off: Institutional Foundations of Economic Reform* (Berkeley: University of California Press, 1999).
44 "Mao Tse-tung's Speeches at the Chengchow Conference," *Chinese Law and Government* 9 (Winter 1976–77), 18.

brigade peasant property without compensation. Mao went so far as to justify peasant resistance, claiming to be on their side. But Mao stuck to the basic ideas of the Leap.

At a party meeting in Lushan in the summer of 1959, the Leap was attacked by Minister of Defense Peng Dehuai as a case of "petty bourgeois fanaticism." Mao, feeling stung, struck back with a purge and launched another, large-scale anti-rightist campaign, which again silenced doubters. In the winter of 1959–60, the "wind of communism" blew anew, leading to expansion of the highly unpopular collective canteens, further centralization by the communes and the resurrection of costly huge projects.[45] Urban communes were also established during this time.

The Leap led to an immense economic crisis in both town and country, but especially in the latter, where an immense famine broke out that took an estimated 36 million lives.[46] It was the product of gross failure of planning and the politicization of statistical reporting. For instance, planners significantly reduced acreage to be sown to grain in winter–spring 1958–59 premised on optimistic hopes of an unprecedented bumper harvest. This was part of the "wind of exaggeration," generated by intense political pressures on local party leaders to come up with huge gains in output. The first projected result for 1959 aggregated to 500 mmt of grain. In the summer of 1959 it was scaled down to 250 mmt, but the actual grain harvest dropped disastrously to 170 mmt, far below the 1958 adjusted grain harvest of 200 mmt.[47] In 1960 and 1961 the harvests were still far below projections. In 1957 China's grain harvest totaled 197 mmt; only in 1965 was this result reached again.

Exaggerated figures seemed to indicate that peasants could afford to part with more grain. Tragically, state procurements in 1959 and in 1960 reached the highest level of the Mao era, 39.7 percent and 35.6 percent of the harvest.[48] Quoting Stalin on peasants' tribute, Mao claimed that the vast majority of peasants were "sending tribute" with a positive attitude. Excessive purchases often enforced by terroristic methods bore distinct similarities to how Soviet

45 *Mao Zhuan*, 1050.
46 Yang Jisheng, *Tombstone: The Great Chinese Famine, 1958–1962* (New York: Farrar, Straus, and Giroux, 2008), 12 and ch. 11. This is an abridged edition of the two-volume Chinese version.
47 Robert Ash, "Squeezing the Peasants: Grain Extraction, Food Consumption and Rural Living Standards, 1949–1966," *China Quarterly* 188 (Dec. 2006), esp. pp. 970–75; and T. Bernstein, "Mao Zedong and the Famine of 1959–1960: A Study in Wilfulness," *China Quarterly* 186 (Jun. 2006), esp. 435.
48 *Zhongguo tongji nianjian 1984* [China Statistical Yearbook] (Beijing: Zhongguo tongji nianjian, 1984), 370.

grain collections had been carried out in famine-stricken Ukraine and elsewhere in 1932–33.[49] They played a key role in unleashing the famine in 1959–60.[50] In 1960 the rural death rate leaped forward from 11 to 27 per 1,000. In Anhui province, the death rate reached 68.6 per 1,000. Unusually high mortality rates continued until 1961 and in some areas until 1962.[51]

Central leaders, including Mao, were deeply shaken when they learned of mass famine in late 1960. In due course, the Leap was dismantled and remedial measures taken, including importing of grain. The goal of creating an advanced socialist society already transitioning to communism was given up. Communes were downsized; their lowest tier, the production team of twenty to forty households, became the operating unit of account. The leap into utopia was short-lived but major damage was done to the economy. China spent years recovering from the catastrophic outcome. During the remainder of the Mao era, agricultural output did grow due to state investments in a "Green Revolution" in seeds, irrigation and fertilizer production. But peasant incomes stagnated mainly because of unfavorable price scissors.[52]

Mao Zedong criticized himself at various points during the Leap and especially during post hoc assessments of what had gone wrong. He acknowledged that the "primary responsibility" for mistakes and shortcomings at the center was his, but at no time did he take responsibility for the famine.[53] Mao admitted that the theoretical underpinnings of the Leap had not been worked out. Not only was there no theory. Since 1953, "we still hadn't had the time or the possibility to formulate a complete set of concrete, general and specific policies and methods which were appropriate to the conditions." He acknowledged having failed effectively to check the wind of communism and the idea of quick entry into communism. The chairman now switched from euphoric optimism to deep pessimism. Fifty or a hundred years or even more might now be required to build a strong socialist economy.

---

49 For a graphic eyewitness account of the Ukrainian famine, see Lev Kopelev, *The Education of a True Believer* (New York: Harper and Row, 1980), 247–306.
50 See Zhou Xun (ed.), *The Great Famine in China, 1958–1962: A Documentary History* (New Haven: Yale University Press, 2012), esp. ch. 2. See also Yang Jisheng, *Tombstone*, chs. 1 and 7.
51 Dali L. Yang, *Calamity and Reform in China: State, Rural Society, and Institutional Change Since the Great Leap Famine* (Stanford: Stanford University Press, 1996), 38.
52 For an overview, see Barry Naughton, *The Chinese Economy: Transitions and Growth* (Cambridge, MA: MIT Press, 2007), ch. 11.
53 Schram (ed.), *Chairman Mao Talks*, 173–80.

In November 1958, Mao commented on and ordered provincial and regional party committees to study Stalin's 1952 pamphlet, *Economic Problems of Socialism in the USSR*.[54] In 1959–62, he wrote lengthy comments on a Soviet *Textbook on Political Economy* published in the 1950s. Mao, it is important to note, did not reject their content out of hand, meaning that he continued to find value in the Soviet model. He admitted that *Economic Problems* contained much that was "correct," but "the basic error is mistrust of the peasantry." The *Textbook* "contains many views that are Marxist-Leninist," but it also deviated "in a good many ways."[55] In his lengthy refutation of Peng Dehuai's critique of the Leap at Lushan in July 1959, Mao insisted that Economic Problems had to be studied "in depth; otherwise we cannot consolidate our cause."[56] By calling for study of this article, Mao invoked Soviet authority for obedience to the objective laws of scientific socialism. During debates about the retreat from the GLF in 1961, Mao acknowledged that "We violated objective laws ... and in the last three years paid a very big penalty." Stalin's textbook needed to be used, he said "since we are not in a position to write our own textbook."[57] In January 1962, he noted that it was the good Soviet experiences that needed to be studied. "As for the bad things ... we should treat them as teachers by negative example and learn lessons from them."[58]

Mao's Alternative Socialism: Uninterrupted Revolution

A second purpose of studying the *Textbook* and *Economic Problems* was to show how far both Stalin and Khrushchev, especially the latter, had gone to subvert the fundamental task of preserving and advancing the socialist system and to highlight what China must do to prevent revisionism and capitalist restoration. Mao's criticisms foreshadowed many of the themes that became prominent in later Chinese anti-Soviet polemics. A summation of these views is in the ninth letter from the CCP to the CPSU Central Committee, "On Khrushchev's Phony Communism and Its Historical Lessons for the

---

54 For Mao's comments on Stalin's pamphlet, see *Critique*, 129–47; for comments on the *Textbook*, see 33–127.
55 *Critique*, 135 and 106–07.   56 Schram (ed.), *Chairman Mao Talks*, 146.
57 *Mao Zhuan*, 1163; Mao, "Zongjie jingyan, jiaoyu ganbu" [Sum Up Experience, Educate Cadres], 12 Jun. 1961, in *Mao Zedong wenji* [Mao's Collected Works], vol. VIII (Beijing: Renmin chubanshe, 1999), 277.
58 Schram (ed.), *Chairman Mao Talks*, 181.

World," which conjured up the "unprecedented danger of capitalist restoration in the Soviet Union."[59]

Chairman Mao offered theoretical criticisms and pointed to specific Soviet failures. He put forth his theory of "uninterrupted revolution" (*buduan geming*), a concept different from Leon Trotksy's "permanent revolution," e.g. with respect to the revolutionary role of peasants.[60] He claimed that contradictions were universal. The struggle to resolve antagonistic ones with enemies is what propels society forward. Moreover, contradictions are absolute, while unanimity and solidarity are temporary. Change proceeds in wave-like fashion from imbalance to balance to imbalance.[61] While granting the need for periods of consolidation and rest, Mao said that "after winning one battle, we must immediately put forward new tasks." This is essential to maintenance of revolutionary enthusiasm of cadres and masses, giving them no time to rest on their laurels.[62] Mao complained that the Soviet *Textbook* denied his concept of uninterrupted revolution, seeing only linear development. It viewed contradictions as "incidental," which was a prescription for stagnation.

Mao criticized Stalin for having claimed in 1936 that, since socialism had been built, there were no more antagonistic classes in the Soviet Union, thereby abandoning his previous insistence that the class struggle would get more fierce as socialism progressed. (Stalin's blood purges started in 1936 but were directed at "enemies of the people" and "anti-Soviet elements rather than classes.")

In their anti-Soviet polemics, the Chinese presented much material derived from Soviet newspapers that in their view demonstrated the existence of class polarization and antagonistic classes. Some originated from the Stalin era but most were from the post-Stalin period.[63] Khrushchev's version of the absence of antagonistic classes meant that the CPSU was now a party of all the people and that the state was no longer a dictatorship of the proletariat but a state of the whole people. This was apostasy for Mao, who proclaimed in 1962, "Never forget class struggle." Such ideas signified that a privileged, bourgeois stratum had been seizing power and was ruling the country in its own interests. Lenin's old question, "who–whom" (*kto kogo*, who wins over

59 "On Khrushchev's Phony Communism and Its Historical Lessons for the World," *Peking Review* 7, 29 (17 Jul. 1964), in William E. Griffith (ed.), *Sino-Soviet Relations, 1964–1965* (Cambridge, MA: MIT Press, 1967), 314–50.
60 Stuart Schram, "The Marxist," in Dick Wilson (ed.), *Mao Tse-tung in the Scales of History* (Cambridge: Cambridge University Press, 1977), 58.
61 *Critique*, 80–82.   62 Schram, "The Marxist," 57.
63 "On Khrushchev's Phony Communism," 321–26.

whom), had to be posed again. A new socialist revolution was needed on the political and ideological fronts which Soviet cadres and masses were said to want.

Mao juxtaposed examples of specific Soviet failings that China must avoid:

– the Soviets failed to put politics in command. Neither the *Textbook* nor *Economic Problems* focused on ideological transformation and the necessity for socialist education;
– the Soviets failed to practice the mass line. Experts and technique were highly valued but workers or peasants did not participate in management. Cadres should be "sent down" to participate in productive labor so as to overcome their overlord mentality;
– the Soviet Union one-sidedly emphasized material incentives rather than nurturing socialist consciousness. Wage differentials should be narrowed to the extent possible rather than widened;
– the Soviet party completely neglected the continuing task of remolding of intellectuals. But this must continue for the entire period of socialism, since even intellectuals of worker–peasant origin could fall under bourgeois influence;
– the *Textbook* claimed that, under socialism, group interests did not conflict with the general interest. But "vested interest groups" (*jide liyi jituan*), "which have grown content with existing institutions," may oppose change. "Building a new system always necessitates some destruction of the old ones";
– training young revolutionary successors in "great storms of revolution" is a most important task absent in the Soviet Union;
– in order for China not to succumb to revisionism and capitalist restoration, the socialist period would require not just decades but one to several centuries during which the dictatorship of the proletariat must be maintained.[64]

In sum, Mao's conception of socialism still borrowed heavily from Soviet ideas and institutions but sought to infuse them with permanent revolutionary commitment. Thus the Cultural Revolution sought to purify and simplify the state but not to abolish it. "There must always be heads," he told radicals who wanted to establish Paris Commune-type governance.[65] In sum, only permanent class struggle could save socialism. It is not surprising that this

64 See *Critique*, various pages; "On Khrushchev's Phony Communism," 346.
65 Schram (ed.), *Chairman Mao Talks*, 277.

cheerless program appealed only to China's leftist radicals and not to most of the elite or the people who wanted stability and a better life.

Conclusion

China's rapid modernization had to await Mao's death in 1976 and the onset of the reform period in 1978. In light of the achievements of the reform era, the preceding era of Mao Zedong is widely regarded as a failure.[66] Some Chinese spoke of twenty lost years from the Great Leap Forward to the Cultural Revolution. Was the Mao era with its modified Soviet model then a giant, extremely costly detour to the current era? Actually, some aspects of the Mao era left a positive legacy. As Ho-fung Hung's important study points out, "many reform measures would not have been successful had it not been for the legacies of the Mao era. The [state-owned industries] and infrastructure constructed in Mao times, though moribund and unprofitable at the advent of reform, were important foundations for the capitalist takeoff during the reform period."[67] In the countryside, alongside several hundred million poverty-stricken villagers, the Mao era bequeathed "a huge reserve army of rural labor with good health and a high standard of literacy," which became available for work in the burgeoning urban sector when migration restrictions began to be eased in the 1980s.[68]

During much of the reform era, some aspects of the Soviet model remained. One was continued state priority for investment in heavy industry at the expense of consumption. Extraction from the rural sector via quotas and price scissors also continued until the early twenty-first century. Most important, China's political institutions continue to resemble those of the former USSR. But China broke sharply with the pre-Gorbachev Soviet model by building a mixed economy consisting of state-owned industries, a large private sector, a foreign-invested sector, a household-based rural sector and a market economy.

Since 1992 this economic construct has been labeled "a socialist market economy with Chinese characteristics." Theoretically, a mixed economy with both capitalist and state ownership is legitimate because China is only

---

66 See Andrew G. Walder, *China Under Mao: A Revolution Derailed* (Cambridge, MA: Harvard University Press, 2015).

67 Ho-fung Hung, *The China Boom: Why China Will Not Rule the World* (New York: Columbia University Press, 2016), 172.

68 Ibid., 48.

at the "initial stage of socialism," which will exist for a very long time, perhaps a century or more.[69] But the fading attractiveness of Marxist-Leninist ideology has led the regime to rely increasingly on legitimation based on performance, on restored national greatness and on reviving Confucian traditions, not just on the image of the "radiant future" promised by the ideology. Many outside observers rightly believe that socialism in China is present more in rhetoric than in reality.

Bibliographical Essay

The end of the Cold War and the collapse of communist regimes led to the opening of archives in Eastern Europe and the Soviet Union to Western and Chinese scholars. Most of the resulting publications focused on the international aspects of Sino-Soviet relations, but the domestic impact on China of the Soviet model and the controversies that it precipitated within China also received a good deal of attention. For instance, Lorenz M. Luthi's excellent book, *The Sino-Soviet Split: Cold War in the Communist World* (Princeton: Princeton University Press, 2008), engages with the conflicts over ideology and politics. It contains a helpful "Essay on the Sources," 353–62. Russian archives have not, however, been fully opened, and access has been further constrained under Vladimir Putin's rule. A major new biography of Mao Zedong by Alexander V. Pantsov with Steven I. Levine, *Mao: The Real Story* (New York: Simon & Schuster, 2012), is based to a significant extent on "unique" access to Soviet archives but Pantsov also notes that he had to rely on "personal relations" with archivists to secure access to closed ones.

Among publications based on Soviet archives and in which domestic issues are treated include *Brothers in Arms: The Rise and Fall of the Sino-Soviet Alliance 1945–1963*, edited by Odd Arne Westad (Stanford: Stanford University Press, 1998). Deborah A. Kaple's chapter on "Soviet Advisors in China in the 1950s," 117–49, is a well-done update of her book, *Dream of a Red Factory: The Legacy of High Stalinism in China, 1949–1953* (Oxford: Oxford University Press, 1994). Sergei Goncharov's chapter examines "Sino-Soviet Military Cooperation," 141–64, while the chapter by Chen Jian and Yang Kuisong is on "Chinese Politics and the Collapse of the Sino-Soviet Alliance," 246–94. Shen Zhihua, a Chinese researcher, published the most detailed available account, *Sulian*

<hr/>

69 See Bao Pu et al. (eds.), *Prisoner of the State: The Secret Journals of Premier Zhao Ziyang* (New York: Simon & Schuster, 2009), 203–06.

chuanjia zai Zhongguo, 1948–1960 [Soviet Advisors in China, 1948–1960] (Beijing: Zhongguo guoji guangbo chubanshe, 2003). Shen and another Chinese scholar, Li Danhui, also edited *Zhan hou Zhong-Su guanxi ruogan wenti yanjiu* [Study of Certain Questions of Postwar Sino-Soviet Relations] (Beijing: Renmin chubanshe, 2006), in which there are three chapters on Soviet advisors and three on Soviet aid, all making extensive use of Soviet and Chinese archives, national and local. Austin Jersild, *The Sino-Soviet Alliance: An International History* (Chapel Hill: University of North Carolina Press, 2014), relies on archives from several East European states and Russia. His book focuses on the more informal aspects of the relationships as well on organizations below the diplomatic horizon, such as the Sino-Soviet friendship societies.

As for Chinese primary sources, during the turmoil of the Cultural Revolution the public assault on "capitalist-roaders" in the leadership enabled Red Guard organizations to publish a wide range of classified documents informally, including speeches by Mao Zedong. When stripped of their polemical editorial content, these materials provide much insight into the politics of the 1950s, including the fate of the Soviet model. A major collection of Mao's hitherto-unpublished writings was made available in Taipei as *Mao Zedong sixiang wan sui* [Long Live Mao Zedong Thought] (Taipei: Institute of International Relations, 1969 and 1974). An entire generation of Western scholars has made use of this and other Red Guard materials. A major example was *Chairman Mao Talks to the People: Talks and Letters, 1956–1971*, edited and introduced by Stuart Schram (New York: Pantheon Books, 1974). The more accurate title of the British edition, *Mao Zedong Unrehearsed*, reflects the fact that Mao spoke to elite audiences, not to the "people." Roderick MacFarquhar's magisterial three-volume study, *The Origins of the Cultural Revolution*, made use of Red Guard material. They are: vol. I, *Contradictions Among the People, 1956–1957* (New York: Columbia University Press, 1974); vol. II, *The Great Leap Forward, 1958–1960* (Oxford: Oxford University Press, 1983); and vol. III, *The Coming of the Cataclysm, 1961–1966* (New York and Oxford: Oxford and Columbia University Presses, 1997). Andrew G. Walder, *China Under Mao: A Revolution Derailed* (Cambridge, MA: Harvard University Press, 2015), is another outstanding book that relies heavily on Cultural Revolution sources. The author, a sociologist, analyzes structural and institutional borrowings from the Soviet Union.

During the reform era that began in 1978 and continues to this day, work on many formerly taboo subjects was allowed, resulting in an immense outpouring of publications on the 1950s and 1960s. These included multivolume works by Mao, Liu Shaoqi, Deng Xiaoping and other leaders; collections of Central Party and government documents, chronologies of leaders' activities (*nianpu*), national and local statistics, and recollections and memoirs by some retired top leaders. An important example of the latter is Bo Yibo, *Ruogan zhongda juece yu shijian de huigu* [Recollections About Some Major Decisions and Events] (Beijing: Zhongong zhongyang dangxiao chubanshe, 1991), 2 vols. A fine book by Chen Jian, *Mao's China and the Cold War* (Chapel Hill: North Carolina University Press, 2001), analyzes – using the new sources – Mao's domestic goals in the emerging conflict with the Soviets.

The ruling communist party restricts what can be said in mainland publications. Its legitimacy is bound up with how CCP history is presented to the Chinese public. Mao Zedong's image as the great leader of the revolution, the founding father of the state and the builder of socialism must, in its view, be protected. But, in order to justify the break with radical Maoism, reform leaders also found it necessary to blame Mao in broad terms for the twin disasters of the Great Leap Forward (GLF) and the Cultural Revolution.[70] His individual role in these tragic events can be scrutinized but not in depth. An example is a two-volume official biography, *Mao Zedong Zhuan, 1949–1976* [Biography of Mao Zedong, 1949–1976], edited by two party researchers, Pang Xianzhi and Jin Chongji (Beijing: Zhongyang wenxian chubanshe, 2003). Certain topics such as his responsibility for precipitating the Sino-Soviet conflict also continue to be taboo. Wu Lengxi, a top-ranking journalist, published *Shinian lunzhan, 1956–1966 – Zhong-Su guanxi huiyi lu* [Ten Years of Recollections of the Polemics in Sino-Soviet Relations] (Beijing: Zhongyang wenxian chubanshe, 1999), 2 vols. This important source offers a straightforward account of meetings of Chinese leaders and between the two sides. Several authors have used Soviet, Chinese and Hungarian archives. Foreign Ministry archives for the 1950s have become accessible to foreign scholars. Some have also been able to use subnational, provincial government and party archives.

Informal factors play a role. Informal access to knowledgeable party historians greatly helped Frederick C. Teiwes with Warren Sun to write their excellent books on top-level politics. See their *China's Road to Catastrophe: Mao, Central Politicians, and Provincial Leaders in the Unfolding of the GLF, 1955–1959* (Armonk, NY: M. E. Sharpe, 1999), for example. The

---

70 See *Resolution on Certain Questions in the History of Our Party Since the Foundings of the PRC, 1949–1981* (Beijing: Foreign Languages Press, 1981).

political status of researchers and their *"guanxi"* – personal relationships – also affect access. Yang Jisheng, a senior journalist and long-time party member was able to gain access to rich material on the famine during the Great Leap in a dozen provincial party archives. This led to the publication of an authoritative two-volume study: Yang Jisheng, *Mubei: Zhongguo liushi niandai da jihuang jilu* [Tombstone: A Record of China's Great Famine] (Hong Kong: Cosmos Books, 2008), but it could only be published in Hong Kong. An abridged version was published in English, edited by Edward Frieman et al. (New York: Farrar, Straus and Giroux, 2012).

Finally note should be taken of a conference volume edited by Thomas P. Bernstein and Hua-yu Li, *China Learns from the Soviet Union, 1949–Present* (Lanham, MD: Lexington Books, 2010). Three chapters cover Sino-Soviet relations; sixteen are on Soviet influences on Chinese ideology, the military, the Soviet economic model, society, science and education, and the lessons Chinese leaders drew from the Soviet collapse.

9

The Chinese Cultural Revolution

ANDREW G. WALDER

According to official communist party historiography, China's Cultural Revolution began in May 1966 and ended with the arrest of Maoist radicals labeled the "Gang of Four" in October 1976. Mao Zedong launched it as a radical and somewhat delayed reaction to de-Stalinization in the Soviet bloc and to the political fallout from his own disastrous Great Leap Forward. It began shortly after the ideological polemics that led to the final break with the Soviet Union in 1964. The Cultural Revolution defined the Chinese branch of revolutionary Stalinism known as Maoism.

Ideological Origins

The origins of the Cultural Revolution can be traced to de-Stalinization in the Soviet bloc in the mid 1950s, and in particular to Nikita Khrushchev's "Secret Speech" to the Twentieth Congress of the Communist Party of the Soviet Union (CPSU) in February 1956. Khrushchev denounced Stalin for the mass executions and imprisonments during party purges in the late 1930s, for the slavish worship of him as a genius promoted by his "cult of personality" and for building socialism as if it were a matter of waging class warfare against internal and domestic enemies. These charges caught China's leaders off guard, and especially Mao, who had built up a personal cult of his own in imitation of Stalin's, and who had carried out a series of large repression campaigns against alleged class enemies and other "anti-party elements" after seizing power in 1949.

Mao consciously modeled himself on Stalin as he consolidated his personal power in the wartime capital of Yan'an in the late 1930s. He had previously excelled as a guerrilla strategist and political infighter, but he had little exposure to Marxism-Leninism, and in particular to the development of Soviet doctrine during the decade after 1927, during which the Chinese communists were driven into rural base areas by Nationalist forces. When Mao set about consolidating his leadership and burnishing his ideological credentials, his primary texts were Soviet materials written in the wake of Stalin's "revolution from above" and the subsequent Great Terror. Particularly influential in the creation of "Mao Zedong Thought" was the Stalinist textbook *History of the Communist Party of the USSR: Short Course*, which portrayed the building of socialism as a successful struggle by Stalin against class enemies and representatives of the bourgeoisie in the party leadership (Leon Trotsky, Nikolai Bukharin and others).[1]

The core idea that Mao took away from these materials – and one that he would not abandon for the rest of his life – was that socialism could be built only through continuous class struggle, and through a revolution from above that mobilized the masses to transform China as rapidly as possible. Central to Mao's understanding of Marxism-Leninism was Stalin's novel claim that class struggle does not abate with the socialist transformation of the economy, but that it actually intensifies, because representatives of former exploiting classes, aided by foreign intelligence services, make a last-ditch effort to derail the attainment of communism. This required a long period of harsh repression, and purges of individuals in the party leadership who offered policy positions that deviated from this understanding – especially those who argued for a slower transition to socialism that tolerated market mechanisms and certain kinds of private enterprise. This also meant that it was essential to have a Great Leader to keep the transition on track, and to condemn dissenting policy opinions as expressions of class struggle waged by the enemies of socialism.[2]

The ideas that Mao absorbed from the Stalinist *Short Course* resonated strongly with his own past understanding of China's revolution. In a series of essays that he penned during the final months of the communist party's alliance with the Nationalists in 1926 and 1927, Mao had argued forcefully for the idea that China's revolution had to be a peasant revolution, and that it was the pent-up energy of the oppressed rural masses that would provide the

1 Hua-Yu Li, *Mao and the Economic Stalinization of China, 1948–1953* (Lanham, MD: Rowman & Littlefield, 2006), 91–102; Commission of the Central Committee of the Communist Party of the Soviet Union, *History of the Communist Party of the Soviet Union (Bolshevik): Short Course* (New York: International Publishers, 1939).

2 See Hua-Yu Li, "Instilling Stalinism in Chinese Party Members: Absorbing Stalin's *Short Course* in the 1950s," in Thomas P. Bernstein and Hua-yu Li (eds.), *China Learns from the Soviet Union, 1949–Present* (Lanham, MD: Lexington Books, 2010), 107–30; and Raymond F. Wylie, *The Emergence of Maoism: Mao Tse-tung, Ch'en Po-ta, and the Search for Chinese Theory, 1935–1945* (Stanford: Stanford University Press, 1980).

force necessary to sweep away foreigners, capitalists and landlords. Mao's views were very radical, and they alienated many of the leaders of the Nationalist Party, most of them from property-owning families. Many in Mao's own party also viewed them as too extreme because they threatened their coalition with the much larger Nationalist Party. Mao vigorously defended his views in several essays, including his famous "Report on the Peasant Movement in Hunan," in which he contended that peasant rebellion was essential, and that individuals in his own party who recoiled from its violence were siding with the forces of reaction. Mao argued that revolutionaries should never recoil from violence, for it is only through violence that lasting change can come about after centuries of exploitation and class repression.[3]

Mao therefore came to the Stalinist texts of the late 1930s primed to accept the idea that the building of socialism involved a vigilant struggle against class enemies. Because he read these materials as part of an effort to bolster his personal authority, he was also receptive to the idea that a revolution depended on an unchallengeable Great Leader. For Mao, this meant that the revolution did not end with the seizure of power, and it did not end with the abolition of private property and the liquidation of the former exploiting classes. It continues indefinitely, requiring a leader who continues to wage class struggle against policies and ideas that hamper progress toward socialism.

Khrushchev's denunciation of Stalin took aim at the core of these ideas. He argued that the severe repressions of the Stalin era were unnecessary, and that the claims of prosecuting them in the name of class struggle were simply a cover for personal tyranny. Personality cults of the kind cultivated by Stalin, moreover, were signs of backwardness and theoretical crudity, and had no place in modern Marxist-Leninism. As Khrushchev redefined Soviet doctrines in the years to follow, Soviet socialism moved far from the doctrines that Mao absorbed in the late 1930s. Khrushchev stated flatly that the era of class struggle was over, and that the building of socialism required a focus on developing the "productive forces" and raising the living standards of the people. The victory of socialism over capitalism would be won by demonstrating the superiority of the socialist system in meeting the material needs

---

3 Mao Zedong, "Report on the Peasant Movement in Hunan" (Feb. 1927), in Stuart R. Schram (ed.), *Mao's Road to Power: Revolutionary Writings 1912–1949*, vol. II (Armonk, NY: M. E. Sharpe, 1994), 429–64; and Benjamin Schwartz, *Chinese Communism and the Rise of Mao* (Cambridge, MA: Harvard University Press, 1951).

of the people, through peaceful competition in an era of relaxed superpower tensions.[4]

China's leaders, especially Mao, objected to Khrushchev's denunciation of Stalin. They felt that his attack on Stalin was far too negative, and ignored his contributions to the building of Soviet socialism and to the defeat of fascism in World War II. They also felt that the criticisms in the speech dwelled too much on Stalin's personal failings and were thereby *ad hominem* and atheoretical. They attributed the upheavals in Poland and Hungary later in 1956 to what they termed the "excessive" denigration of Stalin, which in their view aided the designs of imperialist powers.[5]

Nonetheless, China's party did scale back some its Stalinist features. Mao Zedong Thought was removed from the party constitution as its guiding theory, and Mao briefly experimented with political liberalization during the "Hundred Flowers" campaign of 1956–57. Mao put himself forward as a theorist of "contradictions" in socialist society and called for an open airing of criticisms of the behavior of the party's cadres. Criticisms of the party are not necessarily the work of class enemies, he declared, and the airing of "nonantagonistic contradictions" could improve party rule and stabilize socialism. The Hundred Flowers was soon dropped, however, as criticisms escalated into denunciations of the essential features of single-party dictatorship, accompanied by a rapidly developing student democracy movement, a wave of industrial strikes, and the dismantling of recently established collective farms by disgruntled farmers.[6]

Mao reversed himself and struck back hard in a massive "anti-rightist campaign" that labeled virtually all of the critics as anti-socialist and antiparty, condemning roughly half a million people to rural exile or labor camps, and in some cases to imprisonment or execution.[7] The harsh campaign against political criticism was still underway when Mao launched the "Great Leap Forward" – a frenetic political mobilization to catch up with

---

4 See Archie Brown, *The Rise and Fall of Communism* (New York: Ecco, 2009), 236–43; and William Taubman, *Khrushchev: The Man and His Era* (New York: W. W. Norton, 2003), 271–73.

5 See Daniel Leese, *Mao Cult: Rhetoric and Ritual in China's Cultural Revolution* (Cambridge: Cambridge University Press, 2011), 30–36; Lorenz Lüthi, *The Sino-Soviet Split: Cold War in the Communist World* (Princeton: Princeton University Press, 2008), 49–50; and Roderick MacFarquhar, *The Origins of the Cultural Revolution*, vol. I, *Contradictions Among the People, 1956–1957* (New York: Columbia University Press, 1974), 43–48.

6 See Lüthi, *The Sino-Soviet Split*, 50–53; MacFarquhar, *Contradictions Among the People*, 43–48; and Andrew G. Walder, *China Under Mao: A Revolution Derailed* (Cambridge, MA: Harvard University Press, 2015), 135–48.

7 MacFarquhar, *Contradictions Among the People*, 261–310; and Walder, *China Under Mao*, 148–51.

more advanced countries through an exponential increase in the output of grain, steel and other key agricultural and industrial products.

The Great Leap was a spectacular failure in industry, disrupting enterprises, disorganizing the transportation network, causing industrial accidents and breakdowns, and exhausting scarce supplies of materials and fuel in producing substandard and unusable products. Industrial output plummeted in 1960 and did not recover until four years later. But the greatest damage was in agriculture, where hugely inflated reports of gigantic harvests, submitted by party officials who had pledged enormous increases in output, led to excessive procurement of grain from collective farms, leaving farmers with little to eat. This continued for two years, even as unmistakable signs of famine spread throughout rural China. By the time Mao was finally willing to admit failure in late 1960, China was in the midst of a famine that would claim the lives of roughly 30 million people.[8]

Political Origins

The Cultural Revolution was Mao's eventual response to the political fallout from the Great Leap. He yielded control of economic policy to other senior officials, in particular his second-in-command Liu Shaoqi, Premier Zhou Enlai and Vice-Premier Deng Xiaoping. Mao agreed that the Leap had failed in its objectives, but he bridled at Liu Shaoqi's blunt assessment of the damage caused. Mao was never directly blamed for the Great Leap's outcome, nor was he challenged for the party leadership. But Mao sensed – accurately – that many of his senior colleagues were not enamored of his radical initiatives, and he detected ideological backsliding in their efforts to revive the economy. He was particularly upset by the division of collective farms into household units in hard-hit famine regions, which he equated with a reversion to capitalism.[9]

Mao's political unease over domestic politics dovetailed with growing estrangement from the Soviet Union. The relationship, strained since Khrushchev's denunciation of Stalin, deteriorated further during the Great Leap, which the Soviets viewed with open skepticism. Mao objected to the USSR's leadership of the world communist movement, especially over the desirability of relaxing superpower tensions. The final break came in 1963,

8 Walder, *China Under Mao*, 152–79.
9 Roderick MacFarquhar, *The Origins of the Cultural Revolution*, vol. III, *The Coming of the Cataclysm, 1961–1966* (New York: Columbia University Press, 1997), 13–19, 158–68 and 209–48.

and the exchanges between the two sides dramatically illustrated the doctrinal differences between the two communist powers. In these polemics the Chinese side articulated a vision that was essentially a rationale for the coming Cultural Revolution.

The emerging Maoist view, published in July 1963, asserted that American imperialism was pursuing worldwide aggression and that world peace could be achieved only through armed struggle, not appeasement and naive calls for universal disarmament. Socialism would not triumph simply through a peaceful competition with the capitalist world system. Class struggle and the dictatorship of the proletariat must inevitably persist for a long time. A party that curtailed its vigilant hunt for internal class enemies and spies was falling prey to bourgeois concepts. Attacks on the personality cult were simply an excuse for the Soviet Union to force other communist states to change their leaders.[10]

The Soviets responded with an open letter to the world communist movement. They expressed surprise that any modern communist party would advocate a "personality cult," which they labeled a "petty bourgeois" notion. The clear implication was that the Chinese were defending Mao's anachronistic cult of personality. The Soviets charged that China's position on militant confrontation with imperialism in an era of nuclear weapons treated callously the lives of hundreds of millions of individuals in the working class who would perish in nuclear war. Shortly after issuing this statement, the Soviets signed a partial test ban treaty with the United States, leading to the final split.[11]

The relationship broken, China geared up for a massive propaganda campaign against the Soviet Union. Mao gave the task to Kang Sheng, who had been involved in internal security work dating to the Yan'an base area. Kang presided over more than 100 writers who produced a stream of polemics against Soviet policies, the most important of which was the last, the "ninth polemic" of July 1964.[12] The essay expressed what was to become the ideological justification for the Cultural Revolution.

The polemic portrayed a "revisionist Khrushchev clique" that promoted policies that harmed the working class. They employed material incentives, widened income differences by giving high salaries to educated experts,

10 Lüthi, *The Sino-Soviet Split*, 236–45; and MacFarquhar, *The Coming of the Cataclysm*, 353–54.
11 Lüthi, *The Sino-Soviet Split*, 260–72; and MacFarquhar, *The Coming of the Cataclysm*, 349–50.
12 MacFarquhar, *The Coming of the Cataclysm*, 360–62.

defamed the dictatorship of the proletariat by attacking the personality cult and substituted capitalist for socialist methods of management. "The revisionist Khrushchev clique are the political representatives of the Soviet bourgeoisie, and particularly of its privileged stratum," and they had taken control of the party and government after purging genuine communists. As a result, "the first socialist country in the world . . . is now facing an unprecedented danger of capitalist restoration."[13]

The essay then argued that the crucial question for China was how to train a generation of revolutionary successors who would continue to "march along the correct road laid down by Marxism-Leninism" and prevent the emergence of Khrushchev-style revisionism in China. This was "a matter of life and death for our Party and our country."[14] This soon became the ostensible goal of the Cultural Revolution.

Preparing the Campaign's Launch

Mao prepared carefully for the coming assault on his own party. His colleagues were unfailingly deferential to him personally, but he could not be certain that there would be no coordinated resistance if his intentions were known in advance. Not until his loyalists were in place would he show his hand. Mao intended not merely to remove from the party leadership prominent communists from the revolutionary generation – starting with the second-ranking official, his designated successor Liu Shaoqi. He also intended to mobilize a massive purge of the party apparatus, to root out officials at all levels who in word or deed showed a tendency toward "revisionist" thought and behavior. Mao's charge – it would soon become clear – was that a massive conspiracy of revisionist officials was underway, influenced by remnants of former exploiting classes and their ideas. He planned to wipe the party clean in a massive upheaval of undetermined form.

In this effort Mao relied on individuals whose loyalty to him personally transcended their loyalty to the party organization. These individuals had proven themselves utterly loyal to him in past conflicts and could be relied upon to do his bidding without question. From late 1964 to mid 1966, he laid the groundwork for seizing control of the party apparatus, the government, the army and the security services, cementing his unquestioned personal control. The most important of these loyalists were his wife, Jiang Qing, who

13 Ibid., 363.   14 Ibid., 363–64.

had not previously been active in Chinese politics, held no government or party post and had not appeared in public for many years, and Marshall Lin Biao, who as head of the People's Liberation Army had promoted Mao as a "genius" and propagated Mao Zedong Thought in the armed forces by ordering the compilation and publication of a small handbook, *Quotations from Chairman Mao Zedong*, which later achieved fame as the *Little Red Book*.[15] Two other important Mao loyalists were Kang Sheng, who had directed the party's ferocious purge campaign in the Yan'an base area in the early 1940s and the polemics against the Soviet Union, and Chen Boda, who as Mao's political secretary in Yan'an played a key role in developing the Mao cult and Mao Zedong Thought. The party's theoretical journal, *Red Flag*, founded under his editorship in 1958, was Mao's mouthpiece during the 1960s.

In a series of coordinated moves beginning in November 1965 Mao removed potential sources of resistance to his plans to upend China's political order. In November, he abruptly purged the official who headed the Central Committee's General Office, which controlled the flow of documents at the top of the party apparatus, and replaced him with the head of his personal security detail.[16] In January 1966 he ordered the removal of the chief of staff of the Military Affairs Commission, an official who had a history of conflict with Lin Biao over the politicization of the military.[17] Shortly after Liu Shaoqi left for an extended trip abroad in late March 1966, Mao ordered the disbanding of the Beijing Party Committee and the CCP Propaganda Department.[18] On 2 April 1966, *People's Daily* denounced a "black line" in the Beijing propaganda establishment and the purge of these leading officials as heads of an extensive "anti-party group." Their subordinates were arrested and several prominent figures committed suicide.[19] The moves consolidated Mao's personal control over the national propaganda apparatus, the armed forces and the communication flow to the national party apparatus.[20] By the time Liu Shaoqi returned from his foreign trip, resistance was futile.

---

15 Leese, *Mao Cult*, 94–107, and 108–22 for a full account of the compilation, printing and distribution of the *Little Red Book*.
16 MacFarquhar, *The Coming of the Cataclysm*, 447–48; Roderick MacFarquhar and Michael Schoenhals, *Mao's Last Revolution* (Cambridge, MA: Harvard University Press, 2006), 19–20, 36–37.
17 MacFarquhar, *The Coming of the Cataclysm*, 448–50; MacFarquhar and Schoenhals, *Mao's Last Revolution*, 20–27.
18 MacFarquhar and Schoenhals, *Mao's Last Revolution*, 34–35.
19 MacFarquhar and Schoenhals, *Mao's Last Revolution*, 37–44.   20 Ibid., 48–51.

Political Features

Mao appears not to have had a clear plan for the Cultural Revolution. During its course, he repeatedly improvised and shifted direction after he was frustrated by events and by the behavior of his loyal subordinates. The struggles that he set in motion repeatedly moved in directions that he had not anticipated, forcing him to react and reconsider. What the Cultural Revolution eventually became was probably not anticipated by Mao or anyone else in the party leadership.

From one perspective the Cultural Revolution was a massive purge designed to remove "people in authority taking the capitalist road," Maoist code for "revisionists." Starting with Liu Shaoqi and Deng Xiaoping at the top, and eventually down to the level of party secretaries of rural communes and state factories, party cadres lost their positions on an enormous scale. As in the Soviet Union in the late 1930s, vast numbers were ejected from their posts. In the Soviet Union those purged were unfailingly sent to labor camps or executed. In China they might be imprisoned for a period, sometimes dying in custody or committing suicide, but the standard treatment was public humiliation and beatings, brief imprisonment in makeshift cells and later long stints of manual labor in factories or the countryside. Unlike Stalin's victims, the vast majority of victims survived and later returned to office.

But the Cultural Revolution was much more than a leadership purge. It sought the destruction of the bureaucratic system that China had copied from the Soviet Union. In its place would be a much simpler network of committees that merged civilian and military cadres with rebel representatives, working with office staffs that were only a fraction of the size of the former bureaucratic departments. Eventually, between 70 and 90 percent of the employees of central ministries were sent for sustained periods to rural reeducation centers, where they performed manual labor.[21] The Central Committee's established structures were gutted by purges and paralyzed; its bureaucratic departments were downsized and merged, and decision-making authority shifted to informal committees staffed by Mao loyalists who reported directly to him. Committees of Mao loyalists at the apex of the party-state carried out the destruction and dismemberment of the national bureaucracy, on Mao's authority.

The truly distinctive feature of the Cultural Revolution was the mobilization of a mass insurgency from below. In scope and scale, there was no

---

21 Ibid., 156–60.

parallel to this in the Soviet experience or in any other communist regime. The ostensible rationale was to train "revolutionary successors" from the younger generation. The insurgency targeted officials at all levels who were deemed insufficiently loyal to Mao Zedong Thought. On the surface, the student "Red Guard" movement that burst onto the scene so dramatically in August 1966 appeared to be chaotic and disorganized. In fact, it was monitored and guided by fulltime liaison personnel stationed on campuses who reported on local developments while relaying advice, encouragement and instructions to student rebels. These networks of influence steered the student movement in the summer and fall of 1966, and later the rebel campaigns that also included workers in 1967 and 1968.[22]

A new ad hoc committee, the Central Cultural Revolution Group (CCRG), established at the end of May 1966, directed the unfolding campaign. By the end of 1966, it had replaced the Politburo, its Standing Committee and the party's bureaucratic departments. The key players on the CCRG were familiar figures whose loyalty to Mao was beyond question, and whose positions depended entirely on Mao's patronage. These figures had worked almost exclusively in the fields of propaganda or internal security, and had distinguished themselves in earlier struggles against liberalization and "bourgeois" tendencies.

The CCRG became Mao's staff headquarters for conducting the campaign and, as the central bureaucracy of the party-state was decimated and downsized, the CCRG grew in scale and power. By all accounts the CCRG was a chaotic and poorly organized entity that was beset by internal conflicts and an obvious lack of coordination. Many of the members were openly antagonistic toward one another, and there were few clear lines of authority and no division of labor. There were no formal reporting lines and no system of regular reports. Mao kept aloof, rarely attending meetings, often living in provincial villas far from Beijing. Neither Jiang Qing nor Chen Boda was a capable or experienced administrator, and both had erratic and difficult personalities. The CCRG was typically convened by Premier Zhou Enlai, who was not formally a member of the group, but who set the agenda for meetings.[23] Zhou had very different political leanings from these radical figures, and he tried subtly to blunt the impact of their more destructive

---

22 Andrew Walder, *Fractured Rebellion: The Beijing Red Guard Movement* (Cambridge, MA: Harvard University Press, 2009), 17–18.
23 MacFarquhar and Schoenhals, *Mao's Last Revolution*, 100–01; Walder, *China Under Mao*, 202–05.

initiatives. The CCRG radicals understood this, viewed Zhou with considerable distrust and frequently tried to undermine and block him.

In August 1966 Mao reshuffled the party leadership, sidelining and demoting Liu Shaoqi and Deng Xiaoping, promoting senior members of the CCRG and elevating Lin Biao to the position of first party vice-chairman and Mao's designated successor. Zhou Enlai, who convened an informal "central caucus" on an irregular basis that assumed the functions formerly handled by the Politburo Standing Committee and party Secretariat. Mao and Lin Biao almost never attended.[24] This placed Zhou at the center of the new structure of power, and made him an indispensable cog in the Cultural Revolution power machine. Because virtually all decisions and their implementation went through his hands, he was able to influence the course of events.

Also founded during this period was the Central Case Examination Group, which grew out of the investigation of the Beijing party apparatus in May 1966. The group's purpose was to investigate, unmask, arrest and imprison "revisionists" and "traitors" in the CCP. As the purges of the Cultural Revolution expanded, the group's activities and size also grew. In a clear throwback to the Soviet purges of the 1930s, the main charges against "revisionists" had little to do with policy positions they had taken or their public activities. Instead, the victims of these investigations faced implausible charges of treachery: underground anti-party activity, spying on behalf of the Nationalists or foreign intelligence services or betraying the revolutionary movement before 1949.

The Central Case Examination Group eventually employed thousands in scores of investigations into underground traitor groups. They coordinated their work with quasi-independent mass organizations across China which performed local investigations on their behalf. By 1968 a total of eighty-eight members of the Central Committee were under investigation for suspected "treachery," "spying" or "collusion with the enemy." The group's activities spread through a nationwide network of "case groups." In gathering their evidence these committees, especially those at the grassroots, relied heavily on coercive interrogations, employing threats and both mental and physical torture.[25]

---

24 MacFarquhar and Schoenhals, *Mao's Last Revolution*, 98–99.
25 Ibid., 277 and 281–84; Michael Schoenhals, "The Central Case Examination Group, 1966–1979," *China Quarterly* 145 (Mar. 1996), 87–111; and Michael Schoenhals, "Outsourcing the Inquisition: 'Mass Dictatorship' in China's Cultural Revolution," *Totalitarian Movements and Political Religions* 9, 1 (2008), 3–19.

The Cultural Revolution also mobilized a mass insurgency that targeted bureaucratic structures from below. For almost two years, students and eventually industrial workers were given nearly free rein to form organizations to criticize and "drag out" officials who in their view exhibited tendencies that marked them as "revisionists." This aspect of the Cultural Revolution bore a certain resemblance to Mao's insistence on "open door rectification" of the party in 1956 and 1957. But in 1957 Mao did not sanction independent organizations or attacks on officials by ordinary citizens. Mao's assessment of the party by this point was fundamentally different.

The popular insurgency was not left to its own devices. One of the primary functions of the CCRG was to monitor insurgent groups, instigate and support rebellion, and actively undermine serving officials through back-channel communication and encouragement. As the Red Guard movement grew rapidly in August 1966 hundreds of reporters from *Liberation Army Daily* and the New China News Agency were dispatched as "liaison personnel" on college campuses throughout the country. They established relationships with Red Guard leaders, submitted regular reports to their superiors in Beijing and provided information and advice to student activists about imminent shifts in Cultural Revolution politics. The reports that they submitted to the CCRG were distilled into the *Cultural Revolution Bulletin*, which was printed in fewer than twenty copies and distributed to Mao and a selected group of other leaders.[26]

Mao and the CCRG utilized this intelligence network to monitor trends in the student movement, steer it in desired directions, identify and promote promising and cooperative student leaders and warn off those who were saying and doing things that were not approved. Near the end of 1966 the network was crucial in identifying dissident Red Guards who were critical of the CCRG, and in orchestrating their arrest and denunciation. Some of the liaison personnel became permanent fixtures on campuses, inserting themselves into the deliberations of the leading rebel groups, and were treated as authoritative sources of intelligence. As the CCRG consolidated its ties with favored student factions in the nation's capital, the Beijing students in turn established "liaison stations" in provincial capitals throughout China, providing advice and direction to local Red Guards. By the fall of 1966 the CCRG regularly invited favored Red Guard leaders for consultations.[27]

26 MacFarquhar and Schoenhals, *Mao's Last Revolution*, 79–81; and Walder, *Fractured Rebellion*, 169–70.
27 Walder, *Fractured Rebellion*, 154–71.

Mao and the CCRG actively facilitated student rebellion in other ways. The mass media consistently encouraged student rebels, praising them in an unrestrained fashion. Beginning on 18 August, Mao and other leaders hosted a series of twelve gigantic Red Guard rallies held on Tiananmen Square, all of which were lavishly covered in the national media.[28] All classes were suspended and final exams canceled in mid June, along with the conferral of degrees, job assignments and college entrance examinations. Dormitories and meal services stayed open into the summer vacation and beyond. In late August the Public Security Bureau and armed forces were forbidden from interfering in Red Guard activities.[29]

A Disordered Decade

Party historians refer to the Cultural Revolution as "ten years of turmoil," but the decade went through several distinct and very different phases. These events did not unfold in a logical or seemingly preplanned pattern, but instead appeared to lurch from one direction to another as improvisational responses to unanticipated and unwelcome developments.

In the first period, from June 1966 to the end of that year, a mass insurgency was mobilized, first of students and later of industrial workers, leading to the paralysis of the party organizations of most cities.[30] In June and July 1966, leadership purges of purported anti-socialist elements were carried out under the direction of party organizations, which sent "work teams" of party officials to government offices, schools and state enterprises. The work teams mobilized students in universities and high schools to attack school administrators and faculty, but they also fell into conflict with a minority of students who challenged their authority.

The work teams were abruptly withdrawn from schools at the end of July and were denounced for suppressing the student movement, but Red Guards were divided from the outset between student militants who had cooperated with the work teams and those who had clashed with them. The former became known as the "majority" faction, and the latter the "minority" faction, and they fought for control over their own campuses in the wake of the work teams' withdrawal. Throughout August and September, different Red Guard groups wrought havoc on their campuses and in nearby

---

28 Leese, *Mao Cult*, 129–34.   29 Walder, *Fractured Rebellion*, 148–50.
30 This first period is described in Walder, *China Under Mao*, 205–30.

neighborhoods, unleashing a wave of violence against school officials, faculty and members of former "exploiting class" households. Thousands died in a wave of beatings and suicides. Further splits in the Red Guard movement developed after the wave of violence was denounced as "fascist" by some of the earliest high school Red Guards, who formed "picket corps" to protect some of the defenseless victims.

The clashes between the majority and minority factions divided the movement and sidetracked it from what the CCRG saw as its ultimate goal – higher party officials. After the minority faction began to attack government ministries that had sent work teams to their schools, and after the "picket corps" moved to guard these offices against invasions by rebel students, the CCRG ceased calling for student unity and threw its weight behind the "minority" faction. Leaders of minority factions at major universities were called together by members of the CCRG and anointed as a new "rebel" faction that was showered with favorable media attention and CCRG patronage. Majority faction rebels were pushed aside as "conservative" and lost control of their campuses, and the picket corps were denounced as reactionary, their criticisms of Red Guard violence portrayed as an excuse for trying to protect revisionist officials.

The leaders of the spurned majority faction and the picket corps did not go quietly. During November and December, they mobilized a defiant campaign that denounced the CCRG for manipulating the student movement and for suppressing student rebels, similar to the alleged errors of the work teams of June and July. In response, the CCRG reversed its prohibition against the use of the security services and ordered a wave of arrests. There followed a propaganda campaign that denounced these Red Guards as reactionary tools of revisionists who were determined to hold onto power.

The troubles in the student movement led Mao to shift his hopes to the working class as an instrument of the party-state's destruction. For several months industrial workers were discouraged from forming rebel groups and alliances across factories. This changed dramatically in November 1966 when Mao decreed that the ban on worker and peasant rebel organizations was lifted. This exponentially increased the scale and scope of popular political mobilization as there were close to 70 million industrial workers vs. 600,000 university students. Many large cities, most notably the industrial center of Shanghai, became ungovernable as workers rapidly mobilized, divided into factions and engaged in street battles.

The first week of 1967 initiated the second distinctive period of the Cultural Revolution.[31] The rapid deterioration of public order led to calls for a seizure of power by rebel forces in provinces and large cities. The national model was a leadership coup carried out on 6 January by CCRG members from Shanghai, who ousted the party leadership in coordination with a large alliance of rebel workers, declaring a "power seizure" by rebel forces. After receiving strong public support from Mao and the CCRG, the new leaders of this "Shanghai Commune," later renamed a "Revolutionary Committee," moved rapidly to force workers back to work and to curtail the street battles that had paralyzed the city. They did not hesitate to use the security services and armed forces to suppress rebel groups who denounced the power seizure as a sham.

Shanghai's "January Storm" was praised in the national media as an example for rebels throughout the country, and on 22 January 1967 central radio broadcasts and national newspapers issued an urgent call for rebels nationwide to seize power. Within ten days, half of all government jurisdictions in China down to the county level experienced power seizures by rebel groups that deposed incumbent party officials. By the end of February close to two-thirds had done so.[32] The CCRG and Central Military Commission ordered the armed forces to step in to "support the left" where power seizures had occurred and consolidate public order and buttress the authority of new claimants to power.

This effort to bring the Cultural Revolution to a victorious conclusion after only six months failed spectacularly. Instead of the consolidation of new leading bodies ostensibly more loyal to Chairman Mao, another eighteen months of intensified factional conflict and street fighting ensued. After Shanghai's power seizure, only a handful of provincial power seizures gained the approval of Mao and the CCRG. In most other regions, the Beijing authorities hesitated to sanction new claimants to power, either because they could not identify ranking officials that they trusted, or because the rebel forces were too evenly divided and lacked the critical mass and relative unity that had been apparent in Shanghai. Instead of approving new revolutionary committees, Mao and the CCRG stalled and placed the vast majority of regions under military control while they sorted out the local political situation. Without political settlements at the province level, there could be

---

31 This second period is described ibid., 231–62.
32 Andrew G. Walder, "The Rebellion of the Cadres: The 1967 Implosion of the Chinese Party-State," *China Journal* 75 (Jan. 2016), 102–20.

no settlements in the subordinate cities and counties, which were also eventually all put under military control.[33]

This proved to be a recipe for intensified factional conflict. When armed forces moved to enforce order and consolidate their control over government buildings, railway stations, newspapers, radio stations and banks, they frequently clashed with rebel groups who had only recently declared a power seizure. Predictably, military units detained those who resisted, and in many cases banned the organizations that had resisted military control. In almost all localities, as in Shanghai, there were rebel groups which had been excluded from the power seizure. These groups welcomed military control. This had the effect of drawing the armed forces inadvertently into the middle of local factional conflicts, as the armed forces suppressed rebel groups who resisted them and supported those who cooperated.

When the armed forces suppressed opposition to approved new revolutionary committees, they had the full support of Mao and the CCRG. But when local army units fell into conflict with rebel groups that claimed to have seized power, arresting their leaders and banning their organizations, Maoists in Beijing began to worry that the army was suppressing rather than supporting local rebels. In April 1967 the Beijing authorities called for the army to release arrested rebels, restore banned rebel organizations and forbid further actions of this kind. This unleashed a mobilization by suppressed rebel groups to oppose the further consolidation of military control, but it also stimulated new factional conflicts between these groups and rebels who had supported the actions of the armed forces. In Chinese regions under military control, the axis of conflict now centered on rebel opposition to, and rebel support for, local military forces. When news reached Beijing that local military commands were favoring some rebel groups in struggles with their factional opponents, Mao and the CCRG leaned increasingly for support on the beleaguered anti-army forces. This trend reached a peak in the summer of 1967, which saw an upsurge in armed battles between local rebels, both sides of which by this time had been able to obtain military-grade weaponry.[34]

33 See, for example, Dong Guoqiang and Andrew G. Walder, "Nanjing's Failed 'January Revolution' of 1967: The Inner Politics of a Provincial Power Seizure," *China Quarterly* 203 (Sep. 2010), 675–92.
34 See, for example, Dong Guoqiang and Andrew G. Walder, "Local Politics in the Chinese Cultural Revolution: Nanjing Under Military Control," *Journal of Asian Studies* 70, 2 (May 2011), 425–47.

By September 1967, with much of China in a state resembling civil war, and with signs that army units themselves were splintering into factions, Mao lurched sharply back to support for military forces. After reshuffling local military commands and purging CCRG officials who had strongly advocated rebellion against army commands, Mao ordered Zhou Enlai to negotiate ceasefires and oversee negotiations in Beijing between delegations from local military forces and rebel groups. The negotiations were prolonged and conflict-ridden, and recalcitrant individuals were purged as coercion was increasingly applied to achieve some semblance of rebel unity. By mid 1968 the process had been completed for almost all provinces, and in almost every case the new revolutionary committees, unlike the first handful that had received approval early in 1967, were completely dominated by military commanders.[35]

This ushered in the Cultural Revolution's third distinctive period.[36] By the fall of 1968 most Chinese regions were under a thinly disguised military dictatorship, and the Cultural Revolution entered a strikingly new phase. Military control committees were established in all government jurisdictions and were the power behind the new revolutionary commit-tees, which included nominal representation of rebel leaders and former civilian officials, along with ranking military officers, who held the key positions. Although in some respects this marked the restoration of order, in many other ways the Cultural Revolution was now entering its most extreme and radical phase. The new revolutionary committees proceeded to stamp out all potential sources of opposition, unleashing a wave of campaigns against perceived dissidents and suspected class enemies in a campaign referred to as the "Cleansing of the Class Ranks." In this campaign, local case groups were established to investigate the loyalty not only of former rebels but also of individuals with foreign connections and "reactionary" class backgrounds. Coercive interrogations, often employing physical torture, were routinely used to extract confessions. This period saw a massive escalation in the number of arrests, imprison-ments and executions, and was responsible for the majority of the political casualties that occurred during the entire decade.

This period also marked the intensification of the Mao cult into its more extreme forms. Statues, busts and posters of Mao's image appeared

---

35 See, for example, Dong Guoqiang and Andrew G. Walder, "From Truce to Dictatorship: Creating a Revolutionary Committee in Jiangsu," *China Journal* 68 (Jul. 2012), 1–31.

36 This third period is described in Walder, *China Under Mao*, 263–86.

seemingly everywhere, and parades, assemblies and group meetings proliferated, mobilizing adulation for the Great Helmsman. New rituals were
introduced in workplaces: the reading of Mao quotations and bowing to
Mao portraits at the beginning and end of the workday; the performance of
a "Loyalty Dance" accompanied by a song whose lyrics extolled the love of
millions of beating hearts for the Chairman. In one notorious case, retrospectively perhaps the most embarrassing, a batch of mangoes that Mao had
given as a gift to several model Beijing units (and later fabricated replicas after
the originals rotted) traveled around the country in a celebrity tour that
mobilized hundreds of thousands of adoring masses in ways that resembled
the procession of religious relics. Because the loyalty campaign coincided
with the Cleansing of the Class Ranks, there were few who failed to understand that not complying enthusiastically with these activities could easily be
viewed as disloyalty of the worst kind.[37]

This period also saw the appearance of some of the distinctive practices
associated with Maoism. During 1968, university students who had been
enrolled in 1966, and who had not attended classes since that spring, were
all declared to have graduated and were sent to remote regions to work as
farmers, or in some cases as industrial workers. Universities were closed, and
large portions of their faculty and administrators were sent to perform
manual labor in the countryside or in factories. High school graduates were
all sent to villages to work indefinitely as farmers, and subsequent cohorts of
graduates were treated similarly. Large percentages of white-collar government personnel were also dispatched for reeducation through manual labor,
most of them in rural camps known as "cadre schools."

College entrance examinations, canceled since 1966, were formally abolished. After the universities reopened in 1972, reduced numbers of "worker-
peasant-soldier" students were recruited based on political recommendations
of leaders of villages, factories or army units. These radical educational
policies remained in force until after Mao's death. By the end, close to
18 million urban students were relocated to the countryside, and an entire
generation of college-trained individuals had been lost. Scientific research
ceased almost completely, and the social sciences and humanities largely
ceased to exist in their previous forms.

This phase of the Cultural Revolution, which spanned from 1968 to 1971,
was a period of "high Maoism." Military-dominated revolutionary committees gave the army unprecedented political power. The end of this phase

---

37 See also Leese, *Mao Cult*, 187–231.

began in 1969 and 1970, with a sharpening rivalry between civilian radicals and military commanders who had risen into the top leadership after 1968. Mao decided to scale back the army's power, and the first sign was the purge of Chen Boda, the nominal head of the CCRG who had aligned himself with the military commanders in Politburo controversies. In early 1971 Mao ordered self-criticism for political errors by several of Lin Biao's lieutenants, a sign that Lin Biao himself might be in political trouble.

The tensions between civilian radicals and military officers came to a spectacular end with the death of Lin Biao in a plane crash over Mongolia in September 1971. Lin was charged with trying to flee China and defect to the Soviet Union after a failed military coup that included a plan to assassinate Mao. The evidence for the alleged coup is weak, but it is clear that Lin and his close family members were attempting to flee and did die when their plane crashed.[38]

Lin's flight and death initiated a decisive shift in Chinese politics and ushered in the fourth and final phase of the Cultural Revolution.[39] Military commanders in the national leadership who were closely associated with Lin Biao were purged and arrested, and Mao ordered the withdrawal of the armed forces from civilian administration, a process largely completed by 1974. He also ordered Zhou Enlai to rebuild the national party organization and return many purged officials to prominent posts. The new party committees gradually supplanted the revolutionary committees, whose authority steadily ebbed. After Zhou lost favor in 1974, the task of rebuilding was handed to Deng Xiaoping, who pushed vigorously to restore the economy, to return former officials to leading positions and to assert the authority of the resurgent party organizations.

This period, however, also saw the revival of factional conflicts that had been firmly suppressed under military dictatorship. As military commanders were removed from civilian posts, conflict arose over who should replace them. There were two claimants – former officials who had been purged earlier in the Cultural Revolution and who were now returning to leading posts, and rebel leaders who had been marginalized and often imprisoned under military control. As the army was withdrawn from power, former rebel groups reestablished themselves and in many regions resumed the

38 See MacFarquhar and Schoenhals, *Mao's Last Revolution*, 325–26; and Frederick Teiwes with Warren Sun, *The End of the Maoist Era: Chinese Politics During the Twilight of the Cultural Revolution, 1972–1976* (Armonk, NY: M. E. Sharpe, 2007), 31–35.
39 This fourth period is described in Walder, *China Under Mao*, 287–314.

factional rivalries of the 1967 and 1968. These conflicts reached a climax in 1974, when resurgent rebels again mobilized and threatened public order in ways reminiscent of the earlier period.[40]

Mao, rapidly aging and beset by illness, was of two minds about these developments. He wanted order and discipline to consolidate what he saw as the positive accomplishments of the Cultural Revolution, but he did not want a restoration of the policies and institutions of the status quo ante. Mao shifted his support from one side to the other, trying to reach a balance between these two objectives. Zhou Enlai, suspected of leaning too far toward restoration, was sidelined at the end of 1973, and Deng Xiaoping also lost favor in early 1976 after even more vigorous moves to suppress resurgent rebels and rebuild China's educational and scientific capacities.

Mao, however, did not anticipate a new development during this period – increasingly vocal public hostility to a continuation of Cultural Revolution policies and to the civilian radicals upon whom Mao relied. In the spring of 1976, this led to public demonstrations against the radicals, expressed as public commemoration of Zhou Enlai, who had died in January 1976. In early April of that year massive demonstrations of support for Zhou turned into outspoken denunciations of Politburo radicals, and indirectly of Mao himself, first in Nanjing and then on Tiananmen Square in Beijing. In reaction, Mao removed Deng Xiaoping from his posts for the second time and elevated the relatively young centrist official Hua Guofeng, previously the minister of public security, to the top post.[41] Mao intended Hua to mediate between rival wings in the Politburo but, less than one month after Mao's death in early September 1976, Hua conspired with veteran cadres to arrest the Politburo radicals and denounce them as a "Gang of Four." This marked the end of the Cultural Revolution, leading eventually to political liberalization and a radical shift in economic policy after the return of Deng Xiaoping to power in 1979.

---

40 See, for example, Dong Guoqiang and Andrew G. Walder, "Nanjing's 'Second Cultural Revolution' of 1974," *China Quarterly* 212 (Dec. 2012), 893–918. See also MacFarquhar and Schoenhals, *Mao's Last Revolution*, 358–73; and Teiwes and Sun, *The End of the Maoist Era*, 146–78.

41 See also Frederick Teiwes and Warren Sun, "The First Tiananmen Incident Revisited: Elite Politics and Crisis Management at the End of the Maoist Era," *Pacific Affairs* 77, 2 (Jun. 2004), 211–35; and Dong Guoqiang and Andrew G. Walder, "Foreshocks: Local Origins of Nanjing's Qingming Demonstrations of 1976," *China Quarterly* 220 (Dec. 2014), 1092–1110.

The Impacts of the Cultural Revolution

Although the ideological pedigree of the Cultural Revolution can be traced back the 1930s-era Stalinism, its manifestation in China has no clear parallels in the politics of any other communist regime. Party purges and campaigns against class enemies were common in a range of communist regimes, but none of them relied on the one truly distinctive political feature of the Cultural Revolution: the mobilization of citizens to form independent political organizations and attack the party hierarchy from without.

The Cultural Revolution had a devastating impact on China's economic development. Net per capita growth in the economy was below 2 percent for the decade after 1966. Chronic hunger remained a fact of life for almost one-quarter of China's farmers. The supply of consumer goods and urban housing had declined since the mid 1960s, and rationing was in force for a wide range of staple foods and other commodities. The damage to the economy was less dramatic than the Great Leap Forward but was more systemic and deeply rooted. The universities were in a shambles, and an entire generation of college graduates was missing. Scientific research and technological development had stagnated, falling farther behind other countries. The extreme isolation of China that began in 1966 – cutting China off not only from the West but also from the Soviet bloc – further intensified the damage to both the physical and human capital upon which economic development is based.[42]

The human costs of the Cultural Revolution were also severe. The number of "unnatural deaths" occasioned by the political events of the period range from 1.1 to 1.6 million. This is less than the estimated 2 million killed in Cambodia under Pol Pot, but considerably more than the estimated 400,000 to 800,000 who died in the Soviet purges of the late 1930s. Most of the deaths – well over half – occurred during the period of military control. In evaluating these numbers, it is useful to keep in mind China's total population. On a per capita basis, the death rates during the Cultural Revolution were only a small fraction of those observed in the Soviet Union under Stalin and in a wide range of other notorious cases. What is most distinctive about the human costs of the Cultural Revolution are the extremely large numbers of those who were persecuted in some way – expelled from their jobs, demoted, driven into rural exile, humiliated and beaten in public denunciation meetings, or accused of imaginary political

---

42 A more detailed assessment is in Walder, *China Under Mao*, 220–33.

crimes. An estimated 26 to 30 million individuals were directly victimized in this fashion – some 4 to 5 percent of the total population. What is striking about this number – and a major contrast with purges in the Soviet Union or Cambodia – is the very large percentage of political victims who survived. With 26–30 million accused of political crimes, and 1.1–1.6 million resulting deaths, well over 90 percent of political victims survived. The Cultural Revolution brutalized its victims, but it did not kill them with the efficiency so evident in Stalin's Soviet Union or Pol Pot's Cambodia.[43]

The long-term impact of the Cultural Revolution is somewhat paradoxical. Launched as an effort to stem revisionism and avert the restoration of capitalism, it arguably created conditions that facilitated a shift to a capitalist economy and the survival of communist party rule. It devastated the party organization and bureaucracy that in other socialist states had vested interests that were threatened by market reform along with a strong capacity to undermine reform initiatives. At the time of Mao's death these organizations were still recovering. This put China on a historical path utterly different from the Soviet Union – the rebuilding of the party and state occurred alongside the shift to a market economy. The Cultural Revolution also promoted the authority of a senior leader – Deng Xiaoping – as someone who tried to rescue China from Maoist radicalism during Mao's final years. The historical circumstances facing Deng Xiaoping were therefore much more favorable than those facing Mikhail Gorbachev in the late 1980s – a leader only recently elevated to national leadership and who faced a powerful bureaucracy and conservative party with enormous vested interests and the ability to defend them. In this sense, the Cultural Revolution not only failed to achieve its ostensible objectives, but it inadvertently facilitated China's post-Mao attempt to forge a completely new path out of twentieth-century communism.

Bibliographical Essay

Prior to the 1990s publications on the Cultural Revolution relied heavily on émigré interviews in Hong Kong, scattered copies of student and worker handbills and newspapers, national newspapers and other official publications, and a great deal of supposition. In the post-Mao era much larger

---

43 This paragraph draws on Andrew G. Walder, "Rebellion and Repression in China, 1966–1971," *Social Science History* 38, 3–4 (Fall–Winter 2014), 513–39.

volumes of unofficial publications and inner-party documents found their way abroad, even though the national and regional archives remained inaccessible to all but the most trusted party historians. In the 1980s many individuals published memoirs of their experiences in China, shedding new light on personal experiences. Notable examples in English include Rae Yang's *Spider Eaters: A Memoir* (Berkeley: University of California Press, 1997), by a high school student in Beijing subsequently sent to the country-side, and Gao Yuan's *Born Red: A Chronicle of the Cultural Revolution* (Stanford: Stanford University Press, 1987), by a Red Guard in a provincial high school. Yue Daiyun's *To the Storm: The Odyssey of a Revolutionary Chinese Woman* (with Carolyn Wakeman; Berkeley and Los Angeles: University of California Press, 1985) chronicles the decade from the perspective of a faculty member at Peking University. One of the first studies to draw extensively on materials in municipal archives was Elizabeth Perry and Li Xun, *Proletarian Power: Shanghai in the Cultural Revolution* (Boulder: Westview, 1997). The currently definitive account of national politics during the entire decade, drawing deeply on the full range of new documentation that became available in the post-Mao era, is Roderick MacFarquhar and Michael Schoenhals, *Mao's Last Revolution* (Cambridge, MA: Harvard University Press, 2006). Andrew Walder's *Fractured Rebellion: The Beijing Red Guard Movement* (Cambridge, MA: Harvard University Press, 2009), chronicles the influential Red Guard movement in the nation's capital, drawing extensively on large runs of newspapers and handbills produced by students across a range of universities. Chinese historians have also made notable contributions. Two recent examples are Bu Weihua, *Zalan jiu shijie: Wenhua da geming de dongluan yu haojie (1966–1968)* [Smashing the Old World: The Chaos and Catastrophe of the Cultural Revolution (1966–1968)] (Hong Kong: Chinese University of Hong Kong Press, 2008), and Li Xun's monumental study of Shanghai, *Geming zaofan niandai* [Decade of Revolutionary Rebellion], 2 vols. (Hong Kong: Oxford University Press, 2015). A condensed overview and narrative of the Cultural Revolution can be found in chapters 10 to 13 of Andrew Walder, *China Under Mao: A Revolution Derailed* (Cambridge, MA: Harvard University Press, 2015), which also covers the earlier years of the People's Republic as a prelude to this final decade of Mao's life.

10

The Rise and the Fall of the Sino-Soviet Alliance 1949–1989

SERGEY RADCHENKO

On 14 February 1950, the Soviet foreign minister Andrei Vyshinskii and the Chinese prime minister Zhou Enlai signed a thirty-year Treaty of Friendship, Alliance and Mutual Aid, as Joseph Stalin and Mao Zedong looked on. The pact, negotiated in Moscow over the previous two months, marked one of the turning points in the history of the twentieth century, a geopolitical earthquake of the highest magnitude. The Sino-Soviet alliance helped shape the Cold War in Asia: It led to the Korean War; it energized revolutionary wars in Southeast Asia; it spurred US efforts to support its Asian allies through increased economic and military commitments. Many of the faultlines set in place by the Sino-Soviet alliance in fact outlived the alliance itself, while some (for instance, the division of Korea) are still in place. But the partnership between Moscow and Beijing was more than just a fact of geopolitics. It created space for an unprecedented transfer of technologies, for transplanting concepts and models from the Soviet Union to China. It interlinked the two countries' domestic politics. It also infused the entire global communist project with a deep degree of legitimacy. The alliance of the first socialist country, the Soviet Union, with the world's most populous country, China, not only significantly strengthened the socialist camp but also highlighted prospects for further revolutions elsewhere in the Third World. Communism was no longer just a Russian aberration: It was proven to have a truly global reach.

But soon Sino-Soviet relations soured. By the early 1960s, China and the Soviet Union were openly accusing each other of betraying socialism. They were also engaged in an increasingly bitter global competition for influence. Just as the rise of the alliance legitimized the global communist project, its demise undermined this project by destroying the political and ideological unity of the international communist movement and by setting the socialist camp against itself. This chapter explores the reasons for this failure. It argues that there was nothing preordained about the split. There were many points of attraction in the Sino-Soviet relationship, even as there were also tensions present from the very beginning. The chapter shows why and how these tensions built up to the point of spinning out of control. In the process, it looks at the politics of leadership and recognition, at the interplay between ideology and national interests and at the relationship between domestic politics and foreign policies of China and the Soviet Union.

The Origins of the Sino-Soviet Alliance 1945–1953

The establishment of the Sino-Soviet alliance in February 1950 was unexpected even for those directly involved. The alliance followed the Chinese Communist Party (CCP) victory in the civil war against the Guomindang, a victory that was as swift as it was unanticipated. Who could have thought that the communists – an ill-equipped force of peasant guerrillas holed up in the remote reaches of China's north and northwest – would deliver a crushing blow to the Chinese national government headed by Generalissimo Chiang Kai-shek, who not only reigned supreme in China but also enjoyed international recognition as the legitimate leader of the Chinese state? In 1945 Stalin advised Mao Zedong to come to a peaceful accommodation with Chiang, as a junior partner in a Guomindang-led coalition government. Stalin misread the situation and underestimated Mao. Here he was, in Moscow, a guerrilla revolutionary turned most important Soviet ally. "Victors shall not be judged," Stalin grudgingly acknowledged. "Victors are always right."[1]

In 1945 it was Stalin who was counting the blessings of victory. At the Yalta conference in February he had promised President Franklin D. Roosevelt of the United States that the Soviet Union would join the war against Japan. The grateful Roosevelt agreed to Stalin's demands, including a lease of the Chinese port of Lüshun on the tip of the strategically situated Liaodong peninsula, joint Sino-Soviet operation of the Chinese Eastern (trans-Manchurian) railway and the vaguely defined "status quo" for Outer Mongolia, which on later examination turned out to be Stalin's euphemism for Mongolian independence from China. Chiang Kai-shek, who was presented with a *fait accompli*, could do little but seek an

---

1 Liu Shaoqi's report on a conversation with Stalin, 27 Jul. 1949, in Zhonggong zhongyang wenxian yanjiushi (ed.), *Jianguo yilai Liu Shaoqi wengao*[Liu Shaoqi's Manuscripts Since the PRC's Formation], vol. I (Beijing: Zhongyang wenxian chubanshe, 2005), 41.

agreement with Stalin that would rubberstamp these Soviet gains. Chiang entrusted the task to his brother-in-law T. V. Soong. The rancorous affair played out in Moscow in July–August 1945, with Soong making the most of the concessions. On 14 August 1945, the Chinese and the Soviet governments signed a treaty of alliance.

Now that his gains in East Asia were recognized by the United States and guaranteed through a legal agreement with Chiang, Stalin rested on his laurels. The Soviet Union became a status quo power. Until then Stalin had been more or less actively involved in subverting Chiang's rule in parts of northern and northwestern China, backing Xinjiang's Uighurs and Kazakhs in an anti-Chinese insurgency and tacitly encouraging secessionist sentiments among the Mongol-speaking tribes of Inner Mongolia. But the new Sino-Soviet treaty prompted a rethink. The Soviets now curbed support for secessionist movements and endorsed China's national unity, a grave disappointment for Stalin's clients in Xinjiang and Mongolia. As Stalin explained in February 1946 to the downhearted Mongolian leader Khorloogiin Choibalsan, sponsorship of breakaway states at China's expense "would require a new war with China. Do we need it now?!"[2] In China, as elsewhere, Stalin favored great-power accommodation. He had no qualms about disregarding someone else's liberation struggle to protect and advance the Soviet Union's security interests.

Stalin's approach to the CCP followed the same logic, though there was a nuance. The Chinese communists were not driven by ethnic grievances and did not want to secede from China. They were committed revolutionaries, seeking China's socialist transformation. Many of the leading communist cadres strategizing at Mao's headquarters in Yan'an (in the Chinese northwest) had spent years in training in Moscow. From its establishment in 1921, the Chinese Communist Party was closely linked with Soviet Russia through the Communist International (Comintern) and followed Soviet-prescribed revolutionary strategies, occasionally with disastrous results. Mao Zedong had not always seen eye to eye with Stalin and resented the Comintern's interference. Stalin, too, had certain doubts about how "communist" the Chinese communists really were, privately calling Mao, with a degree of derision, a "cave Marxist" (Mao, like many other CCP cadres, spent the war in caves dug in the loess hillsides of

---

2 Conversation between Joseph Stalin and Khorloogiin Choibalsan, 22 Feb. 1946, in Rossiiskii gosudarstvennyi arkhiv sotsial'no-politicheskoi istorii (RGASPI), f. 558, op. 11, d. 352, l. 88.

Yan'an).[3] "Mao Zedong is a peculiar kind of a person and a peculiar kind of a communist," Stalin observed in early 1946 – he did not mean it as a compliment.[4] Even so, Mao was more than just another warlord. He – and the Chinese communists – were ideological allies who believed themselves to be a part of the international communist movement and looked to Moscow for guidance and support.

The 1945 treaty committed Stalin to supporting Chiang Kai-shek as the Chinese leader. Accordingly, in late August the Soviet leader cabled Mao Zedong to proceed to the wartime Chinese capital of Chongqing for peace talks with Chiang. Mao complied: He had little choice in the matter. In later years he blamed Stalin for a lack of faith in the Chinese Revolution. He was right in the sense that Stalin did not think the communists would have a chance in a civil war, should one break out. And if one did break out, would it not endanger Soviet gains in China? The Soviet leader would rather not have put this possibility to the test. Still, he never fully reneged on his support for the CCP. Stalin was a master of playing both sides of the game.

Soviet support for the CCP manifested itself in the double-handed policy Stalin pursued in Manchuria, following Soviet military occupation of the region in August 1945. On the one hand, by agreement with Chiang, he promised to surrender the region to the Guomindang as the Soviet forces withdrew. On several occasions in the fall of 1945 Soviet military authorities barred the communists from acquiring footholds in major cities. On the other hand, the Soviets obstructed Chiang Kai-shek's efforts to land forces on the Liaodong peninsula, which would have immeasurably eased the Guomindang's takeover of Manchuria. Stalin was concerned that, with the Soviet armies withdrawn, he would have a much more difficult time looking after his assets in the Chinese northeast. He was particularly worried that Chiang Kai-shek would open Manchuria to a US military presence. "This is a Soviet zone," Stalin warned Chiang's son Chiang Chingkuo in December 1945. "American, British or any other foreign troops should not be allowed in Manchuria."[5] In the meantime, the Soviet military command generally tolerated the communists' quiet expansion in the countryside, vindicating their hopes that, even if the

---

3 N. S. Khrushchev, *Vremia, liudi, vlast'* (Moscow: Moskovskie novosti, 1999), 652.
4 Conversation between Joseph Stalin and Chiang Chingkuo, 3 Jan. 1946, in A. M. Ledovskii, R. A. Mirovitskaia and V. S. Miasnikov (eds.), *Sovetsko-kitaiskie otnosheniia*, vol. IV, book 2 (Moscow: Pamiatniki istoricheskoi mysli, 2000), 554.
5 Conversation between Joseph Stalin and Chiang Chingkuo, 30 Dec. 1945, ibid., 338.

Soviets could not be counted on to provide outright support, they would still treat the CCP forces with "great sympathy."[6]

The CCP's Manchurian gambit proved crucial to their victory in the civil war. But even when the tides of war changed in the communists' favor (from mid 1947), Stalin remained circumspect. He rebuffed Mao's requests for an early meeting in Moscow, refusing to commit himself fully to the CCP's cause. As much as he resented Stalin's duplicity, Mao continued to defer to the Soviet leader, calling himself Stalin's pupil and seeking his views on the trajectory of the Chinese Revolution.[7] In June 1949 he proclaimed that henceforth communist China would "lean to one side" – the Soviet side. The same month Mao sent his second-in-command Liu Shaoqi to Moscow with a special report for Stalin, which stressed that as the Communist Party of the Soviet Union was the "main headquarters of the international communist movement," the CCP would "subordinate" itself to Soviet decisions, even when it disagreed with them.[8] Mao wanted to dispel Stalin's doubts about the character of the Chinese Revolution. This was especially important after Stalin's quarrel with the Yugoslav leader Josip Broz Tito, who had refused to toe Moscow's line. With Mao on the verge of victory in China, how would Stalin see the future of his relationship with the "cave Marxist," soon to be ruler of the world's most populous nation? Years later Mao still joked that Stalin held him to be "half Tito."[9]

In December 1949 Mao and Stalin met at last. Mao's two-month sojourn in Moscow was far from pleasant. Stalin at first refused to give up on his 1945 treaty with China, citing the Yalta decisions. Did Stalin fear losing his hard-won privileges in China? Did he fear American intervention? Or perhaps he felt that violating the Yalta framework would delegitimize Soviet gains elsewhere in Europe and Asia? Even more surprisingly, Stalin eventually changed his mind, endorsing a new treaty. We may never know why. Mao had his own theory. Stalin, he thought, was concerned that unless he came around to embrace communist China as an ally, Mao could go it alone by

---

6 CC CCP Instruction, "On Quickly Entering the Northeast and Controlling the Wide Countryside and Small and Medium-Sized Cities," 29 Aug. 1945, in Zhongyang dang'anguan (ed.), *Zhonggong zhongyang wenjian xuanji* [Selected Documents of the CCP Central Committee], vol. XV (1945) (Beijing: Zhonggong zhongyang dangxiao chubanshe, 1991), 257.

7 See, for example, conversation between Anastas Mikoian and Mao Zedong, 30 Jan. 1949, in A. M. Ledovskii, R. A. Mirovitskaia and V. S. Miasnikov, *Sovetsko-kitaiskie otnosheniia*, vol. V, book 2, *1946–February 1950* (Moscow: Pamiatniki istoricheskoi mysli, 2005), 33–37.

8 Liu Shaoqi's report to Joseph Stalin, 4 Jul. 1949, RGASPI, f. 558, op. 11, d. 328, l. 50.

9 Conversation between Pavel Yudin and Mao Zedong, 31 Mar. 1956, in Rossiiskii gosudarstvennyi arkhiv noveishei istorii (RGANI), f. 5, op. 30, d. 163, l. 92.

obtaining Western (especially, American) recognition – perhaps even American aid.[10] True, there was no prospect of American recognition of the People's Republic of China (PRC) in 1950. Also – as scholars generally agree – Mao had no intention of engaging with the West because, true to his ideological proclivities, he wanted to "clean the house before entertaining guests," that is to say, purge China of Western influence in order to pursue the communist revolution.[11] But Stalin did not know that. By locking China in an alliance relationship, he could ensure that he would not lose Mao to American scheming.

Even as the signing of the treaty signaled a new stage in the Sino-Soviet relationship, Stalin was unable to reconcile his ideological commitments and his imperial impulses. He managed to impose quasi-imperialist conditions on his new ally, including joint-stock enterprises, joint ownership of the Chinese Eastern railway and, most unpleasantly from Beijing's perspective, a secret deal to keep Manchuria and Xinjiang closed to foreigners (other than the Soviets). Stalin even managed to keep the Soviet naval base at Lüshun, even though he had himself earlier labeled the agreement "unequal."[12] True, the terms of the lease were altered – the Soviets were supposed to withdraw by the end of 1952 at the latest. But it was not until after Stalin's death that the Soviet military presence was wound down and China's sovereignty in the port fully restored. The first (and only) Mao–Stalin summit thus attained mixed results. On the one hand, Mao obtained much of what he wanted – political legitimacy, military guarantees and economic aid. These were very important for his fledgling regime. On the other hand, Stalin managed to preserve and even expand his quasi-imperialist prerogatives at China's expense, giving Mao cause to complain years later that Stalin had made him "swallow bitter fruits" in Moscow.[13] By failing to control his appetites, Stalin thus inadvertently sowed seeds that yielded a poisonous harvest down road, when the Chinese accused their erstwhile "elder brothers" of social imperialism.

Even as Stalin and Mao negotiated their relationship in Moscow, the Soviet leader made an important decision that had a lasting impact on global politics and, specifically, on the course of the Cold War in Asia.

10 Ibid., l. 93.
11 See discussion in Chen Jian, *Mao's China and the Cold War* (Chapel Hill: University of North Carolina Press, 2001), 40, 44.
12 Conversation between Anastas Mikoian and Mao Zedong, 6 Feb. 1949, in *Sovetsko-kitaiskie otnosheniia*, vol. V, book 2, 82.
13 Conversation between Andrei Gromyko and Mao Zedong, 19 Nov. 1957, Arkhiv vneshnei politiki Rossiiskoi federatsii (AVPRF), f. 0100, op. 50a, pap. 423, d. 1, l. 15.

On 30 January 1950 he, for the first time, responded positively to North Korea's leader Kim Il Sung's request to attack South Korea.[14] Kim had been asking Stalin for months but the cautious Soviet leader rebuffed his pleas. Now he changed his mind. Was there a link between this decision and the emerging Sino-Soviet alliance? It could be, for instance, that Stalin, aware of having to give up on the strategic base of Lüshun down the road, eyed similar bases in South Korea.[15] It could be that he counted on the Chinese to help the North Koreans if it came to the worst and the United States intervened. More likely, he believed that Washington would not intervene in China or in Korea. Emboldened by the geopolitical advantages conferred by the Sino-Soviet alliance and (after August 1949) boasting a rudimentary nuclear deterrent, Stalin played it tough. He miscalculated: Kim Il Sung's invasion of South Korea on 25 June 1950 triggered US intervention, leading to a protracted, bloody conflict that ended inconclusively in 1953.

When in the fall of 1950 Kim Il Sung's armies tottered on the brink of defeat, China joined the fighting in Korea by sending hundreds of thousands of "people's volunteers" across the Yalu River. Mao overruled his skeptical colleagues. Perhaps he was concerned about China's security as US-led forces edged toward the Sino-Korean border or felt that it was his revolutionary duty to help a "fraternal" communist regime. Perhaps, too, he wanted to prove to Stalin that he could be relied upon, that he was not another Tito. As with Stalin, historians remain at odds over interpretations of Mao's decisions. Regardless, China's participation in the Korean War was the first serious test of the Sino-Soviet alliance. Beijing and Moscow closely coordinated their military and political activities, emerging from the war as real comrades-in-arms. In relative terms, Mao's stock in the alliance improved dramatically. By fighting on the front lines of the war against "imperialism," the Chinese raised their standing in the socialist camp, proving their worth as an ally and acquiring moral capital to address the Soviets on equal terms. After all, it was the Chinese who did most of the fighting in Korea, shedding rivers of blood in the name of a common communist cause. The Korean War thus marked the beginning of the golden age of the Sino-Soviet alliance.

---

14 Cipher from Joseph Stalin to Terentii Shtykov, 30 Jan. 1950, AVPRF, f. 059a, op. 5a, d. 3, pap. 11, l. 92.
15 For exposition of this argument, see Shen Zhihua, *Mao, Stalin, and the Korean War: Trilateral Communist Relations in the 1950s*, trans. Neil Silver (London: Routledge, 2012), 6.

The Golden Age 1954–1957

Stalin died on 5 March 1953. His successor, the relatively unknown Nikita Khrushchev, set out to rid the Sino-Soviet relationship of the unpleasant Stalinist legacies. He abandoned Stalin's special privileges in China, gave up the Soviet stake in joint-stock enterprises and withdrew Soviet forces from Lüshun. Eager to court favor with Mao, whose support was important for Khrushchev's legitimacy, both internationally and in domestic power struggles, the new Soviet leader extended generous economic aid to China, including a new credit of 520 million rubles for purchase of industrial equipment. Soviet specialists were dispatched to China in their thousands, working at factories and in the ministries and advising on cultural and educational matters. Soviet universities and research institutes opened their doors to Chinese students and scientists pursuing a variety of technical subjects, including in sensitive areas such as nuclear physics. For example, in 1956 – arguably the peak of the Sino-Soviet alliance – China sent 1,349 undergraduates, 520 postgraduates and 300 teachers to the USSR for study and training.[16] The same year China became a founding member in the Joint Institute for Nuclear Research in Dubna, a Soviet counterpart to Dwight Eisenhower's "Atoms for Peace" program. The following year Khrushchev, in a sign of his confidence in China – and perhaps also as a quid pro quo for Mao's continued support for the Soviet leader in his internal power struggles – agreed to a secret deal to give China a prototype nuclear bomb. What could be a better proof of the closeness of the Sino-Soviet relationship?

China and the Soviet Union also stood shoulder to shoulder in questions of global politics. In 1949 Stalin offered Mao a division of labor: The Soviet Union would look after Europe (and the world, broadly speaking); the Chinese would develop ties with Asian communist parties, specifically, the Koreans and the Japanese.[17] To this end, Stalin proposed to set up an Asian Cominform, modeled on the Soviet-sponsored Cominform, the successor to the Communist International, which worked to align member states' policies with Stalin's priorities. The Asian Cominform never took shape, and in 1956 Khrushchev, in another jab at Stalinism, disbanded the Soviet-led Cominform as well. But a kind of a division of labor did develop between China and the

---

16 T. Yu. Krasovitskaia (ed.), *Vozvratit' domoi druz'iami SSSR. Obuchenie inostrantsev v Sovetskom soiuze, 1956–1965* (Moscow: Mezhdunarodnyi fond demokratiia, 2013), 23.

17 Shen Zhihua and Xia Yafeng, "Leadership Transfer in the Asian Revolution: Mao Zedong and the Asian Cominform," *Journal of Cold War Studies* 14, 2 (May 2014), 195–213.

USSR, with the Chinese taking the lead in advancing the cause of socialism in Southeast Asia and elsewhere in what became known, in the 1950s, as the "Third World." Describing imperialism as a "lion," Mao said in 1949 that, even as the Soviets were holding down the lion's head, "we, the Chinese communists, pinched the lion's tail and are trying to cut it off. We suppose that the cutting of the tail will in turn weaken the power of the imperialists, concentrated in the head of the lion."[18] The Soviets and the Chinese worked closely during the 1954 Geneva talks to end hostilities in Korea and Vietnam, in the latter case bringing pressure to bear on the reluctant North Vietnamese to agree to the division of the country. The Soviets often deferred to Chinese expertise, especially in relation to Southeast Asia.

The big question about Sino-Soviet cooperation in the Third World is when it stopped being cooperation, becoming instead competition for influence. This question goes to the heart of the debate about the nature of the Sino-Soviet relationship, and the causes of the Sino-Soviet split. One approach is to see Mao's engagement with countries such as India, Burma and Indonesia as an effort to redefine the Cold War in Sinocentric terms. Mao, the argument goes, perceived the main global contradiction of his day to be that between imperialism, headed by the United States, and the struggling, poor, underdeveloped nations of the postcolonial world. China's revolutionary experience and anti-imperialist rhetoric struck a relevant tone with the fledging states of Asia and Africa, which formed the major part of what Mao called the "intermediate zone" between the capitalist and socialist worlds. It is possible to interpret Mao's engagement with these countries not as some kind of auxiliary operation to cut off the lion's tail but, by contrast, as an effort to put China in the front and center of the global revolutionary struggle. That is to say, even as Mao coordinated China's approach to the Third World with the Soviet leadership, there was also an element of competition or even an implicit struggle for leadership between Moscow and Beijing. Taking this line of argument would lead to the conclusion that, even at the height of its glory, the Sino-Soviet alliance was riven by internal contradictions over leadership that would eventually drive the two countries apart.

Such an explanation is unduly simplistic, however. Mao did see himself as more of an expert than Khrushchev on the question of Third World revolutions. But projecting their disagreements back to the mid 1950s would

18 Cable from Ivan Kovalev to Joseph Stalin, 17 May 1949, in *Sovetsko-kitaiskie otnosheniia*, vol. V, book 2, 130.

understate the degree of policy coordination between Moscow and Beijing. Mao fully realized that, even as the Chinese Revolution was objectively more relevant to the needs of much of the postcolonial world, it was the Soviets who had the ability to extend economic aid, provide sophisticated weaponry and challenge Western preponderance in far-flung theaters around the world. Mao saw himself as something of a strategic thinker, the philosopher of the socialist camp, directing Soviet policies with insight and experience that Khrushchev could never hope to muster. (There is a remarkable parallel here with the British policymakers who, in the early postwar years, credited themselves with the ability, even the responsibility, to guide inexperienced Americans in opposing Stalin's ploys.) In his meetings with the leaders of the Third World in the mid 1950s, Mao often highlighted Soviet generosity and Soviet aid to China.[19] This was not some hideous hypocritical maneuver. Rather, Mao believed the two countries were engaged in a common revolutionary endeavor: building communism at home and supporting revolutionary struggles around the world.

Still, there was a qualitative change in Sino-Soviet relations. One could trace this change back to the Korean War, when China proved itself a match for the Americans on the battlefield and gained a degree of moral superiority over the Soviet Union, or to 1953, when, with Stalin's death, Mao Zedong assumed the mantle of the most senior revolutionary-philosopher of the socialist camp, towering over hapless Khrushchev. But it is more appropriate to take 1956 as the real turning point of the alliance. That year was important for a number of reasons. It is most prominently remembered as the year when Nikita Khrushchev unleashed de-Stalinization. In his "Secret Speech" to the Twentieth Party Congress, on 25 February, Khrushchev delivered a shocking indictment of the Soviet dictator's domestic and foreign policies and condemned Stalin's personality cult. The details of this Secret Speech were soon leaked to the outside world, causing shock and disillusionment in the international communist movement. Could it be that the Great Teacher Stalin was actually a murderous criminal who perverted communism, suppressed party democracy and substituted blind worship of himself for teachings of Marx and Lenin?

Mao, like many others, was taken by surprise by Khrushchev's speech. In many ways, the Soviet Union had been "de-Stalinizing" since 1953 but quietly, without the *Sturm und Drang* of Khrushchev's denunciation.

---

19 E.g. conversation between Mao Zedong and Jawaharlal Nehru, 26 Oct. 1954, in People's Republic of China Foreign Ministry Archives (PRCFMA), 204-000017-1.

Some historians have traced the Sino-Soviet split to Mao's disagreement with Khrushchev over Stalin's legacy. Drawing on Mao's subsequent complaints that Stalin had been a "sword" that Khrushchev had abandoned, leaving the socialist camp exposed to enemy attacks, these accounts stress the ideological sources of the Sino-Soviet quarrel. To be sure, Moscow and Beijing soon developed a range of ostensibly ideological disagreements, including different views on whether it was possible to avoid war (as Khrushchev thought) or that war was inevitable (Mao); whether communism could be achieved by parliamentary means (Khrushchev) or only by violent struggle (Mao); and whether class struggle was no longer necessary under socialism (Khrushchev) or still essential, even in communist states (Mao). Most of these ideological disagreements could be reduced to a basic disagreement about Stalin and his legacy. When Chinese propaganda accused Khrushchev of "revisionism," as it did with gusto in the early 1960s, it was building on the notion that Khrushchev had betrayed Stalin and so abandoned revolution.

But these ideological quarrels should not be taken at their face value or projected back to 1956 to claim that there was some kind of unbridgeable gap that emerged between China and the USSR because Khrushchev criticized Stalin. Mao did think that Khrushchev had committed a blunder by this sudden exposure but he also welcomed the Soviet leader's speech because, in Mao's words, it "removed the lid," allowing each communist party to act in accordance with its own needs and circumstances, freeing itself from imposed "superstitions." As Mao poetically explained at an extended Politburo meeting on 24 March 1956, Khrushchev had broken "the golden hoop."[20] He was referring to the golden hoop on the head of the Monkey King, the supernatural being who accompanied the monk Xuanzang in the classical Chinese novel *Journey to the West*. By a special spell, the monk tightened the golden hoop on Monkey's head at the slightest sign of disobedience, causing excruciating headaches. With the hoop removed at last, the Monkey King – that is, Mao – was free to strike out on his own path rather than blindly follow Soviet experience.

Mao held his own grudges against Stalin. He was not happy with the way Stalin had treated him in Moscow when he was there in 1949–50. He did not approve of Stalin's interference in CCP politics in the 1920s and the 1930s and accused the late dictator of lacking faith in the Chinese

20 Wu Lengxi, *Shinian lunzhan, 1956–1966: Zhong-Su guanxi huiyi lu* [Ten Years of Debate: Recollections from Sino-Soviet Relations], 2 vols. (Beijing: Zhongyang dangxiao chubanshe, 1999), vol. I, 15.

Revolution (which was all quite true). The bottom line for Mao was that there could not be equality for the two countries under Stalin. "At that time," Mao explained in 1957, "the words 'fraternal parties' were only a pretty phrase. Practically, Stalin was a father and the rest of us sons."[21] Now, Mao felt, the relationship had become more equal: China would have a greater voice in the alliance and in shaping the overall strategy of the socialist camp. Mao's efforts to arrive at a measured assessment of Stalin's legacy, his pronouncements on war, peace and revolution, were all in line with his post-1956 self-perception as the strategist-in-chief of the communist world. Mao's new confidence was on display in October 1956, when Khrushchev, faced with anti-Soviet uprisings in Poland and Hungary, asked the Chinese for advice. Mao identified the problem as a Soviet tendency toward great-power chauvinism and was unquestionably satisfied when on 30 October Khrushchev agreed to publish a declaration on sovereign equality of socialist states.[22] When a few days later the Soviets violated this declaration and invaded Hungary, Mao, again, was quite pleased, because in doing so they followed his advice to crush counterrevolution. Khrushchev, it seemed, was not beyond redemption.

In November 1957, Mao traveled to Moscow for a conference of the world's communist and workers' parties. The Chinese played the key role at the conference, which took place at a time of serious disarray in the international communist movement caused by the Soviet invasion of Hungary the previous year. Mao spent much of his time in the Soviet capital persuading delegations of other communist parties to back the Soviet Union as the leader of the socialist camp. "We are faced by the fairly strong imperialist camp," Mao declared on 14 November from the conference podium. "It has a head. If we are disunited, we are powerless." China, Mao continued, could not head the socialist camp, because it was economically backward, while the Soviets had just launched the first earth-orbiting satellite, Sputnik.[23] On 18 November Mao made one of the most famous speeches of his career, announcing that the East Wind was prevailing over the West

21 Conversation between Andrei Gromyko and Mao Zedong, 19 Nov. 1957, in AVPRF, f. 0100, op. 50a, pap. 423, d. 1, l. 18.
22 For the declaration, see Csaba Békés, Malcolm Byrne and János M. Rainer (eds.), *The 1956 Hungarian Revolution: A History in Documents* (Budapest: Central European University Press, 2002), 188–89.
23 Mao Zedong's comments during a conference session, 14 Nov. 1957, in N. G. Tomilina (ed.), *Nasledniki Kominterna: mezhdunarodnye soveshchaniya Predstavitelei kommunisticheskikh i rabochikh partii v Moskve (noiabr' 1957 g.)* (Moscow: ROSSPEN, 2013), 147.

Wind. He meant that the socialist camp was in the advantageous position. The West, by contrast, was in irreversible decline. Mao was thus effectively setting direction for the socialist camp. Even in recognizing the leadership of the Soviet Union, Mao was implicitly raising his own profile as the authority who could bestow such leadership on others. After advising Khrushchev during the Polish and Hungarian events, and now defending Khrushchev's position as the "head," Mao set himself up above Khrushchev as the ultimate arbiter of disputes of world communism. Ideological disagreements were decidedly secondary to these emerging relationships of authority.

Hidden Tensions

Soon thereafter Mao suffered the biggest setback since assuming power. In 1958 he announced a new stage of China's socialist construction, the Great Leap Forward. This campaign entailed breakneck industrial development and sweeping changes in agriculture, characterized by the creation of the infamous "people's communes." The first of these, suggestively called "the Sputnik commune," was established in Henan province in April 1958. The idea was that these rural organizations, complete with communal kitchens and nurseries that supposedly freed up peasant labor, would unleash the creative energies of the countryside and for the first time implement in practice the communist goal: "from each according to his ability, to each according to his needs." The establishment of communes, massive public works and, notoriously, production of steel in "backyard furnaces" signified to Mao that China was well on its way to overtaking the United States in economic terms, and jumping to communism ahead of the Soviet Union.[24] The utopian schemes of the Great Leap Forward were a practical test of China's ability to stand at the forefront of innovation in the socialist camp. This was a bid for China's leadership, and Mao's personal leadership. Mao, no longer content with the role of the chief communist strategist, eyed the mantle of the chief communist practitioner.

The results were disastrous. Low-quality steel produced in backyard furnaces proved useless. Many of the public works projects had to be abandoned. Most tragically, radical experiments in the countryside caused an unprecedented famine in China, resulting in the deaths of 30–45 million people. In 1959 Mao himself was criticized by his defense minister Peng

---

24 Publicly the Chinese leaders proclaimed the goal of overtaking the United Kingdom; however, privately, the United States was identified as the target.

Dehuai. Mao purged the challenger but, implicitly accepting some of the blame, stepped back from the "first line" of leadership, letting other CCP leaders, including his second-in-command Liu Shaoqi and eventual successor Deng Xiaoping, sort out the mess. For Mao this debacle meant a colossal loss of face, something that could perhaps be covered up in China but not internationally. In August 1958 Mao boasted to Khrushchev about China's exceptional pace of growth. "Amazing achievements," Khrushchev remarked, astounded.[25] But already in late 1958 the Soviet leader had publicly criticized people's communes as "reactionary." Later he commented, acidly: "[T]hey wanted to show us how to build communism. Well, all they got was a stink, nothing else."[26] The failure of the Great Leap Forward delivered a severe blow to China's international prestige and to Mao's self-perception as the leading theoretician and practitioner of the socialist camp.

Mao blamed the debacle on the lack of faith in the party ranks. There were people in authority, he concluded, who were dragging China back toward capitalism, the "capitalist-roaders." By early 1965 Mao identified the most important of these people – Liu Shaoqi and Deng Xiaoping. But this was just the tip of the iceberg. The problem went deeper. It was about bourgeois ideology and bourgeois culture. In 1966, to rid China of these poisonous influences, Mao plunged the country into the chaos of the Cultural Revolution. He imagined, too, that Chinese "revisionism" had allies abroad, among the Soviet leadership. Mao linked his domestic opponents with alleged Soviet sponsors: "They [the Soviets] colluded with the defense minister Peng Dehuai to topple the regime, but were unsuccessful. They had long been colluding with Liu Shaoqi, but were also unsuccessful," Mao later said.[27] What was this – just a convenient excuse for the purge or did the Chinese leader really believe in the international "revisionist" conspiracy? It is hard to say, but this linkage between the Soviets and Mao's domestic opponents is very important as it reveals another dimension of the Sino-Soviet relationship: its close connection to China's domestic political struggles. Weakened domestically and embarrassed on the global stage, Mao had to push back on both fronts. In this

---

25 Conversation between Mao Zedong and Nikita Khrushchev, 2 Aug. 1958. The author is grateful to Shen Zhihua for providing a copy of this document.
26 Nikita Khrushchev's closing remarks to the December (1963) CC CPSU Plenum, 13 Dec. 1963, in RGANI, f. 2, op. 1, d. 679, l. 131.
27 Conversation between Mao Zedong and S.R.D.B. Bandaranaike, 28 Jun. 1972, in Chinese Central Archive.

sense, one could argue that the failure of the Great Leap Forward led not only to the intensification of domestic class struggle, and ultimately to the Cultural Revolution, but also to international class struggle, i.e. the Sino-Soviet split.

But although Mao's domestic struggle against "revisionism" certainly played into worsening Sino-Soviet relations, it was neither the only reason for the split nor, perhaps, the most important. Problems were developing in other areas. Mao felt that his relationship with Khrushchev continued to fall short of the sort of equality he now had every right to expect. This was demonstrated particularly well in the Moscow–Beijing exchange in July–August 1958 concerning Soviet proposals to build a longwave radio station on the island of Hainan and the Sino-Soviet "joint fleet." The longwave radio station had been discussed since January 1958: It was needed to help the Soviets communicate with their blue-water fleet. Moscow insisted on joint ownership but Mao resisted. The "joint fleet" issue arose following the 28 June 1958 request to the Soviet leadership from Premier Zhou Enlai to help China in the construction of its navy.[28]

On learning of Soviet proposals, Mao was livid. In a conversation with Pavel Yudin on 22 July 1958 he accused the Soviets of trying to impose their control on China:

> You do not trust the Chinese, only the Russians. Russians are superior while the Chinese are inferior and careless. So you want a joint venture? Since you want a joint venture, let us discuss everything – army, navy, air force, industry, agriculture, culture and education. Is this okay? Maybe we should give you the entire Chinese coastline of over ten thousand kilometers, while we only keep a guerrilla army. You possess only a little nuclear power, yet you want to control [us].[29]

Informed of Mao's rage, Khrushchev flew to China for talks, part of which famously took place in the Zhongnanhai swimming pool.[30] Historians have argued that this was Mao's way of humiliating Khrushchev. After he heard

---

28 See detailed discussion in Shen Zhihua and Xia Yafeng, *Mao and the Sino-Soviet Partnership, 1945–1959: A New History* (Lanham, MD: Lexington Books, 2015), 308–21. For Khrushchev's denials, see "First Conversation Between Nikita Khrushchev and Mao Zedong," 31 Jul. 1958, digitalarchive.wilsoncenter.org/document/112080, trans. Vladislav Zubok, and Presidium CC CPSU meeting on 24 Jul. 1958, in A. A. Fursenko (ed.), *Prezidium TsK KPSS 1954–1964*, vol. I, *Chernovye protokol'nye zapisi zasedanii Stenogrammy* (Moscow: ROSSPEN, 2003), 326.
29 Cited in Shen Zhihua and Xia Yafeng, *Mao and the Sino-Soviet Partnership*, 314.
30 Only the second of the four Mao–Khrushchev conversations took place in the swimming pool. See Second Conversation between Mao Zedong and Nikita Khrushchev, 1 Aug. 1958, in Chinese Central Archives.

Khrushchev's explanations (the Soviet leader emphasized that he, unlike Stalin, was always against "concessions" in China), Mao declared that the "black clouds have dispersed."[31] But the whole affair left a sour taste both for Khrushchev (who later lamented that he underestimated Chinese nationalism) and for Mao, who continued to suspect the Soviets of imperialist impulses. With the outbreak of public polemics in the 1960s, these suspicions were articulated as Soviet "great-power chauvinism" and, somewhat later, as "social imperialism." Unlike accusations of "revisionism" and "betrayal of the revolution," the labels of Soviet chauvinism and imperialism were retained well into the 1980s, suggesting to many contemporary observers that the "real" reason for the Sino-Soviet split was some kind of deep divergence of national interests between the Soviet Union and China.

The difficulty with the "national interests" explanation is that it holds that China and the Soviet Union had primordial contradictions, that the Soviets were imperialist in their foreign-policy behavior, while the Chinese, in view of their previous experience with Western (including Russian) imperialism, were perennially sensitive to slight. Although the Soviets undoubtedly had quasi-imperialist proclivities (though much more so under Stalin than under Khrushchev), and although the Chinese were clearly sensitive, these generalizations explain very little about the rise and the fall of the alliance. Thus, in 1958–59, the fortunes of the Sino-Soviet relationship definitely took a turn for the worse. Khrushchev was no more imperialist during these years than he was before or after. Mao, though sensitive to slight, was more sensitive on account of the blow to his reputation as the informal leader of the socialist camp, and this had little to do with China's ancient grievances and everything to do with the disasters that had befallen the country in the Great Leap Forward.

One of the spheres where the personal rivalry between Khrushchev and Mao played out in the late 1950s was foreign policy. After claiming in 1957 that forces of socialism were winning worldwide, Mao decided to put some of his foreign-policy conceptions into practice, in part to prove to the socialist camp and the international communist movement that he was right in doubting the imperialists' capabilities and perhaps also to energize his radical domestic programs with robust, even reckless, moves on the global stage. On 23 August 1958 the People's Liberation Army (PLA) began bombarding Taiwan-held islands of Jinmen and Mazu in what at first seemed like preparation for an invasion of Taiwan. Yet it is unlikely that Mao contemplated

---

31 "First Conversation Between Khrushchev and Mao Zedong."

an invasion. All of his actions were in fact calibrated to avoid American retaliation, which would certainly come if the PLA launched a cross-Strait operation. One way of looking at the decision is to bring the domestic factor into play: This was Mao's way of whipping domestic revolutionary enthusiasm into line with the priorities of the Great Leap. Mao's own explanation centered on foreign policy: He wanted to pin down US forces in East Asia to help the Iraqi Revolution of 14 July 1958.[32] It is possible that the Chinese hoped to force Chiang Kai-shek off the islands; this would have bolstered Mao's position that playing it tough paid off.[33]

Khrushchev, who had not been consulted about the bombardment of the offshore islands, felt compelled to issue a statement of support for China. Privately, he was very worried. Mao had already established a reputation for himself as having a rather cavalier attitude toward war. At the November 1957 Moscow meeting, he claimed that it was fine even if half of the world population perished in a nuclear war as long as imperialism was defeated. Mao was, to use his own expression, "shooting empty cannons" but Khrushchev had no way of knowing whether the Chinese leader really meant what he said. On occasion Khrushchev, too, engaged in nuclear bluster and brinksmanship. He felt, though, that he always knew where to stop. But with Mao, who could tell? The Chinese attack on Jinmen and Mazu raised the prospect of a general war that would involve Moscow as well. Eager to avoid hostilities, Khrushchev offered to hold a multilateral summit in New Delhi, bringing together Mao, Khrushchev, Eisenhower, Nehru and several regional politicians.[34] By way of response, Mao assembled socialist ambassadors on 2 October to lecture them on how they (the Chinese) "should not allow them [the Americans] to escape … Maybe we can keep them [in Taiwan] for a longer time. And this can be the means of educating peoples of the entire world and also the entire Chinese people."[35] It was hard to know when Mao was serious and what he really intended. It was this sense of uncertainty about Mao's intentions that prompted Khrushchev in 1959 to scrap the agreement to provide China with a prototype nuclear device.

32 Wang Yan (ed.), *Peng Dehuai nianpu* [Chronological Biography of Peng Dehuai] (Beijing: Renmin chubanshe, 1998), 692.
33 This possibility is mentioned in Zhou Enlai's conversation with S. Antonov on 27 Sep. 1958, in RGANI, f. 5, op. 49, d. 131, ll. 255–263.
34 A. A. Fursenko (ed.), *Prezidium TsK KPSS 1954–1964*, vol. II, *Postanovleniia 1954–1958* (Moscow: ROSSPEN, 2006), 892.
35 Mao Zedong's Conversation with Ambassadors of Six Socialist Countries, 2 Oct. 1958, in RGANI, f. 5, op. 49, d. 131, l. 286.

Mao and Khrushchev had very different assessments of the risks of war. Both leaders were quite keen to avoid war but Mao was certain that in the final analysis the "imperialists" were more afraid of war than the socialist camp. Therefore, it was not only permissible but even necessary to take a tough line in foreign policy. This was hard to do if one was afraid of a nuclear conflict, so this fear had to be cast aside, even if in practice it was advisable to tread carefully. Mao called this "despising the enemy strategically while taking a full account of him tactically," a notion that he had formulated years earlier, in the course of the Chinese Civil War.[36] Khrushchev's frame of reference was different. He was the leader of a superpower; his finger was, figuratively speaking, on the nuclear button. Although the Soviet Union proclaimed in 1956 (in the words of its defense minister Georgii Zhukov) that the next war would of necessity see the use of nuclear missiles, and the Soviet military preparations contained detailed provisions to this effect, Khrushchev felt the risk of an all-out destructive war was simply too grave to be contemplated, which was why in 1956 he also proclaimed the policy of peaceful coexistence.[37] Mao, however, perceived this policy as a case of the Soviet Union ingratiating itself with the United States – indeed, colluding with the latter at China's expense. Mao was especially incensed when Khrushchev, visiting China in the fall of 1959, tried to mediate the release of American prisoners and advised the Chinese to "relax" things with Taiwan. Mao wanted no one, least of all Khrushchev, to place himself between Beijing and Washington.[38]

Khrushchev's 2 October 1959 conversation with the Chinese leaders became so heated that it degenerated into something of a shouting match. The worst quarreling occurred in the course of the discussion of the Sino-Indian conflict (in 1959 there were border clashes between China and India). Khrushchev accused the Chinese of spoiling relations with India, while the Chinese foreign minister Chen Yi announced that Moscow's actions – the USSR maintained strict neutrality in the conflict – were an example of time-serving. Outraged, Khrushchev shouted at Chen Yi not to "spit" at him: "You don't have enough spit!" Mao even had to mediate in a meeting that gives an impression of falling just short of a brawl.

36 For the earlier formulation, see Mao Zedong, "On Some Important Questions of the Party's Present Policy," 18 Jan. 1948, in Mao Zedong, *Selected Works*, vol. IV (Beijing: Foreign Languages Press, 1961), 181.

37 On Zhukov's statement, see *XX S"ezd Kommunisticheskoi partii Sovetskogo soiuza. Stenograficheskii otchet* (Moscow: Gospolitizdat, 1956), 480.

38 Conversation between Nikita Khrushchev and Mao Zedong, 2 Oct. 1959, digitalarchive .wilsoncenter.org/document/112088, trans. Vladislav Zubok.

The Sino-Soviet split – still mostly hidden from the public eye – had already become obvious to its immediate participants. There was no one overriding reason for this. The split was rather a combination of factors – some that had to do with China's domestic politics and with Mao's ideological proclivities, some with China's resentment of perceived Soviet "great-power chauvinism." The timing, though, was clearly related to Mao's failed bid for informal leadership in the socialist camp and the communist movement as a result of the disaster of the Great Leap Forward. Having lost face, and having been subjected to what he thought was Soviet "bullying," Mao fought back. He increasingly compared himself to the founders of Marxism: "In the beginning, Marx and Engels were alone. They were just two people, but with what speed their ideas spread!"[39] By 1962, having rebounded from the political malaise of the previous two to three years, Mao sought to prove himself right: not just domestically but also internationally. The Sino-Soviet split was about to take a whole new turn.

Toward an Open Conflict

The first half of the 1960s was characterized by fierce Sino-Soviet competition for influence in the socialist camp and in the Third World. Elements of this competition were already in place in the mid 1950s, but there was much more cooperation than conflict and Mao endorsed overall Soviet leadership. Now he openly challenged it. In Eastern Europe, the Chinese had only very modest success. The only country to follow Beijing's lead was Albania. In the late 1950s relations between the Soviet Union and Albania worsened sharply (in 1961 there was an actual rupture in diplomatic relations), and the Albanian leader Enver Hoxha turned to China for support, which Mao was keen to offer "because you [the Albanians] live under very difficult circumstances, and you fight in defense of Marxism–Leninism ... You did not fall under the strikes from the batons of others."[40] Romania also struck an independent line from Moscow, and Mao tried to exploit that. But the Romanians were more interested in raising their own profile by mediating the Sino-Soviet split than in following China's leadership. On the whole,

---

39 Conversation between Hysni Kapo and Mao Zedong, 29 Jun. 1962, in Central State Archive, Tirana, AQPPSh-MPKK-V.1962, L. 14, D. 7, obtained by Ana Lalaj, trans. for the Cold War International History Project by Enkel Daljani.
40 Ibid.

then, China's efforts to play on contradictions between Moscow and its satellites in Eastern Europe failed from the very start.

It was different in Africa, Asia and Latin America. Here, objectively, China's revolutionary leadership had greater appeal. Many of the former colonies were still embroiled in war and revolution, and for this reason did not buy into Nikita Khrushchev's peaceful coexistence. Some, such as North Vietnam and North Korea, were closely linked to China by revolutionary ties. The latter two supported China's criticism of Soviet "revisionism" (even though the Vietnamese, in particular, also tried to mediate in the split). The Sino-Soviet split played out in Cuba, especially after the October 1962 Cuban Missile Crisis when, in the face of US pressure, Khrushchev withdrew nuclear-tipped missiles from the island. The Cubans were outraged by what they perceived as Soviet betrayal, and the Chinese exploited the situation to the fullest, accusing Moscow of "capitulationism" in the face of enemy threats. Communist parties around the world had to make up their mind as to whom to follow: the Soviets or the Chinese. A few (most importantly, perhaps, the Indonesian Communist Party led by D. N. Aidit) sided with Mao. Most did not. But in many cases these debates were followed by organizational splits within communist parties, followed by the formation of radical Maoist factions. Some of the leaders of these factions continued to pay homage to Beijing even during the turbulent years of the Cultural Revolution, invariably receiving instructions from Chairman Mao on how to persevere in revolutionary exploits and win battles against "revisionism" and "imperialism."

Mao saw the underdeveloped world as the global equivalent of China's countryside. Just as the Chinese Communist Revolution succeeded in the countryside before "encircling" cities, so the world countryside would encircle the rich and powerful nations of the "First" and "Second" Worlds. Mao felt confident that the war in Vietnam, war and revolution in Africa, and growing unrest in Latin America (in particular, in Brazil) were precursors to global revolution. One of the most prominent themes of Chinese foreign policy was therefore support for the "Afro-Asian solidarity movement." China also made an effort to convene a second Bandung conference (building on its successful performance in 1955) with an eye to excluding Soviet participation. Moscow condemned these efforts as anti-Marxist and, in the sense that the Chinese emphasized solidarity of the "colored peoples," essentially racist. In the meantime, Khrushchev privately emphasized that the problem with Sino-Soviet relations was not that there were ideological disagreements between the two countries but that the Chinese wanted to "play first fiddle." "This is a question of nationalism, a question of egoism."[41]

Khrushchev fell from power in October 1964 for reasons unrelated to the Sino-Soviet conflict. The new Soviet leaders – General Secretary Leonid Brezhnev and Prime Minister Aleksei Kosygin – sought to mend fences with Beijing but met with a rebuff from Mao (in February 1965 Mao promised Kosygin that their struggle would continue for 10,000 years).[42] But the Soviets also had no intention of giving up on their own claim to the "first fiddle." It was even more important for Brezhnev and Kosygin than it had been for Khrushchev to be seen as supporting the revolutionary forces of the Third World, because they needed to establish their own legitimacy on the global stage. Khrushchev had already regained some of the lost ground with Cuba by offering Soviet aid. However Fidel Castro or Che Guevara felt about Soviet "revisionism," China simply could not replace Moscow's economic and military support. Brezhnev and Kosygin also increased Soviet support for the Vietnamese war. They were eager to rebuff Chinese allegations of having sold out an ally in need.

But what really tipped the scales in the Third World in favor of the Soviets was not so much the renewed Soviet assertiveness as the failure of the Chinese-supported revolutionary movements. The biggest setback for Beijing was the failure of the communist insurgency in Indonesia in the fall of 1965, followed by the destruction of the Indonesian Communist Party and the death of its leader Aidit. Even earlier, the spring 1964 military *coup d'état* in Brazil, followed by a rout of leftist forces, significantly reduced the prospects for a Chinese-style revolution. In 1965 Mao still harbored hopes that right-wing violence in Brazil would lead to a revolutionary situation there and encouraged the Maoist splinter faction of the Brazilian Communist Party to head to the countryside and organize peasants – but these hopes were never realized.[43] The Chinese encountered similar frustrations with their African clients. Already in 1965 Beijing began moving away from supporting radical forces in Africa, instead backing military regimes: not because they were revolutionary (many were in fact counterrevolutionary) but when they appeared anti-Soviet.[44] As Mao explained to the Congolese dictator

41 Fursenko, *Prezidium TsK KPSS*, vol. I, 720.
42 Conversation between Mao Zedong and Aleksei Kosygin, 11 Feb. 1965, in AAN, KC PZPR, XI A/10, 517, 524, obtained by Douglas Selvage, trans. Malgorzata Gnoinska.
43 Conversation between Mao Zedong and Carlos Nicolau Danielli, 20 Jul. 1965, in PRCFMA, 111–00637–01.
44 Odd Arne Westad, *Restless Empire: China and the World Since 1750* (New York: Basic Books, 2012), 352.

Mobutu Sese Seko when he met him in January 1973, "It's not that we don't want a revolution, but they [the Congolese revolutionaries] were a disappointment. What can I do if they can't defeat you?"[45] By the 1970s Beijing was backing anti-Soviet forces worldwide, even when doing so put the Chinese on the side of the vilest right-wing dictators. It made sense strategically. Ideologically, though, it was a jarring turnaround. The Chinese-style revolution in the Third World was dead.

One of the major developments that undercut China's position in the global Sino-Soviet competition for influence was the beginning of the Cultural Revolution. As chaos unfolded across China, Beijing withdrew all but one of its ambassadors stationed overseas for "reeducation." Remaining diplomats spent their time in criticism and self-criticism, and distributing Mao's *Little Red Book* to the local population in the face of often bitter opposition of the host countries' authorities. But Beijing's debacle was hardly Moscow's victory. Although by 1969 the Soviets were able to rally their supporters in the socialist camp to the anti-Chinese banner, the unity of the global communist movement never recovered. In the meantime, the legacies of the split in the form of increased Soviet involvement in the Third World proved to be a huge drain on the Soviet economy. It was not until the late 1980s that massive Soviet economic and military commitments to countries such as Vietnam, Cuba, Syria and North Korea were scaled down or abandoned altogether.

The Cultural Revolution took its toll on the Sino-Soviet relationship. The explicit link between Mao's struggle against domestic "revisionism" and its alleged Soviet sponsors fed unprecedented anti-Soviet feeling in China. In 1967 the Soviet embassy in Beijing came under attack, and the lynching of Soviet diplomats was only narrowly averted by Zhou Enlai's eleventh-hour intervention. The Soviet leaders, deeply confused by China's internal situation, came to see their neighbor as a security threat. Their response was to build up forces in the border area while also sending troops to Mongolia. Beijing in turn felt threatened by the Soviet buildup, all the more so after the August 1968 Soviet invasion of Czechoslovakia that proved that the Soviet "social imperialists," far from being a "paper tiger," could and did act decisively to defend their turf in Eastern Europe. If in Eastern Europe, why not also in China? Thus, by the late 1960s the Sino-Soviet relationship faced a classic security dilemma, which was only worsened when

---

45 Conversation between Mao Zedong and Mobutu Sese Seko, 13 Jan. 1973, in Chinese Central Archive.

in March 1969 the Chinese decided to fight a limited border engagement at Zhenbao/Damanskii, a minor islet on the Ussuri River that separated China's northeast from Russia's Far East. The Soviets retaliated and later hinted at a preemptive nuclear strike. Historians agree that Beijing's fear of Soviet invasion was the main reason why Mao Zedong decided to turn to the United States. The era of triangular diplomacy had begun.

Conclusion

By the end of 1969, the Chinese and the Soviets stepped away from the brink, though not very far. The relationship remained deeply antagonistic for more than a decade. It was only in the 1980s that Moscow and Beijing began to warm to each other. In 1989, thirty years after Khrushchev's passionate quarrel in Beijing, a Soviet general secretary at last returned to the Chinese capital. In his meeting with Mikhail Gorbachev (who was only in his late twenties when the Sino-Soviet alliance crashed), the elderly Chinese leader Deng Xiaoping promised to "close the past and open the future." This was an important milestone for Deng: He had been personally and very deeply involved in the polemics, in his time accusing the Soviets of all kinds of ideological sins. Deng thought differently now: "[W]e no longer think that everything we said at that time was right," he told Gorbachev, referring to the late 1950s–early 1960s. "The basic problem was that the Chinese were not treated as equals and felt humiliated."[46] The Soviet leader did not contradict Deng. Ever since relations with China had begun to improve, he had emphasized that there would be no return to the past, no relationship of "brothers" – just equality and mutual interest. "We have so many problems of our own, we would be mad to want a younger brother like China," he said later, explaining his logic.[47]

What, then, was the Sino-Soviet split really about? Historians will not cease debating this issue. There are several alternative explanations, ranging from China's domestic politics, to divergence over ideology, to the so-called clash of national interests. More nuanced explanations would also highlight cultural differences, historical grievances and, of course, the clash of personalities between Mao Zedong and Nikita Khrushchev. None of these explanations stands very well on its own. But they provide a useful set of lenses for understanding the complexities of this relationship. One thing that is quite

---

46 Deng Xiaoping, *Selected Works of Deng Xiaoping*, vol. III (Beijing: Foreign Languages Press, 1994), 287.
47 Author's interview with Mikhail Gorbachev, Moscow, 16 Dec. 2015.

clear about the Sino-Soviet relationship is that, much as with the general pattern of relations in the socialist camp, it required hierarchy and subordination, that is – an international form of what communist propaganda called "democratic centralism." In the late 1950s Mao Zedong challenged this hierarchy. Within a few years, the alliance was in tatters.

Historically, China was not the only country to have challenged the Soviets: At different times, the Yugoslavs, Albanians, Romanians, Poles, Hungarians, Czechoslovaks, Vietnamese, North Koreans – that is, practically all the socialist allies – questioned or defied Moscow's preponderance. Some got away with it, while others were crushed. By this measure, the split was by no means unique. Yet, there was also something particularly significant about the collapse of the Sino-Soviet alliance. This was not just an alliance of two countries; it was a crucial component of the socialist camp. This was not just another bilateral relationship; it was the driving force of the global communist project. The demise of the alliance therefore dealt a most severe blow to the legitimacy of the international communist movement and the socialist camp, a blow from which they never recovered. This implosion of the communist project drained the Cold War of much of its ideological content. By the mid 1970s China had abandoned its revolutionary agenda, prioritizing domestic development. The Soviet Union, saddled with increasingly expensive global commitments, struggled on for another decade before finally giving up. The end of the Cold War opened the way to the renewal of friendship between Moscow and Beijing, this time without the shackles of ideology that had once tightly bound the Sino-Soviet relationship and, by binding it, made it all the more fragile.

Bibliographical Essay

Few Cold War topics have received more generous scholarly attention than the Sino-Soviet relationship. There has been sustained interest in the subject since the early 1960s, when the split between Moscow and Beijing first became public knowledge. Among the early treatments were the classic studies by Donald Zagoria, *The Sino-Soviet Conflict, 1956–1961* (Princeton: Princeton University Press, 1962) and by John Gittings, *Survey of the Sino-Soviet Dispute* (London: Oxford University Press, 1968). The former sought the middle ground between the proponents of the "they are just faking it" school and the sober-minded camp that deemed the split as final and irreversible. The latter dissected the Sino-Soviet polemic under as good a microscope as Western Kremlinology could muster. The 1970s and the 1980s witnessed the rise of theoretical approaches to the troubled relationship. Partly because the deep hostility between two ostensibly communist powers offered such a useful case study for billiard-ball conceptions of international politics, realists of all stripes embraced the subject with gusto. Examples include Jonathan D. Pollack, *The Sino-Soviet Rivalry and Chinese Security Debate* (Santa Monica, CA: RAND, 1982), and Herbert J. Ellison, *The Sino-Soviet Conflict: A Global Perspective* (Seattle: University of Washington Press, 1982). Improvements in Sino-Russian relations in the 1990s prompted scholars to reassess previous approaches, with some – e.g. Elizabeth Wishnick, *Mending Fences: The Evolution of Moscow's China Policy from Brezhnev to Yeltsin* (Seattle: University of Washington Press, 2001) – striking a cautiously positive note, while others, such as Bobo Lo in his *Axis of Convenience: Moscow, Beijing, and the New Geopolitics* (Washington, DC: Brookings Institution Press, 2008), maintained a degree of skepticism about the relationship, which, in just half a century, went from unbreakable friendship, to primordial enmity, to friendship once again.

In the meantime, the study of Sino-Soviet relations – formerly the subject of diplomatic gossip and conferences of political scientists – was handed over to historians. Armed with newly released archival documentation, they scrutinized the story of the rise and fall of the alliance and came up with answers to please theorists of all persuasions. One of the earliest was the still relevant Odd Arne Westad (ed.), *Brothers in Arms: The Rise and Fall of the Sino-Soviet Alliance, 1945–1963* (Washington, DC, and Stanford: Woodrow Wilson Center Press and Stanford University Press, 1998), which, being an edited volume, offered a usefully multicausal explanation but specifically emphasized ideology as an important factor. Coming in the wake of many a realist study that perceived ideology as a cover-up for "real" national interests, *Brothers in Arms* represented an important new departure for Cold War historiography. By contrast, Dieter Heinzig's *The Soviet Union and Communist China 1945–1950: The Arduous Road to the Alliance* (Armonk, NY: M. E. Sharpe, 2004) erred on the side of geopolitics. Some of the same themes were picked up in Lorenz Luthi's seminal *Sino-Soviet Split: Cold War in the Communist World* (Princeton: Princeton University Press, 2008), which put great stress on ideological factors in the alliance and in Sergey Radchenko's *Two Suns in the Heavens: The Sino-Soviet Struggle for Supremacy, 1962–1967* (Washington, DC, and Stanford: Woodrow Wilson Center Press and Stanford University Press, 2009), which rehabilitated realist ideas about Sino-Soviet relations, diluting them in anecdotes about pride, arrogance and cultural prejudice. A similar approach was adopted also in Zhihua Shen and Yafeng Xia, *Mao and the Sino-Soviet Partnership, 1945–1959: A New History* (Lanham, MD: Lexington Books, 2015), a panoramic overview of the early years of the relationship, which highlights the struggle for leadership between Mao Zedong and Nikita Khrushchev.

Matters of culture and ideology were broached in Austin Jersild, *The Sino-Soviet Alliance: An International History* (Chapel Hill: University of North Carolina Press, 2014) – which looks at, among other things, the low politics of cultural, scientific and economic exchange between China and the USSR – and in Mingjiang Li, *Mao's China and the Sino-Soviet Split: Ideological Dilemma* (London: Routledge, 2012), which highlights the centrality of Chinese domestic politics in the Sino-Soviet relationship. Meanwhile, Jeremy Friedman opens new vistas to scholars of Sino-Soviet relations by exploring why and how Moscow and Beijing competed for influence in the Third World. His *Shadow Cold War: The Sino-Soviet Competition for the Third World* (Chapel Hill: University of North Carolina Press, 2015) highlights the divergence between Chinese and Soviet revolutionary experiences. Still, for all the new evidence that has come to light since the 1990s, scholars remain as deeply divided as they have ever been. Every new study tilts the pendulum of opinion this way or that; yet it seems to be destined to swing perpetually between fuzzy conceptions such as "national interests," "ideology," "culture," "equality" and "leadership," dismaying and delighting generations of historians who today know so much and yet so little about the inner dynamics of the love/hate relationship between Beijing and Moscow, which never fails to surprise.

11

Mao Zedong as a Historical Personality

DANIEL LEESE

In the aftermath of the "Great Leap Forward" in August 1961, realizing that his attempted industrial-agricultural transformation of the Chinese countryside had failed and resulted in the deaths of millions of peasants, Mao Zedong in a self-critical mood confided to his guard Zhang Xianpeng that he had three remaining aspirations. First, he wished to spend a year each working in industry and agriculture, as well as half a year in commerce, in order to get a better grasp of the situation and to set an example against bureaucratism for other party cadres. Second, in an outburst of romantic sentiment, he revealed that he would like to ride a horse along the banks of the Yellow River and the Yangzi with a geologist, a historian and a novelist, in order to conduct "on-the-spot investigations" to gain a better understanding of China's geological conditions, a field in which he found himself lacking knowledge. Yet the trip would not be conducted for scientific purposes only – hence the historian and the novelist. He wanted to learn more about how history had shaped and been shaped by the geographic environment and to compare it with his personal life experiences. The third and final aspiration was to transform the results of these investigations into a book that would include a biographical sketch of his life. While he had relayed a version of his remembrances to American journalist Edgar Snow back in Yan'an in 1936, these stopped short of his most crucial successes: the consolidation of power within the Chinese Communist Party (CCP), the victory against Chiang Kai-shek's troops during the Civil War and the founding of the People's Republic of China in 1949, along with the early stages of socialist transformation. While these achievements were to become part of his yet-to-be-written biography, the book was not to shy away from discussing his shortcomings: "Let the people of the whole world then decide whether I am a good or a bad person in the end. Me, I would be very satisfied if the good parts accounted for 70 percent and the bad parts for 30 percent. I do not conceal my own viewpoints; I am just this kind of person. I am not a saint."[1]

Shortly after Mao's death, his ultimate successor Deng Xiaoping would freely quote these considerations in May 1977, on the eve of his second return to power, as he battled with the alleged "two whatevers" faction that emphasized the eternal correctness of the deceased chairman's policy decisions and instructions: "Comrade Mao Zedong said that he himself had also committed errors ... He said: 'If someone can be assessed at a ratio of 70 percent achievements and 30 percent mistakes, this is very good already, not bad at all. If I were to be assessed 70/30 after my death, I would thus be very happy, very satisfied.'"[2] While the "70/30 assessment" never became part of an official party document, in public parlance it has come to stand for the official evaluation of Mao as a historical personality. By the time of his death in 1976, this type of schematic evaluation had become a well-established trope with regard to judging the performance of living or historical personalities as well as important political events. Mao himself had established the equation as a rule of thumb at the Second Plenum of the Seventh Party Congress in March 1949. He had repeated it multiple times, for example when referring to the achievements of Stalin in the wake of Nikita Khrushchev's Secret Speech (1956), when assessing Deng Xiaoping's past behavior (1973) and when commenting on the political achievements of his last political experiment, the Cultural Revolution (1975). The practice of official evaluation harked back to a tradition of two millennia of Chinese historical writing that had continuously passed moral judgement on historical personalities as a guide for future political action.

The following overview will place changing evaluations and self-perceptions of Mao Zedong in historical context by analyzing three topics. The first section, "Mao Zedong as History," highlights facets of his personality that had a lasting influence on political developments. The second, "Mao Zedong and History," traces Mao's policies against the background of his complex engagement with China's tradition and envisioned socialist modernity. The final section, "Mao Zedong in

---

1 Zhonggong zhongyang wenxian yanjiushi (ed.), *Mao Zedong nianpu 1949–1976* [Chronological Biography of Mao Zedong 1949–1976], vol. V (Beijing: Zhongyang wenxian chubanshe, 2014), 15.
2 Zhonggong zhongyang wenxian yanjiushi (ed.), *Deng Xiaoping nianpu 1975–1997* [Chronological Biography of Deng Xiaoping 1975–1997], vol. I (Beijing: Zhongyang wenxian chubanshe, 2004), 159.

History," returns to the question of historical evaluation. It analyzes different standards of measurement to reveal the changing cycles of ascribing historical merit.

Mao Zedong as History

The historical-geological project and the accompanying biography never materialized, and Mao Zedong did not commission any other account of his later years. Even Cultural Revolutionary hagiographies generally consisted of unofficial reprints regarding his childhood and youth taken from Snow's *Red Star over China*. References to his post-1949 career tended to be very general or emphatically emotional. Little was known about the personal life of the seemingly omniscient ruler inside the old imperial palaces of Zhongnanhai, except for rumors. Therefore, public interest remained high, even after Mao's death. Starting in 1989 with Quan Yuanchi's *Mao Zedong: Man Not God*,[3] which was based on interviews with Mao's former bodyguard Li Yinqiao, a wealth of Chinese publications have appeared that shed light on even the most mundane aspects of Mao Zedong's personality. The officially sanctioned spread of "Mao-literature"[4] served the aim of countering the larger-than-life cult image of the late Chairman by commenting on his eating habits or his inattentiveness to questions of adequate clothing or social etiquette. As of the mid 1950s, Mao was famous for holding meetings with foreign ambassadors in his sleeping gown, as well as for conducting Politburo sessions in his private quarters, while lying on his huge bed littered with historical works and recent policy documents. Not even questions regarding his bowel movements were deemed beneath public interest. The Western equivalent of this literature was represented by the memoirs of one of Mao Zedong's personal physicians, Li Zhisui, published in English with heavy editorial assistance in 1994. While the memoirs have been rightly criticized for claiming that Li was a witness to or even consulted by Mao on basically every major policy decision, they nevertheless offered insights into the workings of "Group One," as the cocoon of Mao's personal attendants and staff was termed, notably absent from Chinese Mao-literature. These most famously included Mao Zedong's promiscuous sex life in his later years and his

---

3   Quan Yuanchi, *Zouxia shentan de Mao Zedong* [Mao Zedong: Man Not God] (Beijing: Zhongwai wenhua chubanshe, 1989).
4   See Thomas Scharping, "The Man, the Myth, the Message: New Trends in Mao-Literature from China," *China Quarterly* 137 (Mar. 1994), 168–79.

lack of personal hygiene as reported by Li Zhisui ("I wash myself inside the bodies of my women"),[5] as well as the bouts of depression that had first appeared during periods of interparty rivalry in the mid 1920s and were to return sporadically after major political disappointments such as the defection and death of his chosen successor Lin Biao in 1971.

This shift in biographical writing about Mao, with its inclination toward gossip and the nonpolitical aspects of the man's personality, has in part shrouded the facets of his character that made him a skilled political leader in the first place, who secured longstanding loyalty and admiration among his followers, even after his death. It also fails to explain how a formerly idealist middle-school teacher came to view violence as a crucial means of achieving political success and grew increasingly indifferent, even cynical, about the human toll that his policies caused.

Mao Zedong was not born a psychopath back in 1893. He grew up in the last years of the waning Qing dynasty as the eldest son of a fairly well-off peasant family in Shaoshan, a rural hamlet located in the mountainous province of Hunan in southern China. Conflicts with his stern, dictatorial father characterized his childhood and youth, as he came of age during the tumultuous years of the early Republic of China. Mao quickly achieved a reputation among his classmates and teachers as a bold and unconventional thinker with outstanding literary skills. His early writings reveal a multitude of intellectual influences. He strove for Confucian self-cultivation, tried to strengthen his physical body in order to make up for the weakness of the Chinese body politic, studied Western philosophy textbooks and admired political leaders and thinkers as diverse as George Washington, Kang Youwei and Napoleon. The few contemporary self-reflective letters or scribbled reading notes reveal a passionate, nationalistic youth, who clearly placed egoism before altruism. Yet despite narcissistic tendencies, he was still capable of critical self-appraisal ("I have a very great defect, which I feel ashamed to reveal to others: I am weak-willed")[6] at the time. Mao would remain an avid reader and a passionate writer throughout his life. He craved any type of information available, but he despised learning for learning's sake. Books and newspapers were important sources of information, yet they had to be complemented by personally conducted on-the-spot investigations and

5 Li Zhisui, with Anne F. Thurston, *The Private Life of Chairman Mao*, trans. Tai Hung-chao (New York: Random House, 1994), 364.
6 Mao Zedong, "Letter to Peng Huang" (28 Jan. 1921), in Stuart R. Schram (ed.), *Mao's Road to Power: Revolutionary Writings 1912–1949*, vol. II (Armonk, NY: M. E. Sharpe, 1994), 38.

ultimately lead to political action. He was a political animal and wanted to realize his political ambitions rather than to simply describe the current malaise of early Republican China.

In his late twenties, after having unsuccessfully agitated for the independence of his home province Hunan, Mao Zedong came to understand the value of a tight-knit organization, united by a common ideal, to achieve political success: "We really must create a powerful new atmosphere . . . it requires an 'ism' that everyone holds in common. Without an ism, the atmosphere cannot be created . . . An ism is like a banner; when it is raised the people will have something to hope for and know in what direction to go."[7] Socialism became the banner he had been looking for. It has been argued that it had not been ideas of universal justice or equality that attracted Mao to the communist cause but rather the "apologia of violence, the triumph of will, and the celebration of power."[8] There is considerable truth to this. Mao wanted to achieve tangible results instead of simply "talking big." However, this functional perspective underestimates the importance Mao Zedong attached to socialist ideology as such. Although during the foundational period of the CCP he had a limited understanding of socialist theory and was to immerse himself in the philosophical details of historical materialism only in the late 1930s, his ongoing engagement with Marxist-Leninist ideas crucially shaped his perception of history and politics. This held true for Leninist principles, where the concepts of the avant-garde party, the dictatorship of the proletariat and the coercive function of the state apparatus (until its withering away, as envisioned by Lenin in *The State and Revolution*) provided him with important tools to frame his views on political leadership until the end of his life. It applied less to the field of Marxist economics, where Mao frankly confessed his own incompetence. Yet even in his late sixties, during the high tide of the Great Leap Forward, he would conscientiously work through standard Soviet economy textbooks. Knowing about his weak side, he took criticism of his failed economic policies personally and rated them as political attacks. The "little leap" of 1955–56 and the quelling of party internal critics, which included high-ranking leaders such as Zhou Enlai, is one of many examples of his reaction to criticism.[9]

---

7 Mao Zedong, "Letter to Luo Aojie" (25 Nov. 1920), in Stuart Schram (ed.), *Mao's Road to Power: Revolutionary Writings 1912–1949*, vol. I (Armonk, NY: M. E. Sharpe, 1992), 600.
8 Alexander V. Pantsov with Steven I. Levine, *Mao: The Real Story* (New York: Simon & Schuster, 2012), 94.
9 Andrew Walder, *China Under Mao: A Revolution Derailed* (Cambridge, MA: Harvard University Press, 2015), 153.

There has been a longstanding and, at times, fiercely polemical debate about the question of whether Mao Zedong was a Marxist thinker at all. In 1972, Aleksei Rumiantsev, at the time vice-president of the Soviet Academy of Sciences, in a book-length rebuttal of the philosophical foundations of Mao's adaptation of socialist theories, claimed that Mao "did not master Marxism as an integral science but understood it only fragmentarily and in a coarse and primitive form."[10] The main point of contention was related to doctrinal purity. By having unduly emphasized the role of the peasantry, by nurturing a lavish cult of personality in his later years and by claiming the primary importance of national conditions over international precedents, Mao accordingly had proven himself to be a supporter of "petty bourgeois," "idealist" and "subjectivist" ideas; in short, he was a sham Marxist. Later researchers have continued this debate *ad nauseam*, counting the number of quotations from either the Marxist-Leninist canon or Chinese tradition in order to quantify their relative importance in Mao's thinking.[11]

Recent scholarship has come to reemphasize Mao's continuing acceptance of the underlying key elements of Marxist-Leninist epistemology. Given his doctrinal inferiority to those competitors for power, who had either studied in Moscow or who had mastered foreign languages, Mao placed particular attention on local circumstances ("No investigation, no right to speak!" he would say) and the necessity of adapting Marxism-Leninism to national conditions. This "Sinification" of socialist theory freed him from having to bow to other sources of authority or universally applicable standards of measurement and turned what came to be termed "Mao Zedong Thought" into a flexible guiding principle that left considerable leeway for tactical compromise, most clearly visible in his championing of "New Democracy" and coalition government in the 1940s.

However, power politics was not the only factor behind Mao Zedong's call for local adaptations. He had painfully experienced the limited value of schematically transplanting foreign experiences to the Chinese domestic setting. The Comintern advice to organize the numerically minuscule Chinese proletariat in the cities turned out to be an unrewarding strategy for the CCP, especially as the National People's Party (Guomindang, GMD) under Chiang Kai-shek in April 1927 killed and imprisoned its former united front allies. The same applied to many of Joseph Stalin's interventions in

10 Translated from the German edition, Alexej M. Rumjanzew, *Quellen und Entwicklung der Ideen Mao Tse-tungs* (Berlin: Dietz, 1973), 23.
11 For an overview, see Nick Knight, *Rethinking Mao: Explorations in Mao Zedong's Thought* (Lanham, MD: Lexington Books, 2007).

Chinese domestic politics, for example when forbidding the CCP to take advantage of the capture of Chiang Kai-shek during the 1936 Xi'an incident, when Mao opted for execution but ultimately had to bow to Stalin's authority, who did not believe the Chinese communists were capable of leading a socialist revolution yet. While Mao accepted Stalin's supremacy as leader of the world communist movement, he was often deeply frustrated about the lack of support provided by the Soviet Union. Things came to a head during the negotiations about the Sino-Soviet Friendship Treaty in early 1950, when Mao threatened to leave without having reached an agreement if he were not treated with sufficient respect. It was only after Stalin's death that Mao defended him against Khrushchev's criticism in 1956 as an "outstanding Marxist-Leninist fighter," to be assessed on a 70/30 ratio.

The intense struggles against external enemies as well as leadership rivalries within the CCP shaped Mao Zedong's attitude toward violence. According to Mao, the success of a political movement depended on answering two key questions: "Who are our enemies? Who are our friends?" The distinction remained at the heart of Mao's understanding of politics, irrespective of periods of alliances and coalitions.[12] He had experienced and supported the use of violence during investigations into the problem of peasant mobilization in his early party career. His famous Hunan investigation report from February 1927 featured many of the elements he would later continue to champion: By creating and publicly humiliating a limited number of enemies, often former elites, public passion could effectively be roused and, ideally, be channeled for political purposes. The ensuing revolutionary atmosphere was an effect Mao craved to sustain.

According to Mao, revolution was "not a dinner party" and sacrifice for a higher good remained a crucial tenet of his rhetoric. It has often been argued that Mao, unlike Stalin and Hitler, did not revel in brutality, but rather stressed an approach christened "curing the sickness to save the patient." While Mao did not display openly sadistic traits, he became increasingly oblivious, even cynical, about the value of human life. This holds true for the struggle with interparty rivals, for example during the Futian incident in Jiangxi in late 1930, when several thousand communists were tortured and killed, or his bragging about having had ten times more scholars killed than the infamous first emperor of China. For the sake of agitation and mobilization, he valued the passion aroused by public acts of violence. This is best

---

12 Michael R. Dutton, *Policing Chinese Politics: A History* (Durham, NC: Duke University Press, 2005).

documented for the early 1950s, when he not only personally ordered executions ("If in some regions some corrupt individuals need to be killed in order to mobilize the masses, a few can be killed"),[13] but actually established regional "killing quotas."[14] He also consciously used the threat of violence or his indifference to human suffering in order to unsettle supposedly complacent, bureaucratic or even revisionist communist party leaders, such as when claiming the ultimate victory of socialism, even if half of the world population would perish in the course of a nuclear war. Metaphors of violence also pervaded his vocabulary in other policy fields, such as the economy. These, however, should not always be taken at face value. As a ruler, Mao was ruthless in his dealings with political allies and enemies alike. He loved to upset party comrades and foreign adversaries by making unpredictable utterances that made it hard for others to pin down his actual standpoint.

The bleak view of human life as struggle rendered human relationships subordinate to political struggles. This also held true for his personal life. His wife Yang Kaihui, whom he had left behind in Changsha when he fled to the mountains, and whom he had already replaced by marrying He Zizhen, was shot by GMD troops in 1930, as were several other close relatives over the course of the next years. Only four of his ten children by three wives would live to adulthood, with his eldest son being killed during the Korean War, and his second eldest being driven to insanity due to the ordeals of his childhood. We have to imagine the aging Mao Zedong as an increasingly isolated person, comforted by a number of personal attendants. Unlike during his youth, Mao did not cherish friendships or relationships based on equality when he became a political leader. The climate of suspicion and distrust, which pervaded the party and state organs especially as of the late 1950s, was an immediate consequence of his style of leadership and mirrored the rhetorical trope of the Chinese emperor's self-description as "lonely ruler" (*guaren*).

Mao Zedong and History

When CCP secretary-general Jiang Zemin visited the United States in November 1997, he delivered a speech at Harvard University and presented the local library with a special gift: a multivolume copy of Mao Zedong's

---

13 *Mao Zedong nianpu*, vol. I, 463.
14 Yang Kuisong, "Reconsidering the Campaign to Suppress Counterrevolutionaries," *China Quarterly* 193 (Mar. 2008), 102–21.

comments on China's twenty-four traditional dynastic histories. This "rich heritage of philosophy" was to provide US academics with help in "understanding and drawing useful lessons from Chinese history."[15] Three decades after his *Selected Works* and especially the *Little Red Book*[16] had come to represent the essence of Mao Zedong's contribution to the development of anti-imperialist and socialist theory, the reading notes were to signify the wealth and continuity of Chinese patriotic heritage, not least by way of reproducing them (at least in the case of costly state presents) as a thread-bound facsimile of the Qing dynasty *Wuyingdian* edition in large font, as originally used by Mao between 1952 and his death.

Mao Zedong's relation to Chinese history in particular and traditions more generally, even socialist ones, was far from straightforward. Historical figures such as Napoleon had fascinated him early on and the question of whether great men or the masses were to be considered as creators of history remained a constant issue, despite his acceptance of the fundamental laws of historical materialism, which placed social classes at the center of historical change. He came to adopt Georgii Plekhanov's view of a dialectical relationship between leaders and the masses. Some outstanding individuals accordingly were capable of both synthesizing past developments and recognizing present social needs within the framework of a determinist historical worldview. According to Plekhanov, great men existed, yet this type of individual "is a hero not in the sense that he can stop or change the natural course of things, but in the sense that his activities are the conscious and free expression of this inevitable and unconscious course. Herein lies all his significance; herein lies his whole power. But this significance is colossal, and the power is terrible."[17]

Mao would return to ponder the role of great men in history at various stages during his political career and there could be no mistaking that he counted himself among them. However, his claim to political leadership was not accepted uncontested. He was first sidelined by Comintern representatives or party leaders such as Li Lisan, Qin Bangxian and Zhou Enlai, later by a group of Moscow-trained cadres. These so-called Twenty-Eight Bolsheviks around Wang Ming claimed authority in terms of their theoretical grasp of

---

15 Steven Erlanger, "China's President Draws Applause at Harvard Talk," *New York Times* (2 Nov. 1997).

16 Alexander C. Cook, *Mao's Little Red Book: A Global History* (Cambridge: Cambridge University Press, 2014).

17 Georgii Plekhanov, *Lun geren zai lishi shang de zuoyong* [On the Role of the Individual in History] (Moscow: Waiguowen shuji chubanju, 1950), 43–44.

Marxism-Leninism and emphasized their close relation to Stalin. Mao Zedong's slow rise to power proceeded in piecemeal fashion. He became a master of political infighting and intrigue, as well as a seasoned guerrilla commander, whose strategic and military skills outranked his rivals, most obviously during the disastrous flight from GMD encirclement, christened by Mao in December 1935 retrospectively as the "Long March."

This period is highly illuminating for understanding Mao's perception and instrumentalization of history. In a famous poem entitled "Snow," written in February 1936, which came to be published only ten years later in the context of coalition talks with the GMD in Chongqing, Mao rated the great emperors of old, such as Qin Shihuang, Han Wudi and Genghis Khan and found all of them lacking either in literary style or poetic imagination: "All are past and gone! For truly great men, look to this age alone!" While Mao would later claim that "great men" here referred to the proletariat, contemporary critics had little doubt that the metaphorical reference concealed a far-reaching, vainglorious claim to leadership.[18] The fact that he was still tutored in the intricacies of literary Chinese, the style of expression cultivated by the ruling elites of the Chinese empire, and additionally was a talented poet himself, was to contribute to his lofty image as philosopher-king. The classical idiom lent itself particularly well to ambiguous statements and lyrical expressions that left most of his fellow party-leaders, who often had received little more than primary school educa-tion, either in awe of Mao's erudition or guessing what his actual intentions were. By cultivating an aura of ambiguity, Mao Zedong enjoyed the liberty of watching others trying to make sense of his statements and, as the situation unfolded, either assuming control or quietly retreating from positions that turned out not to work favorably.

While history, in the case of the poem, provided the canvas, against which the present could be positively compared, he also engaged in a more sys-tematic analysis of Chinese history, most famously in his essay "The Chinese Revolution and the Chinese Communist Party." Although he adopted the Marxist framework of class struggle as the crucial mechanism propelling history forward and applied catchphrases such as "feudalism" to vast stretches of time,[19] he devoted particular attention to analyzing "national

---

18 See Geremie R. Barmé, "For Truly Great Men, Look to This Age Alone: Was Mao Zedong a New Emperor?," in Timothy Cheek (ed.), *A Critical Introduction to Mao* (Cambridge: Cambridge University Press, 2010), 248–53.

19 On the adoption of Marxism in Chinese historiography during the years, see Arif Dirlik, *Revolution and History: The Origins of Marxist Historiography in China, 1919–1937* (Berkeley: University of California Press, 1978).

conditions" (*guoqing*), a phrase Deng Xiaoping would also heavily rely upon decades later. Mao therefore placed great emphasis on peasant insurrections in Chinese history, calling them "the real motive force of the progress of Chinese history."[20] However, given the absence of an advanced social class and the correct leadership of an advanced political party, the peasant wars had only come to strengthen the dynastic cycle. With the invasion of foreign imperialists, China had accordingly transformed into a semi-colonial, semi-feudal country in the wake of the opium wars, which after the Xinhai revolution ("old democratic revolution") now needed a "new democratic revolution" under CCP leadership.

Despite his emphasis on China's particular national condition, Mao was careful to speak out against an essentialist view of Chinese traditions and insufficient study of socialist theory. In an anecdote he would frequently retell in the 1960s, Mao mentioned that during the Long March he had been accused by fellow party members of not having grasped key aspects of Marxism-Leninism and of solely conducting his military strategies based on Sun Tzu's classical treatise *The Art of War* and the Ming-dynasty novel *Romance of the Three Kingdoms*. Mao retorted that he had not even read the works of Sun Tzu at this point, with the exception of a few fragments at school; and who could earnestly believe that warfare could be conducted based on a novel?[21] He would read the classical works on Chinese military theory shortly after, alongside Clausewitz as well as Japanese and Soviet treatises, combing them effectively for his military writings of the late 1930s.

Most famously he would spell out his views on war and tactics in *On Protracted Warfare* in 1938, in which he among other things propagated asymmetric, mobile warfare against a stronger enemy such as the Japanese invaders and the importance of political agitation among the soldiers to create revolutionary consciousness. Despite current setbacks for the Chinese forces, he believed history to be on his side. The oppressive and dictatorial nature of Japanese politics would give rise to internal and external contradictions that would bring forth alliances among suppressed classes and nations of the world and ultimately result in Japan's defeat.[22] These insights

---

20 Stuart R. Schram (ed.), *Mao's Road to Power: Revolutionary Writings 1912–1949*, vol. VII (Armonk, NY: M. E. Sharpe, 2005), 283. The reference to China's specific national conditions is on p. 301.
21 *Mao Zedong nianpu*, vol. IV, 504.
22 Stuart Schram (ed.), *Mao's Road to Power: Revolutionary Writings 1912–1949*, vol. VI (Armonk, NY: M. E. Sharpe, 2004), 328.

continued to characterize Mao's perception of conflicts in the international arena, although he would shed the belief that a period of "perpetual peace" was within reach. He would thus liken US imperialism to a "paper tiger" several times in the mid 1940s and 1950s and define the Soviet Union as a "socialist imperialist" nation in the 1960s and 1970s. Imperialism and brute military strength in the long run would always lose out to a just cause such as socialism, which by rallying national and international support of the oppressed would ultimately achieve victory.

He famously illustrated the need for perseverance with a story taken from the classical text *Liezi* entitled *The Foolish Old Man Removes the Mountains*, about how an old man had embarked on a seemingly impossible venture of removing two mountains in his garden, conscious of the fact that within his lifetime this task would not be completed. But there would be future generations to carry on this work. This dedication in the original story moved celestial beings to help him remove the mountains. In a brilliant move that found immediate resonance with the largely illiterate Chinese audience, Mao declared the two mountains to represent "imperialism" and "feudalism," which would have to be removed not by celestial beings but by "the people" under CCP leadership.

Chinese history thus provided him with a reservoir of characters and stories, which he used to exemplify his current aims. Yet, these traditions needed to be reinterpreted, such as in the case of a series of major articles drafted by his political secretary Chen Boda in the 1930s on major philosophical traditions in Chinese history. Otherwise, former legacies could become ideological shackles which had to be undone by force, as Mao Zedong demonstrated in the Hunan investigation report, where not only the castigation of social elites had been depicted but also the destruction of religious heritage. Here influences of the May Fourth heritage of iconoclasm and the striking down of the Confucian tradition remained potent.

As the *Liezi* story reveals, the ability to frame historical events convincingly in a larger narrative that gave meaning to specific incidents and made the present appear as the logical outcome of overarching historical forces counted among Mao's most outstanding leadership skills. The Long March is another case in point. Instead of rendering the horrendous loss of men and material as what it was, a defeat, he transformed it into a tale of extraordinary endurance of a chosen people against foreign and domestic enemies:

Speaking of the Long March, one might ask, "What is its significance?" We say that the Long March is unprecedented in the annals of history, that the Long March is a manifesto, a propaganda team, a seeding machine. Since the time when Pan Gu divided the heavens from the earth and the Three Sovereigns and Five Emperors reigned, has history ever witnessed such a Long March as ours? . . . No, never.[23]

The linkage between national revolution and the historical necessity of the communist victory, which also included a reinterpretation of Chinese tradition, proved to be a highly potent narrative. Mao Zedong would continuously elaborate on and systematize this linkage as a series of necessary steps to finally attain socialism. This narrative and its multifold later applications, for example by having carefully chosen model heroes compare the bitterness of the past with the "sweetness" of the socialist present, provided a forceful means of persuasion that even after decades continued to shape memories of the recent past.[24] Mao perfected his storytelling craft, backed up with disciplinary force, during the Rectification Campaign in Yan'an, when his texts and viewpoints came to constitute the party's standard narrative.[25] Classical anecdotes and recent incidents of heroism or international solidarity such as the example of Canadian physician Norman Bethune were rephrased effectively to spread socialist ideals. Even in the late 1990s, many people who had grown up in the Maoist era were still able to recite these stories by heart. However, the problem of whether the new content fundamentally altered the messages provided by the older narratives and aesthetic forms themselves remained unresolved. Prior to the Cultural Revolution Mao would call for a thorough revolution of traditional forms in the field of opera, yet many cultural continuities remained.[26]

History also served as a means to establish Mao Zedong's intra-party predominance. By the late 1930s, Mao Zedong had secured Moscow's backing and established himself as the party's primary theoretician and political leader, although he was to be elected party chairman only in 1945. In the context of competition with Chiang Kai-shek for national leadership, his erstwhile competitors such as Wang Ming had bowed to his claim of

23 Stuart R. Schram (ed.), *Mao's Road to Power: Revolutionary Writings 1912–1949*, vol. V (Armonk, NY: M. E. Sharpe, 1999), 92.
24 Gail Hershatter, *The Gender of Memory: Rural Women and China's Collective Past* (Berkeley: University of California Press, 2011).
25 David E. Apter and Tony Saich, *Revolutionary Discourse in Mao's Republic* (Cambridge, MA: Harvard University Press, 1994).
26 Barbara Mittler, *A Continuous Revolution: Making Sense of Cultural Revolution Culture* (Cambridge, MA: Harvard University Press, 2013).

dominance, and fellow party leaders such as Liu Shaoqi or Zhu De helped to fashion a leader cult around Mao Zedong that offset key elements of Leninist organizational control.[27] This victory was also enshrined in the party's first resolution on party history, propagated in April 1945, which defined a series of "line struggles" waged prior to Mao's leadership. Although he still publicly claimed that China lacked "a great man,"[28] like Marx or Lenin, and that especially he would have to immerse himself further in the study of Marxist-Leninist theory, Mao Zedong used the resolution as a means of retelling party history in teleological fashion, as a series of "line struggles" that ended with the adoption of correct policy measures under his leadership. The destiny of China as a nation thus was indissolubly linked with Mao's personal claim to leadership and lifted him above the constraints of party discipline. In the early 1940s, a model of charismatic leadership emerged, which centered on Mao Zedong as the party's most prominent symbol.[29] The potency of this symbolism could not be easily offset or routinized, especially after the victory in the civil war, as Mao Zedong turned from revolutionary to ruler. Yet only during the Cultural Revolution would Mao use his cult as an instrument to mobilize the populace against bureaucratic party rule as such.[30]

With the establishment of the People's Republic of China in 1949, the CCP had accomplished a historical achievement. The narratives of national unification and resistance against foreign aggression had mainly served their purposes. Now the tasks of building a modern, socialist nation and debates on the complex present and envisioned future assumed priority. Historical topics occasionally resurfaced, as political conflicts or contested works of art questioned the dominant party narrative. It was after Khrushchev's Secret Speech in 1956, which questioned Stalin's historical legacy and contributed to the ensuing rift between China and the Soviet Union, that history became a crucial issue for Mao Zedong again. Mao increasingly came to ponder his historical legacy and perceived the danger

27 Frederick C. Teiwes and Warren Sun, "From Leninist Party to a Charismatic Party: The CCP's Changing Leadership, 1937–1945," in Tony Saich and Hans van de Ven (eds.), *New Perspectives on the Chinese Communist Revolution* (Armonk, NY: M. E. Sharpe, 1995), 339–87.
28 Stuart R. Schram and Timothy Cheek (eds.), *Mao's Road to Power: Revolutionary Writings 1912–1949*, vol. VIII (Armonk, NY: M. E. Sharpe, 2014), 742.
29 Gao Hua, *Hong taiyang shi zenyang sheng qilai de. Yan'an zhengfeng yundong de lailong qumai* [How the Red Sun Rose: A History of the Yan'an Rectification Movement] (Hong Kong: Chinese University Press, 2000).
30 Daniel Leese, *Mao Cult: Rhetoric and Ritual During China's Cultural Revolution* (Cambridge: Cambridge University Press, 2011).

of a Khrushchev-style critique and complete policy reversal after his death. The policy failures of the Hundred Flowers campaign and the Great Leap Forward also led to an increasing feeling of vulnerability on the domestic front, which Mao countered with increasing separation from his erstwhile colleagues and reliance on nonconstitutional bodies of governance that catered to his wishes alone. The narrative that as of mid 1962 came to dominate his speeches emphasized the continuing importance of class struggle to fend off revisionist tendencies. Given the victory of the revolutionary movement, this argument was much less convincing to a larger audience than the previous call for national resistance against Japanese aggression. Charges against the Soviet Union and domestic enemies had to be exaggerated and, again, Mao relied on historical metaphors to communicate his political aims.

The example of the upright Ming dynasty official Hai Rui perfectly illustrates the instrumental dimension of what Mao Zedong termed "using the past to serve the present." In 1959, he had advised party members to follow Hai Rui's example and to speak the truth, even if this meant "tearing the emperor from his horse," an only half-ironical self-referential description. Once criticism of the disastrous policies of the Great Leap was voiced, most prominently by Minister of Defense Peng Dehuai, Mao changed the signals. He stubbornly clung to a belief in the correctness of his policies and on spurious grounds punished those who had criticized him. He would also twist historical metaphors. When the figure of Hai Rui resurfaced at the outset of the Cultural Revolution, it was in a polemical essay. The essay charged those who still upheld Hai Rui with historical distortion, by claiming that the Ming official could speak up on behalf of the peasants while representing the landholding gentry society, thus transgressing his class boundaries and impeding open class struggle. Critical questions about how the CCP leadership, many of whom (including Mao) came from well-off social backgrounds, managed to transgress the limitations of their own social heritage, were deemed heretical during the Cultural Revolution. It was only Mao who held the privilege of interpreting history and judging historical actors. Criticism was to be directed at the targets specified and within the narrative realms staked out by Mao.

With the outset of the Cultural Revolution, Mao had come to perceive two main dangers for the future prospects of socialism in China: the continuing weight of tradition, especially remnants of bourgeois or feudal thinking, and the emergence of bureaucratic rule from within the party ranks. Both in turn became key targets of the campaign, with symbols of Chinese traditions or carriers of classical learning bearing the brunt of the onslaught in the early stages. Using his cult of leadership, Mao galvanized the masses to attack the "Four Olds." His shock troops, the Red Guards, went on an iconoclastic rampage, destroying supposedly feudal heritage in order to establish a socialist future in complete accordance with Mao Zedong Thought, the contours of which remained hazy at best. While providing easy targets for mobilization, history and historical objects shifted to the background as party leaders came under attack. The objects, if not looted or taken into possession by Cultural Revolution leaders and connoisseurs such as Kang Sheng, were stored in government repositories and later partly restored to their previous owners. Some of these artifacts also provided the basis of state collections, such as in case of the Shanghai Museum.[31]

The politicized use of historical metaphors characterized Mao's rule until the end. He would temporarily single out specific individuals, schools of thought or particular works for praise, such as the first emperor of China and the school of legalism, or proclaim unlikely comparisons between past and present, such as between Lin Biao and Confucius. A body of loyal supporters would provide the relevant articles linking current political leaders with historical events, suggesting linkages at some deeper level only to be perceived by the Great Helmsman, Chairman Mao. Yet, despite Mao's attempts to secure his historical legacy during his lifetime, the instrumental usage of history and cultural symbols to obtain political goals resulted in thorough disillusionment among party members and the populace regarding the sagacity of at least parts of the chairman's policies.

Mao Zedong in History

Mao had been keenly aware of the fact that with the Cultural Revolution he had placed a wager on his political future that might cause severe damage to his reputation among contemporaries and later generations. But, as he famously stated in a letter to his third wife Jiang Qing, which exists only as a copy that was later redacted, he was willing to take this bet. He perceived a revisionist threat to socialist rule in China and, not without reason, feared the reestablishment of capitalist modes of production after his death. If the fashioning of a leader cult around his persona was the only way to mobilize the populace to support his aims, he acceded to its creation, while remaining aware of the fact that he would not be able to live up to these inflated

---

31 Denise Ho, *Curating Revolution: Politics on Display in Mao's China* (forthcoming).

expectations. In the letter, Mao also quoted an entry in the *History of Jin*, a work he would consult right up to his death. He commented on the eccentric third-century poet Ruan Ji, one of the illustrious seven sages of the bamboo grove, who defied all social conventions. Ruan had derided the founding emperor of the Han, Liu Bang, as a "lackey," who had assumed the throne only because "there were no true heroes at the time." Mao famously applied the evaluation to his own rule, when describing the shifting tides of self-confidence: "I always believed that, if there are no tigers in the mountains, the monkey may become king. I have become this type of king."[32] These self-doubts, however, only temporarily tarnished his self-appraisal, as he found himself to be predominantly constituted of "tiger-spirit" with some minor monkey attributes. Mao further anticipated that, after his death, his legacy might be repudiated and vilified. Yet, he remained assured that his writings would always provide sufficient ammunition for true revolutionaries and that reactionary rule was bound to fail in the long run.

Questions on Mao's historical status commenced directly after his death in September 1976. After the radical faction around Mao Zedong's wife had been purged, short-term party chairman Hua Guofeng tried not to question Mao's historical role due to his own frail claims to legitimacy. Deng Xiaoping, on the other hand, who had been expelled by Mao in early 1976, had to break the absolute truth claim attached to Mao's sayings if he wanted to reclaim power. As Deng regained influence, the party leadership decided on a two-pronged approach to deal with the historical legacy of Mao Zedong and his policies. While the "Gang of Four" and military leaders associated with Lin Biao were tried by a special court on grounds of attempting to hijack state power and persecuting hundreds of thousands of innocent people,[33] Mao in an official resolution on party history was held accountable for severe political and ideological errors but not for criminal acts. The resolution of June 1981 was drafted by a small group around Mao's former secretary Hu Qiaomu. Key aspects were settled upon after several personal interventions by key leaders such as Chen Yun and Deng Xiaoping. While Deng perceived the implementation of the "Four Modernizations" to be the most pressing task ahead, he was clearly aware of the fact that, without

---

32 Zhonggong zhongyang wenxian yanjiushi (ed.), *Jianguo yilai Mao Zedong wengao* [Mao Zedong's Manuscripts Since the PRC's Formation], vol. XII (Beijing: Zhongyang wenxian chubanshe, 1998), 72.

33 Alexander C. Cook, *China's Cultural Revolution on Trial: Justice in the Post-Mao Transition* (Cambridge: Cambridge University Press, 2016).

a comprehensive evaluation of Mao as a historical actor, the CCP faced the danger of following the path of the Soviet Union in the wake of Khrushchev's de-Stalinization policies in the mid 1950s, leading to domestic and international turbulence. He therefore impressed three main tasks upon the drafting committee: first, to firmly establish Mao Zedong's place in history and to uphold and further develop "Mao Zedong Thought"; second, to evaluate the correctness of major policies including the respective responsibility of leading party cadres; and, finally, to reach a basic conclusion on the past that would stand the test of time and allow the current leadership to focus on present issues without having to deal with recurrent problems and personal feuds dating from China's revolutionary history. The resolution was to offer a conclusion "in broad strokes and without too many details."[34] It represented an attempt at wiping the historical slate clean once and for all and at providing party and populace with a standard narrative on how to judge the recent past.

After an extended discussion process, which included more than 4,000 political and military cadres, who in part came to voice harsh criticism of both Mao and his policies,[35] the resolution affirmed Mao Zedong's historical merits and the continuing importance of Mao Zedong Thought, now understood as the party's collective wisdom, as guiding theory. While after 1957 Mao was said to have increasingly deviated from the "correct" path of Chinese socialism and the Cultural Revolution represented an outright disaster, the resolution emphasized that, although Mao was clearly to blame for these policy failures, others, including the current leadership, were to share responsibility. On the whole, Mao's errors were outweighed by the contributions he had made to the Chinese Revolution in terms of both policy formulation and implementation.[36] He thus was to remain a crucial figure in party history, not infallible but of outstanding stature.

The resolution, to the present day, provides the framework in China for how to judge the recent Chinese past. Yet despite the limitations on publishing critical research on the Maoist era in China that were instituted in the

34 *Deng Xiaoping wenxuan* [Selected Writings of Deng Xiaoping], vol. II (Beijing: Renmin chubanshe, 1994), 292.
35 Compare Guo Daohui, "Si qian lao ganbu dui dangshi de yi ci minzhu pingyi" [An Instance of Democratic Criticism and Discussion of Party History by Four Thousand Old Cadres], *Yanhuang Chunqiu* 4 (2010), www.yhcqw.com/html/qlj/20 10/49/F998.html.
36 The text of the revolution is "On Questions of Party History: Resolution on Certain Questions in the History of Our Party Since the Founding of the People's Republic of China," *Beijing Review* 27 (6 Jul. 1981), 10–39.

wake of the 1981 resolution, historical evaluation has been much more complex than might be expected. Especially since the 1990s, a plethora of different opinions has been voiced, not least facilitated through publication channels in Hong Kong and Taiwan. Recently, the Bo Xilai affair has revealed once again the twisted legacies of the Maoist era, when nostalgic memories of a supposedly egalitarian era were used to mobilize those left behind by China's economic reforms. Then Premier Wen Jiabao in March 2012 even felt the need to warn against the possible reoccurrence of movements similar to the Cultural Revolution. By November 2013, the CCP officially interdicted the use of pre-1978 historical examples to criticize the present and vice versa.[37] The document presents another attempt at freezing the ambiguous legacies of the Maoist era through an officially mandated *Schlussstrich* – thus closing off further debates.

Historical writings in other parts of the world have gone through different cycles of ascribing blame and merit to Mao Zedong.[38] In the Western media, a crucial role is currently played by bestselling biographies and histories of the early People's Republic of China, which present Mao as a demonic psychopath, who created a system of totalitarian suppression and enslaved the Chinese populace through a rule of terror. In many ways, the narratives of Mao as monster serve the aim of destroying a latently romanticized image of a modern-age Chinese philosopher-king among Western audiences, which is said to have lingered, even among educated elites, since the late 1960s. Despite the conscious distortions of historical sources, these portrayals have stimulated critical discussions about the life and legacies of the former CCP chairman. Depending on the political standpoint, Mao Zedong has left sufficient evidence to be portrayed as a ruthless tyrant, as champion of social justice, as national leader or as gifted poet. He was, in his own words to Edgar Snow in 1970, a "lone monk with a leaky umbrella," the first half of a traditional couplet that continues with a pun on the homophonous characters for "hairlessness" and "lawlessness." While neither the contemporary translator nor Snow understood the allusion, Mao was saying that he felt increasingly unrestrained by social norms or the criteria of future biographers.

---

37 Zhonggong zhongyang dangxiao yanjiushi (ed.), "Zhengque kandai gaige kaifang qianhou liang ge lishi shiqi" [On How to Correctly Assess the Two Historical Periods Before and After Reform and Opening], *Renmin Ribao* (8 Nov, 2013), 6.
38 Compare Charles Hayford, "Mao's Journey to the West: Meanings Made of Mao," and Alexander C. Cook, "Third World Maoism," both in Cheek (ed.), *A Critical Introduction to Mao*, 313–31 and 288–312.

Mao Zedong was a highly complex and at times contradictory historical personality, who came to deliberately shroud his views in ambiguous analogies to retain political leverage. Without doubt, he was China's most important leader in the twentieth century and was, simultaneously, responsible for more casualties in peacetime than any other leader in world history. He facilitated China's return as an important actor on the international stage and discredited the very idea of state socialism he had intended to uphold for future generations. Historical verdicts are never final, as each generation continues to debate its identity by way of relating to the past. It is doubtful, however, that Mao's wish for a predominantly positive assessment after his death will prevail without state censorship in China. The lofty rhetoric of great democracy and mass mobilization does not restore the countless lives that were ruined or ended because of Mao Zedong's policies to create a future utopia.

Bibliographical Essay

The biographical literature on Mao Zedong has assumed gigantic proportions. The most up-to-date account with unique Russian sources, especially for the pre-1949 period, is Alexander V. Pantsov with Steven I. Levine, *Mao: The Real Story* (New York: Simon & Schuster, 2012). A collective biography of Mao Zedong and his times by Chinese and Western researchers is presented in Timothy Cheek (ed.), *A Critical Introduction to Mao* (Cambridge: Cambridge University Press 2010). Jung Chang and Jon Halliday's widely popular *Mao: The Unknown Story* (London: Jonathan Cape, 2005) presents a wealth of sources, the interpretation of which has been severely criticized; see Gregor Benton and Lin Chun (eds.), *Was Mao Really a Monster? The Academic Response to Chang and Halliday's* Mao: The Unknown Story (New York: Routledge, 2009).

The authoritative Chinese biography is Pang Xianzhi and Jin Chongji, *Mao Zedong zhuan (1949–1976)* [Biography of Mao Zedong (1949–1976)], 2 vols. (Beijing: Zhongyang wenxian chubanshe, 2003); for the earlier years, see Jin Chongji (ed.), *Mao Zedong zhuan (1893–1949)* [Biography of Mao Zedong (1893–1949)], 2 vols. (Beijing: Zhongyang wenxian chubanshe, 1996). Indispensable information on Mao Zedong's day-to-day activities is provided by Zhonggong zhongyang wenxian yanjiushi (ed.), *Mao Zedong nianpu 1949–1976* [Chronological Biography of Mao Zedong 1949–1976], 6 vols. (Beijing: Zhongyang wenxian chubanshe, 2014). For the earlier period, see Zhonggong zhongyang wenxian yanjiushi (ed.), *Mao Zedong nianpu 1893–1949*

[Chronological Biography of Mao Zedong 1893–1949], 3 vols. (Beijing: Zhongyang wenxian chubanshe, 2003).

In English translation, Mao Zedong's writings are best documented for the pre-PRC period. A monumental translation project, which is expected to span ten volumes, is Stuart R. Schram et al. (eds.), *Mao's Road to Power: Revolutionary Writings 1912–1949*, 8 vols. (Armonk, NY: M. E. Sharpe, 1992–). The official *Selected Works of Mao Tse-tung*, 5 vols. (Peking: Foreign Languages Press, 1965–77), covers important texts and speeches between 1926 and 1957, partly in heavily redacted versions, and has been complemented by various unofficial reprints of Mao speeches by Red Guard organizations from the Cultural Revolution. A selection is presented by Stuart R. Schram (ed.), *Mao Tse-tung Unrehearsed: Talks and Letters, 1956–1971* (New York: Penguin, 1974). A project on publishing Mao's post-1949 writings includes the years 1949–57, but has remained unfinished: Michael Y. M. Kau and John K. Leung (eds.), *The Writings of Mao Zedong, 1949–1976*, 2 vols. (Armonk: M.E. Sharpe, 1986–92). The most comprehensive collection in Chinese is Zhonggong zhongyang wenxian yanjiushi (ed.), *Jianguo yilai Mao Zedong wengao* [Mao Zedong's Manuscripts Since the PRC's Formation], 13 vols. (Peking: Zhongyang wenxian chubanshe, 1987–98).

On Mao Zedong's political thought, see especially Frederic Wakeman, Jr., *History and Will: Philosophical Perspectives of Mao Tse-tung's Thought* (Berkeley: University of California Press, 1973), as well as Nick Knight, *Rethinking Mao: Explorations in Mao Zedong's Thought* (Lanham, MD: Lexington Books, 2007). Still informative is Stuart R. Schram, *The Political Thought of Mao Tse-tung*, rev. edn. (Harmondsworth: Penguin, 1969). On the political context of the "Sinification" of Marxism and the rise of the Mao cult, see especially Raymond Wylie, *The Emergence of Maoism: Mao Tse-tung, Ch'en Po-ta, and the Search for Chinese Theory, 1935–1945* (Stanford: Stanford University Press, 1980). On post-1949 developments, see Daniel Leese, *Mao Cult: Rhetoric and Ritual in China's Cultural Revolution* (Cambridge: Cambridge University Press, 2011). On Mao as storyteller, see the influential analysis by David E. Apter and Tony Saich, *Mao's Revolutionary Discourse in Mao's Republic* (Cambridge, MA: Harvard University Press, 1994). Daniel F. Vukovich, *China and Orientalism: Western Knowledge Production and the PRC* (London: Routledge, 2012), critically revisits Western writings on Mao Zedong.

A preliminary assessment of Mao Zedong's historical role is presented by Dick Wilson (ed.), *Mao Tse-tung in the Scales of History* (Cambridge: Cambridge University Press, 1977). The politics of history in modern China is discussed in Jonathan Unger (ed.), *Using the Past to Serve the Present: Historiography and Politics in Contemporary China* (Armonk, NY: M. E. Sharpe, 1993), and Li Huaiyin, *Reinventing Modern China: Imagination and Authenticity in Chinese Historical Writing* (Honolulu: University of Hawai'i Press, 2012). On Mao as a historian, see Wang Zijin, *Lishi xuezhe Mao Zedong* [The Historian Mao Zedong] (Beijing: Xiyuan chubanshe, 2013); for a typical appraisal of his historical contributions by a party historian, see Li Jie, *Mao Zedong dui xin Zhongguo de lishi gongxian* [Mao Zedong's Historical Contributions to the New China] (Beijing: Shehui kexue wenxian chubanshe, 2015). The multifold afterlives of Mao are covered by Zheng Yushuo (ed.), *The Use of Mao and the Chongqing Model* (Hong Kong: City of Hong Kong University Press, 2015), and Geremie R. Barmé, *Shades of Mao: The Posthumous Cult of the Great Leader* (Armonk, NY: M. E. Sharpe, 1996). Finally, the multivolume thread-bound edition of Mao Zedong's comments on China's traditional histories, Zhongyang dang'anguan (ed.), *Mao Zedong pingdian ershisi shi* [Mao Zedong's Punctuations and Annotations to the Twenty-Four Histories] (Beijing: Zhongguo dang'an chubanshe, 1996), is highly recommended for bibliophiles.

12

Cold War Anti-Communism and the Impact of Communism on the West

FEDERICO ROMERO

As the polarization of the Cold War began to shape strategic and ideological alignments – first in Europe and then rapidly, albeit haphazardly, on other continents – anti-communism rose to prominence as a key political language throughout the West. As such, postwar anti-communism was not intrinsically different from its interwar predecessor. It still embraced liberals who praised individualism and markets, social democrats who entrusted progress to state planning and collective bargaining, Christian democrats who prioritized family, community and religion, and authoritarian anti-Bolshevist nationalists. There were, however, two key differences. The first was the marginalization of the fascist version of anti-communism, epitomized by the isolated regime of Francisco Franco in Spain. The second and more important one was the replacement of destabilizing rivalries among the various anti-communist political families with an uneven but robust, resilient operational unity.

Ubiquitous and obsessively propagated, anti-communism never congealed into a single, unified ideology. It was rather a lowest common denominator, providing the main Western political cultures with a shared language. In a telling definition, it was "the ideological glue that . . . held often fractious political coalitions together."[1] Although different, and often clashing on policy recipes, anti-communists of various hues coalesced under the banners of anti-Soviet containment and Western unity. For the first two postwar decades they shared a powerful narrative of their epoch as a fundamental conflict between "freedom" and "totalitarianism," Western "democracy" and

---

1 Jan-Werner Muller, 'The End of Christian Democracy," *Foreign Affairs* (15 Jul. 2014), www.foreignaffairs.com/articles/141638/jan-werner-mueller/the-end-of-christian-democracy.

Soviet "tyranny." In Western societies, "totalitarianism was the great mobilizing and unifying concept of the Cold War ... It provided a plausible and frightening vision of a Manichean, radically bifurcated world in which the leaders of the free world would have to struggle ... or perish."[2]

This binary representation of an ominous clash between good and evil entailed a call for Western unity, embodied at the strategic level in the Atlantic alliance. It left room, though, for different policy solutions, especially in the domestic sphere. Thus, anti-communism could be spelled out in multiple vernaculars and very different, even contrasting actions. It fueled strategies of political repression, with restrictions on civil liberties and cultural pluralism, in the United States and West Germany in the early 1950s. There, conservative elites emphasized the danger of an allegedly subversive ideology in order to buttress traditional values of order, family and religion. Anti-communism's rationale, however, could also emphasize social cooperation rather than class conflict, and therefore legitimize strategies of social inclusion, welfare reforms, democratic agency and representation of working-class interests, as would gradually become the case in most of Western Europe. Thus, anti-communism was deployed by different social and political actors to pursue their specific and divergent agendas in the cultural and social spheres no less than in the political realm.

Anti-communism responded to the dual pressures that arose from postwar Western societies, for security *and* enlarged democratic participation, for stability *as well as* growth, social mobility and democratized consumption, although it did not often reconcile these conflicting goals. Its aggressive language usually extolled the defense of a conservative, elitist social order. But its logic pivoted on the strengthening of Western societies, and the championing of democracy and freedom helped to legitimize moderate reformism as an antidote to radicalism. Thus, anti-communism derived its hegemonic command from its permeability to multiple agendas, and ultimately to its promotion of a more prosperous, open, dynamic society. As the latter became entrenched, new agendas and struggles arose in the 1960s, and anti-communism lost traction as a key political factor.

Outside the industrialized West, anti-communism was mostly deployed by authoritarian elites who evoked the Cold War polarity to justify regimes of despotism and violence. Colonial administrations from Vietnam to Malaysia used it to rationalize their repression of independence movements. Regional

---

2 Abbott Gleason, *Totalitarianism: The Inner History of the Cold War* (New York: Oxford University Press, 1995), 3.

allies of the United States such as Iran, Brazil and South Africa used anti-communism to suppress domestic opposition and emphasize their alignment with the West, so as to secure its aid and support. In some cases, such as Indonesia or Guatemala, it led to murderous policies of large-scale extermination. The United States and the West by and large condoned or even encouraged such policies for the sake of imperial control and Cold War priorities, even though the actual strength of communist forces was in most cases limited and feeble.

Anti-communism in Asia and Latin America had multiple, different roots steeped in local culture, political traditions and social cleavages. This chapter cannot explore them; instead it will focus on Western Europe and the United States. However, its circumscribed narrative should always be seen within a global framework in which anti-communism operated as a powerful barrier against nationalist and radical movements that could endanger Western preeminence, US leadership and the international capitalist order.

Containing Soviet Communism

The dawning of peace in Europe was an uncertain, at times turbulent affair. If the victorious powers' agreements and occupation zones redrew physical borders, political configurations across the continent remained for a while indeterminate. The anti-fascist partnership was beginning to show cracks and frictions at the international level and in national contexts. The Allies could not agree on the management of occupied Germany, their occupation zones gradually solidified in separate areas, and by 1948 the building of two distinct German states was well under way. In the coalitions that had emerged from the resistance – in Italy or France – the communist parties were soon at loggerheads with their conservative or reformist partners. In elections and debates everywhere the questions were similar. What kind of democracy would be built on the ashes of fascism and occupation? What mix of individual and social rights would be enshrined in the new constitutions and practices? How much planning and regulation were needed to avoid the markets' failures so painfully experienced in the 1930s, or to overcome capitalism altogether? How could peace be secured, domestically as well as internationally?

The resistance had nurtured radical yearnings for egalitarian, cathartic transformations, which the communists hoped to capture and represent. Yet, those turned out to be the desires of committed minorities. When votes were counted, most Europeans opted for conservative or social-democratic parties preaching stability or cautious change. After the shock of the war they yearned for peace and quiet, and spurned the frightening prospect of further upheaval. Perhaps most alarming was the possibility that more turmoil could once again lead to war.

These fears were further stoked by the increasingly quarrelsome relationships among the great powers and the perception of what was taking place in the Central and East European countries, where communists were using the forbidding presence of Soviet power to secure a preeminent role and direct the reconstruction effort with scant regard for democratic pluralism. Although initially bound to a coalition strategy aimed at establishing "people's democracies," the communist parties were systematically taking over the levers of state power, and would soon start building full-fledged Stalinist regimes. In combination with the Soviet state's awesome military might, communist practices of repression and discourses of ideological struggle cast an ominous sense of fear over most Europeans.

It was precisely this knot of anxieties that Winston Churchill (no longer prime minister of the United Kingdom, but still a most prominent voice as one of the war's great victors) addressed, and turned into a set of public tropes, in a speech delivered in the United States in March 1946. Speaking just a few weeks after Stalin had revived the notion of a paramount conflict between communism and capitalism, Churchill dramatically announced that "an iron curtain [had] descended across" Europe as communist parties were trying "to obtain totalitarian control" over East European countries. They aimed at the "indefinite expansion of their power and doctrines." Together with communism's "fifth columns" in the West, they constituted "a growing challenge and peril to Christian civilization." Capitalizing on his credibility as the critic of prewar appeasement toward Nazi Germany, Churchill warned that "war and tyranny" were once again the key threats, to be faced squarely by the "Western democracies" and particularly by the unified strength of "the English-speaking peoples."[3]

It was not yet a call to arms, as Churchill still advocated a diplomatic settlement, but it set a new tone for public debate in the West. It raised the anti-communist banner in a most authoritative way and anchored it to the powerful, enduring image of the "iron curtain." Meanwhile, the US government was also reconsidering its strategic outlook in the light of

3 Winston Churchill, 'The Sinews of Peace," speech at Fulton, Missouri, 5 Mar. 1946, www.winstonchurchill.org/learn/speeches/speeches-of-winston-churchill/120-the-si news-of-peace.

increasing estrangement from, and hostility toward, the Soviet Union, whose diplomacy appeared intractable to Washington. One of the United States' most insightful diplomats, George Kennan, provided a powerful rationale for a policy shift. The Russian leadership, he wrote, was "committed fanatically to the belief that with [the] US there can be no permanent *modus vivendi*, that it is desirable and necessary that the internal harmony of our society be disrupted, our traditional way of life be destroyed . . . if Soviet power is to be secure." Yet the Soviet Union was much weaker than Western societies, and just as opportunistically ready to exploit frailties as to withdraw when faced by superior strength, since its design for communism was set in a long-term, historical timeframe. The issue, then, was to unite, organize and energize the West under US leadership, since "communism is like [a] malignant parasite which feeds only on diseased tissue."[4]

As relations with the Soviet Union continued to deteriorate, with increasing clashes over Germany and other diplomatic fronts, the language of anti-communism acquired prominence in Western media and domestic debates. In November 1946 the Republican Party won control of the US Congress on a platform that intertwined anti-Soviet language with criticism of New Deal policies as akin to socialism. Kennan's counsel for a tougher attitude gained further credit; an open anti-communist stance could be not only diplomatically helpful but also electorally effective.

In March 1947 President Harry S. Truman of the United States decided to provide aid to Greece's conservative government in support of its war against a domestic communist insurgency. In order to justify this, he dramatically raised the stakes with a speech that many historians consider as the Cold War's opening salvo. "At the present moment in world history," Truman said, "nearly every nation must choose between alternative ways of life." One was defined by "freedom," the other by "terror and oppression." The United States, he proclaimed, was engaged in helping "free peoples . . . against aggressive movements that seek to impose upon them totalitarian regimes."

In a few sentences, Truman constructed the scenario that would dominate Western imagination for a generation. The world was fundamentally divided along moral, ideological and strategic lines. Communism embodied the ultimate totalitarian threat. It was inherently expansive. Thus, it had to be confronted and stopped before it could threaten other countries. The key to

---

4 George Kennan, Telegram from Moscow to the US Secretary of State ("Long Telegram"), 22 Feb. 1946, www.trumanlibrary.org/whistlestop/study_collections/cold war/documents/pdf/6–6.pdf.

doing this was the buildup of Western unity and solidarity, particularly economic strength since "the seeds of totalitarian regimes are nurtured by misery and want."[5] Vigilance was also required at the domestic level, and Truman launched a program of investigation into the loyalty of civil servants, while Congress expanded its inquiries on allegedly subversive "un-American activities."

Truman's rhetoric was soon turned into a strategy, pivoting on the extension of massive American financial aid to Western Europe with the Marshall Plan, to secure its reconstruction and consolidation along anti-Soviet lines. And George Kennan articulated it as a doctrine of "containment" in a learned essay that was subsequently reproduced in mass-circulation magazines such as *Life* and *Reader's Digest*. The USSR, he argued, saw its struggle with capitalism as a historical one and was engaged in a "quest for absolute power." It would exercise "unceasing constant pressure" but it would also be ready to retreat "in the face of superior force." Thus, the United States and the West must exercise a "long term, patient but firm and vigilant containment" in order to frustrate "Russian expansive tendencies" and eventually induce "the break-up or the gradual mellowing of Soviet power."[6]

As the international scene grew sharply polarized, centrist forces in most West European countries took advantage of this new notion of a Western alignment, and of the alluring promise of growth embodied in the Marshall Plan, to strike emblematic victories against the communist parties, as in the 1948 Italian elections. The stalemate over Germany was broken by the decision to proceed with the establishment of a Federal Republic in the Western zones, while the Soviets rapidly imposed Stalinist regimes throughout Eastern Europe. Within a couple of years, Europe was divided in two separate spheres that exemplified the antagonistic East–West divide. Communism was effectively confined in "a pro-Soviet ghetto," and the West unified around "a conformist politics of the centre ground" whose shared lexicon was anti-communism. For Western Europe, it was the beginning of a long era of "uniformity and stability" based on "parliamentary representation, corporatist negotiation and a somewhat depoliticised individual freedom."[7] The communist parties, on the other hand, came to embody the dark prospect of further turmoil extended into the future.

---

5 "Truman Doctrine" speech, 12 Mar, 1947, avalon.law.yale.edu/20th_century/trudoc.asp.
6 X (George F. Kennan), 'The Sources of Soviet Conduct," *Foreign Affairs* 25, 4 (Jul. 1947), 566–82.
7 Martin Conway, "The Rise and Fall of Western Europe's Democratic Age, 1945–1973," *Contemporary European History* 13, 1 (2004), 68–69 and 73.

At the international level, this new compact pivoted on Western Europe's alliance with the United States. Its proclaimed rationale was the need to defend Western freedoms from "totalitarian" expansionism. This was the argument for the Cold War, a term that from 1948 gained widespread currency in Western discourse and replaced the wartime image of anti-fascist unity, which remained the preserve of the communists and their fewer and fewer allies.

The political and ideological success of Western anti-communism derived from various sources. The frightening image of the Stalinist regime was no doubt crucial, as was its pattern of extension to Central Europe via the power of the Red Army. The enticing prospect of American capital and technologies for European reconstruction was another power-ful factor. Even more cogent were the reassuring promises of moderate, cautious and yet forcefully growth-oriented policies advanced by Christian democratic and social-democratic parties that could plausibly point to a future of high employment and rising standards of living. One of anti-communism's key polarities was the contrast between Western material prosperity and the hardship of daily life in the Soviet Union. At a deeper, probably decisive level operated the fear of renewed violence and another war. The insistence on the "totalitarian" nature of communism – so aptly reiterated by every anti-communist voice – efficaciously played on the lesson of appeasement. Soviet power and communist ideology had to be contrasted with the firmness that had so tragically not been deployed against Hitler. For all its ugliness, the Cold War could be accepted and indeed espoused by many, if it was an effective way to avoid a slippery slope into World War III. For the generations who had experienced depression and total war, this was the bedrock of their widespread anti-communist consensus.

The point of no return in the geographical and ideological partition of Europe was reached in June 1948 with the Berlin blockade. It was the Soviets' last, desperate attempt to prevent the formation of a Western-oriented Federal Republic of Germany. It failed in operational terms, as the blockade was overcome by an airlift, and it backfired in the political and symbolical realm, as it hardened the unity of the Western coalition while providing its propaganda with the invaluable image of a city callously besieged by the Soviets and generously saved by the United States. It was the first crisis of the Cold War, the whiff of war was again in the air, and anti-communist discourse rapidly escalated from an ideological stance to the alarmed repre-sentation of an existential threat.

The US foreign-policy establishment concluded that "the ultimate objective of the leaders of the USSR [was] the domination of the world"[8] and in 1949 signed up to the founding of the Atlantic alliance, the key strategic pact linking the United States to the defense of Western Europe. Containment morphed from an eminently political notion to a security strategy aimed at deterring and, if necessary, defeating the aggression that Western analyses considered inherent in Soviet ideology and behavior.

In 1949 Moscow tested its first atom bomb, and the Chinese Revolution brought communism to power in the largest Asian nation. While right-wing Republican senator Joe McCarthy launched a campaign against alleged domestic communist conspiracies, the Truman administration reassessed the strategic equation in the most alarming terms. To its analysts, the Soviet Union appeared "animated by a new fanatic faith" which sought "to impose its absolute authority over the rest of the world." In messianic language resonating with the irreconcilable polarity at the core of US history, the USSR was described as a "slave state" that could not tolerate the "existence of freedom in the world." Thus, the world was confronted with an "endemic" struggle of "the slave society with the free." It was a conflict with no clear boundaries, since in "the present polarization of power a defeat of free institutions anywhere is a defeat everywhere." The United States had to sustain its economic superiority and decisive military preponderance, deploy the best means of propaganda and psychological warfare against communism, and build up all the resources needed to "reduce the power and influence of the USSR to limits which no longer constitute a threat."[9]

In short, the United States was now engaged in a total war that, short of a direct military confrontation between the great powers, was deploying all instruments of conflict against an enemy – international communism – deemed to be a monolithic entity directed by the Kremlin and engaged in subversion on a global scale. In June 1950, when communist North Korea attacked South Korea's US-supported regime, National Security Council (NSC) Report 68's sinister assumptions seemed vindicated, and they dictated the US military response. Containment was transcending its European origins and its initial political nature to become a strategy of unrestrained,

---

8 "US Objectives with Respect to the USSR," NSC 20, 4 (23 Nov. 1948), www.mtholyoke .edu/acad/intrel/coldwar/nsc20-4.htm.
9 "United States Objectives and Programs for National Security," NSC 68 (14 Apr. 1950), www.trumanlibrary.org/whistlestop/study_collections/coldwar/documents/pdf/10-1 .pdf.

universal confrontation. Defeating communism at the polls in Europe, in the propaganda war for public opinion and on the battlefield in Korea (and in Vietnam, where the United States supported the French campaign against a communist-led independence movement) became connected elements of a worldwide struggle between the "free world" and "totalitarianism."

Western Civilization vs. Totalitarianism

Anti-communism in Western Europe and the United States comprised distinct political cultures and projects, often engaged in fierce competition for votes, influence and power. Yet from the late 1940s to the early 1960s it corralled these different voices in a shared representation that structured public narratives and intellectual discourse no less than official propaganda. At its core stood a fundamental dichotomy that opposed an allegedly unitary "Western civilization" to a monolithic "Soviet totalitarianism."

Neither of these terms was self-explanatory, much less obvious. They both carried dense, diverse connotations and implications. The notion of a unitary West, in particular, had little meaning except in an imperially and racially constructed opposition to peoples who were not white and Christian, or to societies that were not industrialized and modern. Yet, in the discourse of anti-communism it acquired internal consistency, conceptual authority and powerful emotional traction precisely by virtue of its opposition to totalitarianism.

The latter term had a convoluted history. Italian fascists first used it to hail their "totalitarian state" in contrast with the liberal society it was meant to supplant. In the 1930s it was used by Catholic thinkers such as Jacques Maritain to designate the danger of an anti-humanist, atheist modernity, or by liberal ones such as Raymond Aron who decried a new, aggressive technique of domination based on amoral rationalism. By the late 1930s, the consolidation of the Nazi and Stalinist regimes provided the concept of totalitarianism with its chief meaning: a new form of dictatorship structured around a single party with an official, exclusive ideology; a modern state machinery wielding violence, propaganda and intrusive controls on its atomized, helpless subjects; and an industrialized economy geared to war. The Nazi–Soviet Pact of 1939 and the ensuing assault on Poland gave credibility to this reading of totalitarianism as the apocalyptic antithesis of peace and civility, and the term took off in public usage in Europe and North America.

At the end of the war, as we have seen, President Truman as well as his conservative opponents revived the concept to indict Soviet communism as the ultimate, impending threat to liberal democracy. In this new permutation as shorthand for dictatorial communism, totalitarianism soon saturated public discourse throughout the nascent Western coalition. In its most widely propagandized meaning, based on the analogy with Nazi Germany, it stood for the alleged external aggressiveness of the Soviet state. At a deeper level, it influenced the lexicon of political debate, which began to revolve around it. Liberal conservative Austrian economist Friedrich von Hayek saw totalitarianism as the end result of any form of social or economic planning, and hailed market freedom as its antidote. Progressive liberals such as American historian Arthur M. Schlesinger, Jr., advocated a centrist repositioning of reformers, who should jettison any delusion of anti-fascist unity in favor of an uncompromising struggle against the totalitarian menace embodied by communism. And the latter's violent, conspiratorial nature was exposed by former sympathizers who belied communism's claims to social progress in order to focus on the antithesis between freedom and tyranny as the defining issue of the era.[10]

In the construction of the imagery and vocabulary of totalitarianism, and its symbiotic identification with Soviet communism, few voices were more widely influential than that of independent socialist British writer George Orwell, whose images – such as "Big Brother" or the "thought police" – became popular staples in the Western representation of communism. His novels *Animal Farm* (1945) and *Nineteen Eighty-Four* (1949) dramatized the tragedy of despotic control and caricatured the pretensions of communist egalitarianism. Translated into more than 60 languages, those two books sold around 40 million copies worldwide. In the 1950s they were often part of school curricula throughout the British empire and the United States, and were repeatedly dramatized in films and television productions. UK and US government agencies promoted the distribution of Orwell's works as part of their propaganda efforts in the early Cold War.

Around and against the dark shadow of the totalitarian enemy, the West built its own self-image. It would rely, of course, on Western societies' long-held assumption of being the apex of civilization and historical progress. But if the United States could plausibly see its triumphant modernity,

10 See respectively Friedrich A. von Hayek, *The Road to Serfdom* (London: Routledge, 1944); Arthur M. Schlesinger, Jr., *The Vital Center: The Politics of Freedom* (Boston: Houghton Mifflin, 1949); Richard H. S. Crossman (ed.), *The God That Failed: Six Studies in Communism* (New York: Harper, 1949).

international supremacy and messianic universalism as signs of a dawning "American Century,"[11] things looked far less radiant in mid-twentieth-century Europe. Its own modernity was too deeply intertwined with the experiences of imperial domination, violence and war that defined the image of totalitarianism. And its domestic cleavages – on issues of democratic inclusion, social reforms and economic planning – ran so deep and wide as to elicit responses that were not only different from, but often also contiguous to communist proposals, as evidenced by a resilient culture of anti-fascist unity.

Thus, the emphasis on a totalitarian other (often associated with ethno-cultural tropes of Russian cruelty, Oriental despotism and Asian barbarism) served multiple functions. It explained the intertwined traumas of crisis and war as the result of an unprecedented assault on the very nature of European civilization. Totalitarianism was represented as a deep "caesura in [the] European political experience,"[12] associated with the rise of unruly masses and a loss of control by the elites. Its enduring threat thus required a constrained, disciplined form of democracy, capable of integrating different social groups on the basis of economic growth, but also stabilized by strong institutions that marginalized radical ideals and demands. In particular, the emphasis on the totalitarian threat challenged, and eventually eroded, the legitimacy communists had gained with their wartime resistance, facilitating their sidelining on the margins, or even beyond the boundaries, of the constitutional arena.

The sense of a shared totalitarian menace also helped to reduce the traditional authority of nationalism as a key organizing principle, in favor of larger dimensions of collaborative interdependence. This did not lead simply to the establishment of effective institutions of international coordination, such as NATO, the European Community and the International Monetary Fund. It also breathed life into broader, emblematic spheres of identification of a civilizational nature: the "West," "Europe," the "free world." Within them, liberals and social democrats could imagine new paths to economic and social progress, while conservatives – particularly in Germany and Italy – could cleanse the stain of their collaboration or contiguity with fascism, and relegitimize themselves as actors, often key protagonists, of the new democratic West.

11 Henry R. Luce, *The American Century* (New York: Time Inc., 1941).
12 Jan-Werner Müller, *Contesting Democracy: Political Ideas in Twentieth-Century Europe* (New Haven: Yale University Press, 2011), 126.

One further, important aspect in the construction of this anti-totalitarian, supranational West was provided by religion. The very notion of a Western civilization had historically been coterminous with Christianity. And Christian institutions, movements and thinkers had long spearheaded the struggle against communism. Now Protestant theologians and Catholic thinkers, in the United States and Europe, took up a specific role in defining totalitarianism around its suppression of religious life. The Catholic Church mobilized worldwide for a firm opposition to international communism, and facilitated the rapprochement between Europe and the United States in spite of its deep reservations about the materialist modernity the latter embodied. Christian-democratic parties became the pivots of Cold War governing coalitions in most of continental Western Europe.

Furthermore, Western statesmen decried the persecution of religious faith and practice in the "godless" Soviet Union not only as evidence of its immoral nature, but specifically as a core feature of totalitarianism. It epitomized the suppression of individual conscience by an all-powerful state bent on eliminating any space for personal autonomy. The presence of religion thus came to be seen – for instance by President Dwight D. Eisenhower of the United States – as a prerequisite to freedom and democracy, a bulwark against totalitarianism. The promotion of religious freedom became a key component of the West's self-representation, and not merely for its propaganda value among the peoples of the Soviet empire. More importantly, it harmonized the key liberal and materialist claims that defined the West – freedom of thought and the pursuit of individual self-interest – with the Christian emphasis on community, hierarchy and allegiance to the church.

The antithesis of totalitarianism – synthesized in the West's self-image as the "free world" – was a wide-ranging, adaptable, amorphous notion of freedom that could encompass authoritarian as well as liberal Catholics, social-democratic planners and business conservatives, communitarian Christians and secular individualists. By the early 1960s, when the specter of a totalitarian threat was waning, their different readings of the West and its promise would diverge, and eventually clash, with entirely new cultural and social dynamics. In the early years of the Cold War, though, the fundamental contrast between a *free*, pluralist West and its *totalitarian* Soviet antagonist shaped the moral, cultural and political universe of anti-communism. In particular, it remodeled the intellectual landscape in Western Europe, precipitating a deep rupture of the anti-fascist consensus that had seemed briefly to prevail at the end of the war.

The most probing, sophisticated analyses of totalitarianism emphasized terror and the absolute suppression of liberty while rooting the phenomenon in crucial elements of Europe's modernity – anti-Semitism, imperialism, racism – thus building a complex, nuanced historical account.[13] Other academic studies focused more specifically on the Soviet experience and formalized the typology of a pervasive and immutable regime that could not be changed from within, but only destroyed.[14]

In the wider public debate, however, even more simplified categories prevailed, and the political urge to redraw alignments and build allegiances dominated. As Cold War antagonism peaked, anti-communist intellectuals came to fear the residual lure of anti-fascist unity, particularly as the communist parties were using it to reach out for allies in their "peace" offensive against the Atlantic alliance. At the time of the Korean War, in particular, their propaganda offensive against Western rearmament appeared to have some traction. What worried American liberals and their European socialist or liberal interlocutors was the appeal of a neutral position, of the refusal to side fully and irrevocably with one of the two nascent blocs. The image of the totalitarian enemy, inherently aggressive and impervious to change, proved particularly useful in this respect, as it projected an existential antagonism between freedom and oppression, with the consequent need for an equally absolute choice between the West and Soviet communism.

It was in order to precipitate and consolidate such a choice that in June 1950 a Congress for Cultural Freedom (CCF) gathered in West Berlin. It was promoted by American liberals, such as Sidney Hook and Arthur Schlesinger, Jr., and a coalition of European liberal intellectuals – such as Bertrand Russell, Benedetto Croce, Raymond Aron and Karl Jaspers – together with socialists and ex-communists such as Arthur Koestler and Ignazio Silone. Its goal was to rally the world of culture and the arts in an Atlantic community hailed as the bastion of freedom, engage in an open fight against Marxist ideas and promote an optimistic faith in a new age of democracy best exemplified by the United States. To these ends, the identification of communism with totalitarianism provided the most useful rationalization, since "in the face of a totalitarian threat, either you decide to oppose or to appease."[15]

13 See, in particular, Hannah Arendt, *The Origins of Totalitarianism* (New York: Harcourt Brace, 1951).
14 Carl J. Friedrich and Zbigniew K. Brzezinski, *Totalitarian Dictatorship and Autocracy* (Cambridge, MA: Harvard University Press, 1956).
15 Sidney Hook quoted in Marc J. Selverstone, *Constructing the Monolith: The United States, Great Britain, and International Communism, 1945–1950* (Cambridge, MA: Harvard University Press, 2009), 171.

The Congress operated as a spearhead in the burgeoning "cultural Cold War" that was to accompany the strategic and political one for years to come (the CIA understood its importance and secretly funded the CCF). It coordinated a set of cultural periodicals – such as *Encounter, Preuves, Der Monat* and *Tempo Presente* – that would engage the battle of ideas against communism from a Western, anti-totalitarian, liberal point of view. Together with less prestigious but equally dedicated organizations, it connected European and American elites in networks of collaboration that gradually built up a powerful sense of trans-Atlantic identity. In particular, it helped to counter the distrust many European intellectuals felt toward the United States as a materialist, uncultivated society. It contributed to dispelling their postwar pacifist expectations and reconciling them with a militarized strategy of containment. It strove to relegitimize liberal ideas in the new framework of democratic politics and mass consumption.

Thus, anti-communism functioned as the catalyst of a complex process of cultural and political foundation of the West. If forming the military and economic alliance was a relatively straightforward, though far from easy, political task, the building of an Atlantic community with a shared sense of destiny and identity required composite cultural tools. It needed to supersede traditions of exclusive nationalist allegiance, to build up a perception of (West) European as well as trans-Atlantic interdependence, and promote the acceptance of US leadership around shared values and policies.

Mass anti-communist propaganda would not have sufficed. To be sure, there was a lot of it, targeted on the population of the socialist regimes via broadcasts such as those of Radio Free Europe and Radio Liberty, or on specific, crucial sections of West European societies such as youth, women and workers, by means of all the most modern and traditional media. The US government (and, to a lesser extent, its European counterparts) spent considerable resources on promoting the idealized image of a free, prosperous West and contrasting it to the misery of life under Soviet tyranny.

Its most significant and successful effort in the cultural Cold War, though, concentrated on shaping and educating a transnational, Western and Atlantic elite. By means as diverse as the secret CIA funding of the Congress for Cultural Freedom, the networking of economic and cultural elites across the Atlantic promoted by wealthy American foundations, or the massive Fulbright fellowship program to educate and socialize young Europeans in American universities, the United States successfully leveraged the anti-totalitarian battle against communism to construct an Atlantic West structured around an unprecedented American cultural hegemony.

Containing Communism or Suppressing It? Domestic Contexts

Within the shared matrix of the anti-totalitarian discourse, the battle against communism was articulated along different priorities and tactics in each distinctive national setting. The variables were many, but the main ones related to each country's political traditions and layout, especially the range and depth of an organized communist presence; the degree to which communism was publicly perceived (or could be plausibly portrayed) as an alien rather than a homegrown actor; the depth and constitutional relevance of the legacy of anti-fascist unity; and the political configuration of key social players, particularly organized labor.

The range of anti-communist strategies and politics was rather wide. In Spain and Portugal, communism had already been crushed with violent, authoritarian means by the right-wing dictatorships established in the 1930s. Here, communist militants who had not been killed struggled either to survive clandestinely or to organize in exile abroad. A similar fate befell Greek communists after they lost the 1946–49 civil war. It was the only postwar case of a communist armed insurgency in the West, and its defeat showed in no uncertain terms the hopelessness of communist subversion on the western side of the Iron Curtain.

In the democratic regimes of the West, whether long established or newly created on the ashes of fascism, two broad strands of anti-communist policies can be typified. The first one – pivoted on the representation of communism as an alien, subversive fifth column directed by the Kremlin – aimed at suppressing the phenomenon altogether by outlawing its organized activities and criminalizing its culture. Most prominent in the United States, this approach was also pursued in West Germany, where the existence of a German communist state next door generated a uniquely territorialized polarization of politics and ideology.

The second strand concerned those countries, such as France and Italy, in which large communist parties, legitimized by their role in the resistance and the postwar constitutional pact, enjoyed considerable electoral support and represented robust social interests and demands. Here, anti-communist strategies entailed an open electoral, cultural and socioeconomic competition within the democratic arena, and were pivoted on the overarching goal of keeping communists outside government. They included judicial and administrative repression of some communist activities, particularly in the field of labor, but the party's organized existence was never seriously challenged. In the remaining Western countries in which communism had a small organized presence, such as Britain, its existence was tolerated but also tightly controlled by a vigilant state, while the prevalence of social democracy in the labor movement made sure that the communists never reached a critical mass.

In each of these different cases, the state had a major, driving role. It shaped the ideological and strategic arena around the notion of an existential threat. It drew the boundaries of legitimacy for domestic communist activities. And it brought its repressive powers to bear. However, anti-communism's influence and efficacy derived also, and in no small extent, from the active mobilization of civil society and private actors, be they corporations or intellectuals, the media or labor unions, the churches, universities or voluntary organizations. Whether in pursuit of their own specific agendas or directly connected to the wider national campaign, these proactive players gave anti-communism a far wider reach, a deeper multifaceted legitimacy and a self-sustaining momentum that crowded out more nuanced opinions and options.

This dynamic was particularly relevant in the United States, where Cold War anti-communism grew into pervasive conformity. Conservative anti-communism had deep roots in the country. It had already engaged in a repressive campaign after World War I, based on a nativist identification of communism with foreign infiltration and subversion. And the Communist Party of the USA (CPUSA) – tiny but with some influence in labor unions and among intellectuals and artists – had made itself vulnerable by a supine adherence to the twists and turns of Soviet foreign policy, particularly at the time of the Nazi–Soviet Pact. As the Cold War polarity began to define the international and domestic horizon, Republicans redeployed anti-communism as a successful tool of electoral mobilization. Liberals within and outside the Truman administration responded, as we have seen, with the anti-Soviet strategy of containment and their own repositioning as the anti-totalitarian middle of the political spectrum. Thus, political competition turned into a race to prove one's credentials as communism's more determined and effective foe.

The language of anti-communism soon saturated public discourse as it merged rather seamlessly with a surging nationalist rhetoric of patriotism.

Communism appeared as the external totalitarian enemy *and* an insidious domestic agent of treason, subversion and spying. Public anxieties about the uncertain postwar world in which the United States was taking an unprecedentedly central role coalesced into fears of contamination, societal degeneration and a weakening of the body politic. A masculine rhetoric of militant patriotism, mingled with a celebration of the traditional family, engendered obsessive fears about hidden pathologies, "deviant" sexuality and especially homosexuality, which was harshly persecuted.

In this fraught cultural context, communism become the epitome of "un-American" behaviors to be suppressed. The federal government led the charge with a protracted anti-communist crusade that peaked in the early 1950s, during the Korean War. The FBI launched massive investigations not only of espionage but also of perfectly legitimate political opinions or trade union activities. Congressional committees aggressively questioned the patriotic loyalty of civil servants, journalists, teachers and activists. Communist leaders were tried and sentenced for advocating revolutionary changes. A crescendo of ever-tighter laws established security boards against subversion and made membership of the CPUSA a crime.[16]

The impact of McCarthyism (as this state-sponsored assault on communism came to be known) was multiplied by a cascading effect. Individuals publicly shamed in congressional hearings as disloyal and dangerous were often fired from their jobs. Employers used anti-communist accusations to get rid of unionists and radicals. Conservative groups assailed activists for racial equality, civil rights and other progressive causes as subversives. In the labor movement, moderate leaders purged communist officials and expelled entire unions. Churches, ethnic groups and a variety of voluntary associations redefined themselves around an intolerant patriotic identity. Thus, within a few years, not only was the CPUSA disabled, its culture and activism effectively banished, but the axis of American politics moved sharply to the right, while public discourse came to be dominated by a suffocating anti-communist consensus.

In Europe the anti-communist offensive did not focus so pervasively and obsessively on the equation of communism with anti-patriotic treason. However, the Federal Republic of Germany offered a comparable case of widespread societal rejection of communism coupled with resolute state repression, culminating in the federal prosecution of the Communist Party

---

16 See Phillip Deery, "American Communism," 642–66 in this volume.

of Germany (Kommunistische Partei Deutschlands, KPD) as an unconstitutional enemy of democracy, with its eventual banning in 1956. There too the KPD was "shunned by an overwhelmingly hostile society with a long pedigree of anti-Communist behaviour."[17] Several strands converged to shape this attitude. There was, of course, the powerful legacy of Nazi anti-Bolshevism. But also the Christian criticism of atheism, coupled with its defense of the "natural" order of family and society, was translated by the Christian Democratic Union (Christlich Demokratische Union Deutschlands, CDU) into a conservative culture of stability, domesticity and social cohesion protected by a strong state. Chancellor Konrad Adenauer denounced communism as totalitarian, Asian and barbaric, and magnified its threat to compel support for the CDU's domestic policies as well as his strategy of integration in the West. He used anti-communism to incorporate conservative nationalists into the new republic, marginalize neutralist tendencies, discipline social conflict and woo the millions of refugees from the East who of course personified, and propagated, a most potent anti-communist message of their own. At the other end of the political spectrum, deep-rooted hostilities and memories of Weimar failure drove the Social Democratic Party (Sozialdemokratische Partei Deutschlands, SPD) to a tough, uncompromising stance often expressed in anti-totalitarian language (an SPD slogan in 1949 was "A vote for the communist party is a vote for the concentration camp").

A key catalyst for this anti-communist consensus was the presence of the Red Army and a rival communist state in East Germany. First, it constituted a palpably sinister alternative as well as a scapegoat. For years, "every form of critique in West Germany was countered and discredited with a scathing: 'Why don't you go over there … if you don't like it here?'"[18] Second, the East German regime and Soviet power on the Elbe embodied the totalitarian menace with an immediacy that had no equivalent elsewhere in Western Europe. The threat was close, palpable and directly encroaching on national soil and emotions. Thus, it provided West Germany with a double legitimization as the defender of national interest *and* a champion of anti-totalitarian rebirth after the Nazi experience. Germans could avoid a full reckoning with their past, and eschew an inevitably controversial process of de-Nazification, because their painful

17 Patrick Major, *The Death of the KPD: Communism and Anti-Communism in West Germany, 1945–1956* (Oxford: Clarendon, 1997), 3.
18 Hanna Schissler, "Introduction," in Hanna Schissler (ed.), *The Miracle Years: A Cultural History of West Germany, 1949–1968* (Princeton: Princeton University Press, 2001), 9.

experience of Soviet warfare and occupation – and now of Soviet power next door – refocused blame away from them, allowed for an "exculpatory identity of victimhood"[19] and buttressed the self-perception of a new Germany at peace with Europe and the West. Thus, anti-communism functioned as the "integrating ideology of the Federal Republic."[20]

The tropes of anti-totalitarianism were of course deployed also in France and Italy. Images of communism as a vast prison camp run by a despotic party, or of a barbaric horde descending on St. Peter's Square, were recurring staples of electoral propaganda. And yet in those two countries their power was relatively stunted, since a representation of communism as a foreign fifth column had limited plausibility. The communist parties were popular (throughout the postwar period they represented between 20 and 30 percent of the voters), legitimized by their role in the resistance and in the constitutional foundation of the new republics, deeply rooted in working-class institutions and culture, appreciated as a vehicle for progress by many intellectuals and fully engaged in the national debate on planning, economic governance and the role of the state to improve welfare and employment. Thus the war metaphor that equated communism with the anti-national external enemy had less relevance, and was used to some effect only during the Korean War, to ward off the communist offensive against NATO rearmament.

In the early years, the prevailing register of anti-communist discourse was the religious one, with the Catholic Church and Christian democratic parties leveraging the ugly image of the atheistic Soviet Union to project their own counterimage as defenders of tradition, the family and a harmonious national community that repudiated the divisive prospect of class struggle and civil warfare (here, too, this permitted the quiet reintegration of conservative nationalists, whose fascist or collaborationist experiences were conveniently silenced).

Liberal and social democrats lived uncomfortably with this clerical emphasis of their main ally, but rationalized it in the name of the common struggle for Western democracy, and balanced it with a materialist insistence on economic prosperity as the main anti-communist weapon. The latter in fact became the key variable as the postwar boom gathered speed. The political strategy was focused not on crushing communism

---

19 William I. Hitchcock, *Liberation: The Bitter Road to Freedom, Europe 1944–1945* (London: Faber & Faber, 2009), 370.
20 Eric D. Weitz, "The Ever-Present Other: Communism in the Making of West Germany," in Schissler (ed.), *The Miracle Years*, 229.

(the Italian government resisted US pressures to outlaw the Italian Communist Party) but on containing, and eventually pushing back, its electoral reach and particularly its influence among industrial and agricultural workers. To this end, the state policies for growth successfully pursued throughout Western Europe – aimed at building a high-employment society with rising incomes, increasing consumption, mounting levels of economic security and upward mobility guaranteed by expansive welfare states – turned out to be the most effective.

Conclusion

By the late 1950s a prolonged economic boom was changing the face and self-perception of Western Europe. Unprecedented levels of prosperity ushered in an optimistic culture of modernization that blunted the appeal of ideological and class warfare. Based on the assumption that the postwar model of state-regulated, affluent capitalism could offer technical solutions to social and economic problems, it spread an ethos of class cooperation rather than confrontation. The integration of labor movements into practices of collective bargaining provided growing sections of the working class with a modicum of economic security, while educational paths to a middle-class future were opening up for their children. Thus, an individualist, consumerist ideology made inroads even among the communist core constituencies, which began to partake of a mass culture of prosperity and social accommodation.

To be sure, the boom was not so uniformly rosy as advertised by the new medium of television. Poverty was far from eliminated. Italy and France were still riven by a higher level of social conflict than West Germany or the Scandinavian countries. And yet, their communist parties – even if still relatively large – were suffering a manifest relegation to a ghetto of decreasing cultural and societal influence. In particular, the communists' belief system, which was centered on collective identities, was being visibly eroded by the individualizing trends inherent in mass consumerism.

This Western consolidation was substantially strengthened by the simultaneous transformations of Soviet communism. With the 1956 invasion of Hungary and the construction of the Berlin Wall in 1961, the Soviet sphere validated anti-communism's most persuasive tenets. It presented itself as a beleaguered self-enclosure, governed only by force, where people rebelled or tried to escape, and which could not sustain any comparison or contact with the West. Even among its erstwhile supporters in the West, the brief hopes raised by the thaw were replaced by disillusionment, and the communist parties' moral authority and progressive charisma suffered a final blow.

Furthermore, the Cold War's international confrontation was becoming less bellicose. After the Cuban Missile Crisis of 1962, coexistence and diplomatic negotiations prevailed, and the East–West rivalry took a far less frightening shape. Rather than the totalitarian ogre, the Soviet Union was increasingly coming across as a military superpower interested in stability, beset by a shoddy economy and plagued by the difficulty of managing its own bloc and a fractious international communist movement.

The faultline of global change moved to the "Third World," where decolonization challenged the West's positions and exposed the self-serving hypocrisy of its culture of freedom and democracy. For the generations that were coming of age in this transformed context, the Manichean dichotomy of anti-totalitarianism appeared preposterous or simply irrelevant, while criticism of Western affluence and imperialism took new forms quite distant from traditional Marxism.

Thus, in the 1960s anti-communism did not disappear, but it became less significant and relevant. To a large extent, this was due to the fact that it had won its key Cold War challenge of stabilizing the West, containing Soviet power and reducing communist influence. But it had also grown far less pertinent to the new trends and tensions that redefined both the international environment and the West's own domestic transformations.

The vastly exaggerated threat of postwar communism had engendered the stabilization of conformist democracies. It had also sustained the unprecedented state regulation of capitalism aimed at promoting income growth and its less unequal distribution. Western societies had been redefined as socially more inclusive and economically more dynamic formations. Over the long term, anti-communism's historical success in the West came to rely less on its McCarthyite repression than on this new, affluent social citizenship. The latter grew increasingly robust and attractive on its own merits, but these were considerably magnified by the persistently unappealing nature of the Soviet challenge, which gradually lost any residual ability to present itself as an alternative model.

Of course, anti-communism did not die. Though at the margins of public discourse in Western democracies, in the late 1960s and 1970s it remained a pillar of conservative identity worldwide. In particular, right-wing dictatorships in Latin America and elsewhere consistently deployed it to justify the suppression of their opponents. Then, the language of anti-communism experienced an intense revival in the early

1980s, when US president Ronald Reagan retrieved the tropes of anti-totalitarianism to exalt a policy of renewed confrontation with the USSR. The lexicon was vintage 1950s, but the implications and function of anti-communist discourse had changed. No longer an appeal for all-out mobilization in a life-and-death conflict, it now conveyed the triumphant belief that Western capitalism had overwhelmed its adversary. "The West," Reagan claimed, "[wouldn't] contain communism, it [would] transcend communism . . . as some bizarre chapter in human history whose last pages are even now being written."[21] Rather than the appeal to an existential struggle, his anti-communism was a tool to restore the rhetoric of American greatness, reengineer its hegemony around a neoliberal vision of economy and society, and entrench an anti-statist culture of individual, rather than social and economic rights. The struggle against communism was being reenacted with neoconservative zeal, but it had been won decades earlier with very different values and instruments.

Bibliographical Essay

The various strands that contribute to the history of postwar anti-communism are rarely joined together in a single study. Many of them can be explored in various essays in *The Cambridge History of the Cold War*, edited by Melvyn P. Leffler and Odd Arne Westad (Cambridge: Cambridge University Press, 2010), and in Richard H. Immerman and Petra Goedde (eds.), *The Oxford Handbook of the Cold War* (Oxford: Oxford University Press, 2013). See also Marc J. Selverstone, *Constructing the Monolith: The United States, Great Britain, and International Communism, 1945–1950* (Cambridge, MA: Harvard University Press, 2009).

The literature on anti-communism in the global South is vast and diversified. For broad overviews, see Odd Arne Westad, *The Global Cold War: Third World Interventions and the Making of Our Times* (Cambridge, MA: Cambridge University Press, 2005), and Robert J. McMahon (ed.), *The Cold War in the Third World* (Oxford: Oxford University Press, 2012).

On Western strategic analyses of the Soviet Union and communism, and the ensuing policy of containment, see Melvyn P. Leffler, *For the Soul of Mankind: The United States, the Soviet Union, and the Cold War* (New York: Hill & Wang, 2007); Anders Stephanson, "The Cold War Considered as a US

---

21 Ronald Reagan, "Address at the University of Notre Dame," 17 May 1981, reaganlibrary.archives.gov/archives/speeches/1981/51781a.htm.

Project," in Silvio Pons and Federico Romero (eds.), *Reinterpreting the End of the Cold War: Issues, Interpretations, Periodizations* (London: Frank Cass, 2005), 52–67; John Lewis Gaddis, *Strategies of Containment: A Critical Appraisal of Postwar American National Security Policy* (Oxford: Oxford University Press, 1982).

The most comprehensive historical investigations of the meanings, permutations and usage of the concept of totalitarianism are Enzo Traverso, *Le totalitarisme. Le XXe siècle en débat* (Paris: Éditions du Seuil, 2001), and Abbott Gleason, *Totalitarianism: The Inner History of the Cold War* (New York: Oxford University Press, 1995).

The "cultural Cold War" waged for the consolidation of an anti-communist Western identity has been explored in many recent studies. Among the most illuminating are Volker R. Berghahn, *America and the Intellectual Cold Wars in Europe: Shepard Stone Between Philanthropy, Academy, and Diplomacy* (Princeton: Princeton University Press, 2001); Patrick Major and Rana Mitter (eds.), *Across the Blocs: Exploring Comparative Cold War Cultural and Social History* (London: Frank Cass, 2004); Marco Mariano (ed.), *Defining the Atlantic Community: Culture, Intellectuals, and Policies in the Mid-Twentieth Century* (New York: Routledge, 2010); Giles Scott-Smith and Hans Krabbendam (eds.), *Cultural Cold War in Western Europe, 1945–1960* (London: Frank Cass, 2004); Giles Scott-Smith, *The Politics of Apolitical Culture: The Congress for Cultural Freedom, the CIA and Post-War American Hegemony* (New York: Routledge, 2002).

On anti-communism in the United States, see Larry Ceplair, *Anti-Communism in Twentieth-Century America: A Critical History* (Santa Barbara, CA: Praeger, 2011); Ellen Schrecker, *Many Are the Crimes: McCarthyism in America* (Boston: Little Brown, 1998); Richard M. Fried, *Nightmare in Red: The McCarthy Era in Perspective* (Oxford: Oxford University Press, 1990); Andrea Friedman, *Citizenship in Cold War America* (Amherst: University of Massachusetts Press, 2014); Douglas Field (ed.), *American Cold War Culture* (Edinburgh: Edinburgh University Press, 2005).

On the politics and culture of postwar Europe, see Tony Judt, *Postwar: A History of Europe Since 1945* (New York: Penguin Press, 2005); Dan Stone, *Goodbye to All That? A History of Europe Since 1945* (Oxford: Oxford University Press, 2014); Jan-Werner Müller, *Contesting Democracy: Political Ideas in Twentieth-Century Europe* (New Haven: Yale University Press, 2011); Mark Gilbert, *Cold War Europe: The Politics of a Contested Continent* (Lanham, MD: Rowman & Littlefield, 2014); Dan Stone (ed.), *The Oxford Handbook of Postwar European History* (Oxford: Oxford University Press,

2012); Patrick Major, *The Death of the KPD: Communism and Anti-Communism in West Germany, 1945–1956* (Oxford: Clarendon, 1997); Hanna Schissler (ed.), *The Miracle Years: A Cultural History of West Germany, 1949–1968* (Princeton: Princeton University Press, 2001); Konrad Hugo Jarausch, *After Hitler: Recivilizing Germans, 1945–1995* (Oxford: Oxford University Press, 2006); Mario Del Pero, *L'alleato scomodo. Gli USA e la DC negli anni del Centrismo (1948–1955)* (Rome: Carocci, 2001); Andrea Mariuzzo, *Divergenze parallele. Comunismo e anticomunismo alle origini del linguaggio politico dell'Italia repubblicana (1945–1955)* (Soveria Mannelli: Rubbettino, 2010); Philippe Buton, Olivier Buttner and Michel Hastings (eds.), *La Guerre froide vue d'en bas* (Paris: CNRS Éditions, 2014).

PART II

*

BECOMING GLOBAL, BECOMING NATIONAL

13

Communism, Decolonization and the Third World

ANDREAS HILGER

By the time Stalin dissolved the Comintern (Communist International) in 1943, the organization had long abandoned its erstwhile national liberation momentum. At the beginning, the October Revolution had not only embol- dened and strengthened the world's communist circles, but had also inspired colonial and dependent peoples with new hopes. Nevertheless, national movements under bourgeois leadership did not necessarily pursue commu- nist conceptions regarding the content and reality of independence. In short, while communism was not thinkable without overcoming foreign domina- tion, national self-determination and state-building without communism were.

Due to the constitution of, first, a socialist state and, afterwards, a socialist camp and socialist world system, relations between communism and national liberation were never a question of domestic affairs alone. They always possessed significant international dimensions and implications. In this global context, it seems to be appropriate to conceptualize contacts or interactions between the Third and Second Worlds as relationships between emerging nations of the "East" and a Soviet empire. The USSR by all historical standards qualified for categorization as an empire. Its vast territory and multiethnic population were organized in a distinct center–periphery hier- archy and ruled by a metropolitan elite. As in other empires, brute force was considered to be the last resort of its power. Finally, Marxism-Leninism provided Moscow with a "civilizing mission" in domestic and international affairs.[1] Independent of formal or informal types of integration, imperial

---

1 For discussion of terminologies, see B. R. Tomlinson, "What Was the Third World?" in *Journal of Contemporary History* 38 (2003), 307–21; special number of *Third World Quarterly* 1 (2004), "After the Third World"; Jürgen Osterhammel, *Die Verwandlung der Welt. Eine Geschichte des 19. Jahrhunderts* (Munich: Beck, 2009), 606–16; Ronald Grigor Suny and Terry Martin (eds.), *A State of Nations: Empire- and Nation-Making in the Age of Lenin and*

extension implies fundamental reorganization as well as reorientation of political, social, economic and cultural ideas and constellations of peripheral parts. Therefore, the process of empire-building basically runs counter to aspirations of nation-building that aim for self-determined structuring of these central aspects.

In theory, ultimate dissolution of national confines in an all-encompassing communist world seemed to offer the possibility of reconciling different visions. During a transitional period of indefinite duration, however, tensions between noncommunist movements or states and Moscow's empire appeared to be unavoidable. These international tensions interacted with communist–nationalist dynamics on the national level.

The given constellation provided for a complex trilateral relationship between national noncommunist movements, their communist counterparts and the emerging center of world communism, Moscow. In the prewar years, the anti-imperialist thrust of all three sides could at least allow for temporary alliances, diverging perspectives on nation-building after liberation notwithstanding. Since the very beginning, however, cooperation was pragmatic rather than amicable. Finally, the activities and reactions of the alleged common enemy always had the potential to influence the cohesion of the anti-imperialist pact. Perceived changes in size, solidarity, motivations or the overall threat of the opposite camp affected international as well as domestic priorities of members of the anti-imperialist front, with adjustments by one section altering the balance of the whole. In the final analysis, the communist–Third World relationship was always an integral part of a web of interrelated connections among multiple centers of all the three worlds.

Postwar Orientations

Since the 1920s, in the context of fierce power struggles, the Kremlin elite had enforced its ideological hegemony in the world communist community. Increasing domination went hand in hand with the unconditional orientation of organized socialist internationalism toward the needs of the Kremlin.

Stalin (Oxford: Oxford University Press, 2001); Dominic C. Lieven, Empire: The Russian Empire and Its Rivals (London: Murray, 2000); Tania Raffass, The Soviet Union: Federation or Empire? (London: Routledge, 2012); and Hannes Adomeit, Imperial Overstretch: Germany in Soviet Policy from Stalin to Gorbachev (Baden-Baden: Nomos, 1998). Vladislav Zubok and Konstantin Pleshakov, Inside the Kremlin's Cold War: From Stalin to Khrushchev (Cambridge, MA: Harvard University Press, 1996), seem to overrate friction between geopolitics and ideology in imperial approaches.

Consequently, communist activists – inside and outside Europe – were expected to recognize the USSR's leadership as the highest authority in questions of methods and goals of their own anti-imperialist activities. In practice, Moscow's tactical and strategic guidance more often than not was prone to ignoring local conditions. During World War II, the Soviet Union's cooperation with imperial powers additionally exacerbated contradictions between national liberation ambitions and communist pro-Soviet politics. The standing of the Communist Party of India (CPI) is a case in point: Indian communists' backing of British war efforts completely estranged the party from the national mainstream and denied the CPI any influence during the most important decision-making processes after the war. At that time, Soviet observers themselves considered the CPI to be nothing more than an occasional source of information.[2] Anyway, the Comintern's successor, the Cominform (Communist Information Bureau), established in 1947, remained an exclusively European affair, thus reflecting the Soviet Union's immediate concerns of the postwar period.

Echoing Khrushchev's criticism, historical analyses often tend to interpret Stalin's considerable reservations about involvement outside Eastern Europe after World War II as indifference toward developments and possibilities in the rest of the world. Certainly, Stalin's knowledge about Asian and African, let alone Latin American, developments was outdated and sketchy at best. Nevertheless, beginning in 1943–44, Soviet state and party functionaries had developed a distinct interest in changes looming in Asia and Africa. The USSR had virtually no possibility of influencing accelerating processes of decolonization, but the leadership was determined to take advantage of the situation. From Stalin's point of view, under conditions of socialist–imperialist bipolarity, adequate reactions were likely to promote recognition of Soviet great-power status and to enhance geopolitical security in critical adjacent regions. In addition, all kinds of disturbances in the colonial world would test the coherence of the opposing, imperialist camp and restrict both its power and its maneuverability. On the other hand, the Soviet Union and its potential allies, while closing ranks and consolidating strength, had to avoid direct confrontation with overwhelmingly powerful adversaries for the time being.

2 Gene D. Overstreet and Marshall Windmiller, *Communism in India* (Berkeley: University of California Press, 1959); Purabi Roy, Sobhanlal DattaGupta and Hari Vasudevan (eds.), *Indo-Russian Relations: 1917–1947*, Part II, *1929–1947* (Kolkata: Asiatic Society, 2000); Andreas Hilger, "The Soviet Union and India: The Years of Late Stalinism" (2008), www .php.isn.ethz.ch/collections/coll_india/intro_stalin.cfm?navinfo=56154#F6.

These fundamental calculations explain Moscow's concrete activities in the Third World at that time: A Soviet voice in former Italian colonies, sponsorship of Kurdish and Azerbaijani national sentiments in the Middle East, backing of the foundation of the state of Israel, propagandistic encouragement for anti-colonial movements in Southeast Asia and diplomatic pinpricks regarding South Asian independence as well as support for Chinese communists in Manchuria had to serve these interconnected goals.

As in preceding years, Moscow believed that a skillful combination of Soviet state interests with anti-imperialist perspectives depended on undisputed Soviet leadership of world communism. Radicalization of South and Southeast Asian communist parties from 1947–48 heralded growing differences within the socialist camp. In fact, they did not follow Moscow's instructions: To a certain degree they reflected Yugoslav combativeness as well as local susceptibilities to communist Chinese successes.[3] In the light of Mao's advance, Stalin himself had to acknowledge that Mao's independent revolutionary calculus "proved to be right, and we were wrong."[4] Nevertheless, the concession was not to be mistaken for Moscow's renunciation of overall leadership. Ideas and plans for an Asian Cominform were never realized.

New Possibilities

At the end of the 1940s, postwar Soviet economic reconstruction, nuclear successes and Mao's proclamation of the People's Republic of China, as well as consolidation of Soviet power in Eastern Europe, combined to increase the Kremlin's international capacity to act. Given the contrast between the freezing of the correlation of forces in Europe on the one hand, and Asian dynamics on the other, Asia seemed to be the obvious choice for further socialist moves. From the point of view of Moscow, the combined activities of local and international forces still had to serve the USSR's international priorities. They had to curtail imperialist vigor while undermining imperialist positions and cooperation. Yet in doing so, the chosen maneuvers had to avoid an escalation to general war, thus furnishing socialist countries with additional time for stabilization. Besides, the chances of success of selective

---

3 Special issue of *Journal of Southeast Asian Studies* 40, 3 (2009), "The Origins of the Southeast Asian Cold War."

4 Memo of conversation of Stalin, Molotov, etc. with Bulgarian leadership, 10 Feb. 1948, in Ivo Banac (ed.), *The Diary of Georgi Dimitrov 1933–1949* (New Haven: Yale University Press, 2003), 443.

anti-imperialist probing had to be carefully calculated lest these probes unnecessarily exhaust socialist resources. Strengthening the socialist camp and affirming Moscow's socialist hegemony still seemed to be quasi-identical goals. The definition of promising courses of action in concrete situations, deployment of socialist forces and balancing national and international concerns were all aspects of policy that were expected to remain Soviet prerogatives. So, by downplaying Chinese military successes and rejecting Beijing's ideological relevance and usefulness as a model, Stalin in the early 1950s aimed to curb revolutionary-minded but ineffective Indian and Indonesian communists.[5] Although Moscow diminished Mao's significance for world communism, it nevertheless requested and appreciated the deployment of Chinese resources for the common cause in Korea and Vietnam. To be sure, Soviet military, economic and diplomatic aid did bolster Mao's China, but there was a price to be paid for it. The so-called liberation of Taiwan remained out of Beijing's reach. In contrast, China's rapid, violent integration of Tibet had Moscow's unconditional support.

Sino-Soviet consensus in regard to relations with Tibet underlined the socialist camp's lack of sympathy for noncommunist national liberation movements and nonsocialist states alike. Beijing's intervention not only ran contrary to distinct Tibetan hopes, but unsettled the expectations of neighboring independent India as well. In Stalin's and Mao's final analysis, bourgeois or feudal self-determination meant nothing less than continuation of oppression of the masses. According to socialist assessments, in global terms Indian apprehensions once again seemed to reveal an anti-socialist nature as well as the obedience to imperialism of Nehru's and similar nationalist governments.

Against the background of Stalin's understanding of international relations, limited cooperation with such new countries appeared to be a useful instrument to augment perceived intra-imperialist inconsistencies. At the same time, attracting broader leftist circles to Soviet international positions was regarded as helpful in undermining corresponding nonsocialist governments. Mobilization for Soviet-guided peace campaigns in Asia, the International Economic Conference in Moscow (3–12 April 1952) with its noticeable presence of guests from nonsocialist countries, first Soviet trade offers to the Third World and Soviet anti-Western engagement in United

5 Hilger, "The Soviet Union and India"; Larisa M. Efimova, "Stalin and the Revival of the Communist Party of Indonesia," *Cold War History* 5 (2005), 107–20.

Nations discussions concerning noncommunist crisis regions such as Kashmir demonstrated Stalinism's new flexibility in international affairs. However, they signaled neither an abandonment of communist claims to leadership in questions of national liberation nor recognition of autonomous positions of nonsocialist governments in decolonized countries. Consequentially, the Kremlin demonstrated benign interest in Asian attempts to find negotiated solutions in Korea, but ultimately let the bloody conflict simmer. Moscow contemplated the destruction of the "American" United Nations, but brusquely rejected proposals to liquidate the Soviet Cominform.[6] According to Stalin, communist and workers' parties had to raise the "banner of national independence and national sovereignty [which] has been thrown overboard" by the bourgeoisie, thus becoming "leading powers" of their nations – and making their countries reliable allies of the USSR.[7]

The Emerging Third World and Khrushchev's Offensive

Following Stalin's death, reevaluation of his foreign policy took place under conditions of merciless power struggles and disputes about economic and domestic politics. Finally, Nikita Khrushchev overcame proponents of a continuation of the Stalinist course. For years to come, although Khrushchev never achieved a Stalin-like position in the USSR or in the broader socialist camp, he would be able to shape Soviet international relations decisively.

One argument of the Khrushchev camp for redesigning foreign policy had been the virtual isolation of socialism, leading to ignorance regarding the current situation in different corners of the world. Accordingly, in February 1956 Soviet Oriental studies once again came under harsh criticism for its failures to provide appropriate information.[8] In reality, however, all Soviet international actors – from the Ministry of Foreign Affairs and Ministry of Foreign Trade to the Intelligence Service, Society for Cultural

---

6 Memo of conversation, Stalin with Zhou Enlai, 19 Sep. 1952, in S. L. Tichvinskii (ed.), *Sovetsko-kitaiskie otnosheniia,* vol. V, part 2, *1949–fevral' 1950 gg.* (Moscow: Pamiatniki istoricheskoi mysli, 2005), 331; Memo of conversation, Stalin with Indian ambassador Sarvepalli Radhakrishnan, 5 Apr. 1952, *Revolutionary Democracy* 12 (2006), no. 1, www.revolutionarydemocracy.org/rdv12n1/3convers.htm.
7 Stalin at Nineteenth CPSU Party Congress, 14 Oct. 1952, in Iosif V. Stalin, *Werke,* vol. XV (Dortmund: Roter Morgen, 1979), 247.
8 Anastas Mikoian on the Twentieth Party Congress, 16 Feb. 1956, in *XX s"ezd Kommunisticheskoi partii Sovetskogo soiuza 14–25 fevralia 1956 goda. Stenograficheskii otchet,* vol. I (Moscow: Politicheskaia literatura, 1956), 324–25.

Relations, Intourist and the Foreign Commission of the Union of Soviet Writers – had very limited access to and scant understanding of foreign regions, let alone the Third World.

In the meantime, the term "Third World" was acquiring its distinct quality. Decolonization was becoming an irreversible process. In 1955 the Bandung conference demonstrated a new sense of Afro-Asian solidarity and cohesion. Shared pasts of foreign oppression and exploitation constituted one pillar of their claimed collective identity. In addition, representatives were convinced that current international structures tended to perpetuate traditional hierarchical political and economic relations, to the detriment of the peoples of Asia, Africa and Latin America. In the following years, the rather vague commitment to self-determination, equality and development was substantiated by both more concrete and more far-reaching demands, as demonstrated at the Non-Aligned Conference in Belgrade (1961) and the UNCTAD (United Nations Conference on Trade and Development) in Geneva (1964). At the same time, the Third World was becoming more differentiated and more discordant. Leftist governments and movements agitated for socialist-informed solutions to all problems of political and economic nation-building and against the lasting inertia of colonial power. Other influential parts of the Third World acted as counterbalances. Ongoing diversification was illustrated by the sequence of Third World forums from the formation of the Casablanca and Monrovia groups (1961), disunity concerning the followup to Bandung and Belgrade (1964–65), to the First Solidarity Conference of the Peoples of Africa, Asia and Latin America in Havana (1966). To a certain degree, divisions corresponded to political-ideological Cold War contradictions. For all that, Third World right- or left-leaning leaderships did not duplicate the "two camps" argumentation, nor their fundamental goals. Instead, they attempted to adapt Cold War considerations to their own nation-building programs.

At first the Third World's anti-imperialist grounding seemed to offer the socialist world promising contact points, all the more so as the new leadership in Moscow was ready to adjust to the evident dynamics of decolonization entangled with Cold War developments. The Kremlin introduced several important innovations in its traditional calculations of the correlation of power in the domestic and international spheres. In contrast to Stalin's uncompromising bipolar view on the world, post-Stalinism acted on the assumption that new, emerging political actors of the Third World could and would achieve real independence from their former hegemons. Under these conditions Khrushchev affirmed a quasi-natural identity of Third World and communist interests in overcoming Western imperialism, in peacekeeping and in the general progress of mankind. This interconnected global process would be promoted by the new societies' transition to socialism and vice versa. In the domestic sphere, Moscow equated industrialization and economic improvements with the awakening and strengthening of political awareness among the masses. This trend was to be supported by constructive cooperation with socialist countries, the assumed increasing attractiveness of socialist living standards and the continuous downward spiral of Western capitalism. Altogether, these ingredients would facilitate nonrevolutionary, parliamentary paths to socialism, thus more or less automatically implementing historical laws.

During the transition period, socialist countries had to shield at the lowest possible cost both domestic and international progress from imperialist encroachments. Analogous to domestic affairs, on the international level the supposedly reinforcing processes of decolonization and socialism had to master corresponding challenges: An economically successful and militarily strong socialist world system with the assistance of growing anti-imperialist forces in the Third World (and supported by peace movements in the First World) would be able to peacefully defend ongoing advances toward communism by deterring imperialism from desperate wars. War on a global scale no longer was regarded to be inevitable. Instead, in view of the balance of nuclear terror, the prevention of general war proved to be a new necessity for world communism's blossoming.

Undoubtedly, this vision of a socialist perpetual-motion machine rested upon fragile premises. On the international level, the dynamic polygon of Three Worlds demanded careful balance between systemic Cold War competition and anti-imperialism. A preponderance of superpower considerations could impair socialist–Third World relations, since Cold War aggravations or détente tended to eclipse either the Third World's security needs or its equal rights and development concerns. On the other hand, too radical an anti-imperialism could provoke undesired imperialist aggressiveness, while laxity risked opening new gateways for imperialist machinations. Bilaterally, diplomatic as well as economic, cultural and military cooperation between socialist and Third Worlds continuously had to reconcile fundamental imperial and national orientations. Aside from international uncertainties, envisaged domestic developments likewise were far from being certain. It remained to be seen whether bourgeois leaders of the Third World would readily accept their evolutionary replacement, or if socialism would prove to be the choice of the Third World masses. Finally, congruence of domestic and international positioning was no foregone conclusion either. Basically, in cases of future incongruities, Soviet international relations would prefer to retain foreign-policy advantages, thus to a certain degree neglecting contradictions in their partners' domestic affairs.

In the final analysis, it was Khrushchev's optimism that had to compensate for any conceptual shortcomings of his theory. From his point of view, there seemed to be no ambiguities when Gamal Abdel Nasser, Jawaharlal Nehru, U Nu and Sukarno proclaimed socialist leanings and plans. His confidence was strengthened in 1955 – during his Asia trip the socialist leader claimed to have experienced the "trust and love of the masses in the countries of the East."[9] According to Khrushchev, socialism "has started to conquer the mind of mankind."[10]

Soviet elites and functionaries set to work on supporting this development by all thinkable peaceful means in every sphere of international and domestic life. The dissolution of the Cominform (1956) signaled Moscow's attention to Third World apprehensions concerning foreign interference in domestic affairs. Visits and invitations; the organization of conferences, meetings and institutions; economic, diplomatic and military cooperation as well as cultural and scientific exchange; propagandistic self-portrayals or demonstrations of military power and of technical and social achievements – all ceaselessly depicted the advantages of the socialist order. The growing participation of Central Asian and Caucasian emissaries was supposed to lend the Soviet model additional credibility and persuasiveness. Besides, it was understood that fellow socialist countries would share the work of winning hearts and minds in the Third World. Khrushchev, by riding elephants in Asia, lecturing African, Asian and Latin America leaders about correct development policy or peaceful coexistence, and pounding the UN lectern, literally epitomized the complex mixture of communist openness, solidarity, condescension and aggressiveness. But we should note that Moscow's activities were contextualized in peaceful competition for socialist hegemony and designed less as interaction than as a one-way street.

9 Khrushchev at the Twentieth CPSU Party Congress, 14 Feb. 1956, in *XX. Parteitag der Kommunistischen Partei der Sowjetunion. Bericht des Zentralkomitees der KPdSU* (Düsseldorf: KPD, 1956), 22.
10 Khrushchev at Party Meeting Factory No. 23, 11 Aug. 1955, in N. G. Tomilina (ed.), *Nikita Sergeevich Khrushchev*, vol. I (Moscow: Demokratiia, 2009), 556.

Economic Cooperation and National Developments in the Third World

In this general context, the Soviet Union inevitably paid special attention to economic cooperation. In 1955, Khrushchev's close associate Anastas Mikoian put the Kremlin's new calculations in a nutshell: "We have to help some states, if we want to start a more serious competition with the USA."[11] Purposeful promotion of Third World industrialization was expected to bolster alienation of decolonized states from the West and propel their domestic transition to socialism at the same time. Implementation of this economic dual-track offensive revealed its inconsistencies as well as its limits. Cooperation achieved mixed results at best. To be sure, the Soviets may have contributed to establishing new sectors of industry in several countries. The long-term impacts of partial industrialization, of minor foreign trade diversification or reorientation, and of possible temporary foreign reserve savings were uneven, and there is still no consensus on the results. With regard to the principal goals or expected implications of socialist development aid, the broader picture turned out to be disappointing. In terms of peaceful competition with the West, Third World planners never could realize their ambitions by socialist aid alone. During the 1950s and 1960s, Western financial, trade and educational cooperative projects far outnumbered socialist contributions. The resources of Comecon (Council for Mutual Economic Assistance) members were limited, and the coordination of their foreign economic projects remained incomplete. Besides, some East European junior partners proved to be reluctant imperial missionaries. In addition, Third World commercial partners from time to time prioritized prestige projects without a positive development impact. More elaborate cooperative projects suffered from limited intake capacities on the receiving end and serious supply difficulties on the donor end, with regard to quantity as well as quality. General debt service restricted cooperation as well. In addition, in nonsocialist countries industrialization efforts tended to remain isolated from broader economic and domestic politics, since such governments shied away from radical land, social, educational and administrative reforms. Trade relations added to the complications of socialist–Third World economic relations. Traditional trade patterns, with the USSR exporting machines and other heavy industrial goods while importing raw materials

11 Protocol, CC Presidium, 16 Dec. 1955, in A. A. Fursenko (ed.), *Prezidium TsK KPSS 1954–1964*, vol. I, *Chernovye protokol'nye zapisi zasedanii Stenogrammy* (Moscow: ROSSPEN, 2003), 71–72.

and selected products from unsophisticated light industries, ran the risk of undermining plans for all-encompassing industrialization.

Finally, domestic leftist forces in former colonies had problems playing a decisive role. Obviously, the transition to socialism did not constitute a self-fulfilling prophecy. Neither perceptions of socialist reality nor propaganda were able to shape developments decisively in accordance with Khrushchev's early concept. As before, Third World representatives were determined to pursue independently defined national goals by selecting autonomously from foreign partners and offers. The alleged pro-socialist countries from 1955 were a case in point. By 1960, Nehru's central administration had dismissed the first elected communist state government in Kerala. In addition, Delhi had decided to shelter anti-Chinese refugees from Tibet. In Egypt, Nasser had imprisoned indigenous and foreign communists alike. Burma's U Nu had given way to a self-declared military caretaker government that detained and deported members of the communist party. In Indonesia the fragile relationship between the army and communist supporters of Sukarno had collapsed temporarily, while several communist functionaries had been arrested. The question of whether "socialism can be built by persons who do not take up Marxist positions" must have been on the minds of Soviet elites long before 1964.[12] At the end of the 1950s, corresponding academic debates started filling more and more pages of journals specializing in area studies. They did not exert a noticeable influence on the Kremlin's decision-making, although the global situation had become more complicated than either Khrushchev or his experts had expected.

Socialist Countries, the Third World and Global Cold War

Indeed, from Moscow's point of view the chain of events demonstrated unanticipated volatility and, above all, reckless imperialist attempts to stem the socialist tide. Suez, Anglo-American intervention in the Middle East, French cancellation of all aid programs for newly independent Guinea, alleged foreign involvement in the Tibetan rebellion, Patrice Lumumba's Congo disaster, Gary Power's U-2 surveillance flight from Pakistan, the American embargo and unconcealed violence against Cuba,

---

12 Dictation, Khrushchev, 27 Jun. 1964, in A. N. Artizov et al. (eds.), *Nikita Khrushchev 1964. Stenogrammy plenuma TsK KPSS i drugie dokumenty* (Moscow: Demokratiia, 2007), 43–44.

fighting in Vietnam and almost incomprehensible embroilments in Laos as well as continuing racism and colonialism in southern Africa and Algeria refreshed memories of pre-1955 imperialist incursions into Iran and Guatemala. These events also underlined the alleged peace-threatening characteristics of pro-Western alliances in Southeast Asia (SEATO, Southeast Asia Treaty Organization) and the Middle East (CENTO, Central Treaty Organization).

A dialectic interpretation could consider imperialist maneuvers to be reflex actions in the face of continuous advances of the anti-imperialist alliance. Indeed, decolonization was gaining momentum, culminating in the emergence of seventeen newly independent African states in 1960. Cuba had planted the seeds of socialism in Latin America. The famous Declaration 1514 of the United Nations General Assembly "On Granting Independence to Colonial Countries and Peoples" was adopted by an overwhelming majority and isolated abstaining Western powers from world opinion.

Nevertheless, these processes did not result in a convergence of Third World self-determination and socialist advances. The genesis of this UN declaration provides an illuminating example. Noncommunist representatives prevented Soviet utilization of original Third World concerns for simplistic Cold War benefits. Equally, Soviet ideas to substitute a West-East-Third World troika for the UN's secretary-general did not find understanding among African, Asian and Latin American delegations. In contrast, increasing superpower tensions at that time lent new impetus to Third World efforts to elude the dangerous logic of Cold War. In 1961, the Belgrade Non-Aligned Conference formulated independent international positions which ran counter to the USSR's international activities. Against the background of obvious differences on international questions, Khrushchev started to blame Third World countries for their "anti-communism."[13] Moreover, the Soviet leadership deliberately demonstrated that it had learned different lessons from international developments from Suez to Congo. The Kremlin's decision to restart nuclear tests at the very beginning of the Belgrade conference highlighted discrepancies regarding international priorities and approaches. "[O]ne cannot by adjurations, speeches and prayers wrest peace from the enemy," Khrushchev declared; "One has to wrest it from him by struggle, and

---

13 Khrushchev at Presidium CC CPSU, 26 May 1961, in Fursenko (ed.), *Prezidium TsK KPSS*, vol. I, 506.

therefore we do not shy away from that struggle nor from carrying out tests." In this general context, Khrushchev regarded the new test series to be "necessary for cleaning the brains of some pacifists" in Third World countries.[14]

In view of a certain dissatisfaction and impatience regarding anti-imperialist developments and with unrelieved tensions of the Cold War in mind, Moscow had to adjust its underlying concepts of socialist–Third World relations. In doing so, the socialist community under Soviet guidance refined attributes that would allow Third World domestic orders to be qualified as auspicious starting points for the future construction of socialism. Such postindependence "states of national democracy" had to permit, among other things, leftist activities, reforms and economics. In November 1960, the authoritative declaration of the Moscow meeting of delegates from eighty-one communist and workers' parties therefore, once again, underlined the decisive importance of communist activities in achieving real national progress. Significantly, however, the conference started its definition with foreign-policy categories such as defense of national economic and political sovereignty and "struggle against imperialism and its military blocs, against military bases on Third World territories" and "against penetration by imperialist capital" alike.[15] All in all, the conference assessed the potential of noncommunist movements and states with more restraint than the overoptimistic Khrushchev of 1955, but stuck to his general line. Although criticizing previous deviations from the straight course toward socialism, the conference affirmed the fundamentally progressive nature of anti-imperialist, nonsocialist leaderships in the Third World for the time being.[16] Therefore, domestic nonrevolutionary paths to socialism remained a promising option. With regard to global developments, such nonsocialist governments still seemed to offer possibilities for both long-term transitions as well as immediate opportunities in the context of the USSR's superpower competition.

Moscow's leader also formulated a more differentiated understanding of war prevention, to balance his main objectives in the context of decolonization and the Cold War. As before, the USSR considered World War III to be

---

14 After-dinner speech Khrushchev, Crimea, 27 Aug. 1961, in Gerhard Wettig (ed.), *Chruschtschows Westpolitik 1955–1964. Gespräche, Aufzeichnungen und Stellungnahmen*, vol. III (Munich: Oldenbourg, 2011), 415–16.

15 Declaration, Conference of Communist and Workers' Parties, 5 Dec. 1960, in *Erklärung der Beratung von Vertretern der kommunistischen und Arbeiterparteien. November 1960* (Berlin: Dietz, 1961), 44–45.

16 Ibid., 43–44.

avoidable and was determined to avoid it in any circumstance. As demonstrated by their nuclear test series, the Kremlin considered shows and positions of strength to be necessary instruments to achieve peaceful objectives. With regard to the Third World, determination to prevent a global war could not and should not indefinitely restrict the "sacred" rights of people worldwide to freedom, self-determination and progress. In fact, national liberation wars appeared to be the last resort of defense against imperialist intransigence. "Where a people will lose their patience and rise in arms," "the Communists fully support such just wars."[17] In doing so, however, Moscow would continue to pay due attention to prevention of unlimited escalation. In any case, the USSR's "most positive" attitude to such wars was not automatically translated into extensive military support.[18]

Military Cooperation and Third World Conflicts

Military aid constituted a classic instrument of both superpower geopolitics and strengthening anti-imperialist bonds. In 1955, arms deliveries to Egypt had fit into Moscow's new determination and optimism in the Third World. In principle, given the complex interconnection between socialist–Third World relations and superpower antagonism, military cooperation led to ambivalent results at best and dangerous ones at worst. Inevitably, military expenditures would impede Third World economic development plans. Moreover, arming the Third World tended to increase regional militarization. The growing military potential ran the danger of exacerbating regional conflicts as well as radicalizing regional anti-imperialists, with violent reactions from local and global counterparts looming large. As in the case of economic cooperation, military contacts did not necessarily translate into lasting big-power influence or socialist reorientation of Third World recipients. Therefore, in implementing military cooperation Moscow had to weigh possible advantages against the rising danger of becoming implicated in regional conflicts or even of finding itself face to face with the Western adversary. Local conflagrations could reveal certain Soviet weaknesses with

---

17 Nikita Khrushchev, "For New Victories of the World Communist Movement," speech at meeting of Party Organizations of Higher Party School et al., 6 Jan. 1961, quoted in translation in *Hearing Before the Subcommittee to Investigate the Administration of the Internal Security Act and Internal Security Laws*, 16 Jun. 1961 (Washington, DC: US Government Printing Office, 1961), Appendix III, 64–65.
18 Khrushchev, "For New Victories of the World Communist Movement."

regard to the USSR's capability to project military power globally. Escalating embroilment would force a choice between peaceful competition and anti-imperialist leadership – a choice the Kremlin preferred to avoid lest it estrange its allies or risk a nuclear showdown.

Soviet attempts to capitalize on the Third World's need for self-defense vis-à-vis the imperial powers, without promoting incalculable aggressiveness was like walking a tightrope. In the final analysis, the USSR acted on the assumption that the imperialist rival would duly give in for reasons of caution, rationality or exhaustion, thus allowing for peaceful solutions. In the meantime, to keep the balance, the Kremlin resorted to a mixture of propagandistic abrasiveness in the media and international forums, diplomatic initiatives and conservatively calculated military aid in the form of weapons, money, training and advice. This approach shaped Soviet reactions to Congo, Laos, Algeria, Vietnam, the Sino-Indian border conflict, southern African liberation movements and the Egyptian intervention in Yemen in the early 1960s.

To be sure, deployment of nuclear weapons in Cuba was a contribution to the defense of Havana's revolution. Nevertheless, Khrushchev could not overcome the temptation to exploit the situation in favor of pure superpower considerations. By launching an "aggressive policy" in Cuba, he strove for decisive improvements in the overall Soviet strategic position vis-à-vis the USA.[19] As events unfolded, Soviet withdrawal of its missiles clearly demonstrated Khrushchev's preferences when he had to choose between unconditional anti-imperialism and peaceful competition. The more radical wing of world communism did not lose time in venting its anger. Che Guevara, the co-leader of the Cuban Revolution, assured the world public that he would have fired the missiles had he been in control.[20]

The Sino-Soviet Split and the Third World

Since 1945, Soviet predominance in world communism and its Third World policies have been repeatedly contested. As mentioned above, Yugoslav representatives had pleaded for more activism as early as 1948. Later, Belgrade's nonaligned cooperation with Third World countries posed a strong challenge to Moscow's hegemonic style. North Vietnam's route to forced unification under the socialist banner, as well as Cuba's

19 Khrushchev at Presidium CC CPSU, 21 May 1962, in Fursenko (ed.), *Prezidium TsK KPSS*, vol. I, 556.
20 Jon Lee Anderson, *Che Guevara: A Revolutionary Life* (New York: Grove Press, 1997), 545.

combativeness, represented left radicalism that consciously questioned Moscow's foreign-policy recipes. Nevertheless, the main challenge came from Mao's China – which had achieved its socialist great-power status with the aid of considerable diplomatic, economic and military support from the USSR. Since the late 1950s, Chinese criticism had undoubtedly increased at least Soviet verbal radicalism and contributed to Moscow's growing dissatisfaction with the results of its foreign policy. This criticism also complicated Soviet attempts to balance its relations with both the Third and First Worlds.

From the very beginning, the Sino-Soviet relationship had been ambivalent. During Stalin's lifetime, hierarchies in the socialist camp appeared to be uncontroversial. Then, Beijing took advantage of increasing Soviet aid, and the peaceful environment after the Korean War encouraged the rise of China's international role. Mao, however, while not questioning the Soviet-determined orientation of world communism, forgot neither Chinese national aspirations nor his claim to socialist self-determination. China's Anti-Rightist Movement and Great Leap Forward, the shelling of disputed islands in the Taiwan Strait and increasing hostility toward India all signaled distinct Chinese positioning in the most important aspects of domestic and international socialist politics.

Soviet–Chinese disagreements came to the fore in the late 1950s and intensified thereafter. China began to present itself as the most reliable ally, the most consequent fighter for national liberation and the most appropriate developmental model in the socialist world. According to China, Soviet policy was fearful opportunism at best, betrayal of socialist imperatives at worst. Finally, Beijing's basic assumptions of inherent contradictions between the Chinese-inspired global village and the white global metropolis fundamentally challenged Moscow's position within the communist world and its foreign-policy conception alike.

From Moscow's point of view, Beijing's ambitions were imbued with Chinese racism and chauvinism. Therefore, they could not but weaken socialist unity and progressive developments in the noncommunist part of the Third World. In particular, uncompromising Chinese radicalism was said to spur alarmed noncommunist countries to seek Western shelter. Finally, Moscow observers were convinced that Mao was playing with fire and likely to provoke dangerous consequences, all the way to global war.

Again and again, Soviet–Chinese disputes revolved around assessments and chances of Third World developments. In addition, both socialist centers attempted to find local allies. China developed its own full-fledged Third

World offensive by propagandistic, diplomatic, cultural, economic and military means, with clear disadvantages in material capacities. Chinese radicalism, however, obviously attracted certain leftist circles.

Third World representatives could perceive Chinese international assertiveness as alternative support, as a complication of socialist–Third World relations or as an outright challenge to cherished national goals. For a start, Soviet–Chinese antagonism sharpened internal contradictions in Third World communist and leftist movements as well as in their international organizations. Governmental Third World reactions appeared to be divided and reflected more often than not simply the necessity of gaining support for their own national programs and needs.

The Sino-Indian border war in 1962 demonstrated all the implications of the Sino-Soviet clash of ideas and interests. Consequently, it raised the level of escalation. For the rest of Khrushchev's reign, Chinese attacks on and qualified Soviet support for India constituted a *cause célèbre*. Whereas Moscow considered the domestic and international consequences of the fighting to be evidence of Chinese political irresponsibility and ideological miscalculation, Beijing kept bemoaning Soviet collaboration with anti-socialist forces. Restoration of a cohesive communist Third World policy would need a common new approach to anti-imperialism under conditions of Cold War superpower competition. Khrushchev's successors seemed to be willing to undertake corresponding adjustments, as they stated in late 1964: "China is a socialist country, India – its neutralism notwithstanding – is a bourgeois state, and we should not have equipped it with weaponry against socialist China."[21]

After Khrushchev: Continuities and Escalations

The anti-Khrushchev conspirators produced several foreign-policy issues to substantiate their fundamental complaints about Khrushchev's capriciousness, ideological deficits and autarchy. With regard to Third World contacts, Leonid Brezhnev and Aleksei Kosygin did not want to alter the fundamentals of Soviet approaches, but emphasized the necessity of more reserved, more constant and more stable relations. Their demand for closer attention to enlightened self-interest in concrete political and economic cooperation was presented as a new class and economic consciousness. Equally, while stating

---

21 Draft report, Presidium CC CPSU, for Plenum CC CPSU, [not later than 13 Oct. 1964], in Artizov et al. (eds.), *Nikita Khrushchev 1964*, 200.

continuing willingness to support just wars, they placed even more emphasis on the need to prevent the unforeseeable consequences of anti-imperialist radicalism and to stabilize the peaceful framework of superpower relations. Idle threats such as those issued during the Suez Crisis or blind adventures in indefensible regions such as Cuba were declared to be excesses of the past. It remained to be seen, however, whether declarations of intent would stand the test of time.

As in previous years, Soviet decision-making took place in the intertwined contexts of domestic economic and social developments, internal power struggles, and international processes partially beyond Soviet control. With regard to promises of more productive economic competition in the Third World, the new leadership ordered its economic bureaucracies to assess former approaches and to design corresponding adjustments. In this context, the Twenty-Third Party Congress singled out Third World states with a clear socialist orientation for "especially friendly" cooperation and aid.[22] At the same time, however, the Kremlin's messengers assured previous leftist and bourgeois partners alike that the change in Soviet leadership would not alter concrete economic cooperation. As late as summer 1968, Brezhnev was still brooding over problems of foreign economic relations that had plagued Soviet decision-makers since Stalin's death. "Today, we give everybody a little bit and therefore we are not able to endure 'competition' with the imperialist enemies," reads his draft memo. "Perhaps we have to define zones of the most important interests and have to focus on ensuring these interests."[23]

Moreover, Moscow's continuing adherence to former trade patterns corresponded even less to development goals in Asia, Africa and Latin America than in previous years. This undermined conceptions of socialist–Third World cooperation, with its expected long-term ideological as well as economic benefits. Significantly, Third World representatives with different regional and political backgrounds such as Che Guevara or India's Lal Bahadur Shastri noticed identical deficits: "Too many countries wished merely to assist exports of their own plant machinery: This was not genuine aid."[24] All in all, the global South directed its criticism of colonial-like trade

22 Report, Brezhnev to Twenty-Third Party Congress, 29 Mar. 1966, in L. I. Breshnew, *Auf dem Wege Lenins. Reden und Aufsätze*, vol. I (Berlin: Dietz, 1971), 302.
23 Draft memo, Brezhnev to Politburo, 6 Jul. 1968, in *General'nyi sekretar' L. I. Brezhnev, 1964–1982*, Special issue, *Vestnik arkhiva prezidenta* (Moscow: Germanskii Istoricheskii Inst., 2006), 76.
24 Shastri, Commonwealth Prime Ministers' Conference, 11th Meeting, 23 Jun. 1965, The National Archives, Kew, UK, CAB 133/254.

relations against both capitalist and socialist governments. Obviously, the assumed anti-imperialist identity of interests of the Second and Third Worlds continued to erode.

In the meantime, several events once again revealed the fragility of leftist advances in the Third World, while "imperialist" aggressiveness seemed to reach new dimensions. In 1965–66 promising prospects in the Dominican Republic, Indonesia and Ghana were brusquely interrupted by domestic "reactionary" forces with more or less support or inspiration from Western governments.[25] Above all, American escalation of the Vietnam War again raised questions about the adequate mixture of nonviolent and violent instruments in world communism's repertoire.

Socialist China's answers had not changed. Within a few months after Khrushchev's fall, Soviet hopes for reconciliation had evaporated. Mao's Cultural Revolution provided for new levels of radicalization of Beijing's international positions, although domestic upheaval virtually undermined China's capacity to act globally. Meanwhile, Soviet socialism basically resembled previous balancing acts, now oscillating between purposeful anti-imperialist solidarity and pursuit of stable superpower détente. In this general framework, probing and augmenting imperialist weak points by peaceful military cooperation with appropriate Third World candidates such as Egypt was intended to undermine Western positions and promote the Soviet empire's geopolitical and ideological influence. Providing appropriate assistance for alleged self-defense of beleaguered allies such as North Vietnam continued to be a matter of course. In doing so, however, the escalation of regional crises had to be prevented, and local and just wars alike had to be reasonably terminated as soon as possible. All in all, successful maneuvering was expected to promote Soviet-style socialism in its competition with Western adversaries as well as with socialist or anti-imperialist deviations in the Third World and above all in China. Corresponding outcomes still would depend on imperialist concessions and Third World compliance.

In fact, instead of determining the course of world events, during the turbulent late 1960s Moscow was almost constantly compelled to react to challenges from intertwined Third World and Cold War developments. The Kremlin again and again had to weigh anti-imperialist and détente considerations. It had to adjust to upcoming opportunities or challenges, in due consideration of the demands of desirable long-term socialist

---

25 In 1968, Modibo Keïta's government in Mali was toppled.

empire-building. In practice, inherent ambivalences as well as the limits of influence led to a wide spectrum of Soviet reactions. So, while engaged in mediation – however short-lived – to foster rapprochement between India and Pakistan, the Kremlin started to provide Rawalpindi with military equipment. Meanwhile, East Pakistan's secessionist movements were ignored and the leftist uprisings in East India were condemned. Equally, Cuba was strongly criticized for its "adventurous" experiments in the export of revolution to African countries and Latin American neighbors.[26] In contrast, the southern African indigenous anti-Portuguese struggle as well as Nigeria's campaign against Biafra's independence were supported. In addition, increasing Soviet aid for North Vietnam was accompanied by fruitless endeavors to bridge the gap between Washington's and Hanoi's ideas about the future of an independent South Vietnam. Finally, the USSR continued to arm Egypt and Syria but at the same time hoped for deescalation of the Arab–Israeli confrontation. When that proved to be illusory, Moscow activated the hot line with Washington during the Six-Day War to prevent possible superpower involvement – and started rearming the defeated Arab states against Israel.

All in all, the new Kremlin team's good intentions of 1964 did not fundamentally alter Soviet socialist–Third World relations during the second half of the 1960s. In November 1967, in a speech at the central meeting on the occasion of the fiftieth anniversary of the October Revolution, Brezhnev depicted mixed processes. Algeria, Burma, Guinea, North Vietnam and southern Africa were presented as success stories. However, socialist and anti-imperialist advances notwithstanding, according to Brezhnev, conniving representatives of imperialism, disunity within the socialist world, and incomplete, contested domestic developments in the majority of Third World countries constituted serious challenges. Altogether, the speech mixed dutiful optimism with an observant and cautious mood.[27]

26 Report, Kosygin at Conference of Communist and Workers' Parties, Budapest, 11–12 Jul. 1967, in *Cold War International History Project Bulletin* 17/18, (2012), 795–8, www .wilsoncenter.org/sites/default/files/CWHIP_Bulletin_17–18_Cuban_Missile_Crisi s_v2_COMPLETE.pdf.

27 Leonid I. Brezhnev, *50 let Velikoi oktiabr'skoi sotsialisticheskoi revoliutsii. Torzhestvennoe zasedanie Tsentral'nogo komiteta KPSS, Verkhovnogo soveta SSSR, Verkhovnogo soveta RSFSR, 3.–4. noiabria 1967 g. Stenograficheskii otchet* (Moscow: Politicheskaia literatura, 1967).

Plate 1 A Soviet propaganda poster from the "Great Patriotic War," circa 1942. Aleksandr Nevskii, Aleksandr Suvorov and Vasilii Chapaev are depicted behind the troops. Galerie Bilderwelt / Contributor / Getty

Plate 2 Red Army soldiers preparing to fly a red flag over the Schlisselburg Fortress near Leningrad, to mark the first breaking of the siege of the city, January 1943. Leningrad was besieged by the German armies from September 1941 until January 1944. The blockade, in which about half of the population lost their lives, became one of the symbols of the "Great Patriotic War." Daily Herald Archive / Getty

Plate 3 Joseph Stalin and Franklin D. Roosevelt at the first conference of the leaders of the Grand Alliance, the anti-fascist war coalition, held in Tehran, 28 November–1 December 1943. Granger Historical Picture Archive / Alamy

Plate 4 Writer Ilia Ehrenburg in Vilnius with Jewish partisans who entered the city with the Red Army, July 1944. Sovfoto Universal Images Group / Getty

Plate 5 The Yugoslav communist ruling group near the end of World War II, 1944: left to right, Vladimir Bakarić, Ivan Milutinović, Edvard Kardelj, Josip Broz Tito, Aleksandar Ranković, Svetozar Vukmanović, Milovan Djilas. The communist resistance movement in Yugoslavia developed a strong organization after the Nazi invasion of April 1941, growing to almost 1 million men and women by the end of the war. ullstein bild / Getty

Plate 6 Italian partisans, December 1944. After the fall of the fascist regime in July and the armistice in September 1943, the resistance in northern Italy, occupied by Nazi Germany, became a mass movement in which communists achieved significant influence. Keystone Hulton Archive / Getty

Plate 7 Greek National Liberation Front (EAM) poster, 1944. The communist resistance organization achieved hegemony over the Greek resistance on the model of Yugoslav communists. But the civil war that broke out in December 1944 led to British military intervention and the communists' defeat. De Agostini Picture Library / Getty

Plate 8 Joseph Stalin and Winston Churchill at the second major conference of the leaders of the anti-fascist war coalition held in Yalta, 4–11 February 1945. Photos 12 / Alamy

Plate 9 Red Army soldiers reach the Reichstag, Berlin, 1945. Sovfoto Universal Images Group / Getty

Plate 10 "Glory to the Red Army!" The poster on the wall is the famous wartime image: "We will get to Berlin." Written in red on the wall: "We made it to Berlin." Copy. *Zvezda*. Hoover Archives Poster Collection

Plate 11 Ho Chi Minh meeting Marius Moutet, French minister for overseas affairs, for negotiations in 1946 in Paris. These negotiations did not prevent the outbreak of the French–Viet Minh War later that year. Gamma-Keystone / Getty

Plate 12 The Korean communist leader Kim Il Sung (center) at the founding of the North Korean Workers' Party, 1946. Charles Armstrong's personal archive

Plate 13 The general secretary of the French Communist Party, Maurice Thorez, speaking at the May Day celebration, Place de la Concorde, Paris, 1 May 1947. The French (and Italian) communists would soon be ousted from government after a three-year coalition as a consequence of early Cold War tensions. INTERFOTO / Alamy

Plate 14 Prague 1948: communist demonstration with Soviet flags. In February 1948 the Communist Party of Czechoslovakia organized a *coup d'état* and established its own dictatorship. Subsequently, Eastern Europe underwent the full Sovietization of political, social and economic life. CTK / Alamy

Plate 27 Soviet tanks in the streets of Budapest, November 1956. World History Archive / Alamy

Plate 28 Imre Nagy surrounded by crowds of people while leaving the Hungarian parliament, 4 November 1956. On that same day, Soviet troops intervened in Hungary. ullstein bild / Getty

Plate 29 Mao Zedong and Nikita Khrushchev, 8 August 1958. This photo of the two smiling communist leaders in Beijing belies the problematic nature of their relationship, which would soon break down, as the Sino-Soviet split became public in 1960. Keystone-France / Getty

Plate 30 Mao Zedong with Deng Xiaoping, 1959. Bettmann / Getty

Plate 49 Soviet tanks on the streets of Prague in August 1968 were met by nonviolent resistance, but this did not prevent the Soviet forces from asserting control over Czechoslovakia and ending the Prague Spring. AFP Stringer / Getty

Plate 50 On 24 January 1969, citizens pay tribute at Prague's Wenceslas Square to Jan Palach, the day before his funeral. Palach, a Czechoslovak student, burned himself to death in January 1969 to protest the Soviet occupation of his country. GERARD LEROUX / Getty

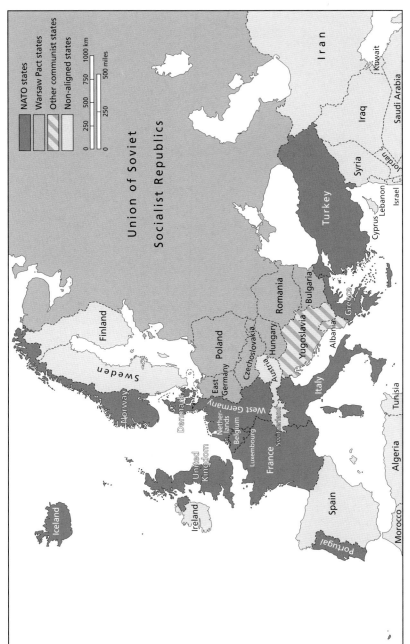

NATO states
Warsaw Pact states
Other communist states
Non-aligned states

0   250   500   750   1000 km
0   250   500 miles

Union of Soviet
Socialist Republics

Iran

Kuwait
Saudi Arabia
Iraq
Syria
Jordan
Lebanon
Israel
Cyprus
Turkey

Greece
Bulgaria
Romania
Albania
Yugoslavia
Hungary
Austria
Czechoslovakia
Poland
East Germany
Italy
West Germany
Switzerland
Luxembourg
Belgium
Nether lands
France
Denmark
Norway
Finland
Sweden
United Kingdom
Ireland
Iceland
Spain
Portugal
Morocco
Algeria
Tunisia

Plate 51 Divided Europe in the Cold War

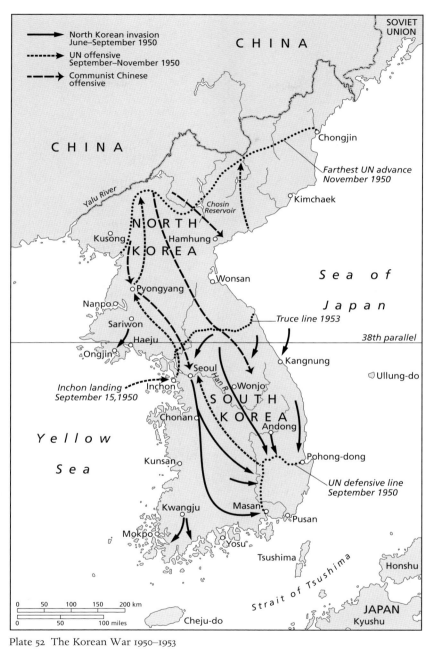

Plate 52 The Korean War 1950–1953

North Korean invasion
June–September 1950

UN offensive
September–November 1950

Communist Chinese
offensive

SOVIET
UNION

CHINA

CHINA

Chongjin

Farthest UN advance
November 1950

Yalu River

Chosin
Reservoir

Kimchaek

NORTH

Kusong

Hamhung

KOREA

Wonsan

Sea of

Japan

Nanpo

Pyongyang

Sariwon

Truce line 1953

38th parallel

Haeju

Ongjin

Kangnung

Ullung-do

Seoul

Inchon landing
September 15, 1950

Inchon

Han R.

Wonjo

SOUTH

Chonan

KOREA

Andong

Yellow

Pohong-dong

Kunsan

UN defensive line
September 1950

Sea

Kwangju

Masan

Mokpo

Pusan

Yosu

Tsushima

Honshu

Strait of Tsushima

0   50   100   150   200 km

JAPAN

0   50   100 miles

Cheju-do

Kyushu

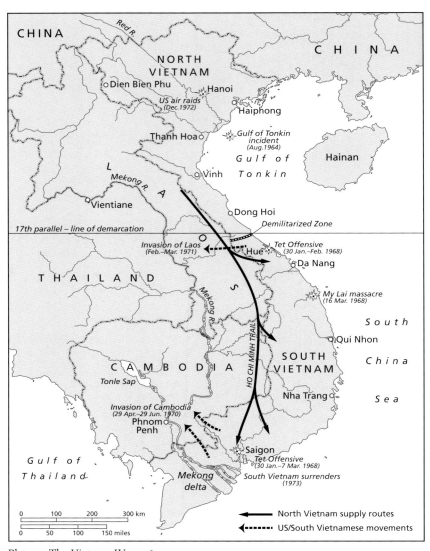

CHINA

NORTH
VIETNAM

Red R.

Dien Bien Phu

Hanoi

US air raids
(Dec. 1972)

Haiphong

Thanh Hoa

Gulf of Tonkin
incident
(Aug. 1964)

C H I N A

Gulf of
Tonkin

Hainan

L

Mekong R.

A

Vientiane

Vinh

Dong Hoi

Demilitarized Zone

17th parallel – line of demarcation

O

Invasion of Laos
(Feb.–Mar. 1971)

Hue

Tet Offensive
(30 Jan.–Feb. 1968)

T H A I L A N D

Mekong R.

S

Da Nang

My Lai massacre
(16 Mar. 1968)

South

Qui Nhon

China

HO CHI MINH TRAIL

SOUTH
VIETNAM

C A M B O D I A

Tonle Sap

Nha Trang

Sea

Invasion of Cambodia
(29 Apr.–29 Jun. 1970)

Phnom
Penh

Gulf of

Thailand

Mekong
delta

Saigon

Tet Offensive
(30 Jan.–7 Mar. 1968)

South Vietnam surrenders
(1973)

0   100   200   300 km

0   50   100   150 miles

North Vietnam supply routes

US/South Vietnamese movements

Plate 53 The Vietnam War 1964–1975

Within eighteen months, restraint was gone. The United States definitely was losing its way in Southeast Asia. Latin America experienced new waves of social unrest. In the meantime, Third World disapproval of the Kremlin's violent termination of the Prague Spring had proved to be short-lived. Equally, the superpowers' relations had not been deeply affected by Warsaw Pact intervention. Time seemed to be ripe for a new, "broader offensive against imperialism, against forces of reaction and of war" – under the guidance of the USSR, as the declaration of the 1969 third global Conference of Communist and Workers' Parties implied.[28] Significantly, while Cuba had sent observers, Beijing did not participate in the conference.

During the subsequent years, socialist victories in Southeast Asia, the emergence of southern African independent states, strongholds in the Middle East (outside Egypt), emerging new prospects in the Horn of Africa and economic shocks in the First World could be regarded as justification of the proclaimed offensive. The combination of superpower détente and socialist benefits from Third World developments finally seemed to function in favor of the Soviet empire. "The world was going our way," First Deputy Head of the Central Committee's International Department, Karen N. Brutents, in retrospect summarized Soviet expectations of that time.[29] Nevertheless, during the 1970s Egyptian–Soviet clashes, Chinese–American rapprochement, fighting in the Horn of Africa and Cambodian-Vietnamese-Chinese embroilment demonstrated the changeability of socialist–Third World relations. These reversals resulted from divisions within both worlds, their inextricable interconnection with Cold War relations, and inherent contradictions between imperial and national concerns. Liaisons between the Second and the Third Worlds remained fragile and contentious. Throughout the period, the concrete translation of ideological certainties and vague hopes into practical relations led to mixed, ambivalent results. Some years later, in 1979 the dynamics of multipolar interrelations between different communisms, Third Worlds and imperialisms would culminate in the Soviet intervention in Afghanistan.

---

28 Declaration, Conference of Communist and Workers' Parties, 17 Jun. 1969, in *Internationale Beratung der kommunistischen und Arbeiterparteien. Moskau 1969* (Prague: Frieden und Sozialismus, 1969), 12.

29 Quoted in Odd Arne Westad, "Moscow and the Angolan Crisis, 1974–1976: A New Pattern of Intervention," *Cold War International History Project Bulletin* no. 8/9 (1996), 21, www.wilsoncenter.org/publication/bulletin-no-89-winter-1996.

Bibliographical Essay

Until the end of the 1980s, historiography and its counterpart, political science, had to rely on official documents, press reports and autobiographies. As a rule, communist relations with the Third World were interpreted through Cold War lenses. Exemplary accounts include, among others, Alvin Z. Rubinstein, *Moscow's Third World Strategy* (Princeton: Princeton University Press, 1988); Elizabeth Kridl Valkenier, *The Soviet Union and the Third World: An Economic Bind* (New York: Praeger, 1983); Dietrich Geyer (ed.), *Sowjetunion. Aussenpolitik 1955–1973* (Cologne: Böhlau, 1976). The end of the USSR was accompanied by a remarkable decline in interest in socialist–Third World relations in general. In recent years, by using stimuli from modernized history of international relations and new Cold War history as well as by integrating approaches from postcolonial studies, historians are rediscovering, extending and partially reinventing the field. New evidence from previously inaccessible archives in former socialist or Third World countries lends additional impetus, although declassification processes are still incomplete or may even appear to be erratic. Latest important editions of documents are T. Yu. Krasovitskaia (ed.), *"Vozvratit' domoi druz'iami SSSR . . ." Obuchenie inostrantsev v Sovetskom soiuze 1956–1965* [To Return Home as Friends of the USSR: The Education of Foreigners in the Soviet Union 1956–1965] (Moscow: Demokratiia, 2013); N. G. Tomilina (ed.), *Naslediniki Kominterna. Mezhdunarodnye soveshchaniia predstavitelei kommunisticheskikh i rabochikh partii v Moskve (noiabr' 1957 g.)* [Heirs of the Comintern. International Conference of Representatives of Communist and Workers' Parties in Moscow (November 1957)] (Moscow: ROSSPĖN, 2013). Most recent bibliographical overviews are included in David C. Engerman, "The Second World's Third World," *Kritika* 12 (2011), 183–211; Andreas Hilger (ed.), *Die Sowjetunion und die Dritte Welt. UdSSR, Staatssozialismus und Antikolonialismus im Kalten Krieg 1945–1991* (Munich: Oldenbourg, 2009); and Stephen A. Smith (ed.), *The Oxford Handbook of the History of Communism* (New York: Oxford University Press, 2014). The seminal post-1989 study (with emphasis on the period since the late 1960s) is Odd Arne Westad, *The Global Cold War: Third World Interventions and the Making of Our Times* (Cambridge: Cambridge University Press, 2007). In addition, many in-depth studies of bilateral relations and biographies of relevant actors on both sides are available. Unfortunately, a comprehensive study on general Comecon–Third World relations until the late 1960s remains a desideratum.

Under these general conditions, entangled histories of Cold War and decolonization developments in the economic, diplomatic, military, cultural and propaganda spheres will remain an important aspect of research. In this context, they will continue to integrate case studies about bilateral relations of an increasing number of socialist and Third World countries into a broader picture. Detailed descriptions of the contradictory interplay between super-power competition, splits within the communist (and capitalist) camp, and differentiation of the Third World significantly enhance understanding of the importance and multidimensionality of corresponding interdependencies. They underline the ability of Third World representatives to pursue their own domestic as well as foreign-policy agendas. Likewise, they actively shaped designs and outcomes of cultural and economic interactions. The following selection may illustrate the diversity and main directions of research: Irina Filatova and Apollon Davidson, *The Hidden Thread: Russia and South Africa in the Soviet Era* (Johannesburg: Jonathan Ball, 2013); Andreas Hilger, *Die sowjetisch-indischen Beziehungen 1941–1965/1966. Kommunismus, Dekolonisierung und Kalter Krieg* (2017); Tobias Rupprecht, *Soviet Internationalism After Stalin: Interaction and Exchange Between the USSR and Latin America During the Cold War* (Cambridge: Cambridge University Press, 2015); E. I. Beliakova, *"Russkii" Amadu i brazil'skaia literatura v Rossii* [The Russian "Amadu" and Brazilian Literature in Russia] (Moscow: Institut Latinskoi ameriki, 2010); Oscar Sanchez-Sibony, *Red Globalization: The Political Economy of the Soviet Cold War from Stalin to Khrushchev* (Cambridge: Cambridge University Press, 2015); Martin Aust (ed.), *Globalisierung imperial und sozialistisch. Russland und die Sowjetunion in der Globalgeschichte 1851–1991* (Frankfurt am Main: Campus, 2013); Michael Kemper and Stephan Conermann (eds.), *The Heritage of Soviet Oriental Studies* (London: Routledge, 2011); Natasha Mishkovich, Harald Fischer-Tiné and Nada Boshkovska (eds.), *The Non-Aligned Movement and the Cold War: Delhi–Bandung–Belgrade* (London: Routledge, 2014). Finally, general accounts of history of communism or of Soviet history include chapters on Third World dimensions; see, for example, Silvio Pons, *The Global Revolution: A History of International Communism 1917–1991* (Oxford: Oxford University Press, 2014).

In taking into account the perceptible impact of Third World societies and states on both international relations as well as on world metropolises, current studies widen historical perspectives on the relations between Second and Third World countries. In doing so, they allow for the integration of twentieth-century history of communist international relations into questions and interpretations that cover global interconnections and processes beyond Cold War dichotomies, such as modernization and urbanization, developmental and population policy, and youth protest and culture – future research will add other fascinating themes.

The Socialist Camp and the Challenge of Economic Modernization in the Third World

SARA LORENZINI

In 1957 one of the most important, albeit controversial figures in Soviet intellectual history, economist Yevgenii Varga, explained the orthodox view on decolonization and modernization. The end of the colonial system, he maintained, was shaking imperialism at its foundations, providing a net contribution to the general crisis of capitalism. Given that underdevelopment was a consequence of colonial domination, it would persist as long as the structures of capitalism were there. The recipe for economic modernization was therefore simple: cutting relations with the West and introducing planning, nationalization, industrialization and close relations with the Eastern bloc.[1] In terms of sectorial priorities, modernizing agriculture, with collective farms owned by the state, came first. Then came investments in infrastructure and industrial facilities. The state had to be the only promoter of development and had to limit the participation of foreign capital to a minimum. Socialist aid had to function to promote economic liberation. Developing modern industries and forming a working class were a condition for moving toward socialism: This was the reason behind Soviet aid, rather than compensation for a past of colonial plundering.

In the socialist camp, the promotion of socialist modernity was imbued with a discourse of anti-imperialistic solidarity.[2] As a backward country that had been able to transform itself into an advanced one, the Soviet Union had

---

1 Evgenij Varga, "Of the Tendencies of Development of Contemporary Capitalism and Socialism," *World Economy and International Relations* 4 (Oct. 1957), quoted in United States Department of State, *The Sino-Soviet Economic Offensive in the Less Developed Countries* (Washington, DC: Government Printing Office, 1958), 13.
2 See Berthold Unfried and Eva Himmelstoss (eds.), "Die eine Welt schaffen. Praktiken von 'Internationaler Solidarität' und 'Internationaler Entwicklung' – Create One World: Practices of 'International Solidarity' and 'International Development,'" *ITH Conference Proceedings* 46 (Leipzig: Akademische Verlagsanstalt 2012), 57–72.

huge political capital to spend, which it aspired to translate into trade relations and the systematic adoption of its economic model.[3] However, this did not happen very often.

Indeed, the socialist side of Cold War economic competition has on the whole been described as unsuccessful. Rough estimates produced by Western analysts during the Cold War testify to a clear Western predominance in aid and trade with the South. The story of the involvement of the socialist camp in the South is often told as a series of uncoordinated actions, an extemporary policy dictated by the Soviet Union, driven by an attempt at seizing any opportunity to induce political reversals in developing countries, and characterized by clumsy investments in costly prestige projects or arms deals, without any knowledge of the local situation or of the real needs of the recipient. Elements of this grotesque picture are obviously true. This chapter on the political economy of East–South relations, however, aims to reassess the engagement of the Soviet bloc with the South, presenting it as a coherent strategy to deal with the challenge of promoting political change, new trade patterns and ideas of socialist modernity in the South. It shows that from the very beginning trade opportunities and considerations of economic sustainability were part and parcel of relations with the South. Far from being a political crusade, the socialist bloc's commitment to the South needed to be delicately handled.

This chapter adopts a very specific angle: The view from the Council for Mutual Economic Assistance, commonly referred to as Comecon or the CMEA, the international organization for economic cooperation in the socialist bloc, which shows how the different national interests were fused to form a comprehensive strategy. In doing so, it does not conceal the structural and political weaknesses of the organization. Constituted in 1949, Comecon was in the beginning not much more than an annual reunion of representatives of the member states, who met to define common orientations and common projects. Only in 1954 was a Secretariat established, with the task of conducting economic research based on the data collected by the single countries, while only in 1956 were the first sectoral permanent commissions set up.[4] The base was in Moscow, the language of operation Russian. Comecon represented an idea of a real alternative system, in terms of political economy. It became a laboratory for ideas on how to promote

---

3 Tobias Rupprecht, "Die sowjetische Gesellschaft in der Welt des Kalten Kriegs. Neue Forschungsperspektiven," *Jahrbücher für Geschichte Osteuropas* 58 (2010), 381–99.
4 Council for Mutual Economic Assistance, Secretariat, *Experience of the CMEA Activities over 25 Years* (Moscow: CMEA, 1975).

socialist modernity. From the 1960s it developed a transnational potential and its own social capital. Delegates working for Comecon were experts in national planning. Given the necessity of fluency in Russian, they were either war immigrants to the Soviet Union (first generation) or students at the Foreign Trade Academy in Moscow. They formed a knowledge community, sharing values and ideas on how to promote socialist modernity, which they identified with the goals of the bloc more than with those of individual member states.[5] Like other international officials, they were internationally socialized and lived within a complex relationship, juggling the good of the organization with the idea that experts were expected to serve their own national interest.[6] At times, the USSR, Comecon and individual countries in Eastern Europe were at variance as to how to structure relations with developing countries, and political action did not always coincide with the evolution of economic or political thinking.

The history of how the Eastern bloc dealt with economic modernization in the South is plain to read in the documents of Comecon. Although clearly thin as regards the ideological content or implications of the policies envisaged, the Comecon documents still show how the Eastern bloc's strategy underwent a complete reversal, as it changed from the dream of forming a closed system with selected countries in the South which could form an alternative to the West, to the acknowledgement of economic interdependence and of the desirability of East–West cooperation in economic development.

The Two World Markets: Prescribing Separateness from the West

It was in the mid 1950s that East–South relations became a topic of interest for the whole socialist camp. Soviet opening up to the world is usually associated with Nikita Khrushchev, and with his ideological shift at the Twentieth Congress of the Communist Party of the Soviet Union (CPSU), with the introduction of the concept of national democracy as a tool to deal with the awakening of the South. In the 1950s and 1960s, the terms used to define

---

5 Simon Godard, "Construire le bloc de l'Est par l'économie? La délicate émergence d'une solidarité internationale socialiste au sein du Conseil d'aide économique mutuelle," *Vingtième Siècle. Revue d'histoire* 109 (Jan. 2011), 45–58.
6 For a study on Comecon's expert community, see Simon Godard, "Construire le 'bloc' par l'économie. Configuration des territoires et des identités socialistes au Conseil d'Aide Économique Mutuelle (Caem) 1949–1989," Ph.D. dissertation (Université de Genève and Université Paris 1 – Panthéon Sorbonne, 2014), 368–91, 468–75, 493–524.

the newly independent countries emerging from the process of decolonization were either "backward areas" or "underdeveloped areas." Otherwise, the regional description (Arab, African or Latin American countries) was widely preferred. Conversely, the expression "Third World" was not welcome, since it suggested the existence of a third way, outside the option of the two world-systems, capitalism and communism. Although sometimes used in the years of détente, after 1967–68 and until the mid 1970s, "Third World" was then fully abandoned in the second half of the 1970s, when other formulas prevailed such as "newly free countries" or "developing countries."[7]

The idea promoted by Khrushchev was to offer a clear alternative to the West. The two-camps theory had its political economy corollary: the theory of the two world markets. Newly independent countries in the South could be partners either with the West or with the socialist countries. Mostly, the first was the case, and relations with the South were dubbed relations with a special kind of capitalist country. Nevertheless, the socialist camp was open to political and economic relations. Khrushchev's speech at the Twentieth Congress of the CPSU was clear on this point: The socialist countries offered their aid to former colonial territories in order to help them build an independent national economy without the need to "go begging to their former oppressors for modern equipment."[8] The Soviets rejected the term "aid," because they felt that it was charged with a moral obligation they did not accept. They mostly spoke of long-term credit and of technical assistance, of trade agreements and scientific-technical cooperation. Only partially did they adopt the international jargon used in the UN system, more specifically in the UN Expanded Technical Assistance Program, in which the Soviet Union actively took part starting in 1953. In the Soviet discourse, socialist aid was an alternative to Western practice. It promoted the growth of the public sector and centralized economic decision-making. It fostered independence and granted equality. It took place in the form of balanced trade and for the mutual benefit of the trading partners. It was also a cooperative action: Socialist economic assistance to developing countries had common

---

7 For a discussion of the expressions "Third World," and "South," see Marie Lavigne (ed.), *East–South Relations in the World Economy* (Boulder: Westview Press, 1988), 10–11. See also, for example, Karen N. Brutents, *The Newly Freed Countries in the Seventies* (Moscow: Progress, 1983; first Russian edn. 1979).

8 Quoted in Robert S. Walters, *American and Soviet Aid: A Comparative Analysis* (Pittsburgh: University of Pittsburgh Press, 1970), 30.

features. Most of these elements are characteristic of the Eastern bloc aid throughout the Cold War.

The attempt to create a cohesive bloc strategy was especially important in the years of competitive coexistence. In the Eastern bloc, Comecon soon became the ideal setting for institutionalized cooperation among socialist donors.[9] In September 1957 the Permanent Commission for Foreign Trade was put in charge of coordinating trade relations with underdeveloped countries. It constituted a working group, which dealt specifically with developing countries and with the harmonization of conditions in agreements for the export of machinery and complete plants in exchange for goods and raw materials. The working group discussed proposals for multilateral trade agreements and for the founding of an international bank of socialist countries, which would be able to guarantee an independent pricing system totally detached from world market dynamics.

From the very beginning, gaining access to new sources of raw materials was crucial, and the socialist countries were well aware of the extent of Western control over natural resources in formerly colonized territories. Nevertheless, as early as 1956 a research group in the Soviet Academy of Sciences proposed that Eastern Europe should begin to import raw materials directly from Africa.[10] In 1958, Soviet foreign trade officials pointed out the problems of balancing trade with developing countries and the need to pay attention to hard-currency reserves when negotiating plans for foreign trade.[11] This kind of concern did not fail to trickle down in Comecon discussions. In September 1960, Comecon cooperation with underdeveloped countries was considered unsatisfactory. With few exceptions (like the case of Iraq) coordination was not effective, either in the construction of bigger plants or in the supply of smaller machinery. Comecon members were fully aware that developing countries tended to submit the same "shopping list" to several potential donors and accepted aid for the same development project from different sources.[12]

---

9 The documents of Comecon and its Commission for Technical Assistance (CTA) used for this article are held by the Bundesarchiv Berlin (BArchB), Ministerium für Außenwirtschaft (DL2). Reports on the CTA meetings were a part of the dossiers used by the East German delegation and cover the years 1960–74.

10 Christopher Coker, *NATO, the Warsaw Pact, and Africa* (Basingstoke: Macmillan, 1985), 158.

11 Oscar Sanchez-Sibony, *Red Globalization: The Political Economy of the Soviet Cold War from Stalin to Khrushchev* (Cambridge: Cambridge University Press, 2014), 111.

12 "Bericht, Konsultation der Stellvertretenden Minister für Außenhandel, Moskau, September 1965," in BArchB, DL2 VAN 57. On this, see David C. Engerman, "The Second World's Third World," *Kritika* 12, 1 (2011), 196.

Therefore, in June 1961 the matter was entrusted to a brand new, very specialized and very little-known permanent commission, the Commission for Technical Assistance. The documents of the CTA tell a story of great differences within the Eastern bloc regarding the strategy envisaged toward the Third World. They illustrate the problems encountered during negotiations within Comecon and the doubts that emerged in the framing of common policies, evidence of both the limits and the strength of Soviet power vis-à-vis its European partners. The Soviet Union was undoubtedly the engine of the CTA. From the very first meeting it came with drafts for working plans, statutes and rules of procedure. "In the interest of good relations between the GDR [German Democratic Republic] and the Soviet Union it is not expedient to express any critical observation on this point."[13] These words from the first East German directive to its delegation in the CTA give a clear idea of the paramount role of the Soviet Union in the commission. They also anticipate how narrow the space for discussion on strategies would be. Notwithstanding these unsurprising limits, the CTA proceedings do expose differences and clashing priorities among the members.

In the early 1960s, there was no doubt that technical assistance to developing countries meant fostering industrialization. This largely reflected the requests from the South, and matched the natural inclination of the socialist countries and their economic structure. Soviet ideas on development were well known, and were promoted whenever possible. At an early meeting of the UN Economic and Social Council (ECOSOC), when the UN discussed multilateral technical aid, the Soviet representative, Platon D. Morozov, maintained that technical assistance should promote the expansion of heavy industry.[14] However, financing heavy industry had huge costs. Therefore, smaller countries in Central and Eastern Europe insisted, instead, on meeting the requests of developing countries. For them, this more nuanced strategy should include a different kind of industrialization: smaller projects that were intended to develop manufacturing rather than heavy industry. Among East European experts, there was a general agreement on the fact that small was better.

13 Sara Lorenzini, "Modernisierung durch Handel. Der Ostblock und die Koordinierung der Entwicklungshilfe in der Ständigen Kommission für Technische Unterstützung," in Martin Aust and Julia Obertreis (eds.), Osteuropäische Geschichte und Globalgeschichte (Stuttgart: Steiner-Verlag, 2014), 225.
14 Alvin Z. Rubinstein, "Soviet Policy Toward Under-Developed Areas in the Economic and Social Council," International Organization 9 (1955), 233.

Discussion in the CTA focused on how to organize the joint creation of complete plants to be built in developing countries. Some members, such as Hungary and Czechoslovakia, identified an interesting model for Comecon in the trade policies of the European Economic Community (EEC); others looked at the consortia strategy engineered by the World Bank and by the OECD.[15] For the Soviet Union, the issue of avoiding interbloc competition was crucial. Competition on the same project was not implausible, nor was double funding. There had been precedents, as in the case of India, where Czechoslovak offers exceeded Soviet ones.[16] The CTA discussed at length the case of Guinea, where duplication of commitments was likely to occur.[17]

Discussions on how to deal with East–South relations were intertwined with thoughts on economic reform within the socialist bloc. Although the domestic reforms of the late 1950s were pursued independently from debates on the regional and multilateral level, they did not fail to influence Comecon as a whole. The first attempt to organize a socialist division of labor, following on from the drafting of the "Basic Principles of the Social International Division of Labor" agreed upon in 1962, was not able to promote Comecon as an instrument of multilateral cooperation, but confirmed the strength of bilateral links and the dependence of East European countries on trade with the Soviet Union.[18] Nevertheless, a regional monetary unit and a settlements bank were established in 1963. A general scheme for the political and economic coordination of relations with less developed countries was discussed thoroughly and agreed upon in the same year. It adopted common standards for trade with the developing countries and focused especially on the harmonization of credit conditions. However, the conditions agreed upon were not binding. Therefore, its members rarely followed the decisions and recommendations of the CTA.

East European countries were not a monolithic bloc and resisted more constraining rules. A division of tasks nonetheless emerged, and anticipated the more effective bloc policy described in the "Comprehensive Program for

---

15 This was especially the case of Czechoslovakia; see "Gespräch David/Stibi," in Politisches Archiv des Früheren Ministeriums für Auswärtige Angelegenheiten, Berlin (MfAA), A17085.

16 Andreas Hilger, "The Soviet Union and India: The Khrushchev Era and Its Aftermath Until 1966," in Andreas Hilger et al. (eds.), *Indo-Soviet Relations Collection: The Khrushchev Years* (Parallel History Project on Cooperative Security, 2009), 5, www.php.isn.ethz.ch/.

17 "Bericht, Konsultation der Stellvertretenden Minister für Außenhandel, Moskau, September 1965."

18 Jozef M. van Brabant, *The Planned Economies and International Economic Organizations* (Cambridge: Cambridge University Press, 1991), 95–101.

the Further Extension and Improvement of Cooperation and the Further Development of Socialist Economic Integration by Comecon Member Countries," of August 1971. The 1960s division of labor saw Czechoslovakia offering projects for the energy sector, the steel industry and light industries (leather, shoes, textiles, sugar); Hungary specializing in light machinery, hydroelectric power and pharmaceuticals; East Germany in telecommunications and electronics; Poland in the mining sector, naval construction and wood processing; and Romania in oil-processing technology and petrochemical production.[19]

In the 1950s and early 1960s, coordination plans mostly resulted in failures. It is astonishing how discussions in the CTA, highly technical regarding trade prospects, failed to mention political or ideological factors. The discourse of solidarity, so typical for the Eastern bloc, was absent. Staging socialist modernity in developing countries was a complex action, which was carefully organized, but this happened outside the Comecon setting. It involved, rather, the social organizations: trade unions, youth and women's associations, specific solidarity actions or institutions. Very rarely did Comecon discuss progress in education and in health care. Ideas that might have promoted the social capital of socialist countries were succumbing to the pressure of trade concerns.

Yet, in some wider and less technical arenas, the priority was different. Rather than focusing on how they could build superior systems in the "backward" lands, the socialist countries united behind the language of solidarity, of socialist humanism, of willingness to cooperate with the Third World to dramatically change power relations worldwide. The United Nations Conference on Trade and Development (UNCTAD), which opened in Geneva in March 1964, was considered the ideal stage for this kind of propaganda. Socialist countries made specific efforts to coordinate their strategy and their rhetoric, identifying with newly independent countries' demands and showing a willingness to comply with the requests of less developed countries.

Disappointments and the Concept of Mutual Advantage

Whereas until the early 1960s Comecon wanted to constitute a radical alternative to the West, in the late 1960s the attitude changed dramatically.

19 Heinrich Machowski and Siegfried Schultz, *RGW-Staaten und Dritte Welt. Wirtschaftsbeziehungen und Entwicklungshilfe* (Bonn: Forschungsinstitut der Deutschen Gesellschaft für Auswärtige Politik e.V., 1981), 43. On the common system for collection of statistical data introduced in October 1963, see BArchB, DL2 VA 6767.

Disillusionment on the part of socialist countries with socialism's prospects in the South was widespread. Developing countries did not fulfill the expectations. Some exploited the state-building instruments offered by Soviet and East European advisors and described themselves as socialist, mostly with some sort of qualification, such as African socialists or Arab socialists. Archive sources testify very clearly that Soviet and East European diplomats were skeptical about the socialist character of these countries and of their leaders.[20]

As regards the political economy aspect of this developmental model, Comecon members increasingly felt the Third World to be a burden. The indebtedness of developing countries was having a disastrous impact. The CTA discussed at length a way out of the crisis. The 1950s rule of sticking to the principle of balanced trade to circumvent the possibility of insolvency had proved ineffective. In October 1963, at the fifth meeting of the CTA, the Soviet appeal was especially clear-cut: Developing countries had to make clear how they intended to pay back their debts if they were to be granted new credits. Several East European partners argued that a strategy focused on the promotion of small business was an available option to facilitate the repayment of loans.[21] The fourteenth meeting, held in Minsk in June 1968, decided to write off loans which had no proven economic advantage.[22]

In the early Brezhnev years, while economic relations with the West were influenced by "depoliticized" concepts, which allowed the pursuit of modernization in the Eastern bloc through Western credit and knowhow, East–South economic relations were still governed by the old ideologies. Yet, economic thinking did go through some change. Participation in specialized agencies of the United Nations granted exposure to Western theories and "contaminated" the thinking of Soviet scholars. The first open attack on orthodoxy is to be found in a 1963 article written by Leonid Goncharov, deputy director of the Soviet Institute of Africa, who criticized the rhetoric on the disintegration of capitalism under the blows of national liberation movements. Others reinforced his view: The world capitalist economy had adapted successfully to new conditions, due to changes in policy and in structure. Neocolonialism

---

20 See for example the reports on the trip to Africa of East German minister Otto Winzer, and his conversations with Soviet ambassadors, Stiftung Archiv der Parteien und Massorganisationen der DDR im Bundesarchiv, Berlin (SAPMO), DY 30 IV A 2/20, 795.
21 BArchB, DE1 VA 42175.   22 BArchB, DL2 VAN 76.

was a new policy, carried out with new methods.[23] Socialist countries had to act accordingly.

In addition to questions on its orthodoxy, doubts on the appropriateness of the Soviet model of industrialization also emerged in the 1960s, when the debt problem became overwhelming. The direct involvement of the state was not enough to produce progress. Georgii Mirskii, a leading Third World specialist at the Institute of World Economics and International Relations (IMEMO), criticized both the emphasis on heavy industry and the strategy of nationalization.[24] Officially, however, the failure of the Soviet model was attributed to local problems, essentially corruption and the inability to form an efficient bureaucracy. The new formula maintained that the state did not need to be burdened with an unnecessary expansion of functions and that developing countries should try to turn to advantage their traditional role as raw materials producers. Strategists in Comecon suggested that less developed countries "no longer need to build up heavy industry, for they can quite simply import the necessary manufactured or semi-manufactured products from socialist states and pay for them with their own export earnings."[25]

The reasons for disappointment on the recipient side often were very down to earth. Unable to quickly adapt their technology and general aid to the requests of the recipients, socialist bloc countries slipped on the classic banana peel of their own carelessness. Too often equipment was incompetently delivered, with delays that compromised economic and political effectiveness. The poor quality of Soviet and East European aid resulted in recipients voicing their disappointment. They encountered problems operating machinery due to the lack of instructions, complained about delays in supply, the lack of spare parts and poor service in general. They rejected outdated or inappropriate technology.[26] Although typical for aid supplies from all East European countries, this issue was not discussed in the broader Comecon community, as if no one wanted to wash their dirty linen in public. Each trade representation or diplomatic post dealt with this

23 V. Rybakov, Dec. 1965, quoted in Jerry F. Hough, *The Struggle for the Third World: Soviet Debates and American Options* (Washington, DC: Brookings Institution Press, 1986), 79.
24 Ibid., 78–81.
25 The change in Soviet attitude was signaled in a series of articles in *Voprosy ekonomiki*, starting with G. Prokhorov, "Mirovaia sistema sotsializma osvobodivshiesia strany," *Voprosy ekonomiki* 11 (1965), 85.
26 For case studies, see Sanchez-Sibony, *Red Globalization*, and Young-Sun Hong, *Cold War Germany, the Third World, and the Global Humanitarian Regime* (Cambridge: Cambridge University Press, 2015).

kind of practical problem on a bilateral level. For example, in the East German Foreign Ministry records, reports on problems with trade and aid abound.[27] Occasionally they were the topic of discussion with other Eastern bloc diplomats. Generally, though, East German trade representatives reacted dismissively or, when the problems resurfaced cyclically, with puzzlement. Although aware that practicalities could amount to huge problems, they grossly underestimated the disruptive potential of inefficient completion of GDR projects, in the conviction that ideological support, together with sustained solidarity campaigns, including medical aid and generous educational schemes, could compensate.

Rationality or the Obsession with Raw Materials

The documents of the CTA offer strong evidence for Roger Kanet's thesis on the Soviet bloc moving away from ideology and toward realism.[28] In the 1970s, there was a sharp turn toward economic rationality, and mutual advantage became the new catchphrase. The developmental discourse of the 1960s almost vanished. Trade became crucial, and the Eastern bloc became obsessed with importing strategic raw materials. The new approach was to construct "stably founded, mutually advantageous relations."[29]

Economic rationality was characteristic for the "new line" after the Twenty-Third Congress of the CPSU in 1966. The chairman of the Council of Ministers, Aleksei N. Kosygin, maintained that relations with less developed countries could help to make better use of the international division of labor. There was a new effort to expand economic relations beyond the circle of socialist-oriented countries, including those rich in raw materials that were of interest to the Eastern bloc, such as Morocco (phosphates) and Nigeria (oil). The joint procurement of raw materials was given increasing relevance by the CTA. The sixth meeting of the Commission in 1964 was the first specifically devoted to the organization of the joint import of strategic raw materials.[30] After 1967 the Soviet Union made it clear that its European allies

27 For full details, see Sara Lorenzini, *Due Germanie in Africa. La cooperazione allo sviluppo e la competizione per i mercati di materie prime e tecnologia* (Florence: Polistampa, 2003).
28 Roger Kanet, *The Soviet Union and the Developing Nations* (Baltimore: Johns Hopkins University Press, 1974).
29 *Pravda*, 1971, quoted in Elizabeth Kridl Valkenier, *The Soviet Union and the Third World: An Economic Bind* (New York: Praeger, 1985), 17.
30 "Vorstellungen der Delegationen der Mitgliedsländer des RGW in der SKTU bei der Frage einer möglichen Beteiligung an der Organisierung und Erweiterung der Produktion von Kupfer, Nickel, Kautschuk, und Baumwolle in den EL (1964)," BArchB, DE1 VSII 12720.

were expected to secure other sources of raw materials in the Third World. In April 1971, at the Moscow meeting of the deputy ministers for foreign trade of Comecon, the issue was clearer than ever: The Soviet Union declared that it was not able to satisfy the demand for oil from its partners. It offered instead to mediate the purchase of oil from other sources.[31] From then onward, capital investments had to be designed to achieve considerable growth in the supplies of fuel, raw materials and metals. Industrial modernization in the developing world was now a secondary goal.[32] The Soviet Union offered to help. Details on how to get better conditions for the import of fuel and other raw materials were discussed during the twenty-second meeting of the CTA, in November 1970. The USSR was willing to sign agreements with the producers and then provide subcontracts to the other socialist countries.[33]

As for the exploration of new sources of strategic raw materials, East European countries were in a predicament that is well documented in the Comecon sources: Unable to finance huge projects on an individual basis, they were left with no alternative but to enter bigger projects financed by the Soviet Union.[34] In turn, the Soviet Union was very keen to embark on cooperative and multilateral initiatives. Its experts contended that "great opportunities reside in multilateral cooperation," which meant building joint export enterprises, jointly providing technical assistance and pooling resources in training personnel. Indeed, the CTA meetings in the years 1971–74 focused exclusively on the joint imports of raw materials. They mentioned Africa and the Arab countries as especially promising areas that could offer access to new sources of oil and phosphates, which were much needed for the production of fertilizers. Discussion revolved around specific projects, for example on oil in the deserts of Libya, on phosphates in Egypt's Western Desert (Abu-Tartur) and on the Kindia project in Guinea for the extraction of bauxite.[35]

In order to improve relations with Third World countries, which complained about Soviet and East European aid, the Comecon countries

---

31 BArchB, SKAH, DL2 VAN 57.
32 Yurii Konstantinov in 1977, quoted by David R. Stone, "CMEA's International Investment Bank and the Crisis of Developed Socialism," *Journal of Cold War Studies* 10, 3 (2008), 66.
33 BArchB, SKAH, DL2 VAN 56.   34 BArchB, SKAH, DL2 VA 1225.
35 See the meeting of foreign trade representatives of Comecon (21–23 Apr. 1971, Moscow), BArchB DL2 VAN 57; on the 23rd meeting of the Permanent Commission for Technical Assistance (Ständige Kommission für Technische Unterstützung) in 1972, see BArchB, DE1 VA 52248.

introduced intergovernmental commissions into their cooperation agreements. Originally a way to overcome the gap between expectations and offers and solve the problems of aid, joint committees involving experts from socialist donors and from recipient countries became an instrument for aid planning and a way to implement a more comprehensive approach to aid.[36]

Efforts were also made to deepen financial relations with Third World countries. The economic integration plan of August 1971 foresaw the gradual adoption of the convertible ruble to settle accounts among Comecon countries and with developing countries as well. The old project of a socialist countries' development bank was also on the agenda and was implemented in January 1974, when Comecon set up an international investment bank with a 1 billion transferable ruble fund to promote economic and technical assistance to developing countries.[37] This, the socialist bloc maintained, was a great opportunity for the developing countries, which could finance projects in the extractive industries. Once again, the hunger for raw materials drove the aid offers from the bloc.

Debating Concepts of Development: Comecon as an Alternative to the New International Economic Order

The ranking of socialist countries according to development indicators became an issue of contention for Comecon in the mid 1960s, when the Eastern bloc was confronted with developmental issues within the UN system. This required a whole reframing of the concept of backwardness.[38] In the orthodox view, socialism was going hand in hand with progress and modernity. As a logical consequence, no socialist country could possibly be identified with underdevelopment or backwardness, nor would the path of development of socialist countries align with the capitalist stages of growth.[39]

---

36 Konstantin Ivanovich Mikulsky, *CMEA: International Significance of Socialist Integration* (Moscow: Progress, 1982), ch. 9. The authors of this chapter are V. Kves (Czechoslovakia), I. I. Orlik and G. M. Prokhorov (USSR), and M. Simai (Hungary).
37 BArchB, DL2 1894. See also Stone, *CMEA's International Investment Bank*.
38 See Simon Godard, "Framing the Discourse on 'Backwardness': Tension About the Development Issue Considered Within the Socialist Bloc or on a Global Scale," paper presented at the conference "Development and Underdevelopment in Post-War Europe," Columbia University, 10 Oct. 2014.
39 Instead, the prospect was that of a technological jump, *"überholen ohne einzuholen"* in the East German discourse; see André Steiner, *Von Plan zu Plan. Eine Wirtschaftsgeschichte der DDR* (Munich: Deutsche Verlags-Anstalt, 2004), 142.

The attainment of socialism could happen by bypassing or at least drastically curtailing industrial and monopoly capitalism.[40]

Yet this view was not universally accepted in the Eastern bloc. In the mid 1960s, Romania identified politically with the developing countries and their requests, and claimed status as a developing country. Together with Bulgaria, it challenged the principles of the socialist international division of labor, claiming that specializations determined by relative labor costs would result in perpetuating backwardness.[41] In the early 1970s, Romania became even more resolved, and Nicolae Ceaușescu constructed an identity as a "socialist developing country," aiming to create a bridge between the Third World and the socialist countries. This included embracing the rhetoric of the new international economic order (NIEO), in the years 1975–78, with the prospect of creating stronger connections with countries with a similar development level, as opposed to existing links to countries having the same political systems.[42]

The discussion on the concept of development should be read in connection with the broader effort to discuss the standardization of statistical measures, which at the time were being promoted in the international arena, especially within the Economic Commission for Europe. This was opposed by the Soviet Union because it could be used as a way to expose the economic failures of the Eastern bloc. Therefore, the Soviets disregarded the notion of "development," something they defined narrowly as a legacy of colonialism that did not concern socialist countries.

This definition no longer worked in the 1970s, however, when Comecon discussed the prospects for non-European members, Mongolia (admitted in 1962), Cuba (1972) and the newly admitted Vietnam (1978), or the special cooperation agreements with the countries with observer status: Afghanistan, Angola, Ethiopia, Laos, Mozambique, Nicaragua and the People's Republic of Yemen.[43] The quarrel over recognizing a socialist country as a developing country was rekindled, with Romania asking for a ranking based on the economic criteria acknowledged by international organizations.

40 R. Ulyanovsky, *Socialism in the Newly Independent Nations* (Moscow: Progress, 1974).
41 John Michael Montias, "Background and Origins of the Rumanian Dispute with Comecon," *Soviet Studies* 16, 2 (Oct. 1964), 132.
42 Thomas P. M. Barnett, *Romanian and East German Policies in the Third World: Comparing the Strategies of Ceausescu and Honecker* (Westport, CT: Praeger, 1992).
43 Klaus Fritsche, *Sozialistische Entwicklungsländer in der "internationalen sozialistischen Arbeitsteilung" des RGW. Zum Forschungsstand* (Cologne: Bundesinstitut für Ostwissenschaftliche und Internationale Studien, 1991), 27.

In Comecon, debates revolved around the likelihood of the cohesion of the socialist world-economy.[44]

In the mid 1970s, relations with developing countries constituted a fundamental dimension of Comecon activities. The self-portrait published by the Comecon Secretariat in 1975 repeatedly mentions the importance of developing countries. It describes the increase in Comecon trade turnover (seventeen-fold between 1950 and 1975) and lists the products exchanged, pointing at the preference given to commodities manufactured in developing countries. It stresses the constant attention to economic relations, the expansion of multilateral assistance, including a scholarship fund to help train national cadres and a credit-financing fund established within the framework of the International Investment Bank.[45] To be sure, the significant increase praised by Comecon sources does not imply a significant change or, even less, a reversal in trends in world trade. The West still had the lion's share of trade with the South. Comecon, however, wanted to stand out as an alternative model to the NIEO. The future of North–South relations lay in the formula of "integration through equality," socialist countries claimed. Comecon's less developed members, argued one East German specialist, were the "incontrovertible" proof that such a prospect was possible.[46]

The Comecon countries, with their own "Campaign to Restructure International Economic Relations in a Progressive Way," refused to read reality through the lens of a North–South divide: "It is of immense importance for the successful and consistent struggle for a genuine democratisation of international economic relations that the countries in the socialist community, like many developing countries, should refute the false Maoist notion of world partition into North and South, into rich and poor countries; this has to be replaced by the scientifically grounded notion of the partition of the world into two social systems."[47] In September 1975 Yakov Malik, the USSR's representative at the UN General Assembly, officially rejected any definition of a North–South conflict in which the

---

44 "Information über die 60. Tagung des Executivkomittees des RGW," in SAPMO, DY 3023–1311, *Zusammenarbeit mit dem Rat für Gegenseitige Wirtschaftshilfe*, 1972–73. See also Giovanni Graziani, "The Non-European Members of the CMEA: A Model for Developing Countries?," in Roger E. Kanet, *The Soviet Union, Eastern Europe and the Third World* (Cambridge: Cambridge University Press, 1988).
45 CMEA Secretariat, *Experience of the CMEA Activities*, 18.
46 See Heinz Joswig, "Zur Perspektive der ökonomischen Zusammenarbeit zwischen den Ländern des RGW und den Entwicklungsländern," *Deutsche Aussenpolitik* 20, 3 (Mar. 1975), 331–39.
47 Mikulsky, *CMEA*, 316.

Soviet Union was put on the same side as the capitalist North. The Soviet view of dependency theorists was harsh, and among them specifically Samir Amin, the personification of the theoretical radicalism of the Third World establishment; they were especially disliked because they placed socialist countries on the same level as the capitalist North.[48] Never fully convinced by the concept of the Third World as a homogeneous group, in the second half of the 1970s Soviet and East European experts openly declared that the unity of the Third World was a myth and that the idea of a special role for the Third World in the world economy needed to be rejected. The Third World was not acting as one, nor were national liberation movements. Internal divisions, they argued, were to be acknowledged as a success for imperial strategies.

International organizations did not buy Comecon's view. UNCTAD, for example, did not accept the self-representation of the socialist countries as a system, only partially applying the principle according to which political orientation trumped economic development. In the 1970s, for instance, Cuba, Vietnam and Mongolia figured in the developing countries of Africa, Asia and Latin America, whereas socialist countries of Eastern Europe constituted a separate bloc, according to UNCTAD.[49]

In government circles and in the academic community within the Soviet Union, the recognition began to emerge that the establishment of an alternate, worldwide economic order patterned on integration agreements set up in Comecon was not realistic.[50] Nonetheless, this optimistic view was still being voiced in 1980, when Oleg Bogomolov, head of the Institute of Economics of the World Socialist System (IEMSS), stated: "the practice of international division of labour and cooperation within Comecon sets an example of [a] balanced and just solution to many of the problems posed by the movement for the NIEO." He went on to say that Comecon was the "real experience of restructuring world economic relations on the principles of equality, respect for the interests of all the cooperating countries and friendly mutual assistance for the sake of common progress."[51] In the 1970s, this more dogmatic view coexisted with another more open-minded view, which

48 See Elizabeth Kridl Valkenier, "Revolutionary Change in the Third World: Recent Soviet Assessments," *World Politics* 38, 3 (1986), 415–34; and Kridl Valkenier, *The Soviet Union and the Third World*, 136.
49 Godard, "Framing the Discourse."
50 Kridl Valkenier, *The Soviet Union and the Third World*, 26.
51 Oleg Bogomolov, "The CMEA Countries and the NIEO," in Christopher T. Saunders (ed.), *East-West-South: Economic Interaction Between Three Worlds* (Basingstoke: Macmillan, 1983), 250.

praised the economic and technological advantages of cooperation with the West.

If You Can't Beat Them, Join Them

"If you can't beat them, join them," is how Aroon K. Basak, deputy director of the World Bank responsible for the United Nations Industrial Development Organization (UNIDO) cooperative program, described the Socialist bloc strategy of the 1970s and especially the move toward tripartite industrial cooperation (TIC).[52]

At the end of the 1970s, interstate agreements for joint activities in third countries and joint East–West companies that operated in Third World markets experienced steady growth. Typically, tripartite projects originated in tenders from the developing country. Western firms provided management and the most advanced technology and equipment and the Eastern bloc provided the intermediate level of machinery and knowhow, while developing countries supplied labor and raw materials. Another, less common version saw the Soviet Union teaming up with the more advanced among the less developed countries for the construction and design of industrial projects, the extraction of raw materials and the provision of consulting services in other developing states. Especially common in the energy sector and in oil refining, tripartite projects experienced a dramatic increase after 1975.[53] East European countries were from the start very keen on trilateral cooperation, less so the Soviet Union. Here, debates had been going on since the second half of the 1960s, when the problem of exporting to the developing world was discussed and some of the reasons for the Soviet predicament (the quality of machinery or the lack of spare parts and service) were also mentioned.[54] Despite these initial doubts, however, the Soviet share in trilateral projects soon topped that of Eastern Europe.

Trilateral cooperation looked more like cooperation "in" rather than cooperation "with" the developing countries. It was proof that socialist

52 Aroon K. Basak's comments in Saunders (ed.), *East-West-South*, 369.
53 Patrick Gutmann, "Tripartite Industrial Cooperation and Third World Countries," in Saunders (ed.), *East-West-South*, 346. Gutmann analyzes a sample of 226 TIC operations, completed or in progress (principally for the years 1976–79), and an additional 199 protocol agreements for 1965–79 that show clearly that 1975 constitutes a break. See also Patrick Gutmann, "West-östliche Wirtschaftskooperationen in der Dritten Welt," in Christian Th. Müller, Claudia Weber and Bernd Greiner (eds.), *Ökonomie im Kalten Krieg* (Hamburg: Hamburger Edition, 2010), 395–412.
54 Hough, *The Struggle for the Third World*, 81.

countries were rethinking the role of capitalism in the world economy. Capitalism had been on the whole successful in its relations with the developing countries, Mirskii stated at the end of the 1970s. Karen Brutents, an expert on African and Asian matters and a prominent member of the International Department of the Central Committee of the CPSU, in a 1978 article in *Pravda* on "Imperialism and the Liberated Countries," authoritatively restated that capitalism had adapted well to the new conditions after decolonization and now used more sophisticated forms of exploitation.[55]

Partly, this revised approach had to do with the failure to establish a socialist international division of labor with developing countries. In the 1970s socialist aid was still aimed at fostering economic integration between Comecon and the countries of the South, with a special role for cooperation in prospecting for minerals. Tripartite agreements were considered a key strategic step in the immediate future. East European economists no longer believed in the complementarity of East and South economies. They tended to think that the South was already moving toward competition. Both groups, they contended, had similar supply-led and investment-hungry economies. Their structures were therefore not sufficiently complementary, and a broader trade basis, one that included the West, would be ideal.[56] Some scholars argued that, since developing countries were capitalist, the socialist countries should not offer handouts, but instead organize remunerative economic relations. The goal of economic relations was now described as "mutual benefit," because the use of the word "profit" was a problem both domestically and abroad.

At the Sixth Workshop on East–West European Economic Interaction, organized by the Vienna Institute for Comparative Economic Studies in Dubrovnik in May 1980, speakers from Eastern Europe still insisted that their ideal was a new order whose goal was radical change within the structures of national societies. Development was an integrated process, they contended – recalling the Comecon wording – and stressed the importance of an educational system designed for the needs of the future. They rejected an overarching formula for "appropriate technology": neither "small is beautiful," nor "big is wonderful," but rather the analysis of what could be in each case the appropriate mix of technologies. Although still promoting autonomy, they contended that it was no longer synonymous with autarky,

55 Kridl Valkenier, *The Soviet Union and the Third World*, 59 and 65.
56 See Michal Kalecki, *Essays in Developing Economies* (Hassocks, UK: Harvester, 1976), 36.

as Christopher Saunders observed in his concluding remarks, summing up the lessons of the symposium.[57]

The Myth of Socialist Modernity Fades Away

In the 1970s, the new approach to East–South relations was linked to a different perception of the global.[58] Under the multiple blows of the economic and social crisis and of perceived new threats such as energy dependence and ecological problems, the paradigm of progress and the grand narratives of industrialization were questioned, in the West and the East alike. Soviet modernity was transformed by the technocratic ideas of economic governance. Marxist intellectuals had gone a long way in criticizing the thesis of convergence advanced in the 1960s, linked especially with John K. Galbraith's book on *The New Industrial State* (1968).[59] In the mid 1970s, though, socialist countries eventually accepted a concept of interdependence. Soviet intellectuals, often high-ranking officials, participated in international networks and came into contact with Western ideas. One of them, Djermen Gvishiani, deputy chairman of the USSR's State Commission on Science and Technology, epitomizes this thinking. As head of the International Institute for Applied Systems Analysis founded in Vienna in 1976, he was in touch with the Club of Rome and developed similar views on global concerns. At the Twenty-Fifth Congress of the CPSU, Brezhnev admitted that the development of science and the challenge of environmental degradation could not be solved without East–West cooperation.[60] Margarita Maksimova, head of the Soviet Scientific Council of Philosophy and Global Problems, remarked that "despite all the differences and contradictions," the two world markets found themselves "in a definite mutual interaction," and

57 This is Saunders's synthesis of the views that emerged during the conference, in Saunders, *East-West-South*, 3.
58 See Niall Ferguson et al. (eds.), *The Shock of the Global: The 1970s in Perspective* (Cambridge, MA: Belknap Press of Harvard University Press, 2010).
59 See Neil MacFarlane, "Moscow's New Thinking," in Joan Barth Urban (ed.), *Moscow and the Global Left in the Gorbachev Era* (Ithaca: Cornell University Press, 1992), 127–59. See also Elizabeth Kridl Valkenier, "The USSR, the Third World, and the Global Economy," *Problems of Communism* 28 (1979), 17–33. For a discussion, see Istvan Dobozi, "Patterns, Determinants, and Prospects of East–South Economic Relations," in Brigitte Schulz and William W. Hansen (eds.), *The Soviet Bloc and the Third World: The Political Economy of East–South Relations* (Boulder: Westview Press, 1989), 111–36.
60 Yakov Feygin, "Détente Economics: The Soviet Union and the Global Dream of a Technocratic Political Economy, 1960–1987," paper presented at the conference "Cold War Economics," London 14–15 Dec. 2015, 1.

showed common tendencies that operated in the world economy as a whole.[61]

This change in approach did not fail to influence East–South relations. Increasingly, among East European and Soviet economists, the issue was to promote a mixed economy in developing countries with a role for both domestic and foreign private capital.[62] The growth in international cooperation suggested the possibility of agreeing on solutions for the problems connected with backwardness in the developing countries.[63] Many, like Leon Zalmanovich Zevin, Director of the Division for Relations with Developing Countries at the Institute for the Socialist World Economic System of the USSR Academy of Sciences, insisted that for developing countries cooperation with developed countries, "including those with different social systems," was the key to success. Tripartite cooperation, where the socialist country could help the developing nation to get rid of the one-sided attachment to the world capitalist economy, was the preferred form.[64] The most striking manifestation of the change in strategy emerged in 1981, when Mozambique was refused entry into Comecon. This event signaled the collapse of the rhetoric of a special East–South solidarity: Not all Third World countries were equal; not all possessed the right level of development to integrate with the socialist system. Radical leaders in the Third World perceived the new line as a betrayal.

Conclusions

In the early phase of the Cold War, socialist bloc relations with the newly independent countries were characterized by the prospect of building an alternative system. The political priority was overwhelming, though not exclusive: In order to win their allegiance, in explicit opposition to both Western Europe and the United States, the socialist bloc, especially the Soviet Union, was ready to comply with the majority of less developed countries' requests. Comecon documents reinforce the argument based on the documents of the international departments of the communist parties, make sense of the political and ideological motivation behind East–South economic

61 M. Maximova, quoted by Kridl Valkenier, *The Soviet Union and the Third World*, 55.
62 "Soviet Policy in Southern Africa: An Interview with Viktor Goncharev by Howard Barrell," *Work in Progress* 4, 7 (1987), 140–41.
63 N. N. Inozemtsev, quoted in Kridl Valkenier, *The Soviet Union and the Third World*, 68.
64 Anatoli Olshany and Leon Z. Zevin, *CMEA Countries and Developing States: Economic Cooperation* (Moscow: Progress, 1984), 91.

relations and provide evidence of the efforts to coordinate agreements of balanced trade. They show that the Comecon community of experts tried to organize a coherent socialist model. They also confirm the predicament in which the whole bloc ended up being burdened with the unexpected consequences of trade reorientation.

In the years of détente, the political element became less marked and the South was seen as a trading partner that could cooperate with the East only on special, mutually advantageous terms. The socialist bloc's desperate craving for resources increasingly resembled the typical center–periphery pattern. Some dependency theorists did not fail to point their finger at the East, and developing countries, often disappointed with the quality and quantity of socialist aid, did not fail to stress the similarities. Ideology, however, was always there to remind the Comecon countries of the distinctive nature of East–South relations, and of the desirability of involvement in the socialist camp for those newly independent countries that were deemed to be ideologically mature and strategically important.

With the 1970s crisis in industrial society, however, the myth of socialist modernity as a variant of industrial modernity had definitely faded.[65] The European state socialist regimes could no longer function as a closed system, and ceased to promote, in Comecon and elsewhere, the prospect of an exclusive East–South cooperation in economic modernization.

Bibliographical Essay

This bibliographical essay only includes works with a specific focus on East–South economic relations. As for the political economy of East–South relations, scholarship generally tends to equate Soviet strategy with bloc strategy, due to the undeniable primacy of the Soviet Union within the bloc. Given the centrality of ideology in Eastern bloc policy-making, the relevant literature often covers both the economic and the social side of the construction of socialist modernity.

A compelling review of the historiography of East–South relations is David C. Engerman, "The Second World's Third World," *Kritika* 12, 1 (2011), 183–211. The standard work on the intellectual history of East–South relations is Jerry F. Hough, *The Struggle for the Third World: Soviet Debates and American Options*

---

65 See Marie-Janine Calic, Dietmar Neutatz and Julia Obertreis, *The Crisis of Socialist Modernity: The Soviet Union and Yugoslavia in the 1970s* (Göttingen: Vandenhoeck & Ruprecht, 2011), 7–27.

(Washington, DC: Brookings Institution Press, 1986). The study by Elizabeth Kridl Valkenier, *The Soviet Union and the Third World: An Economic Bind* (New York: Praeger, 1985), is also essential reading. Her articles are insightful, especially Elizabeth Kridl Valkenier, "The USSR, the Third World, and the Global Economy," *Problems of Communism* 28 (1979), 17–33, and Elizabeth Kridl Valkenier, "Revolutionary Change in the Third World: Recent Soviet Assessments," *World Politics* 38, 3 (1986), 415–34. More recently, Oscar Sanchez-Sibony's *Red Globalization: The Political Economy of the Soviet Cold War from Stalin to Khrushchev* (Cambridge: Cambridge University Press, 2014) offers interesting reflections on the Soviet involvement in the international economy.

With their focus on the economic history of East–South relations, the works of Marie Lavigne are fundamental: Marie Lavigne, *East–South Relations in the World Economy* (Boulder: Westview Press, 1988); Marie Lavigne, *Economie internationale des pays socialistes* (Paris: Colin, 1985). Also important are Christopher T. Saunders (ed.), *East–West Cooperation in Business: Inter-Firm Studies* (Vienna and New York: Springer Verlag, 1977); Christopher T. Saunders, *East-West-South: Economic Interaction Between Three Worlds* (Basingstoke: Macmillan, 1983); Carol R. Saivetz and Sylvia Woodby, *Soviet–Third World Relations* (Boulder: Westview Press, 1985); Brigitte Schulz and William W. Hansen, *The Soviet Bloc and the Third World: The Political Economy of East–South Relations* (Boulder: Westview Press 1989); Christian Th. Müller, Claudia Weber and Bernd Greiner (eds.), *Ökonomie im Kalten Krieg* (Hamburg: Hamburger Edition, 2010).

Earlier accounts dealing with the effort to build economic ties with the Third World are often highly ideological but still useful. The most balanced is Robert S. Walters, *American and Soviet Aid: A Comparative Analysis* (Pittsburgh: University of Pittsburgh Press, 1970). Other works include Halina Araszkiewicz and Pavel Apostol, *Osteuropa und Afrika. Ökonomische und soziokulturelle Aspekte des Technologietranfers zwischen Ost und Süd* (Munich: Wilhelm Fink Verlag, 1986); Klaus Billerbeck, *Soviet Bloc Foreign Aid to the Underdeveloped Countries: An Analysis and a Prognosis* (Hamburg: Verlag Weltarchiv, 1960); Reinhold Biskup, *Sowjetpolitik und Entwicklungsländer. Ideologie und Strategie in der sowjietischen Politik gegenüber den Entwicklungsländern* (Freiburg i. Br.: Rombach, 1970); Robert Cassen (ed.), *Soviet Interests in the Third World* (London: Sage Publications, 1985); Klaus Fritsche, *Entwicklungshilfe der Sowjetunion* (Cologne: Bundesinstitut für Ostwissenschaftliche und Internationale Studien, 1986); Emilio Gasparini, *Rubli e sottosviluppo. Analisi e quantificazione dell'aiuto sovietico*

(Milan: CESES, 1972); Roger Kanet, *The Soviet Union and the Developing Nations* (Baltimore: Johns Hopkins University Press, 1974); Andrzej Korbonski and Francis Fukuyama, *The Soviet Union and the Third World: The Last Three Decades* (Ithaca: Cornell University Press, 1987); Anatoli Olshany and Leon Z. Zevin, *CMEA Countries and Developing States: Economic Cooperation* (Moscow: Progress Publishers, 1984); Michael Radu (ed.), *Eastern Europe and the World: East vs. South* (New York: Praeger, 1981); and Leon Z. Zevin, *Economic Cooperation of Socialist and Developing Countries: New Trends* (Moscow: Nauka Publishing House, 1976).

Suggested specific studies on Comecon include Klaus Fritsche, *Sozialistische Entwicklungsländer in der "internationalen sozialistischen Arbeitsteilung" des RGW. Zum Forschungsstand* (Cologne: Bundesinstituts für ostwissenschaftliche und internationale Studien, 1991), Konstantin Ivanovich Mikulsky, *CMEA: International Significance of Socialist Integration* (Moscow: Progress Publishers, 1979; translation, 1982); Venelin I. Ganev, *Comecon and the "Third World": Problems of Cooperation and Division of Labour* (Moscow: Ekonomika, 1976). More recent contributions on Comecon and developing countries include David R. Stone, "CMEA's International Investment Bank and the Crisis of Developed Socialism," *Journal of Cold War Studies* 10, 3 (2008), 48–77; Sara Lorenzini, "Modernisierung durch Handel. Der Ostblock und die Koordinierung der Entwicklungshilfe in der Ständigen Kommission für Technische Unterstützung," in Martin Aust and Julia Obertreis (eds.), *Osteuropäische Geschichte und Globalgeschichte* (Stuttgart: Steiner-Verlag, 2014), 221–40; and Sara Lorenzini, "Comecon and the South in the Years of Détente: A Study on East–South Economic Relations," *European Review of History: Revue européenne d'histoire* 21, 2 (2014), 183–99.

15

The Cuban Revolution: The First Decade

PIERO GLEIJESES

José Martí, the father of Cuban independence, dreamed of a Cuba in which the peasants would own land and racial discrimination would not exist; a Cuba that would be free – not only from decaying Spain, but also from the new giant, the United States, which had sought to annex the island since Thomas Jefferson's time. In 1895, as Cuba's revolt against Spanish rule began, Martí wrote "What I have done, and shall continue to do is to . . . block with our [Cuban] blood . . . the annexation of the peoples of America to the turbulent and brutal North that despises them . . . I lived in the monster [the United States] and know its entrails – and my sling is that of David."[1] The next day he was killed on the battlefield.

In 1898, as the Cuban revolt entered its fourth year, the United States joined the war against an exhausted Spain, ostensibly to free Cuba. After Spain surrendered, Washington forced on the Cubans the Platt amendment, which granted the United States the right to send troops to the island whenever it deemed necessary and to establish bases on Cuban soil. (Today, the Platt amendment lives on in the US naval base at Guantánamo Bay.) Cuba became, more than any other Latin American country, "an American fiefdom"[2] – until 1959, when Fidel Castro came to power.

Unlike his two closest associates – his younger brother Raúl and Che Guevara – Fidel Castro was not a communist when he overthrew the dictator Fulgencio Batista. "I always thought of Fidel as an authentic leader of the leftist bourgeoisie," Che wrote in December 1957.[3] Fidel Castro had a magnetic personality; he was extremely intelligent and a spell-binding

---

1 José Martí to Manuel Mercado, 18 May 1895, in José Martí, *Epistolario* (Havana: Editorial de ciencias sociales, 1993), vol. V, 250.
2 Tad Szulc, *Fidel: A Critical Portrait* (New York: HarperCollins, 1987), 13.
3 Che Guevara to Daniel, 14 Dec. 1957, in Carlos Franqui (ed.), *Diary of the Cuban Revolution* (New York: Viking Press, 1980), 269.

orator. He wanted to rule, but he was also an idealist. "He is clearly a strong personality and a born leader of great personal courage and conviction," US officials noted in April 1959, and a few months later a National Intelligence Estimate reported, "He is inspired by a messianic sense of mission to aid his people."[4] Even though he did not have a clear blueprint of the Cuba he wanted to create, Castro dreamed of a sweeping revolution that would uproot his country's oppressive socioeconomic structure. He dreamed of a Cuba free of the United States.

La Fête Cubaine

The first three years of the revolution were, as historian Louis Pérez writes, "euphoric times. Expectations ran high, were met, and then raised again."[5] In the cities, the poor benefited: On the government's orders, rents were cut and electricity rates slashed; labor contracts were renegotiated and wages raised; pensions were increased, and health and educational services expanded. In the countryside, the government established People's Stores which offered cheaper goods and liberal credit; it built schools and provided teachers; it erected low-rent houses; and it began programs to take health services to rural areas. Furthermore, the first Agrarian Reform Law in May 1959 expropriated estates larger than 1,000 acres; the owners would be compensated with twenty-year bonds bearing an annual interest rate of 4.5 percent; the law was not harsher than the agrarian reform the United States had imposed on Japan during the occupation or that it had promoted in Taiwan, but it was an unprecedented affront to Cuba's large landowners and also to the many US citizens who owned land in Cuba. (No Americans had owned land in Japan or Taiwan.) President Dwight D. Eisenhower's administration demanded prompt and effective compensation.

It was the first time in the history of Cuba that the government had improved the lot of the rural masses, and the masses responded. After noting that Castro had given the peasants higher incomes, literacy programs,

4 "Unofficial Visit of Prime Minister Castro of Cuba to Washington – A Tentative Evaluation," enclosed in Herter to Eisenhower, 23 Apr. 1959, US Department of State, *Foreign Relations of the United States* [hereafter *FRUS*] *1958–1960* (Washington, DC: US Government Printing Office, 1991), vol. VI, 483; Special National Intelligence Estimate (NIE), "The Situation in the Caribbean Through 1959," 30 Jun. 1959, National Security Archive, Washington, DC (NSA).
5 Louis Pérez, *Cuba Between Reform and Revolution* (New York: Oxford University Press, 1988), 320. For the relevant secondary sources about Cuba in the 1960s, see the Bibliographical Essay, 385–87.

housing and health care, US intelligence concluded: "Above all Castro has given the guajiro [peasant] the sense of having a stake in the nation." The revolutionary government moved decisively to abolish racial discrimination, in dramatic contrast to the United States of John F. Kennedy. The revolution had promised "much" in the sphere of racial equality and it had achieved "much," the same intelligence report noted. "Negroes have achieved greatly enhanced status."[6]

These years of redistribution and reform were capped in 1961 by an extraordinary event: the literacy campaign. By the end of 1961 the government claimed that adult literacy rate had risen from 75 percent to 96.1 percent. As Jorge Domínguez notes, "there is some doubt" about the statistics, "but the reduction of illiteracy was real." The campaign mobilized the urban youth of the country: 100,000 schoolchildren aged 13–18 went to live for several months with the peasants to teach them to read; in the process, urban youths were exposed to a new world.[7]

If the lower classes benefited in this dawn of the revolution it was not because the economic pie had become significantly larger, but because it had been redistributed at the expense of the country's upper class, as well as foreigners, notably US citizens. This bred resistance. In the fall of 1959 unidentified planes began flying from Florida to attack economic targets on the island, leading the US embassy in Havana to warn the State Department that the Cuban people were "becoming aroused" against the United States.[8] Anti-Castro guerrillas sprang to action in the cities and in the countryside. The CIA urged them on with money and weapons. Armed rebels, and the growing threat from the United States, reinforced the new leaders' authoritarian bent. Multiparty elections, initially promised within eighteen months, never took place, and room for dissent was increasingly restricted until in early 1961 all opposition newspapers were shuttered.

The Break with the United States

It was not Castro's record on political democracy that bothered the US officials. Washington had consistently maintained good relations with

6 Hughes to Johnson, "A Cuban Balance Sheet: Batista and Castro," Spring 1963, National Security Files (NSF), Meetings and Memoranda, box 315, John F. Kennedy Library, Boston.
7 Jorge Domínguez, *Cuba: Order and Revolution* (Cambridge, MA: Harvard University Press, 1978), 165.
8 Braddock to Secretary of State, 1 Feb. 1960, *FRUS 1958–1960*, vol. VI, 778.

the worst dictators of the hemisphere, as long as they had accepted US hegemony.

Castro, however, was not willing to bow to the United States. Many of the opponents of the Batista regime had wanted to accommodate the United States, either because they admired its culture or had a fatalistic respect for its power. Castro, on the other hand, represented the views of those anti-Batista youths who were repulsed by Washington's domination and paternalism. Eisenhower was baffled, for he believed, as most Americans still do, that the United States had been the Cubans' truest friend, fighting Spain in 1898 to give them independence. "Here is a country," he marveled, "that you would believe, on the basis of our history, would be one of our real friends." As US historian Nancy Mitchell has pointed out, "our selective recall not only serves a purpose, it also has repercussions. It creates a chasm between us and the Cubans: we share a past, but we have no shared memories."[9] Ethnocentrism and ignorance – the pillars of the City on the Hill – complicated US relations with Castro's Cuba.

The United States responded to Castro's challenge in the way it always dealt with nuisances in its backyard: with violence. It imposed a very strict embargo and applied strong pressure on third countries not to trade with Cuba. The CIA began planning the overthrow of Castro. In April 1961, 1,300 CIA-trained insurgents stormed a Cuban beach at the Bay of Pigs – only to surrender en masse three days later.

Flushed with this victory, Castro tendered an olive branch. On 17 August 1961, Che Guevara told a close aide of Kennedy that Cuba wanted to explore a *modus vivendi* with the United States. Kennedy was not interested. A few months later, on the president's orders, the CIA launched Operation Mongoose, a program of paramilitary operations, economic warfare and sabotage designed to visit what Kennedy's aide Arthur Schlesinger has called the "terrors of the earth"[10] on Fidel Castro. Meanwhile the CIA was hard at work trying to assassinate the Cuban leader.

Relations with Moscow

Castro understood that only strong Soviet backing could protect his fledgling revolution from the wrath of the United States. In January 1959, the Soviets

9 Eisenhower press conference, 28 Oct. 1959, in United States, General Services Administration, *Public Papers of the Presidents of the United States, 1959* (Washington, DC: US Government Printing Office, 1961), 271; Nancy Mitchell, "Remember the Myth," *News and Observer* (Raleigh) (1 Nov. 1998), G5.
10 Arthur Schlesinger, *Robert Kennedy and His Times* (New York: Ballantine, 1979), 516.

knew very little about him. For several months their only contact was through leaders of the Cuban Communist Party visiting Moscow to vouch for the revolutionary credentials of the new government. In October 1959, a KGB official arrived in Havana, establishing the first direct link between the Kremlin and the new Cuban leadership. Soon, the tempo accelerated: In March 1960 Moscow approved a Cuban request for weapons. Diplomatic relations were established the following May. In 1961, the relationship grew close and even ebullient as Soviet bloc arms and economic aid arrived. Castro was charismatic, he seemed steadfast, he worked well with the Cuban communists and he had humiliated the United States at the Bay of Pigs. The Soviet Union would transform the island into a socialist showcase in Latin America.

It was the Missile Crisis that brought the romance to an abrupt end. Thirty years later, in 1992, Kennedy's defense secretary Robert McNamara finally understood why the Soviets and the Cubans had decided to place missiles in Cuba: "I want to state quite frankly with hindsight, if I had been a Cuban leader, I think I might have expected a US invasion ... And I should say, as well, if I had been a Soviet leader at the time, I might have come to the same conclusion."[11] Kennedy's reckless policy meant that Castro had legitimate concerns for his country's security. Added to this was the Kremlin's desire to close the "missile gap," the well-publicized overwhelming superiority of the United States in strategic weapons.

Kennedy learned that there were Soviet missiles in Cuba on 16 October 1962. On 24 October, the US Navy blockaded the island. Four days later, when Nikita Khrushchev agreed to remove the missiles, he did not ask for Castro's opinion – "I don't see how you can say that we were consulted in the decision you took," Castro wrote Khrushchev.[12] The honeymoon was over.

In the wake of the Missile Crisis, the United States continued paramilitary raids and sabotage operations against Cuba, trying to cripple its economy and assassinate Castro. US officials were no longer confident that they could topple Castro, but they were determined to teach the Latin Americans that the price of following Cuba's example would be high. "Cuba was the key,"

---

11 McNamara, in Laurence Chang and Peter Kornbluh (eds.), *The Cuban Missile Crisis, 1962: A National Security Archive Documents Reader* (New York: New Press, 1992), xi–xii.
12 Castro to Khrushchev, 31 Oct. 1962, in James Blight, Bruce Allyn and David Welch (eds.), *Cuba on the Brink: Castro, the Missile Crisis and the Soviet Collapse* (New York: Pantheon, 1993), 491.

the Director of Central Intelligence told Kennedy. "If Cuba succeeds, we can expect most of Latin America to fall."[13]

While Kennedy promoted subversion in Cuba, Castro promoted revolution in Latin America. Self-defense and idealism motivated the Cubans. "The United States will not be able to hurt us if all of Latin America is in flames," Castro explained.[14] Revolution in Latin America was also, Cubans believed, in the interest of the people. Only through armed struggle could Latin Americans attain social justice and national sovereignty. Castro, the CIA said, was a man with a "fanatical devotion to his cause."[15] He believed that he was "engaged in a great crusade" to help free the people of the Third World from the misery and the oppression that tormented them.[16]

Cuban leaders and US officials agreed on one key point: The objective conditions that gave rise to revolution – misery, ignorance, exploitation – were present in Latin America. As Thomas Hughes, the director of the State Department's Bureau of Intelligence and Research (INR), pointed out, the Cubans viewed Latin America "as a tinder box to which one merely had to apply a spark ... to set off the revolutionary explosion."[17] This spark would be created by what the Castroites called the *foco*, the small guerrilla vanguard that would launch armed struggle in the countryside.

Castro wanted the armed struggle to start immediately. He explained: "In the course of the struggle the revolutionary conscience [the people's awareness that they could and should fight] will surge forth." The war against Batista had shown that the *foco* could create this awareness and set the forest ablaze. One of Che Guevara's closest aides recalled: "We were absolutely convinced that we had discovered an infallible method to free the people." Because the objective conditions were present, a handful of dedicated revolutionaries could triumph against impossible odds. "We have demonstrated," Che wrote, "that a small group of men

13 McCone, memo of meeting with president, 23 Aug. 1962, *FRUS 1961–1963* (Washington, DC: US Government Printing Office, 1997), vol. X, 955.
14 Castro, quoted in Aleksandr Fursenko and Timothy Naftali, *"One Hell of a Gamble": Khrushchev, Castro and Kennedy, 1958–1964* (New York: W. W. Norton & Company, 1997), 141.
15 CIA, Directorate of Intelligence (DI), "Cuban Subversive Policy and the Bolivian Guerrilla Episode," May 1968, National Security File Country File (NSFCF), box 19, Lyndon B. Johnson Library, Austin, Texas (LBJL).
16 NIE, "The Situation in Cuba," 14 Jun. 1960, NSA.
17 Hughes to Secretary of State, "Cuba in 1964," 17 Apr. 1964, Freedom of Information Act (FOIA) 1996/668.

who are determined, supported by the people and not afraid of death . . . can overcome a regular army." This was, he believed, the lesson of the Cuban Revolution.[18]

It echoed throughout Latin America. "The Cuban Revolution . . . was like a continental detonator," a member of the Central Committee of the Venezuelan Communist Party remarked. "It justified revolutionary impatience, and it ended the old discussion about geographic fatalism – the belief that no revolution in Latin America could ever succeed because it was in the backyard of the US empire. In one fell swoop, the Cuban Revolution swept away that old ghost."[19] Fired up by the Cuban example and by Castro's call to the true revolutionaries to fight, guerrillas became active in Venezuela, Guatemala, Nicaragua, Honduras, the Dominican Republic, Peru and Argentina.

Castro argued that "the virus of revolution is not carried in submarines or ships. It is wafted instead on the ethereal waves of ideas . . . The power of Cuba is the power of its revolutionary ideas, the power of its example." The CIA agreed. "Castro's shadow looms large because social and economic conditions throughout Latin America invite opposition to ruling authority and encourage agitation for radical change," it noted in mid 1961.[20] Cuba, however, did not rely just on the power of its example. "By 1961–1962, Cuban support [for revolution] began taking many forms," the CIA noted, "ranging from inspiration and training to such tangibles as financing and communications support as well as some military assistance." The most important was military training. The CIA estimated that between 1961 and 1964 "at least" 1,500 to 2,000 Latin Americans received "either guerrilla warfare training or political indoctrination in Cuba."[21]

Very few Cubans, however, joined the guerrillas in Latin America. Havana's revolutionary fervor was tempered by self-preservation. Castro did not want to give the United States a pretext to invade Cuba, and sending Cuban guerrillas to fight in Latin America would be far more provocative

18 Quotations from Castro, 26 Jul. 1966 speech, *Granma*, 27 Jul. 1966, 3; author's interview with Oscar Fernández Mell, Havana, 2 Jul. 1994; Guevara, "Proyecciones sociales del Ejército Rebelde," 27 Jan. 1959, in Juan José Soto Valdespino (ed.), *Ernesto Che Guevara. Escritos y discursos* (Havana: Editorial de Ciencias Sociales, 1977), vol. IV, 20.
19 Alfredo Maneiro in Agustín Blanco Muñoz, *La lucha armada: hablan 6 comandantes* (Caracas: Universidad Central de Venezuela, 1981), 349.
20 Castro, *Revolución* (Havana) (23 Feb. 1963), 4; NIE, "Latin American Reactions to Developments in and with Respect to Cuba," 18 Jul. 1961, NSF, NIE, box 8/9, LBJL.
21 CIA, DI, "Cuban Subversive Activities in Latin America, 1959–1968," 16 Feb. 1968, NSFCF, box 19, LBJL.

than bringing hundreds of Latin Americans to train on the island. As a result, between 1961 and 1964 only two Cubans fought in Latin America (both in Argentina). The same caution governed the dispatch of weapons. Cuba, the CIA noted in 1964, "generally has avoided sending arms directly to other Latin American countries."[22]

From 1961 to 1964 the degree of Cuban involvement in the guerrilla wars of Latin America varied. At one extreme was Argentina, where the Cubans prepared the 1963–64 insurgency and selected its leader; at the other, the 1963 uprising in the Dominican Republic, where Cuban involvement was virtually nonexistent.[23]

Tilting at a *Modus Vivendi*

While supporting guerrillas in Latin America, Castro also explored the possibility of some form of accommodation with the United States. He had tried in August 1961, and he tried again, repeatedly, in 1963. Finally in late 1963 there was, a senior US official noted, "a very tenuous, sensitive, and marginal" beginning:[24] Kennedy responded to yet another Castro overture by stipulating that, before he decided whether to engage in substantive talks, the Cubans had to present a list of the concessions they were willing to make. Kennedy was assassinated before the Cubans had time to respond and President Lyndon Johnson chose not to pursue the talks.

It is impossible to know what price Castro would have been willing to pay for a *modus vivendi*. Ending Cuba's support for armed struggle in Latin America would have violated his sense of mission, but a *modus vivendi* with the United States had a powerful attraction. Castro's foremost biographer stresses "the obsession of Fidel Castro to do away with human, social, and economic underdevelopment in Cuba ... To eradicate underdevelopment ... was indeed Castro's magnificent obsession from the beginning."[25] INR director Hughes wrote insightfully in the spring of 1964:

22 CIA, Office of Current Intelligence, "Survey of Latin America," 1 Apr. 1964, NSFCF, box 1, LJBL.
23 For the Dominican Republic, see Piero Gleijeses, *La Esperanza Desgarrada. La rebelión dominicana de 1965 y la invasión norteamericana* (Santo Domingo: Editora Búho, 2012); for Argentina, see Pierre-Olivier Pilard, *Jorge Ricardo Masetti. Un révolutionnaire guévarien et guévariste de 1958 à 1964* (Paris: L'Harmattan, 2007).
24 National Security Advisor McGeorge Bundy quoted in Chase, "Meeting with the President, December 19, 1963," *FRUS 1961–1963, 1963* (Washington, DC: US Government Printing Office, 1996), vol. XI, 907.
25 Szulc, *Fidel*, 593–94.

> On the one end, they [Cuba's leaders] are still dedicated revolutionaries, utterly convinced that they can and must bring radical change in Latin America some day. Many would rather be remembered as revolutionary martyrs than economic planners. Yet on the other hand these same men are aware that the current pressing problems demand amelioration that can only be brought by muting the call to revolution, by attempting to reach live and let live arrangements with the US, and by widening trade and diplomatic contacts with the free world.
>
> Tensions between the two paths, between peaceful coexistence and the call for violent revolution, will continue to exist within the Cuban hierarchy, both within and between individuals, for the foreseeable future.[26]

In the months that followed this report, Castro tried again to open conversations with the United States but was rebuffed. Finally he gave up, in the fall of 1964, "because of the lack of US interest in his proposal," Hughes noted.[27] There would be no more attempts at a dialogue, on either side, for a decade.

Setbacks in Latin America

Spurned by the United States, Castro continued to support armed struggle in Latin America. But by 1964 he faced a string of defeats. The most notable was the spectacular failure of the guerrillas in Venezuela to disrupt the country's December 1963 presidential elections. Guerrilla uprisings in Peru, Argentina, Nicaragua and the Dominican Republic had been swiftly crushed. Castro's belief that a small band of guerrillas could set the forest ablaze had been wrong. The security forces of the various Latin American countries were strong enough to annihilate the handful of guerrillas, and the modest aid Cuba could afford – a few weapons, a little money, some training – paled in comparison with the massive aid Washington gave the Latin American security forces.

Castro also faced Soviet disapproval. The Kremlin was unhappy because his policies complicated its relations with the United States and Latin American governments. Castro was unbending. At a meeting of communist parties in Moscow in March 1965, Raúl Castro, who was Cuba's defense minister, stressed that it was imperative "to organize a global movement of solidarity with the guerrillas in Venezuela, Colombia and

26 Hughes to Secretary of State, "Cuba in 1964," 17 Apr. 1964, FOIA 1996/668.
27 Hughes to Secretary of State, "The Cuban Revolution: Phase Two," 10 Aug. 1965, NSFCF, box 18/19, LBJL.

Guatemala who ... are fighting heroically for the independence of their countries."[28]

As Raúl spoke in Moscow, secret preparations were underway in Havana to organize another guerrilla offensive. On 26 April the *Uvero*, the largest ship of the Cuban merchant fleet, steamed from the port of Matanzas. Its destination was Africa.

Cuba Turns to Africa

When US officials thought of communist subversion in Africa, they pictured Moscow and Beijing, not Havana. They could not imagine that a poor Caribbean island whose only link to Africa was the blood of hundreds of thousands of slaves could play a role on that faraway continent.

Fidel Castro, however, could imagine it. Two years after his victory over Batista, his emissaries crossed the ocean to offer Cuba's help to the Algerian rebels, fighting for independence against France. A few weeks later, in December 1961, a Cuban ship unloaded weapons at Casablanca for the Algerians and returned to Havana with seventy-six wounded guerrillas and twenty children from refugee camps. Cuba's African journey had begun. This single ship represented the dual thrust of Cuban internationalism: military aid and humanitarian assistance.[29]

In May 1963, after Algeria had gained its independence, a 55-person Cuban medical mission arrived in Algiers to establish a program of free health care for the Algerian people. The following October, when Algeria was threatened by Morocco, the Cubans rushed a force of 686 men with heavy weapons to the Algerians, jeopardizing a contract Morocco had just signed with Havana to buy Cuban sugar worth US$ 184 million, a considerable amount of hard currency at a time when the United States was trying to cripple Cuba's economy.

History, geography, culture and language made Latin America the Cubans' natural habitat, the place closest to Castro's and his followers' hearts, the first place where they tried to spread revolution, but Latin America was also where their freedom of movement was most circumscribed. Castro was,

---

28 Raúl Castro, "Discurso pronunciado en la reunión consultiva de los Partidos Comunistas y Obreros que se celebra en Moscú," 3 Mar. 1965, Oficina Secreta 2do Sec. CC PCC, Havana (OS).

29 This section on Cuba in Africa is based on Piero Gleijeses, *Conflicting Missions: Havana, Washington, and Africa, 1959–1976* (Chapel Hill: University of North Carolina Press, 2002). The author had access to the closed Cuban archives.

as the CIA observed, "canny enough to keep his risks low" in the United States' backyard.[30] Hence, fewer than forty Cubans fought in Latin America in the 1960s, and Cuba exercised extreme caution before sending weapons to Latin American rebels.

In Africa, Cuba incurred fewer risks. Whereas in Latin America Havana aided guerrillas who were challenging legal governments, in Africa either the rebels it aided were confronting colonial powers or, in some cases, it defended established states. Above all, in Africa, there was much less risk of a head-on collision with the United States. In the 1960s US officials barely took notice of the Cubans in Africa.

Moreover, the Cuban leaders were convinced that their country had a special empathy for and a special role to play in the Third World beyond the confines of Latin America. The Soviets and their East European allies were white and, by Third World standards, rich; the Chinese exhibited the hubris of a great and rising power and were unable to adapt to African and Latin American culture. By contrast, Cuba was nonwhite, poor, threatened by a powerful enemy and culturally both Latin American and African. It was, therefore, a unique hybrid: a socialist country with a Third World sensibility. This mattered in a world that was dominated, as Castro rightly understood, by the "conflict between privileged and underprivileged, humanity against imperialism,"[31] and where the major faultline was not between socialist and capitalist states but between developed and under-developed countries.

In December 1964 Che Guevara went to Africa on a three-month trip that signaled Havana's quickening interest in the continent. This was the moment of the great illusion when the Cubans, and many others, believed that revolution beckoned in Africa. Guerrillas were fighting the Portuguese in Angola, Guinea-Bissau and Mozambique. In Congo Brazzaville, a new government proclaimed its revolutionary sympathies. Above all, there was Congo Leopoldville, the former Belgian Congo, where rebels threatened the corrupt pro-American regime that Eisenhower and Kennedy had labored to put in place. To save the Leopoldville regime, the Johnson administration raised an army of 1,000 white mercenaries in a major covert operation that provoked a wave of revulsion even among African leaders friendly to the United States. Che pledged, on Castro's behalf, Cuban military instructors to

30 Special NIE, "Castro's Problems and Prospects Over the Next Year or Two," 27 Jun. 1968, NSF, NIE, box 8/9, LBJL.
31 United States Department of State (DOS), "National Policy Paper – Cuba: United States Policy," draft, 15 Jul. 1968, Declassified Documents Reference System.

the rebels; they accepted, he wrote, "with delight."[32] In April 1965 a column of 120 Cubans led by Che began infiltrating Congo Leopoldville from Tanzania. In August, a second column, led by a man destined to play a key role in Cuba's policy in Africa, Jorge Risquet, arrived in neighboring Congo Brazzaville at the request of that country's leftist government, which feared an attack by the CIA's mercenaries; the column would also, if possible, assist Che in Congo Leopoldville. In the summer of 1965, there were 400 Cuban soldiers in Central Africa.

Many writers, including Jorge Castañeda, Che's major biographer, have argued that Guevara went to Congo because his growing criticism of the Soviet Union had led to a clash with Fidel's brother Raúl and, ultimately, with Fidel himself. Castañeda describes an incident in March 1965 when Raúl and Che argued violently while Fidel watched in embarrassed silence.[33] The tale is poignant, but the meeting is fiction – as US, Cuban and East German documents prove. In March 1965, Raúl could not have been in Havana insulting Che because he was in Moscow upbraiding the Soviets for their failure to provide adequate assistance to North Vietnam. Raúl and Che were never in the same country from December 1964 to July 1966. And while it is true that Che had become very critical of the Soviet Union, Fidel Castro had also become critical, and almost as outspoken.[34]

Guevara went to Congo in April 1965 not because of an alleged estrangement from Fidel, but because he believed, as did Fidel, that sub-Saharan Africa was ready for revolution and that the Congo was the epicenter of the struggle. He had toured the continent from December 1964 to March 1965 as Castro's emissary. He was moved by what he saw. "I have found here in Africa . . . entire populations that are, if you'll allow me this image, like water on the verge of boiling," he told a journalist.[35] Under Castro's guidance, Che Guevara had orchestrated Cuban assistance to insurgencies in Latin America. Now sub-Saharan Africa had moved to center stage. The Congo operation was Cuba's most daring move yet in the Third World; it was not Che's personal escape.

Central Africa, however, was not ready for revolution. By the time the Cubans arrived in Congo Leopoldville, the CIA's mercenaries had broken the

---

32 Che Guevara, "Pasajes de la guerra revolucionaria (Congo)" [Dar-es-Salaam, Dec. 1965 or early 1966], 13, Private Collection, Havana.
33 Jorge Castañeda, *Compañero: The Life and Death of Che Guevara* (New York: Vintage, 1997), 296–97.
34 Gleijeses, *Conflicting Missions*, 101–06.
35 Hamadi Ben Milad, "Che Guevara: l'avenir de l'Afrique c'est le socialisme, puis le communisme," *Jeune Afrique* (21 May 1965), 22–23.

resolve of the rebels, leaving Che no choice by November 1965 but to withdraw. In Congo Brazzaville, Risquet's column saved the host government from a military coup, carried out the first vaccination campaign against polio in the country's history and trained the rebels of Agostinho Neto's Popular Movement for the Liberation of Angola before withdrawing in December 1966.

The late 1960s were a period of deepening maturity in Cuba's relationship with Africa. "Fidel is a little pessimistic about Africa," a senior Cuban official admitted in January 1967.[36] No longer deluded that revolution was around the corner, the Cubans were learning about the continent. The focus of Havana's attention in Africa shifted to Guinea-Bissau, where rebels fighting for independence from Portugal asked for Cuba's assistance. Cuban military instructors and doctors joined the rebels there in 1966 and remained through the war's end in 1974 – the longest and most successful Cuban intervention in Africa before the dispatch of troops to Angola in 1975. In the words of Guinea-Bissau's first president: "We were able to fight and triumph because other countries helped us . . . with weapons, medicine and supplies . . . but there is one nation that, in addition to material, political and diplomatic support, even sent its children to fight by our side, to shed their blood in our land. This great people, this heroic people, we all know that it is the heroic people of Cuba; the Cuba of Fidel Castro."[37]

The Revolutionary Offensive in Latin America

By the mid 1960s the government had consolidated its control in Cuba. The last groups of anti-Castro guerrillas were wiped out in 1965. And while the Americans' embargo and their attempts to force third countries not to trade with Cuba continued with full venom, US paramilitary operations against the island virtually ended in 1965, in part because the CIA had run out of Cubans willing to serve as cannon fodder, in part because the results had been increasingly meager and in part because Washington's attention was shifting to Vietnam. Castro, however, was not mollified. "For more than a year Castro has maintained an attitude of passionate and resentful hostility toward USA," the Canadian embassy in Havana noted in a perceptive March 1966 report. "Hurt by rejection of overtures

---

36 Osmany Cienfuegos, quoted in "Versión taquigráfica de la reunión en el EMG con el comp. Risquet (Enero 18/1967)," enclosed in Ulises to Tomassevich, 18 Jan. 1967, Archives of the Central Committee of the Cuban Communist Party, Havana.
37 President Luís Cabral, Nõ Pintcha (Bissau) (22 Jan. 1977), 4.

[for a *modus vivendi*] in 1964 and infuriated by American activities in Vietnam and Dominican Republic [the US invasion in April 1965] Castro apparently saw no alternative other than to throw himself into forefront of revolutionary activity directed largely against 'American imperialism.'"[38] In 1966–67 Cuba made its strongest attempt to launch armed struggle in the hemisphere. It was concentrated on four countries: Venezuela, Guatemala, Colombia and Bolivia. Four Cuban officers landed in Venezuela in July 1966; more followed in May 1967. Sixteen Cubans went to Bolivia with Che Guevara. Cuba had put its "first team" there, the CIA wrote.[39]

Bolivia was the linchpin of an ambitious plan hatched in Havana: It would be the beachhead from which the guerrillas would spread to neighboring countries. The CIA pointed out that Bolivia – "a land of chronic political and economic instability" with a combative labor movement and security forces notorious for their ineptitude – "seemed to present an ideal background for a liberating guerrilla movement."[40]

The Bolivian insurgency lasted only a few months – from March to October 1967. Che was wounded and captured on 8 October. The following day he was murdered on the orders of the Bolivian president. The US government said that his fate should be left to his Bolivian captors, knowing full well that he would be killed. As a senior CIA official pointed out, Che "would have been hopeless to debrief" because he was such a "committed and dedicated man."[41]

Perhaps the best epitaph to the relationship between Che Guevara and Fidel Castro was written by Régis Debray, the prominent French intellectual who in 1967 was a trusted aide of Castro. By 1996 he had become a fervent critic, but he remembered: "I listened [in 1967] to Fidel – the two of us alone – talk for an entire night about Che, with that mixture of tact, pride and concern that an older brother might feel for his youngest brother who is setting off on an adventure, knowing his faults all too well, and loving him for them. [In Bolivia] I heard Che ... speak to me of Fidel ... with unquestionable devotion."[42]

---

38 Canadian embassy, Havana, to External, 7 Mar. 1966, Cuba 8849, pt. 4, Bibliothèque et Archives Canada/Library and Archives Canada, Ottawa (Canada).
39 CIA, DI, "Cuban Subversive Activities in Latin America: 1959–1968," 16 Feb. 1968, NSFCF, box 19, LBJL. See Gleijeses, *Conflicting Missions*, 455, n. 15.
40 CIA, DI, "Cuban Subversive Policy and the Bolivian Guerrilla Episode," May 1968, NSFCF, box 19, LBJL.
41 Henry Ryan, *The Fall of Che Guevara: A Story of Soldiers, Spies, and Diplomats* (New York: Oxford University Press, 1998), 132.
42 Régis Debray, *Loués soient nos seigneurs* (Paris: Gallimard, 1996), 176–77.

Growing Tensions with the USSR . . . and China

Cuba's renewed focus on armed struggle in Latin America in 1966–67 created strains in its relationship with the Soviet Union. Moscow was trying to expand its commercial and diplomatic ties with Latin American governments – the same governments that Castro was trying to overthrow. Castro was blunt. "It is absurd," he said, referring to Soviet offers of aid to Colombia, "loans in dollars to an oligarchical government that is . . . persecuting and murdering guerrillas . . . This is absurd."[43] Castro criticized the Soviet Union as dogmatic and opportunistic, niggardly in its aid to Third World governments and liberation movements and overeager to seek accommodation with the United States. He made no secret of his displeasure with the inadequacy of Moscow's support of North Vietnam. "If they gave us any advice, we'd say that they were interfering in our internal affairs," Raúl Castro later remarked, "but we didn't hesitate to express our opinions about their internal affairs."[44]

While US policymakers publicly lambasted Castro as a Soviet puppet, US intelligence analysts quietly pointed to his refusal to accept Soviet advice and his open criticism of the Soviet Union. "He has no intention of subordinating himself to Soviet discipline and direction, and he has increasingly disagreed with Soviet concepts, strategies and theories," a 1968 study concluded, reflecting the consensus of the US intelligence community.[45] To explain why the Soviets put up with "their recalcitrant Cuban ally,"[46] a 1967 US intelligence report noted that the Kremlin still saw advantages in its alliance with Cuba; it was a symbol of Soviet ability to support even "remote allies," and it had a "nuisance value vis-à-vis the US." Above all, the Kremlin drew back from the political and psychological cost of a break: "How could the Soviets pull out of Cuba and look at the world or themselves in the morning? It would be a confession of monumental failure – the first and only socialist enterprise in the New World abandoned – and it would seriously damage Soviet prestige and be widely interpreted as a victory of sorts for the United States."[47]

43 Castro, 10 Aug. 1967 speech, *Granma* (11 Aug. 1967), 4.
44 Memcon (Raúl Castro, Mengistu), 7 Jan. 1978, OS.
45 DOS, "National Policy Paper."
46 Hughes to Secretary of State, "Soviet Intentions Toward Cuba," 12 Mar. 1965, NSFCF, box 33/37, LBJL.
47 CIA, Board of National Estimates, "Bolsheviks and Heroes: The USSR and Cuba," Nov. 21, 1967, FOIA 1993/1807.

In early 1968 the Cubans publicly accused Soviet officials of interfering in Cuba's domestic affairs and announced that the Cuban Communist Party would not attend the forthcoming Budapest meeting of communist parties sponsored by the Soviet Union. In July 1968 a senior Soviet official remarked, "At present . . . there is unfortunately absolutely no contact whatsoever at a high level between the CPSU [Communist Party of the Soviet Union] and the Cuban Communist Party."[48]

If Cuba's relations with Moscow were strained, its relations with China were execrable. In 1960 Cuba and China had established warm relations, and Beijing had provided Havana a modest amount of economic and military aid.[49] As the quarrel between Beijing and Moscow exploded in public in 1960 and grew ever more bitter, the Cubans were in a fix. "We felt," President Osvaldo Dorticós told the Soviet ambassador in 1963, "that both sides wanted us to take a position that would strengthen our relations with one of them and hurt our friendship with the other."[50]

Moscow "handled" the prickly Cubans "adroitly," the CIA remarked. It made no frontal assaults to force its views on its nettlesome ally.[51] China was less patient. When pro-Chinese factions broke from the communist parties of Brazil (in February 1962) and Peru (in January 1964) to create pro-Chinese communist splinter groups, Beijing expected Havana to recognize them. This did not happen. Nor did Havana invite the two pro-Chinese parties to a conference of Latin American communist parties that met in Cuba in late 1964. Worse, the communiqué of the conference, published in *Pravda* on 19 January 1965, stated that "any factional activity, no matter what its nature or source, must be categorically condemned."[52] For Beijing, this was a serious offense.

Since the early 1960s the Chinese and the Soviets had been disseminating propaganda in Havana attacking each other. "The Chinese were much more aggressive," a well-informed scholar notes, "and they often sent such materials directly to the homes of Cuban party officials and military officers." In mid 1964 Cuba requested that China and the Soviet Union restrain their

---

48 Axen to Ulbricht, 26 Jul. 1968, quoting Soviet ambassador Piotr Abrasimov, DY30 IVA 2/20/265, Stiftung Archiv der Parteien und Massenorganisationen der DDR im Bundesarchiv, Berlin (SAPMO).

49 CIA, Office of Current Intelligence, "Bloc Economic Support for Cuba," 14 Jun. 1963, CREST, National Archives, College Park, MD.

50 Alekseev, "Zapis besedi s Osvaldo Dorticom," 7 Dec. 1963, NSA.

51 CIA, DI, "Castro and Communism: The Cuban Revolution in Perspective," 9 May 1966, NSFCF, box 19, LBJL.

52 *Pravda* (Moscow) (19 Jan. 1965), 3.

propaganda, but Beijing paid no heed, and it intensified its efforts in 1965 "despite Cuban objections," as the Canadian embassy reported.[53] In early 1966 the quarrel between Havana and Beijing exploded in public when Castro accused the Chinese of committing a "criminal act of economic aggression": They had reduced the amount of rice they had promised to send to Cuba in an effort – Castro believed – to blackmail him into siding with them against Moscow. The Chinese responded with equal vehemence, accusing Cuba of being a Soviet satellite.[54] Relations between the two countries remained tense until the late 1980s.

Relations with Moscow, which by early 1968 were under great strain, were far more important. Having reached the brink, Castro drew back. He may have been motivated by the desire not to jeopardize Soviet aid at a moment when he was trying desperately to improve the Cuban economy but, above all, the approach of the November 1968 US presidential elections stirred anxiety in Havana. Richard Nixon, whose personal animus toward Castro was notorious, was pledging to enact a tougher Cuban policy. If Nixon won, Castro told the Soviet chargé d'affaires in October 1968, "[US] military actions [against Cuba] could not be excluded." "The time had come," he added, "for an improvement of the friendly relations between the USSR and Cuba."[55]

The Soviet invasion of Czechoslovakia provided the opportunity. On 23 August 1968, two days after Soviet tanks had entered the Czech capital to stifle the Prague Spring, Castro addressed the Cuban nation. Many in Cuba and abroad expected him to condemn the Soviet Union. As a prominent journalist said, Castro was the leader of "a nation with a maximum concern for national independence, for the sovereignty of small nations."[56] Instead, however, Castro almost endorsed the invasion. The Soviet action was a "flagrant" violation of Czech sovereignty but, he added significantly, it had been absolutely necessary because the country's leader, Alexander

53 Yinghong Cheng, "Sino-Cuban Relations During the Early Years of the Castro Regime, 1959–1966," *Journal of Cold War Studies* 9, 3 (Summer 2007), 98–99; Canadian embassy, Havana, to Secretary of State for External Affairs, 22 Sep. 1965, Cuba 8849, pt. 4, Canada.
54 See Castro: 2 Jan. 1966 speech, 6 Feb. statement and 13 Mar. speech, in *Granma*: 3 Jan. 1966, 4–7; 6 Feb., 4–5; 14 Mar., 7 quoted. See also *Peking Review*: 14 Jan. 1966, 21–23; 4 Feb., 15–16; 25 Feb., 23–25.
55 Naumann to Markowski et al., 29 Oct. 1968 (quoting the Soviet chargé), DY30 IVA 2/20/265, SAPMO.
56 K. S. Karol, *Guerrillas in Power: The Course of the Cuban Revolution* (New York: Hill & Wang, 1970), 506.

Dubček, had been "heading toward capitalism and was inexorably heading toward imperialism."[57]

This struck many observers as an abject surrender to Soviet economic pressure. Castro, however, had his own reasons to welcome the invasion. "The worst thing that could have happened," he later said, "was chaos in the socialist camp."[58] Dubček had allowed political freedoms – free speech, a free press, independent trade unions – that clashed with the Marxist-Leninist model established in Cuba. Furthermore, these reforms were bound to lead to free elections, the defeat of the Communist Party of Czechoslovakia and the rupture of the Warsaw Pact. Therefore, Soviet pressure on Castro to endorse the invasion was not necessary. Castro saw in Dubček not the champion of a small socialist nation's sovereignty but a demagogue who was wrenching his country from the socialist camp.

On 5 November 1968, Nixon was elected president of the United States. A few days later, a high-level East German delegation arrived in Havana. "Our Cuban comrades," it reported, "stressed repeatedly that Nixon's election ... means an acceleration of US aggression against Cuba ... Comrade Castro repeatedly pointed to its implications for Cuba's security" and was forthright about his desire to improve relations with the Soviet Union.[59] By 1969 Cuban public criticism of the Soviet Union had ceased.

The improvement in relations with Moscow was made easier by a shift in Cuban policy in Latin America. The guerrillas had been crushed in Bolivia in October 1967, had been virtually wiped out in Guatemala by 1968 and had suffered cruel setbacks in Venezuela and Colombia. No other insurgent groups were active in the hemisphere. These defeats and, above all, Che's death, forced Castro to reevaluate the *foco* theory. He finally accepted that a handful of brave men was insufficient to ignite armed struggle in Latin America. "By 1970 Cuban assistance to guerrilla groups and other efforts to export revolution had been cut back to very low levels," US officials remarked.[60] Cuba's new approach to armed struggle

---

57 Castro, 23 Aug. 1968 speech, *Granma* (24 Aug. 1968), 2.
58 Castro, quoted in "Aussprache mit einer Delegation der Kommunistischen Partei Kuba," 8 Dec. 1968, DY30 IVA 2/20/265, SAPMO.
59 Verner, "Bericht über die Reise der Delegation des Zentralkomitees der SED nach Kuba von 11 bis 22 November 1968," 29 Nov. 1968, DY30 IVA 2/20/265, SAPMO.
60 DOS, "Cuban Presence in Africa," 28 Dec. 1977, enclosed in US House, Committee on International Relations, Subcommittee on Inter-American Affairs, *Impact of Cuban-Soviet Ties in Western Hemisphere* (Washington, DC: US Government Printing Office, 1978), 57.

in Latin America – more subtle, more discriminating – eliminated a major source of tension with the Soviet Union.

The Revolutionary Offensive at Home

Fidel Castro had announced on 1 December 1961 that he had become a Marxist-Leninist. Following the Soviet model, the land expropriated by the Agrarian Reform of May 1959 and the Second Agrarian Reform Law of October 1963 (which affected all medium-sized holdings) was transformed into state farms. Only 30 percent of Cuban agricultural land remained in private hands; it would turn out to be the only efficient sector of Cuban agriculture.

In 1961 the government launched an ambitious program of industrialization, even though the country lacked the necessary raw materials and skilled workers. Agriculture would be diversified, and Cuba's dependence on sugar, which was associated with underdevelopment, would be reduced. The number of acres devoted to sugar fell from 3,494,070 in 1958 to 2,629,201 in 1963.

As US intelligence noted, the government's plans "quickly ran aground on the shoals of economic reality."[61] The industrialization program sank in chaos, waste and mismanagement. Sugar production – the mainstay of the country's economy – decreased sharply. Bowing to reality, in 1964 Cuba returned to sugar as the center of its economy and abandoned the industrialization plans. The Soviet Union offered a reliable market for sugar at favorable prices, and Cuba accepted its place within the socialist community as the producer of a single raw material – sugar. After the dreams of the first years, this was a return to economic realism.

But the young Cuban Revolution still sought a new path. Cuba would build communism and socialism at the same time, Fidel Castro announced in August 1966. Unlike the Soviet Union, henceforth it would rely only on moral incentives, such as badges and flags, to motivate workers. Material incentives (such as trips, refrigerators and motorcycles) as well as overtime pay and bonuses for overfulfillment of work quotas were eliminated. "It is possible for a country to think it is building communism when in fact it is building capitalism," Castro said, in a clear swipe at Moscow and its East European allies.[62] Communism required a New Man and this could never be

---

61 Hughes to Secretary of State, "Cuba in 1964," 17 Apr. 1964, FOIA 1996/668.
62 Castro, 29 Aug. 1966 speech, *Granma* (30 Aug. 1966), 4.

achieved by appealing to individual ambition, selfishness and greed. "Today we cannot abolish money – but someday, if we want to establish a communist state, we will get rid of money," he pledged in March 1968.[63] By the late 1960s, no fees were charged for education, health care, day care, funeral services, sports events, utilities, local bus transportation and local telephone services. Rents would be abolished "by 1970 at the latest," Fidel Castro promised.[64] Cuba, he explained, aspired to embody the classic communist formula of "from each according to his ability, to each according to his need." He said: "Just as books are distributed now to those who need them, just as medicines and medical services are distributed to those who need them, education to those who need it, so we shall gradually reach the day when adequate food will be distributed to those who need it; adequate clothing and shoes will be distributed to those who need them."[65]

On 13 March 1968, the government suddenly launched a "Revolutionary Offensive" that completed the total collectivization of the nonagricultural sector: the 55,600 nonagricultural small businesses still in private hands – small stores, handicraft shops, cafés, craftsmen and street vendors – were nationalized. Cuba, *Granma* boasted in a front-page editorial on 29 March 1968, had become "the socialist country with the highest percentage of state-owned property."[66] It was a costly error.

A 1968 US State Department study noted that "Castro retains his magnetism and political skill . . . He still has great appeal for important elements of society, especially among the youth . . . His personal popularity as a revolutionary caudillo have [sic] proved durable."[67] He used his charisma to urge a tired population forward, promising a better future with just one more sacrifice. Staking the "honor of the revolution"[68] on a grandiose goal, he pledged that in 1970 Cuba would reap the largest sugar harvest in history – 10 million tons, almost double the 1968 harvest. Mobilizing the nation as if for war, he diverted scarce resources to attain the impossible goal. In the end, he failed dismally: The harvest fell short and the economy went into freefall. On 20 May 1970, Fidel Castro spoke to the nation. "The Battle of the Ten Million [tons of sugar] was not lost by the people. We lost it. We,

63 Castro, 13 Mar. 1968 speech, *Granma* (14 Mar. 1968), 7.
64 Castro, 29 Aug. 1966 speech, *Granma* (30 Aug. 1966), 6.
65 Castro, 26 Jul. 1968 speech, *Granma* (27 Jul. 1968), 3.
66 *Granma* (29 Mar. 1968), 1 (editorial).   67 DOS, "National Policy Paper."
68 Castro, 13 Mar. 1968 speech, *Granma* (14 Mar. 1968), 4.

the administrative bureaucracy of the revolution, we, the leaders of the revolution, lost this battle."[69]

The gamble had failed, and Castro drew the lesson. Cuba returned to the Soviet economic model. It was inefficient and wasteful, yet it was a dramatic improvement. The Cuban government abandoned its emphasis on moral incentives, accepted the central importance of money, admitted that wage differentials were inevitable and renounced its dream of forming the Communist Man and the communist society in the near future. This sobriety paid off. Through the 1970s the economy – and the living standards of the population – continued to improve. Soviet economic aid increased and was used more rationally, with better results. "The Cubans are on the verge of making their system work – that is to say, of constructing a socialist state in the Western Hemisphere," Pat Holt, the chief of staff of the Senate Foreign Relations Committee, reported after visiting the island in June 1974.[70]

Looking Back

By 1970 Cuba was a paradox. On one hand, its economic performance was very poor. This had many roots. The very serious economic mistakes of the revolutionary leadership in the 1960s were compounded by the dearth of trained personnel: Most middle- and upper-level managers had left the country. But there were other reasons as well. Foremost was the bitter hostility of the United States, bent on overthrowing the regime or at least ensuring that it fail, in order to teach the Cuban people and the people of Latin America the price of revolution. Through the first years of the revolution the US embargo had a disastrous effect because the Cuban economy had been reliant on the US market. Directing trade toward the Soviet bloc took time and was expensive. Furthermore, the fear of US aggression forced the regime to divert resources to military preparedness.

But even though the economy was by 1970 in dire straits, the standard of living of a significant number of Cubans had improved, and the revolution could boast of impressive achievements in education and health. Rationing, introduced in March 1962, ensured that every Cuban had the necessary nutritional minimum; for middle-class Cubans this was a definite loss, but for the poor – a much larger group – it was a definite gain. The fact that Cuba could achieve this despite the economy's weakness was due to generous

---

69 Castro, 20 May 1970 speech, *Granma* (21 May 1970), 5.
70 US Senate, Committee on Foreign Relations, *Cuba: A Staff Report* (Washington, DC: US Government Printing Office, 1974), 1.

Soviet economic aid as well as to the commitment of the revolutionary leadership to use such aid to improve the lot of the population.

In foreign policy the revolution's successes were both meager and immense. Cuba survived the onslaught of the United States – an unprecedented feat for a country in the US backyard. It had become a symbol of hope for millions in the Third World. The yoke imposed by the United States in 1898 had been broken. For the first time in its history Cuba was truly independent. Of course, it depended on the Soviet lifeline for its survival, but it was no satellite: The Soviets did not dictate Cuban domestic or foreign policy.

The Cuban Revolution enjoyed immense prestige throughout the Third World, but its tangible foreign-policy successes in the 1960s were slim. The revolutionary offensive in Latin America had failed because it was based on a false premise, the *foco* theory. It was in Africa that Cuba had achieved some success. As the decade of the 1960s ended, almost 1,000 Cuban aid workers had rendered valuable assistance to a dozen African countries. And in Guinea-Bissau, Cuban doctors and military advisors provided crucial assistance to the guerrillas fighting against Portuguese rule.

Still, it seemed to many observers looking at Cuba in the early 1970s that the revolution had been tamed, that Cuba had become a well-behaved Soviet client rather than a fiery revolutionary outpost. Suddenly, however, this perception would be proven false. In late 1975, 36,000 Cuban soldiers poured into Angola to defeat a South African invasion that had been encouraged by the United States. In sending his soldiers, Fidel Castro foiled a major US covert operation and also challenged the Kremlin, which opposed the intervention. The Cubans who went to Angola were following in the footsteps of those who had gone in the 1960s to Algeria, Congo Leopoldville, Congo Brazzaville and Guinea-Bissau. The Cuban Revolution had come of age. Over the next fifteen years, against Washington's bitter opposition and defying the Soviet Union, Cuba would help change the course of history in southern Africa.[71]

Bibliographical Essay

The Cuban archives for the post-Batista period are closed. The study of the Cuban revolutionary era has consequently suffered. Unless otherwise noted, none of the studies listed below uses Cuban documents.

---

71 See Piero Gleijeses, *Visions of Freedom: Havana, Washington, Pretoria and the Struggle for Southern Africa, 1976–1991* (Chapel Hill: University of North Carolina Press, 2013).

The best biography of Fidel Castro, by far, is Tad Szulc's *Fidel: A Critical Portrait* (New York: HarperCollins, 1987). Two more recent works should be noted: Leycester Coltman's *The Real Fidel Castro* (New Haven: Yale University Press, 2003) combines insights with factual errors; Ignacio Ramonet's *Cien Horas con Fidel*, 3rd rev. edn. (Havana: Consejo de Estado, 2006), is a very lengthy interview with Fidel Castro, but Ramonet's limited knowledge of Cuba renders him a superficial interviewer.

For perspectives on Cuba's domestic politics in the period covered by this chapter, see Louis Pérez, *Cuba Between Reform and Revolution* (New York: Oxford University Press, 1988); Jorge Domínguez, *Cuba: Order and Revolution* (Cambridge, MA: Harvard University Press, 1978); Marifeli Perez-Stable, *The Cuban Revolution: Origins, Course and Legacy*, rev. edn. (New York: Oxford University Press, 2012); Carmelo Mesa-Lago (ed.), *Revolutionary Change in Cuba* (Pittsburgh: University of Pittsburgh Press, 1971); Edward Gonzalez, *Cuba Under Castro: The Limits of Charisma* (Boston: Houghton Mifflin, 1974); K. S. Karol, *Guerrillas in Power: The Course of the Cuban Revolution* (New York: Hill & Wang, 1970); Richard Fagen, *The Transformation of Political Culture in Cuba* (Stanford: Stanford University Press, 1969); and Lillian Guerra, *Visions of Power in Cuba: Revolution, Redemption and Resistance, 1959–1976* (Chapel Hill: University of North Carolina Press, 2012).

Three accounts of Cuban foreign policy in the 1960s written by Cuban protagonists are particularly valuable: Ernesto Che Guevara's *Pasajes de la guerra revolucionaria. Congo*, edited by Aleyda March (Barcelona: Grijalbo-Mondadori, 1999), is the history Guevara wrote for Fidel Castro of the Cuban column he led in the former Belgian Congo in 1965; Jorge Risquet, *El segundo frente del Che en el Congo. Historia del batallón Patricio Lumumba*, 2nd rev. edn. (Havana: Abril, 2006), is a very well-documented account of the activities of the Cuban column that Risquet led in the former French Congo in 1965–66; José Gómez Abad, *Como el Che burló a la CIA* (Sevilla: RD editores, 2007), which is written by a member of the Cuban intelligence services, is the only study of Cuban support for armed struggle in Latin America based on Cuban documents.

Aleksandr Fursenko and Timothy Naftali, *"One Hell of a Gamble": Khrushchev, Castro and Kennedy, 1958–1964* (New York: W. W. Norton, 1997), is the only study of Cuban–Soviet relations that relies on an important number of Soviet documents, but unfortunately it is marred by serious factual mistakes about the Cuban revolutionary process. The best books on

US relations with Cuba are Lars Schoultz, *That Infernal Little Cuban Republic: The United States and the Cuban Revolution* (Chapel Hill: University of North Carolina Press, 2009); William M. LeoGrande and Peter Kornbluh, *Back Channel to Cuba: The Hidden History of Negotiations Between Washington and Havana* (Chapel Hill: University of North Carolina Press, 2014).

The best accounts of the Sino-Cuban clash are Yinghong Cheng, "Sino-Cuban Relations During the Early Years of the Castro Regime, 1959–1966," *Journal of Cold War Studies* 9, 3 (Summer 2007), 78–115 and Cecil Johnson, *Communist China and Latin America, 1959–1967*, (New York: Columbia University Press, 1970), 129–80.

The best book on armed struggle in Latin America in the 1960s is Richard Gott, *Guerrilla Movements in Latin America* (London: Seagull Books, 2008). Boris Goldenberg, *Kommunismus in Lateinamerika* (Stuttgart: Kohlhammer, 1971), offers a superb analysis of the impact of the Cuban Revolution on the communist movement in Latin America.

Since 1994, I have conducted research in the closed Cuban archives and photocopied thousands of documents, mainly on Cuban policy in Africa, but also on Cuba's relations with the Soviet Union. See especially Piero Gleijeses, *Conflicting Missions: Havana, Washington, and Africa, 1959–1976* (Chapel Hill: University of North Carolina Press, 2002), and Piero Gleijeses, *Visions of Freedom: Havana, Washington, Pretoria and the Struggle for Southern Africa, 1976–1991* (Chapel Hill: University of North Carolina Press, 2013).

For a comprehensive annotated bibliography of the Cuban Revolution, see Piero Gleijeses, "The United States and Castro's Cuba in the Cold War," in Ben Winson (ed.), *Oxford Bibliographies on Line in Latin American Studies*, www.oxfordbibliographies.com.

16

Latin American Communism

VICTOR FIGUEROA CLARK

Introduction

Latin America is one of the areas of the world where left-wing and particularly Marxist ideas have remained a strong source of inspiration and social identity into the twenty-first century. Although in the wake of the Soviet Union's collapse communist parties suffered a serious loss of influence – and in some cases disappeared – in other countries they remain influential, whether through political representation or their presence in broader social movements. The history of communism in the region is therefore not just of historical interest.

Charting the development of communism in Latin America is a complex task, in part because much of the historiography is anti-communist in its perspective, which has had the effect of entrenching multiple misconceptions about communists and communist parties, and in part because of a dearth of material due to repression and the clandestine nature of some communist activities.

Given the diversity and geographic expanse of the region, and the substantial time period covered, this chapter will provide an overview of the historical conditions prevalent at the time communist ideas and organizations developed in the region, and then a brief description and analysis of the fundamental challenges communists faced during and after the Cold War. The case studies chosen reflect considerations of the importance of the local communist movement, its access to power loosely defined. I discuss several important issues that remained relevant until the collapse of the Soviet Union, including the tensions arising from being sections of an international whole whose ideological model and material basis were located in Europe, the diverse experiences of repression and occasional political opportunities, and the struggle to understand how, when and in what forms it was appropriate to develop armed forms of struggle, and whether these ought to carry a defensive or offensive character. This debate also relates to a series of theoretical issues around the forms of organization, the nature of the struggle and the character of the revolution itself.

Latin America is an area of the world marked by similarities of language, culture and social structure, as well as a shared history of colonialism and resistance, and similar economic ties to the rest of the world. Within this picture there were and are areas of regional socioeconomic, racial, cultural and political similarity – Mexico and Central America, the Caribbean, the Bolivarian nations (Colombia and Venezuela), the Andean nations (Peru, Ecuador and Bolivia), the Southern Cone (Argentina, Chile, Uruguay, Paraguay and southern Brazil) and Brazil. Each region also has somewhat different relations with the outside world, with Central America and the Caribbean marked more by the direct and indirect domination of the United States. The Southern Cone countries were more economically developed and had stronger state and political structures with some democratic traditions. Elsewhere, at least until the 1960s, largely rural societies were governed by caudillos or military strongmen connected to liberal or conservative political tendencies, often with highly repressive political systems. Across the region the growing presence of the United States in economic affairs, or through direct military and political interventions, created a highly unequal US–Latin American relationship in which Washington's actions served to strengthen Latin American elites.

The Communist "Experience"

In understanding and evaluating communism in Latin America, we have to bear in mind that communism provoked a systemic anti-communist response. While the repression of subaltern challenges by Latin American elites was not new, and while communists were not the only targets, their presence in all of the key points and moments of conflict combined with elite fear of communism to ensure that communists were particularly hard hit by repression. As a result, communist parties were illegal throughout much of the twentieth century, forced to work through front organizations or clandestinely. Even when legal they were subjected to violent attacks, judicial harassment and the constant hostility of landowners, business, the church and the media. The history of Latin American communism is marked by murder, torture, imprisonment and blacklisting. Thus, most communists and their families suffered significant material deprivation and emotional suffering over long periods of time. These experiences mean that communism in Latin America was not just an ideology or a form of organization; it was also a lived experience and an expression of counterculture.

Another widespread form of repression that contributed to the communist identity was exile. While exile was a painful reality, it also enabled communists to experience and extend "proletarian internationalism," which was further facilitated by a common language and similar culture across the region. Early communists forced into exile carried out a feverish internationalist activism, as in the cases of Luis Emilio Recabarren, Farabundo Martí, Gustavo Machado and Julio Antonio Mella, who between them were active in Chile, Argentina, El Salvador, Guatemala, Mexico, the United States, Cuba, Venezuela and Colombia. In later years exiles sought sanctuary in the few countries with more democratic or progressive traditions, such as Mexico, Chile and Uruguay – but also Costa Rica during the 1930s and 1970s, Guatemala in the late 1940s and early 1950s and Cuba after 1959. The experience of exile was also reinforced by interactions within a global communist movement – during conferences of the Communist International (Comintern) or later through attendance at congresses of the Communist Party of the Soviet Union (CPSU), periods of study spent in Moscow, working for Soviet publications, for Revista Internacional in Prague or in the Casa de las Américas in Cuba, membership of organizing committees for World Youth Festivals and so on. Together with the communists' internationalist ideology, and their cultural similarities, exile helped to forge a Latin American communist identity.[1] Exile also provided the space within which the conciliation of communists and the "new left" began to occur. Together with anticommunist propaganda, repression was one of the main factors limiting communism's development in the region.

However, it was not just repression that hampered the development of communist parties there. Latin America's communists were unable to build stable alliances with other political sectors, despite this being a central plank of their political strategy throughout their existence. This was partly due to the requirements of remaining ideologically monolithic, and the memory among other leftists of the sectarianism of the "Third Period," but it was also affected by the complexity of communist relations with the Soviet Union. This relationship was not one of domination, but it

---

1 Particularly after the Cuban Revolution became more identifiably "communist" in the mid 1970s.

did entail loyalty to certain ideas along with the willingness to sometimes subordinate local interest to international (Soviet) priorities. This combined with anti-Soviet propaganda to significantly affect communist ability to build sustainable alliances with other political groups. These were occasionally happy to take political advantage of communist support, but were all too willing to forget their commitments when pressured by the United States.

Faced with such difficult conditions, what attracted Latin Americans to communist parties? While much work remains to be done to explain this, it is clear that socioeconomic and political conditions across the continent played an important role as a push factor. There were also significant pull factors, such as the profound sense of camaraderie experienced by communists engaged in "the struggle." Another was the ability of communists to connect and explain sectoral struggles within a broader national and global context amid the growing aura around the achievements of the Soviet Union as a workers' state, particularly between 1945 and the late 1960s. Communists also made significant efforts to provide entertainment and sources of information for ordinary working people long before the existence of mass literacy and mass media, as was the case with the Brazilian samba schools or Recabarren's popular theaters.[2] Communists also emphasized the importance of education and subsequently made important contributions to the study of the history of their countries and to a subaltern reinterpretation of their struggles for independence, which allowed workers, campesinos (Latin American peasants) and indigenous people to reenvision themselves as protagonists of history and social development. Another – unintended – pull factor was the tendency of elites, particularly before the 1960s, to label all social demands as "communism," thereby legitimating communists in the eyes of those making the demands. These factors, alongside the efforts made by communists to connect their struggles to those of the recent and more distant past ensured that communist parties were always able to attract new members, despite the many problems that becoming a communist entailed.

The Comintern and Early Communism

Marxist and anarchist ideas arrived during the nineteenth century alongside new industrial methods of production. They transformed the way that

2 John Joe Bardsley, "Contestation and Co-option: Brazilian State Policy and Discourse in the Regulation of Rio De Janeiro's Samba Schools from the 1930s to the 1970s," MA thesis (University of London, 2007).

working-class people understood themselves and opened the way for an overt struggle for power, but they did not arrive as a coherent and system-atized body of work. They came through multiple channels – the arrival of socialist or anarchist immigrants from Europe, through Latin Americans who had lived or worked in Europe and North America and via political materials published in Europe. They found fertile soil, particularly in Brazil, Mexico and the Southern Cone. The gradual opening of the political systems in much of Latin America created spaces in which the working class could organize, and by the time of the October Revolution in 1917 there were already several parties influenced by Marxism in existence, notably Chile's Partido Obrero Socialista (est. 1912), and Uruguay and Argentina's socialist parties (1910 and 1895 respectively), with smaller parties in Cuba, Bolivia, Brazil and Mexico.[3]

The region's first communist parties were organized in Mexico and the Southern Cone, but it was only in the latter that they developed from established socialist parties. Through the 1920s groups calling themselves communist were established in most countries, but even by the end of that decade the Comintern only recognized the parties of Brazil, Uruguay and Argentina as "real" communist parties (Chile was not included probably because it did not attend the First Conference of Latin American parties and it was unclear if its leadership was alive or not).[4] Seeking out interna-tional contacts was not a new phenomenon, with the Uruguayan, Brazilian and Argentinean socialist parties all members of the Second International. In Chile the predecessor of the Socialist Workers' Party had also applied to join the Second International in 1908, and there were chapters of the International Workers of the World (IWW) across the region.[5] There were therefore well-established precedents for the development of international connections, particularly with the European "center." Once the Second International became discredited, the parties sought out contact with the headquarters of the new revolution.

However, the new International knew little about Latin America and in its early days saw the entire "colonial and neocolonial world," which Latin America was understood to be part of, as important largely in relation to the imperialist centers in Europe and the United States. Despite this, the 1920s

---

3 Luis Vitale, *De Martí a Chiapas* (Santiago: Síntesis, 1995), 30.
4 Report of Jules Embert Droz to the South American Secretariat, 12 Jul. 1929.
5 Luis Sicilia, *Luis Emilio Recabarren: el sueño comunista* (Buenos Aires: Capital Intelectual, 2007), 62.

saw a relatively rapid development of the International's knowledge of the situation in the Americas, which was the result of Comintern agents traveling out to the region, and the joining of new parties and their participation in Comintern congresses and other international events. This learning process is evident in the increased differentiation of its regional sections: a Pan-American section, then a Latin American section under the Executive Committee in 1921, a South American Bureau based in Buenos Aires in 1924 and a Secretariat in Moscow in 1925. Finally, in 1931 a separate Caribbean bureau was created.[6] The Comintern also assisted in the planning of several regional meetings of communists – the 1929 conferences in Buenos Aires and Montevideo, the 1930 conference in Moscow and the October 1934 conference in Montevideo.

The Comintern's role in Latin America was to help create parties that would be recognizably communist in both structure and ideology in order to lead the revolutions that would assist in undermining the major imperialist powers, while also emancipating the peoples of the region. This was an objective that Latin American communists shared, but with the priorities reversed. The Comintern's mission was complicated by the heterogeneous ideological composition and organizational forms of the Latin American parties. According to the Comintern's agents, Latin American parties suffered from a series of ideological "deviations" that led them to adopt dangerously incorrect political positions. For example, as far as the Comintern was concerned, the anarchosyndicalist influence evident in Colombia, Brazil and Argentina led to a propensity for insurrection and violence, an overreliance on workplace activism alone and a rejection of political alliances (symptoms of "leftist" deviation), which led to the division of the workers' movement. Meanwhile, the "reformist" deviations evident in Chile and Argentina threatened to abandon the goal of revolution.[7] Parties that lacked an experienced and well-versed leadership could even swing from one extreme to the other, as occurred in Colombia during the 1930s.[8]

The parties that became communist parties agreed to the notorious twenty-one conditions of membership adopted by the Comintern's Second

6 N. P. Kalmykov (ed.), *Komintern i Latinskaia Amerika. Sbornik dokumentov* (Moscow: Nauka, 1998), 7–8.
7 To simplify, the "infantile" "leftist deviation" emphasized subjective and voluntarist factors, while the "rightist deviation" rejected them, leaving only the materialist and economistic interpretation.
8 *Treinta años de lucha del partido comunista de Colombia* (Bogotá: Minerva, n.d.).

Congress, and later to subsequent instructions on the organizational structure and tasks of a communist party. These were intended to allow a party to survive repression and at the same time take advantage of political opportunities when they opened. They incorporated a decision-making process that allowed broad discussion to be followed by disciplined action, and measures to allow parties to struggle effectively in all spheres, both legally and illegally. All of these measures were intended to help bring about the revolution. However, a party's activity depended upon its judgement of the objective and subjective conditions and its analysis of class structures and contradictions. A "correct" judgement was understood to depend upon a solid Marxist (later Marxist-Leninist) education. The problems for the Comintern were that early Latin American communists lacked that solid Marxist education and that the Comintern knew very little about Latin America. This situation created a dynamic whereby the Comintern and its agents, who were assumed to have a superior knowledge of Marxist ideology, revolutionary theory and the correct methods of organization, were "teaching" the Latin Americans how to be communists. While this may have been useful in reorganizing the communist parties, not least to enable them to withstand repression, and helped systematize the uneven understanding of Marxism-Leninism within the parties, it had a negative side. Lacking local knowledge, the Comintern's agents guided themselves using their previous experiences in Europe and a schematic analysis of Latin America's socioeconomic structures, which hid important differences with the European situation.

The Bolsheviks' initial political line had coincided with the views of local revolutionaries – the revolution would be immediately socialist. However, it altered during the 1920s in response to changes in the European situation. The emphasis shifted toward an intermediate phase that was called the "bourgeois democratic revolution." This posited a progressive role for the "national bourgeoisie" and therefore proposed that communists build alliances with it. This position required what Michael Löwy called a significant "stretching" of Latin American reality over the "procrustean bed" of Eurocentric Marxism-Leninism.[9] The new line was opposed by many Latin American communists, some of whom had already creatively applied Marxism to their reality – with Josè Carlos Mariátegui (Peru) and Ricardo Paredes (Ecuador) arguing that in Latin America the revolution should

---

9 Michael Löwy (ed.), *Marxism in Latin America from 1909 to the Present: An Anthology* (New York: Humanities Press, 1992), xiv.

immediately pursue socialism. The debates were important because the definition had implications for how the party ought to work, the identification of allies and what they ought to do once power was achieved.

The impassioned discussions pitted different understandings of Latin American reality against each other. The Eurocentric view saw Latin America as a semi-feudal region moving toward capitalism, as if it were a few decades "behind" Europe in its development.[10] Those Latin Americans who had most successfully adapted the Marxist method to their reality argued that this was not the case. Perhaps the most important differences lay in the understanding of Latin American campesinos. In the European experience and according to classical Marxism, the peasant farmer was generally seen as a conservative, proto-bourgeois concerned with private property, market access and the acquisition of greater material wealth. In Latin America, meanwhile, although the campesinos lived in conditions that bore a superficial resemblance to feudal structures, they were also often indigenous and therefore held a different worldview, particularly toward private property and the land. In many countries there were also racial differences between campesinos and their usually white overlords, alongside a social memory of resistance to colonial conquest. Furthermore, in many countries, campesinos also worked on modern large-scale, foreign-owned agricultural enterprises, such as sugar cane, rubber or banana plantations, which created a somewhat "proletarianized" rural workforce. The Latin American campesinos were therefore rather unlike European peasant farmers, and consequently their role in processes of social change was different.

Nor was the Latin American bourgeoisie similar to its European counterparts. Outside the Southern Cone, the bourgeoisie, rather than being a productive capitalist class, tended to be dependent upon large foreign-owned enterprises and foreign capital. The role or existence of a "national bourgeoisie" as a potential ally of the proletariat was much debated in the Comintern and among Latin American communists prior to the 1930s. For the Comintern, the national bourgeoisie would develop contradictions with imperialism as it sought to realize its own development, but many Latin American communists thought otherwise, with Paredes emphasizing that the bourgeoisie's dependent relationship with imperialism meant that its "solidarity with the imperialists must be very

10 Eurocentrism was and is a phenomenon that affected Latin American society as a whole, as evinced by various neofascist, and indeed liberal and Christian democratic, movements.

strong."[11] However, following the Comintern's Seventh Congress, the existence and progressive role of the "national bourgeoisie" were largely accepted.

These debates connected to political questions within the Comintern, whose leaders were themselves engaged in a bitter struggle over the "correct line'" to follow. During the mid to late 1920s, the Comintern-defined period of capitalist stabilization and the struggle against Trotskyism, the "rightist" deviation was seen as more dangerous, which therefore justified a policy that highlighted class differences. The Comintern's new policy was a rather abrupt leftward shift. Combined with a process of ideological and organizational homogenization, it created chaos in Latin America. The result was to splinter relatively new and untested parties, at a time when in Latin America, a continuation of the previous "united front" policy and a slower process of homogenization would have been more effective. The Comintern's leftward shift was counterproductive in a region where social democracy was itself weak, and where the working class, although militant, was small and politically inexperienced.

It was therefore something of a misfortune that the Comintern began to seriously organize in Latin America precisely during this Third Period. The external conduit for the political line was reinforced, and in some places, such as Brazil and Argentina, the Comintern's agents were even allowed to temporarily take control of parties that had become disorganized because of the changes. When this circumstance combined with a small membership and a national leadership often still feeling its way toward a comprehensive understanding of Marxism, it was perhaps inevitable that foreign revolutionaries would play a dominating role. Further from the Comintern's Latin American center, or where local parties were better developed, the Comintern's influence was weaker. This lack of influence was also magnified by significant logistical constraints produced by widespread repression and lack of manpower and resources. For example, while communications with Argentina, Uruguay and Brazil seem to have been regular, contacts with the rest of the region were, as expressed by a Comintern agent in early 1930, "carried out completely unsatisfactorily."[12] In the rest of Latin America the Comintern's role was largely undertaken by communists working through

11 Ricardo Paredes, speech on Comintern report on Latin America, 25 Sep.1928, in Eduardo Paredes Ruíz, *Ricardo Paredes Romero y la antorcha revolucionaria* (Quito: CCEBC, 2014), 66.
12 Letter from "Rustico," 7 May 1930, in Kalmykov (ed.), *Komintern i Latinskaia Amerika. Sbornik dokumentov*, 59.

the Anti-Imperialist League of the Americas and International Red Aid, but there is little evidence that their communications were any better.[13]

Poor communications was just one of the obstacles that faced the Comintern and its sections in Latin America. Revolts and insurrections across the region during the late 1920s and early 1930s showed the difficulties of transforming even seemingly fertile revolutionary situations into successful seizures of power. In Chile (1931–32) and Cuba (1933) military mutinies were accompanied by social uprisings. Although their respective communist parties participated in these events, they did not lead them, and both fizzled out. Efforts to create soviets and Red Guard units were largely unsuccessful. In El Salvador in 1932 the communist party had led a mass movement for several years and was forced to prepare for an insurrection that was already beginning in many areas. In Brazil in 1935 the government made the rapidly growing communist-led Aliança Nacional Libertadora illegal, prompting the party to try a military insurrection in November that year. In all these cases efforts at insurrection failed, although only in El Salvador and Brazil did communists plan for a seizure of power. Generally, though, these insurrections were less planned attempts at seizing power, and more reactions to existing social ferment. Nevertheless, the lesson communists took from these failures was to reject the sectarianism of the Third Period and seek broader political alliances, but also, in a less obvious fashion, to avoid revolutionary audacity and violence.

In Chile by 1933 the party had returned to its "Recabarrenista" positions, which the Comintern had earlier categorized as "reformist," opening the way for a successful alliance between communists, socialists and radicals. Elsewhere there were also moves toward a "popular front" policy. In Costa Rica, although the rhetoric remained fiery, the party's activism came to be based upon the struggle for gradual reforms. In Colombia, too, the communists formed an alliance with the Liberal Party. By launching the "popular front" strategy, the Seventh Comintern Congress therefore put a seal of official approval on a set of policies that was already in train across the region, an example of the dialectic that existed between the Comintern's center and its national sections.

With their reorganization complete and the existence of an alliance-building line ratified by the International, communist parties entered a long period of ideological stability. By the end of the 1930s there were communist

---

13 Roque Dalton, *Miguel Mármol. Los sucesos de 1932 en El Salvador* (Bogotá: Ocean Sur, 2007), 172.

parties and communist-influenced labor movements of greater or lesser importance in most countries. Communists were part of a government coalition in Chile and were influential in Costa Rica, Cuba, Uruguay and Ecuador. While the "Bolshevization" of 1928–35 had split existing movements, sometimes at quite significant cost to the popular movement, it had also ensured that parties could endure long periods of repression; furthermore, the adoption of a systematized version of Marxism, whatever its shortcomings, made it easier to educate new members with a coherent political message. With its global revolution no longer imminent, and its party-building task completed, the Comintern faded away – the Caribbean bureau was dissolved in 1935, the South American bureau soon afterward – and Stalin dissolved the Comintern itself in 1943.

Overall, the Comintern's agents brought with them a harsh sectarianism made worse by confusing policy shifts, alongside a Eurocentricity that distorted the communist interpretation of local reality. They were unable to effectively synthesize Marxist theory and local knowledge. However, they also provided Latin America's communists with the discipline and methods that enabled them to survive long periods of vicious repression, and they helped develop a systematized way of studying Marxism that created a coherent political line. They also acted as a living example of the international character of the working-class struggle. Therefore, it is an exaggeration to say that "the agents of the International were perfectly unnecessary," but nor was their role completely beneficial.[14]

During World War II a number of Latin American countries began to industrialize in earnest, leading to a substantial growth in the size of the urban population and the working class. Latin American support for the Allies, with the exceptions of Argentina and Chile, led to a triple process of democratization, the opening of diplomatic relations with the USSR and the legalization of communist parties and trade unions. As in Europe, this wartime thaw, alongside the prestige gained by the USSR resulting from its leading role in defeating both Nazi Germany and Japan, prompted substantial growth of communist parties and a rise in working-class mobilization.[15] In Brazil, Venezuela, Costa Rica, Cuba, Peru, Colombia, Chile and

---

14 Volodia Teitelboim, *Un muchacho del siglo XX* (Santiago: Ed. Universitaria, 2006), 297.
15 See Leslie Bethell and Ian Roxborough, "Latin America Between the Second World War and the Cold War: Reflections on the 1945–1948 Conjuncture," *Journal of Latin American Studies* 20, 1 (May 1988), 167–89; and "Kommunisticheskoe dvizhenie," in V. V. Vol'skii (ed.), *Entsiklopedicheskii spravochnik. Latinskaia Amerika* (Moscow, 1979). In the latter it states that the number of communists in Latin America "was higher than 380,000."

Ecuador, communists had representatives elected to national or subnational parliaments.[16] In Cuba (1943–44), Ecuador (1944–46) and Chile (1946–47), communists participated in government. In Brazil the communist party grew to some 200,000 members in 1946 with dozens of elected representatives at regional and national levels; Fernando Claudin estimates that membership across the region stood at around 500,000 by 1947, up from 25,000 in 1935.[17] However, their political influence was greater than their numbers and electoral support in most countries, partly as a result of their strength in the labor movement, partly because electoral systems across the region were imperfect, biased against the poor and subject to high levels of fraud.[18]

Cold War and Cuban Revolution

This brief period of growth ended with the onset of the Cold War and the overthrow of democratic governments across Latin America (with the notable exception of Guatemala, whose leftist government, which included some communists, was not overthrown until 1954). Communist parties across the region were made illegal once more, and a new repressive cycle began. Civil wars in Costa Rica and Paraguay saw communists forced underground and into exile. However, this time the communist parties were generally better organized and better known than during the prewar period, and they were better able to weather the repression. Subsequently communists participated in the Bolivian Revolution of 1952 and played an important role in the fall of dictatorships in Peru, Colombia and Venezuela in the late 1950s. In 1957 Latin American communists participated in the world conference of communist and workers' parties in Moscow, where they ratified the conclusions of the CPSU's Twentieth Congress with regard to peaceful coexistence and the possibility of a peaceful transition to socialism, which was particularly welcome for parties in Chile and Uruguay, where communists had in effect already been pursuing this path. Communists also played an important, albeit secondary, role in the overthrow of Fulgencio Batista in Cuba, the event that

16 "Kommunisticheskoe dvizhenie."
17 Fernando Claudin cited in Bethell and Roxborough, "Latin America," 173.
18 During the same period most Latin American parties were temporarily affected in some measure by "Browderism," an extreme interpretation of popular frontism led by the Communist Party of the USA that ultimately proposed the dissolution of communist parties. The Mexican, Colombian and Cuban parties were most affected. The onset of the Cold War was marked by a swift turn away from this policy.

marked a deepening of Latin America's internal cold war and the full-scale interference of the United States in the region's affairs.

For Latin America's communists the Cuban Revolution was both a boon and a challenge. The revolution, alongside anti-colonial struggles in the rest of the world, acted to stimulate a radicalization of the region's population, in particular its youth. But the revolution also implied a profound criticism of Latin American communists, who had in forty years not managed a single significant seizure of power. The Cuban Revolution therefore put this question of power at the center of the revolutionary agenda for the first time since the 1920s, but also, once it adopted an overtly socialist goal, it challenged the "stageist" approach to the revolution prevalent among communist parties.[19] This was exacerbated by Cuban assistance to and legitimization of guerrilla groups inspired by the revolution. The activities of these groups undermined communist efforts to build alliances with more centrist political groups as well as serving to justify the deployment of state coercion against the left as a whole. The Cuban example also combined with the bitter debates provoked by the Sino-Soviet split, pointing toward ideological weaknesses in Soviet-style Marxism-Leninism, and in the way Latin American communists were implementing its teachings, particularly with regard to the debate over the use of violence in the seizure of power. Communists therefore faced several challenges from Cuba – ideological and methodological, but also a challenge to what could be called the heroic ideal of the revolutionary. These challenges led to bitter debates during the late 1960s which led to notable, albeit temporary, rifts between the Cubans and most Latin American communist parties.

It was partly because of the Cuban example and the subsequent rift that the issue of violence and armed struggle became such an important one for Latin American communists. It became the issue that defined their external and internal political context. It is not that communists overtly rejected the use of violence in the overthrow of capitalism – since their Bolshevization in the 1920s, the region's communist parties had to varying degrees given a handful of political cadres some military training. Some of these cadres came through their national armies, others were given some training in the USSR and in the late 1930s a large number of Latin American communists gained military experience in the Spanish Civil War. The Argentinian party had even engaged in guerrilla warfare in the Chaco region, and a bombing campaign

19 Gerardo Leibner, *Camaradas y compañeros: una historia política y social de los comunistas del Uruguay* (Montevideo: Trilce, 2012), 478.

against Nazi infrastructure in Argentina during the world war.[20] However, most parties did not do much, if anything, to develop their military capacity. For communists, violence played a defensive role, enabling them to defend popular mobilizations or their own organizations from state or para-state violence or, perhaps, in a prerevolutionary situation it might enable them to assist insurgent units of the armed forces and the mobilized masses. Communist party military preparations, where they existed, were not, as in the *"foquista"* proposal, to create the spark for revolution through the armed struggle of a select group, the *"foco."* Therefore, the communist perspective on violence differed significantly from that of the Cubans and the "new left."

The Cuban Revolution and the Sino-Soviet split heralded the end of the almost complete monopoly of Marxism that communists had held since the 1920s, and led to the rapid creation of large numbers of Cuban-inspired "political-military organizations" such as the several MIRs (movimientos de izquierda revolucionaria) which in their name implied the nonrevolutionary reformism of communists, as well as several national liberation armies and fronts, such as those founded in this period in Nicaragua, Brazil, Bolivia, Colombia and Chile. Many of them received backing from Cuba. Liberation theology also entered the fray, inspiring large numbers of the region's Catholics with revolutionary ardor. In some countries, Maoist groups also splintered from communist parties and formed guerrilla organizations such as the EPL (Ejército Popular de Liberación) in Colombia or Shining Path in Peru.

Communists and Armed Struggle

The issues around power and armed struggle defined much of the late Cold War for all Latin American Marxists and were also reflected within the region's communist parties. Proponents of armed struggle temporarily won control of their parties in Paraguay, where the leadership, inspired by the Cuban example, launched an ill-prepared and short-lived guerrilla war against the dictatorship of Alfredo Stroessner at the end of 1959; and in Venezuela, where a large part of the PCV (Partido Comunista de Venezuela) leadership was heavily influenced by the success of the Cuban Revolution. The PCV's Third Congress in March 1961 had approved the now-traditional line of mass

---

20 Alberto Nadra, *Secretos en rojo: un militante entre dos siglos* (Buenos Aires: Corregidor, 2012), 48–52.

struggle and anti-imperialism. However, shortly afterwards, enthused by the Cuban example, and in response to violent repression and pressure from other left-wing groups, some of the party's leaders began to carry out armed actions – infected, in the words of the then general secretary – "by the warlike frenzy that had invaded the party."[21] The party then helped create the FALN (Armed Forces of National Liberation) along with rebel officers and members of the MIR. The rebels were subsequently crushed, and the defeat bred division inside the PCV and between it and its erstwhile allies in the FALN. In late 1965 the communist party leadership decided to abandon armed struggle, and the "militarists" then left the party. The effect was that in 1969 the PCV was significantly smaller than it had been in 1958. The Venezuelan case showed the dangers of adopting armed struggle inspired by foreign experiences, whose superficial similarities to the local situation obscured important differences. It exacerbated serious tensions between Venezuelan communists and the Cuban Revolution. It served as a negative example for communists in the rest of the region, whose opposition to armed "adventurism" and "voluntarist" interpretations was reinforced.

The Cuban Revolution also transformed the political, and more specifically, the military context of the region. The region's elites suddenly felt much less secure than at any point since the 1930s, and the United States embarked upon, on the one hand, a rhetorical commitment to social justice and democracy and, on the other, a very practical commitment to strengthening the region's coercive institutions. The massive expansion of US training to Latin American security forces helped to systematize and broaden existing anti-communist ideas among officers, but also helped to provide the technical means through which to break down clandestine organizations through improved intelligence sharing and collection, gained through the calculated use of terror. The systematization of "dirty war" tactics led to widespread use of torture, assassination and disappearances, hitting communist parties hard. The traditional propensity of Latin American elites to use violence was now married to twentieth-century technology to create repressive machines of terrifying brutality. The 1960s saw democratic or civilian governments fall to military rule across the region. In some countries, communists also had to face the political challenge of new centrist parties with reformist agendas and flush with foreign money, or the seizure of power by military regimes that had nationalist and broadly progressive programs – as occurred in Panama

---

21 Jesús Faría, *Mi línea no cambia, es hasta la muerte* (Caracas: COFAE, 2010), 222.

and Peru in 1968 – and which encouraged communists to search for "demo-cratic elements" within the region's armed forces. Despite these challenges, in countries where they were able to operate legally or semi-legally – and in the light of the military defeat of most of the Cuban-inspired guerrillas – communist parties grew in size, voter support and political importance, as in Bolivia, Chile, Uruguay, Costa Rica, Peru and Argentina.

Communist parties responded to the increased threat of coups and violent repression by requesting that the USSR and other socialist countries provide training in clandestine forms of struggle, known as "military combative work" courses. These included some military theory and the use of firearms. It seems that a small number of Chileans, El Salvadoreans, Argentinians, Uruguayans and Costa Ricans were also given specifically military training, usually in the USSR. It is important to underline that the rationale of these courses was not to allow communist parties to undertake armed forms of struggle, but to create a nucleus of members who could, in time of need, such as a coup, ally with sectors of the armed forces to provide a "popular" military alternative. It also allowed parties to create self-defense groups that could protect offices and senior leaders. In other words, the rationale for the military training of communists was still essentially defensive and was by no means the main focus of party efforts.

The development of some military capacity by the Uruguayan Communist Party during the 1960s illustrates this. The PCU (Partido Comunista del Uruguay) went into the 1960s with a political line that was a flexible inter-pretation of the post-1956 "peaceful road" to socialism. Its leader, Rodney Arismendi, rather uniquely among Latin American communists, had a vision of revolution as a continental phenomenon and thought that the Cuban Revolution had led to a sharpening of class contradictions and transformed what had hitherto been largely theoretical issues concerning violence and the seizure of power into important practical issues. This perspective was rein-forced by the 1964 and 1966 coups in Brazil and Argentina, which Arismendi thought communists had a duty to resist.[22] Therefore, under Arismendi, the PCU developed an understanding that violence would be necessary at some point in the transition to socialism, whether offensively or defensively, although the PCU would prefer to struggle in democratic conditions. Following this analysis, in 1964 the PCU set up a small armed apparatus whose role would be to resist any coup (which seemed increasingly likely after 1966) and potentially create a kernel around which the PCU could, if

22 Leibner, *Camaradas y compañeros*, 481–82.

necessary, shift from unarmed forms of mass struggle to armed forms.[23] The key issue here was to ensure that the masses supported the use of violence. This interpretation was more nuanced and flexible, yet more easily confused with the Cuban position than that of most of the region's communist parties, and therefore one that they generally struggled to understand. Yet even in Uruguay the communist party never fully utilized its "military cadres." While the PCU's apparatus carried out a few armed or violent actions of "international solidarity" during the 1960s, it did not offer military resistance to the 1973 coup because of the hope that a progressive nationalist wing of the army would take over, replicating events in Peru after 1968.[24] The Uruguayan case demonstrates that, even where the ideological rationale and the military apparatus existed, it was highly unlikely that communists would consider the use of violence.

Yet where the impetus toward armed struggle came from historic factors, rather than theoretical constructs, as in Colombia, communists did accept the use of violence. The Colombian Communist Party (PCC, Partido Comunista Colombiano) had inherited a strong rural tradition from the Partido Socialista Revolucionario (PSR). In the 1930s, while its urban structures were heavily repressed, this tradition translated into a differentiated approach toward the campesino world, one which understood "its different social, economic, cultural and political scope," and which allowed the PCC to develop specific forms of struggle. Among these was the development of defensive strategies to confront landholder and state violence, including mass forms of "self-defense." By the late 1950s, more than 40 percent of the PCC membership was of campesino origin.[25] This was highly unusual for a Latin American communist party. During the increasing violence of the 1940s and into the 1950s, this rural membership enabled the PCC to foster rural forms of organization that paralleled state functions, but with socialist and campesino goals that emphasized education, participatory democracy and shared ownership. The government called the areas where this process was most developed "independent republics."

23 Ibid., 480–81; Sergio Marquez Zacchino, *La revolución estafada. PCU y aparato armado: un reportaje a Elizardo Iglesias ex-integrante de la Cuarta Dirección del Partido Comunista de Uruguay* (Montevideo: Ed. Juan Darien, 1991), 18.
24 Alfonso Lessa, *La Izquierda y el golpe militar de febrero de 1973* (Montevideo: Ed. Sudamericana, 2012). This search for a democratic or progressive wing within Latin American militaries was a feature of communist parties during the period, and was part of an effort not to repeat mistakes of the Third Period.
25 James J. Brittain, *Revolutionary Social Change in Colombia* (London: Pluto, 2010), 3.

Once again made illegal and suffering repression in both cities and rural areas, in 1961 the PCC celebrated its Ninth Congress, at which it adapted its political line toward the possibility of "the combination all forms of struggle," in which armed forms of struggle could become the main, although not the only form.[26] Therefore the communists sought to continue building social organizations and the union movement, while at the same time continuing to support their rural self-defense groups. In the same period conservative politicians began a campaign to destroy the campesino enclaves, and in 1962 and then in 1964 the government undertook massive US-backed counterinsurgency campaigns designed to eliminate them, which inflicted significant civilian casualties and led to the temporary displacement of the defenders. In the wake of the "Marquetalia" operation by the Colombian army, the campesino forces decided to form mobile guerrilla columns and proclaimed an agrarian reform program. Two years later a second conference established the FARC (Fuerzas Armadas Revolucionarias de Colombia) and set out its mission as the seizure of power together with other downtrodden sectors of the population.

Yet, while for the PCC leadership the FARC created a haven from repression and a tool with which to pressure Colombia's political elite, the armed struggle was not seen as the method through which power would be seized.[27] This created a tension between the leaders of the FARC and the rest of the PCC. For a long time, the FARC was part of the PCC, its leaders members of the Central Committee, largely sharing its ideological line and participating in its conferences and congresses. Nor did the FARC have any independent international connections. Yet the establishment of the FARC effectively created an autonomous sector of the party, one that operated in guerrilla columns and rural settlements and that, by dint of its military strength and geographic remoteness, was able to set itself the task of creating a parallel revolutionary social order without much need to worry about repression. Paradoxically, what was arguably the most successful insurgency of the 1960s and 1970s was not one inspired by the Cuban example, but instead by the semi-autonomous branch of a Soviet-aligned communist party. Yet, precisely because it did not fit comfortably in the

---

26 Luis Fernando Trejos and Roberto González Arana, "El Partido Comunista Colombiano y la combinación de todas las formas de lucha. Entre la simpatía internacional y las tensiones locales, 1961–1981," *Izquierdas* 17 (2013), 70.

27 Ibid., 75.

ideological frameworks of the time, it remained relatively unknown outside Colombia.

Furthermore, following the death of Che Guevara, the early 1970s appeared to show the potential of the peaceful road to socialism when Salvador Allende's Popular Unity won elections in Chile, and the Frente Amplio (Broad Front) made a strong showing in Uruguay – both with strong communist participation. However, brutal coups in both countries in 1973 put the issue of revolutionary violence at center stage once more, leading to a reevaluation of violence, particularly by the Chilean Communist Party, hitherto one of the least inclined toward violence, marking an important step in the further reconciliation between Cuba and Latin American communists.

In Chile the Partido Comunista de Chile (PCCh), although it did not arrive at the same conclusions as the PCU about the role of violence, had begun to train some "military cadres" in 1963, mainly with a view to defending a future popular government. The Popular Unity victory in 1970 led the party to train a handful of members with Cuban support. The party did not use them after the coup in the absence of a split in the armed forces. However, defeat prompted the PCCh leadership to accept a Cuban proposal to train professional military officers who could be incorporated into future democratic armed forces.[28] As the years wore on and the dictatorship's political project developed, the party reevaluated its forms of opposition, arguing that the closure of political spaces and Augusto Pinochet's plans to remain in power created the need for more active forms of resistance that would produce the space within which mass opposition to the regime could develop. The party subsequently reinterpreted its mass struggle to include violence and created an armed apparatus – the Frente Patriótico Manuel Rodríguez (FPMR). Between 1983 and 1986 the FPMR and the PCCh developed an increasingly sophisticated struggle that combined defensive mass actions with spectacular offensive actions. These contributed to the development of mass opposition, destabilizing the Pinochet regime and prompting it to accept the pressure from the administration of President Ronald Reagan to initiate a transition to civilian rule.[29] Along with the El Salvadoran case, Chile showed that many communists, facing severe repression and political exclusion, came to

---

28 Rolando Alvarez, *Arriba los pobres* (Santiago: LOM, 2011), 174.
29 See Victor Figueroa Clark, "The Forgotten History of the Chilean Transition: Armed Resistance Against Pinochet and US Policy Towards Chile in the 1980s," *Journal of Latin American Studies* 47, 3 (Aug. 2015), 491–520.

reevaluate the use of violence during the late 1970s and early 1980s, influenced by their interactions with Cuba, but also by the examples of Nicaragua and national liberation struggles further afield. The problems the PCCh encountered in deploying its new strategy also highlighted the complications inherent in overturning entrenched traditions, and the failure to achieve participation in the post-Pinochet regime showed the political risks involved in such a change.

Slightly earlier, during the late 1970s, the El Salvadorean Communist Party (Partido Comunista de El Salvador, PCS) also reevaluated its position on armed struggle. The party had members who had gained experience fighting counterrevolutionary bands in Cuba during the early 1960s, but the party cut short its military development amid the challenge of Guevarist *"foquismo,"* also seeing the "absorption" of its cadres by military tasks as one of the reasons for its weakness in the trade unions.[30] Then in 1970 the party split after a debate that began over forms of leadership but ended on disagreement over the forms of struggle. Shortly afterward, the opposition alliance had electoral victories in 1972 and 1977 overturned, prompting a radicalization of the population.[31] Other revolutionary groups undertook violent resistance to the regime and following the repression of mass demonstrations protesting electoral fraud in 1977, the PCS Political Commission also decided to undertake armed struggle.[32] The PCS subsequently joined other rebel groups in creating the FMLN (Farabundo Martí National Liberation Front). For El Salvador, too, state repression was an important factor pushing the party to take up arms, alongside the influence of the Cuban and Sandinista revolutions. It is also another example of the difficult ideological tightrope that needed to be mastered in order to adopt the "correct" form of struggle at the right time, and the tension between violence as a revolutionary means vs. violence as a political tool.

These examples show the different ways that communist parties approached the issue of violence in the wake of the Cuban Revolution. They highlight that communists were not quite the reformist pacifists seen by the "new left" of the 1960s, although communists did largely understand violence as a defensive form of struggle. They also emphasize that, far from

---

30 See Marta Harnecker, *El Salvador: Partido Comunista y guerra revolucionaria, entrevista a Schafik Handal* (Buenos Aires: Ediciones Dialéctica, 1987), 13–15.

31 For a description of these events, see José Luis Merino, *Comandante Ramiro: revelaciones de un guerrillero y líder revolucionario salvadoreño* (Mexico City: Ocean Sur, 2011), 37–47.

32 Schafik Handal, "Consideraciones acerca del viraje del partido comunista de El Salvador hacia la lucha armada," *Fundamentos y Perspectivas* 5 (Apr. 1983), 6–8.

being static dogmatists, communists were generally able to change their tactics and interpret their ideology with flexibility – albeit with difficulty and after long discussions – as long as they did not cause significant problems for Soviet foreign policy and did not violate certain key tenets.

The Late Cold War

The issue of violence was only one of many challenges that communists faced during the late Cold War. The continuation of dictatorial rule in Chile, the civil wars in Central America and the election of the Reagan administration initially obscured some of the more important changes that began to take place. Societies had begun to transform after the imposition of neoliberal economic reforms, particularly after the 1982 debt crisis. These devastated industries drastically reduced the size and role of the state in the economy, and handicapped organized labor, a traditional bastion for communist parties. They also created a large underclass of impoverished former workers. Simultaneously, the international context began to change, with US–Soviet rapprochement and a transformation of US foreign policy away from overt support for dictatorial regimes toward a policy of "democratization," although still with a strongly anti-communist bias. US foreign policy also became partly "privatized" through nongovernmental organizations, corporate foundations and other institutions. Together these phenomena transformed the international environment, the socioeconomic structures and the domestic political environment across the entire region, a disorienting process that affected communists no less than other political groups.

However, the effect of these changes was not particularly noticeable during the early 1980s, an important period in the deepening of communist "internationalist" activism. During the early 1980s, the tradition of mutual support developed into military backing for Central American revolution-aries, particularly the Fuerzas Armadas de Liberación (Armed Forces of Liberation, FAL) in El Salvador and the Sandinistas in Nicaragua. For the first time since the Spanish Civil War, substantial numbers of Latin American communists became engaged in military conflict, where they fought along-side leftists more inspired by liberation theology and the Cuban Revolution. Cuba played an important role in supporting this internationalism, which helped seal Havana's place as the regional center for Latin America's communists. The 1980s also saw a gradual process of conciliation between communist parties and Latin America's "new left," in which Cuba again played an important role. Examples of this process were the creation of the FMLN in El Salvador in 1980, the creation of an alliance between the Chilean Communist Party and the MIR in 1983, the Mexican decision to dissolve into a new broad leftist party called the PSUM (Partido Socialista Unificado de México) in 1981, the alliance between the PCA (Partido Comunista de la Argentina) and Trotskyists in Argentina after 1989, and the Tupamaro guerrillas joining the Frente Amplio in Uruguay in the latter half of the 1980s. The 1980s therefore saw Latin American communists increasingly involved in international struggles, more at home with their erstwhile challengers and more connected to Cuba.

The mid 1980s were also the period when Mikhail Gorbachev's reforms began in the USSR. Although initially focused on the economy, these then expanded into the political system, and eventually led to a substantial questioning of the ideology of the Soviet state. Among the concepts questioned was "internationalism," the solidarity of the Soviet Union toward revolutionaries and liberation struggles around the world. Although Soviet assistance to communist parties continued, particularly to those struggling against dictatorships, the ideological debates, the trend toward limiting of aid to friendly regimes and the rapprochement with Reagan's United States unsettled many Latin American communists. Some communists found their doubts about Soviet-style socialism reinforced, and began a process of moving away from traditional communist positions. Toward the end of the decade some founded new organizations, while others stopped being active. Meanwhile, those skeptical of Gorbachev's reforms found an ally in Fidel Castro, reinforcing Havana's existence as an alternative pole for the region's communists.

The Soviet Union had been at the center of communists' revolutionary identity, the source of their interpretation of Marxism, the example of a "successful" socialist society and the invincible bastion of the global workers' movement. The collapse of the Soviet Union was therefore a devastating blow. For it to collapse as it did, with an abject ideological surrender, was akin to all their "cathedrals falling," as the title of one communists' memoir suggests.[33] In Brazil and Honduras the communist parties voted to dissolve, although in Brazil a fraction soon took up the mantle. Elsewhere, communist parties suffered a hemorrhage of members and a decline in their political relevance.

---

33 Luis Guastavino, *Caen las Catedrales* (Santiago: Hachette, 1990).

The subsequent development through the 1990s of mass consumer societies funded by cheap credit and fueled by a new internationalized media also transformed the political environment. It seemed the end of history had indeed arrived. However, there were three exceptions to this process. In El Salvador the PCS, as part of the FMLN, was able to negotiate a peace accord that guaranteed it a place in the nation's political future. In Colombia, while the PCC and the FARC split in 1993, the FARC went on to become a serious challenger for power – a challenge that was averted only by peace talks between 1998 and 2002, during which time Washington provided massive funding to retrain and reequip the Colombian military. Altogether, the 1990s were hard years for the region's communists, during which parties became noticeably more "Latin Americanist" and Cuba-centered, reevaluating some of their past beliefs, particularly with regard to the USSR. They have therefore become more similar to the organizations that originated in the "new left."

Conclusion

Communists were Latin America's first Marxist revolutionaries, and they succeeded in articulating the demands of broad sections of society, creating or contributing to strong trade unions and social movements in many countries. As a result, they were an important democratizing influence, for not only did they participate in the creation of democratic political systems, they were also crucial to the overthrow of most dictatorships, and their presence played an important role in provoking the US-backed reformism of the 1960s and 1980s. However, while the struggle for democracy was one aim of communist activism, there were internal debates over whether it was an aim in itself, as the basis for a bourgeois democratic revolution, or whether it was a way of mobilizing the masses around an outright revolutionary goal. Communists tried to bridge the gap between subjective revolutionism and practical politics, marrying the pursuit of power with an effective form of organization and analysis of society, but they struggled to deal with repeated transitions from illegality to legality and back again, since each bout of legality exposed leaders and members who were then repressed when communism was proscribed. Their expansion during legal periods also created problems – the influx of new members brought with it the danger of infiltration by intelligence services, and also diluted the ideological cohesion of the membership – a particular problem during the 1960s, for example. Illegality created problems related to survival and also placed huge obstacles in the path of the parties' efforts to reach out to the masses, in some cases stimulating a negative "bunker mentality."

Perhaps the most significant achievement of the region's communists has been to survive as a political force. Today, while communist parties have not recovered the numeric strength of yesteryear, they remain present in most of the key countries of the region. In Chile, Bolivia and Uruguay they are part of governing coalitions. In El Salvador the PCS, through the FMLN, is in government. In Venezuela the PCV has a handful of deputies in the National Assembly. In Argentina the communist party is strongly connected to the unions and social movements. In Colombia the FARC remains a communist organization and is currently negotiating a peace accord with the government, which will alter that country's political landscape. Furthermore, in all these countries communists retain influence in trade unions and in social movements. This level of political representation and social strength marks a high point not seen in many decades. It is interesting to note that the left movements in the region today are, in the absence of any superpower ally, leading processes that bear remarkable similarities to the project of the bourgeois democratic revolution of pre-1991 communist parties. Recent electoral defeats may raise questions about the sustainability of these projects, but there is no doubt that the history of Latin American communism is a long way from having come to an end.

Bibliographical Essay

While numerous works on communism in Latin America were published during the Cold War period, up until the mid 1990s the majority approached the topic from overtly ideological positions. Thankfully recent years have seen a range of more objective treatments, many originating from the region itself. Given the region's complexities, many works focus on individual countries, or subregions, while only a handful of texts attempt to deal with communism in Latin America as a whole. For excellent bibliographic reviews of communism in the region, see Elvira Concheiro Bórquez, "Repensar a los comunistas en América Latina," *Revista Izquierdas* 3, 7 (2010), 1–19; and Gerardo Leibner and James N. Green, "New Views on the History of Latin American Communism," *Latin American Perspectives* 35, 3 (Mar. 2008), 3–8.

Historians have increasingly begun making use of archival materials, particularly those located in Russia, but also some local party archives where available. There are now also numerous memoirs of communist party members and leaders available, which are usually nationally focused. Naturally, the largest collection of Comintern documentation is located in Moscow, with the Center of Latin American Research, Russian Academy of Sciences, documentary collection *Komintern i Latinskaia Amerika: sbornik dokumentov* [The Comintern and Latin America: A Collection of Documents] (Moscow: Nauka, 1998) being one of the most useful. This collection also benefits from an introduction with a very complete analysis of the political, ideological and other problems that beset the Comintern, something that is less adequately covered in other studies of the Comintern in the region, which have tended to be written by Latin Americanists.

Jaime Massardo's *Investigaciones sobre la historia del marxismo en América Latina* (Santiago: Bravo y Allende, 2001) examines the arrival of Marxist ideas in the region, as do Luis Vitale in *De Martí a Chiapas: balance de un siglo* (Santiago: Síntesis, 1995); Mely González in *Lo latinoamericano en el marxismo* (México: Ocean Sur, 2012); and Sheldon Liss in *Marxist Thought in Latin America* (Berkeley: University of California Press, 1984). Vitale and González are also concerned with the development of Marxist ideas through the twentieth century from a post-Soviet vantage point, as are Omar Acha and Débora D'Antonio, in their "Cartografía y perspectivas del 'marxismo latinoamericano,'" *A Contra Corriente* 7, 2 (Winter 2010), 210–56. Roberto Regalado's edited volume, *La izquierda latinoamericana a 20 años del derrumbe de la Unión Soviética* (México: Ocean Sur, 2012), examines the history of the Latin American left generally, from the vantage point of the present. Analyzing communism more specifically, Elvira Concheira and Massimo Modonesi's tome *El Comunismo: otras miradas desde América Latina* (Mexico City: UNAM, 2007), contains a comprehensive introduction to the problems of the study of communism in the region, as well as chapters that examine some of the fundamental issues across several countries.

There are several important histories of the Comintern's interactions with Latin America as a region, chief among them Manuel Caballero, *Latin America and the Comintern, 1919–1943* (Cambridge: Cambridge University Press, 1986); Michael Löwy, *Marxism in Latin America from 1909 to the Present: An Anthology* (New York: Humanities Press, 1992), especially its extended 2007 Spanish edition; Rodolfo Cerdas Cruz, *The Comintern in*

Central America, *1920–1936* (London: Macmillan, 1993); and Robert J. Alexander, whose *Communism in Latin America* (New Brunswick, NJ: Rutgers University Press, 1957) has been influential particularly in drawing out the frames of reference for understanding the early history of communism in the region.

There are numerous texts that illustrate the dynamics of relations between the Comintern and specific countries during the early period; for example, see Olga Ulianova's two-volume *Chile en los archivos soviéticos* (Santiago: LOM, 2009); Marc Becker, "Mariátegui, the Comintern, and the Indigenous Question in Latin America," *Science and Society* 70, 4 (2006), 450–79; and Klaus Meschkat, "Helpful Intervention? The Impact of the Comintern on Early Colombian Communism," *Latin American Perspectives* 35, 2 (2008), 39–56, along with the later documentary collection on the Comintern and Colombia that he edited with José María Rojas: *Liquidando el pasado: la izquierda colombiana en los archivos de la Unión Soviética* (Bogotá: Fescol-Taurus, 2009).

Meanwhile, Karen Brutents, a former high-ranking official in the International Department of the Communist Party of the Soviet Union, has left a fascinating memoir of Soviet relations with communist parties in the postwar period, which has a global perspective on the Soviet–Latin American aspect of that relationship: *Tridtsat' let na Staroi ploshchadi* [Thirty Years on Staraia Ploshchad] (Moscow, Mezhdunarodnye otnoshenie, 1998).

17

The History of the Vietnamese Communist Party 1941–1975

SOPHIE QUINN-JUDGE

Introduction

Communism in Vietnam grew out of the search for foreign allies to support this French colony's quest for independence. The Western rebuff to the Vietnamese nationalists who petitioned the Paris Peace Conference in 1919 for greater freedom set Ho Chi Minh on his path to Moscow in 1923. But by the time the party was founded in 1930 there were already signs of conflict over the degree of influence that foreign patrons should wield. Vietnamese communist history until 1992 would be characterized by a continuing struggle for balance in the party's relations with socialist allies.

The party's official narrative is one of political unity focused on winning freedom from French rule and subsequent US interference. However, a more historical narrative has emerged with the opening of archives in postcommunist nations, as well as in China and Vietnam itself. This is a history of frequent schisms and of competing outside influences from the Soviet bloc and China. The image of Ho Chi Minh as founder and guide of the Vietnamese Communist Party (VCP)[1] has provided the Vietnamese communists with a facade of strong solidarity, and it is true that the fight for independence forced them to conceal internal ideological disagreements. But at intervals this facade cracked to reveal the dual origin of the communist movement, in urban, European communism and Chinese peasant resistance and secret societies. In the Vietnamese context, the major division between

---

[1] The Vietnamese Communist Party was the official party name from February to October 1930, when the Communist International (Comintern) advised that it should be changed to Indochinese Communist Party, to include all the countries in French Indochina. This name remained until March 1951, when a purely national party was formed, the Vietnam Workers' Party (Dang Lao Dong). This name was changed to the Vietnamese Communist Party in 1976, once the country had been unified.

these two groups was the desire of the first to create a nationalist coalition to defeat imperialism and the strong commitment to violent methods and class struggle of the second faction.

This chapter is divided into four sections: (1) a brief sketch of the foundations of the VCP up to the end of the popular front in 1938; (2) the World War II alliance between the Vietnamese united front and the OSS (US Office of Strategic Services, precursor to the CIA) up to the 1946 outbreak of the Franco-Vietnam War; (3) 1946–56 – independence and unification delayed; (4) 1957–68, the US war up to the Tet Offensive, when the Cultural Revolution would lead to the first break with China. The conclusion ties together some of the themes running through this history, underlining the fact that the Vietnamese Communist Party, under its various titles, functioned as the leader of an armed resistance movement until 1975, and even then did not become a peacetime party until the Third Indochina War (against Pol Pot's Democratic Kampuchea and China) was drawing to a close in 1989.

The Party's Origins

The May 1941 creation of the Viet Minh alliance is one of the foundational moments in the history of Vietnamese communism. Ho Chi Minh, still known to most of his comrades at that time as Nguyen Ai Quoc, Nguyen the Patriot, had summoned a handful of party leaders to meet on the Chinese border, near the town of Jingxi. Here he asserted his belief that the outbreak of war in Europe and Asia made this the opportune moment to unite a patriotic coalition of Vietnamese to oust the colonial French.

The Vietnamese communists, still part of the Indochinese Communist Party (ICP) founded in Hong Kong in 1930, had followed the twists of Moscow's "New Course" from 1928 to 1935. Ho had begun recruiting members of his communist group among émigrés in southern China in the years when the Comintern advocated united fronts between nationalists and communists in colonial countries. But by 1930 this policy had been overtaken by the Sixth Congress's "class against class" leftism. After his arrest in Hong Kong in 1931, Ho had spent more than two years in British custody. When he finally reestablished his links with the Comintern in 1934, after being expelled from Hong Kong, he was out of step with the younger leaders returning to Asia from training in Moscow. He made his way back to the USSR that summer but, like others involved in the 1931 arrests in southern China, did not return to a hero's welcome. He had to spend five years as a student and low-level instructor in the Comintern's schools until he was cleared to return to Asia in the fall of 1938. From then until the 1941 Eighth Plenum on the Vietnamese–Chinese border, he had worked to reestablish an official relationship with the ICP leadership in Vietnam.

The communists within Vietnam had restored the party under the leadership of "Moscow returnees" and maintained their critical attitude toward "bourgeois nationalists" until the late 1930s. They had broken off an informal, perhaps unique, partnership with local Trotskyists in 1937, at the prodding of the French communists. But after their active and influential role in the popular front era, when union organizing and the left-wing press flourished, two attempted uprisings in 1940 had reduced their numbers. By 1941 many party veterans had been imprisoned or executed, especially in the southern part of the country. The movement of Japanese troops into Vietnam over the course of 1940, following the French accommodation with Japan, had not resulted in the Japanese support to the independence revolution that many Vietnamese had hoped for. Although some communist party members and a number of Trotskyists in the south allied themselves with the Japanese, the communists in the north remained loyal to the Allied coalition that brought the nationalist Guomindang (GMD) into a brief united front with the Chinese Communist Party (CCP).

Ho, having established contact with the Overseas Bureau of the ICP by late 1940, brought the promise of outside support and cohesion to the struggling ICP; the timing of this formal contact with the in-country leaders to some extent restored his authority. But it should not be forgotten that he had been far away, studying in Moscow since mid 1934, and had been criticized for his "petty bourgeois nationalism" after the collapse of the high tide of peasant uprisings in 1930–31. So his resumption of party leadership was not a foregone conclusion. Nor was the provision of aid from Moscow or Mao's base in Yan'an, both cut off from easy contact with the Vietnamese party by the summer of 1941.

World War II and Independence

The decisions made at the 1941 meeting, known as the Eighth Plenum of the First Congress (1935), shaped the public identity of the Vietnamese movement – the nationalist, revolutionary incarnation. Ho insisted that it was time to abandon slogans of class struggle and focus on the contradiction between the Vietnamese nation and the imperialist French and Japanese occupiers. The party "must align their policy with the hopes of all the people of Indochina," he declared. The mission to defeat the French and push out the Japanese "was not just the duty of the proletarians and peasants," but the common duty of the entire nation.[2] The formation of a united front of anti-colonial Vietnamese, the Viet Nam Doc Lap Dong Minh Hoi (Association of Vietnamese Allies for Independence, Viet Minh for short) was a victory for the China-based Overseas Bureau of the party, which had been promoting the inclusion of the Vietnamese communists in an anti-fascist coalition. The arrival of the acting party head, Truong Chinh, at the border to accept the authority of Ho Chi Minh and the Comintern apparently unified the diverging factions within the ICP. It also confirmed Truong Chinh, a native of the Red River delta, in his position as general secretary of the party.

As the latter stages of World War II would demonstrate, however, there were still many communists within Vietnam who rejected the change of goals. There were, for example, a number of influential Trotskyists in Cochinchina who supported the Japanese and bitterly opposed what they referred to as the "Stalinists" in the ICP. Ho Chi Minh and his closest comrades, including Pham Van Dong and Vo Nguyen Giap, spent the early years of the war promoting military training courses sponsored by the Guomindang for Vietnamese in southern China. Only a few Vietnamese communists spent time in Yan'an with Mao's troops, among them the legendary Nguyen Son, who – after several years with the Viet Minh fighting the French – in 1949 would return to China, his ideas on party "rectification" rejected by his Vietnamese comrades as premature.[3]

Relations with the Chinese Guomindang became more difficult as the war progressed, and Ho himself was arrested on suspicion that he was a spy in 1942. He was held in several GMD prisons until his release in 1944. He demonstrated his own aptitude for accommodation during his imprisonment by translating into Vietnamese the writings of Sun Yat-sen (the father of nationalist China). His colleagues' lobbying finally secured his release. After that Ho began to haunt the US Office of War Information (OWI) in Kunming, where he read US publications, helped create psywar materials

---

2 Ngô Đăng Tri, *80 năm (1930–2010) Đảng Cộng Sản Việt Nam, những chặng đường lịch sử* [Eighty Years (1930–2010) of the Vietnamese Communist Party] (Hanoi: NXB Thông Tin và Truyền Thông, 2010), 83–84.

3 Georges Boudarel, "L'idéocratie importée au Vietnam avec le Maoisme," in Georges Boudarel, *La bureaucratie au Vietnam* (Paris: L'Harmattan/Vietnam-Asie-Débat 1, 1983), 62–63.

for use in Vietnam and finally made contact with Americans who could discuss joint actions to oppose the Japanese.[4]

The Viet Minh gained new importance in US eyes after the March 1945 Japanese coup that removed the French from power in Indochina, when much of the French army was interned. French information networks on Japanese troop movements went silent after the coup – at that point the OSS was ready to turn to any Vietnamese resistance groups with contacts inside Vietnam for help in intelligence gathering. Ho took advantage of this opportunity by using his Viet Minh to send information out to the border. The Viet Minh also rescued at least one downed US pilot and made sure that General Claire Chennault, commander of the Flying Tigers, knew about it. By June Ho had negotiated a training program for his small guerrilla army in the highlands above Hanoi. Known as the Deer Mission, this OSS training in guerrilla warfare had lasted only two weeks, when it was cut short by news of the Japanese surrender in early August. Unlike in 1941, when the Viet Minh had hoped for aid from the USSR and the Chinese united front, in the autumn of 1945 the United States was now the most promising patron of newly independent states in Southeast Asia.

It is important to recall that at the moment of Ho Chi Minh's Declaration of Independence in Hanoi, 2 September 1945, he saw his communist-led movement as part of the Allied coalition that had defeated the Japanese. From then until mid-1947 he made continued approaches to the United States, including letters to President Truman that went unanswered, requesting recognition of his government and cooperation for economic development. The United States, on the other hand, listened more closely to France: The Americans were persuaded that if the French lost their colony in Indochina they might fall into the orbit of the Soviet Union. The US focus on Europe thus shaped its response to the Viet Minh independence movement; this lack of support by 1947 would force the Viet Minh to renounce their earlier optimistic assessment of US anti-colonial thinking. Concurrently, the United States would increasingly view Ho Chi Minh and the Viet Minh as a purely communist movement, committed to Marxist-Leninist thinking and controlled by the Soviet Union. Still, the Soviet and Chinese recognition of the Democratic Republic of Vietnam (DRV), formed in 1945, would not come until January 1950, after the Chinese communists' 1949 victory in their civil war.

4 Archimedes L. A. Patti, *Why Viet Nam? Prelude to America's Albatross* (Berkeley: University of California Press, 1980), 82–88, 102.

While many analysts saw this evolution of the DRV into a communist satellite as the inevitable outcome of communist domination of Vietnam's anti-colonial movement, there is evidence that the state of Vietnamese communism in the mid 1940s was fluid and contested. Those Viet Minh leaders aligned with Ho were willing to accept US support if it meant independence from France. Ho's view that Vietnam could have developed successfully in alliance with the United States, or even within a freely constituted French Overseas Union, was a pragmatic response to the lack of Soviet influence in Southeast Asia, not to mention the apparent weakness of the Chinese communists in 1945–47.[5]

In fact, Ho had dissolved the ICP in October 1945, turning it into a Marxist study group; it would not resurface as an officially constituted party until 1951. However, in a 1947 exchange with a Soviet interlocutor in Switzerland, Ho's envoy insisted that, although the ICP was an underground movement, it was still the strongest party in the country. Of the Vietnamese government's eighteen members, the envoy said, twelve were communists, although only three had announced their membership of the party. The ICP had been dissolved in 1945 to avoid arousing US opposition, he explained.[6]

1946–1956: Independence and Unification Delayed

By the end of 1946, the Viet Minh were forced out of Hanoi and back into the underground by constant French encroachments on their prerogatives and zone of control. As vicious battles broke out in the city, the DRV became a government in exile, with Ho continuing to serve as president of the Council of Ministers, attempting to negotiate peace with foreign heads of state and maintain control of the economy. By 1947–48, however, the underground ICP, with Truong Chinh at its head, was gradually assuming control of economic policy, security and the military. The growth of ICP power within the resistance is little understood, but there are signs that Ho would have preferred to retain control of government power within the broader Viet Minh alliance. According to the diary of Le Van Hien, the

5 Pierre Brocheux, *Ho Chi Minh: A Biography* (Cambridge: Cambridge University Press, 2007), 121.
6 Rossiiskii gosudarstvennyi arkhiv sotsial'no-politicheskoi istorii (RGASPI), f. 17 (Central Committee), zapis' 128, d. 404, to CC from First European Section, Ministry of Foreign Affairs, 20 Sep. 1947, "Beseda s Fam No Makh, zamestitelem sekretaria pri prezidenture soveta ministrov Respubliki Viet-nam, iz dnevnika Poslannika SSSR v Shveitsarii A. G. Kulazhenkov."

DRV minister of finance and an ICP member, Ho attempted to maintain the authority of the Council of Ministers, as opposed to the ICP Central Committee, over the resistance. By 1948, however, the communist party was expanding its membership and beginning to criticize the bourgeois members of the Viet Minh government. At the party's "Central Cadres meeting" in August 1948, the ICP revealed itself as the organization with the highest level of secrecy and resources within the resistance.[7]

Ho Chi Minh 's efforts to control the DRV's decision-making machinery would end in early 1951, with the introduction of the renamed Vietnam Workers' Party (VWP, Dang Lao Dong Viet Nam) at the Second Party Congress. Given the DRV's diplomatic isolation and the CCP's presence on Vietnam's northern border after their 1949 victory, those communists most closely allied with China became the dominant force in the DRV. By the Second Party Congress in February 1951, the number of party members had reached 766,349. The VWP was also building up its new political front, known as the Lien Viet, ostensibly with a broader reach than the Viet Minh. The Lien Viet would officially replace the Viet Minh in March 1951, although the old name continued to be used for the members of the resistance until 1954.

The Aftermath of Communist Victory in China

After the Chinese communists' victory in October 1949, the Viet Minh saw their fortunes change. Chinese military and political advisors helped the Vietnamese to stage a successful border campaign in the fall of 1950. The Chinese began printing Viet Minh money and supplying advice on the wartime economy, which had been slipping out of Viet Minh control. Ho Chi Minh and his trusted general, Vo Nguyen Giap, retained key roles in the leadership of the resistance, but now they were obliged to heed the thinking of Chinese advisors, whose logistical and material aid was so essential to their military success.

This was the start of the most intense period of Chinese communist influence on the Vietnamese, and it occurred with complete Soviet acquiescence. Stalin had already agreed with Liu Shaoqi in 1949 that the Chinese were in a better position to advise Asian communist parties than the USSR and, so long as the Soviets and Chinese agreed on doctrine and tactics, this

---

7 Lê Văn Hiến, *Nhật Ký của một Bộ Trưởng* [Diary of a Cabinet Minister], vol. I (Danang: NXB Đà Nẵng, 1995), 382, 397, 401, 463.

outsourcing of the advisory role worked.[8] The French Communist Party (Parti communiste français, PCF) at the same time began to increase its interest in the DRV and in 1950 sent a former resistance leader, Léo Figuères, on a mission to gather information there. Part of his role was to defend the Viet Minh's decision-making to his comrades in Moscow and Beijing, who still harbored doubts about Ho's policies.[9]

The Second Party Congress saw the division of the ICP into three national movements for Cambodia, Laos and Vietnam. The Vietnam Workers' Party now acquired the official leading role to direct the resistance, while Truong Chinh as the party general secretary delivered the report on the Vietnamese Revolution and its progress toward socialism.[10] Ho Chi Minh gave the "Political Report" on the world situation and the history of the Vietnamese Revolution in the first part of the twentieth century, but biographies in the new party newspaper *Nhân Dân* (The People) stated that Truong Chinh was now "the builder and commander of the Vietnamese Revolution," while Ho was described as its "soul."[11] These designations would seem to show that Ho Chi Minh was already being assigned a more symbolic place in the leadership, in spite of his title as "chairman of the party." The report on the "organization and rules" of the party was given by Le Van Luong (Nguyen Cong Mieu), who had been playing an important role in party meetings since 1947, but who in 1951 was still listed as a "candidate" member of the Politburo. Luong, a long-time prisoner on Con Son Island, would become known for his role in the party's "Rectification Campaign" after 1952.

In an effort to mobilize the peasantry for a long war, the party began a land reform in 1952 in the "free zone," building on an earlier program of rent reductions and the distribution of land left vacant by the French and wealthy landlords. The party Rectification Campaign that accompanied the land reform was designed to educate the 90 percent of party members who came from petty bourgeois or peasant backgrounds. The land reform, carried out by a special committee on the model of China's own agrarian reform, became a divisive phenomenon in the villages, where in order to satisfy the quota of landlords to be arrested a substantial number of middle peasants were wrongly classified as landlords, and an unknown number of

8 Chen Jian, *Mao's China and the Cold War* (Chapel Hill: University of North Carolina Press, 2001), 44.
9 Céline Marangé, *Le communisme vietnamien (1919–1991)* (Paris: Presses de Sciences Po, 2012), 184.
10 Ngô Đăng Tri, *80 năm*, 138.   11 *Nhân Dân* [The People] (21 Mar. 1951).

patriotic landlords supporting the Viet Minh were among those executed by people's tribunals. The May 1954 communist victory at the Battle of Dien Bien Phu on the Lao border brought a hiatus to these campaigns, as the Geneva conference finally demonstrated the French desire to end the Indochina War.

Intensive negotiations and strong pressure from both China and the USSR resulted in a set of Geneva Agreements that divided Vietnam at the 17th parallel north of Hue, to create regroupment zones for the two sides until nationwide elections for a new government could be held, within two years. A 300-day period of free movement between the two zones allowed almost 1 million people, mainly Catholics, to take refuge in the southern zone, while in theory the communist forces south of the 17th parallel regrouped to the north. Many members of the Viet Minh political infra-structure remained in the south, believing that the Geneva Agreements protected them from retribution and waiting for the national elections, due to be held by July 1956. Ho Chi Minh had persuaded the party to accept the Geneva Agreements, even though the division left several Viet Minh strongholds on the wrong side of the border. He clearly hoped that the peace would bring not only elections, but also reconciliation and trade with France, as he said in a July speech to the Central Committee. Whereas in the past, "we called for the extermination, the wiping out of the puppet forces in order to unify, now we are using the policy of generosity [khoan đại], the method of a nationwide general election, to arrive at national unity," he explained.[12]

The French, however, had to withdraw their military forces from Vietnam by 1955 for lack of funds and US support. Their role as guarantors of the Geneva final statement on elections became impossible to implement. This probably made it more difficult for the FCP to play a clandestine role in supporting the communists. The United States and the southern regime established with their backing had not signed the Geneva Agreements and had no intention of holding nationwide elections. The US military saw it as their obligation to aid and advise the new Republic of Vietnam (RVN), established under President Ngo Dinh Diem in 1955. Meanwhile in the DRV the communist party campaigns of Land Reform and Party Rectification picked up steam, accompanied by a campaign to "socialize" the urban economy of Hanoi and other cities. Thus, what had briefly seemed

12 Đảng Cộng Sản Việt Nam [Vietnamese Communist Party], Văn Kiện Đảng 1954 [Documents of Party History 1954], vol. XV, "Báo Cáo của Bộ Chính Trị tại Hội Nghị Trung Ương lần thứ 6" [Report to the Sixth Party Plenum], 15 Jul. 1954, 167–68.

a time of hope became one of extreme suspicion and polarization on both sides of the 17th parallel. Although government laws on the Land Reform appeared to soften the program in early 1955, the Seventh Plenum of the VWP in March 1955 declared that the "implementation of the Land Reform had been 'too moderate, too rightist,'" although it admitted that there had also been some leftist errors."[13] Both the Land Reform and the Party Rectification became witch-hunts for class enemies by mid 1955, placing greater trust in poor peasants who had fought for the French than in landlords and well-off peasants who had become members of local Viet Minh Committees and even party members.

The effects of de-Stalinization finally caught up with the Workers' Party in October 1956, at their Tenth Plenum. By this time the CCP had also declared a change in course and denounced cults of personality. Ho Chi Minh apologized for his failure to control the excesses of the Land Reform campaigns, and his surrogate Vo Nguyen Giap gave the official speech that made a full analysis of the errors committed. He criticized the overwhelming focus on the anti-landlord struggle and class background. The search for "enemy organizations" within the party had gone too far. "The deeper our attacks on the enemy went, the more they were misdirected; when we attacked the landlord despots and saboteurs, we attacked within our own ranks at the same time," he claimed. In Giap's analysis, "The errors in the rectification of organizations were the most serious errors in the whole land reform."[14]

The "correction of errors" began immediately, and by the start of December more than 12,000 people had been freed from prison. The approximately 7,000 victims who had been executed in many cases had their reputations cleared.[15] While the Central Committee as a whole took responsibility for the excesses, those most directly involved in the Central Land Reform Committee were the ones disciplined. Truong Chinh was removed as general secretary of the party, although he remained in the Politburo and Central Committee Secretariat. Ho Viet Thang, the immediate

13 Edwin E. Moise, *Land Reform in China and North Vietnam* (Chapel Hill: University of North Carolina Press, 1983), 196–97.

14 Moise, *Land Reform*, 246–47, citing Giap's speech to a public meeting in Hanoi, 29 Oct. 1956, printed in *Nhân Dân* (31 Oct. 1956), 2.

15 Đặng Phong, *Lịch Sử Kinh Tế Việt Nam 1945–2000* [Vietnam's Economic History 1945–2000], vol. II, *1955–1975* (Hanoi: NXB Khoa Học Xã Hội, 2005), 85–87, gives a figure of 26,453 people classified as "cruel and bullying landlords," of whom 77 percent or 20,493 were judged to have been misclassified. He does not give a number of landlords executed, but estimates range from 7,000 to 15,000.

overseer of the work, was demoted to become an ordinary party member. Finally, Le Van Luong lost his key posts as chairman of the party's Central Organization Committee, deputy minister of the interior and member of the Politburo and Secretariat.

The "correction of errors" of the Land Reform was judged to have restored some faith in the VWP. General Giap's reputation grew accordingly – he was now not just the hero of Dien Bien Phu but also the conscience of the party. In 1954–56 the army briefly became involved in artistic and intellectual liberalization as well. But the platform the writers put before the army's political commissar, Nguyen Chi Thanh, was not greeted with sympathy; it led to accusations that the artists had been infected by capitalist ideas. In early 1956, one of the demobilized writers persisted in the quest for freedom by publishing an uncensored collection of literary works to celebrate the New Year. After the Twentieth Party Congress of the Communist Party of the Soviet Union, a few issues of an independent journal, *Nhân Văn*, were printed, bringing to the public eye problems such as the need for a legal system instead of rule by decree. But the thaw at the end of 1956 was very short in Vietnam, as the Hungarian Uprising and the growing confrontation with the Diem government unsettled the leadership. By 1958 all seeds of intellectual dissent were cleared away, with self-criticisms in *Nhân Dân* and prison terms for some of the prominent gadflies.[16]

1957–1968: The US War up to the Tet Offensive

The year 1956 remains a clear turning point in Vietnam's communist history: It marks the first time that the Stalinist–Maoist orthodoxy of party policies was questioned and rejected. Afterwards, the Vietnamese communists would never again place themselves so completely under Chinese tutelage, although there would be long periods of strong Chinese influence, especially as the US–Vietnam War heated up in 1963. The level of Soviet influence was, on the other hand, quite variable, with periods of distance between the two nations alternating with extreme dependence and doctrinal convergence, especially when the USSR followed more orthodox policies, as it did from the end of 1968 to 1985.

16 Kim N. B. Ninh, *A World Transformed: The Politics of Culture in Revolutionary Vietnam, 1945–1965* (Ann Arbor: University of Michigan Press, 2002), 158–60. Her chapter "Intellectual Dissent," 121–63, is a good summary of this episode.

After the DRV sent its negotiating team to Paris in 1968, the French communists would also play a stronger supporting and advisory role.

The removal of Truong Chinh from the top leadership in 1956 did not result in the rise of Vo Nguyen Giap, as many observers had expected. The Maoists in the VCP remained influential, and the compromise candidate found to succeed Truong Chinh, after Ho Chi Minh's temporary appointment as party general secretary in 1956, was Le Duan. Le Duan, a cadre from the province of Quang Tri, just south of the demilitarized zone, had been assigned to work in the Mekong delta in the 1940s and early 1950s. His great virtue in 1957 was that he was not linked to the Land Reform. His elevation to party First Secretary (the title of general secretary was temporarily retired), made official at the Third Party Congress in 1960, also reflected the growing importance of the resistance in the south. As a leader during the popular front era in Saigon, he had learned how to operate in a united front. This became his hallmark as a leader of the southern revolution and armed resistance.

One of his early contributions to communist policy was his program for the revolution in the south, *Theses on the Path of Revolution in South Vietnam* [*Đường lối cách mạng miền nam Việt Nam*]. He advocated an active political struggle by the front groups that still existed in the RVN, including the student and labor movements. The *Theses* were approved by the Southern Party Committee at the close of 1956.[17] At this time neither of the DRV's communist allies was eager to support a violent struggle in South Vietnam; the Soviet Union even suggested in 1957 that the two sections of Vietnam be admitted to the UN separately, a suggestion that outraged the southern revolutionaries and the northern leadership alike.

However, the Diem government's communist suppression campaigns and anti-communist law of 1959 made it impossible for the southern communists to continue avoiding armed conflict if they wanted to preserve their dwindling ranks. By January 1959, at the Fifteenth Plenum, a resolution was drawn up that changed the path of the revolution in South Vietnam, now defining it as "that of violent struggle."[18] But it was "only with reluctance," as William

17 See *Đường lối cách mạng miền nam* [Theses on the Path of Revolution in South Vietnam], in Gareth Porter's *Vietnam: The Definitive Documentation of Human Decisions*, vol. II (Stanfordville, NY: Earl M. Coleman Enterprises, Inc., 1979), 24–30. Porter's translation was made from the document captured in Long An Province in 1957.

18 William J. Duiker, *The Communist Road to Power in Vietnam*, 2nd edn. (Boulder: Westview Press, 1996), 200.

Duiker says, that Hanoi was forced to accept this change of strategy.[19] At the 1960 Party Congress the leadership drew up a clear division of strategy for the DRV and the communists south of the 17th parallel. This emphasized the "building of socialism" in the north, with the understanding that there would be a rapid march to communism, jumping over the phase of capitalism with the aid of more advanced communist nations. In the southern part of the country, the "national democratic revolution" would continue, with the assumption that armed struggle would be necessary to finally unify the country.[20] There was as yet no awareness of the sacrifices that would be required to defeat the US effort to end the southern communist insurgency, but one should not assume that the northern leadership was uninterested in this problem. The return of the south's rice-growing delta to the national economy was an urgent need for food self-sufficiency.

Agriculture was a key challenge for the DRV, and in 1958, as plans to create a centrally planned economy were being laid, the party's Fourteenth Plenum decreed that the northern economy henceforth would be composed of two sectors: the state-controlled and the collective.[21] From that point a program to collectivize farming began, gathering speed in 1960.[22]

The 1960 Party Congress marked a gradual return of the leaders who had been demoted in 1956. Whether this can be attributed to Le Duan's leadership or the deeply entrenched position of this faction in the northern bureaucracy is debatable. Be that as it may, Ho Chi Minh and Giap both gave up their seats on the Secretariat, which they had attained only in October 1956. Le Van Luong reclaimed his and became a full member of the Central Committee. Truong Chinh remained a Politburo member, and once again took charge of the Nguyen Ai Quoc training school for Marxism-Leninism, a post he held from 1956 to 1957 and again from 1961 to 1966.[23] He also became chairman of the Standing Committee of the National Assembly, a position that gave him the power to issue government decrees. Le Duc Tho, a long-time member of the northern party and protegé of Le Van Luong, became the chairman of the party's Organization Committee. This position would give him a long-term hold on party personnel decisions and make him arguably its most powerful member.

19 Ibid., 213.   20 Ngô Đăng Tri, *80 nam*, 155.   21 Ibid., 163.
22 Benedict J. Tria Kerkvliet, *The Power of Everyday Politics: How Vietnamese Peasants Transformed National Policy* (Ithaca: Cornell University Press, 2005), 67.
23 My source on the leadership of the Nguyen Ai Quoc School is the list displayed in the "Memory Room" of what is now called the Ho Chi Minh National Academy of Politics and Administration in Hanoi.

Although ostensibly a loyal proponent of Nikita Khrushchev's policy of "peaceful coexistence," Hanoi turned to Beijing in the summer and fall of 1962 with an alarmist message. A delegation led by Ho Chi Minh and Nguyen Chi Thanh, soon to become the chief military strategist and political commissar in South Vietnam, pointed out that with the escalating conflict in the South, the United States might use air and/or land forces to attack the North. At an October meeting with General Giap, Mao Zedong admitted that, "in the past several years, we did not think much about whether or not the imperialists might attack us, and now we must carefully think about it."[24]

1963: The Turn Toward China

By 1963, with American military assistance to the RVN expanding yearly, Le Duan and his southern comrades were understandably eager for a more serious military commitment from their allies in the USSR and China. The Soviet Union would largely stand aside from the Vietnam conflict until 1965, following Khrushchev's 1964 overthrow. This would lead to a deep cooling of DRV–Moscow relations until early 1965, when the USSR began supplying heavy weapons. But the Chinese took the buildup of American forces in South Vietnam under President John F. Kennedy as a threat to their own security – in the summer of 1962, they decided to send Hanoi enough weapons for 230 infantry battalions, with no repayment required.[25] High-level visits to Hanoi began in early 1963, by Luo Ruiqing, chief of staff of the People's Liberation Army, in March and President Liu Shaoqi in May. But the discussions held by Liu Shaoqi in Hanoi involved more than promises of military hardware. The final communiqué from this visit "denounced 'revisionism' and 'rightist opportunism' as the main threat to the international communist movement and emphasized that the DRV should mainly rely on its own strength when building up socialism and carrying out the revolution in South Vietnam."[26]

Signals in Hanoi remained mixed throughout the first part of 1963. A January communiqué praising peaceful coexistence "as the most correct policy," signed by the visiting Czech president Antonín Novotný and Ho Chi Minh, demonstrated that the DRV was still sympathetic to the Soviet

24 Chen Jian, *Mao's China and the Cold War*, 207.
25 Roderick MacFarquhar, *The Origins of the Cultural Revolution*, part III, *The Coming of the Cataclysm 1961–1966* (Oxford and New York: Oxford University Press and Columbia University Press, 1997), 368.
26 Martin Grossheim, "Revisionism in the Democratic Republic of Vietnam: New Evidence from the East German Archives," *Cold War History* 5, 4 (Nov. 2005), 453.

position in the polemics dividing the communist bloc. However, a report from an East German newspaper correspondent based in Hanoi underlined the tension that existed among party members at that moment: "they were not allowed to discuss 'problems within the international workers' movement,'" he noted.[27] A clear sign of the direction the party was moving came in March, when Le Duan gave a speech at the Nguyen Ai Quoc Party School. In this he emphasized the Chinese struggle as the model for the VWP and made the point that "the revolutionary war in the south promoted, rather than undermined, the defense of world peace because it weakened American imperialism."[28] Before Liu Shaoqi's visit in May, a number of middle-ranking cadres working in the DRV press were replaced, in particular a number who wrote on foreign-policy issues. Foreign Minister Ung Van Khiem, a long-time party member from the south, was made to bear the responsibility for the Novotný–Ho Chi Minh communiqué and would be replaced at the end of the year.[29]

Hanoi's campaign against revisionists in the party's ranks gathered pace in the summer and fall, and was institutionalized by a November decree issued by the Secretariat, signed by Le Duc Tho. Sources from the German Democratic Republic (GDR) say that two of the targets were Vo Nguyen Giap and Ho Chi Minh. General Giap was put under house arrest in June, GDR diplomats reported. Prime Minister Pham Van Dong's private secretary was arrested, on the charge of passing confidential information to the Soviet embassy, and Dong was powerless to intervene on his behalf. The director of the party's Su That press was removed from his post and returned to his home province to spend the next twelve years in isolation.[30]

The GDR chargé d'affaires passed on the information that Ho Chi Minh was being subjected to criticism for his past policies, in the form of a "theory of two mistakes." According to this theory, Ho's first mistake was to have compromised with the French in 1945–46, allowing them to return to Vietnam; the second mistake was to have accepted the partition of the country in 1954. (The fact that the Chinese had advised accepting the Geneva arrangement and that Truong Chinh had given it his backing was not discussed, apparently.)[31] With Le Duc Tho's decree announcing a new

---

27 Ibid.
28 Qiang Zhai, *China and the Vietnam Wars, 1950–1975* (Chapel Hill: University of North Carolina Press, 2000), 48, citing Gareth Porter.
29 Grossheim, "Revisionism in the DRV," 453.
30 Nguyễn Văn Trấn, *Viết cho Mẹ và Quốc Hội* [Writing for Mother and the National Assembly] (Westminster, CA: Văn Nghệ Press, 1995), 326.
31 Grossheim, "Revisionism in the DRV," 454–55.

campaign to "protect the party" by investigating questions regarding members' pasts, the pressure to conform was ratcheted up. It is not surprising that Ho Chi Minh was politically neutralized at this point, as party dissident Hoang Minh Chinh has maintained.[32] In December Ho also announced to the Soviet ambassador his withdrawal from day-to-day politics.[33]

Secretariat decree number 68 was issued on 19 November 1963, apparently just before the Ninth Plenum; its long title was for convenience shortened to "Campaign to Defend the Party." The text refers to "the enemy's plot and tricks to destroy the inner core [*nội bộ*] of the party, from the time that peace was reestablished to the present."[34] Nowhere in Decree 68 is there any explanation of the "mistaken viewpoints" that were most troubling party unity, but the unpublished resolutions of the Ninth Plenum, ending in December, made clear that revisionism was the target. In the description of the Moscow-trained philosopher Hoang Minh Chinh, at a meeting for high-level cadres in January 1964, Truong Chinh announced that, "All comrades must pay special attention to one point: Resolution 9 cannot be written down, due to the complex situation within the international communist movement. You must pay attention to the fact that the content of Resolution 9 can be made known only by word of mouth. The point is this: the international and internal policies [*đường lối*] of our party and government are in basic unity with the international and internal policies of the CCP and government of China."[35]

It is clear from reading Le Duc Tho's decree of November 1963 that the fate of the revisionists in the VWP had been predetermined. After the Ninth Plenum they would no longer be free to express disagreement with the new party line. The plenum was held in circumstances that guaranteed the passing of the resolutions, after those in disagreement had been isolated and put on notice that any sympathies for the Soviet Union, even in the cultural world, would not be tolerated. This campaign would run out of steam after relations

32 In author's interview with Hoang Minh Chinh in 1995, he said that Ho Chi Minh had been "*vô hiệu hóa*" or "made powerless" or "ineffective."
33 Mari Olsen, "Changing Alliances: Moscow's Relations with Hanoi and the Role of China, 1949–1964," Ph.D. dissertation (University of Oslo, 2005), 224.
34 *Văn Kiện Đảng Toàn Tập* [Full Collection of Party Documents], vol. XXIV, 1963, Chỉ Thị của Ban Bí Thư, Số 68-CT/TW, 19–11-1963, "Về việc mở cuộc vận động nâng cao tinh thần cảnh giác cách mạng, vv" [Secretariat Decree, no. 68/CC 9–11-1963, "On the Opening of the Campaign to Raise the Spirit of Revolutionary Vigilance, etc."] (Hanoi: NXB Chính Trị Quốc Gia, 2003), 655–68.
35 Hoàng Minh Chính, "Thư ngỏ của công dân Hoàng Minh Chính" [Open Letter from Citizen Hoàng Minh Chính], dated Hanoi, 27 Aug. 1993, printed in the journal *Diễn Đàn/Forum* (1993), www.diendan.org/tai-lieu/bao-cu/so-023/thu-hoang-minh-chinh.

with the Soviet Union improved in 1965–66, following the USSR's entry into the Vietnam War as suppliers of heavy weapons and military training. But the anti-revisionist struggle heated up again in 1967, and this time around resulted in long prison sentences for the accused.

The interpretation of the 1963 Ninth Plenum as the moment when the DRV declared war on the United States exaggerates its importance in the history of the Vietnam War. DRV support for armed conflict and for northern aid to the South had already been established by that time. Le Duan would, in fact, continue to argue in favor of ways to help the United States leave Vietnam without losing face, into 1964–65.[36] What the plenum did do was to reestablish a strong alliance with the CCP and put pressure on the Soviets to support the Vietnamese fight for reunification.

The power of the Ninth Plenum resolution decreeing Vietnam's ideological unity with the People's Republic of China (PRC) seemed to be waning by 1966, as the necessity for Soviet anti-aircraft technology to defend the DRV became clear. The Vietnamese maintained an even-handed approach in public toward their two socialist patrons, although one senior political advisor, Tran Quynh, maintained that the majority in the Vietnamese Politburo continued to favor China.[37] However, the Soviet chargé in Washington believed that there existed "forces of moderation in the DRV" that wanted to start negotiations with the United States, but that "they could not be active while bombs were falling on Hanoi."[38]

The Anti-Party Affair and the Tet Offensive

In mid 1967 Hanoi again swung away from the Soviet Union and entered a renewed phase of the campaign against "revisionism." This time around, the attack on those deemed to be ideologically out of step led to arrests and imprisonment. The official Hanoi explanation of these arrests portrays them as the reaction to a supposed anti-government plot referred to as the "Anti-Party Affair." The controversy arose in part from fear that some Vietnamese leaders close to the Soviet Union were encouraging negotiations to end the war, an issue discussed at the June superpower summit in Glassboro, New Jersey, between President Lyndon Johnson and Soviet premier Aleksei

---

36 Lê Duẩn, *Thư vào Nam* [Letters to the South] (Hanoi: NXB Sự Thật, 1985), 68–93, letter to Nguyễn Chí Thanh, Feb. 1965.
37 Trần Quỳnh, *Hồi Ký về Lê Đuẩn (1960–1986)* [Memoirs of Le Duan (1960–1986)], 30 (unpublished draft manuscript, copy in author's possession).
38 Ilya V. Gaiduk, *The Soviet Union and the Vietnam War* (Chicago: Ivan R. Dee, 1996), 94.

Kosygin. These talks especially disturbed the Chinese leadership, who were becoming ever more suspicious of Soviet intentions.

By 1967 China had slipped into chaos, as the Cultural Revolution grew into pitched battles between rival factions. The growing radicalism began to affect foreign relations as well as internal stability. When Indonesia expelled the Chinese ambassador Yao Tengshan in April, he returned to a hero's welcome in Beijing and took control of the Foreign Ministry from the Minister Chen Yi. The spillover from this radicalization provoked crises in Hong Kong, Cambodia and Burma in April and May. China's diplomats were called home in the spring and returned to their posts in June, when a major escalation in the export of the Cultural Revolution began.[39]

The actions of Chinese diplomats in spreading Maoist propaganda in Burma and Cambodia are well documented; in Vietnam we do not have a clear idea of how active the Chinese were in promoting this new phase of "permanent revolution." But certainly the political temperature rose in Hanoi in the middle of the year, something that may have been connected to the recall of Hanoi's diplomatic corps in July. Another event that rattled the leadership in July 1967 was the death in Hanoi of General Nguyen Chi Thanh, the chief advocate of strong offensive tactics against the United States, and usually thought of as a rival of General Giap. His death may have upset the balance in the Politburo.

At the end of August 1967, as preparations for a new stage in the war, the general offensive, were getting underway, a number of VWP members believed to be pro-Soviet began to be arrested. Among these was a former personal secretary to Ho Chi Minh, Vu Dinh Huynh. Another of the victims was Hoang Minh Chinh, until late 1963 head of the Institute of Philosophy in Hanoi. Although he had been removed from this post, he was still known as one of the Vietnamese proponents of "peaceful coexistence." Another group of people, not all members of the party, were arrested in October and December. The arrests of these men and the subsequent accusation that they were involved in a pro-Soviet plot against the VWP became known as the "Hoang Minh Chinh Affair" or the "Anti-Party Affair."[40]

---

39 Roderick MacFarquar and John K. Fairbank (eds.), *The Cambridge History of China*, vol. XV, *The People's Republic*, part 2, *Revolutions Within the Chinese Revolution, 1996–1982* (Cambridge: Cambridge University Press, 1991), 232–47.

40 See Judy Stowe, "'Revisionism' in Vietnam," paper delivered at Association for Asian Studies Conference in Washington DC, 1998, for a summary of the Anti-Party Affair. Her paper was published in French in *Communisme* 65–66 (2001), 233–49. Georges Boudarel wrote an earlier account in *Cent fleurs écloses dans la nuit du Vietnam. Communisme et dissidence 1954–1956* (Paris: Jacques Bertoin, 1991), 256–64.

Around 30 high-level figures were arrested, and perhaps as many as 300 altogether, including generals, theoreticians, professors, writers and television journalists trained in Moscow. The memoir of Vu Dinh Huynh's son, Vu Thu Hien, arrested just before Christmas in 1967, has become a major source on this affair. His account of his arrest and interrogation has not been published in Vietnam. But its basic themes are corroborated by the petitions for restitution of civic rights from other victims of the affair, in particular by Hoang Minh Chinh himself, who finally passed away in 2008, after many years in prison, solitary confinement and house arrest.

There were multiple causes of these events in late 1967 and 1968. The obvious conclusion is that party members considered as hostile to the escalation of the war were being incarcerated to quell any dissent within the regime. In November, a decree from the Standing Committee of the National Assembly, headed by Truong Chinh, prescribed "death sentences, life prison terms and lesser penalties for a long list of 'counterrevolutionary crimes,' including espionage, sabotage, security violations and the crime of opposing or hindering the execution of national defense plans."[41]

The fact that those arrested were held in prison until 1972 and rearrested if they made an effort to gain redress leads one to believe that some faction of the leadership considered them a long-term threat. Vu Thu Hien, a nonparty member, offers his own explanation for the wave of arrests. During his prison interrogation he was closely questioned about his father's relations with General Vo Nguyen Giap.[42] He concludes that Le Duc Tho and Le Duan viewed Giap as a rival for power, and thus concocted the story of a coup plot to discredit him, along with other influential, second-tier cadres who were considered to be pro-Soviet. At another point in his narrative, Hien writes that Le Duc Tho may have led Le Duan astray with his story of a Soviet plot. The only formal accusation against the "modern revisionists" came four years later, at a Central Committee plenum in January 1972, when Le Duc Tho announced that there had been a conspiracy to overthrow the party leadership. The Soviet ambassador Ilia Shcherbakov and his Second Secretary were accused of links with the plotters.

Peace talks with the United States that were in the very early phases in June 1967 were cut short by late August. The fact that on 20 August American planes bombed targets around Hanoi may have been linked to the breakdown in talks. The British consulate reported that the bombing of

41 Don Oberdorfer, *Tet!* (New York: Doubleday, 1971), 66.
42 Vũ Thư Hiên, *Đêm giữa ban ngày* [Darkness in the Daytime] (Westminster, CA: Văn nghệ, 1997), 271–79.

targets close to Hanoi, including the power station and the main bridge over the Red River, was inducing "spy fever" in Hanoi.[43] At the same time, the decision to stage an offensive in the future had already been made; clearly, whatever support for immediate peace talks had existed in July had collapsed. From 20 to 24 October 1967 the Politburo met and decided that they could carry out the offensive earlier than they had initially planned, as the 1988 official history of the People's Army of Vietnam states.[44] This meeting was chaired by Truong Chinh and included Pham Van Dong, Nguyen Duy Trinh, Le Thanh Nghi, Van Tien Dung, Tran Quoc Hoan and Le Duc Tho. Three Politburo members were absent from Hanoi at the time, including Ho Chi Minh, Vo Nguyen Giap and Le Duan. Ho was in China for medical treatment; Giap had flown to Hungary for medical treatment as well and did not return until late in the year.[45] Le Duan had departed for the celebrations of the fiftieth anniversary of the October Revolution in Moscow.[46] Although Le Duan is usually presented as the key proponent of the Tet Offensive, the military planning was carried out by General Van Tien Dung.[47] (By this time, Le Duan himself seems to have been willing to countenance the idea of peace talks. The Chinese leadership in June 1966 included him among the "pro-Kremlin revisionists" whom they accused of infiltrating the DRV leadership, "producing a struggle between those who backed fighting until military victory ... and those who favored talks to end the war quickly." Zhou Enlai referred explicitly to Le Duan as someone who had "changed course." "Until now he had been a leftist," Zhou said.[48])

43 The National Archives, Kew, UK, FCO, 15/481, 1014/67, Confidential Report from Consul Brian Stewart to DF Murray, FO, Hanoi, 9 Nov. 1967.

44 Military History Institute of Vietnam, *Victory in Vietnam: The Official History of the People's Army of Vietnam, 1954–1975*, trans. Merle L. Pribbenow (Lawrence: University of Kansas Press, 2002), 214.

45 Documents from the Hungarian archives confirm Giap's presence in Hungary, e.g. "Memorandum: The Visit of Vietnamese Ambassador Hoàng Lương to Dep. Foreign Minister Erdelyi, Hungarian Foreign Affairs Archives," VTS 1967.93.doboz, 146,001025/ 19/1967. Thanks to Balázs Szalontai for his translation.

46 A 2001 Hanoi source confirms that both Giap and Le Duan were absent from the Politburo meeting of 20–24 October 1967: These "comrades were absent for health reasons, as both were receiving medical treatment abroad." See *Lịch Sử Kháng Chiến Chống Mỹ Cứu Nước, 1954–1975* [History of the Resistance War Against the Americans to Save the Nation, 1954–1975], vol. V, *Tổng Tiến Công Và Nổi Dậy Năm 1968* [The 1968 General Offensive and Uprising] (Hanoi: NXB CTQG, 2001), 32.

47 Hội Đồng Chỉ Đạo Biên Soạn Lịch Sử Nam Bộ Kháng Chiến (ed.), *Lịch sử Nam bộ kháng chiến* [The History of the Southern Resistance], vol. II (Ho Chi Minh City: NXB Chinh Tri Quoc Gia, 2013), 575.

48 James G. Hershberg, *Marigold: The Lost Chance for Peace in Vietnam* (Washington, DC, and Stanford: Woodrow Wilson Center Press and Stanford University Press, 2012), 158.

The Tet or Lunar New Year's Offensive that swept into towns throughout the RVN in late January had a strong shock value in the United States, where the public had been led to believe that the war was being won. It led to President Johnson's decision to halt US bombing north of the 20th parallel and to agree to peace talks in Paris. In the end, however, Tet was a military defeat for the communist forces, which in three different phases of attack suffered heavy casualties and lost some of their zones of control in the Mekong delta. After this, the southern forces became more dependent on regular troops from the DRV. But the political balance of forces within the VWP Politburo did not change significantly. Although the pressure on General Giap eased, the strong leftist views of the dominant leaders remained intact. Even as relations with China deteriorated, once the DRV entered serious peace negotiations in Paris, the national communists such as General Giap remained outnumbered.

In August 1968 another shift in the balance of the socialist bloc occurred when the Soviet Union sent troops into Czechoslovakia to end the Prague Spring. The Vietnamese hardliners welcomed this demonstration that Moscow was at last supporting orthodox communist policies and moving away from revisionism. With the rise of Leonid Brezhnev to preeminence, the USSR would slide back to more Stalinist economic and political positions; at the same time, it would continue to be a reliable source of arms.

After the invasion of Czechoslovakia, a major speech by Truong Chinh was broadcast by Hanoi and printed in the party's journal in September and October. The Vietnamese now appeared to feel secure enough to publicize their orthodox views. One of Truong Chinh's points was that only violent revolution could bring about an end to the Saigon government. He insisted that the southern revolution must rely on "nonpeaceful means" to make the transition to socialism.[49] This stood in direct opposition to Le Duan's 1968 plan to create a coalition government of nationalists in South Vietnam, to replace the government of Nguyen Van Thieu. As someone who had supported Kosygin's controversial ideas on economic reform, Le Duan at least temporarily lost some of his political clout at the end of 1968. He had been a supporter of experiments with family-based work units on farms in

---

49 These excerpts come from a US analysis of the speech circulated by the French embassy in London. See Paris, La Corneuve, Ministère des Affaires Etrangères (MAE), Série Conflit Vietnam, 11 (FNL), Extraits d'un rapport de Trường Chinh, diffusé par Radio Hanoi du 16 au 20 sept. 1968.

Vinh Phuc province, but the Politburo decreed that these must be ended in late 1968.[50]

Conclusion: Peacemaking, Unification and Reform

Peace negotiations made progress in the last months of the Johnson administration, but the deal was not closed because RVN president Thieu refused at the last moment to sign on. Richard Nixon's administration presented the DRV leadership with new challenges: Although publicly committed to ending the Vietnam War, the new president at first tried a variety of strategies to weaken the communist side. These included more aggressive operations in the Mekong delta, the bombing of National Liberation Front (NLF) sanctuaries in Cambodia, a military incursion into Cambodia in 1970 and an effort to cut the Ho Chi Minh Trail in Laos in early 1971. At the same time the gradual withdrawal of US troops began, as the policy known as "Vietnamization" took effect. US military actions in the long run had little influence on the DRV's determination to fight on, but did increase the casualty numbers for all sides. The Army of the Republic of South Vietnam suffered heavy casualties resulting from the incursion into Laos; these induced the White House to return to the Paris talks, but also intensified Henry Kissinger's contacts with the PRC. The US–Chinese rapprochement, formalized by Nixon's 1972 visit, was in the end more effective in bringing an end to the war than all of Nixon's military bluster.

The year 1969 was said by foreigners present in Hanoi to be a low point for the DRV. The VWP had to close ranks to deal with the death of Ho Chi Minh in September. Even though Ho had become a symbolic, inspirational leader, the party knew the dangers of losing his legitimizing presence. They consented to the Soviet offer to embalm him, and the Soviet specialists were already in Hanoi by the time Ho died. Truong Chinh oversaw the writing of his official biography, a vague and hagiographic document.

The Politburo was persuaded by Soviet pressure to wait for the outcome of the October 1971 presidential election in Saigon, duly won by the single candidate, Nguyen Van Thieu, before undertaking a new offensive. The 1972 "Easter Offensive" was the final military play for the DRV – the US détente with China meant that the latter no longer had a vital interest in Hanoi's

---

50 Đặng Phong and Melanie Beresford, *Authority Relations and Economic Decision-making in Vietnam* (Copenhagen: NIAS, 1998), 61–62.

success and would no longer be a reliable ally, while the Soviet Union had long wished for a negotiated peace to eliminate this obstacle to détente with the United States. With Soviet tanks now supporting DRV main force units, the offensive scored major victories until US airpower stopped their advances. The stalemated war brought the key negotiators, Henry Kissinger and Le Duc Tho, back to Paris in the leadup to the US presidential election. Concessions on each side, including the DRV agreement to Thieu's continuation in power, and the US acceptance of a ceasefire in place, with no withdrawal of DRV troops, solved the key issues. Nixon was able to declare that "peace is at hand." But once again Thieu balked at signing the agreement and, after the November election, the United States indulged in a final round of "Christmas bombing" – this time of industrial sites and military installations around Hanoi. The final agreement was identical on most points to the one agreed upon in October, but the bombing allowed Nixon and Kissinger to claim that their boldness had brought a "recalcitrant" Hanoi back to the negotiating table. In fact, the delay provided a window for the United States to accelerate the reequipping of Saigon's forces before the peace agreement took effect, to placate the unhappy RVN leaders.

The January 1973 Agreement on Ending the War in Vietnam created some hope for a peaceful resolution of the civil war in the South. The agreement's political provisions mandated the formation of a Council of Peace and National Reconciliation, an organ that would be composed of representatives of the Saigon government, the NLF's Provisional Revolutionary Government (PRG) and neutralists. However, President Thieu rejected all of the political aspects of the peace agreement and continued to fight to take back the communists' zones of control. In response, a July resolution by the Hanoi Politburo stated that the DRV would prepare for a military offensive to end the war. This final act came more quickly than anyone could have imagined. Nixon's resignation in August 1974 prompted an outbreak of protests against Thieu's corruption and his failure to implement any of the political articles of the Paris Agreement. As Thieu grew politically weaker, the communist forces gained ground on all the battlefronts of the south. A surprise attack on the central highlands town of Banmethuot in March 1975 led Thieu to withdraw the RVN's forces from the highlands. By early April the DRV Politburo had opened its final offensive; the fall of Saigon came on 30 April, as an exodus of Vietnamese linked to the United States was ended.

The glory of victory did not long endure for the VCP – much reduced aid from the PRC and border conflict with the Khmer Rouge (KR) regime in Cambodia made the peace precarious. The economy was already devastated, and the nation had fallen far behind its neighbors. (For this reason, the Vietnamese now speak of the Vietnam War era as the time of "resistance" as opposed to a "communist revolution.") A November 1975 conference of representatives from North and South decreed that the two parts of Vietnam would reunify in 1976, while attempts at economic transformation of southern agriculture and urban business would quickly follow. With the return of pragmatist Deng Xiaoping to power in China in 1977, the Hanoi Politburo hoped that they could reestablish normal relations with the Chinese. But they were disappointed, as China opted for a stronger relationship with the KR and pressured Vietnam to end its close relations with the Soviet Union. As border incursions by the KR became a serious threat, the Vietnamese were persuaded in late 1978 to sign a long-term friendship treaty with the USSR in order to balance what they now saw as China's attempts to destabilize them. The 1978–79 Vietnamese offensive to remove the KR from power resulted in a ten-year occupation of Cambodia by Vietnamese troops. This left Vietnam isolated from most forms of international aid and dependent on the USSR, until the collapse of the Soviet Union in 1991. The nation's dire economic situation forced the beginning of reforms in agriculture by 1979. By the early 1980s a variety of economic experiments were underway in agriculture and foreign trade, which were institutionalized by the Sixth Party Congress in 1986.

Since the deaths of the first-generation leaders, the VCP has settled for rather anonymous leadership, clinging to its power by delivering economic progress but little moral leadership. Overall, in contrast to North Korea, China and Cuba, no single member of the Politburo has ever developed a true cult of personality, to the extent that he could rewrite party history to glorify his own role or claim to be the source of all theoretical wisdom. Ho Chi Minh has posthumously been turned into the leading theoretician, as the VCP has elaborated a system of "Ho Chi Minh Thought," mainly since 1991. The Vietnamese leadership has presented itself as a collegial body, with the clairvoyance to correct its mistakes before they became too serious. Unofficially, however, since the end of the Soviet Union, Le Duan has been singled out as the leader who took Vietnam into war with the United States and into a dependent relationship with the Soviet Union after 1975. This view reflects that of the Chinese leadership and the fact of the party's closer relations with the CCP since 1990. This use of Le Duan to explain past mistakes in fact does much to obfuscate the real history of the war era – perhaps for this reason it has been well received by both the United States and Hanoi's current leaders.

Bibliographical Essay

The Vietnamese Communist Party has never agreed on a Resolution on Party History, such as the Chinese Communist Party has issued at intervals. There is thus no unified view on many problems of VCP history. We see changing emphases over time, but never the sort of rejection of past policies that leads to the opening of archives on a wide scale. The main periods of opening were influenced by upheavals in the Soviet Union. In 1956 a short literary and ideological thaw allowed criticism of the Land Reform to be published in the party newspaper, *Nhân Dân* (The People). The second period of real opening occurred from roughly 1986 to 1989, when General Secretary Nguyen Van Linh encouraged criticism of the party and state as part of the early *Đổi Mới* (reform) process. Economic reforms would continue after the collapse of European communism, but the ideological thaw began to cool down between 1989 and 1991. Over the past two decades, many volumes of *Văn Kiện Đảng Toàn Tập* (Complete Collection of Party Documents) have been published, but these have been carefully edited, leave out key decisions and rarely attribute responsibility. For 1968, for example, see *Nhà Xuất Bản Chính Trị Quốc Gia* (National Politics Publishing House, 2004); the volume covering 1930 was published in 2005.

To supplement these volumes, researchers turn to histories compiled by committees of ministries and institutes, for example the Military History Institute of Vietnam, or the Institute of Marxism, Leninism and Ho Chi Minh Thought, now renamed the Ho Chi Minh Academy of Politics and Administration. *80 năm (1930–2010) Đảng Cộng Sản Việt Nam: Những chặng đường lịch sử* [80 Years (1930–2010) of the Vietnamese Communist Party: Its Historical Path] (Hanoi, 2010) by Ngô Đăng Tri is a reliable source of dates, meetings and memberships. Much can be gleaned from the diaries and memoirs of communist party members and their relatives, those published both in Vietnam and overseas. In particular, I have found these memoirs useful for the 1950s–60s: Vũ Thư Hiên, *Đêm giữa ban ngày* [Darkness in the Daytime] (Germany, 1997) and Nguyễn Văn Trấn, *Viết cho mẹ & Quốc Hội* [Writing for Mother and the National Assembly] (Westminster, CA: Nhà Xuất Bản Văn Nghệ, 1996). The two-volume *Nhật Ký của một Bộ Trưởng* [The Diary of a Cabinet Minister] by Lê Văn Hiến (Danang: Nhà in Báo Nhân

Korean Communist Movements 1918–1945

From the beginning, Korean communist organizations were focused more on questions of national liberation and autonomy than on ideology and social reform, although these were always more or less linked. Korean communist organizations were established by émigrés in Russia less than a year after the Bolshevik Revolution, when Korea had been a colony of Japan for nearly a decade.[4] In June 1918, the first Marxist-oriented party organized by Koreans, the Korean People's Socialist Party, was established with financial assistance from Moscow under the leadership of the independence fighter Yi Tonghwi. Many of its members were longtime residents of the Russian Far East, where Koreans had been immigrating in increasing numbers since the 1860s. In 1919, Yi moved his organization to Shanghai, where it joined forces with the newly established Korean Provisional Government, and was renamed the Korean Communist Party. At the same time, a rival All-Russian Korean Communist Party was established in Irkutsk, and the two vied for Comintern backing. In the summer of 1921, members of the Shanghai and Irkutsk groups came into armed conflict in the city of Alekseevsk.

The first domestic Korean communist party was organized in Seoul in 1925. Under constant Japanese police pressure, the party was dissolved and reconstituted three times, until it broke up for good in 1928. Some Korean communists went underground and engaged in organizing farmers and factory laborers; many were imprisoned by the colonial regime and were "converted" to denounce communism and support Japanese rule. By the time Korea was liberated in August 1945, at the end of World War II, few active Korean communists remained in the country. Although there were some Korean communists active in Japan until the early 1930s, particularly students, the main hub of Korean communist activity in the 1930s and early 1940s was China, especially the northeast area near the Korean border. Under the leadership of the Chinese Communist Party, Korean fighters joined the Northeast Anti-Japanese United Army (NEAJUA), which waged a guerrilla campaign against the Japanese authorities from the early 1930s until the last units were crushed or driven into exile in the Soviet Union in 1941. Among the Korean members of the NEAJUA was a young unit commander from the Pyongyang region named Kim Song-ju, who took on the *nom de guerre* Kim Il

---

4 Much of the following section is adapted from Dae-sook Suh, *The Korean Communist Movement, 1918–1948* (Princeton: Princeton University Press, 1967), and Dae-sook Suh (ed.), *Documents of Korean Communism, 1918–1948* (Princeton: Princeton University Press, 1970).

Sung. Kim and his unit fled to the vicinity of Khabarovsk sometime in late 1940, and were reorganized into a reconnaissance brigade of the Soviet Far Eastern Army. Other Korean communists joined Mao Zedong's group in Yan'an, and the two groups had little contact with each other until after the war. Following liberation from Japanese colonial rule, Korean communists resurfaced in Korea and many returned from exile in China and the Soviet Union. Attempts to reestablish a viable communist movement in Seoul faced violent opposition from anti-communist Korean elements in the South as well as the distrust of and eventual proscription by the US occupation authorities. Pyongyang, the headquarters of the Soviet occupation in the North, became the new center of Korean communist activity and ultimately the capital of a new Soviet-oriented Korean state.

Formation of the Democratic People's Republic
1945–1948

Following the Japanese defeat in World War II, the Soviet Union occupied North Korea from 1945 to 1948, according to their 11 August agreement with the United States, which occupied the southern half of the peninsula. Neither the United States nor the USSR intended Korean division to be permanent, and neither had planned for a long-term occupation. Nevertheless, once a decision was made to remain in Korea, the Soviets quickly set up a central administrative structure in Pyongyang. The Soviet Civil Administration (SCA), established on 3 October, was organized by General Terentii Fomich Shtykov, a member of the Military Council of the Far Eastern First Front, vice-commander for military affairs of the 25th Army and later ambassador to the DPRK. The Five-Province Administration, created as a temporary government in Pyongyang in November, had Soviet advisors for each of the ten departments, and Red Army officers worked as advisors to the Provincial People's Committees.[5] Officers of the 25th Army held all the important posts in the SCA, which oversaw provincial and county *komendaturas* (military commands).

With the support and encouragement of the Soviet occupation authorities, Korean communists in the North emerged from underground and rapidly began to rebuild a communist party. The first step toward a centralized northern party was the Northwest Five-Province Korean Communist Party

---

5 Eric Van Ree, *Socialism in One Zone: Stalin's Policy in Korea, 1945–1947* (Oxford: Berg, 1989), 111, 104. The following is based in part on my books *The North Korean Revolution, 1945–1950* (Ithaca: Cornell University Press, 2003) and *Tyranny of the Weak: North Korea and the World, 1950–1992* (Ithaca: Cornell University Press, 2013).

Member and Enthusiasts' Alliance Conference, held in Pyongyang on 10–13 October. The conference resulted in the creation of the North Korean Bureau of the Korean Communist Party, which became the foundation of a separate northern party.[6] The day after the conference ended, on 14 October, Kim Il Sung made his first public appearance at a Soviet-sponsored rally in Pyongyang, introduced by the conservative nationalist leader and Pyongyang native Cho Mansik. In August 1946 communist parties in the North united to form the North Korean Workers' Party (NKWP), and in June 1949 the North and South Korean Workers' Parties were merged into the Korean Workers' Party (KWP), which remains the ruling party of the DPRK. The NKWP in theory led a coalition of parties that included the Korean Democratic Party, led by Cho Mansik and other conservatives, including many Protestant Christians; and the Young Friends' Party of the native Korean Ch'ondogyo religion. In practice, the latter two groups became, in classic Leninist fashion, merely "transmission belts" for the policies of the Workers' Party.

Resistance to the Soviet occupation and the emerging communist-dominated state reached a peak in late 1945 and early 1946, declining sharply thereafter. The home of Soviet 25th Army commander General Ivan Chistiakov was firebombed; Kang Ryanguk, vice-chairman of the KDP, was attacked by terrorists; and at the commemoration of the March First Movement in Pyongyang in 1946, a grenade was thrown onto the podium where Soviet and North Korean officials were standing. Although the scale of overt violence never approached that of South Korea in the late 1940s, in which thousands were killed in the suppression of uprisings in Seoul and the provinces, protests were sometimes met with armed force. Soviet and North Korean security forces shot and killed several dozen demonstrators in the city of Sinuiju in December 1945 and in the eastern industrial city of Hamhung in March 1946.

Nor was the creation of a political coalition in the North without its share of violence. As in South Korea, political struggles in the North sometimes took a bloody turn, beginning with the assassination of the prominent communist Hyon Chunhyok in September 1945. The Soviet attempt to work with Cho Mansik, the most popular nationalist figure in the North, ended in failure. Cho, a conservative Protestant Christian whose Korean Democratic Party had its main constituency among the landlord and

---

6 Chosôn sanôp nodong chosaso (ed.), *Orûn nosôn* [The Correct Line] (Tokyo: Minjung sinmunsa, 1946), 30–48.

capitalist classes, never saw eye to eye with the Soviet occupation authorities or the communists. After the Moscow Foreign Ministers' Conference in December 1945 established Soviet–American agreement for extended trusteeship over Korea, Cho rebuffed repeated Soviet attempts to win his support for trusteeship. Cho strongly opposed trusteeship, along with other conservative nationalists in the North and the South, and was placed under house arrest in January 1946. He was replaced as head of the Korean Democratic Party by Kim Il Sung's Manchurian colleague Ch'oe Yonggôn and was apparently killed in the early stages of the Korean War. The removal of Cho and the flight of upper-class and conservative elements to the South meant the end of effective noncommunist political organization and opposition to the regime by mid 1946.

In the spring of 1946, the nascent North Korean government (officially the Provisional People's Committee), dominated by communists, initiated a series of social and economic reforms. These included land redistribution, new labor regulations, a law on gender equality and the launching of a centralized economic plan for industrialization and development in 1947. New "mass organizations," including youth, women's, farmers' and workers' groups, were set up under central directive and mobilized a large majority of the population. As part of the reform process, the class origin, religious affiliation and political background of each North Korean resident were recorded in detail by Workers' Party branches and social organizations. The recorded status, or *songbun*, of every North Korean thus became a matter of record and an important factor for determining one's occupation, residence, educational opportunities and other matters. Eventually *songbun* would become hereditary, shaping the life chances of North Koreans for generations to come.[7]

Following the collapse of US–Soviet talks on Korea in 1947, the "Korean Question" was handed over to the United Nations. UN attempts to supervise nationwide elections in the spring of 1948 were rebuffed by the North Korean leaders and their Soviet backers, who decried the elections for excluding the communists and promoting only pro-US interests in Korea. In the end, elections were held in the South alone, and the American-educated Syngman Rhee became the first president of the Republic of Korea

7 The *songbun* system has persisted into the twenty-first century and is strongly criticized in the 2014 United Nations human rights report on the DPRK. See "Report of the Commission of Inquiry on Human Rights in the Democratic People's Republic of Korea," www.ohchr.org/EN/HRBodies/HRC/CoIDPRK/Pages/ReportoftheCommissionofInquiryDPRK.aspx.

in August 1948. The North held its own elections and declared the establishment of the Democratic People's Republic of Korea, under the leadership of Kim Il Sung, on 9 September. With two governments on the peninsula, each claiming to be the legitimate authority over the whole of Korea, each backed by one of the Cold War superpowers, civil war was all but inevitable.

The Korean War and Its Aftermath

The North Korean invasion of 25 June 1950 was widely perceived by the West to have been masterminded by Stalin as part of a global strategy of Soviet expansion. Later, scholars challenged this standard interpretation by focusing on the civil nature of the war and the possible role of South Korea and the United States in provoking the conflict.[8] Newly accessible evidence from Soviet and Chinese sources in the 1990s suggest that Kim Il Sung planned the invasion of the South, with the knowledge and support of the Soviet and Chinese leadership, well in advance of June 1950.[9] The degree of collusion among Kim, Stalin and Mao is still quite speculative, but it appears that Stalin agreed to support North Korea in "liberating" the South after Kim convinced him that the war would be won quickly and decisively, before the United States had time to intervene. Mao apparently agreed to deploy Chinese troops in North Korea's defense should the need arise.

The war, launched with a Blitzkrieg attack in the early hours of 25 June, initially went well for the North. The KPA overwhelmed South Korean and the remaining American forces, taking Seoul in three days; by August, the North Koreans had taken all but a small corner of the southeastern part of the peninsula, the so-called Pusan perimeter. In mid September the tide was reversed, after US general Douglas MacArthur's now-famous landing at the port of Inchon near Seoul. Under the flag of the United Nations, US, ROK and other allied troops retook Seoul and crossed the thirty-eighth parallel into

---

8 See especially Bruce Cumings, *The Origins of the Korean War*, vol. II (Princeton: Princeton University Press, 1990). A good summary of competing explanations for the origins of the war can be found in John Merrill, *Korea: The Peninsular Origins of the War* (Newark: University of Delaware Press, 1989), ch. 1.

9 See Kathryn Weathersby, *Soviet Aims in Korea and the Origins of the Korean War, 1945–1950: New Evidence from the Russian Archives*, Cold War International History Project Working Paper no. 8 (Washington, DC: Woodrow Wilson International Center for Scholars, Nov. 1993); Sergei Goncharov, John W. Lewis and Xue Litai, *Uncertain Partners: Stalin, Mao and the Korean War* (Stanford: Stanford University Press, 1993); and Chen Jian, *China's Road to the Korean War: The Making of the Sino-American Confrontation* (New York: Columbia University Press, 1994).

North Korea on 30 September. UN forces continued to march toward the
Yalu River dividing North Korea from China. In November, thousands of
Chinese People's Volunteers crossed into Korea, pushing UN forces back
across the parallel. Throughout the war China sent hundreds of thousands of
troops and suffered immense casualties, including the death of Mao's son,
Mao Anying.

While the Chinese contributed by far the most important outside
assistance to North Korea, the USSR contributed fighter pilots for combat
over the northern part of North Korea and prepared as many as five
divisions of Red Army soldiers to enter the war, which were never sent.
Stalin's priority was to avoid a direct confrontation with the United States
and the possible global war that would result, and engagements with
UN forces were seriously hampered by the need to keep Soviet involvement limited and discreet. Soviet reluctance created strains in the USSR's
relations with both China and the DPRK, which helped lead to the Sino-
Soviet split and the relative increase of Chinese influence in North Korea
after the war.[10]

The physical and human destruction of the Korean War was awesome in
both North and South, but the North suffered the greater devastation. Much
of this was due to the tactics and technological superiority of the UN forces,
especially the US Air Force. The United States sought to use massive and
prolonged aerial bombardment as a means of breaking the morale of the
North Korean population, despite evidence from World War II – particularly
the Allied bombing of Dresden – that such tactics were counterproductive.
In one two-day period the United States dropped 700 bombs on Pyongyang,
which according to North Korean sources had only one building left standing
at the end of the war.[11] Virtually every city in North Korea was leveled,
thousands of factories were destroyed and much of North Korea's industrial
production, as well as the political leadership and population as a whole, were
forced underground to avoid the bombing. The new and horrifying weapon
of napalm was used on a wide scale for the first time, and at one point in
the spring of 1951 the United States considered the use of atomic bombs.
Finally, toward the end of the war North Korea's major dams and hydroelectric plants were bombed, creating massive flooding and destroying food
crops. Of perhaps 3 million killed in the war, North Korean civilian deaths

10 Robert R. Simmons, *The Strained Alliance: Peking, P'yŏngyang, Moscow and the Politics of
the Korean Civil War* (New York: Free Press, 1975).
11 *Postwar Rehabilitation and Development of the National Economy* (Pyongyang: Foreign
Languages Publishing House, 1957), 8.

numbered more than 2 million, or 20 percent of the population. Millions more were injured, uprooted or separated from their families.

Despite the war's destructiveness, the effect of the war on the regime was ambiguous. Although many KWP members relinquished or "lost" their party identification cards in the autumn of 1950, when UN and South Korean forces occupied the North, the party was rebuilt through strenuous efforts of recruitment and education during the remainder of the war and beyond. In particular, the war seems to have strengthened the position of Kim Il Sung and his partisans. Many opponents of the regime, especially Christians, fled south during the war or were executed or otherwise eliminated. The war helped to consolidate and intensify certain policies that had previously been pursued, including the mass line, anti-Americanism, self-reliance and the Kim Il Sung leadership.[12] By April 1956, at the time of the Third Party Congress, the KWP claimed that membership had increased from 725,762 at the Second Congress in 1952 to a current total of 1,164,945 – making the KWP, representing 12 percent of North Korea's total population, proportionately the largest Marxist-Leninist party in the world.[13]

Purges of the KWP and the DPRK leadership had begun during the war itself, after the UN assault had pushed North Korean forces to the far north of the peninsula. At the Third Plenum of the KWP Central Committee in December 1950, held in the city of Kanggye, Kim Il Sung chastised other DPRK leaders for their conduct in the war, and many were expelled from the party. Mu Chông, a Yan'an veteran and one of the most experienced military men in the leadership, came under particularly severe criticism for failing to defend Pyongyang, and for indiscriminate killing during his retreat to Mukden in Manchuria when the UN forces attacked. Unlike most other purged leaders, Mu Chông was not reinstated in the party and disappeared soon after the war, possibly going into exile in China.

In September 1951 Kim Il Sung clashed with Hô Kai, the most prominent of the so-called Soviet-Koreans, over the organization of the Workers' Party. Hô, taking a more orthodox Leninist line and concerned with the number of party members who had collaborated with the US/UN/ROK occupation forces, ordered a widescale purge of the party and insisted on giving priority to industrial workers for new membership. Kim, consistent with the

---

12 Kang Chông-gu, "Hanguk chônjaeng kwa Pukhan ûi sahoejuûi kônsôl" [The Korean War and the Construction of Socialism in North Korea], *Hanguk kwa kukje chôngch'i* 6, 2 (Autumn 1990), 95–137.
13 Kim Il Sung, *On the Building of the Workers' Party of Korea*, vol. II (Pyongyang: Foreign Languages Publishing House, 1978), 233–34.

mass-party approach he had taken before the war, demanded the party be kept open to large numbers of peasants. Kim ordered the reinstatement of most of the expelled party members, and Hô Kai himself was purged in November. Hô is alleged to have committed suicide in August 1953.

Kim's most important rival had been Pak Hônyông, one of the few Korean communists to survive in Korea throughout the colonial period with his wellbeing and political integrity intact. Pak commanded enormous respect among Korean communists, especially those from South Korea, many of whom (like Pak himself) had come north before or during the war. He had been named vice-premier and foreign minister in the first DPRK cabinet, and was second only to Kim in power, a situation apparently not viewed favorably by many of Pak's supporters.

On 10 July 1953, three days after the Korean War armistice, Pak's close ally Yi Sûng'yôp and eleven other conspirators were charged with attempting to overthrow the DPRK government. The men were put on trial of spying for the United States, destroying "democratic forces" during the war and attempting to unseat the present leadership and replace Kim with Pak Hônyông. Pak was stripped of his party membership but not tried. Like the victims of Stalin's show trials in the 1930s, the accused admitted to all the charges, however outrageous and fabricated some of them clearly were. All were sentenced to death and presumably executed.[14]

Pak himself was brought to trial in December 1955. His list of alleged crimes was even lengthier and more incredible than that of the twelve co-conspirators, and included responsibility for the failure of a guerrilla uprising in the South during the war and collusion with American soldiers, business-men and missionaries going as far back as 1919. Pak was given the death sentence after a one-day trial.

The biggest postwar leadership challenge to Kim came in 1956, shortly after the Soviet Union's "de-Stalinization" campaign began at the Twentieth Congress of the CPSU. While Kim was away on a trip to the USSR and other Soviet-bloc states in June and July, an alleged conspiracy led by Ch'oe Ch'ang'ik and other members of the "Yan'an group" attempted to eliminate Kim and his growing cult of personality, intending to replace him with a collective leadership. Kim scathingly attacked the Yan'an group at the August plenum of the KWP Central Committee; most leading members

---

14 Dae-Sook Suh, *Kim Il Sung: The North Korean Leader* (New York: Columbia University Press, 1988), 130–34; Koon Woo Nam, *The North Korean Communist Leadership, 1945–1965: A Study of Factionalism and Political Consolidation* (Tuscaloosa: University of Alabama Press, 1974), 92–95.

of this group and other accused conspirators were expelled from the party, some fleeing to China and the USSR. In a widespread purge lasting until the spring of 1958, virtually all real or potential threats to the supremacy of Kim and his partisan comrades were removed from their positions of authority, some sent into forced labor, some killed, others going into exile.[15] From then on, the core of the DPRK leadership remained a group of loyalists with close personal ties to Kim Il Sung, either through their shared Manchurian guerrilla experience or later through family connections. The final purge of members of the Manchurian group itself came in the late 1960s, and there has not been any evidence of a serious political challenge to Kim from that time until his death in 1994.

Power struggles at the top of the political system were not reflected in political and social unrest on the part of ordinary North Koreans. After the war, the social environment in North Korea was remarkably stable, with few signs of political discontent and opposition, or indeed of crime and violence.[16] Most opponents of the regime had left during the war, and what opposition remained seems to have been eliminated by the mid to late 1950s through improved living standards, intense ideological indoctrination, and extensive networks of surveillance and control. Most importantly, the energies of the North Korean people were channeled into the enormous project of postwar economic reconstruction.

By any measure, economic growth in the first decade after the war was nothing short of astonishing. This was the period of greatest economic success for the DPRK, not matched before or since. The advantages of the North Korean variant of the socialist command economy in the beginning stages of development, including opportunities for extensive growth, a high degree of popular mobilization, a preexisting industrial base upon which to build and an educated and organized workforce, put the DPRK well ahead of South Korea in economic growth until at least the mid 1960s.[17] Reconstruction was also helped by economic aid from the USSR and other socialist countries, amounting to US$ 550 million according to North Korean

---

15 Lim Un, *The Founding Of a Dynasty in North Korea: An Authentic Biography of Kim Il Sung* (Tokyo: Jiyu-sha, 1982), ch. 6. "Lim Un" is the collective pseudonym for three North Korean exiles residing in the former Soviet Union.

16 Glenn D. Paige and Dong Jun Lee, "The Post-War Politics of North Korea," in Robert A. Scalapino (ed.), *North Korea Today* (New York: Praeger, 1963), 19.

17 For a comparison of the two economies, see United States Central Intelligence Agency, *Korea: The Economic Race Between the North and the South* (Washington, DC: US Government Printing Office, 1978).

estimates,[18] as well as the labor and assistance of Chinese People's Volunteer troops, who remained in North Korea until October 1958.

Targets for the first Three-Year Plan (1954–56) were officially reached well before the end of three years, in August 1956; quotas for the first Five-Year Plan, launched in December 1956, were completed in 1960, one year ahead of schedule. Even if one accounts for probable exaggerations in official DPRK estimates, North Korea's economic growth in this period was one of the highest in the world.[19] Economic development was not merely a priority in itself; development was also a means of "consolidating the democratic base" and strengthening Korean socialism. In that regard, two of the most significant goals in postwar reconstruction were the collectivization of agriculture and the appropriation of all remaining private industry by the state. Both of these goals were accomplished by 1958, completing a process of socialist transformation that had begun with the reforms of 1946.

Collectivization – or "cooperativization" (hyôpdonghwa) as the North Koreans generally called it – had been enshrined as a goal in the 1948 constitution and promulgated as state policy shortly before the war, but was not put into widespread practice until 1954, after being launched on an "experimental" basis in August 1953. As a land-to-the-tiller policy, the 1946 land reform had actually increased the number of private landowners, so that by 1953 95 percent of agricultural land in North Korea was privately owned.[20] The regime quickly set about reversing this process, bringing the entire rural population into farming cooperatives by August 1958, with 13,309 cooperatives each averaging 79 households with 134 chongbo of land. In October these cooperatives were amalgamated into 3,843 larger units, averaging 275 households and 456 chongbo. In addition, administrative districts were redrawn so that the ri or village, the lowest-level administrative unit, was identical with the cooperative farm.[21] Thus, the cooperative corresponded roughly with the "natural" village (or collection of neighboring villages) of traditional Korea, unlike large Soviet state farms. Some private farming was allowed for personal use, but in practice all

18 Cited in Ellen Brun and Jacques Hersh, *Socialist Korea: A Case Study of the Strategy of Economic Development* (New York: Monthly Review Press, 1976), 165.
19 Charles Armstrong, "'Fraternal Socialism': The International Reconstruction of North Korea, 1953–1962," *Cold War History* 5, 2 (May 2005), 161–87.
20 Joseph Sang-Hoon Chung, *The North Korean Economy: Structure and Development* (Stanford: Hoover Institution Press, 1974), 10.
21 Mun Woong Lee, *Rural North Korea Under Communism: A Study of Sociocultural Change* (Houston: Rice University Press, 1976), 27. A *chongbo* is roughly equivalent to a hectare.

farms were state-run collectives.[22] In 1958 "complete socialization" of all industries was declared, and all enterprises became either state-owned operations or industrial cooperatives, with the vast majority belonging to the former category.[23] Privately owned industry ceased to exist, signaling the "complete victory of the socialist revolution."

Deepening the Revolution 1958–1972

The political and economic consolidation of the late 1950s set the basic patterns of organization, behavior and ideology that were deepened and routinized in the 1960s, and that characterized the DPRK for the following three decades or more. These included the unassailable position of Kim Il Sung at the center of political power, surrounded by individuals linked closely to him by a common experience of anti-Japanese guerrilla struggle in Manchuria or (as became increasingly important over the years) family ties; the concept of *chuch'e* – self-identity or self-reliance – as the overarching philosophical principle guiding all areas of life, from education to foreign policy; the sacralization of "Kim Il Sung Thought" (in practice indistinguishable from *chuch'e*) as the "monolithic ideology" (*yuil sasang*) of the DPRK; the frequent use of mass mobilization and "speed campaigns" in large-scale economic projects; and a foreign policy that emphasized independence and the delegitimation of South Korea, while at the same time attempting to maintain support from both the USSR and China throughout the sometimes-acrimonious Sino-Soviet split.

Ch'ŏllima, Chuch'e and the Cult of Kim Il Sung

By 1958, the DPRK was on a "high tide of socialist construction,"[24] and North Korea launched a new campaign that became the primary symbol of economic, political and cultural development until the 1970s, enshrined in the

22 The North Korean cooperative movement was likely influenced by the People's Commune campaign being launched simultaneously in China, especially in the second stage of amalgamation. However, the DPRK had begun the formation of large cooperatives well before the commune movement, and did not simply copy the Chinese model, as some observers have suggested. See Chong-Sik Lee, "Land Reform, Collectivisation and the Peasants in North Korea," *China Quarterly* 4 (Apr.–Jun. 1963), 76.
23 Chung, *North Korean Economy*, 62.
24 Glenn D. Paige, "North Korea and the Emulation of Russian and Chinese Behavior," in A. Doak Barnett (ed.), *Communist Strategies in Asia: A Comparative Analysis of Governments and Parties* (New York: Praeger, 1963), 242.

DPRK constitution between 1972 and 1992.[25] The purpose of this campaign was "socialist construction," the slogan was *chuch'e*, the technique was mass mobilization through both material and moral incentives, and the symbol was *Ch'ŏllima*, or the "Thousand-*li* Winged Horse." The Ch'ŏllima movement was first announced at the December 1956 plenum of the KWP Central Committee but not put into practice until 1958.[26] It bore a resemblance to both the Soviet Stakhanovite movement of the 1930s and the Chinese Great Leap Forward of the late 1950s, although the latter was declared after Ch'ŏllima and was more of a coterminous influence than a direct inspiration. Workers in both agriculture and industry were exhorted to overfulfill their quotas, for which individuals would be decorated with the Order of Ch'ŏllima and particularly successful groups would be designated Ch'ŏllima Work Teams; an outstanding few received Double Ch'ŏllima awards.

The economic impact of Ch'ŏllima is difficult to assess. It certainly seems to have been less disruptive than the Great Leap Forward, which resulted in disaster and famine for millions. The North Korean economy performed well through the early 1960s, and the Five-Year Plan was declared fulfilled a year ahead of schedule in 1960. Whether or not this was the direct result of the Ch'ŏllima movement, the DPRK declared the movement a great success, and by 1961 2 million workers were said to be members of Ch'ŏllima Work Teams.[27] One favorable assessment of the movement credits Ch'ŏllima for its balance between industry and agriculture and its emphasis on collective performance and innovation.[28]

In the early 1960s Ch'ŏllima was supplemented by two new models of economic management, both allegedly the creation of Kim Il Sung: the Chŏngsalli Method in agriculture and the Taean Work System in industry. Both were "mass-line" techniques which attempted to devolve decision-making to the local level and incorporate workers into the management process.[29] Economic administration was partly shifted from the central

25 Ryu Kiljae, "The 'Ch'ŏllima Movement' and Socialist Economic Construction Campaigns: Focusing on Comparison to the Stakhanovite Movement and the 'Great Leap Forward,'" in Ch'oe Ch'ŏngho et al., *Pukhan sahoejuûi kônsôl ûi chôngch'i kyôngje* [The Political Economy of North Korean Socialist Construction] (Seoul: Kyungnam University Far East Institute, 1993), 75. The 1972 constitution referred to the Chŏllima movement as the "general line [*ch'ong nosôn*] of socialist construction in the DPRK."
26 Robert A. Scalapino and Chong-Sik Lee, *Communism in Korea*, vol. I, *The Movement* (Berkeley: University of California Press, 1972), 540.
27 Ibid., 575. 28 Brun and Hersh, *Socialist Korea*, 187.
29 See Chŏng Sang-hun (Joseph S. Chung), "Nongŏp kwa sanŏp kwalli ch'eje: Ch'ŏngsalli pangbŏp kwa Taean saŏp ch'eje" [Agricultural and Industrial Management Systems: Ch'ŏngsalli Method and Taean Work System], in Ch'oe Ch'ŏngho et al., *Pukhan sahoejuûi kônsôl*, 81–104.

government to the county (*kun*), and the input of local farmers and factory workers was brought into a collective leadership system through local party committees. Cadres were sent to provincial and county workplaces to propagate government policies as well as elicit comments and suggestions from local workers.[30] Kim Il Sung himself was the model of this practice, regularly going to farms and factories throughout the DPRK for well-publicized "on-the-spot guidance" tours.

In the course of the 1960s, the term *"chuch'e,"* meaning literally "self-mastery" but often translated as "independence" or "self-reliance," became canonized as the foremost principle of DPRK ideology. Kim Il Sung's first-known reference to *chuch'e* was in 1955, although later North Korean texts claimed the term originated in Kim's guerrilla days of the 1930s. Significantly, Kim's original *"chuch'e"* speech was concerned with ideological work.[31] *Chuch'e* has been the preeminent expression of North Korea's emphasis on the ideological over the material, thought over matter, super-structure over base. Portrayed as a supplement to and improvement on Marxism-Leninism, *chuch'e* in fact reverses the historical materialism of Marx; rather than superstructural transformation resulting from changes in relations of production, in North Korea's official ideology "thought revolution" is the first step in transforming individuals and society, out of which comes "correct" political organization and finally increased economic production.[32] As a philosophical concept and political principle *chuch'e* has been extremely flexible, at times nearly indefinable, but at its core *chuch'e* reflects a deep sense of Korean nationalism and "putting Korea first." Kim's 1955 speech emphasized the need to know Korea's unique history, geography and culture in order "to educate our people in a way that suits them and to inspire in them an ardent love for their native place and their motherland."[33] Everyone must "have *chuch'e*," which does not mean that individuals themselves are "self-reliant" (although the term may imply flexibility and adaptation to local circumstances), but on the con-trary that individuals submerge their separate identities into the collective subjectivity of the Korean nation.

30 Ilpyong J. Kim, *Communist Politics in North Korea* (New York: Praeger, 1975), 85–86.
31 Kim Il Sung, "On Eliminating Dogmatism and Formalism and Establishing Juche in Ideological Work," in *Kim Il Sung Works*, vol. IX (Pyongyang: Foreign Languages Publishing House, 1982), 395–417.
32 Pak Hyŏngjung, *Pukhanjŏk hyŏnsang ŭi yŏn'gu: Pukhan sahoejuŭi kŏnsŏl ŭi chŏngch'i kyŏngjehak* [The North Korean Phenomenon: The Political Economy of North Korea's Socialist Construction] (Seoul: Yŏn'gusa, 1994), 172.
33 Kim, "On Eliminating Dogmatism and Formalism," 396.

The term itself is not unique to the DPRK; Koreans from the early twentieth century nationalist Shin Ch'aeho to South Korean president Park Chung Hee have used the term *chuch'e* to refer to the national subjectivity, political independence and self-identity of the Korean people, often in contradistinction to *sadae* or "serving the great," the traditional Confucian expression for Korea's subordinate relationship to China that came to be roundly condemned by nationalist intellectuals.[34] In the DPRK of the 1960s *chuch'e* became the key concept for an increasing range of activities, and was portrayed as an original North Korean contribution to revolutionary ideology as well as a model for other emerging Third World societies to emulate. At a speech in Indonesia in 1965, during his first official visit outside the communist bloc, Kim Il Sung declared, "Juche in ideology, independence in politics, self-sustenance in the economy and self-defense in national defense – this is the stand our Party has consistently adhered to."[35] In 1972 *chuch'e* became enshrined in the DPRK constitution as the guiding principle of politics.

Simultaneous with the elevation of *chuch'e* to the commanding heights of North Korean ideology was the explosive growth of the cult of personality surrounding Kim Il Sung. Kim had been revered before, but by the late 1960s his words, deeds and guerrilla experiences (real and fictitious) had become the overwhelming, indeed nearly exclusive, subject of mass education and indoctrination. This partly reflected the unchallengeable position of power Kim and his fellow Manchurian guerrilla veterans had achieved. By the Fourth Party Congress in September 1961, the KWP Central Committee was completely dominated by Kim and others associated with the anti-Japanese struggle in Manchuria, with only three members of the Yan'an group and one "Soviet-Korean" (the Kim loyalist Nam Il) remaining.[36] The Manchurian guerrilla experience was held up as the sole legitimate liberation movement during the colonial period, and North Koreans were taught to emulate this heroic struggle and be like the guerrillas – incorruptible, self-sacrificing, nationalistic and devoted to the Great Leader.[37]

34 See Michael Robinson, "National Identity and the Thought of Shin Ch'aeho: *Sadaejuûi* and *Chuch'e* in History and Politics," *Journal of Korean Studies* 5 (1984), 121–42.
35 Kim Il Sung, *On Juche in Our Revolution* (Pyongyang: Foreign Languages Publishing House, 1977), 428–29.
36 Wada, *Kin Nichisei to Manshu konichi senso* [Kim Il Sung and the Anti-Japanese War in Manchuria] (Tokyo: Heibonsha, 1992), 372–73.
37 Yi Chongsôk, *Chosôn Nodongdang yôn'gu: chido sasang kwa kujo pyônghwa rûl chungsimûro* [A Study of the Korean Workers' Party: Focusing on Ruling Thought and Structural Change] (Seoul: Yôksa pip'yôngsa, 1995), 291.

The term *Suryŏng* ("Great Leader") for Kim Il Sung, though it had been in occasional use since the 1940s, became widespread during this time.[38] Previously, the term had been generally reserved for Stalin as the Great Leader of the world communist movement; in part, the appellation of Kim as *Suryŏng* reflected North Korea's independent socialist line. More fundamentally, North Korea's new "monolithic ideology" stressed the absolute identification of the DPRK state, the Workers' Party and the person of Kim Il Sung, the latter embodying the whole nation and society as the paramount leader. Everything associated with Kim became an object of popular study and veneration: his speeches, his revolutionary past, his birthplace of Mangyôngdae near Pyongyang and his family. Kim's mother Kang Pansôk, for example, was upheld for the first time as a "model of womanhood" in 1967.[39] Similarly, his father's "revolutionary activities" during the colonial period were venerated from the late 1960s onward.[40]

North Korea and the World

After the heady years of rapid reconstruction, economic expansion and quota overfulfillment in the 1950s and early 1960s, the North Korean economy slowed down markedly in the late 1960s. The 1961–67 Seven-Year Plan was the first economic plan to fail to meet its deadline. In 1967 the plan was extended to 1970, becoming a de facto ten-year plan. Like other centralized command economies, North Korea had difficulty shifting from extensive to intensive growth and to the demands of a more complex economy, facing the common problems of bottlenecks and structural inefficiencies. Much of the spectacular economic growth of the post-Korean War years was a result of economic reconstruction and the continued movement of people from farms to factories in the early stages of industrialization. While a planned economy could be quite successful at this early stage of development, the very success of North Korea's early growth made it difficult for the DPRK to alter its policies for a more complex stage of economic development.[41] The DPRK lost outside assistance by the sharp reduction in foreign aid after 1958 and

---

38 For an early reference to Kim as *Suryŏng*, see Han Chaedôk, *Kim Ilsông changgun kaesôn'gi* [Record of the Triumphant Return of General Kim Il Sung] (Pyongyang: Minju Chosônsa, 1947), 8.
39 Yi Chongsôk, *Chosôn Nodongdang yôn'gu*, 302.
40 Kim's "revolutionary lineage"' had appeared in North Korean texts at least as early as the Korean War, but not as extensively or as systematically. See RG 242, SA 2009 8/32, *Chôngch'i kyobon* (n.p., n.d., probably 1950 or 1951), 1–2.
41 Chung, *North Korean Economy*, 99.

strained relations with the Soviet Union in the early 1960s. Its policy of self-reliance and hostility toward the United States, Japan and other Western countries hindered the DPRK from establishing strong economic ties to the capitalist West.

Another source of economic slowdown was the diversion of civilian resources to the military after the mid 1960s. Between 1965 and 1967 military expenditure nearly tripled, to 30 percent of total government expenditure.[42] The relative balance between heavy industry on the one hand, and light industry and consumer goods on the other, shifted markedly in favor of heavy industry and defense. Critics of this move, who advocated slower and more balanced growth, were removed from power in the last major DPRK purge of 1968–70.[43] After 1963, the DPRK stopped releasing economic production figures.

DPRK planners, emboldened by the success of the reconstruction years after the Korean War, had overestimated the potential for economic growth in the 1960s. Nevertheless, North Korea was hardly an economic basket case by the beginning of the 1970s. Outside estimates put North Korea's GNP growth from 1961 to 1967 at a respectable 8.6 percent overall.[44] By the 1970s the DPRK had become nearly self-sufficient in energy and food, with an annual increase in grain production well ahead of population growth, according to CIA estimates.[45] Though falling behind South Korea, the DPRK's economy grew at an estimated 7.4 percent annually between 1965 and 1976, while South Korean growth approached 11 percent.[46]

A number of outside factors, including the economic rise of South Korea, the 1965 Japan–South Korean normalization treaty and the acceleration of US military involvement in Vietnam, contributed to a new mood of militarization in North Korea. Kim Il Sung spoke of the need "to turn the whole country into an impregnable fortress" to combat "American imperialism."[47] Equal weight was to be given to economic development and military preparedness. In the central government, military figures rose to prominence, including Oh Chin'u, who became army chief of staff and later defense minister. Hostility toward South Korea shifted from rhetoric

42 Byung Chul Koh, *The Foreign Policy Systems of North and South Korea* (Berkeley: University of California Press, 1984), 59.
43 Kim, *Communist Politics*, 87.   44 Scalapino and Lee, *Communism in Korea*, 617.
45 Tai-sung An, *North Korea in Transition: From Dictatorship to Dynasty* (Westport, CT: Greenwood Press, 1983), 86, 93.
46 Ralph N. Clough, *Embattled Korea: The Rivalry for International Support* (Boulder: Westview Press, 1987), 87.
47 Ibid., 50.

to action, indicating perhaps a North Korean attempt to emulate the North Vietnamese example of internal subversion. In 1968 several teams of North Korean guerrillas infiltrated the South, including a group of some thirty commandos who came within a few hundred meters of the South Korean presidential palace in a failed attempt to assassinate Park Chung Hee on 21 January. Two days later, on 23 January, the DPRK Navy seized the USS *Pueblo* off the North Korean coast, bringing tensions with the United States to their highest level since the Korean War.

Probably the most sensitive foreign-policy issue from the 1960s until the 1980s was North Korea's relations with China and the USSR in light of the tense – at times openly hostile – relationship between the two communist giants. During the roughly thirty years of Sino-Soviet estrangement, from the withdrawal of Soviet technicians from China in 1960 to Gorbachev's visit to Beijing in 1989, no other small communist country managed so skillfully to balance between the two. North Korea was able to maintain political, economic and military ties with both countries throughout most of this period because of its strategic value to the USSR and China, neither of whom was willing to lose the DPRK to the other camp. For its part, North Korea insisted on an independent course: Unlike Vietnam, the DPRK never joined the Soviet-dominated Council for Mutual Economic Assistance; unlike Albania, North Korea was never excommunicated from the communist bloc. On the whole, however, North Korea was politically and ideologically closer to China, while the Soviet Union was more important as a military ally and source of economic assistance. Except for a period of mutual slandering and border clashes in the late 1960s, Sino-North Korean relations have been portrayed by both countries as more cordial and "fraternal," and Soviet–North Korean relations as somewhat cooler and more distant. China and North Korea shared a common East Asian culture, intertwined histories, a revolutionary leadership with roots in anti-Japanese guerrilla struggle and a similar world outlook opposed to Western imperialism in general and the United States in particular. Kim Il Sung himself had spent many of his formative years on Chinese territory, fought alongside Chinese soldiers as a member of the Chinese Communist Party and spoke Mandarin. Not least, thousands of Chinese troops had lost their lives during the Korean War, creating what the North Koreans and Chinese called a "friendship sealed in blood," a relationship "as close as lips and teeth." The USSR conspicuously had failed to make such a commitment to defending the DPRK, and the Soviet–North Korean bond was never as intimate.

When the Sino-Soviet rift first became public in 1960, North Korea attempted to remain neutral, and for a time benefited from Chinese and Soviet competition for North Korea's support. In October 1960 the USSR agreed to defer repayment of North Korean loans and offered scientific and technical assistance. In the summer of 1961 the DPRK signed treaties of "Friendship, Cooperation and Mutual Assistance" with both the USSR and China.[48] However, by 1962 North Korea showed signs of "leaning toward" China, with a concomitant decline in relations with the USSR. North Korea supported China in its border dispute with India, by then an ally of the USSR, and indirectly criticized Soviet "revisionism" and accommodation with the West (albeit in milder language than China). Ch'oe Yonggôn visited Beijing in June 1963, for which China reciprocated by sending Liu Shaoqi to Pyongyang later that year, and the two men spoke glowingly of the friendship between their nations. Finally, in June 1964 Pyongyang held the Second Asian Economic Seminar, at which China and North Korea dominated the proceedings, while the Soviet Union and India were visibly excluded. The event became a platform for espousing national economic self-reliance – the Chinese and North Korean model – and criticizing the USSR. The seminar was sharply attacked by the Soviets.[49]

After the fall of Nikita Khrushchev in 1964, toward whom the North Korean leadership had held mixed feelings at best since the late 1950s, Soviet–North Korean relations improved again as Sino-North Korean relations deteriorated. Soviet premier Aleksei Kosygin visited Pyongyang in February 1965, the first high-ranking Soviet official to arrive since 1961, and the DPRK's criticism of the USSR and "modern revisionism" diminished. By mid 1966, North Korea and the USSR had signed new agreements on trade and military assistance.[50] Meanwhile, China descended into the isolation and chaos of the Great Proletarian Cultural Revolution and its relations with most of the outside world, North Korea included, became militant and hostile. China snubbed North Korea diplomatically at the twentieth-anniversary celebrations of Korean liberation in Pyongyang in August 1965, and the Chinese press began to accuse North Korea of collusion with the "revisionists" and a lapse of revolutionary faith.[51] By the end of the 1960s Red

48 Chin O. Chung, *P'yôngyang Between Peking and Moscow: North Korea's Involvement in the Sino-Soviet Dispute, 1958–1975* (Tuscaloosa: University of Alabama Press, 1978), 55–57.
49 Ibid., 100–04.
50 Wayne Kiyosaki, *North Korea's Foreign Relations: The Politics of Accommodation, 1945–1975* (New York: Praeger, 1976), 78.
51 Ibid., 71.

Guard posters in Beijing labeled Kim Il Sung a "fat revisionist" and "Korea's Khrushchev"; according to Western sources, armed skirmishes occurred on the disputed Sino-North Korean border at Mt. Paektu.[52]

By the end of 1969 Sino-North Korea relations were on the mend, signified by Ch'oe Yonggôn's visit to Beijing for the twentieth anniversary celebrations of the People's Republic of China (PRC) in October. Zhou Enlai visited Pyongyang in turn in April 1970, the first high-ranking Chinese official to do so since 1963. The PRC and the DPRK once again exchanged ambassadors, and relations were normalized.[53] North Korea would remain relatively balanced between (or at least never again estranged from) both China and the USSR until the end of the 1980s and the beginning of the 1990s. At that time, first Moscow and then Beijing moved toward closer ties with South Korea over the strenuous objections of the DPRK.

Toward Dynastic Socialism

The problem of political succession has been acute in communist states, as in other authoritarian systems. Kim Il Sung seemed determined to avoid the struggle for power and lapse into "revisionism" that had, in his view, been so detrimental to the Soviet Union after Stalin's death. Over the course of the 1970s, while China experienced its own succession crisis with the death of Mao, Kim's eldest son Kim Jong Il was gradually built up as the leading, and finally only, candidate for succession to top leadership in the DPRK. With Kim Il Sung's death in 1994 North Korea became the only socialist state to transfer leadership from father to son. In 2011, after Kim Jong Il's death, power was transferred to the third generation.

As early as 1963 Kim Il Sung had complained of the lack of revolutionary fervor among North Korea's youth.[54] As the 1970s began Kim spoke more openly of the need for a generational transfer of power. For a time, it seemed that Kim Yôngju, younger brother of Kim Il Sung and chief DPRK negotiator for North–South talks in the early 1970s, was the leading candidate for succession. However, Kim Yôngju's rapid ascent abruptly ended in 1975, when he was removed from the Politburo and faded into obscurity, until

---

52 Chung, *P'yôngyang Between Peking and Moscow*, 130.
53 Kiyosaki, *North Korea's Foreign Relations*, 84.
54 Chong-Sik Lee, "Evolution of the Korean Workers' Party and the Rise of Kim Chông-il," in Robert A. Scalapino and Chun-yǒp Kim, *North Korea Today: Strategic and Domestic Issues* (2nd edn., Berkeley: Institute of East Asian Studies, University of California, 1983), 71.

his sudden reemergence as vice-president shortly before Kim Il Sung's death.[55] By the late 1970s Kim Jong Il had been unquestionably designated successor to the Great Leader.

The first clear indication of Kim Jong Il's rise to prominence was his election as secretary in charge of organization, propaganda and agitation in the Central Committee of the Korean Workers' Party in 1973. He was said to be personally directing the Three Revolutions Campaign, the DPRK's new mass-mobilization movement to revolutionize ideology, technology and culture. The Three Revolutions Campaign sent teams of twenty to fifty young party cadres to factories and farms to discuss with and guide local leaders.

In 1974 the North Korean media began to refer to a mysterious "Party Center" (*tang chung'ang*) said to be in charge of much of the day-to-day politics of the DPRK and second only to Kim Il Sung in power. At the Sixth Congress of the Korean Workers' Party in October 1980, this Party Center was revealed to be Kim Jong Il, and the younger Kim attained positions in the Secretariat, the Politburo and the Military Commission. Only Kim Il Sung held higher positions in all three bodies. Kim Jong Il had clearly "come out" as the number-two leader in North Korea.[56]

The choice of Kim Il Sung's son as successor evoked disdain and ridicule from the DPRK's critics and less-than-enthusiastic endorsement from its allies. The North Koreans justified the choice of Kim Jong Il as the only candidate able to fulfill the qualities of leadership succession: youth, absolute loyalty to Kim Il Sung, thorough familiarity with Kim Il Sung's ideas, and superior intellect and ability.[57] Above all Kim Jong Il represented continuity and stability for a system increasingly threatened by events in the outside world and changes within the communist bloc. Over the next fourteen years the two Kims became in effect joint leaders of the country. Following Kim Il Sung's death in July 1994, the younger Kim assumed the chairmanship of the National Defense Council in addition to his position as general secretary of the Korean Workers' Party. The position of president, however, was reserved for the deceased Kim Il Sung, who was named "Eternal President" in 1998. As the twentieth century came to an end,

55 Shim Jae Hoon, "Kith and Kim: President's Family to the Fore in Major Reshuffle," *Far Eastern Economic Review* (23 Dec. 1993), 25.
56 Morgan E. Clippinger, "Kim Chông-il in the North Korean Mass Media: A Study of Semi-Esoteric Communication," *Asian Survey* 21, 3 (Mar. 1981), 289–309.
57 Byung Chul Koh, "The Cult of Personality and the Succession Issue," in C. I. Eugene Kim and B. C. Koh (eds.), *Journey to North Korea: Personal Perceptions* (Berkeley: Institute of East Asian Studies, University of California, 1983), 34–36.

North Korea completed its transition from a communist state modeled on the Soviet Union to a full-fledged family regime that barely acknowledged its Marxist-Leninist origins.

After his own death in December 2011, Kim Jong Il was succeeded by his son Kim Jong Un. Just as his father Kim Il Sung had been elevated to "Eternal President," Kim Jong Il was posthumously named "Eternal General Secretary." North Korea in the twenty-first century is a unique family state, led in theory by two dead men and one living one, in an unbroken dynastic succession. The DPRK had emphasized autonomy and independence over socialism and internationalism since the 1960s, and for all its weaknesses and flaws managed to survive the collapse of global communism, confrontation with the United States and South Korea, and international isolation under the nationalistic, inward-looking leadership of the Kim family line.

Bibliographical Essay

Korean Communist Movements

Korean communism has diverse and multiple origins in Russia, China and Korea, and there are few studies covering the entire Korean communist movement – or rather movements, in the plural – predating the founding of the Democratic People's Republic of Korea in 1948. Part of the reason for this paucity is the remoteness and diversity of these movements, which – unlike the Chinese and Vietnamese movements – had almost no connection to the West. A history of Korean communism before 1948 would have to engage with material in multiple languages across far-flung places in Russia, Manchuria, the Korean peninsula and Japan. The most comprehensive works in English are now a generation old: Dae-sook Suh, *The Korean Communist Movement, 1918–1948* (Princeton: Princeton University Press, 1967), and Robert Scalapino and Chong-Sik Lee, *Communism in Korea*, vol. I, *The Movement* (Berkeley: University of California Press, 1972).

North Korean scholarship on the subject is highly biased, to put it mildly, focusing overwhelmingly on Kim Il Sung's guerrilla activities in Manchuria (northeast China) in the 1930s and early 1940s, which were not insignificant but hardly central to the Korean communist movement at the time. South Korean scholarship was once equally biased, although in the opposite direction, but since political liberalization in the late 1980s serious research on Korean communism and the history of North Korea has vastly increased quantitatively and improved qualitatively. Among the notable South Korean studies of Korean communism is Sim Chi-hyŏn, *Chosŏn kongsanjuŭijadŭl ŭi insik kwa nolli* [Understanding and Logic of Korean Communists] (Seoul: Paeksan Sŏdang, 2015). The best work on Kim Il Sung's Manchurian guerrilla activities is by the Japanese historian Wada Haruki. Wada's *Kin Nichisei to Manshū kōnichi sensō* [Kim Il Sung and the Anti-Japanese War in Manchuria] (Tokyo: Heibonsha, 1992) has been translated into Korean but not yet into English. A rare first-hand account of Korean communist activity in China in English is Nym Wales (Helen Foster Snow) and Kim San, *Song of Ariran: A Korean Communist in the Chinese Revolution* (New York: Ramparts, 1972), now unfortunately out of print.

The Formation of the DPRK and the Korean War

The period of the founding of the DPRK in the late 1940s and the Korean War of 1950–53 are the areas in which the greatest amount of new material has emerged since the 1980s, with the declassification of North Korean documents captured by the United States in the Korean War, the opening of archives from the former Soviet Union, and the publication of memoirs and document collections from the People's Republic of China. Bruce Cumings's *The Origins of the Korean War*, 2 vols. (Princeton: Princeton University Press, 1981–90), was the first study to make use of these "captured enemy documents" (known collectively by their National Archives designation as Record Group [RG] 242), although his work deals with more than just North Korea. Charles Armstrong's *The North Korean Revolution, 1945–1950* (Ithaca: Cornell University Press, 2003) and Suzy Kim's *Everyday Life in the North Korean Revolution, 1945–1950* (Ithaca, NY: Cornell University Press, 2013) rely extensively on RG 242 to explore the political and social history of the early DPRK. Andrei Lankov's *From Stalin to Kim Il Sung: The Formation of the North Korea, 1945–1960* (New Brunswick, NJ: Rutgers University Press, 2002) covers the early history of the DPRK mainly based on Russian-language sources.

Major studies of the Korean War relying on Soviet and Chinese materials include Sergei Goncharov, John W. Lewis and Xue Litai, *Uncertain Partners: Stalin, Mao and the Korean War* (Stanford: Stanford University Press, 1993); Chen Jian, *China's Road to the Korean War: The Making of the Sino-American Confrontation* (New York: Columbia University Press, 1994); and Shen Zhihua, *Mao, Stalin and the Korean War: Trilateral Communist Relations in the 1950s* (London: Routledge, 2012). The history of the DPRK and the Korean War continues to be revised based on newly available documents from the Soviet Union, Eastern Europe, China, South Korea and other countries. Many thousands of such documents have been collected and translated by the Cold War International History Project (CWIHP) at the Woodrow Wilson Center for Scholars in Washington, DC. The North Korea International Documentation Project, a spin-off of CWIHP (www.wilsoncenter.org/pro gram/north-korea-international-documentation-project), has become the central clearing house for North Korea-related documents.

North Korea After the Korean War

The DPRK is rightly known as one of the most closed societies on earth, and there is little access to domestic primary sources for the post-Korean War period. Balázs Szalontai's *Kim Il Sung in the Khrushchev Era: Soviet–DPRK Relations and the Roots of North Korean Despotism, 1953–1964* (Stanford: Stanford University Press, 2006) relies mostly on Hungarian documents; Andrei Lankov's *The Real North Korea: Life and Politics in the Failed Stalinist Utopia* (New York: Oxford University Press, 2013) is based largely on first-hand observation, combined with work in the Soviet materials; Charles Armstrong's *Tyranny of the Weak: North Korea and the World, 1950–1992* (Ithaca: Cornell University Press, 2013) brings research in various post-communist archives to bear on the study of North Korean foreign relations. Dae-Sook Suh's *Kim Il Sung: The North Korean Leader* (New York: Columbia University Press, 1988) remains the most thorough biography of North Korea's founding leader, and *inter alia* a useful history of the DPRK to the late 1980s. Notable studies of North Korean politics, economy and society include Stephan Haggard and Marcus Noland, *Famine in North Korea: Markets, Aid, and Reform* (New York: Columbia University Press, 2007); Heonik Kwon and Byung-Ho Chung, *North Korea: Beyond Charismatic Politics* (Lanham, MD: Rowman & Littlefield, 2012); and Hazel Smith, *North Korea: Markets and Military Rule* (Cambridge: Cambridge University Press, 2015).

Finally, recent scrutiny of North Korea's human rights practices (or lack thereof) by the United Nations, along with a surge in defectors leaving the DPRK since the 1990s, has led to a new interest in human rights in the DPRK. The UN Commission of Inquiry Report is the most extensive review of the subject to date: www.ohchr.org/EN/HRBodies/HRC/CoIDPRK/Pages/Co mmissionInquiryonHRinDPRK.aspx. David Hawk, *The Hidden Gulag: Exposing North Korea's Prison Camps* (Washington, DC: Committee for Human Rights in

North Korea, 2012), and Robert Collins, *Pyongyang Republic: North Korea's Capital of Human Rights Denial* (Washington, DC: Committee for Human Rights in North Korea, 2016), also deal extensively with North Korea's human rights violations, particularly its treatment of political prisoners. Whether these issues are aspects of "Korean communism" may depend on whether North Korea today is still to be considered a communist state or a *sui generis* form of family dictatorship far removed from its Marxist-Leninist origins.

19

Indonesian Communism: The Perils of the Parliamentary Path

JOHN ROOSA

When 27-year-old D. N. Aidit took over the leadership of the Communist Party of Indonesia (Partai Komunis Indonesia, PKI) in January 1951, the party was a semi-clandestine organization. The Republic of Indonesia, which had just gained independence from Dutch colonial rule two years earlier, was under the control of anti-communists. The president and vice-president of the new republic, Sukarno and Mohammad Hatta, had ordered the brutal repression of the party in 1948, in the midst of their war against the Dutch, and continued to view the PKI as a pernicious internal enemy. The meetings of the PKI's Central Committee, such as the one that chose Aidit to be the chairman, were held in secret locations, with attendees taking elaborate precautions to avoid being followed.

It would have been understandable if Aidit had opted for an armed struggle against the Republic of Indonesia. Some party members who had fought against the Dutch from 1945 to 1949 still held onto their guns. But Aidit did not support an armed struggle. He did not even support an armed struggle after August 1951 when the government attacked the PKI yet again, arresting about 2,000 members. His adamant rejection of armed struggle was anomalous in the region; every other communist party in Southeast Asia – in Burma, Malaya, the Philippines and Vietnam – was engaged in guerrilla warfare in the late 1940s and early 1950s. It is remarkable that Aidit and his fellow party leaders – the oldest of whom was thirty – formulated a distinct strategic vision for the party. They neither blindly followed tradition nor imitated the party line of another communist party.

This chapter examines the origins of the PKI's legal, parliamentary strategy in the early 1950s, the strategy's spectacular success over the 1950s and early 1960s, and its ultimate demise in the horrific violence of 1965–66 when hundreds of thousands of unarmed members of the PKI were slaughtered by the Indonesian army. The PKI had a unique trajectory among communist parties in the latter half of the twentieth century. It rose close to the summits of state power through above-ground struggles, grew into the largest communist party in the world outside the USSR and the People's Republic of China (PRC) and then quickly collapsed. Every aspect of that trajectory has been puzzling. Why did the PKI adopt a legal, parliamentary strategy in the first place? How did it expect to defend itself? Why were so many Indonesians attracted to the party? How did party activists adapt Marxism-Leninism and the paradigms from the Russian and Chinese Revolutions so that they made sense to ordinary Indonesians? What influence did the USSR and the PRC have on the PKI? How could such a large organization with millions of supporters be destroyed so quickly and thoroughly, with so little resistance? Did not the PKI leaders understand their vulnerability and prepare some way of protecting themselves? Was the slaughter proof that the legal, parliamentary strategy was mistaken, that the success of fourteen years of mass mobilization was illusory? Or was it proof that Aidit's particular implementation of that strategy was mistaken?

The scholarly literature on the PKI, largely based on the party's publications, is very good at documenting the public face of the PKI. The twists and turns of the party line have been carefully chronicled. The literature has been less insightful in answering the questions that pertain to the undocumented sides of the party – such as the motivations of rank-and-file members – and the clandestine side of the party – such as its secret dealings with military officers. Researchers have found it difficult to study these sides of the party given that the army killed so many party leaders in 1965–66 and has continued to terrorize the survivors up to the present day. Many former members have felt slightly freer to discuss the PKI's history since the fall of the Suharto dictatorship in 1998, but they remain reluctant to narrate their pre-1965 political activism. With the recent publication of oral histories, memoirs and formerly classified documents from Soviet and Chinese archives, researchers are now in a better position to reassess the history of the party.

Origins of the "New Road" Strategy

The PKI was founded in Jakarta (then called Batavia) in May 1920 as the first communist party in Asia. The founders, largely Dutch citizens living in the colony and Dutch-educated Javanese men, had been active in the trade union movement and campaigns to make the colonial state more democratic. They had been in contact with the social-democratic parties of Europe during the 1910s and decided to affiliate with the Comintern because of their perception of the Russian Revolution as a new, more effective paradigm for gaining state power.[1] By organizing a bloc within a large political organization for Muslims (Sarekat Islam) in the early 1920s, the PKI was able to recruit many new members, including devout Muslims. Some key party organizers thought of Islam as a form of communism, as a religion of the oppressed fighting against capitalism.[2] The PKI's delegates to the Comintern, such as Tan Malaka, argued against adopting an antagonistic policy toward pan-Islamism. Sukarno, who later became Indonesia's first president (1945–66), began his political career in the 1920s by proposing a *modus vivendi* between communism and Islam. The youthful nationalist leader, when trying to unite all anti-colonial tendencies, wrote a booklet titled *Nationalism, Islam and Marxism* (1926).[3]

The top state officials of the Dutch East Indies had allowed greater freedoms for "the natives" (*inlanders*) after World War I in the hopes of coopting them. Seeing the PKI call for revolution and organize a series of strikes, they decided to crack down on the party in 1925. The PKI leaders, captives of the paradigm of the Russian Revolution, saw no way of responding other than with a revolt. The Comintern urged the PKI not to revolt but its message from Moscow arrived too late. The revolt began in November 1926. Crowds of people in cities throughout Java and Sumatra besieged police stations and government offices. Islamic scholars played a key role by mobilizing their followers.[4] Lacking weapons and large numbers of people, the insurgents were quickly defeated. The colonial state arrested about 18,000 suspected PKI members and exiled 1,300 of them to a concentration camp, called Boven Digul, in the middle of the jungle on the island of Papua. Out of this defeat, however, came a kind of victory: The communists became national heroes for their assault on the colonial state and their fortitude in facing the repression. Their writings from Boven Digul, with stories of escape attempts and adventures of survival in the jungle, became bestsellers

1 Ruth McVey, *The Rise of Indonesian Communism* (Ithaca: Cornell University Press, 1965), 34–75.
2 Takashi Shiraishi, *An Age in Motion: Popular Radicalism in Java, 1912–1926* (Ithaca: Cornell University Press, 1990).
3 Soekarno [Sukarno], *Nationalism, Islam and Marxism*, trans. K. H. Warouw and P. D. Weldon (Ithaca: Cornell University, Modern Indonesia Project, 1970).
4 Michael Williams, *Communism, Religion and Revolt in Banten* (Athens, OH: University Center for International Studies, 1990).

back in Java.[5] While the communists were unable to organize in the 1930s – they were either in prison, in hiding or in exile – they gained a reputation as self-sacrificing patriots. The Dutch persecuted noncommunists as well. Even the conservative nationalist leader, Hatta, was sent to Boven Digul.

PKI members who had survived Dutch colonial rule were subjected to even more intense repression during the Japanese occupation from early 1942 to August 1945. Given the international communist movement's anti-fascism, Japanese military officers in Indonesia prioritized the hunting down of communists.[6] The remaining Boven Digul prisoners – some 300 of them – were safely out of reach; they were evacuated to Australia in 1943. But the PKI members still in Indonesia struggled to avoid being apprehended by Japan's secret police. The split between the communists and noncommunists widened as many among the latter, such as Sukarno and Hatta, became collaborators.

The communists were able to regroup only once Japan lost the war. After Sukarno and Hatta proclaimed the Republic of Indonesia on 17 August 1945, Indonesian communists scattered throughout the globe headed for Jakarta: The "Digulists" arrived from Australia and the exiles from Europe. Those who had been in hiding or in prison in Indonesia reemerged for party meetings. Still worried about being attacked by right-wing forces, they refused to work above ground immediately. As a result, the PKI did not become a single, unified party during the very years when the nationalist movement was rapidly expanding. Having spent the previous twenty years in an illegal organization, the communists had made a habit of disguising themselves as noncommunists. PKI supporters were deeply involved in the organizing of trade unions, peasant associations, youth groups and armed militias in the fight against the Dutch recolonization campaign in the latter half of the 1940s. But the PKI was more of an informal, fractious network than a unified party.[7]

To consolidate the different factions, Musso, who had led the party in the 1920s, returned from the USSR in August 1948 with a program he called the "New Road." The intention was to take the PKI into the open and wrest

5 Pramoedya Ananta Toer (ed.), *Cerita dari Digul* [Stories from Digul] (Jakarta: Kepustakaan Populer Gramedia, 2001).
6 Anton Lucas (ed.), *Local Opposition and Underground Resistance to the Japanese in Java, 1942–1945* (Melbourne: Centre of Southeast Asian Studies, Monash University, 1986).
7 Lembaga Sejarah PKI, *Manuskrip Sejarah 45 Tahun PKI, 1920–1965* [The Manuscript of the History of 45 Years of the PKI, 1920–1965] (Bandung: Ultimus, 2014), 249–76.

control of the nationalist movement from "bourgeois" politicians such as Sukarno and Hatta. It was Musso's misfortune to attempt this reorganization at a time when the tension between left-wing and right-wing groups in Java was reaching breaking point. The left was organizing militias and soldiers opposed to Hatta's decision to reduce the number of the republic's troops. PKI-led trade unions were organizing large-scale strikes at factories owned by the republic. Sukarno and Hatta, viewing the communists as traitors, decided in September 1948 to use an uprising in a city in East Java, Madiun, as an excuse to suppress them. Some militias and military units fought back, but the PKI was unprepared for the attack. Thousands of PKI supporters were killed and arrested. Most of the top PKI leaders were captured without a fight, though Musso, carrying a revolver, was shot dead after a lengthy gunfight with better-armed police.[8] The republic's military commander summarily executed eleven PKI leaders in December.[9]

Anti-communist writers have cultivated elaborate myths about the Madiun revolt as a "stab in the back."[10] In the history textbooks still used today in Indonesia, the PKI is cast as the aggressor and the republic as the hapless, unsuspecting victim. According to this storyline, the PKI acted on direct orders from Moscow, which, in accordance with Andrei Zhdanov's "two camps" line, was instigating a worldwide revolt against capitalist states. The timing of the communist revolts in India, Burma, the Philippines and Indonesia in 1948 led some analysts to conclude that they were all the result of a Soviet conspiracy. Ruth McVey rebutted this conspiracy theory years ago, and more recent research has confirmed her analysis.[11] The Russian scholar, Larissa Efimova, working from newly declassified Soviet documents, has concluded that Musso himself formulated the New Road strategy over the first half of 1948 on the basis of discussions and correspondence with the communist parties of China and the Netherlands, not just the Comintern.[12] Musso's strategy was very much *his* strategy.

---

8 Ibid., 295–96.
9 Harry Poeze, *Madiun 1948: PKI Bergerak* [Madiun 1948: The PKI in Motion] (Jakarta: KITLV and Obor, 2011), 255–303.
10 For example: Pusat Sejarah ABRI, *Bahaya Laten Komunisme di Indonesia: Penumpasan Pemberontakan PKI (1948)* [The Latent Danger of Communism in Indonesia: The Crushing of the PKI Revolt, 1948] (Jakarta: Pusat Sejarah ABRI, 1992).
11 Ruth T. McVey, *The Calcutta Conference and the Southeast Asian Uprisings* (Ithaca: Department of Far Eastern Studies, Cornell University, 1958).
12 Larissa Efimova, "Who Gave Instructions to the Indonesian Communist Leader Musso in 1948?," *Indonesia and the Malay World* 31, 90 (Jul. 2003), 171–89.

Ironically, the Republic of Indonesia won its independence in 1949 because of its war on the PKI. The republic's armed forces were unable to drive out the Dutch, despite having an overwhelming numerical superiority. But, by attacking the PKI, Sukarno and Hatta had proven their anti-communist credentials to US officials, some of whom had harbored doubts about the wisdom of bankrolling the Dutch recolonization campaign. Just at the moment when the Dutch were winning a decisive military victory, the Americans forced them to transfer power to the Indonesian nationalists.[13]

After the withdrawal of Dutch troops in December 1949, the communists, many of whom had gone underground, started reemerging and reorganizing the party. There was no new Musso to arrive from abroad with a program that could unite the different factions. Instead, the role of unifier this time was to be played by a group of youths who had joined the party in the 1940s and had no connection to the internal feuds that went back to the 1920s. Gaining their political experience during the anti-colonial struggle from 1945 to 1949, what was then known as the "Indonesian Revolution," they were able to connect the party to a new generation of nationalists. The youth (*pemuda*) played an outsized role in the Indonesian Revolution.[14] For the PKI to remain relevant in national politics, it had to be led by youths of the "1945 generation." As a product of a mass upsurge of many different social groups, these youths, unlike the communists of the 1920s, saw no need to marry communism with Islam and no need to conceal their identities as communists.

The core group that assumed control over the party during the course of 1950 consisted of D. N. Aidit, Lukman, Njoto and Sudisman. With diverse skills, they made a remarkably effective team. Aidit, as a student activist in Jakarta associated with the Free Indonesia Hostel at Menteng 31, had worked closely with the top nationalist leaders since 1945. He was known as a quick study and brilliant strategist who had dedicated himself to nationalist politics. His first two names – Dipa Nusantara (the Fortress of the Archipelago) – were names he gave himself, with expectations of greatness, much as Nguyen Sinh Cung had named himself Ho Chi Minh ("Ho, the Most Enlightened"). Lukman, the oldest among them at thirty, provided some continuity to the 1920s generation of communists; as the son of a PKI leader (who was a devout Muslim), he had spent part of

13 Robert McMahon, *Colonialism and Cold War: The United States and the Struggle for Indonesian Independence, 1945–1949* (Ithaca: Cornell University Press, 1981).
14 Benedict Anderson, *Java in a Time of Revolution: Occupation and Resistance, 1944–1946* (Ithaca: Cornell University Press, 1972).

his childhood in the prison camp of Boven Digul. Njoto was the most intelligent and bookish of the group. He was a naturally talented musician and an accomplished writer who appreciated fine art and literature. Sudisman had been the leader of the Socialist Youth (Pesindo), which had been one of the most important youth groups in the Indonesian Revolution. With impeccable self-control and a dignified demeanor, he became the party's secretary general, handling personnel issues. One reason the party did not suffer any splits from 1950 to 1965 was the cohesiveness of this team.

Aidit and his close comrades, elected leaders of the PKI in January 1951, strenuously argued against those PKI members who advocated an armed struggle like that waged by the Chinese communists. They argued that Indonesia, as an archipelago of islands, offered no place that could serve as a liberated zone. Any place used for concentrating the PKI's armed forces could be easily isolated and surrounded. There was no rear base, like Yan'an in China or the Viet Bac in Vietnam, that was adjacent to a neighboring country from which the PKI could obtain supplies. Moreover, the vast bulk of the PKI's supporters were on the island of Java, where there was no large upland or forested area.

For the new leadership under Aidit, there could be no imitation of the Chinese Revolution, just as there could be no return to the Bolshevik paradigm behind the 1926–27 urban insurrections. The PKI would have to forge its own path. Aidit was convinced that a legal, parliamentary strategy was viable in an independent Indonesia that was meant to be a constitutional democracy. Sukarno and Hatta, amid the post-Madiun repression of the PKI, did not ban the party, and the constitution of the new state made it difficult for them to place a blanket ban on any political party. For veteran PKI members, who had known only exile, prisons and summary executions for twenty-five years, and had just suffered another round of terror, Aidit's group was proposing a leap into uncharted territory. But Indonesia was a new nation-state that offered signs of hope.

In the parliament of the early 1950s, with its complicated constellation of political parties, the PKI found an ally in the Nationalist Party (Partai Nasionalis Indonesia, PNI) associated with Sukarno. The PNI needed the PKI's support to battle the right-wing Muslim party, Masjumi. When the Masjumi prime minister, Sukiman, ordered mass arrests of PKI members in August 1951, Aidit obtained the help of other political parties. The some 2,000 members who had been arrested were released without charge within months. The freer media of postcolonial Indonesia revealed the grounds for the arrests to have been fraudulent.[15] The repression of the PKI was not going to be as easy as it had been during the years of Dutch and Japanese colonialism.

The Growth of the PKI and Its Mass Organizations

In rebuilding the party according to Musso's New Road program in the early 1950s, the youthful quadrumvirate in the Politburo was committed to the idea of making the PKI the center of a "national front." The party would ally with a large variety of classes, including the "national bourgeoisie" (as opposed to the "comprador bourgeoisie"), to continue the fight against the vestiges of Dutch imperial rule – such as the massive, odious debt the Dutch had imposed on Indonesia as a precondition for independence – and the growing influence of the United States. The PKI, seeing Indonesia as "semi-colonial and semi-feudal," set its immediate task to be the defense of electoral democracy and democratic rights.[16]

The PKI faced a dilemma when expanding its membership: It wanted rapid growth but did not want to relax its strict selection process for membership. If the PKI quickly inducted millions of people, then it risked diluting the quality of the party's cadres. It was not easy to become a party member: One had to prove that one had organized some kind of action, like a strike or a demonstration. But if the PKI maintained strict criteria for membership, then the party's growth would be excruciatingly slow. The solution to the quantity-vs.-quality dilemma was to create two tiers. Following Musso's program of 1948, the PKI allied itself with a wide variety of "mass organizations" (*organisasi massa*) that represented different sectors of the population, such as workers, peasants, women, university students, artists, intellectuals and youth.

The PKI's relationship to these mass organizations was complicated. Only one – the People's Youth (Pemuda Rakjat) – was directly under the party. The others retained a great deal of autonomy. The party ensured that its personnel were among the top leaders and that resolutions at the

15 Siswoyo, *Siswoyo Dalam Pusaran Arus Sejarah Kiri: Memoar Anggota Sekretariat CC PKI* [Siswoyo in the Vortex of Left History: A Memoir of a PKI Central Committee Member] (Bandung: Ultimus, 2014), 118–19; Francisca Fanggidaej, *Memoar Perempuan Revolusioner* [A Revolutionary Woman's Memoir] (Yogyakarta: Galang Press, 2006), 179–84; Lembaga Sejarah PKI, *Manuskrip Sejarah 45*, 325–31.
16 The most important articulation of the party line was at the Fifth Congress of the PKI in 1954: *Kongres Nasional Ke-V Partai Komunis Indonesia* [Fifth National Congress of the Communist Party of Indonesia] (Jakarta: Yayasan Pembaruan, 1954).

periodic conferences were in accordance with the party line. For all other matters, the party did not intervene. Indeed, for the party's national front strategy to be effective, the PKI leadership had to allow the mass organizations to operate according to the basic nationalist principles that many noncommunists supported. These organizations did not insist on ideological conformity; members were not required to support the PKI.

In the early 1950s, the party, rather than dominating the trade unions, was greatly dependent upon them, especially the Railway Workers' Union, which was the oldest and wealthiest union.[17] The PKI had controlled the leadership of the union since the 1920s. The Railway Workers' Union hall, built in the early 1950s near the main station in Jakarta, Manggarai, contained a large auditorium that served as the venue for all manner of left meetings, including PKI conferences, until it was confiscated by the military in late 1965. The expansion of the party membership in the early 1950s – from about 8,000 in 1951 to 165,000 in 1954 – appears to have been accomplished principally by recruiting people from the trade unions.[18]

PKI leaders, while serving the interests of organized workers, lamented the preponderance of urban members. For the Comintern and the PKI, the lesson of the 1926–27 revolts was that the PKI could not rely solely upon an urban base of support. Stalin's basic message to the party in the early 1950s was that organizing in the rural areas had to be prioritized, given the largely rural character of Indonesia.[19] The new party leadership under Aidit had some success extending the party's chapters into the countryside by amalgamating existing, locally based peasant unions, usually controlled by young activists from middle-class backgrounds.[20] The PKI claimed that the membership in its mass organization for peasants, Barisan Tani Indonesia (BTI), grew from 400,000 at the time of its founding in 1953 to 3.5 million in 1959. The party was also affiliated to a union for plantation workers, Sarbupri, that grew rapidly in the rural areas over the 1950s. The party tended to inflate figures but there was no doubt substantial growth.

17 Jafar Suryomenggolo, *Organising Under the Revolution: Unions and the State in Java, 1945–1948* (Singapore: NUS Press, 2013), 94–129.
18 Donald Hindley, *The Communist Party of Indonesia, 1951–1963* (Berkeley: University of California Press, 1966), 64, 70, 79.
19 Larissa Efimova, "Stalin and the New Program for the Communist Party of Indonesia," intro. Ruth T. McVey, *Indonesia* 91 (Apr. 2011), 131–64.
20 Syamsir (a former BTI leader), oral interviews, Bandung, 12 May 2000 and 31 Mar. 2001. All oral interviews cited in this essay were conducted by me; the recordings and transcripts are held at the Indonesian Institute of Social History in Jakarta.

One reason the PKI and the mass organizations were able to grow so quickly was the lack of competition. The other political parties were dominated by middle- and upper-class individuals who were uncomfortable mingling with poor people, traveling long distances on dirt roads and enduring the unhygienic conditions of slums. The PKI's activists, even those from middle-class backgrounds, were required to have an ethos of self-sacrifice. The activists lived among workers and peasants, many of them illiterate, who were desperate for a voice in politics and for support from powerful national organizations that could help them in their local struggles.

In the first elections for the national parliament in 1955, 6 million people voted for the PKI. The party won 16 percent of the vote, placing it only six points behind the party that won the plurality of votes – the PNI. The noncommunist parties were shocked, given that the party had been attacked only seven years earlier. The election results were proof of the behind-the-scenes, unheralded work that PKI activists had been doing since the 1920s among poor communities, especially in Java. Nearly all (89 percent) of the votes for the PKI came from Java, and the votes from the outer islands were largely from Javanese who were living there, such as the Javanese plantation workers in North Sumatra. In the elections for district-level governments in 1957, PKI placed first in many districts of Java and won 1 million more votes than it had won in the 1955 elections.

The PKI was not a generic political party campaigning for votes. It was like a Calvinist religious movement that addressed the ethics of everyday behavior. The communists entered poor communities, where alcoholism and gambling were pervasive among the men, and insisted that they reform their habits. The scholarly literature on the PKI has largely overlooked this side of the party. For many ordinary people, a very powerful aspect of the party was its strict disapproval of what it called the "Five Ms" – five sins that in the Javanese language all begin with the letter M: gambling, alcohol, drugs, womanizing and stealing. To be a proper party member, one could not even smoke cigarettes – in a country that was one of the largest producers of tobacco in the world. The PKI and its mass organizations wanted workers and peasants to be thrifty so they could take care of their families and avoid falling into the grip of moneylenders. The activists set an example by living simply.[21]

---

21 Suryaatmadja (member of the PKI's provincial leadership for West Java), oral interview, Cileungsi, 11 Jul. 2001; Sukamto (head of Pemuda Rakjat for Central Java), oral interviews, Yogyakarta, 12 Jul. 2000 and 24 Jun. 2001; Rusno (grassroots PKI activist in East Java), oral interview, Sidoarjo, 10 May 2001.

The party was also attractive to poor communities because of its emphasis on education. The party and its mass organizations held courses to teach the illiterate to read. They maintained a wide variety of specialized schools. Those who gained an education felt indebted, and many became committed supporters of the party. The PKI ran a People's University (Universitas Rakjat), which was not so much a university but a set of evening classes held at PKI offices throughout the country. For experienced activists, the party ran its own institute for the study of Marxism-Leninism, the Ali Archam Social Science Institute (Akademi Ilmu Sosial Ali Archam), named after a PKI leader of the 1920s who had died of malaria in Boven Digul. As the government invested a lot of money in education in the 1950s, it trained many people from poor communities in Java to become schoolteachers. Many of these new teachers became supporters of the communist party.[22]

Some people from privileged backgrounds were also attracted to the party. It gave them opportunities to become better acquainted with the lives of their fellow Indonesians. Living in a new nation-state in which all citizens held equal rights under the law, they sensed the elite's traditional arrogance was no longer viable. Marxism-Leninism appeared to be a rigorous science that could lead, if properly understood and implemented, to a more modern and egalitarian society.[23]

The party's mass organizations for artists, Lekra, attracted many of the country's best painters (such as Hendra Gunawan), best writers (such as Pramoedya Ananta Toer) and best filmmakers and dramatists (such as Bachtiar Siagian and Utuy Tatang Sontani). Njoto, a Politburo member who was himself a musician and writer, had helped establish Lekra in 1950. He earned the respect of many artists by giving them a free hand to create what they wished while urging them to be inspired by the experience of the Indonesian national revolution and the struggles of workers and peasants.[24] Lekra artists did not produce propagandistic art on orders from the Politburo. One famous painter, Sudjojono (whose paintings today, like Hendra's, command high prices at Sotheby's auctions), represented the party in the parliament. The party allowed for some

22 Ruth T. McVey, "Teaching Modernity: The PKI as an Educational Institution," *Indonesia* 50 (Oct. 1990), 5–28; Siswoyo, *Siswoyo Dalam Pusaran*, 157–67.
23 Siswoyo, *Siswoyo Dalam Pusaran*, 26–29.
24 Oey Hai Djoen (a leader of Lekra and PKI member of parliament), oral interviews, Jakarta, 14 Jul. 2001, 16 Jan. 2002, 24 Jan. 2002.

unconventional behavior among artists, but it drew a line when Sudjojono cheated on his wife. He was dismissed from the party in 1957.[25]

As it was organizing millions of people in the 1950s and bringing people of different classes together, the PKI was under constant attack by the army, right-wing political parties and gangsters hired by private companies. Some of its meetings and demonstrations were broken up by force. Its newspaper was repeatedly banned, and its activists were periodically arrested. In adopting the legal, parliamentary path, how did Aidit and his fellow leaders expect the party to defend itself against the elite groups it was challenging?

The PKI leaders understood that large numbers alone would not protect them. Their guiding principle was what they called the "Method for Combining the Three Forms of Struggle." The three forms were: mobilizing (1) peasants in the villages, (2) workers in the cities and (3) soldiers in the military.[26] This third point was the crucial one. It was a "form of struggle" that had to be hidden. The scholarly literature on the PKI rarely mentions it because the PKI leaders in their public formulations rarely mentioned it.[27] Some soldiers and militia members became attracted to the PKI during the armed struggle against the Dutch (1945–49), and a portion of them became incorporated into the military after independence. A clandestine group of PKI stalwarts maintained contact with these military personnel and reported directly to Aidit. The purpose was mainly to share information: The party helped the military personnel and vice versa. It was not a large network, and it faced an uphill battle against the strict anti-communists among the top officers.[28]

The PKI was very similar to the Communist Party of India (CPI) – another communist party in postcolonial Asia that had reconciled itself to electoral democracy. But it did better than the CPI in challenging the hegemonic position of the middle-class nationalist party (which in India was the Indian National Congress). The PKI had much greater influence within Indonesia than the CPI had in India. The CPI never earned more

---

25 Mia Bustam, *Sudjojono dan Aku* [Sudjojono and Me] (Jakarta: Institut Studi Arus Informasi, 2006).

26 Lembaga Sejarah PKI, *Manuskrip Sejarah 45*, 438–39.

27 Mortimer's book mentions it once when quoting an Aidit speech of 1964. Aidit, speaking in public, referred to the third point in vague terms as "the struggle to integrate the apparatus of the state with the revolutionary struggle of the people": Rex Mortimer, *Indonesian Communism Under Sukarno: Ideology and Politics, 1959–1965* (Ithaca: Cornell University Press, 1974), 337.

28 John Roosa, *Pretext for Mass Murder: The September 30th Movement and Suharto's Coup d'État in Indonesia* (Madison: University of Wisconsin Press, 2006), ch. 4.

than 9 percent of the vote. The parliamentary path and the "national front" strategy seemed to be perfectly suited to Indonesia's conditions. The party reported that it had 1.5 million members at the time of its Sixth National Congress in 1959. But the PKI's parliamentary path suddenly reached a dead end. President Sukarno disbanded the parliament and canceled further elections in 1959. The PKI had to improvise.

The PKI's Faustian Bargain with Sukarno 1959–1965

On 5 July 1959, from the steps of the presidential palace, Sukarno pronounced the death of the Constitutional Assembly. The 550 members of the assembly, after working for three years, could not agree on the constitution's basic principle – was it to be Islam or Pancasila, the more or less secular "state ideology" that had been articulated by Sukarno in 1945? Sukarno saw this deadlock as symptomatic of the general failure of what he habitually called "free-fight liberalism." Between 1950 and 1959, the parliament had changed prime ministers and cabinets eight times. On top of this constant squabbling between the political parties came a rebellion by military commanders in the outer islands hoping to create a parallel government in 1957–58.

In the midst of these multiple crises, Sukarno assumed extra-legal powers in 1959 and reinstituted the rudimentary constitution of 1945 that allowed for a presidential system. Sukarno arrogated to himself the authority to choose not just cabinet ministers but all 261 members of the legislature too. He reserved the majority of seats for representatives of "functional groups" (businesspeople, women, youth, etc.). The role of the new legislature, in which the PKI wound up with thirty seats, was to rubberstamp Sukarno's presidential directives. Sukarno's name for this one-man polity, "Guided Democracy," became a world-famous euphemism.

The PKI leaders supported Guided Democracy. They decided their electoral successes would have to be sacrificed. They needed the alliance with Sukarno to fight more dangerous enemies: the anti-communist army officer corps and the right-wing political parties.[29] The US-backed rebellions of

---

29 In his essay explaining the PKI's support for Guided Democracy, Sakirman, a Politburo member, acknowledged some of its negative aspects and the "difficulty which some comrades have in understanding" the party line. See "Apa Arti Sokongan PKI kepada UUD 1945 dan Demokrasi Terpimpin" [What Is the Significance of the PKI's Contribution to the 1945 Constitution and Guided Democracy?], *Bintang Merah* 16 (May–Jun. 1960), 194–219.

1957–58 had posed serious threats to the PKI. In the regions of the rebellion, members of the PKI and its mass organizations were terrorized and arrested *en masse*. The Dulles brothers heading the CIA and the State Department in Washington DC sent money and guns to the rebels in the hopes of removing all the outer islands from the control of Java, which their overheated imaginations led them to believe had become dominated by the PKI after the 1957 elections.[30]

The PKI's abandonment of its parliamentary path had its rewards. Sukarno, who had attacked the party only eleven years earlier, now depended on its support for his improvised polity and wanted to protect it from army repression. The army tried to prevent the PKI's Sixth National Congress from being held in 1959, only two months after Sukarno's declaration of Guided Democracy, but had to relent under pressure from the president. The army attempted another bout of repression in July–August 1960, and again Sukarno intervened. The PKI leaders understood that the party could continue to grow under Guided Democracy even if it could not contest elections. Sukarno's banning of Masjumi, the right-wing Islamic party, in 1960 removed a significant obstacle to the PKI's growth.

The PKI also appreciated the fact that Sukarno's policies had become almost indistinguishable from its own. His "Political Manifesto" for Guided Democracy, his 1959 speech on Independence Day, was in accordance with the PKI's program. Sukarno saw the main enemy of the nation as "the Nekolim" – his neologism standing for neocolonialism, colonialism and imperialism. He returned to his 1926 formulation (from his booklet *Nationalism, Islam and Marxism*) and called for an Indonesian state based upon a combination of "nationalism, religion and communism," a trinity that became abbreviated as Nasakom. The PKI, whose members were routinely denounced as traitors by the right-wing parties, felt honored to be recognized as an essential tendency within Indonesian nationalism. The song most frequently sung at party events was "Nasakom Bersatu" ("Nasakom Unite").

The party's greatest difficulty was to balance its commitment to a crossclass, national front strategy and its commitment to defending workers and peasants. The party's mass organization for peasants, the BTI, encouraged landless villagers in late 1963 to seize land and withhold rents in

---

30 Audrey Kahin and George Kahin, *Subversion as Foreign Policy: The Secret Eisenhower and Dulles Debacle in Indonesia* (New York: New Press, 1995).

accordance with the land reform and sharecropping laws of 1960. That campaign intensified already existing conflicts in villages. The party leadership worried about breaking up the national front behind Sukarno and backed away from the BTI campaign in early 1965.[31]

The PKI's strategy of burrowing within the military met with greater success. Because the PKI militantly supported Sukarno's military campaigns (to suppress the CIA-backed regional rebellions in 1957–58; to seize West Papua from the Dutch in 1960–62; to oppose the formation of Malaysia in 1963–65), its members had a chance to work closely with military personnel. Members of the PKI and its mass organizations participated in military training for volunteer militias. The PKI did its best to prove to military officers that it was more patriotic, reliable and self-sacrificing than any other political party. The party took great pride in the fact that Aidit, as a minister in Sukarno's cabinet and vice-head of the legislature (1962–65), delivered lectures in front of the academies of all four branches of the armed forces in 1963 (army, navy, air force and police).[32]

Sukarno, while protecting the PKI, limited its power. He never appointed a PKI leader to a powerful cabinet post (such as the minister of the interior). Aidit's posts were largely ceremonial. Sukarno had to appease the army generals who were also supporting his Guided Democracy. The generals liked his one-man rule precisely because it blocked the PKI's access to state power through the ballot box. The generals arranged for the legislature to proclaim Sukarno "president for life" in 1963 to ensure that elections would not be held for the foreseeable future. Sukarno, serving as a shield for both the PKI and the army, played an elaborate game of triangulation. By appearances, he was a dictator, but in reality he was just a balancer of two large institutions, neither of which he fully controlled.[33]

By early 1965, the army generals felt that Sukarno's balancing act was failing; they saw him leaning too far to the left. Confrontation, the campaign against Malaysia, was having major repercussions on Indonesia's economy and foreign relations. Britain, which was guaranteeing Malaysia's security, was preparing for war with Indonesia. The nationalization of British firms in 1963–64 made all foreign firms anxious. By 1965, international investors were boycotting Indonesia. In a wave of worker occupations justified in the name

---

31 Mortimer, *Indonesian Communism Under Sukarno*, 276–328.
32 Lembaga Sejarah PKI, *Manuskrip Sejarah 45*, 443–45.
33 Herbert Feith, "President Soekarno, the Army, and the Communists: The Triangle Changes Shape," *Asian Survey* 4, 8 (Aug. 1964), 969–80.

of Confrontation, PKI-affiliated trade unions began taking over many American-owned companies in early 1965. The future of the multinational oil companies in Indonesia, such as Caltex and Shell, was in doubt.[34]

During the years of Confrontation, Sukarno became closer to China, since it enthusiastically supported his anti-imperialist campaigns. Sukarno is still well known today for organizing the Asia-Africa Conference in 1955, which was the germ of the idea of Third World nonalignment. He is less known for abandoning the idea of nonalignment in the early 1960s in favor of an international alliance between what he called "New Emerging Forces." To rival the Olympics, he held the Games of the New Emerging Forces in Jakarta in 1963. China provided a good part of the funding for this international sporting event. To rival the United Nations, he constructed a massive building in Jakarta that was to be the headquarters for the Conference of the New Emerging Forces, again with money from China. Mao Zedong and Zhou Enlai, in September 1965, were even expressing a willingness to help Indonesia build a nuclear bomb.[35] Sukarno, in his annual Independence Day address in August 1965, declared that Indonesia's foreign relations would revolve around an "axis" connecting Cambodia, North Vietnam, China and North Korea.

The PKI was the political party that most strongly supported Sukarno's challenge to the world order. It had expanded under Guided Democracy into the largest, wealthiest, best-organized party in the country. Aidit had pressured the party and the mass organizations to recruit new members as quickly as possible. By 1965 he was boasting that they had a total of 27 million members. That number was no doubt inflated, but everyone saw that the PKI could mobilize more people for demonstrations and rallies than any other party. Sukarno greatly respected the PKI for its crowds. He stood with Aidit in front of packed crowds of PKI supporters in the country's main stadium twice in May 1965 – once for the 1 May rally and once for the party's forty-fifth anniversary – and proclaimed a heartfelt admiration for the party.

As Sukarno became closer to China, the PKI did as well. The PKI dropped the pretense of being neutral in the Sino-Soviet split, though it stopped short of breaking off relations with the USSR. The PKI, unlike the Communist

---

34 William Redfern, "Sukarno's Guided Democracy and the Takeovers of Foreign Companies in Indonesia in the 1960s," Ph.D. dissertation (University of Michigan, 2010).

35 Taomo Zhou, "China and the Thirtieth of September Movement," *Indonesia* 98 (2014), 41–46.

Party of India, did not fracture because of the Sino-Soviet split in the early 1960s. No party leader attempted to set up a rival organization.

The PKI's official history compiled for its forty-fifth anniversary in May 1965 viewed Guided Democracy as a time when "the revolutionary situation quickly intensified." The party saw its alliance with Sukarno as having been entirely beneficial; the "pro-people" side of the state was becoming stronger than the "anti-people" side of the state.[36] The PKI leaders apparently overestimated their strength. One Central Committee member, writing decades later with the benefit of hindsight, concluded that Guided Democracy had "largely benefited the military."[37]

The Massacres 1965–1966

PKI leaders sensed in early 1965 that army officers were contemplating a coup against Sukarno. Many business elites and politicians were secretly meeting with army officers. Foreign trade had collapsed and the currency was in free fall. Sukarno had rejected overtures from the noncommunist parties to reverse his policies. He had intensified the country's isolation by pulling out of the United Nations in early January 1965 over the UN's recognition of Malaysia. He was challenging the world's great powers, the United States and Britain, and neighboring states in Southeast Asia. Sukarno had entitled his Independence Day speech in August 1964 "The Year of Living Dangerously" because he knew that his challenge to what he called the "Old Established Forces" was risky.

The PKI was stuck in early 1965: It had no chance of gaining state power through the ballot – there were no elections to contest. But it could not gain power through the bullet either – it had no armed forces. Its power was greatly dependent on the protection provided by Sukarno, but he was in danger of being overthrown, assassinated (there had been multiple attempts on his life) or debilitated by health problems. By mid 1965, Aidit had formed a small ad hoc committee inside the Politburo for contingency planning. When he was in Beijing on 5 August, he explained some of this planning to Mao. If Sukarno passed away and the right-wing army generals attacked the party, the PKI would use its network of supporters inside the military to foil the attack. These pro-PKI military personnel would trick

---

36 Lembaga Sejarah PKI, *Manuskrip Sejarah 45*, 377–94.
37 Siswoyo, *Siswoyo Dalam Pusaran*, 169.

the generals by creating a seemingly neutral "military committee." Aidit explained:

> Our enemies would be uncertain about the nature of this committee, and therefore the military commanders who are sympathetic to the right wing will not oppose us immediately. If we show our red flag right away, they will oppose us right away. The head of this military committee would be an underground member of our party, but he would identify himself as [being] neutral.[38]

At some point over the two months after this conversation with Mao, Aidit became convinced that the anti-communist army high command was going to stage a coup even before Sukarno died. The question for Aidit was whether to wait for the coup to take place or to launch a preemptive strike. Aidit opted for the latter course of action. The plan for setting up a seemingly neutral "military committee" was put into action on the morning of 1 October. The party supporters inside the military abducted the six generals on the army's General Staff, including the commander of the army, General Yani, and proclaimed the existence of a new "Revolutionary Council." This action, called the September 30th Movement, was designed to appear as if it was an autonomous action by officers wishing to protect Sukarno from a cabal of pro-American coup plotters. The idea was to have Sukarno appoint a new, more left-leaning army commander who would prevent the army from attacking the PKI. With this protection, the PKI could continue to grow. As Aidit explained to Mao, once the "military committee" had been established, "we need to arm the workers and peasants in a timely fashion." The unusual character of this plan – neither mutiny, nor coup, nor mass revolt – reflected the PKI's unusual position.

The plan, with its dissimulations and multiple phases, turned out to be too complicated. The disorganized plotters did not even complete the first phase. The abductions were botched, and Sukarno told the pro-PKI officers to call off the action, which they obligingly did, about eight hours after they started. Sukarno appointed a caretaker army commander who was sympathetic to the PKI, but the anti-PKI generals in the army high command rejected his appointee. Major General Suharto, who had already taken control of the army that morning of 1 October, remained in charge, in flagrant defiance of his commander-in-chief. That was the beginning of the end for both Sukarno and the PKI.

---

38 Zhou, "China and the Thirtieth of September Movement," 51.

As US declassified documents reveal, the army generals were waiting for a pretext to attack the PKI before 1 October. They wanted to provoke the party into some kind of rash action by spreading rumors that they were determined to stage a coup. They planned to justify an assault on the party in the same way they had justified their previous assaults in 1948 and 1951 – as the suppression of a PKI coup attempt. The September 30th Movement, by itself, was not a coup attempt; it was not directed against President Sukarno. But that is what the army generals called it in early October as they initiated the longstanding plan to destroy the PKI and reduce Sukarno to a figurehead president.

Aidit had thought that the party had enough support among military personnel, especially in the air force, to counter any army attack. But he miscalculated the depth of that support. The PKI leaders had assumed that the army would not be able to summon up the logistical wherewithal to suppress a movement that large. Even the anti-communist analyst from the United States, Guy Pauker, who was close to the army officers, thought in 1964 that the officers "would probably lack the ruthlessness that made it possible for the Nazis to suppress the Communist Party of Germany."[39] As it turned out, the generals did become that ruthless. The September 30th Movement was their Reichstag Fire.

Aidit and the party leaders did not issue a call to resist the repression in early October. Instead, they called for calm so that Sukarno could investigate what had happened and find a "political resolution." But Aidit, in a move inconsistent with stated party policy, remained underground in Central Java, where the party was strongest, apparently trying to encourage military personnel there to stage some kind of action. Whatever he was trying to do, nothing came of it. The rest of the party leaders were in Jakarta, confused in the absence of Aidit. They last met in a safe house on 9 October and then went underground themselves.[40] The party had to rely, as it had so many times before, on Sukarno's protection. But this time was different; Sukarno did not have the power to protect it.

It was not inevitable that the army's repression of the PKI would be successful. Party supporters were prepared to take action. The railway workers could have refused to carry the troops. Mechanics in military garages, most of whom were union members, could have sabotaged the vehicles. Villagers could have set up barricades. Workers could have occupied

39 Guy Pauker, *Communist Prospects in Indonesia* (Santa Monica, CA: RAND Corporation, Nov. 1964), 22.
40 Oey Hay Djoen, oral interview, Jakarta, 21 Aug. 2004.

factories. The PKI could have put up substantial resistance if it had wanted to. Except in a few places in Central Java, party members allowed themselves to be detained, believing that they would be soon released since they had done nothing wrong. The death toll was so high because the army had taken the party by surprise and faced no resistance. The most common pattern was for the army to take truckloads of detainees out of prisons and detention camps at night and massacre them in remote areas. Most of the killings were disappearances, which is one reason why still today so little is known about them.[41]

The army, desperate to obtain US economic aid, pointed to the killing of communists as proof of its service to the global war on communism. Suharto and his generals expected to be rewarded by the United States, and they were. The United States and its allies lavished aid on Indonesia as soon as Suharto had clearly sidelined Sukarno in March 1966.[42] Suharto, able to claim that he had engineered an economic recovery, gained a legitimacy for his dictatorship which, to the surprise of many observers, lasted for thirty-two years, until the economic crisis of 1997–98.

The slaughter Suharto orchestrated was proof of a serious failure of the party's strategy. But what exactly went wrong? Some in the PKI believed that their error had been to attempt a legal, parliamentary path to state power in the first place. In 1966, it fell to Sudisman, the sole surviving member of the quartet that had led the PKI since 1951, to explain how the party could have fallen victim to the army's murderous repression – what he called a "white terror" in reference to the White Russians. In his "Self-Criticism" document, Sudisman denounced the leaders of the PKI, including himself, for building an above-ground party that had not clearly distinguished itself from the run-of-the-mill populism and anti-imperialism of other nationalist groups. It had prioritized national unity over class struggle and nationalism over Marxist-Leninist doctrines. For Sudisman, the success of those years of "legal parliamentary struggle" following "national front" policies had been illusory. In the midst of the "white terror," he called for a smaller party of highly committed, well-trained cadres who would lead an armed struggle along Maoist lines.[43]

41 John Roosa, "The State of Knowledge About an Open Secret: Indonesia's Mass Disappearances of 1965–1966," *Journal of Asian Studies* 75 (2016), 281–97.
42 Brad Simpson, *Economists with Guns: Authoritarian Development and US–Indonesian Relations, 1960–1968* (Stanford: Stanford University Press, 2008), ch. 8.
43 Sudisman, *Otokritik Politbiro CC PKI* [The Self-Criticism of the CC PKI Politburo] (Sep. 1966), www.marxists.org/indonesia/indones/1966-SudismanOtoKritik.htm.

Sudisman did not have the chance to organize such an armed struggle. He was captured in his hideout in Jakarta in December 1966. The other surviving leaders congregated in the most remote district on Java, South Blitar, and called upon PKI supporters to join them.[44] The PRC, promising help, gathered the hundreds of Indonesian communists left stranded there and put them in a military training center near Nanjing in 1967 with the plan to infiltrate them back into Indonesia as guerrilla fighters.[45] The army caught wind of the existence of PKI members in South Blitar and raided the area in June 1968, before the armed struggle began. With the collapse of that miniature proto-liberated zone, the PRC abandoned its plan to help the armed struggle.

The Indonesian communists in exile, scattered across the globe, denied passports by the Suharto regime, wrote a number of post-mortems of the party. Their analyses tended to be tendentious and doctrinaire. Some condemned the PKI for not being Maoist enough, echoing Sudisman's laments. Others, aligning themselves with the USSR, condemned the PKI for being too Maoist: The September 30th Movement was evidence, they suggested, of a spirit of "adventurism" among the PKI leaders.[46] These post-mortems searched for structural causes, some deep flaws in the party's theory and practice, to explain the PKI's defeat. It may well have been, however, that contingent factors were more important. With a different series of decisions at the time of the political crisis in 1965, the PKI might well have been able to survive its contest with the army high command.

The PKI no longer functioned after 1968. Everyone of any importance in the party was either dead, in prison, in exile or in hiding. The Indonesian state dedicated itself to identifying and persecuting all members of the PKI and its mass organizations. The Suharto dictatorship (1966–98) treated anti-communism as a state religion. All means of state propaganda – such as films, museums, monuments and textbooks – were deployed to convince the

44 Andre Liem, "Perjuangan Bersenjata PKI di Blitar Selatan dan Operasi Trisula" [The PKI's Armed Struggle in Blitar Selatan and Operation Trisula], in J. Roosa et al. (eds.), *Tahun yang Tak Pernah Berakhir* [The Year That Never Ended] (Jakarta: Lembaga Studi dan Advokasi Masyaraka, 2004), 163–201; Vannessa C. Hearman, "South Blitar and the PKI Bases: Refuge, Resistance, and Repression," in Douglas Kammen and Katherine McGregor (eds.), *The Contours of Mass Violence in Indonesia, 1965–1968* (Singapore: NUS Press, 2012), 182–207.
45 Utuy Tatang Sontani, *Di Bawah Langit tak Berbintang* [Under a Starless Sky] (Jakarta: Pustaka Jaya, 2001), 73–150; Zhou, "China and the Thirtieth of September Movement," 56–57.
46 Rex Mortimer, "Indonesia: Emigré Post-Mortems on the PKI," *Australian Outlook* 28, 3 (Dec. 1968), 347–59.

people that the PKI was evil and that everyone in the party had been collectively responsible for the September 30th Movement. Suharto banned the PKI in March 1966, after finally sidelining Sukarno, and his handpicked parliament banned any expression of Marxism-Leninism five months later. That 1966 law is still in effect and is routinely used by the army to justify suppression of all manner of political organizing. The army, justifying its internal police powers since 1965 by appealing to an ever-present, latent communist threat, continues to have a vested interest in keeping the specter of the PKI stalking the country.[47]

Bibliographical Essay

The three major works of English-language scholarship on the PKI, put together, provide an excellent overview of the party's history. Ruth McVey's 500-page tome, *The Rise of Indonesian Communism* (Ithaca: Cornell University Press, 1965), covers the early years from the founding in 1920 to the 1926–27 revolts. Donald Hindley's book analyzes the growth of the party in the 1950s: *The Communist Party of Indonesia, 1951–1963* (Berkeley: University of California Press, 1966). Rex Mortimer's book focuses on the Guided Democracy period: *Indonesian Communism Under Sukarno: Ideology and Politics, 1959–1965* (Ithaca: Cornell University Press, 1974).

Olle Törnquist's book delves into the theoretical positions of the Aidit era and reflects on the reasons for its demise: *Dilemmas of Third World Communism: The Destruction of the PKI in Indonesia* (London: Zed Press, 1984). The writings of Justus van der Kroef, an anti-communist political scientist who wrote prolifically on the party in the 1950s–60s, are informative though not always reliable in their interpretations. His major work is *The Communist Party of Indonesia: Its History, Program and Tactics* (Vancouver: University of British Columbia, 1965). The controversies over the PKI's relationship to the September 30th Movement in 1965 are analyzed in John Roosa, *Pretext for Mass Murder: The September 30th Movement and Suharto's Coup d'État in Indonesia* (Madison: University of Wisconsin Press, 2006).

---

47 Ariel Heryanto, "Where Communism Never Dies: Violence, Trauma and Narration in the Last Cold War Capitalist Authoritarian State," *International Journal of Cultural Studies* 2, 2 (1999), 147–77; "Indonesia's 'Red Scare' Stokes Unease over Military's Growing Influence," *New York Times* (18 May 2016), www.reuters.com/article/us-indonesia-military-idUSKCN0Y933F].

The period from 1928 to 1945, when members of the PKI were either in prison, in hiding or in exile, has suffered from relative neglect. The Boven Digul prison camp has been studied, most recently by Rudolf Mrázek, "Boven Digoel and Terezín: Camps at the Time of Triumphant Technology," *East Asian Science, Technology and Society* 3, 2–3 (2009), 287–314. Tan Malaka (1897–1949), who spent many of those years in exile, wrote a three-volume autobiography that has been translated into English: *From Jail to Jail*, trans. Helen Jarvis (Athens: Ohio University Center for International Studies, 1991).

The chaos in the party from 1945 to 1950 has made the study of that period extraordinarily complicated. Harry Poeze's three-volume biography of Malaka addresses the broader history of the PKI during that period. It is so far available only in Dutch and in Indonesian translation: *Verguisd en vergeten: Tan Malaka, de linkse beweging en de Indonesische Revolutie, 1945–1949* (Leiden: KITLV, 2007).

Ruth McVey, in a series of articles, has gone the furthest in writing about the PKI in the genres of social and cultural history: "The Enchantment of the Revolution: History and Action in an Indonesian Communist Text," in Anthony Reid and David G. Marr (eds.), *Perceptions of the Past in Southeast Asia* (Kuala Lumpur: Asian Studies Association of Australia, 1979), 340–58; "The Wayang Controversy in Indonesian Communism," in M. Hobart and R. H. Taylor (eds.), *Context, Meaning and Power in Southeast Asia* (Ithaca: Cornell University Southeast Asian Program Publications, 1986), 21–51; and "Teaching Modernity: The PKI as an Educational Institution," *Indonesia* 50 (Oct. 1990), 5–28.

Working above ground after 1951, the PKI published an enormous quantity of material in Bahasa Indonesia: a daily newspaper *Harian Rakjat*, a bimonthly theoretical journal, *Bintang Merah*, and many occasional pamphlets and books. IDC Publishers has placed 332 titles of PKI documents on a microfiche collection that is available at major research libraries. Some of these documents are available online at the Indonesian section of Marxists.org: www.marxists.org/history/indonesia/index.htm. The key documents for members were the party program and constitution adopted at the Fifth National Congress in 1954 and the book published under Aidit's name: *Indonesian Society and the Indonesian Revolution* (1957). Each mass organization issued its own periodicals and occasional publications as well. For instance, the plantation workers's union, Sarbupri, issued a monthly magazine *Warta Sarbupri*. Most of these documents will be found in hard copy or in microform at major research libraries.

The most detailed account of the party's history written by the PKI itself was written in May 1965 for the PKI's forty-fifth anniversary. It has only recently been published: Lembaga Sejarah PKI, *Manuskrip Sejarah 45 Tahun PKI (1920–1965)* [The Manuscript of 45 Years of PKI History] (Bandung: Ultimus, 2014). The most informative memoir written by a high-ranking PKI leader who survived the cataclysm is Siswoyo, *Siswoyo Dalam Pusaran Arus Sejarah Kiri: Memoar Anggota Sekretariat CC PKI* [Siswoyo in the Vortex of Left History: A Memoir of a PKI Central Committee Member] (Bandung: Ultimus, 2014). Other significant memoirs include: Hasan Raid, *Pergulatan Muslim Komunis* [The Struggles of Muslim Communist] (Yogyakarta: LKPSM Syarikat, 2001); Francisca Fanggidaej, *Memoar Perempuan Revolusioner* [Memoir of a Revolutionary Woman] (Yogyakarta: Galang Press, 2006).

The Indonesian Institute of Social History (IISH) in Jakarta holds interviews with more than 400 individuals, most of them ex-political prisoners who had been members of the PKI or one of its mass organizations. One book that grew out of the IISH's oral history research focuses on their experiences of imprisonment, torture and forced labor after 1965: John Roosa, Ayu Ratih and Hilmar Farid (eds.), *Tahun yang Tak Pernah Berakhir: Memahami Pengalaman Korban '65: Esai-Esai Sejarah Lisan* [The Year that Never Ended: Understanding the Experiences of the 1965 Victims: Oral History Essays] (Jakarta: Elsam, 2004).

The history of the PKI's mass organizations, such as Sarbupri, has yet to be written. Lekra, the organization of artists, has received the most attention. See, for instance, Michael Bodden's recent pioneering studies: "Modern Drama, Politics, and the Postcolonial Aesthetics of Left-Nationalism in North Sumatra: The Forgotten Theater of Indonesia's Lekra, 1955–1965," in Tony Day and Maya Liem (eds.), *Cultures at War: The Cold War and Cultural Expression in Southeast Asia* (Ithaca: Cornell University Southeast Asia Program Publications, 2010), 45–80; and "The Dynamic Tensions of Lekra's Modern National Theatre," in Jennifer Lindsay and Maya H. T. Liem (eds.), *Heirs to World Culture: Being Indonesian 1950–1965* (Leiden: KITLV Press, 2012), 453–84. A group of filmmakers and IISH researchers in Jakarta has made a revealing film about Lekra that is available for viewing online with English subtitles: *Jalan Cidurian 19* (2009).

20

Communism in India

HARI VASUDEVAN

Introduction

In 1947, when India became independent, communism in the country was centered on the Communist Party of India (CPI). The party was affiliated before 1943 to the Soviet-backed Comintern; and the CPI's commitment to the overthrow of the British colonial establishment foreclosed a stable legal existence during the interwar years. Party structures, though, developed. This was under the cover of mass organizations and other political groups; it was also through an interface with the Indian National Congress (INC), the main nationalist force. After 1942 the CPI supported the war effort against the Axis and functioned openly.

From 1947, without renouncing its revolutionary character, the CPI became involved in electoral politics. A complex relationship took shape with the ruling INC. The development evolved from the CPI's status as a minor opposition party in provincial assemblies in the 1946 elections. From 1952, the party became an element in the Indian republic's national and state legislatures, based on bicameral structures and universal adult suffrage. Its standing grew as indicated in the tables at the end of the chapter. During the Nehru period, the CPI faced INC measures to integrate the state more effectively, give practical form to its constitution, evolve social goals and establish a system of economic planning. The situation generated challenges to ideology as well as opportunities for the CPI to indulge in political mobilization. The party established perspectives on where the country stood on the path to the construction of socialism and evaluated its priorities; to achieve its goals, the party created disciplined structures, even as it encouraged mass appeal and mass support.[1]

---

1 See Bidyut Chakrabarty, *Communism in India: Events, Processes and Ideologies* (New Delhi: Oxford University Press, 2014), "Introduction"; and Dwaipayan Bhattacharyya, *Government as Practice: Democratic Left in a Transforming India* (New Delhi: Cambridge University Press, 2016), ch. 1, for different aspects of the party.

Soviet communism and its allied parties were reference points for the CPI. It was through the connection that the party linked to global communism. Indian communists were critical of the valorization of national development per se and looked to the Soviet experiment as a model. The USSR and the Communist Party of the Soviet Union (CPSU) saw in Indian communism an instance (like China) of how communism could be meaningful in the postcolonial world and serve the Soviet Union's purposes in the Cold War.

Indian communism was marked by heterogeneity. Communism was not focused on an individual, though specific figures commanded respect. Ideologically communism was adaptive, although it was given structure by communist parties, by the Comintern and by the example of the Soviet Union. Texts and ideas were read according to local circumstances, and developed specificity. Within the CPI, rival positions and groups were not silent. Dissension in the CPI led to a split in 1964 and the formation of the Communist Party of India (Marxist) or CPI(M). In 1967, the CPI(M) itself divided, and the Communist Party of India (Marxist-Leninist), or CPI(ML), was formed. The situation drew from a culture of socialist discourse in India's post-1947 public life. Marxist-inclined groups and parties existed outside the CPI. Discussions and alliances occurred across party boundaries. This encouraged the development of a plurality of formal communisms in India.

Politics, leadership, mobilization and ideology in Indian communism have been subjects of study, especially in areas of regional strength. This chapter builds on the literature to show how communism's scattered presence was consolidated in the 1950s. This established ground-level authority in enclaves, as well as a national and international reputation for Indian communism. When global connections weakened, national strength was maintained at the cost of international awareness within a party; when global links were stronger, this could weaken internal coherence and strength.

Communism in India: The Pre-1947 Background

Socialist Ideals and the Nationalist Movement Before 1917

Before 1917, in British India, anti-colonial nationalism, economic justice and social equality drew attention rather than "socialism" or "communism." Awareness of socialist literature existed, but was not significant. Empathy with notions of equality and cooperative action were associated with prominent public figures such as Narendranath Datta (Swami Vivekananda) and Rabindranath Tagore, institutions such as the Theosophical Society and figures in the INC. Liberalism, radicalism and sectarian religious and communitarian ideas that had arisen independently within the country shaped people's perspectives.[2]

The impact of ideas varied in an India divided into directly governed provinces and princely states under a viceregal administration. Except in the princely states, electoral politics, associative activity and a lively print culture, both in English and in Indian languages, provided the ambience for debate. Egalitarian, anti-colonial and revolutionary sentiments were aggressively asserted in the Swadeshi movement of 1905–06 in Bengal. Revolutionary organizations, focusing on terrorist strategies, developed in Bengal and Punjab. During World War I, these sentiments found expression in a provisional government of India in Kabul, a Berlin group that sought German help for India's independence and the Gadr movement set up in the United States by Hardayal.[3]

The Communist Party of India and the Comintern

After the October Revolution in Russia, Indian communism took shape in a diffused manner. Indian revolutionaries in Kabul and Berlin were attracted by the Bolsheviks' affirmation of principles of national self-determination and the social agenda of a communist regime that thought beyond constitutional reform. M. N. Roy, an Indian revolutionary working in Mexico, attended the second meeting of the Comintern in July 1920. Indians were present at the Bolshevik-organized Baku Congress of Peoples of the East in September 1920. These diverse elements established a Communist Party of India in October 1920 in Tashkent.[4] The party's reference points were Comintern positions on the "colonial question," i.e. the nature of imperialism, its class character and how it was to be overcome, with or without assistance from "bourgeois" nationalism.[5]

---

2 Christopher Bayly, *Recovering Liberties: Indian Thought in the Age of Liberalism and Empire* (Cambridge: Cambridge University Press, 2011).

3 Amales Tripathi, *The Extremist Challenge: India Between 1890 and 1910* (Mumbai: Orient Longmans, 1967); Sumit Sarkar, *The Swadeshi Movement in Bengal, 1903–1908* (New Delhi: People's Publishing House, 1973); Hiren Chakrabarti, *Political Protest in Bengal: Boycott and Terrorism, 1905–1918* (Kolkata: Papyrus, 1992).

4 M. A. Persits, *Revolutionaries of India in Soviet Russia: Mainsprings of the Communist Movement in the East* (Moscow: Progress Publishers, 1973).

5 Sobhanlal Datta Gupta, *Comintern and the Destiny of Communism in India, 1919–1943: Dialectics of Real and a Possible History* (Kolkata: Seriban, 2006).

Those forming this CPI were members of a cosmopolitan set whose "revolutionary" character was shaped within a global defiance of empire located in transnational social spaces.[6] They were not revolutionaries with a specific constituency in India or socialists schooled in debates of the Second International. In India, independent of this, and also unschooled in debates of the International, Singaravelu Chettiar formed a Labour Kisan (Peasant) Party in Madras. Muzaffar Ahmed in Calcutta drew together Muslim activists who read up on Marxism, through books such as Julian Borchardt's *The People's Marx* (1921). Suggestions came from M. N. Roy, and his emissary, Nalini Gupta, who arranged the distribution of Bolshevik literature.[7]

These early developments occurred in isolated enclaves and were not linked to each other.[8] Numbers increased, following the popular politics of the Non Co-operation Movement (1921–22) – substantially inspired by M. K. Gandhi and the INC – and disillusionment with the movement's abandonment by the INC. A conference of communists took place at Kanpur in December 1925. A meeting in Bombay in 1928 established a communist party constitution and Central Committee. The Comintern was the reference; local suggestions for the formation of a National Communist Party were not accepted in 1925. As a party, the CPI had a difficult existence: British authorities defined its activities as seditious and imprisoned communists following the Peshawar conspiracy case (1923), the Kanpur conspiracy case (1924) and, in 1929, the Meerut conspiracy case.

The focus of the party was agitation and strike activity in trade unions, and a role in movements for land rights among peasant bodies. Its social goals and revolutionary strategies, arguably utopian,[9] differed from those of the Congress. The CPI did not participate in local, municipal and provincial British Indian elected bodies. Authority within limits was established in a Workers' and Peasants' Party (until 1929) and other mass organizations. By 1939, the communists dominated the All India Trades Union Congress (AITUC) established in 1920 and the All India Kisan Sabha

6 Kris Manjapra, *M. N. Roy: Marxism and Colonial Cosmopolitanism* (New Delhi: Routledge, 2010).
7 Suchetana Chattopadhyay, *An Early Communist: Muzaffar Ahmad in Calcutta 1913–1929* (New Delhi: Tulika Books, 2011).
8 Muzaffar Ahmad, *Amar Jibani o Bharater Komiunist Parti* [My Life and the Communist Party of India], 12th edn. (Kolkata: National Book Agency, 2012), 85–86.
9 In their *Struggle for Hegemony in India 1920–1947* (New Delhi: Sage, 1992–93), Shashi Joshi and Bhagwan Josh develop arguments already made in this direction by Bipan Chandra, Aditya Mukherjee and Mridula Mukherjee.

(AIKS) peasant body established in 1936, though in neither was their position unchallenged. Members of the Communist Party of Great Britain (CPGB) – Philip Spratt and Ben Bradley – came to organize the party in India and give it some form. Schooled in the USSR's discussion circles, they provided interpretations of Marxist theory generated by the Comintern.[10]

To Indian communists, the Comintern provided a sense of communism as a critique of capitalism based on class analysis and Leninist theories of imperialism. Literature stressed differences between communist parties and organizations with a social agenda.[11] Strategies were suggested for anti-colonial struggles: for collaboration within a framework of alliances before 1928, a strict "class approach" after 1928 and construction of "united fronts" after 1935. Analysis and injunctions were important, since the CPI's own networks, journals and newspapers had a fragile existence. Funds dispatched by the Comintern through international organizations assisted strikes and provided wherewithal for party work.[12]

Communists charted a course through various specific issues toward theory. The issues included regional and linguistic particularism, as in Telugu-speaking areas, divided between the directly administered Madras Presidency and the princely state of Hyderabad – where Telugu had no official standing. Communists threw in their lot with the Andhra Mahasabha, which promoted use of Telugu – and developed a social agenda linked to tenants' rights.[13] Religious issues promoted by the Muslim League were not ignored, nor were caste concerns (focused on inherited disadvantage). Both were major factors in politics, partly promoted by electoral arrangements based on separate electorates after the 1919 reforms. The communist emphasis on class relations as a frame of reference evoked sympathy – but also dissatisfaction. In the case of caste, this drew a line between the "dalit" activist B. R. Ambedkar, who sought affirmative action

10 See Ashoke Kumar Mukhopadhyay (ed.), *India and Communism: Secret British Documents* (Kolkata: National Book Agency, 1997), for the CPGB in India.
11 Communist Party of India (Marxist), *Documents on Party Organization 1964–2009: A Collection* (Kolkata: National Book Agency Pvt., 2015), 9–58. For Moscow discussions, see Purabi Roy, Sobhanlal Datta Gupta and Hari Vasudevan, *Indo-Russian Relations 1917–1947: Select Archives of the Former Soviet Union: An Inventory* (New Delhi: Shipra, 2012), 37–106.
12 E. Mel'nikov, "Kommunisticheskaia partiia i deiatel'nost' sovestskikh sektsii masso-vykh mezhdunarodnykh organizatsii rabochevo klassa (1919–1959)," Ph.D. dissertation (Leningrad University, 1984); Roy, Datta Gupta and Vasudevan, *Indo-Russian Relations*.
13 P. Sundarayya, *The Telangana People's Struggle and Its Lessons*, www.revolutionary democracy.org/archive/Telangana.pdf

for lower castes. Ambedkar developed a critique of communism and formed bodies focused on the emancipation of lower castes.[14] Elsewhere, communist tactics led to dissension, as in trade unions, when "red unions" functioned briefly during 1931–34.[15]

By 1939, the CPI was active in cultural initiatives. Via agencies closely linked to the party, experiments were undertaken in street theater and song production as well as writing, painting and sculpture. The All-India Progressive Writers' Association (AIPWA) was pivotal to this from 1934. The Indian Progressive Theatre Association (IPTA) was established later. Production in many Indian languages found attention.[16] Noncommunists were drawn into debates. In projections of communism, the Soviet experience acquired iconic status and figures such as Lenin aroused intense affective enthusiasm.[17]

Fellow Travelers

Groups outside the CPI were committed to socialist and Marxist perspectives.[18] The Congress Socialist Party (CSP) was concerned with social issues (wage levels, working hours, problems of rent, terms of tenancy etc.) and radical tactics to achieve its agenda. Established in 1934, it was until 1939 a group within the Congress, founded branches throughout the country and acted as an interface between communists and the Congress. The CSP had the approval of Jawaharlal Nehru, who expressed admiration for the Soviet experiment.

Elsewhere, in Punjab, activists of the Gadr party, trained in Moscow, became the core of the Kirti Kisan Party. In 1939, the Forward Bloc (FB) was set up with a strong social agenda by Subhas Chandra Bose, after the sabotage of his presidency of the Congress by M. K. Gandhi. Members of the Bengali revolutionary organization Anushilan turned to Marxism and formed the Revolutionary Socialist Party (RSP) in 1940. Trotskyites[19] and

---

14 See Ishita Banerjee Dube, *A History of Modern India* (Cambridge: Cambridge University Press, 2014), ch. 9, for general accounts of caste and B. R. Ambedkar.
15 V. B. Karnik, *Indian Trade Unions: A Survey* (Mumbai: Manaktala, 1966), 74–75.
16 Anuradha Roy, *Cultural Communism in Bengal, 1936–1952* (New Delhi: Primus, 2014).
17 R. Vaidyanath, "Soviet Studies in India," *Revue Canadienne des Slavistes* 11, 2 (1969), 145–55; Rajarshi Dasgupta, "Rhyming the Revolution: Marxism and Culture in Colonial Bengal," *Studies in History* 21, 1 (2005), 79–98.
18 Satyabrata Rai Chowdhuri, *Leftism in India, 1917–1947* (New Delhi: Palgrave-Macmillan Reprint, 2007).
19 Robert J. Alexander, *International Trotskyism 1929–1985: A Documented Analysis of the Movement* (Durham, NC: Duke University Press, 1991), 516–32.

the Socialist Unity Centre of India would add to the number of Indian communists by 1948, as would M. N. Roy, who broke with the CPI and formed his own party.

With "fellow travelers," the CPI pressed, during the Civil Disobedience Movement (1930–34), for alleviation of the rent burden on various categories of tenants throughout the provinces. When Congress ministries of 1937–39 failed to take adequate measures in this direction, and restrict inroads into forest areas to the cost of tribal populations, the CSP and the CPI launched joint agitations. Compromises regarding class attitudes and other issues associated with Gandhian strategies were deemed unacceptable by the CPI; such compromises drove a wedge between the CSP and the CPI, as well as between the CSP and the FB and RSP.

World War II

During World War II, the CPI followed the Soviet lead. Initial opposition to the "imperial" war effort turned to support for the British government in the "People's War" initiative after 1942. The party refused to boycott the British authorities as part of the Congress Quit India program (1942). The CPI lost support from "fellow travelers," who stood with the Congress view that the time should be utilized to press for independence.

Permission to function legally led to party consolidation. The CPI did not participate in government, but activity was unencumbered by police action. The party intensified control over mass organizations. It staged mass events to draw attention to the Soviet war effort, through the Friends of the Soviet Union.[20] The anti-colonial agenda was not abandoned. Sympathizers on the cultural front drew attention to the famine in Bengal (1943–44). By 1945, party structures had gained in solidity. The first congress was held in 1943. At a time when women were increasingly active in politics, the establishment of the women's Mahila Atma Raksha Samiti (1942) added to the party's profile.[21] Notions of an impending end to British rule inspired suggestions for India's future: as a federation that mirrored the USSR, based on states driven by language and/or culture.[22]

20 L. V. Mitrokhin, *Friends of the Soviet Union: India's Solidarity with the USSR During the Second World War in 1941–1945* (Mumbai: Allied Publishers, 1977).
21 M. Sinha Roy, *Gender and Radical Politics in India* (New Delhi: Routledge, 2010), 28ff.
22 Utpal Ghosh, *The Communist Party of India and India's Freedom Struggle, 1917–1947* (Kolkata: Pearl Publishers, 1996), chs. 4 and 5 for broad politics, and pp. 196–211 specifically for constitutional suggestions.

Communism in India After Independence
1947–1960: The Changing Role of the CPI

A Regional Map of Communism in India

In 1945, the standing of communists in different parts of India varied.[23] In the case of Bengal, Muslims turned to communism, finding Congress, the Muslim League and other parties unacceptable or limited. Workers in tramways, the port and the jute mills formed part of the CPI rank and file. Professionals, recruited by the CPGB while studying in Britain, added to numbers, as did other members of Bengal's *bhadralok* (educated classes). In the case of Bihar, the rank and file came from the AIKS, as they did in the United Provinces and Punjab, although in Kanpur the party was strong among the textile workers. In Telugu-speaking areas of the Madras Presidency, the Andhra Mahasabha was the core, with influence in the Nizam's Hyderabad. In Bombay, under S. A. Dange's and S. V. Ghate's initiatives the unions were the pivot, while in Kerala, between 1934 and 1939, most of the CSP, led by P. Krishna Pillai and E. M. S. Namboodiripad, went over to the CPI.[24]

Early Post-Independence Years

After 1945, in the CPI illusions of opportunity[25] were inspired by Soviet success in the war and communist victories in China. This coincided with postwar scarcity, economic dislocation and announcements that the British Empire in India was to end: phenomena that pointed to a crisis of imperialism and capitalism. Equally, CPI leaders were aware of the party's limited numbers, while the notion was popular that the INC and the class alliances it represented would undermine imperialism and benefit the laboring poor. Meanwhile, INC participants in the Quit India movement were released from prison. In directly governed provinces, after the elections of January 1946, executive authority rested with the Congress and the Muslim League. The two parties shared control over departments

---

23 Unless otherwise specified, the narrative up to 1958 is found in G. Overstreet and M. Windmiller, *Communism in India* (Berkeley: University of California Press, 1959).

24 T. J. Nossiter, *Communism in Kerala: A Study in Political Adaptation* (New Delhi: Oxford University Press, 1982), 73ff.; Dilip Menon, *Caste, Nationalism and Communism in South India: Malabar 1900–1948* (Cambridge: Cambridge University Press, 2007).

25 Sekhar Bandyopadhyay, *Decolonization in South Asia: Meanings of Freedom in Post-Independence West Bengal, 1947–1952* (Hyderabad: Orient BlackSwan, 2009), ch. 4.

of central government after formation of the Interim Government in September 1946. This political reality marked communism's weakness.

Communists were committed to revolutionary and constitutional strategies simultaneously. They were involved in the naval mutiny in Bombay in 1945. At a time when the Congress was in conflict with the Muslim League, the CPI provided support to peasants in Bengal, who, in the Tebhaga movement (1946) sought a more substantial portion of the harvest in sharecropping arrangements. These actions were projected as agitations directed against colonial misrule.

P. C. Joshi, the CPI general secretary, allowed articulation of gestures in support of the Congress through 1947. Conflicts between the Congress and the Muslim League about India's future led to Hindu–Muslim confrontation based on mobilization around religious sensibilities and tropes. Communists asserted their opposition to this "communalism," supporting the Congress where possible in elections in January 1946, when the CPI first entered electoral politics. India's partition in 1947, the persistence of violence thereafter and the arrival of refugees in the newly fashioned states of PEPSU (Patiala and East Punjab States) and West Bengal led to continuities in the CPI focus on anti-communalism, with involvement in rehabilitation of refugees and common cause with Congress administrations.

Uncertainties of the three years that followed mirrored the variety in communist debate internationally. Soviet ideas on colonies were in flux, and Mao's ideas were influential.[26] Doctrinal assistance and resources were sought from international communist bodies, especially the CPGB and the CPSU. Dange was dispatched to Moscow in September 1947 and met Andrei Zhdanov and Mikhail Suslov to discuss whether the CPI should continue to be a party straddling India and Pakistan, along with other issues.[27] In the atmosphere of the early Cold War, the "line" propagated by Zhdanov arguing for militancy among communist parties was foregrounded; but the Soviet establishment was negotiating different arguments,[28] as Zhdanov acknowledged to Dange.

Accepting Soviet advice that the party must divide following partition, the CPI oriented its focus to the new "India." The local standing of the party in different regions slowly altered. Independent of any "line" disseminated by

26 John H. Kautsky, *Moscow and the Communist Party of India* (New York: MIT Press and John Wiley, 1956), 6–30.
27 Roy, DattaGupta and Vasudevan, *Documents*, vol. II, 348–62.
28 Kautsky, *Moscow and the Communist Party*, 28–29.

Moscow, Andhra members of the CPI, acting from positions of strength in the Andhra Mahasabha, built on the party's activities among peasant tenants in the Telangana region to take advantage of a rebellion there. The rebellion began from conflicts between tribal and peasant cultivators and landowners supported by the administration of the Nizam of Hyderabad. The Telangana rebellion grew in scale from its origins in Nalgonda country in January 1946, involved both women and men, and marginal as well as more substantial cultivators.[29] The CPI's involvement gave a sharp revolutionary angle to the party's public profile. This coincided with the party's role in strikes in other parts of India.

The INC worked to consolidate its position in the princely states, through the Praja Mandal initiatives and through reorganization of the states. The CPI took a stand in the complications of reorganization and found support. The party came to be pitted against the INC – especially in Telangana, where rebellion persisted after the nationalist government's military action in Hyderabad in early 1948, and in West Bengal, where fresh rural and urban agitations occurred, driven by shortages of essentials and high prices.

Revisions occurred in the CPI's ideological position toward Nehru's government. The Bombay radical B. T. Ranadive became general secretary in February–March 1948 at the Second Congress of the CPI at Calcutta. He argued for strikes in industrial areas, further radicalization of peasant action and proclamations that "this freedom is a lie." The approach led to police and military action that targeted the CPI, and bans on the party in Telugu country and West Bengal.

Divisions within the party came to the fore over the alliances in Telangana, the Central Committee opposing the Andhra secretariat on the matter. At the same time, the formation of the INTUC (Indian National Trade Union Congress) in 1947 and new Congress peasant initiatives outside the AIKS gave the Congress instruments to undermine the CPI. "Fellow travelers" and their popular organizations added to the party's problems. B. T. Ranadive was replaced by the more moderate Rajeswara Rao and, in 1951, Ajoy Ghosh. Debates in the party were sharp and marked with references to "right" and "left" deviations (pro-Congress and pro-revolutionary respectively) – terms that marked party discussion thereafter.[30]

29 Sundarayya, *The Telangana People's Struggle*; D. N. Dhanagare, *Peasant Movements in India 1920–1950* (New Delhi: Oxford University Press, 1986).
30 T. R. Sharma, *Communism in India: The Politics of Fragmentation* (New Delhi: Sterling, 1984), ch. 2.

Changes in leadership and policy were effected through maneuvers in the Central Committee and the various provincial committees of the party (Andhra, Kerala, West Bengal and Bombay) and mobilization of opinion through the party press organs, *Communist* and *Crossroads*. Even the decision to fight the elections of 1952 was taken at this level. The party congress at Madurai in late 1953 faced a *fait accompli* at many levels. The party acquired a reputation for discipline, intolerance and conspiracy. The impression was circulated by the anti-Soviet Indian Committee for Cultural Freedom and the Democratic Research Service, established in 1948 by the socialist-turned-conservative Minoo Masani, who received support from the home minister, Vallabhai Patel.

Changing policy paid dividends, albeit in a limited manner. The early popularity of Congress postindependence labor policy declined quickly. The latter had been epitomized by legislation of 1948, new tribunals and the triumph of unions therein. Firm action against AITUC strikes and arrests of CPI members undermined goodwill toward the Congress. This coincided with dissension in the Congress. This coalition of those disillusioned with the Congress led to increased support for the communists. In national elections of 1952, the CPI emerged as the single largest opposition party. In states formed from princely entities, the communists gained where there was dissension surrounding the Congress's Praja Mandal initiatives, as in Manipur, where communists focused on the disgruntled Irabot Singh, a pivotal figure in public life. The party emerged strongly in Tripura, where tribal claims and refugee rehabilitation were problems.[31] Trade union activity spread to Mysore and Rajasthan.[32]

The party remained well short of the Congress as a force at the national level in the 1952 and 1957 elections. Its vote share was less than that of the successors of the CSP – the Socialist Party and the Praja Socialist Party (PSP). In 1952, the CPI was authoritative in two provincial legislative assemblies – West Bengal and Madras – and in Andhra and Travancore-Cochin through other organizations. The Congress, though, formed all state governments. Communists had a thin showing in Bihar, Punjab and Bombay – previously reliable areas of support.

31 S. K. Chaube, *Hill Politics in North East India* (Hyderabad: Orient BlackSwan, 1999), 204–10.
32 R. Chatterjee, *Union Politics and the State: A Study of Indian Labour Politics* (New Delhi: South Asian Publishers, 1980).

The Communist Party of India: The Making
of a "Revisionist" Party

The party leadership's decision to focus on electoral politics received support from the Third Congress at Madurai (December 1953–January 1954) and the Fourth Congress at Palghat (April 1956). Continuity prevailed in party structures. Older figures were brought back into active party life (both P. C. Joshi and B. T. Ranadive). This, though, did not resolve tensions that came of a disconnect between parliamentary concerns, established commitment to "revolution" and links with marginal peasants and trade unionists to whom constitutional politics meant little.

In terms of perspective, the slide into electoral politics came of a view, better shaped after 1954, that India was not ready for the construction of socialism; rather, it was argued, the country required to be oriented toward the construction of democracy and the building of a powerful anti-imperialist, anti-feudal coalition based on popular politics.[33] Electoral campaigns, parliamentary politics and organizational matters came to take up a large part of party activity. Central Committee meetings, intermittent party conferences and standard party congresses became further institutionalized.

Subtle changes took place. While overall critical of the Congress – which was presented by communists as the representative of the interests of large landownership and capitalist wealth – the CPI's position in the parliament wavered. In foreign policy, especially after the Korean, Hungarian and Suez crises, party representatives approved government policy. Deeply critical of the First Five-Year Plan (1951–56), the party was less negative about the Second and Third Five-Year Plans, where the extension of state enterprise was foreseen.[34] At other levels the CPI settled down to a piece-by-piece negotiation over official policy, often acknowledging the validity of government stands. This occurred over the reorganization of the states on the basis of language (1956), adding to the party's standing in the Vishal Andhra (Greater Andhra) and Aikya Kerala (United Kerala) movements[35] and other occasions after 1945 when CPI spokespersons pressed for linguistically based states.

33 See Kautsky, *Moscow and the Communist Party of India*, 17ff., for early ideas on these lines after 1947.
34 Pranab Kumar Dalal, "The Communist Opposition in the First and Second Indian Parliaments," D.Phil. thesis (University of Burdwan, India, 1979), ch. 4.
35 Ramachandra Guha, *India After Gandhi: The History of the World's Largest Democracy* (New Delhi: Pan Macmillan, 2011), ch. 9; K. Sreedhara Menon, *Political History of Modern Kerala* (Kottayam: DC Books, 2010), ch. 5.

This case-by-case strategy was applied to positions taken over untouch-ability offences (1955), the press (1954), marriage (1952) and dowry (1953), preventive detention and president's rule. CPI parliamentarians felt the government was inadequately distancing itself from exploitative forces; but they considered that policy was susceptible to pressure. Statements made by the Congress at its Avadi plenum in 1955 concerning "socialistic" goals – however far from communist usage of "socialism" – were regarded posi-tively. The Palghat Congress was enthusiastic about the potential of parlia-mentary action, and members resolved to continue their commitment in this sphere. The consequence of the CPI's electoral focus was improvement in numbers in the second general elections of 1957, when, as the table at the end of the chapter indicates, vote share more than doubled. The party was able to form the government in Kerala.[36]

In the course of the CPI's parliamentary participation in 1952–57, strong awareness of etiquette and procedures was established among CPI represen-tatives – an important change for an underground party. A. K. Gopalan, H. N. Mukherjee, Renu Chakrabarti and Sadhan Gupta, in the Lok Sabha/Lower House, and K. Sundarayya in the Rajya Sabha/Upper House were among those affected. The awareness was consolidated in the third and fourth parliaments of 1957–62 and 1962–67. In the Central Committee and party press, a parliamentary focus evolved. The parliament was treated as a forum for interpellation and one in which to press for legislation, especially during budget presentations or debates on ministry appropriations. In state legislatures, similar initiatives were seen. Party journals and newspapers were used to critique legislation.

The Communist Party of India: Social Concerns

Initiatives outside electoral politics continued. Associative action as well as methods linked with demonstrations, assaults and bombs were a stock in trade. These were practices of a party organization that used a rigid communist lexicon; members cultivated an image of probity and austerity.[37]

---

36 Dalal, "The Communist Opposition," 227–93.
37 For agitation activity, see Susanta Bhattacharya, "The CPI and Radicalization of Politics in West Bengal 1950–1962," D.Phil. thesis (University of Burdwan, India, 2012), ch. 2. For AITUC links, see P. R. N. Sinha, *Industrial Relations, Trade Unions and Labour Legislation* (New Delhi: Pearson International, 2006), chs. 4 and 5. For memoir literature on image-building, see Ritwika Biswas, *The Radical Face of Democratic Liberalism* (Kolkata: Calcutta University Press, 2011), 135–41.

In the cultural sphere, communism was still avant-garde. The AIPWA and IPTA continued to be influential through cultural personalities such as Kaifi Azmi, Balraj Sahni and K. A. Abbas.[38] Romesh Thapar (associated with *Crossroads*) and, later, Nikhil Chakravarty (editor of *Mainstream*) became prominent social figures. In academic circles D. D. Kosambi, S. Nurul Hasan and Mohammad Habib exhibited Marxist leanings among historians, as did a number of political scientists and sociologists. From this kind of engagement, Marxist theoretical debate in India acquired an edge – adding to the quality of "left" political discourse, though not always party discourse.

Language politics was a focus. In the State of Bombay – which had not been reconstructed during the formation of linguistic states in 1956 – the CPI gained support from local intelligentsia and associations standing for a Marathi-language state and a Gujarati-language state to be carved out from old Bombay.[39]

Otherwise, the party acted through mass organizations to achieve social goals. Among the working class, the CPI supported AITUC activities under the first two plans. Authority fluctuated: partly the result of neighborhood politics and recruitment networks;[40] partly the consequence of inroads by the Congress INTUC, the socialist HMS (Hind Mazdoor Sabha) and independent Marxist UTUC (United Trade Union Congress).[41] The party's Price Increase and Famine Resistance Committee was a force in West Bengal during demonstrations of popular outrage at times of food shortage, but the effects of action were temporary. Refugee activism in Bengal through the United Central Rehabilitation Committee was more lasting.[42]

The CPI's stand on land issues was crucial to support for the party. The party was critical of the Congress's response to the J. C. Kumarappa Committee of 1948. The committee argued for ending the variety of tenures prevalent under British rule and paramountcy with benefit to the cultivator. Normative legislation was established by Congress state administrations.

---

38 For a sense of the "set," see Khwaja Ahmad Abbas, *I Am Not an Island: An Experiment in Autobiography* (New Delhi: ImprintOne, 2010).
39 Dalal, "The Communist Opposition," 229–49.
40 E. A. Ramaswamy, *The Worker and His Union: A Study in South India* (Mumbai: Allied Publishing House, 1977).
41 See Chatterjee, *Union Politics*, 58–59, for the Rajasthan case.
42 Bhattacharyya, *Government as Practice*, 8–10; Prafulla Chakrabarty, *The Marginal Men: The Refugees and the Left Political Syndrome in West Bengal* (Kalyani: Lumiere Books, 1990).

This envisaged rights to the cultivator, a ceiling on holdings and the abolition of other rights with due compensation. The legislation made exceptions, though, blunting its redistributive edge. Some laws were passed during 1947–54, when, for most of the time, the CPI-led AIKS, still the main umbrella body for peasant organizations, was banned in the states and no meetings were held. The AIKS, at Cannanore (1953), Moga (1954) and Dahanu (1955) congresses, addressed the limitations of legislation, especially in the case of marginal cultivators and agricultural labor.[43]

The party consolidated a constituency among those discontented with Congress legislation. But achievement was not uniform. The AIKS failed to evolve after 1955 in different states. Conditions of agriculture and landholding changed with Green Revolution policies after 1960. These were designed to improve productivity of cultivation with US assistance focused on technology and new strains of seed.[44] This coincided with revisions in grain-procurement policies and the establishment of the Food Corporation of India and the Agricultural Prices Commission (1965). The variety of issues generated across the country weakened the authority of the AIKS, even if it provided the CPI different constituencies among agricultural laborers and new smallholders. In Uttar Pradesh and Bihar, peasant interests coalesced around the socialist parties. The CPI's approach to the land question changed to use of land reform legislation and state agencies.

The Communist Party of India: Soviet Links

The CPI was guided by Soviet interpretations in its own propaganda regarding socialist construction, as well as its analysis of flaws in capitalism, imperialism and other global trends. The Soviet party's representative was present in the congresses of the CPI and vice versa. Regular references to the Soviet Union were made at party congresses.

The party participated in Soviet-generated international institutions that promoted the communist agenda. The CPI was involved in the Afro-Asian People's Solidarity Organisation, the World Federation of Trade Unions, the World Federation of Democratic Youth, the Women's International Democratic Federation and the World Peace Council. This led to the situation at the end of the 1960s where Romesh Chandra of the CPI headed the World

---

43 H. K. S. Surjeet, *The History of the Kisan Sabha* (Kolkata: National Book Agency, 1996), 92–113, for a partisan resumé.
44 Francine Frankel, *India's Green Revolution: Economic Gains and Political Costs* (Princeton: Princeton University Press, 1971), 3–11 and 74–75.

Peace Council.[45] As host and participant, the CPI played a role in CPSU policies to win "hearts and minds" on a global scale through these organizations in the late Stalin, Khrushchev and Brezhnev eras.[46] Soviet and Chinese achievements indelibly marked the Indian communist's imagination, despite 1956 revelations regarding Stalinist excesses.[47] The party worked with the Soviet establishment's notions of the meaning of communism, with no attention paid to the larger discussions during the thaw in the USSR.

At the time of the Soviet meeting with Dange in 1947 and, when CPI leaders met Joseph Stalin in February 1951, the dependence of the CPI on the CPSU was on display. The pattern was epitomized by the structure and relationships of the Communist Information Bureau (Cominform, 1947–56). But this did not foreclose debate. In the Stalinist establishment itself, risks were taken – as indicated by the case of the first Soviet ambassador to India, K. V. Novikov, who argued, to his cost, for a strong engagement with India.[48] The dispatch by the CPI of the vast range of papers concerning Telangana to Moscow told of such expectation. The Soviet embassy in Delhi was a point of dispatch for regular correspondence. Space for discussion, disagreement and negotiation with the Soviet establishment grew with time. This was also true elsewhere during the Khrushchev era.[49]

In the case of India, the flexibility came from changing Soviet perspectives on roads to socialism. David Engerman indicates that, from 1954, doctrine enunciated in Moscow stressed that the road to socialism in former colonies could bypass capitalist ascendancy.[50] The ideas were "learned" by Moscow from colonial experiences and set as reference for communist parties. Civil war was not necessary for the advancement of socialism; support to constructive forces could lead to the evolution of "state capitalism" in a postcolonial context. The distinction between communist and noncommunist was not

45 Fredrick C. Barghoorn, *Soviet Cultural Offensive* (Princeton: Princeton University Press, 1960), ch. 7; David Engerman, "Learning from the East: Soviet Experts and India in the Era of Competitive Coexistence," *Comparative Studies of South Asia, Africa and the Middle East* 33, 2 (2013), 227–38.

46 Andreas Hilger's introduction in Andreas Hilger (ed.), *Die Sowjetunion und die Dritte Welt. UdSSR, Staatssozialismus und Antikolonialismus im Kalten Krieg 1945–1991* (Munich: R. Oldenbourg, 2009), 7–17.

47 Hiren Mukherjee, *The Stalin Legacy: Ivory Flawed but Ivory Still* (Kolkata: National Book Agency, 1994).

48 P. M. Shastitko and P. M. Charyeva, "Istoricheskii proryv v sovetsko-indiiskikh otnosheniiakh. O vizite N. A. Bulganina i N. S. Khrushcheva v Indiiu v 1955," in *V Indiiu dukha* (Moscow: Vostochnaia literatura RAN, 2008).

49 Ted Hopf, *Reconstructing the Cold War: The Early Years 1945–1958* (New York: Oxford University Press, 2012).

50 Engerman, "Learning from the East."

rejected; but the road to socialism, it was suggested, could be achieved in the developing world through negotiation or parliamentary means. Accommodation came easily to communisms from the developing world that adapted to local requirements.

The Soviet approach had a double edge. It projected the desirability of accommodations with the Congress. Nehru's visit to Moscow (1954) and Nikita Khrushchev's and Nikolai Bulganin's visit to India (1955) were important here as was later Soviet assistance for Indian projects in steel production, heavy engineering and electricals, pharmaceuticals and oil refining.[51] The Nehru state's commitment to "state capitalism" was on show in these ventures. But the Congress regularly refused to play to the Soviet lead. In 1960, cooperation between Nehru's government and the USA over agricultural innovation was initiated. Observers noted attempts to develop links between the Congress trade union organization (INTUC) and US unions.[52] The Congress developed its own youth movement associated with the anti-Soviet WAY (World Association of Youth).[53] Soviet leaders remained convinced, though, that the Congress was not a counterrevolutionary force and might be a contributor to socialist construction.

The CPI's perspectives anticipated the international parties' conference in Moscow in November 1957, where transition to communism in conditions of "peaceful coexistence" was declared possible. The perspective was given concrete shape at the extraordinary congress at Amritsar (1958). This declared the importance of the simultaneous development of electoral profiles and a mass party base to achieve this. The new constitution passed at Amritsar reshaped the party's structures further along the model of the Soviet party.

Communism in India 1957–1968: Toward the Development of Multiple Communisms

Disagreements in the CPI, Sino-Soviet Tensions and the Formation of the CPI(M)

The constitution represented a compromise between two forces in the party: a side willing to compromise with the Congress and a side skeptical of such

51 Hari Vasudevan, *Shadows of Substance: India-Russia Trade and Military Technical Cooperation Since 1991* (New Delhi: Manohar, 2010), ch. 1.
52 David S. Burgess, *Fighting for Social Justice: The Life Story of David Burgess* (Detroit: Wayne State University Press, 2000), 111–13.
53 Joel Kotek, *La Jeune Garde. La jeunesse entre KGB et CIA (1917–1989)* (Paris: Éditions du Seuil, 1998), touches on the complications of the international youth movements.

action, which looked to mass initiatives. [54] Both were involved in party policy in Kerala, where the CPI came to power in 1957. Here, from the start, the communists gave protection to the small cultivator, passing an ordinance that was a stay of eviction proceedings. Land legislation was prepared to redistribute property. The party also undertook legislation on education, and involved itself in appointments in the police and civil service. Large-scale violence erupted around these measures, with the party's general secretary Govindan Nair suggesting the formation of party militias to counter the formation of militias by other groups. However, compromises were established by the moderate figure of E. M. S. Namboodiripad.

From Delhi, the Congress dismissed the communist front in 1959. Radicals in the CPI concluded that peaceful initiatives had failed. In West Bengal, in 1959, the Congress's response to the leftist Food Movement against high prices and shortages contributed to confrontation. The Congress government used police to disperse demonstrators and arrested sympathizers. [55]

Tensions began to surface vigorously with the assessment by the Chinese Communist Party of the Kerala experiment as misguided and its assertion that the USSR was guilty of major ideological mistakes. [56] By the Sixth Congress at Vijayawada (1961), [57] there was a marked lack of unity in the response from the CPI. Ignoring party injunctions, some members visited Beijing to ascertain Chinese views. [58] When the parliamentary debate over Tibet (1959) and Sino-Indian border disagreements took place, though, there was relative agreement. S. A. Dange, a supporter of pro-Congress policy, was firm that the government had to negotiate with China. [59] But debates exacerbated interparty disagreements regarding support for the Congress. Cracks were plastered over at the time of the death of Ajoy Ghosh

54 The most up-to-date narrative is in Biswas, *The Radical Face*, 142–242. This builds on Anjali Ghosh, *Peaceful Transition to Power: A Study of Marxist Political Strategies in West Bengal (1967–1977)* (Kolkata: Firma KLM, 1981), and Marcus Franda, *Political Development and Political Decay in Bengal* (Kolkata: Firma KLM, 1971).
55 Suranjan Das and P. K. Bandyopadhyay (eds.), *Food Movement of 1959: Documenting a Turning Point in the History of West Bengal* (Kolkata: K. P. Bagchi, 2004); and Sibaji Pratim Basu, *The Chronicle of a Forgotten Food Movement*, www.mcrg.ac.in/PP56.pdf.
56 Lorenz M. Lüthi, *The Sino-Soviet Split: Cold War in the Communist World* (Princeton: Princeton University Press, 2008), 141ff.
57 Stanley Kochanek, "The Coalition Strategies and Tactics of Indian Communism," in Trond Gilberg (ed.), *Coalition Strategies of Marxist Parties* (Durham, NC: Duke University Press, 1989), 218.
58 Ross Mullick, *Indian Communism: Opposition, Collaboration, and Institutionalization* (New Delhi: Oxford University Press, 1994), 36.
59 Dalal, "The Communist Opposition," 382–85.

in January 1962: Dange, the major pro-Congress leader, became chairman while Namboodiripad was appointed general secretary.[60]

The war with China, later in 1962, brought matters to a head. Some party members refused to accept the party's condemnation of "Chinese aggression." Under the Emergency Decree of that year, party members were arrested. However, many party organizations continued to operate. The crisis came at a meeting in 1964. CPI members who had lost control of organizations, or suffered from accommodations with the Congress in politics and policy, walked out when a resolution on China came up. Figures such as E. M. S. Namboodiripad, Pramod Dasgupta and the young Jyoti Basu were concerned. They held a congress at Calcutta in October and formed the Communist Party of India (Marxist), which fought the 1967 elections alone, seeking support in "people's democratic fronts."[61]

The close connections with the Soviet "commonwealth" and its international institutions were retained by the CPI. Intellectuals associated with the CPI(M) cultivated links with China and radicals elsewhere without formal institutionalization.

The Radicalism of the CPI(M)

The two branches of the party were disoriented by the split, but developed direction. The CPI survived the split as an electoral force. The party varied its links with the Congress and "left" parties thereafter. The CPI(M) presented itself as the radical edge of communism. Successive party congresses at Kochi (1968) and Madurai (1972) emphasized the "revisionist" nature of the CPI. Challenges were mounted against the AIKS, leading to the formation of the AIKS (Ashoka Road) and other local organizations. Approaches to the workers' movement were piecemeal, leading to formation of the CITU (Centre of Indian Trade Unions) in 1970.[62] The SFI (Students' Federation of India) was the party's student organization.

The party sought to realize its aims through the control of government via coalition politics. An opportunity came through alliances on the eve of the 1967 elections. The outcome was the CPI(M)'s participation in the United Front governments of 1967–68 and 1969–70 in West Bengal and in 1967 in Kerala. Assertion of democratic rights was the watchword in both administrations, along with instructions to the police to remain neutral in cases of

---

60 Bhattacharya, *The CPI and Radicalization of Politics in West Bengal*, 294–98.
61 Sharma, *Communism in India*, ch. 5.   62 See citucentre.org.

land grabbing and politically sponsored affrays and *gherao* (a strategy focused on isolation of an individual physically without violence). All parties in the front participated in these agitations.

The CPI(M) Splits: Formation of the CPI(ML)

The situation was unstable. The CPI(M) consisted of those alienated from the CPI leadership by the priority they gave to the Congress. But, equally, generations and cliques confronted each other. In West Bengal Charu Mazumdar led young members critical of the CPI(M) for faltering steps to advanced land reform even in the aftermath of the split in the party. They rejected CPI involvement in the United Fronts. Critics who took this line came together in the All India Conference of Maoist leaders in Calcutta in 1967, after confrontations between local activists of the CPI(M) and police in Naxalbari in the north of the State of West Bengal. The conference was followed by the formation of the Coordination Committee of Communist Revolutionaries in Calcutta in 1968.[63] The new "group" within the party met with sympathy in a number of states: Andhra Pradesh (Srikakulam), Orissa (Koraput), Uttar Pradesh (Lakhimpur) and a number of places in Kerala, Tamil Nadu and Punjab.

The Chinese Communist Party celebrated the formation of the "Naxalite" group (named after the Naxalbari confrontations). According to Rabindra Ray, the situation also allowed for fresh formulations of ideology – some of it coming from "new left" perspectives. The situation coincided, though, with the inability of the Chinese Communist Party, during the Cultural Revolution, to build an international presence of substance.[64] Contributions to the Naxalite movement were restricted to limited training and distribution of literature.[65]

CPI(M) leaders admitted that the Indian ruling class might have been susceptible to neocolonialism; but they refused, at the party's Madurai Congress, to accept the legitimacy of the radicals. The latter established bases in the countryside, before initiating a wave of guerrilla strikes in urban and rural areas during 1969–71. In Calcutta, the new grouping announced the formation of the Communist Party of India

63 Franda, *Political Development and Political Decay in Bengal*, ch. 6.
64 Ingrid d'Hooghe, "Public Diplomacy in the People's Republic of China," in Jan Melissen (ed.), *The New Public Diplomacy: Soft Power in International Relations* (Basingstoke, UK: Palgrave Macmillan, 2005), 88–105.
65 Sreemati Chakrabarti, *China and the Naxalites* (New Delhi: Radiant, 1990).

(Marxist-Leninist) at a congress in May 1970.[66] The following three years showed that this unity was more apparent than real, with various groups forming an independent presence (e.g. the Nagi Reddy group in Andhra) after the suppression of the urban violence in 1971.[67] Maoism in India developed as a much divided force.

Communism in India After the Mid-Century

National Communisms, the Dispersal of International Perspective and the Ascendancy of Regional Organizations

Both the CPI(M) and the CPI(ML) evolved with Indian politics as their primary focus. The CPI(M) projected a concern with international developments but affirmed a distance from the two major communist parties abroad. The Sino-US entente and Soviet–US détente were noted, but generated no serious debate. The CPI maintained connections with the USSR's global initiatives, but it was drawn into local problems generated by its formal project of building "national democracy" in India.

Regional focus was important all around. In the CPI(M), in 1967, awareness of differences of depth in the party's local authority guided an official focus on West Bengal and Kerala state organizations.[68] In the CPI, a region-specific approach came with the formation of a "mini-front" in Kerala in 1969 with Congress support; this did not involve a similar strategy elsewhere. In the case of the CPI(ML), central organization was seldom strong.

Meanwhile, state assemblies increased in number after legislation in 1963 and 1973 for Tripura, Manipur and Mizoram. Tripura especially attracted CPI(M) attention.[69] Scope for coalition politics grew in all states between 1965 and 1971. Congress hegemony waned. In 1967, the number of the Congress's seats in the parliament fell sharply; non-Congress governments were formed in Uttar Pradesh, Punjab and Bihar. With representatives in several states (see table), communists participated in coalition politics.

The central leaderships of communist parties faced conundrums. In the CPI, the approach to the Congress under Indira Gandhi

66 Rabindra Ray, *The Naxalites and Their Ideology* (New Delhi: Oxford University Press, 1988), 107.
67 Ibid., ch. 5. 68 Communist Party of India (Marxist), *Documents*, 197–203.
69 Chakrabarty, *Communism in India*, ch. 1.

(1965–77) varied. A socialist tenor to policy aroused support. But violent confrontations followed the Congress's electoral victory in 1972 and the party's use of state machinery against opponents thereafter. Decisions to associate with the Indian Emergency (1975–77) came with reservations, and only from a sense of a sharp global confrontation between "imperialist" and socialist forces. A decisive loss of membership and electoral support followed the Emergency.[70]

In the CPI(M) and CPI(ML), the Congress's onslaught on the opposition before and during the Indian Emergency contributed to poor consolidation of central organization. Both parties rallied regional resources to survive, affirming a regional orientation in the parties.[71] The CPI(ML) disintegrated, and its components retreated into local "insurgencies." The CPI(M) focused heavily on West Bengal, Kerala and Tripura, within a framework of regional coalitions and national coordination. Here, after the Congress's defeat in the 1977–78 elections, legislation on land, education and tribal affairs evolved according to state priorities.[72]

Endnote

The "federalized" state of communist parties was unsatisfactory to leaderships.[73] But Congress governments dominated national politics in 1980–88, and communist strength showed only in the regions. National coalitions of 1989–92 afforded an opportunity to communist leaderships to assert themselves; the brevity and turbulence of the occasion, though, and regional electoral compulsions, ensured that party behavior hardly altered.

Internationally, *perestroika* in the USSR and the Chinese reforms presented a chance to utilize ideology as a means for authority in parties. However, while innovative in strategy, Indian communisms adhered to established references in an almost ritual fashion. Innovation in discourse posed problems. Invariably, obsolescence at this level, along with disaggregation and regional focus, came to be defining features of Indian communism by the end of the century.

---

70 David Lockwood, *The Communist Party of India and the Indian Emergency* (New Delhi: Sage, 2016).
71 Communist Party of India (Marxist), *Documents*, 243–73.
72 Bhattacharyya, *Government as Practice*.
73 Communist Party of India (Marxist), *Documents*, 339.

Table 20.1 *Communists in Indian National Election Results (Lower House or Lok Sabha)*

Name	1952		1957		1962		1967	
	Vote Share	Seats	Vote Share	Seats	Vote Share	Seats	Vote Share	Seats
INC	44.99	364	47.78	371	44.72	361	40.78	283
CPI (CPM)	3.29	16	8.92	27	9.94	29	5.11 (4.28)	23 (19)
Socialist Party /Samyukta	10.59	12	(10.41)	(19)	2.69 (6.81)	6 (12)	4.92 (3.06)	23 (13)
Socialist Party (PSP or others)							-	-
RSP	0.44	3	0.26	0	0.39	2		
FB(M)	0.91	1	0.55	2	0.72	2	0.43	2

Name	1971		1977		1981		1984	
	Vote Share	Seats	Vote Share	Seats	Vote Share	Seats	Vote Share	Seats
INC	43.68	352		154	42.69	353	49.1	404
CPI /CPM	4.73/5.12	23/25	2.82/4.29	7/22	2.49/6.24	10/37	2.71/5.87	6/22
Socialist Party /Samyukta	2.13/1.04	5/2	[41.32]	[295]	[9.39]	[41]	[6.89/5.97]	[10/3]
Socialist Party/ PSP	-	-	-	-	-	-	-	-
RSP	-		-		-		-	
FB(M)	-		-		-		-	

Note: CPI: Communist Party of India; CPM or CPI(M): Communist Party of India (Marxist); FB(M): Forward Block (Marxist Group); INC: Indian National Congress; PSP: Praja Socialist Party; RSP: Revolutionary Socialist Party.

Table 20.2 Election Performance of the Communist Party of India (CPI) in Principal Areas of Support Among Indian States (Party Seats/Total Seats, CPM/Front Parties Figures in Brackets)

	1951	1955	1957	1962	1967
West Bengal	28/238		46/252	50/252	16/280 (CPM 43)
Travancore-Cochin/Kerala			60/126	29/126 (1960)	19/133 (CPM 52)
Hyderabad/Andhra Pradesh	[PDF 42/175]	15/196		51/300	11/287 (CPM 9)
Madras/Tamil Nadu	62/292		4/205	2/206	2/234 (CPM 11)
Tripura					1/30 (CPM 2)
PEPSU/Punjab	4/126		6/154	9/154	5/104 (CPM 3)
Bihar	0/330		7/318	12/318	24/318 (CPM 4)
Orissa	7/140		9/140	4/140 (1961)	7/140 (CPM 1)
Bombay	1/315		13/396	6/264	10/270 (CPM 1)
Assam	1/82		4/108	0/105	7/126 (CPM 0)

	1969	1971	1972	1974	1977	1978	1980	1982	1985
West Bengal	30/258 (CPM 80)	13/258 (CPM 113)	35/280 (CPM 14)		2/294 (CPM 178)			7/294 (CPM 174)	
Kerala		16/133 (CPM 29)			23/140 (CPM 17)		17/140 (CPM 35)	13/140 (CPM 26)	
Andhra Pradesh			7/287 (CPM 1)			6/294 (CPM 8)		(1983) 4/294 (CPM 5)	11/294 (CPM 11)
Tripura			1/60 (CPM 16)		0/60 (CPM 51)			(1983) 0/60 (CPM 37)	
Madras/Tamil Nadu		8/234			5/234 (CPM 12)		9/234 (CPM, 11)		(1984) 2/234 (CPM 5)
Punjab	4/102 (CPM 2)		10/104 (CPM 1)		7/117 (CPM 8)		9/117 (CPM 5)		1/117

Bihar	25/294 (CPM 3)	35/301	21/324 (CPM 4)	23/324 (CPM 6)	12/354 (CPM 1)
Orissa	4/140 (CPM 2)		7/146 (CP-M 3) 1/147 (CPM 1)	9/117 (CPM 5)	1/147
Bombay/Maharashtra		2/270 (CPM 1)	1/288 (CPM 9)	2/288 (CPM 2)	2/288 (CPM 2)
Assam		3/114	5/126 CPM 11		(1983) 1/109 (CPM 2)

Source: Election Commission of India, eci.nic.in/eci_main1/ElectionStatistics.aspx

Bibliographical Essay

Collections of communist party documents by Subodh Roy, G. Adhikari et al. and Jyoti Basu et al., remain important for this subject. Soviet archival material and excerpts from it have been published by Purabi Roy, Shobanlal Datta Gupta and Hari Vasudevan, and early intelligence material by Ashoke Kumar Mukhopadhyay. Among memoirs, Jyoti Basu, *Memoirs, a Political Autobiography* (Kolkata: National Book Agency, 1999), and Mohit Sen, *A Traveller and the Road: A Journey of an Indian Communist* (New Delhi: Rupa, 2003), are the best.

Most general and regional histories of mid-century India deal with communism. Essays on the Indian left are numerous. The standard reference for the period up to the 1960s, though, is still Gene D. Overstreet and Marshall Windmiller, *Communism in India* (Berkeley: University of California Press, 1959). Doctrinal change after 1947 is handled in T. R. Sharma, *Communism in India: The Politics of Fragmentation* (New Delhi: Sterling, 1984); and politics with social analysis, at the regional level, by T. J. Nossiter, *Communism in Kerala: A Study in Political Adaptation* (New Delhi: Oxford University Press, 1982), Marcus Franda, *Radical Politics in West Bengal* (Cambridge, MA: MIT Press, 1971), and Marcus Franda, *Political Development and Political Decay in Bengal* (Kolkata: Firma KLM, 1971).

Foundations of communism in India have drawn comment in Sanjay Seth, *Marxist Theory and Nationalist Politics: The Case of Colonial India* (New Delhi: Oxford University Press, 1995); the literature is discussed in Suchetana Chattopadhyay, *An Early Communist: Muzaffar Ahmad in Calcutta 1913–1929* (New Delhi: Tulika Books, 2011). Chattopadhyay's archivally driven work on graduation to communism marks a departure as does the well-documented *Comintern and the Destiny of Communism in India, 1919–1943* (Kolkata: Seribaan, 2006) by Sobhanlal Datta Gupta. D. N. Gupta's *Communism and Nationalism in Colonial India, 1939–1945* (New Delhi: Sage, 2008) is a fair account of the subject.

On the CPI/CPI (M) after 1947, rare archival referencing is found in Sekhar Bandyopadhyay, *Decolonization in South Asia: Meanings of Freedom in Post-Independence West Bengal, 1947–1952* (Hyderabad: Orient BlackSwan, 2009), and Ritwika Biswas, *The Radical Face of Democratic Liberalism* (Kolkata: Calcutta University Press, 2011).

Communist parties after the mid century are covered in Dwaipayan Bhattacharyya, *Government as Practice: Democratic Left in a Transforming India* (New Delhi: Cambridge University Press, 2016), and David Lockwood, *The*

Communist Party of India and the Indian Emergency (New Delhi: Sage, 2016). Among many writings on the CPI(ML) Rabindra Ray, *The Naxalites and Their Ideology* (New Delhi: Oxford University Press, 1988), is the best. Maoism in India thereafter is covered in Bidyut Chakrabarty and Rajat Kumar Kujur, *Maoism in India: Reincarnation of Ultra-Left Wing Extremism in the Twenty-First Century* (New Delhi: Routledge, 2010).

Communism and the trade unions are summed up in P. R. N. Sinha, *Industrial Relations, Trade Unions and Labour Legislation* (New Delhi: Pearson International, 2006), which provides bibliographic references. A basic narrative of communism and the Kisan Sabha can be found in Abdullah Rasul, *A History of the All India Kisan Sabha* (Kolkata: National Book Agency, 1989). Francine Frankel, *India's Green Revolution: Economic Gains and Political Costs* (Princeton: Princeton University Press, 1971), is good on the impact of the Green Revolution on communist support. Mobilization around the food shortages of 1959 is the specific subject of Suranjan Das and P. K. Bandyopadhyay (eds.), *Food Movement of 1959: Documenting a Turning Point in the History of West Bengal* (Kolkata: K. P. Bagchi, 2004).

Studies of post-1947 links between Soviet and Indian communism are rare. John H. Kautsky, *Moscow and the Communist Party of India* (New York: MIT and John Wiley, 1956), remains important. Hari Vasudevan, "New Delhi 1971," sums up literature on Indo-Soviet economic collaboration in Andreas Hilger (ed.), *Die Sowjetunion und die Dritte Welt. UdSSR, Staatssozialismus und Antikolonialismus im Kalten Krieg 1945–1991* (Munich: R. Oldenburg Verlag, 2009), in which Hilger's introduction is important. Otherwise, while David Engerman has summed up implications of doctrinal revisions of the Khrushchev era in articles, there is useful material in *V Indiiu dukha* [To India of the Spirit] (Moscow: Vostochnaia literatura RAN, 2008).

21

Comparing African Experiences
of Communism

ALLISON DREW

African experiences of communism as a twentieth-century global project highlight the importance of national and geopolitical constraints on communist parties. A key debate in communist studies has been the core–periphery question – the varied relationships between the Soviet state and the national communist parties that constituted the communist world. But, in addition to their relationships with the Soviet state, African communist parties were also profoundly influenced by the metropole–colony dynamic. Thus, while World War II's defeat of fascism was critical for the maintenance of Soviet power and prestige, the war impacted African countries very differently, reflecting their varied relationships with European imperial powers. Moreover, precisely because of the metropole–colony dynamic, the periodization of communism in Africa differs from the European communist experience. While the Soviet invasions of Hungary and Czechoslovakia were pivotal events for European communists, this was not so for African communists, who were far more concerned with their own national liberation movements. Nonetheless, communist historiography has generally been silent about the metropole–colony dynamic.

Notwithstanding the primacy of the metropole–colony dynamic for colonized peoples, African communists valued participation in a global communist community that offered possibilities for undercutting international relationships premised on domination. Whether through reading, studying in overseas communist schools or attending international conferences, African communists and their sympathizers learned about conditions across the colonized world, knowledge that became particularly

My thanks to the Institute for European Global Studies, University of Basel, for a fellowship during January–March 2014 that enabled me to develop the ideas in this chapter.

important as the movement for decolonization spread across Asia and Africa.

Indeed, African communists saw communism as intrinsically linked with the anti-colonial struggle. European powers had claimed most of Africa by the early twentieth century. The ensuing anti-colonialist revolts were typically expressed in ethnic, religious and, eventually, national terms. With prospects for revolution in Europe over by the early 1920s, the Communist International (Comintern) – founded in 1919 as an international network of communist parties – stipulated support for anti-colonial movements as a means to weaken imperialism. In practice, the Comintern was far more concerned with Europe and Asia, areas of direct foreign-policy interest to the Soviet Union. Nonetheless, to the varying degrees that African liberation movements were influenced by left-wing doctrines, these were more likely to be communist rather than social-democratic – European social democracy did not normally reject colonialism but instead argued for its reform.

Communist ideas penetrated Africa from the coastal areas, where ports allowed the influx of radical ideas from other parts of the world, and they gained a foothold in areas of European settlement. Communists also had some success in organizing along rail lines, which enabled the dissemination of political propaganda and literature. The prospects for building communist movements were greatest in areas with an urban proletariat, especially at cultural crossroads such as Algeria, South Africa and Sudan. Communism's ability to develop as a movement also depended on its success in forging alliances with democratic and anti-colonial movements. Communist influence was found in the north and south and to a lesser extent in the west, but there was virtually no communist influence in east Africa. Generally, the continent's predominantly rural and peasant population made the diffusion of communist ideas difficult or even impossible.[1]

While a shared communist ideology and participation in a global communist community undoubtedly inspired African communists, national and geopolitical factors were far more important determinants of communist party trajectories. Communism had significant impact in Algeria and South Africa, settler colonies with some industrial development where Europeans introduced left-wing ideas. In both Algeria and South Africa, communism's strength lay in organized labor; indeed, socialists and communists built these

---

1 Allison Drew, "Communism in Africa," in Stephen A. Smith (ed.), *Oxford Handbook of the History of Communism* (Oxford: Oxford University Press, 2013), 285–302, esp. 285–86, 293.

countries' trade union movements. Crucially, South African communists had greater success in forging a long-term alliance with nationalists than did Algerian communists. This chapter examines communist experiences in these two countries, with comparative references to other parts of the continent, to illustrate the unfolding of national and geopolitical influences on the communist parties.

Colonial Conquest and Its Repercussions

These national and geopolitical specificities reflected the social, economic and political changes unleashed by the European colonial conquest of these regions. This conquest radically restructured class relations and pulled them into the international capitalist system, imposing a new form of state that acted on behalf of both capital and settlers. The geopolitical position of each country meant that they were drawn unevenly into this world order. The unfolding and intertwining of several factors – class and social cleavages, state power and geopolitics – underpinned the differing trajectories of Algeria and South Africa and their communist parties.

Both Algeria and South Africa were subjected to protracted military conquest and massive land expropriation. By the early twentieth century the indigenous people were generally small-scale agricultural cultivators, agricultural laborers or land-hungry migrant workers. Yet there were significant differences. Notably, Algeria had a traditional Muslim landed elite that succeeded in retaining its land in the colonial era. Algeria's landed elites therefore comprised both European settler and Muslim Algerian landowners, however small the latter group was compared to the former. In South Africa, by contrast, any possibility for a prosperous black peasantry and landowning class had been eliminated by the mass evictions and expropriations that had followed the 1913 Land Act. Thus, in the absence of a black landed elite, the black South African class structure was flatter than was the case for Muslims in Algeria.

Moreover, the pattern of religious, ethnic and national cleavages varied tremendously between these countries, with political consequences. Islam and Christianity both offered imagined international communities. Algeria was torn by the conflict of these two globalizing religions: European nationality, French citizenship and Catholicism vs. Algerian nationality and Islam. The secular French state and its European settlers imposed an anti-Islamic secularization that attacked local identity; Islam's centuries-old penetration of North African society offered an anti-colonial discourse that Christianity, as the religion of the colonizer, could not provide. With religious and national differences overlaying and reinforcing each other, there was scant common ground allowing contact across the religious divisions. Cultural nationalism was correspondingly stronger, leaving little space for the penetration of secular and communist values.

By contrast, South Africa's localized indigenous religious beliefs were inherently more vulnerable to the globalizing mission of the diverse Christian denominations, and its religious and ethnic cleavages were cross-cutting. Despite the pernicious racial divisions, leading black political activists were educated in Christian mission schools. This provided a common religious and educational framework that cut across the racial divide, allowing greater possibilities for crosscultural communication and for secular rather than cultural nationalism compared to Algeria.

Finally, the nature of the state had profound political ramifications. Indirect rule was paradigmatic for European domination in Africa, Mahmood Mamdani argues. The bifurcated colonial state, in which two forms of power operated under a single authority, ensured that a foreign European minority could rule over an indigenous African majority. Citizenship was reserved for urban, predominantly European civil society; citizens had direct representative government. By contrast, rural subsistence cultivators experienced indirect rule under chiefly authority; they became subjects in a system of decentralized despotism. This pattern of indirect rule can be seen with variations in colonial Algeria and colonial–apartheid South Africa. But unlike South Africa, where indirect rule was under civil authority, however repressive, in Algeria indirect rule had been militarized over centuries of Turkish and French domination.[2]

The bifurcation of the colonial state was never absolute, however. In practice, neither urban nor rural areas were reserved entirely for either Europeans or Africans. Precisely because Algeria and South Africa suffered massive land expropriation, labor migration became structurally embedded in both countries, slowly eroding the urban–rural distinction. Migrant labor became the basis for political movements to undermine the repressive states and a vector for the transmission of ideas between cities and countryside.

---

2 Mahmood Mamdani, *Citizen and Subject: Contemporary Africa and the Legacy of Late Colonialism* (Princeton: Princeton University Press 1996), 17–18; Lungisile Ntsebeza, *Democracy Compromised: Chiefs and the Politics of Land in South Africa* (Cape Town: HSRC, 2006), 16–22; John Ruedy, *Modern Algeria: The Origins and Development of a Nation*, 2nd edn. (Bloomington: Indiana University Press, 2005), 1–2, 10–12, 87–88; Martin Evans and John Phillips, *Algeria: Anger of the Dispossessed* (New Haven: Yale University Press, 2007), 1–25.

In both countries the demand for the extension of democratic rights to all became a rallying cry transmitted by migrant labor.

The Union of South Africa became a politically autonomous member of the British Empire in 1910. Black South Africans demanded democratic rights within the new union. South Africa's migrant workers went to Cape Town, Durban and Johannesburg, and its first worker-based national organization – the Industrial and Commercial Workers' Union – was launched in Cape Town in 1919; working-class nationalism had deeper roots in South Africa than in Algeria. By contrast, although claimed as French by France, Algeria was a de facto colony. Large numbers of Algerian workers migrated to France, creating a displaced proletariat. The first Algerian worker-based national organization – the Étoile nord-africaine (North African Star) – was launched in Paris in 1926. Only in the 1930s was the North African Star's successor organization, the Parti du peuple algérien (Algerian People's Party, PPA) launched in Algeria. Initially Algerians demanded equal rights under the French constitution but, after World War II, they demanded independence.[3]

National and geopolitical specificities shaped communist development from the outset. The autonomous Communist Party of South Africa (CPSA) was formed in 1920; geographic distance insulated it from undue pressure from the British Communist Party and, with some exceptions, from the Comintern. By contrast, communism began in Algeria as a region of the Parti communiste français (PCF), which had an extremely close relationship with the Comintern and the Soviet communist hierarchy. Not surprisingly, the Comintern intervened in Algeria earlier than it did in South Africa. While the CPSA became demographically representative of the black majority by the late 1920s, this was not so in Algeria, where Muslims were subjected to the *Côde de l'indigénat* (Native Code), which imposed harsh punishments for infractions that were not illegal in France but were in Algeria. Thus while Algerians could join the PCF in France, they could not legally do so in Algeria. In Algeria, communism constituted the far left; in South Africa communism splintered and a Trotskyist movement developed. The differences highlight the lack of any uniform communist experience in Africa despite broad parallels linked to global developments.[4] Nonetheless, notwithstanding the enormous distance and

3 Allison Drew, "Bolshevizing Communist Parties: The Algerian and South African Experiences," *International Review of Social History* 48 (2003), 167–202, 173–75.
4 Ruedy, *Modern Algeria*, 89; Allison Drew, *Discordant Comrades: Identities and Loyalties on the South African Left* (Aldershot: Ashgate, 2000; Pretoria: Unisa, 2002), 46–57; Allison Drew, *We Are No Longer in France: Communists in Colonial Algeria* (Manchester:

the language barrier, by 1922 communists in Algeria knew about South African labor struggles. Facilitated by the Comintern's multilingual practice, news traveled across the communist world, enabling African communists to begin their own comparative study of their continent.[5]

Geopolitics was pivotal during the popular front years. But, as George Orwell observed, anti-fascism – based on the popular front – could mask the desire to maintain imperial and colonial privileges over the nationally oppressed. Indeed, just as the Comintern itself increasingly reflected Soviet interests, the anti-fascist movement reflected Soviet and European interests and marginalized the colonial question.[6] The popular front years saw the expansion of urban public space in both countries as rural poverty drove people to the overcrowded urban slums and shanty towns, surviving through formal and informal employment. Significantly, South Africa was more urbanized than Algeria. By 1936, 17 percent of Africans in South Africa were urbanized; including Coloureds and Indians, the black population was even more urbanized. By contrast, only 13 percent of Algerians were urbanized.

This urban public space was sharply divided across national, religious and racial lines. In South Africa the popular front pandered to white racism; white workers would not share a platform with black people, producing two formations, one black and one white. In Algeria the popular front led to a backtracking on the call for independence, a communist demand in the 1920s. The Soviets supported a strong, united France to fight fascism; the PCF saw Algerian nationalism as divisive. An autonomous Parti communiste algérien (PCA) was launched in 1936, but nonetheless followed the PCF's opposition to independence. Geographical proximity tied the PCA closely to French and European politics during the popular front and World War II years.[7]

Manchester University Press, 2014; and Cape Town: South African History Online, 2015), 49, 95–98.
5 Drew, *We Are No Longer in France*, 33; Vadim A. Staklo, "The Comintern," in William J. Chase (ed.), *Enemies Within the Gates? The Comintern and the Stalinist Repression, 1934–1939* (New Haven: Yale University Press, 2001), 10–36, esp. 19–20.
6 Silvio Pons, *The Global Revolution: A History of International Communism, 1917–1991* (Oxford: Oxford University Press, 2014), 75–85; Kevin McDermott and Jeremy Agnew, *The Comintern: A History of International Communism from Lenin to Stalin* (Basingstoke: Macmillan, 1996), 120–57; George Orwell, "Not Counting Niggers," in Sonia Orwell and Ian Angus (eds.), *The Collected Essays, Journalism and Letters of George Orwell*, vol. I (Harmondsworth: Penguin Books, 1970), 434–38.
7 Drew, *We Are No Longer in France*, 81–109; Drew, *Discordant Comrades*, 199–224.

World War II in Africa

When war in Europe broke out on 3 September 1939 the USSR remained neutral; the Comintern defined the war as one of interimperialist rivalry, causing shock waves across the communist world. Like most communist parties, the PCA and CPSA suffered defections, but nonetheless followed the Comintern. There the similarity ended, as the geopolitical position of each country shaped the communist movements. In France and Algeria repression was fierce: The PCF, PCA and PPA were banned. More than 500 French communists and trade unionists were deported to detention camps in Algeria, where government authorities rounded up more than 10,000 alleged opponents and threw them in prison or work or detention camps. The fall of France and establishment of the Vichy regime in June 1940 brought further repression. European settlers were strongly pro-Vichy. Communists were given lengthy prison sentences, tortured and condemned to death. The country became increasingly militarized.

Undaunted, the emaciated and clandestine PCA took advantage of the Comintern's revised position to once again call for Algerian independence to weaken French imperialism. But once Germany invaded the USSR in June 1941, the Comintern endorsed the war. The national sections followed suit: The need to preserve party unity and maintain the belief in the Comintern's legitimacy won the day. The PCA followed the PCF in promoting the unity of France and Algeria. Once again, as they had during the popular front period, the USSR, the PCF and the PCA concurred that Algeria should remain part of France. Yet the repression continued. The Spanish Civil War had led to an exodus of Spanish communists and republicans into Algeria, another indicator of the importance of geopolitics. Some of these were charged with helping the underground PCA. A military tribunal judged eighty-one Spanish communists on 6 February 1942 and meted out severe punishments, some to death and many to twenty-year sentences. More military tribunals followed.[8]

The Anglo-American landing in November 1942 stimulated Algerian nationalism, which grew exponentially during the war. Nationalists demanded not only an extension of democratic rights within a French Algeria but, increasingly, an independent Algeria. The PCA, by contrast, prioritizing Franco-Algerian unity against fascism, downplayed independence. In February 1943 the Soviet victory at the Battle of Stalingrad increased

---

8 McDermott and Agnew, *Comintern*, 191–204; Pons, *Global Revolution*, 91–115; Drew, *We Are No Longer in France*, 113–22.

its leverage within the Allied camp and led to the release of the imprisoned French communist deputies. But PCA prisoners had to wait longer, enabling the French communists to influence PCA policy. Nor did the Comintern's dissolution that year lessen Soviet influence over its national sections. Nonetheless, the dramatic growth in Algerian nationalism – an early sign that colonial authority was under threat – put pressure on Algerian communists. Despite the PCA's official stance for unity with France, local communists highlighted independence.[9]

While Europe celebrated the war's end, in Algeria tensions between European settlers and Algerians skyrocketed. Following nationalist demonstrations on 8 May 1945, settlers massacred many thousands of Muslims in eastern Algeria. Viewing the events through anti-fascist lenses, the PCF and PCA initially believed that the 8 May protests were inspired by fascists and were slow to condemn the massacre. As a result, Algerians were generally ambivalent and often cynical toward communists. Gradually, however, the PCA recognized the massacre's scale and campaigned vigorously against the ensuing repression.[10]

The contrast with South Africa's experience of the war could not have been starker. Despite South Africa's position within the British Empire, the South African state was not directly tied to the European anti-fascist struggle. Many Afrikaners sympathized with the Germans. The South African Parliament was divided, leading to a change in government; the parliament voted for war against Germany by a thin majority. In marked contrast to Algeria, the South African government – more concerned about right-wing than left-wing threats – interned several hundred fascist sympathizers but only a small number of leading left-wing trade unionists.

Once the CPSA joined the war effort it gained white recruits and its relations with African nationalists improved. The CPSA now supported the government that it had previously attacked through its comparison of racial oppression in South Africa with fascism in Europe. Its pro-war position meant an endorsement of the government's domestic war policies; state repression of communists eased measurably. While counseling against strike action, the CPSA supported worker demands for better pay and conditions; communists gained leading positions in both white and black trade unions. Thus, while the PCA emerged from the war scorned by Algerian nationalists, the CPSA had built a solid alliance with African nationalists, as seen in the joint CPSA

9 Drew, *We Are No Longer in France*, 122–38.
10 Jean-Louis Planche, *Sétif 1945. Histoire d'un massacre annoncé* (Paris: Perrin, 2006); Drew, *We Are No Longer in France*, 145–79.

and African National Congress (ANC) support for the August 1946 African mine workers' strike.[11]

The Cold War in Africa

The postwar years saw a global political realignment that culminated in the Cold War. The USSR's role in defeating Nazi Germany relegitimized the communist global project that had been tainted by Stalin's Great Terror. The Soviet state became a superpower presiding over an international network of states and parties that had internalized the primacy of Soviet state interests. This was symbolized by the establishment of the Cominform (Communist Information Bureau) in September 1947. The Comintern's successor, the Cominform, maintained the Soviet position that the world was divided into two antagonistic camps and criticized nationalist movements that did not accept communist leadership.[12]

After the war, imperial powers increased their resource extraction to finance their own reconstruction. Strikes erupted in Bulawayo, Dakar, Dar es Salaam, Johannesburg, Mombasa, Timezrit and Zanzibar and across the Gold Coast, Nigerian, French West African and Sudanese railway systems.[13] The labor unrest fed into anti-colonial and national liberation struggles. The Cold War proved an important ideological tool against left-wing activists seeking support from discontented groups demanding democratic rights. Both Algeria and South Africa experienced an intensification of repression, but the trajectories of the two communist parties diverged even more as they were swept along by national and international developments.

In Algeria the PCA regained the political space it had lost in the aftermath of the Sétif massacre. Nationalist organizations were not interested in socioeconomic issues. Their fiercely competitive leaders were increasingly intolerant of open discussion within their own organizations. As a result, the PCA's Algerian membership grew as Algerian youth joined because of its social justice concerns. The PCA pursued a multipronged strategy, contesting elections, forming amnesty committees against repression and

---

11 Drew, *Discordant Comrades*, 225–40.
12 Pons, *Global Revolution*, 162–67, 235, 317–18; McDermott and Agnew, *Comintern*, 217.
13 Frederick Cooper, *Decolonization and African Society: The Labor Question in French and British Africa* (Cambridge: Cambridge University Press, 1996), 225–27; Gaston Revel, *Un instituteur communiste en Algérie. L'engagement et le combat (1936–1965)*, ed. Alexis Sempé (Cahors: La Louve, 2013), 262–64.

organizing united fronts for democratic rights. However, it still faced pressure from the PCF. Caught between its parent party and the nationalist movement, its divided loyalty made united fronts difficult to sustain. Thus, while August–September 1951 saw the formation of the Front algérien of communist and nationalist organizations, in October the front faltered because the PCA succumbed to pressure from the PCF, which had its own agenda of improving relations with the French Socialist Party. The PCA's relationship with the PCF invariably fanned nationalist skepticism.[14]

In South Africa, the squashing of the 1946 African mine workers' strike set the stage for an intensified attack by the state on the left. In the strike's aftermath, fifty-two individuals – communists, ANC members and trade unionists – were charged with conspiracy and eight members of the CPSA's Central Executive Committee with sedition. The main charges were eventually dismissed, but the common repression to which communists and nationalists were subjected strengthened the relationship that had been forged during their tactical alliances and laid the basis for their postwar strategic alliance. Communists aligned with the ANC, which in 1946 increased the number of seats on its national executive, enabling three communists to win seats without displacing the established leaders.

Political repression was accompanied by racial polarization as the National Party was elected in 1948 on a platform of apartheid. Although white electoral support was fueled by fears of black working-class militancy, black trade unions had been smashed in the aftermath of the war. The National Party tightened racial classification, codified separate racial development and suppressed political dissent. The apartheid project rested on the continued erosion of democratic rights, rationalized by the need to suppress the communist threat symbolized by the USSR's postwar ascendancy. Thus, while reflecting South African specificities, apartheid was also the South African variant of the Cold War.

The 1950 Suppression of Communism Act allowed the South African government to ban the CPSA and other socialists. Unlike the PCA, which had gone underground during World War II and reemerged when the political environment liberalized, the CPSA's Central Committee disbanded the party without consulting the members or preparing for underground work. Three years later communists who were unhappy with that decision

14 Drew, *We Are No Longer in France*, 145–79.

ALLISON DREW

formed the underground South African Communist Party (SACP). The SACP stressed closer collaboration with the ANC, giving primacy to alliance politics over class struggle and eschewing an independent profile. Leading African nationalists joined the SACP; overlapping membership at the leadership level was common. This close relationship had its critics, but South African communists claimed that they had merged with the national liberation movement.[15]

Alongside their intense national struggles, communists in Africa became acculturated into a global communist community. Recruitment programs and party schools fostered the belief in communism as a global project. Thus, in the 1950s Algerians joined the PCA as part of a national recruitment drive known as *la promotion Staline*; Stalin was particularly admired both for the defeat of fascism and for state-led industrial development, which offered a model for African countries. The acculturation was also accomplished through visits to China, the USSR and Eastern bloc countries, where Algerian and South African communists attended world peace movement forums and women's and youth congresses. The success of this acculturation, juxtaposed against the intense repression communists experienced in their own countries, meant that the USSR's 1956 invasion of Hungary, so important for the European left, had very little impact on Algerian and South African communists.[16]

National Liberation and Armed Struggle

Intertwined with the Cold War, another international process was unfolding – the unraveling of colonial empires. Algerian and South African communists had been inspired by the October 1949 Chinese Revolution, which inspired hope for future anti-capitalist revolutions in predominantly agrarian societies. They carefully followed and sought to learn from other national liberation struggles.

The French state resisted the dismantling of its empire with all its might. Moroccan and Tunisian nationalists were demanding independence; the PCA maintained transnational links with Moroccan and Tunisian communists

15 Jack Simons and Ray Simons, *Class and Colour in South Africa, 1850–1950* (London: International Defence and Aid Fund, 1983), 10, 610–25; Drew, *Discordant Comrades*, 249–74.
16 Drew, *We Are No Longer in France*, 166, 182; Revel, *Un instituteur communiste*, 235–60; Chris Saunders and Sue Onslow, "The Cold War and Southern Africa, 1976–1990," in Melvyn P. Leffler and Odd Arne Westad (eds.) *Cambridge History of the Cold War*, vol. III (Cambridge: Cambridge University Press, 2009), 224.

528

throughout the 1940s and 1950s. Vietnam became a symbol of both the Cold War and the international anti-colonial struggle. The French state stepped up military engagement in Vietnam and resisted calls for reform in Algeria, where its limited political concessions came too little, too late. PCA newspapers reported on the Tunisian guerrilla struggle launched in 1952 and the Vietnamese struggle; the Vietnamese victory over the French at Dien Bien Phu in May 1954 was inspirational for Algerians. Despite the PCA's support for the Tunisian and Vietnamese guerrilla struggles, it hesitated to join the armed struggle launched by the Front de libération national (FLN) in November 1954.

Little by little, however, the PCA gave clandestine support to the armed struggle, hoping to remain legal as long as possible. Pushed especially by its rural activists, in June 1955 the PCA's Central Committee agreed to increase its support for the armed struggle, to participate directly wherever it had sufficient numbers and to form its own armed detachments – the Combattants de la libération (Liberation Soldiers, CDL). The FLN categorically refused to tolerate any other independent political organization; it eventually succeeded in capturing most of the political space within the liberation movement. But the PCA refused to give up its organizational autonomy and merge into the FLN. As a result, relations between the PCA and FLN were tense throughout the war.

The Cold War played itself out in Algeria as the French state, keen to placate the Americans, who feared Soviet expansion in North Africa, hounded the underground PCA and CDL. As a result, although the PCA maintained its autonomy, in July 1956 it pragmatically agreed to integrate the CDL into the FLN's Armée de libération nationale (Army of National Liberation). Yet even this failed to ease FLN skepticism toward communists, many of whom were killed during the independence war – by both the French army and Algerian nationalists.[17]

France's relationship with Algeria was central to its imperial identity. Occupied by Germany, defeated by the Vietnamese at Dien Bien Phu, France would not consider another defeat. French forces occupied Algeria, but this did not prevent the FLN's armed struggle from developing into a guerrilla war. However, the French succeeded in cutting off contact between the FLN's internal and exile forces. The internal guerrilla army was starved of resources while Soviet and Eastern bloc military support allowed the growth of the external army of national liberation. But precisely

17 Drew, *We Are No Longer in France*, 180–216.

because it was based outside Algeria the external army did not engage in military activity. By the war's end, the FLN's external military wing was the strongest organization; civil society was exhausted.

Despite the uneasy relationship of Algeria's communists and nationalists, the force of Algeria's war of independence altered the top-down policy direction characteristic of the communist world. Thus, when Algerian communists learned that the PCF had voted for the Special Powers Bill in March 1956, they expressed shock and anger. Moreover, in contrast to the PCF, the PCA supported sabotage and endorsed desertion from the French army. The most telling example is seen in the PCA's recognition of the Gouvernement provisoire de la République algérienne (Provisional Government of the Algerian Republic, GPRA) two months after its establishment by the FLN in September 1958. The USSR recognized the GPRA as the de facto government in late 1960; PCF recognition followed in early 1961. Ultimately, both the USSR and the PCF followed the PCA's stance on the war. The conventional direction in which international communist policy flowed was reversed.

The Algerian independence war unfolded against the backdrop of a continental drive for independence. Morocco, Tunisia and Sudan, which also had a communist tradition, all became independent in 1956. In Sudan Marxist ideas had been introduced by Egyptian communists and Central and East European immigrants working on the railway. Communist influence grew during World War II due to the combined influence of British communist soldiers and Sudanese students returning from Egypt. In 1946 the Sudanese Movement for National Liberation was launched. In 1949 this became the Sudanese Communist Party, which played an important role in the independence struggle.[18]

The year 1960 was a turning point for Africa as seventeen sub-Saharan countries became independent. But the South African government rigidly resisted democratic reforms. On 21 March 1960 unarmed protesters at Pan Africanist Congress (PAC) anti-pass demonstrations in Sharpeville and Langa were massacred – the PAC had split from the ANC citing the undue influence of white communists, among other reasons. Following the massacre, the

18 Ahmad A. Sikainga, "Organized Labor in Contemporary Sudan: The Story of the Railway Workers of Atbara," *South Atlantic Quarterly* 109, 1 (Winter 2010), 31–51; Alain Gresh, "The Free Officers and the Comrades: The Sudanese Communist Party and Nimeiri, Face-to-Face, 1969–1971," *International Journal of Middle East Studies* 21, 3 (Aug. 1989), 393–409; Gabriel Warburg, *Islam, Nationalism and Communism in a Traditional Society: The Case of Sudan* (London: Routledge, 1978), 93–101.

government imposed a state of emergency, banned political organizations and arrested more than 2,000 people. Those not detained went underground or into exile. With nonviolent protest seemingly ineffective in countering the state's increasing repression, anti-apartheid activists studied the Algerian experience.[19]

In contrast to the PCA, which had deliberately remained legal as long as possible, the SACP had been launched as an underground group with no public presence at all. The mounting repression reactivated a debate about issuing propaganda in its own name. In October 1959 it launched its journal *African Communist* as a compromise between those wanting the party to go public and those advocating the status quo to preserve the alliance with the ANC. Although noting that only Algeria and South Africa had "substantial Marxist parties," the *African Communist* gave no hint of its South African origins.[20] In July 1960 the SACP finally issued a flyer in its name.

The SACP studied the relationship between the FLN and the PCA. The two communist parties were in contact. In 1947 the PCA had published an article on South Africa's repressive labor system, and the *African Communist* now carried articles on the Algerian struggle. The FLN, which had launched armed struggle without the PCA's involvement, would not allow dual membership. The PCA refused to disband, and its relationship with the FLN remained tense throughout the war despite the integration of the CDL guerrillas into the FLN's army. For the SACP, this indicated the need for a joint armed struggle from the start. Unlike the FLN, the ANC allowed dual membership, and many of its leaders were communists. This made SACP collaboration with the ANC far easier than had been the case with the PCA and FLN. Thus, SACP and ANC members jointly formed Umkhonto we Sizwe (Spear of the Nation, MK), which launched a sabotage campaign in December 1961. Across much of Africa, however, political leaders were hostile to communism: When Nelson Mandela toured Africa in 1962 to raise funds for MK, he quickly became aware of this hostility and advised his comrades to downplay communist influence, at least publicly. MK's first wave of sabotage ended in July 1963 with the arrest of its top leaders. By November 1965, with its key activists

19 Allison Drew, "Visions of Liberation: The Algerian War of Independence and Its South African Reverberations," *Review of African Political Economy* 42, 143 (Mar. 2015), 22–43.
20 Toussaint, "Marxism – The Science of Change," *African Communist* 1 (Oct. 1959), 16, disa .ukzn.ac.za/sites/default/files/pdf_files/Acn159.0001.9976.000.001.Oct1959.4.pdf.

imprisoned or in exile, the SACP had ceased functioning as an organized body within South Africa.[21]

State-Led Socialism in Africa

Although the independence of much of Africa undermined the metropole–colony dynamic, the authoritarian bifurcated state structure remained. So did economic dependence, which seemingly opened up possibilities for communist influence. With capitalism tarnished by its association with colonialism, the USSR hoped that independent African countries would follow its model. Indeed, six African communist parties attended the CPSU's Twenty-Second Congress in October 1961 – Algeria, Morocco, Réunion, South Africa, Sudan and Tunisia. But the conditions facing African communists were harsh indeed: Only in Tunisia and Réunion were the parties legal, and Egypt's fragmented communist movement was heavily repressed.[22]

Algeria became independent in July 1962. Seventy percent of Algerians still lived in rural areas. The Muslim landed elite had survived; the peasantry, by contrast, had been profoundly proletarianized. The FLN styled itself as a socialist alternative to Soviet-style communism for the Third World, carefully negotiating with both the Soviets and the Chinese as Sino-Soviet tensions undermined the Eastern bloc's seeming unity. Nonetheless, the FLN was resolutely hostile to independent socialist initiatives, banning the PCA in November 1962 and proclaiming itself as the sole legal party the next year. Next it crushed the Kabyle-based Front des forces socialistes (FFS) launched in September 1963.

The military regime that seized power in June 1965 continued this hostility to autonomous socialist groups. The Organisation de la résistance populaire (ORP), formed after the coup by members of the banned PCA and leftists close to the deposed president Ahmed Ben Bella, was crushed within a few months. A successor organization, the Parti de l'avant-garde socialiste (PAGS), was formed the next year and continued the PCA's pro-Soviet orientation. The PAGS saw the FLN's approach to the USSR in an anti-imperialist light. When the military regime took a left turn in 1971, nationalizing Algeria's oil and gas reserves and collectivizing agriculture, the PAGS saw these as further positive moves. Many PAGS members and supporters

21 Drew, *We Are No Longer in France*, 162; Drew, "Visions of Liberation."
22 Walter Kolarz, "The Impact of Communism on West Africa," *International Affairs* 38, 2 (Apr. 1962), 158–59.

worked in the public sector, and in the 1960s and 1970s the party seemed influential beyond its numbers, at least in terms of ideas. But it could hardly dent the military regime.[23]

Nor did other African leaders rush to adopt communism, despite their skepticism about capitalism. China had initially followed a broad anti-imperialist line in Africa, but after the 1963 Sino-Soviet split its policies increasingly reflected its rivalry with the USSR. A nonaligned African socialism led by Ghana and Tanzania became the dominant left-wing approach of the 1960s and early 1970s, indicating the willingness of leftist-inclined state leaders to experiment with non-Soviet alternatives; Tanzania had close relations with the Chinese. Proponents of African socialism argued that Africa's precolonial communal values and relative absence of classes and class struggle should form the basis for an African path of development. However, by the 1970s the doctrine was discredited both by its failed economic projects and by the repressive one-party regimes wielding power in its name.[24]

Military coups and one-party regimes became common across Africa, the subject of a study by South African communist Ruth First, who argued that economic dependence, coupled with the tenuous unity of liberation movements and the artificial nature of colonially imposed states predisposed postcolonial Africa to such a fate. Military leaders often used left-wing discourse to justify their seizure of power.[25] Sudan provides another illustration of the hostility of even left-wing states toward communists. In 1969 Gaafar Nimeiri took power in a military coup, announcing his decision to form a progressive one-party system. The Sudanese Communist Party, which retained its strong labor base, refused to disband despite pressure from both the regime and the Soviets. Drawing lessons from Egyptian communists, who in 1965 had merged into Gamal Abdel Nasser's Arab Socialist Union, in 1970 it called for a national front of progressive organizations. But communist

23 Evans and Phillips, *Algeria*, 76, 80, 90–91.
24 Martin Kilson, "Politics of African Socialism," *African Forum* 1, 3 (Winter 1966), 17–26; Kwame Nkrumah, "Some Aspects of Socialism in Africa," in W. H. Friedland and C. G. Rosberg, Jr. (eds.), *African Socialism* (Stanford: Stanford University Press, 1964), 259–63; J. K. Nyerere, *Ujamaa: The Basis of African Socialism* (Dar es Salaam: Tanganyika African National Union, 1962); A. M. Babu, *African Socialism or Socialist Africa?* (London: Zed Books, 1981); Steven F. Jackson, "China's Third World Foreign Policy: The Case of Angola and Mozambique, 1961–1993," *China Quarterly* 142 (Jun. 1995), 393, 396–98.
25 Ruth First, *The Barrel of a Gun: Political Power in Africa and the Coup d'Etat* (London: Penguin Books, 1970), 411–13; Arnold Hughes, "The Appeal of Marxism to Africans," *Journal of Communist Studies* 8, 2 (Jun. 1992), 13–15.

leaders were arrested in April 1971 and hundreds of communists executed four months later. The USSR, concerned with global hegemony, supported authoritarian left-leaning states that smashed their own socialist movements; it maintained cordial relations with Nimeiri, only reconsidering when he shifted his Cold War allegiances. Only very gradually did the Sudanese Communist Party begin to recover from heavy repression.[26]

Soviet influence in Africa increased in the 1970s as Angola, Benin, Cape Verde, Ethiopia, Guinea-Bissau, Madagascar, Mozambique, the People's Republic of the Congo and Somalia all espoused Marxism-Leninism or "scientific socialism" and, in varying degrees, pursued closer ties with the USSR. Along with anti-authoritarian upheavals in Asia and Latin America, the events precipitated a rethink of US foreign policy – American policy-makers were concerned that the new regimes would be pro-Soviet – along with an increase in US military involvement in the Third World. These developments intensified the Cold War, producing what Fred Halliday called the second Cold War.[27]

The Second Cold War in Africa

The second Cold War was clearly seen in southern Africa, where struggles against settler colonialism and white-minority rule became intertwined with superpower Cold War ambitions. On the one side were the Soviets and the Cubans; on the other were the Americans, South Africans and Chinese, who all supported groups that rejected the USSR.

Alliance politics were crucial for southern African communists, who integrated themselves into armed liberation movements in Mozambique, Angola and South Africa. Although this might suggest communism's relative success in the region, it also signaled its limitations. While some Mozambican and Angolan anti-colonial leaders had embraced communism as students in 1950s Portugal, they were too few in number to sustain autonomous communist parties; the short-lived Angolan Communist Party that had formed in October 1955 later merged with other small groups into the Movimento popular da libertação de Angola (MPLA). In 1957–58 Lusophone activists launched a transnational network that was vital for the struggles against

---

26 Warburg, *Islam*, 125; Gresh, "Free Officers," 400–06.
27 Fred Halliday, *The Making of the Second Cold War* (London: Verso, 1983); Odd Arne Westad, *The Global Cold War: Third World Interventions and the Making of Our Times* (Cambridge: Cambridge University Press, 2005), 331–63; Hughes, "Appeal of Marxism," 10–11.

Portuguese colonialism.[28] Intense repression delayed the development of national liberation movements in Mozambique and Angola; when they emerged in the late 1950s and early 1960s it was to launch guerrilla war. Influenced by the USSR, the leaders of Angola's MPLA and Mozambique's Frente de Libertação de Moçambique (Frelimo) gradually adopted socialism during their armed struggles.

Portugal's April 1974 military coup transformed the southern African political terrain. Mozambique and Angola became independent in June and November 1975 respectively. But the outbreak of civil war in both countries pulled them directly into the Cold War, as rival powers funded rival political movements. South Africa had already invaded Angola a month before independence, fearing that, once independent, Mozambique and Angola would support the South African and Namibian liberation struggles. For the South African government, their alignment with the USSR, along with Cuban military support for the MPLA, raised the specter of communism in southern Africa. China's de facto alliance with the apartheid government against the MPLA proved embarrassing; its role in southern Africa gradually declined, and its relations with Africa became "virtually estranged."[29]

In 1977 Mozambique, Angola and Ethiopia adopted Marxism-Leninism as their state ideology. Unlike other Soviet-aligned African states, however, they also applied Marxism-Leninism as a state-led developmental model. This Afrocommunist approach entailed closer ties with the Soviet bloc, the formation of a vanguard party and state control of the economy to promote industrialization and modernization – a marked contrast to African socialism's concern with tradition. National and geopolitical factors are essential for understanding their diverse experiences. By 1980 the three countries had built political parties, organized peasants and developed state farms. In the Horn of Africa Marxism-Leninism appealed both to Ethiopia's military regime, which aspired to radical change, and to regional opposition movements. But Ethiopia's left turn also reflected regional Cold War dynamics, as Somalia's military regime expelled the Soviets and embraced the Americans and Chinese. By contrast, the left-wing trajectories of Mozambique and

---

28 Joao Manuel Neves, "Frantz Fanon and the Struggle for the Independence of Angola: The Meeting in Rome in 1959," *Interventions* 17, 3 (2015), 417–33.
29 Drew, "Communism in Africa," 295; Saunders and Onslow, "The Cold War and Southern Africa," 225–27; Jackson, "China's Third World Foreign Policy," 413, 420–21; Mark Webber, "Angola: Continuity and Change," *Journal of Communist Studies* 8, 2 (Jun. 1992), 126–44; Jeremy Harding, "Apartheid's Last Stand," *London Review of Books* (17 Mar. 2016), 9–20.

Angola developed out of alliances formed during their anti-colonial struggles.[30]

The SACP pursued alliance politics with great skill and success. Smashed inside the country, its external wing assumed leadership, setting up headquarters in London. Exile strengthened the party's relationship with the Eastern bloc countries, undoubtedly due to financial dependence. Not surprisingly, the Soviet invasion of Czechoslovakia, which sparked a crisis for European communists, had little impact on South African communists, whose response was uncritically pro-Soviet. The SACP hoped to infiltrate MK troops trained in African and East European countries back into South Africa. But repeated military failures compelled the ANC to convene a conference at Morogoro, Tanzania, in April–May 1969. The conference strengthened the political alliance of the SACP, ANC, MK and the South African Congress of Trade Unions (SACTU). The ANC's executive resigned *en bloc*. Communists formed the majority of the new executive, and MK was put under the supervision of a "revolutionary council" that included three communists and answered to the new executive. The ANC's "Strategies and Tactics" document had strong communist input. Yet, although communists were well placed in the ANC and MK, the SACP did not function as a collective entity.

If the Czechoslovakian crisis had seemingly no impact on South African communists, the "global 1968" that coincided with the crisis did have South African – and Algerian – reverberations, especially for students and youth. While the rise of the black-consciousness movement was a response to South African conditions, it also reflected the influence of African-American and student protests internationally. By the 1970s South Africa was bubbling, inspired by the independence of Angola and Mozambique. The black trade union movement grew exponentially, diverse socialist currents challenged the SACP's position on the left and the year-long 1976 Soweto uprising shook the country. The SACP was initially antagonistic toward the new trade union movement – communists figured prominently among exiled SACTU leaders – and cautiously critical of the new socialist currents.

Just as Mozambican and Angolan independence had intensified Cold War rivalries in the region, the revived Cold War had repercussions for the South

---

30 Saunders and Onslow, "The Cold War and Southern Africa," 229–37; Harding, "Apartheid's Last Stand," 9; Jackson, "China's Third World Foreign Policy," 413; David Ottaway and Marina Ottaway, *Afrocommunism* (New York and London: Africana, 1981); Marina Ottaway, "Afrocommunism Ten Years After: Crippled but Alive," *Issue: A Journal of Opinion* 16, 1 (1987), 11–17; Christopher Clapham, "The Socialist Experience in Ethiopia and Its Demise," *Journal of Communist Studies* 8, 2 (Jun. 1992), 105–25.

African liberation struggle. In 1977 the SACP moved its headquarters to Luanda, Angola – closer to home. Yet the armed struggle on which its hopes were pinned was stymied by the difficulty of infiltrating troops back into the country. Reflecting American pressure, the 1984 Nkomati Accord between Mozambique and South Africa precluded MK access to Mozambique and increased pressure on MK troops in Angola. More discontent within MK ranks – culminating in a mutiny in Angola – propelled another ANC conference in June 1985 at Kabwe, Zambia. The Kabwe conference urged the broadening of armed struggle into a "people's war" and opened ANC membership to all South Africans, irrespective of racial category – another SACP victory.[31]

In South Africa popular pressure against apartheid escalated dramatically during the 1980s, a decade of intense socialist debate that raised the possibility of an SACP resurgence inside the country. The 1984–85 Vaal uprising fed into left-wing debates about community and workplace struggles, while the massive growth of the anti-capitalist labor movement led to the formation of the Congress of South African Trade Unions (COSATU) in December 1985. Pragmatically, the SACP wooed COSATU leaders and, after concerted political battles, COSATU aligned itself with the ANC and the SACP. By the late 1980s the SACP had absorbed a range of left-wing intellectuals into its ranks. Despite being banned, it was visible at mass demonstrations across the country.

Cold War dynamics continued to frame southern African developments. As a result of *perestroika* and *glasnost'* the Soviets began decreasing their economic and military involvement in Africa. In December 1986 they announced their intention to curtail their involvement in Angola. Nonetheless, they remained engaged in its military struggles. The 1987–88 battle of Cuito Cuanavale, which the MPLA won with Cuban and Soviet support, led to a shift in the region's balance of power. The South African military was forced to withdraw from Angola. The South African government agreed to negotiate an end to its illegal occupation of Namibia in May 1988; independence accords were signed in December.[32]

---

31 Saunders and Onslow, "The Cold War and Southern Africa," 227, 237. See Stephen Ellis, *External Mission: The ANC in Exile, 1960–1990* (Johannesburg and Cape Town: Jonathan Ball, 2012), 40–204, for a detailed analysis of the shifting SACP-ANC-MK alliances.
32 Saunders and Onslow, "The Cold War and Southern Africa," 240; Harding, "Apartheid's Last Stand," 16–18; Margot Light, "Moscow's Retreat from Africa," *Journal of Communist Studies* 8, 2 (Jun. 1992), 30–38.

Buoyed by events at Cuito Cuanavale and worried that the South African government would pressure the liberation movement into premature negotiations, the SACP clung to the idea of armed struggle. Its seventh congress in Havana, Cuba, in April 1989 stressed armed struggle, underground and mass action, and international pressure. Although it did not foresee the East European uprisings later that year, it recouped quickly. Senior communist Joe Slovo's January 1990 discussion paper "Has Socialism Failed?" criticized Stalinism for bureaucratic and authoritarian leadership and insisted that socialism could function democratically without Soviet "distortions." The South African government, now less worried about Soviet domination, announced the unbanning of political organizations and negotiations in February 1990. The SACP seemed poised to provide substantial direction to the ANC – a far cry from the experience of Algerian communists in 1962.[33]

Algeria likewise experienced a democratic uprising. In October 1988 a conjuncture of events produced what is known as the "first Arab spring," when popular protests compelled the one-party state to introduce democratic reforms and multiparty elections. The elections signaled both the rejection of the dominant party and the salience of nonsecular politics: The Islamist Front islamique du salut won the majority of votes. But a military coup in January 1992 aborted the democratic transition. The PAGS, which had failed miserably in the elections, dissolved later that year. Some of its members formed the left-wing anti-Islamist Ettahaddi (Defiance); others, following the communist tradition, the Parti algérien pour la démocratie et le socialisme. Martial law was followed by a decade of civil war and an eventual return to civilian rule backed by a powerful military–security establishment. Civil society revived, producing a tiny, fragile and fragmented socialist movement.[34]

Conclusion

The Soviet Union's collapse and the end of the Cold War coincided with a wave of change across Africa. A succession of leftist regimes – Angola, Benin, Ethiopia, Mozambique, People's Republic of the Congo and Zambia – either lost power or dramatically shifted their policies. The changes reflected complex combinations of national and geopolitical factors. Generally, the

---

33 Saunders and Onslow, "The Cold War and Southern Africa," 241.
34 Evans and Phillips, *Algeria*, 114, 156–57, 232; Kamel Daoud, "The Algerian Exception," *New York Times*, 29 May 2015.

top-down centralized and collectivist policies followed by these countries had been unsuccessful in promoting sustainable development. This contributed to pressure against authoritarian regimes for democratic change. In the absence of longstanding socialist or communist movements, state policies succumbed more readily to global neoliberal pressures.

The Algerian and South African cases suggest that the periodization of twentieth-century communism in Africa reflects the timing of the resolution of the national liberation struggle, whether through independence or democracy. Communism's development and endurance as a movement were tied to several factors: first, whether there was a class structure that was sufficiently proletarianized to give meaning and credibility to communist ideas; second, whether the pattern of social cleavages allowed or impeded social interaction across the divisions; third, the ability to make and sustain alliances with other social or political movements; and, fourth, the strength of urban civil society relative to the state and the military.

On all four indicators, South Africa showed more potential for the development of a viable communist movement than Algeria. First, South Africa was more proletarianized and urbanized than was Algeria. Second, South Africa's crosscutting cleavages allowed some contact, however limited, across the racial divide. By contrast, Algeria's reinforcing cleavages impeded interaction across religious lines, and the contest between the two globalizing religions, Christianity and Islam, inhibited the diffusion of secular ideas. Third, the SACP was remarkably successful in forging alliances. By contrast, the PCA's relationship with the PCF precluded long-term national alliances during the colonial period, despite occasional short-term alliances. Following independence, authoritarian rule, repression and civil war made such alliances extremely difficult if not impossible.

Finally, South Africa's urban civil society relative to the state and the military was stronger than that of Algeria. The anti-apartheid struggle's long duration facilitated the development of civil society organizations inside the country, while the long-term difficulty of infiltrating armed guerrillas into the country meant that, despite the state's growing militarization, civil society struggles were far more important than the periodic sabotage attacks. Urban political and trade union struggles were paramount in the years leading up to the democratic transition. The SACP's ability to link itself to these urban struggles was critical to its success in reintegrating itself in the country during the democratic transition. Significantly, the struggle's long duration influenced the nature of the SACP's alliances. SACP-ANC-MK financial dependence on the Soviet Union allowed the penetration of Soviet ideology throughout the exile movement through education and training in the Eastern bloc. This strengthened the close relationship of the SACP and ANC. As a result, at the moment of the transition, the civilian state controlled the military, civil society was far stronger than the liberation movement's armed units and the SACP was seemingly extremely influential within the liberation movement.

Yet the SACP's very success at forging this alliance paradoxically signaled an underlying weakness. Since South Africa's democratic transition, the SACP's continued alliance with a dominant party pursuing a neoliberal capitalist agenda has been at the expense of any social justice agenda. This has split the labor movement, whose fortunes have been damaged by deindustrialization. The SACP's membership reflects its proximity to power, not any anti-capitalist commitment. Its 2015 ninety-fourth anniversary at Motherwell, Eastern Cape, was attended by some 600 people – a far cry from the 45,000 claimed at its 1990 relaunch as a legal party.

In Algeria, by contrast, the extreme violence of the war for independence limited the potential of urban political struggle to develop; trade union and women's movement activists were either in exile, in prison or underground. The military side of the liberation struggle dominated at the expense of political organization. At the moment of independence, civil society was not strong enough to contest the cohesive and well-armed external army that ultimately took power. Independent socialist organizations were unable to survive in such an environment. Military rule and civil war hampered the development of a secular civil society.

Africa's rapid urbanization since the 1970s notwithstanding, urban dwellers often live in squatter communities and hold informal sector jobs rather than industrial ones. Thus, the social class base of classical communism remains weak in postcolonial Africa. Nonetheless, the failure of capitalism to produce jobs with living wages suggests that social justice movements will still have a resonance in Africa, particularly in countries with socialist or communist traditions. As with Africa's complex relationship with twentieth-century communism, such twenty-first-century movements will reflect patterns of class structure and social cleavages, prospects for long-term alliances and the relative strength of urban civil society, all shaped by a profoundly altered geopolitical context.

Bibliographical Essay

The historiography of communism in Africa is relatively small, in part reflecting communism's weakness across the continent and in part the fact that historians of twentieth-century Africa have focused on nationalist movements and the role of the left within them rather than communism per se.

Research on communism in Algeria has been constrained by the country's history of violence. The war of independence, military rule and a decade of civil war impeded research on political history; intellectuals were targeted for assassination during the civil war.

The three-volume work by the communist Henri Alleg (ed.), *La guerre d'Algérie* (Paris: Editions Messidor, 1981), discusses communism in the context of the national liberation struggle. René Gallissot (ed.), *Algérie. Engagements sociaux et question nationale de la colonisation à l'indépendance, de 1830 à 1962* (Ivry-sur-Seine and Paris: Éditions de l'Atelier/Éditions ouvrières, 2006), provides an indispensable biographical dictionary. See also Emmanuel Sivan, *Communisme et nationalisme en Algérie, 1920–1962* (Paris: Fondation Nationale des Sciences Politiques, 1976); Hafid Khatib, *Le 1er juillet 1956. L'accord FLN–PCA et l'intégration des "combattants de la libération" dans l'armée de libération nationale en Algérie* (Algiers: Office des Publications Universitaires, 1991); and Allison Drew, *We Are No Longer in France: Communists in Colonial Algeria* (Manchester: Manchester University Press, 2014, 2017; and Cape Town: South African History Online, 2015).

Memoirs and biographies include Pierre Durand, *Cette mystérieuse section coloniale. Le PCF et les colonies (1920–1962)* (Paris: Messidor, 1986); Henri Alleg, *Mémoire algérienne. Souvenirs de luttes et d'espérances* (Paris: Stock, 2005); William Sportisse with Pierre-Jean Le Foll-Luciani, *Le camp des oliviers. Parcours d'un communiste algérien* (Rennes: Presses Universitaires de Rennes, 2012); Gaston Revel, *Un instituteur communiste en Algérie. L'engagement et le combat (1936–1965)*, ed. Alexis Sempé (Cahors: La Louve, 2013); and Mohamed Rebah, *Des chemins et des hommes* (Algiers: Mille-Feuilles, 2010). Maher El-Charif's publication of part one of Mahmoud Latrèche's Arabic-language memoir, *Chemin de la lutte en Palestine et en Orient arabe. Mémoires du leader communiste Mahmoud Latrèche le Maghrébin (1903–1939)* (Beirut: Institut for Palestine Studies, 2015), moves beyond the conventional France–Algeria framework by placing Algeria in an Arab context.

On the Communist Party of South Africa, Edward Roux, *Time Longer than Rope: A History of the Black Man's Struggle for Freedom in South Africa*, 2nd edn.

(Milwaukee: University of Wisconsin Press, 1964 [1948]), and Jack Simons and Ray Simons, *Class and Colour in South Africa, 1850–1950* (London: International Defence and Aid Fund, 1983 [1969]) are histories by activist-intellectuals. See also Sheridan Johns, *Raising the Red Flag: The International Socialist League and the Communist Party of South Africa, 1914–1932* (Bellville: Mayibuye, 1995), and Allison Drew, *Discordant Comrades: Identities and Loyalties on the South African Left* (Aldershot: Ashgate, 2000; and Pretoria: Unisa, 2002). For varied perspectives on the South African Communist Party, see Vladimir Shubin, *ANC: A View from Moscow* (Cape Town: Mayibuye Books, 1999); Eddy Maloka, *The South African Communist Party in Exile, 1963–1990* (East Lansing: Michigan State University Press, 2002); Stephen Ellis, *External Mission: The ANC in Exile* (Johannesburg and Cape Town: Jonathan Ball, 2012); and Irina Filatova and Apollon Davidson, *The Hidden Thread: Russia and South Africa in the Soviet Era* (Johannesburg and Cape Town: Jonathan Ball, 2013). The memoirs and biographies of South African communists are too numerous to list.

Brian Bunting (ed.), *South African Communists Speak: Documents from the History of the South African Communist Party 1915–1980* (London: Inkululeko, 1981) and Apollon Davidson, Irina Filatova, Valentin Gorodnov and Sheridan Johns (eds.), *South Africa and the Communist International: A Documentary History*, 2 vols. (London: Frank Cass, 2003), provide important primary documents. *Socialgerie*, www.socialgerie.net/, the web site of Algerian communist Sadek Hadjerès, includes digitized Algerian Communist Party documents.

Other case studies include Gabriel Warburg, *Islam, Nationalism and Communism in a Traditional Society: The Case of Sudan* (London: Routledge, 1978); Tareq Y. Ismael and Rifa'at El-Sa'id, *The Communist Movement in Egypt, 1920–1988* (Syracuse, NY: Syracuse University Press, 1990); Donald L. Donham, *Marxist Modern: An Ethnographic History of the Ethiopian Revolution* (Berkeley and Los Angeles: University of California Press and Oxford: James Currey, 1999).

On the Comintern in Africa, see Hakim Adi, *Pan-Africanism and Communism: The Communist International, Africa and the Diaspora, 1919–1939* (Trenton, NJ: Africa World Press, 2013). On varieties of socialism see W. H. Friedland and C. G. Rosberg, Jr. (eds.), *African Socialism* (Stanford: Stanford University Press, 1964); A. M. Babu, *African Socialism or Socialist Africa?* (London: Zed, 1981); Barry Munslow (ed.), *Africa: Problems in the Transition to Socialism* (London: Zed, 1986); and the special issue on "African Socialisms and Postsocialisms," *Africa: Journal of the International African Institute* 76,

1 (2006), 1–14. On state-led communism, see David Ottaway and Marina Ottaway, *Afrocommunism* (New York and London: Africana, 1981); Edmond Keller and Donald Rothchild (eds.), *Afro-Marxist Regimes: Ideology and Public Policy* (Boulder: Lynne Rienner, 1987); and Arnold Hughes (ed.), *Marxism's Retreat from Africa* (New York: Frank Cass, 1992).

22

Communism in the Arab World and Iran

JOHAN FRANZÉN

Introduction

The communist movement in the Arab world and Iran has been as complex and multifaceted as the region itself. Since the early modern period, the Ottoman and Qajar Empires had been pressured culturally, socially, militarily and economically by an ever-expanding Europe. By the nineteenth century, the Sublime Porte was reduced to a pawn in a game of European chess. The "Eastern Question" dominated European politics in the long nineteenth century and was arguably one of the chief causes of the Great War. Persia, too, was at the mercy of Western powers, with Britain and Russia having carved up the empire into spheres of influence. The Ottomans, and to a lesser extent the Qajars, decided to modernize and Westernize their empires to try to close the gap that had opened up in the economic, scientific and, not least, military fields. Western experts were brought in to oversee the modernization, and scores of Ottoman subjects were sent abroad to study the new ideas. As the interaction between East and West thus increased, new revolutionary ideas originating from the French Revolution and tested in the uprisings of 1848–49, and again during the Paris Commune, made their way into the Middle East. At first, these ideas were mainly diffused among the large European communities that had settled in cities such as Alexandria, Beirut and Istanbul. In Persia, the new ideas began to spread into Azerbaijan, situated on the border with Russia. The spread of socialist and communist ideas to the Arab world and Iran was thus intimately linked to the modernization process and the region's gradual subjugation to the West. This made for a peculiar situation, in which the social, economic, political and military system that was responsible for the region's subjugation also produced the ideology with which this system could be resisted. Communism, then, was viewed with suspicion as being in essence a European idea. Nationalism and religion acted as bulwarks against its diffusion. Nevertheless, throughout the twentieth century, communism spread across the region and, at times, achieved great popularity. Ultimately, however, it was defeated as idea and movement by nationalism and the self-interests of the Soviet Union.

As essentially a European affair, socialist ideas were initially circulated among communities of French, Italian, Russian and British workers. There were no translations into Arabic, Farsi or other regional languages. This, naturally, prevented the spread of the ideas beyond this narrow group, as most indigenous people were not versed in European languages. There were, however, communities of non-Muslims that, for historical and religious reasons, did speak these languages. The many Christian sects scattered across the region, such as the Copts in Egypt, the Maronites in Lebanon, the Assyro-Chaldeans in Mesopotamia, the Armenians in Anatolia and throughout the region, and Jews living in many of the main cities had long-established links with the Western powers, for religious, cultural or economic reasons. Like their ancestors during the Islamic conquests of the seventh and eighth centuries, who as learned men of the ancient world had translated and transmitted its knowledge, the region's minorities again played a crucial role in the dissemination of new ideas.

An early dilemma for those faced with transmitting the vast literature of socialism, and later communism, was translation of the terms themselves. How could ideas steeped in the philosophical tradition of Europe, and derived from its cultural language, Latin, be rendered into Arabic and other regional languages without losing their meaning? For a while, the problem was left unresolved. The early activists simply transliterated "socialism" into *sūsyālizm*. While this practice was continued in Iran and Turkey, in the Arabic-speaking areas the term *ishtirākiyyah* soon became the established translation of "socialism." *Ishtirākiyyah* is derived from the root *shīn* (sh), *rā'* (r) and *kāf* (k), which in its original denotation means "to share" and in stem form VIII "to cooperate" or "to enter into partnership." This may seem like a suitable translation, as sharing and cooperating could be said to be essential components of the socialist creed. However, the problem with translation or transmittance of philosophical ideas from one sociocultural context to another, and in this case from a completely different language family, is that the connotations are entirely different. In the case of *ishtirākiyyah*, as with most other philosophical terms in Arabic, these connotations are firmly rooted within an Islamic (and Eastern Christian) sociocultural context. Thus, for instance, the word *shirkah* or *sharikah*, which is derived from the same root, could mean either a "commercial business" or, in the Christian tradition, a "communion." Both connotations undoubtedly give off the wrong impression. Moreover, the term *shirk*, again derived from the same root, means "polytheism" or "idolatry," and is derived from stem form IV *ashraka*,[1] which arguably is the worst possible association any concept could have in a Middle Eastern context.

The same type of problem was encountered with the term "communism." In Iran, it was again left untranslated as *kūmunizm*, whereas in the Arab world it was translated as *shuyūᶜiyyah*. The latter derives from the root *shīn* (sh), *yāʾ* (y) and *ᶜayn* (ᶜ), and its basic meaning is "to spread." The term is formed from the verbal noun *shuyūᶜ*, which, depending on context, could mean "spread," but also "publicity" or "circulation [of news]." The political term "collectivism" has also been constructed from the verbal noun of stem form IV, *ishāᶜah*, on the same pattern as *shuyūᶜiyyah*, namely *ishāᶜiyyah*. The reason for this goes back to Islamic history, where *mushāᶜ* was a particular form of joint or collective ownership, in accordance with Islamic law, the *sharīᶜah*. *Mushāᶜ* lands were usually tribal or village lands that were owned collectively. This practice undoubtedly bore some resemblance to Marx's notion of "primitive communism," which he, and Engels, envisaged as a distinct stage in the development of human societies, occurring before more advanced slave-owning societies.[2] However, the religious and tribal connotations of the concept were again something that created the wrong impression. Moreover, the root from which *shuyūᶜiyyah* is derived is also the root that form the term *shīᶜah* – the followers of ᶜAli. The fact that *shuyūᶜī*, "a communist," dialectically is pronounced more like *shūᶜī* makes it almost a homonym of *shīᶜī*, "a Shiite."[3] This linguistic link with the largest Muslim "minority," coupled with the fact that communism became very popular among some Shiᶜah communities in places such as Iraq and Lebanon, added to the sense that communism was a "minority ideology" challenging the dominant Sunni superiority of the region.[4]

---

1 *Ashraka bil-lāhi*, to "attribute associates to God," i.e. to be a polytheist.
2 See, for instance, Friedrich Engels, *The Origin of Family, Private Property and the State* (Zurich, 1884).
3 For the full derivations of these terms, see Hans Wehr, *A Dictionary of Modern Written Arabic* (Beirut: Librairie du Liban, 1980).
4 On this particular point, see Silvia Naef, "Shīᶜī–Shuyūᶜī or: How to Become a Communist in a Holy City," in R. Brunner and W. Ende (eds.), *The Twelver Shia in Modern Times: Religious Culture and Political History* (Leiden: Brill, 2001), 255–67.

Given the dominance of Islam on the political and philosophical planes at the beginning of the modern period, it was to be expected that any terms chosen as translations for "communism" and "socialism" would be problematic and laden with religious connotations. On the other hand, the path chosen in Iran, where the terms were left untranslated, was hardly more conducive to the acceptance of the terms among the population but, at the very least, it avoided the added difficulty of association with religion and Islamic tradition.

Having established these fundamental linguistic, sociohistorical and philosophical differences, our focus now turns to the communist movement itself as it evolved in the Middle East. As will be made clear in this chapter, this movement essentially had a dualist, almost schizophrenic nature. On the one hand, there was the communism of the October Revolution, the Communist International (Comintern) and the universal idea of the world revolution. On the other hand, there was the Middle Eastern reality, with imperialism, nationalism and religion. The former insisted on ideological purity, on the "dictatorship of the proletariat" and on "proletarian internationalism." The latter was mired in tribalism, religious fanaticism and the struggle for modernity. Nationalism, not internationalism, was the watchword of this world. There, it was not the "proletariat" – which hardly even existed – but intellectuals and people from the professional classes, the so-called *effendiyyah*, who were the vanguard of communism. The story of communism in the Arab world and Iran is thus not a single story, but two stories of incompatible movements – one guided and steered from Moscow, seeking in vain to emulate the achievements of the Russian communists, and another more intent on feeling which direction the winds of the Middle East were blowing, and looking not toward Moscow, but toward Cairo, Damascus and Baghdad for its leadership.

World War I had a cataclysmic effect on the Middle East. The Ottoman Empire, which had sided with Germany during the war, was defeated and the "Eastern Question" was forcibly solved once and for all. The empire was dismantled, and in its stead the victorious parties (Britain, France, Italy and the USA) created new states that were to be supervised by a mandate system, under the auspices of the newly established League of Nations. Britain became the mandatory power for the new states of Iraq, Transjordan and Palestine, and, in addition, a British protectorate was declared over Egypt – under British occupation since 1882. France took control over Syria and Lebanon. To the east, Iran managed to retain its empire, but British influence made it a semi-independent state at best. This was clearly illustrated when, in

1925, the Qajar dynasty was ended by a British-supported military coup, carried out by Reza Khan, who later declared himself king (*shah*) and started the Pahlavi dynasty.[5]

In the Arabic-speaking countries, ideas of nationalism were beginning to take firm root.[6] During the war, Britain had instigated the Arab Revolt under the leadership of Sharif Husayn of Mecca, who had been promised an "independent Arab kingdom" at the war's conclusion. However, other pledges to the French, and to the Zionist movement, resulted in a significantly reduced area of Arab control. A compromise solution, which satisfied no one, was found whereby Sharif Husayn's sons, Faysal and ʿAbdallah, became kings in Iraq and Transjordan, respectively, whereas Syria and Lebanon were handed over to the French, and Palestine set apart as a "national home" for the Jews. These machinations created a postwar situation in which resentment toward Britain for its broken promises soon outweighed any goodwill that had been created by the overthrow of the Ottomans. Coupled with hatred of the French for having "stolen" Syria, which in many ways was the epicenter of Arab nationalism, and the Zionists for colonizing Palestine, anti-imperialist nationalism soon emerged as the dominant idea among the politically conscious segments of the population.[7] In Iran, frustration with a struggling modernization process, which had stalled since the days of the Constitutional Revolution of 1905–07, and British meddling in internal affairs, as well as deep resentment about British attempts to secure favorable terms for its capitalist enterprises in the country, meant that the dominant sentiment there was hardly any less anti-British.

Resistance against the new order became legion. A "revolution" broke out in Egypt when in 1919 Saʿd Zaghlul and his followers were refused permission to form a delegation to the postwar peace negotiations at Versailles. The following year, anti-Jewish riots broke out in neighbouring Palestine and, when the Iraqi mandate had been confirmed by the San Remo conference in April 1920, a widespread revolt rocked that country from the summer onward. In Syria, disapproval of the mandate system, and especially the French insistence on "divide-and-rule" tactics – as seen in the division of

5 See Cyrus Ghani, *Iran and the Rise of Reza Shah: From Qajar Collapse to Pahlavi Power* (London: I. B. Tauris, 1998).
6 For a discussion of the development of Arab nationalism, see Albert Hourani, *Arabic Thought in the Liberal Age 1798–1939* (Oxford: Oxford University Press, 1962).
7 See Timothy J. Paris, *Britain, the Hashemites and Arab Rule: The Sherifian Solution* (London: Frank Cass, 2003).

Syria along religious lines – kept unrest simmering until it finally broke out in full-scale rebellion between 1925 and 1927.

The Revolution of the East

With the eruption of these popular revolts across the Middle East, and with the emergence of the nationalist leader Mustafa Kemal (Atatürk) in Anatolia, who was gradually able to unite the Anatolian heartland and thwart Western imperialist plans for its dismemberment, the Russian communists began to take notice of the region. Joseph Stalin himself assumed responsibility for Eastern communists within the Russian Communist Party,[8] and a Department of International Propaganda for Eastern Peoples was set up in 1918. Persia was seen by the Russian communists as having the greatest potential for revolution of all the Eastern lands. The reason for this optimism was to be found in the wartime activities that had been taking place in Persian Azerbaijan. During the latter stages of the war, British troops occupied the western parts of Persia, and a military mission under General Lionel Dunsterville tried to press on toward Baku (in Russian Azerbaijan), and from there to Tiflis (Tbilisi, in Russian Georgia). In Gilan, this was resisted by Mirza Kuchuk Khan, in what became known as the "Jangali movement." This movement was led by a pan-Islamic organization calling itself Ettehād-e-Islām (Islamic Unity), and received funds and arms from the Ottomans and Germans. At the same time, *soviets* were being formed in Enzeli by Russian soldiers who had deserted, along with local communists from Turkestan and the wider Caucasus region. In this endeavor, they were supported by a group of Persian and Azerbaijani workers, calling themselves ᶜAdalat (Justice), which had been formed in 1918. Eventually, the pan-Islamic Jangali movement transformed itself into a patriotic movement and joined forces with the communists.[9]

Meanwhile, on the Russian side of the border, revolutionary troops defeated General Anton Denikin's assault on Moscow in the summer of 1919, after his troops had captured much of the Caucasus earlier in the year. A short-lived Azerbaijani Republic, which had been declared in 1918, was overthrown two years later, following an invasion by the Red Army. On 28 April 1920, the Azerbaijan Soviet Socialist Republic was declared by

8 Or, more correctly, the All-Union Communist Party (Bolsheviks), Kommunisticheskaia partiia Sovetskogo soiuza, hereafter abbreviated as CPSU.
9 See Sepehr Zabih, *The Communist Movement in Iran* (Berkeley: University of California Press, 1966).

the Russian communists. At the occasion, Mirsaid Sultan-Galiev, a Tatar Muslim communist who was the Muslim commissar in the Commissariat for Nationalities, stated the following on the role of Azerbaijan:

> Now Soviet Azarbayjan [*sic*] with its old and experienced revolutionary proletariat and its sufficiently consolidated Communist party will become a revolutionary beacon for Persia, Arabia, and Turkey ... From there it is possible to disturb the British in Persia and stretch friendly hands to Arabia and to lead the revolutionary movement in Turkey until it assumes the form of a class struggle.[10]

Having secured the oil-rich Russian Azerbaijan, Soviet troops continued to advance into Persia. The official reason given was to eliminate the threat from White forces and British troops that were still present in Gilan, fighting the Jangali movement. Soviet troops and navy vessels thus sailed across the Caspian Sea and landed in Enzeli on 18 May. Shortly thereafter, on 4 June, Gilan was declared a republic. The foreign incursion was not accepted by the nationalists and patriots, and in July Mirza Kuchuk Khan resigned from the government and took his supporters into the forest. The Persian and Azerbaijani communists who were helping the Soviets became ever more isolated, as local people turned away from the new republic. The gap widened further when Gilan was declared a Soviet republic on 4 August. In the midst of this turmoil, the First Congress of the Persian Communist Party, which had been formed largely by members of the earlier ʿAdalat group, was held in Enzeli on 23 June – at a time when the city was still occupied by the Red Army.[11]

The establishment of a Soviet republic on Iranian soil, without proper local support, highlighted the basic problem of communism in the East: What should the revolution be, and for whom was it to be carried out? These questions took on more urgency following the postwar failures of European communism. Lenin and other Bolshevik leaders had been convinced that the revolution would triumph first in Western Europe – due to its advanced economic system – and then spread to Eastern lands. The success of the Russian Revolution modified this determinist outlook somewhat, and the defeat of the German Revolution in particular forced a change of view within the Bolshevik leadership. Thus, by 1920, the East seemed the only

---

10 *Zhizn' natsional'nostei* (organ of Narkomindel, the Commissariat of Foreign Affairs), 13 May 1920, 7, quoted in Zabih, *Iran*, 10–11.

11 For an in-depth study of the Soviet adventure in Gilan, see Schapour Ravasani, *Sowjetrepublik Gilan: Die Sozialistische Bewegung im Iran seit Ende des 19. Jhdt. bis 1922* (Berlin: Basis-Verlag, 1973).

opportunity to spread the revolution. Having secured Russian Azerbaijan, and with inroads into Persia, the Comintern held its Second Congress between 19 July and 7 August. At the congress, a lively debate on the Revolution in the East took place between Lenin and M. N. Roy, an Indian communist. Lenin saw the struggle in the East as a mainly anti-imperialist struggle that would weaken the colonial system and thus hasten the revolution in the European mother countries. The basic problem of the East was the lack of a proletariat and the backward economic systems. With an insufficient industrial base, a small capitalist class and a large semi-feudal agricultural sector, Eastern countries were not suited for socialist revolution. Lenin therefore proposed that Eastern communists should form alliances with the "national revolutionary" sections of the "national bourgeoisie." Roy, who had extensive experience of the duplicitous nature of the Indian "national bourgeoisie," thought collaboration would be a recipe for disaster. Sultan Zadeh, a prominent Persian communist who had cofounded the Persian Communist Party (PCP) shortly before the Congress, put forward a compromise solution, arguing that the attitude toward the "national bourgeoisie" needed to be flexible and to adapt to local circumstances. Lenin accepted the compromise and drafted a resolution that stated the following:

> the Communist International should support bourgeois-democratic national movements in colonial and backward countries only on condition that, in these countries, the elements of future proletarian parties, which will be communist not only in name, are brought together and trained to understand their special tasks, i.e., those of the struggle against the bourgeois-democratic movements within their own nations. The Communist International must enter into a temporary alliance with bourgeois democracy in the colonial and backward countries, but should not merge with it, and should under all circumstances uphold the independence of the proletarian movement even if it is in its most embryonic form.[12]

To prepare for the Eastern revolution, the Comintern decided to organize a Congress of the Peoples of the East, to be held in the newly "liberated" city of Baku, the capital of Russian Azerbaijan. Following the conclusion of the Comintern congress, the Baku Congress was thus held in September, and was attended by no fewer than 1,891 delegates from across Asia. The largest delegation was the Turkish, which included 235 delegates, closely followed

---

12 V. I. Lenin, "Preliminary Draft Theses on the National and Colonial Questions," 28 Jul. 1920, in A. Adler (ed.), *Theses, Resolutions and Manifestos of the First Four Congresses of the Third International* (London: Pluto Press, 1983), 80.

by the Persian at 192. However, these delegates were generally not communists, but anti-imperialist nationalists of varying hue. The Congress was
chaired by Grigorii Zinoviev, the head of the Comintern, who in his opening
address called for a holy war against the British Empire. Many of the
delegates gave essentially nationalist speeches, but using a vocabulary
intended to please the communists. This prompted Zinoviev and other
Comintern spokesmen to stress that the core of socialist struggle was the
class struggle, which was not confined by national borders. He did concede,
however, that the Comintern would have to cooperate with nationalist
groups in the current situation. The Congress passed two resolutions, one
calling on the "oppressed masses of the peasantry" to rely on support from
the Comintern and to struggle for soviet power in the East. The other
resolution called for the establishment of "Soviet Government in the East"
as the objective of the revolution. The Congress was important insofar as it
showed a real intent on the part of the Comintern and Western communists
to help the revolution advance in the East but, in terms of real, concrete
impact, the achievements were decidedly more meager. In fact, in both
Turkey and Persia the Congress arguably sowed dissension between communists and nationalists. A year later, at the Third Comintern Congress,
which was held in Moscow from 22 June to 12 July 1921, Javed Zadeh of the
PCP reported that, in Turkey, the communist movement had split into three
different parties and in Persia into two. "If anything, then," commented
Zabih, "the Baku Congress and its aftermath merely emphasized once
again the Bolsheviks' dilemma in the handling of nationalism. The best
they could hope for was the transformation of the revolutionary movements
after their initial, strongly nationalistic stage."[13]

The Comintern and the Foundation of Arab Communism

While the Baku Congress failed to achieve an immediate revolutionary
impulse in the Eastern lands, the long-term commitment by the Comintern
to organize a communist movement in the region was more successful.
The spread of communist ideology, and the eventual creation of communist parties in the Arab world, was largely due to efforts by the Comintern.
The earliest organizational attempts took place in Egypt and Palestine,
almost exclusively by East European Jews who had migrated to these

13 Zabih, *Iran*, 34–35.

countries. However, revolutionary ideas had existed among the large foreign community in Egypt well before the outbreak of World War I. An influx of activist Jews from Eastern Europe, as well as radical Arab intellectuals fleeing the oppressive climate of Sultan ʿAbd al-Hamid's Ottoman Empire, meant that Egypt was a dissident hotspot at the time. Among these refugees was Shibli Shumayyil, an Arab theoretician who was a staunch believer in science and socialism, and one of the first to proffer a "scientific" critique of religion. One of his disciples was Niqula al-Haddad, another recent émigré from Syria, who became one of the pioneers of socialist thought in Egypt. He was influenced by the 1919 revolt, which he analyzed "scientifically" in a study called ʿIlm al-Ijtimāʿ (Social Sciences). He also published a book entitled al-Ishtirākiyyah (Socialism) in 1920. Another of Shumayyil's followers was Salamah Musa, who became one of the most important intellectuals of modern Egypt. There was also a smaller group of Bolshevik Jews, who had escaped to Egypt following the failed 1905 Revolution in Russia. Together they formed Majmuʿat al-Balshafik (the Bolshevik Group), which was active until the 1917 October Revolution, following which most returned to Russia. Thus, on the eve of the war, there were many communist and socialist groups in Egypt, although most of them were to be found in the large community of foreigners, which at its peak counted almost 237,000. With the outbreak of war, however, many foreigners left the country, which meant that the communist movement suffered a heavy blow. Nevertheless, it also meant that the new movement that emerged after the war was dominated not by foreign elements, but by local Arabs and Jews.[14]

One such local Jew was Joseph Rosenthal, who became one of the most important people in early Egyptian communism. He was born in neighboring Palestine in 1872 to Ukrainian immigrant parents. In his teens, Joseph moved to Beirut, where he set up a jewelry shop, which became a place of political debate. At first, he was neither a communist nor even a socialist, yet his activities were sufficient to attract the attention of the Ottoman authorities, which eventually compelled him to move to Alexandria in Egypt. There, he got involved with groups of Italian anarchists and socialists. He soon became disillusioned with these groups, as they were merely interested in conditions back in their own homeland. For Joseph, the conditions of the Egyptian poor, especially the *fellaḥīn* (poor peasants),

---

14 For a more in-depth discussion of the prewar socialist scene in Egypt, see Rami Ginat, *A History of Egyptian Communism: Jews and Their Compatriots in Quest of Revolution* (Boulder: Lynne Rienner, 2011).

were the prime concern. He later moved to Cairo, where he got involved in the early workers' movement, helping to organize strikes at the turn of the century. To demonstrate his commitment to Egypt, he took up Egyptian citizenship and once more moved back to Alexandria, where he worked as a watchmaker. The outbreak of the 1919 revolt, and the accompanying strikes that were carried out by workers in the cities, convinced Rosenthal that Egypt was ripe for a general federation of workers, which he called for with some success. In 1921, he organized the first celebration of May Day in Egyptian history. In an interview given to the *Egyptian Gazette* on that day, he stated that the *fellahīn* and the "millions of agricultural labourers" would be the force to change Egypt. At the same time, however, he expressed skepticism about the possibility of spreading communist ideology to these vast masses: "[T]here is not the slightest chance of the Egyptian fellah ever becoming a communist, and Lenin's recent confession as to the complete failure of the Moscow Government to convert the Russian Moujik to communism is a good lesson for us in our future propaganda among the fellahin of Egypt."[15] This dilemma, it would turn out, was to become the crux of communism in the Arab world, as the conditions of the Egyptian *fellahīn* were replicated throughout the region. In general, the *fellahīn* were the most wretched, uneducated, superstitious and generally backward group in the Middle East. As Arab communists were to find out, transforming the *fellahīn* into disciplined, class-conscious fighters for communism would be a herculean task.

An Egyptian Communist Party (ECP) was founded in March 1920, following a joint meeting in Alexandria of various groups of East European Jews. These activists were in contact with the Comintern and, although the new party was not recognized as a section of the Comintern, it was clear that it had support from Moscow. The ECP had a bureau in Vienna that was attached to the Austrian Communist Party. This bureau helped with "technical needs," such as bringing in printing materials and literature. The Comintern connection could also be seen in the fact that the ECP sent a representative to the Third Comintern Congress in 1921, a certain Kari David Peler. Rosenthal, however, chose not to get involved directly in the ECP (possibly due to its "foreign" character); instead he founded a study circle called La Clarté (al-Wuḍūḥ) in 1921 together with other activists. This study circle was inspired by the French journal with the same name that

15 The National Archives, Kew, UK, FO 371/6297, E6878/260/16, "Letter P. F. 37617 M.I.5. A.," quoted in Ginat, *Egyptian Communism*, 32–33.

had been set up in 1919 by Henri Barbusse, and the Egyptian group corresponded frequently with it.[16]

The Comintern was also instrumental in introducing communism into Palestine. As in Egypt, Palestine had seen a large influx of East European Jews before and after the war. There, of course, the main driving force of migration had been the Zionist movement, and many of the East European Jews belonged to socialist Zionist or labor Zionist schools of thought. One such group was Mifleget Ha-Poʿalim Ha-Sotsialistit (MPS, Socialist Workers' Party), which had broken away from the distinctly Zionist Poʿale Tsiyon (Workers of Zion) party in 1919. Contact between the MPS and the Comintern was established, possibly through Joseph Rosenthal's daughter, Charlotte, who toured Palestine in November 1920. She was also sent to Moscow to pursue revolutionary studies at the Communist University of the Toilers of the East (Kommunisticheskii universitet tru-diashchikhsia vostoka, KUTV) from May 1922 to July 1923 – a path that many regional communist leaders would later follow. The MPS applied for Comintern membership, but this was rejected due to the group's Zionist nature. A split into several factions followed, but eventually, following the unification of the two largest groups in 1923, the party was granted Comintern affiliation on condition that it changed its name to the Palestine Communist Party (Palestiner Komunistishe Partei, PKP) and rejected Zionism. This finally happened in March 1924, and the PKP became the official Comintern section in Palestine. A key organizer during this early phase was Yehiel Kossoy, a Ukrainian Jew who had arrived in Palestine with the Jewish Battalion during the war. Kossoy often traveled under the pseudonym "Constantine Weiss," and wrote in the Comintern organ *Inprecor* (International Press Correspondence) under the name "Avigdor." In 1921, he traveled to Moscow to negotiate Comintern membership on behalf of the MPS. There, he received training and was later sent to Egypt to help organize the ECP. He married Charlotte Rosenthal, and worked with Joseph in La Clarté. The dominance of Jews in the PKP, in a country that was still overwhelmingly Arab, constituted a major obstacle to the spreading of communist influence in Palestine, and so the Comintern instructed the PKP leaders to "Arabize" the party. This direc-tive created much resentment in the rank and file (and eventually a split along ethnic lines in the 1930s), but a few Arab nationalists who were found to be sympathetic to the communist cause were sent for training at the

16 Ibid., 41–45.

KUTV throughout the 1920s. Thus, by its Seventh Congress in 1930, the PKP could eventually present a Central Committee with an Arab majority.[17]

In Syria and Lebanon, too, the Comintern influence was marked. In 1924, Yusuf Ibrahim Yazbak, a local activist, was visited by Joseph Berger-Barzilai of the PKP, who had been tasked with helping to establish a communist movement in Lebanon and Syria. Later in the year, on 24 October, Yazbak, together with Fuʾad al-Shamali, Farid Touma, Ilyas Qashami and Butrus Hishimah, established the Lebanese People's Party (Ḥizb al-Shaʿb). An organization called the Spartacus League (modeled on the Spartakusbund) had been formed earlier by Armenian communists. In 1925, the two groups came together and established the Syrian–Lebanese Communist Party (SLCP, al-Ḥizb al-Shuyūʿī al-Sūrī al-Lubnānī). The new party, however, immediately became embroiled in the fractious politics of the era. In the summer, the great Syrian revolt broke out and, when the SLCP openly supported it, the entire leadership was arrested and remained locked up until a general amnesty in 1928. The Comintern ordered the PKP to take temporary control of the SLCP's affairs. Upon release, the SLCP was able to send a representative to the Sixth Comintern Congress, held from 17 July to 1 September 1928. There, the party received official recognition as a Comintern section, and was released from the PKP guardianship. In the early 1930s, the party was able to expand its activities considerably, and a number of promising young activists joined the party. Among them was Khaled Bakdash, a fierce Kurd who would emerge as the strongman of the party in the 1940s and 1950s. Others included Niqula Shawi and Farjallah al-Hilu, who were also destined to play important roles. As had happened in Palestine, the SLCP was instructed to "Arabize" to move away from its reliance on minorities, primarily Armenians. As with other Arab communist parties, a select number of recruits was sent to Moscow for training, most notably Bakdash, who stayed in Moscow from 1933 until 1937. There, he was appointed by the Comintern as the representative of Arab communist parties.[18]

---

17 For a discussion of the problems caused by this setup, see Johan Franzén, "Communism Versus Zionism: The Comintern, Yishuvism, and the Palestine Communist Party," *Journal of Palestine Studies* 36, 2 (2007), 6–24; for a wider discussion of the PKP, see Musa Budeiri, *The Palestine Communist Party, 1919–1948: Arab and Jew in the Struggle for Internationalism* (London: Ithaca Press, 1979).

18 For a fuller discussion of the SLCP, see Tareq Y. Ismael and Jacqueline S. Ismael, *The Communist Movement in Syria and Lebanon* (Gainesville: University Press of Florida, 1998).

In Iraq, communist ideas had first been introduced by Russian soldiers stationed in the northern parts of the country during the war. These early encounters, however, were not of a lasting nature. Instead, it was Husayn al-Rahhal, a Shiʿi of mixed Arab–Turkoman descent, who first started a Marxist study circle in the early 1920s. Husayn had earlier been living in Germany with his father, an Ottoman officer, who had been stationed there following the war. In 1919, Husayn witnessed the failed German Revolution, led by the Spartakusbund, which made an indelible impression on him. In 1926, he formed Nādi al-Taḍāmun (the Solidarity Club) together with other young activists. While only lasting two years, this club brought together many of the future communist leaders. In southern Iraq, communist ideas were first introduced by Petros Vasili, an Assyrian who had grown up in Tiflis (Tbilisi), Georgia, but who originally stemmed from ʿAmadiyyah in northern Iraq, whence his father had emigrated. Vasili entered the country in 1922 as a professional revolutionary. In the south, he met fellow Assyrian Yusuf Salman Yusuf – soon to be known under his party name, Comrade Fahad – and his brother Daʾud. The two brothers, together with Ghali Zuwayyid, a slave of the wealthy Saʿdun family, set up a communist study circle in al-Nasiriyyah in 1928. Eventually, the two strands came together, and in 1934, the Iraqi Communist Party (ICP, al-Ḥizb al-Shuyūʿī al-ʿIrāqī) was formed. Similarly to the ECP, PKP and SLCP, the Iraqis also sent a number of committed activists for training at the KUTV, most notably Fahad himself, who trained there from 1935 to 1937. He returned to Iraq in early 1938, and, following a period of turmoil in the party – brought about by a failed attempt to organize cells in the army, something that resulted in many arrests of party members and the promulgation of an anti-communist law – he eventually took over the leadership in 1941.[19]

Nationalism and Populism

World War II marked a turning point for the Middle Eastern communist parties. The alliance between the Soviet Union and Britain during the war meant that the repression of communists was considerably relaxed. The Soviets responded by closing down the Comintern in 1943. On the one hand, this decision deprived the local communists of an organizational

19 For an exhaustive discussion of the ICP's early phase, see Hanna Batatu, *The Old Social Classes and the Revolutionary Movements of Iraq* (Princeton: Princeton University Press, 1978); see also Johan Franzén, *Red Star over Iraq: Iraqi Communism Before Saddam* (London: Hurst, 2011).

framework for their activities, but on the other it also removed some of the British and French suspicion that Middle Eastern communists were merely Soviet agents. Following the Seventh, and final, Comintern Congress, which had been held from 25 July to 20 August 1935, and which had endorsed the popular front against fascism line, the Middle Eastern communist parties entered into what might be called a "populist" phase. The Comintern resolution had also established that, in the colonized world, the communists should struggle to achieve "national" rather than "popular" fronts, that is, to seek alliances with the "national bourgeoisie" against imperialism. In Iran, this populism was particularly noticeable. There, the earlier Soviet-led communist movement had largely crumbled following the ascent to the throne of Reza Shah, who went on to ban communist activity in 1931. Yet, in the late 1930s, a more indigenous movement took shape. A group of Iranian communists, most of whom were from a middle-class background, had formed around Dr. Taghi Erani, an Azerbaijani physicist who had been educated in Berlin. In 1937, the group was arrested, which helped their radicalization. Dr. Erani died in prison in 1940 but, when the group's members were released the following year, they went on to set up a new communist organization – Ḥezb-e Tūdeh Īrān (Party of the Masses of Iran). The new party was able to exploit the relative freedom caused by Reza Shah's removal by the Allies the same year, and the fact that the Red Army was once again stationed in the northern parts of the country because of the war. Tudeh was not openly communist, instead stressing that it supported the Iranian constitution and was fighting for its full implementation.[20] The same wartime strategy could also be noticed in neighboring Iraq, where the ICP in 1944 convened its First Conference, which also called for the revival of the constitution and in general offered a populist program.[21] The SLCP, too, held a congress in December 1943–January 1944, which put forward a similarly moderate program. In fact, such was the level of its moderation that the program did not even mention the word "socialism."[22] As part of the populist drive, an effort to set up or expand trade unions was also a feature of the wartime and immediate postwar period.

The period of legality during the war and the first few years thereafter provided the communist parties with an opportunity to expand their operations, and in general this short space of time constituted the only moment in their history when, however briefly, they were able to operate freely.

---

20 Zabih, *Iran*, 65–70.   21 Franzén, *Red Star*, 41.
22 Ismael and Ismael, *Syria and Lebanon*, 36–37.

The Tudeh in particular seized the opportunity and, within a few years of its foundation, it had emerged as a countrywide mass party, largely due to its focused attention on labor questions and support for trade unions. At the time of its First Congress in 1944, the Tudeh counted a membership of some 25,000 people. Bolstered by the Soviet presence (Britain and the Soviet Union effectively occupied the country throughout the war), the party organized large demonstrations to put pressure on the government at a time when central government was at its weakest. A young Mohammad Reza Shah had been installed to replace his father in 1941, and throughout the war he remained a puppet of the Allies. However, before the Tudeh was able to threaten the regime seriously, a reversal of fortunes occurred. In 1949, a failed attempt on the shah's life prompted the regime to clamp down on leftist organizations, banning the Tudeh and generally restricting liberties that had been granted during the previous period. The young shah followed his father's example and transformed his rule to make it more absolutist. To undermine the parliamentary system, he introduced a senate, some of whose members would be appointed by himself. He also strengthened the intelligence apparatus to prevent any further attempts on his life. These measures meant that the honeymoon period was over for the Tudeh, and once more communism was an outlawed activity in Iran.[23]

A similar trajectory was followed by the Arab communist parties, but their postwar experience was overshadowed by the Palestine Question. The temporary boost of communist popularity in the Arab world that followed the Soviet defeat of Nazism was quickly undone when, in November 1947, the Soviet Union voted for partition of Palestine in the newly established United Nations. The Soviet U-turn – and a U-turn it was, for communists had denounced Zionism and its objectives in Palestine for as long as the movement had existed – caused shock and consternation among Arab communists, including the Jews within their ranks (whose numbers at the time were considerable). At first, the ICP and the SLCP, which had separated into a Syrian (SCP) and a Lebanese (LCP) branch in 1943, went against the Soviet position. In Palestine, ethnic tensions had already caused a split of the party in 1943 when the Arab communists had broken away to form ʿUṣbat al-Taḥarrur al-Waṭanī (National Liberation League, NLL). The remaining Jewish communists hailed the partition and changed the name of their party to HaMiflagah HaKomunistit HaʾEretz Yisraʾelit

23 Zabih, *Iran*, 80–165.

(MAKEI, Communist Party of the Land of Israel) in 1947. The NLL was decidedly against partition, as were the ICP, LCP and SCP. In Egypt, the issue was less straightforward. There, the communist movement had developed into a kaleidoscope of different groups of varying size and composition, some of which were less antagonistic to partition. Nevertheless, despite the initial opposition, both the ICP and the Syrian–Lebanese parties eventually toed the Soviet line, and by the summer of 1948 they began advocating an "independent democratic Arab state in the Arab part of Palestine."[24] The NLL, too, came around to the Soviet position and, despite the earlier tension with the Jewish communists, a merger between the NLL and MAKEI eventually took place following the Arab–Israeli War, producing the new Israeli Communist Party (HaMiflagah HaKomunistit HaYisra'elit).

The communist support for partition (and indirectly for Zionism) caused a wave of state repression against the Arab communist parties, and hostile animosity from Arab nationalists in general. Overnight, the communists went from respected anti-imperialist activists within the general fold of Arab nationalism to treasonous pariahs who were beyond the pale. The headquarters of the SCP in Damascus was torched by an angry mob in late November 1947, and at the same time the party's organ, Ṣawt al-Shaʿb (Voice of the People), was banned. In Iraq, a general crackdown on communists that predated the partition vote had resulted in the arrest of much of the party leadership, including the First Secretary, "Comrade Fahad." He and other leaders were sentenced to death but, following international pressure, the death sentences were commuted to life imprisonment. However, following a wave of demonstrations in early 1948, later remembered as al-Wathbah (the Leap), which had been caused by the signing of a new British–Iraqi treaty at Portsmouth, Fahad was retried and once more sentenced to death. The sentence was carried out in February 1949, when he and three other communists were hanged in four different Baghdad squares.[25] In Lebanon, too, repression was relentless, and the LCP was banned in the summer of 1948. The SCP was forced underground, and a decision to move its headquarters from Damascus to Beirut was taken.

Whether because of this repression or perhaps because of an influx of a younger generation of communists in the early 1950s, the communist parties in the Middle East radicalized their positions considerably, and up until the mid 1950s a "revolutionist phase" is clearly noticeable. In Iran, the

24 Statement of the ICP Central Committee, 6 Jul. 1948, quoted in Batatu, *Old Social Classes*, 599.
25 Ibid., ch. 22.

communists joined nationalists and other activists during the widespread protests in 1952 that ultimately helped to reinstate Mohammad Mossadegh to power. Although the Tudeh played a crucial role during this episode, they were eventually betrayed by the nationalists once their common objective had been met. After Mossadegh's ousting in a CIA-sponsored coup the following year, all-out repression of the party and its auxiliary organizations ensued.[26] The party leadership concluded that, had they possessed a trained military apparatus at the peak of the protests, they would have been in a good position to seize power. A decision to militarize the party and prepare it for violent revolution was thus taken. However, over the next year much of the work was undone when the authorities discovered a vast network of Tudeh supporters in the army – some 600 officers, ranging from noncommissioned officers to colonels.[27] In Iraq, too, radicalism was brewing. Despite the repression of 1947–49, which had almost broken the back of the party, the ICP had regrouped and recruited new members by the early 1950s. In 1952, it played a key role in the *Intifāḍah* that rocked the country in a similar way as the 1948 *Wathbah* had done. Revolutionism was evidenced within its ranks as well when in 1954 it created a military organization, al-Lajnah al-Waṭaniyyah li-Ittiḥād al-Junūd wa l-Ḍubbāṭ (National Committee for Unity of Soldiers and Officers).[28]

Violent Revolution, "Arab Socialism" and the End of the Movement

The year 1956 marked a watershed for Middle Eastern communists. Three major events took place during this year: the thwarting of the Hungarian Uprising, the Suez Crisis and the Twentieth Congress of the CPSU. The first of these events did not have much impact on Middle Eastern affairs, but it showed the extent to which the Soviet Union was willing to use force to protect its sphere of influence. The Suez Crisis, on the other hand, had immense impact as it essentially transformed Gamal Abdel Nasser (Gamal ʿAbd al-Nasir) into an "Arab hero" throughout the region, and generally made his strand of pan-Arabist ideology dominant. However, it was the Twentieth Congress and the changes in ideology it brought with it that most transformed Middle Eastern communist parties. The Twentieth Congress, which is perhaps best known for Nikita Khrushchev's "secret

---

26 For an in-depth study of this crucial period in Iranian history, see Sepehr Zabih, *The Mossadegh Era: Roots of the Iranian Revolution* (Chicago: Lakeview, 1982).
27 Ibid., 177–209. 28 Franzén, *Red Star*, 61–68.

speech," introduced significant changes in Soviet ideology. The theories of "peaceful coexistence" in international relations and of a "peaceful road to socialism" were the most radical changes. Undoubtedly, these changes were linked to the Cold War, which was increasingly becoming the dominant feature of the era. The "peaceful road" proposed a theory that essentially rendered the communist party superfluous as it proclaimed that the socialist stage could be reached by relying on the "national bourgeoisie" alone. The role of the communists was therefore not to seize power, but to support "national-democratic" movements and help turn them pro-Soviet. Later, this was further developed in the "noncapitalist path to socialism" theory, which argued that the capitalist stage could be bypassed altogether, so that regimes in the "Third World" could move straight from a semi-colonial, semi-feudal stage to socialism. In reality, what these theories argued was that political, rather than economic liberation was what mattered. It was good enough if a country achieved political independence from imperialism as, with the help and assistance of the Soviet Union, it could now avoid remaining in economic dependence. The irony, of course, was that it created a new type of economic dependence – on the Soviet Union.[29]

Did Cold War logic force these changes in the Soviet outlook? Did Stalin's death and Khrushchev's ambitions play a part? Did the war and its consequences impel Soviet leaders to view international relations through a more realist lens? Did bureaucratization and routinization of Soviet society and the CPSU leadership kill the original revolutionary idea? Alternatively, had Stalin's notion of "socialism in one country" already done that? These are all important questions, albeit very difficult to answer. What is indisputable, though, is that from the outbreak of the Cold War Soviet foreign policy became dominated by concerns of "national interest," rather than "world revolution." From the point of view of Middle Eastern communists, this development was disastrous. The new Soviet policy was put into practice with the Egyptian Revolution in 1952 and the subsequent rise of Nasser from the mid 1950s onward, followed by the Iraqi Revolution in 1958, and other "Arab socialist" revolutions in places such as Yemen, Algeria and Syria. The battle for Nasser's loyalty was the standout feature of the early Cold War in the Middle East. As he was the leader of the largest Arab country, attracting him to one's side was seen as crucial by both superpowers. Egypt

---

29 For a thorough discussion, and rejection, of the noncapitalist theory in the case of Egypt, see Esmail Hosseinzadeh, *Soviet Non-Capitalist Development: The Case of Nasser's Egypt* (New York: Praeger, 1989).

had also long been a pillar of British imperial strategy, with a large British base guarding the Suez Canal. Thus, Nasser's switch from the American sphere to the Soviet, following broken American promises to fund the building of the Aswan dam, was a great victory for the Soviets – at least symbolically. However, for the Egyptian communists it was catastrophic. Nasser was an anti-communist and clamped down on the Egyptian left with menace, banning all political parties except his own officially approved Arab Socialist Union. The Baʿth Party in Syria and Iraq was equally hostile to communism, if not more so. In February 1963, the Iraqi Baʿthists joined ʿAbd al-Salam ʿAref in a coup to overthrow ʿAbd al-Karim Qasim, who had led the country since the 1958 revolution. As a counterweight to Nasser's pan-Arabism, the ICP had put their full support behind Qasim in the early stages of the new regime – only to be betrayed by him later. The 1963 coup saw thousands of ICP members and sympathizers, and Qasim loyalists, killed by Baʿthist "National Guards." The Baʿthists were themselves betrayed by ʿAref later in the year, and he and his brother, ʿAbd al-Rahman, ruled Iraq until 1968, when the Baʿthists once more took power.[30]

The Baʿthist takeover in Iraq in February 1963, and a month later in Syria, marked the beginning of the end for Arab communists. "Arab socialism," the ideology espoused by the Baʿthist regimes and by Nasser proved to be the final undoing of communist ideology. The reason for this was twofold. First, "Arab socialism" took those elements of communist ideology – social justice, land reform, anti-imperialism etc. – that had made it popular in the first place, and combined these with Arab nationalism, which was already immensely popular at the time. Second, the Baʿth Party emulated communist organizational practices, establishing secret and clandestine branches and cells throughout the country. While the physical threat of Baʿthism was indeed very real in Iraq, it was in the ideational sphere in which the battle for the masses was lost. By portraying themselves as socialists and nationalists, the Baʿthists were always at an advantage compared to the communists, who risked being attacked for lacking patriotism. Thus, despite the fact that the Baʿth Party had attempted to physically eliminate the Iraqi communist movement, and

30 For good overviews of Soviet relations with the "radical" Arab regimes, see Oles M. Smolansky, *The Soviet Union and the Arab East Under Khrushchev* (Lewisburg, PA: Bucknell University Press, 1974); and Oles M. Smolansky and Bettie M. Smolansky, *The USSR and Iraq: The Soviet Quest for Influence* (Durham, NC: Duke University Press, 1991).

despite Nasser's increasing authoritarianism, Arab communists thought the spread of "Arab socialism" was working to their advantage:

> As a result of the successes won by world socialism, socialist ideas are becoming increasingly popular among the masses, a fact which is compelling statesmen and public personalities in the Arab countries to speak of socialism as a perspective in the national and social advance of the young sovereign states ... There is no denying that the ideas of so-called "Arab socialism" have exerted their influence on students, intellectuals and also a large section of the peasantry ... Another positive feature of "Arab socialism" is that the word "socialism" has gained currency in the Arab East.[31]

In other words, the lip service being paid to "socialism" by Arab leaders was taken as an indication of communist progression and influence.[32]

Arguably, however, the battle had already been lost at an earlier stage when the communists had attempted to infuse a revolutionary Marxist understanding of Arab nationalism and the pan-Arabist objective to unify the Arabic-speaking world into a unitary state. Such was the dominance of nationalist thought that no political organization could survive without declaring unwavering support for it. For the Iraqi communists, and to a lesser extent the Syrian communists, the clash came to a head in 1959 when attempts by Gamal Abdel Nasser to undermine the rule of ʿAbd al-Karim Qasim by sponsoring a nationalist rebellion in Mosul came to naught. The fact that the Iraqi communists had sided with Qasim in his falling out with Nasser in the aftermath of the Iraqi Revolution of 14 July 1958 meant that the Qasim regime was branded "pro-communist" by Nasser (and by the West). At the height of this battle, ʿAziz al-Hajj, himself ironically a Kurd, but also a prominent member of the ICP, outlined the communist position on Arab nationalism in the following manner:

> Arab nationalism is an evident reality that even its enemies cannot disregard. Arab nationalism is a tangible fact that crystallizes and develops, and is being embodied in a stormy revolutionary movement reflecting the hopes and wishes of 80 million people, and their intense yearning for the return of their usurped rights, and the building of a new Arab life that contributes to the building of a new human civilization ... today, it is not an issue of a number of parties or leaders, but a giant mass movement of all the Arab peoples; it is the reflection of a nation existing in reality, firmly rooted in the Arab land,

---

31 "The Present Stage of the National-Liberation Movement of the Arab Peoples," *World Marxist Review* 6, 10 (Oct. 1963), 72–73.

32 For numerous other examples of the communist position on "Arab Socialism," see Franzén, *Red Star*.

whether the enemy recognizes it or not, and whether this or that is aware of it. This nation possesses all the national characteristics of [being] one nation. That is because its being [is] a firm group of people that was formed historically, and lives on a common land (despite the existing invented borders) and speaks a common language, and it has increasing economic assets that complete each other, and it has a shared psychological basis that finds an expression in the shared Arab culture and traditions, and in the mutual national aspirations toward complete liberation and a happy life, and toward the eradication of the manufactured division. The Sultans of the House of ʿUthman [the Ottomans] and their racist Turkish allies, and after them the new Imperialism in particular, have all tried for tens of years to erase these national traits in order to keep the Arab nation fragmented to facilitate its enslavement and exploitation, but these features were able to resist and preserve their bond because they were original ones.[33]

This passage epitomizes the communist ambivalence on nationalism. While trying to couch their analyses in Marxist-Leninist phraseology, and insisting on the revolutionary nature of the "Arab nation" as justification for their position, even the most cursory glance at the vast Arab communist literature on nationalism gives an indelible impression that in fact there was very little, if anything, to distinguish between the ostensibly "scientific" Marxist interpretation and the highly metaphysical understanding of nationalism put forward by noncommunists.

For obvious reasons, communist views on the Baʿth Party were initially hostile, especially in Iraq. The Baʿthists were dismissed as "fascists" who could not be trusted. However, soon after the Baʿthist takeover in Iraq and Syria, this assessment began to be amended, prompted by a changing Soviet evaluation of the Baʿthist movement. Soviet experts distinguished between an "extremist right wing" and the "healthy forces of the party." Soon, similar positions were echoed by the Arab communists. Despite the fact that thousands of Iraqi communists had been killed and arrested, and communists were banned in Egypt and Syria, the Soviet Union continued to offer unconditional support for Nasser, the Baʿthist regimes and Arab nationalist military regimes in general. This could be seen in Khrushchev's important visit to Egypt in 1964, officially to inaugurate the High Dam at Aswan, when he held meetings with Nasser, Iraq's ʿAref and Yemen's ʿAbdallah al-Sallal. In fact, following that visit, the view of "Arab socialism," and of Nasser in

---

33 ʿAzīz al-Ḥajj, *al-Qawmiyyah al-ʿArabiyyah wa l-Dīmūqrāṭiyyah* [Arab Nationalism and Democracy] (Baghdad, [1959]).

particular, changed considerably. The Iraqi communists especially, who had fallen out with Nasser during the Qasim regime, now made a U-turn, following the Soviet endorsement of the Egyptian regime.[34]

In Iran, the absurdity of the Soviet position was even more plain to see. The shah's Iran was an important US ally against the Soviets, but, despite this, the Soviet Union maintained amicable relations with the country – even when, in 1955, Iran (along with Iraq, Turkey, Pakistan and Britain) formed the so-called Baghdad Pact, a NATO-style military organization tasked with containing the Soviets. In 1962, following a period of worsening Soviet–Iranian relations, the situation again improved when the shah promised that he would not allow American military bases on Iranian soil. This promise, along with the shah's "White Revolution" in the 1960s, was enough to create a positive Soviet image of Iran, which the Iranian communists, despite their misgivings, had to follow. Writing on the topic in the mid 1960s, Zabih commented that, while the Tudeh leadership mostly accepted the situation, particularly as many within that leadership had sought refuge in the Soviet Union, "the lower echelons of the party and the membership at large will probably not remain impervious to the growing Soviet accommodation with the Iranian regime."[35]

That this was the case could be seen in the late 1960s when, following the Soviet–Chinese split on the international level, many communists throughout the region questioned the leaderships of their parties. In 1965–66, some senior Tudeh leaders whose sympathies lay with the Chinese argued that "violent revolution" was "the only way to the liberation of the Iranian masses." As a result, they were thrown out of the Central Committee. Later, in the summer of 1966, the party split along these lines.[36] In Iraq, too, the ICP was threatened by a revolutionary base. There, a full split of the party occurred when ᶜAziz al-Hajj broke away to form the "Central Command" group (al-Qiyādah al-Markaziyyah) in 1967–68. In 1968, this group declared a revolution and began armed struggle in the southern marshes. However, the attempt was quickly crushed by the Baᶜth Party, following its coup in July 1968. The remainder of the ICP came out in full support of the Soviet Union, denouncing the renegades – as did the Tudeh leadership.[37]

In Egypt, Nasser co-opted some communists, who received well-paid jobs in the civil service in exchange for abandoning their struggle. Those that

34 For a closer look at Khrushchev's crucial Egypt visit, see Smolansky, *Arab East*.
35 Zabih, *Iran*, 241.   36 Ibid., 241–45.   37 Franzén, *Red Star*, 173–83.

nationally repressed, but predominantly agrarian southeast – in Montenegro, Kosovo and Macedonia.[3]

The communist electoral showing and excessive self-confidence in the Constituent Assembly provoked official reprisals and the banning of the KPJ in 1921. Rough handling of the communists was the government's way of sending a message to the overall opposition, not just in the 1920s. Whereas the KPJ's numbers dwindled from some 50,000 members in May 1920 to no more than 688 members in 1924, the parties of disaffected nationalities grew significantly during the same period. The recovery of the Yugoslav communist movement was slow in the 1920s. The KPJ's agenda during this decade of rump parliamentarianism was dominated by the internecine conflict between the two underground party factions – the right faction of Sima Marković (1888–1938) and the left faction of Ðuro Cvijić (1896–1938). At the beginning both factions held that the national question and the nationality opposition movements, particularly that of Stjepan Radić's HSS in Croatia, were the handiwork of the Croat capitalists in their competition with the Serb bourgeoisie. Slowly, however, the left faction came to view Serbian oppression as the real problem and national self-determination as the Leninist answer. In time, the left graduated to a federalist program of state organization, and its principals, who were mainly former Croat unitarists, came out in favor of the separate identity of Serbs, Croats and Slovenes and started supporting the non-Serb national movements. The right faction, with its base in Serbia, always kept itself aloof from unitarism. (Marković held that the idea of a "triune" Yugoslav people and the "formula of 'three tribes of a single nation' cannot have any scientific basis.")[4] Its members preferred regional autonomy – though not nationality-based autonomy – to federalism and remained hostile to the non-Serb national movements (Marković wrote that the "equality that the Croats and Slovenes seek is only a political expression of their fundamental economic demand: *the equality of capital*").[5]

The KPJ, like the Comintern itself, steadily moved leftward at the time when the Yugoslav state crisis intensified, following the assassination of Croat peasant leader Stjepan Radić in 1928. In August 1928, the Sixth World Congress of the Comintern ordered a sharp left turn

---

3 Ivo Banac, *The National Question in Yugoslavia: Origins, History, Politics* (Ithaca: Cornell University Press, 1984), 330.
4 Sima Marković, *Tragizam malih naroda: Spisi o nacionalnom pitanju* (Belgrade: Filip Višnjić, 1985), 80.
5 Ibid., 85.

(the "Third Period," 1928–35), which was to last until the victory of world revolution. The KPJ seconded the decisions of the Comintern at its Fourth Congress, which convened clandestinely in Dresden, Germany, in October 1928. The subject at issue was no longer the revolutionary potential of the nationality conflict, but rather how to wrest the leadership in the nationality movements from "national reformists." When King Aleksandar of Yugoslavia proclaimed the royal dictatorship in January 1929, suspending the parliament and banning all political parties, communist leaflets called for the breakup of Yugoslavia, announced their support for the "free and independent Croatia, free, independent and united Macedonia, and free and independent Montenegro and Slovenia," welcomed the defeat of the national opposition's "policy of compromise" and called on the "workers and peasants of Croatia and the other oppressed nations" to respond to the "sabre and riflebutt attacks with lead and armed struggle of the whole people" and not with paper declarations.[6]

Following the assassination of King Aleksandar in 1934, the succeeding regime of Aleksandar's cousin Regent Paul moved away from the excesses of the royal dictatorship and slowly permitted the revival of oppositional activity. This coincided with the Comintern's slow abandonment of confrontation with the moderate left (the Social Democrats in Western Europe and the peasant parties in Central and Southeastern Europe) following the rise of Adolf Hitler in Germany. Milan Gorkić (real name Josip Čižinski), who had headed the KPJ from exile since 1932, took advantage of the new situation and greatly contributed to the restoration of communist activity. Under his leadership, KPJ membership rose from 300–500 (in the middle of 1932) to 2,200 (October 1934).[7] From 1935 Gorkić directed the KPJ toward the new popular front strategy, which in Yugoslavia meant reconciliation with the revived HSS and the rest of the moderate opposition, but also the abandonment of Yugoslavia's breakup in favor of a federal union of seven units (Serbia, Croatia, Slovenia, Macedonia, Montenegro, Bosnia and Herzegovina, Vojvodina). The end of the Gorkić period coincided with the KPJ's mobilization, but also with growing tensions in the KPJ's command structure. In 1937 Gorkić and most members of the KPJ apparatus in

6 Hrvatski državni arhiv (HDA), Zagreb, HR-HDA-1349: ZB-XVIII-L-1/9 (1929).
7 Rossiiskii gosudarstvennyi arkhiv sotsial'no-politicheskoi istorii (RGASPI), Moscow, f. 495 (IKKI), op. 70 (KPIU), 1919–1941 g., d. 103, Izveštaj CK na IV. zem. konf.: III. Partija, Organizaciono stanje, 2.

Moscow were arrested in the Stalinist purges, reopening not only the crisis of leadership, but also speculations on the dissolution of the KPJ.

Tito's "Legal Revolution"

The Comintern's choice for the new head of the KPJ was Josip Broz (1892–1980), better known under his party pseudonym – Tito. This Croat metalworker of peasant origin from the rural Zagorje, northwest of Zagreb, had a long career in illegal party and trade union work and several prison terms to his record. His mission was to establish a fully Bolshevized party by purging all factional leaders. Indeed, in the next few years Tito swept away not only all the old factional adherents, but also all the critical communists, skeptical intelligentsia (the circle of Miroslav Krleža) and those who in the 1938 elections had supported the HSS-led democratic opposition over the weak KPJ proxy party.

Thanks to Tito's purges and his imposition of strict discipline, the KPJ became organizationally stronger but politically more isolated. Its strength of some 6,620 members, with an additional 17,800 members of the SKOJ (Savez komunističke omladine Jugoslavije, Young Communist League), was insufficient for the task of insurrection under the best of circumstances. The Axis invasion and occupation of April 1941, Yugoslavia's military defeat and the flight of the king and government into exile, however, created the conditions for the tightly knit KPJ, with its unique emphasis on armed resistance, to show its mettle. Since the occupiers and the collaborationist regimes pursued very harsh policies, most notably in satellite Croatia where the Serbs were severely persecuted, the KPJ gained the sort of prominence that it had not previously enjoyed. Moreover, since the occupiers appealed to the non-Serbs, the KPJ goal of restoring the Yugoslav state could be advanced only by offering a qualitatively different state – a federation of equal nationalities.[8]

The dilemma was that a federal program would inevitably set the KPJ against the exponents of the old regime – the royal government-in-exile and its predominantly Serb Chetnik guerrillas at home. In addition, since the outcome of the conflict with the Chetniks would unfailingly determine who would rule Yugoslavia after the war, it necessarily took center stage. This was precisely what Moscow wanted to avoid. Stalin's concept of the "Grand Alliance" against fascism not only set aside the long-term communist

8 Josip Broz Tito, "Nacionalno pitanje u Jugoslaviji u svjetlosti narodnooslobodilačke borbe," in Josip Broz Tito, *Sabrana djela*, vol. XIII (Belgrade: Izdavački centar Komunist, 1986), 99.

revolutionary aims, but actually implicitly obliged communists to support the restoration of previous regimes as a matter of national salvation. The concept of "national liberation," which was used during the Third Period as the code name for the KPJ-sponsored nationality struggle against Serbian hegemony and dictatorship, became Moscow's term of choice. Moscow advised sabotage, disruption of communications, withholding of food stuffs and even the fomenting of partisan war in the enemy's rear, but not a communist revolution.

Tito's strategy was markedly different. Even before the attack on the USSR, in the first half of June 1941, Tito promoted the policy of "joint struggle for Soviet power and alliance with the USSR" and "joint struggle against English agents and attempts to restore the old order."[9] Soviet instructions interfered with these goals, making it imperative to conceal the ultimate aim, but there were numerous instances when various members of Tito's Politburo, including Tito himself, showed their colors. Milovan Djilas (Ðilas; 1911–95), the leftmost member of the Politburo, introduced the notion of the "forthcoming anti-fascist revolution, which is nothing other than a necessary stage in the proletarian revolution."[10] The collapse of Tito's first compact liberated territory in southwestern Serbia (the Užice Republic) to the joint German–Chetnik offensive in December 1941 can be attributed in part to the KPJ social radicalism – confiscations of property and projects of land collectivization, which were alien to the partisan peasant base. The Soviet victory over the Germans at Moscow, also in December, convinced the KPJ Politburo that the wartime struggle was entering the "second – proletarian – stage," in which the war against the Axis was secondary to the task of class struggle against the domestic counterrevolution. Hence the adoption of the communist symbols (red five-pointed stars with hammer-and-sickle insignia) and new terminology for elite partisan units (Proletarian shock brigades), which the Comintern saw as a dangerous precedent, creating an impression that the "partisan movement is acquiring a communist character."[11] Equally unhelpful was the red terror in Montenegro and eastern Herzegovina in the winter of 1941–42, which only swelled the Chetnik ranks.

Moscow insisted on a broad united front with the Chetniks even after the royalists started collaborating with the occupiers against the communist partisans. Moreover, Moscow continued to frustrate Tito's plans to

9 Tito, *Sabrana djela*, vol. VII (Belgrade: Izdavački centar Komunist, 1979), 42.
10 Cited in Ðuro Vujović, "O lijevim greškama KPJ u Crnoj Gori u prvoj godini narodnooslobodilačkog rata," *Istorijski zapisi* 20, 1 (1967), 52.
11 Cited in Tito, *Sabrana djela*, vol. IX (Belgrade: Izdavački centar Komunist, 1979), 224.

build communist-dominated governmental structures. When, on
12 November 1942, Tito informed Moscow that they were "now forming
something like a government,"[12] Georgi Dimitrov responded with instructions that the planned committee "should not be considered as some sort of
a government," nor should it "compete with the Yugoslav government in
London." Neither should monarchy be questioned nor republican slogans
advanced.[13] Tito formed the Anti-Fascist Council of People's Liberation of
Yugoslavia (Antifašističko vijeće narodnog oslobođenja Jugoslavije, AVNOJ)
instead, waiting another year before establishing his government (Nacionalni
komitet oslobođenja Jugoslavije, NKOJ) at the Second Session of the AVNOJ
(Jajce, Bosnia, 29–30 November 1943), moreover on an open republican
platform.[14] The KPJ's political advances followed decisive developments
afield.

By the end of 1943, having survived the Axis onslaughts at Neretva
(Operation Weiß, January–March 1943) and Sutjeska (Operation Schwarz,
May–June 1943) and – moreover – having defeating the Chetniks militarily
and benefited greatly from the capitulation of Italy, Tito's movement was
growing despite Tito's rigid leftism. In Slovenia and northern Croatia, however, the KPJ developed a significantly more moderate leadership, which
coexisted with Tito's Politburo, but better reflected Moscow's line. This led
to programmatic differences between the central authority and the local
organs of power (Land Councils) in the future federal republics. Andrija
Hebrang (1899–1949), the secretary of the Communist Party of Croatia
(Komunistička partija Hrvatske, KPH), was a typical moderate. He stressed
the "national-militant and anti-fascist" character of the partisan movement in
Croatia, which meant, among other matters, that economic life on partisan
territory was based on private ownership and free trade, and that catechism
was an obligatory subject in partisan schools. Nor did he shy away from
assuming for Croatia the sovereignty that Tito deemed appropriate to
Yugoslavia alone.[15] This led to his transfer from Croatia as the movement
became more centralized by the end of the war.

Despite these differences in emphasis, the partisans' ascendance was
further advanced thanks to the British decision in January 1944 to abandon
the compromised and disabled Chetniks in favor of Tito's movement.

---

12 Tito, *Sabrana djela*, vol. XII (Belgrade: Izdavački Centar Komunist, 1982), 232.
13 Cited ibid., 297.
14 Paul Ivan Jukić, "Uncommon Cause: The Soviet Union and the Rise of Tito's
   Yugoslavia, 1941–1945," Ph.D. dissertation (Yale University, New Haven, 1997), 318–31.
15 Milovan Djilas, *Wartime* (New York: Harcourt Brace Jovanovich, 1977), 407.

Churchill believed that this would improve Britain's political standing and the royalist Yugoslav cause. In reality, with the backing of an increasingly self-confident Stalin (who, Dimitrov insisted, ought to be referred "in future [coded] telegrams as Friend"), Tito held out for the elimination of the government in exile, the recognition "by England and the other Allies" of his own (AVNOJ) government, to whose laws "the king must submit."[16] This in effect happened through the signing of the Vis agreement (16 June 1944), whereby the government-in-exile recognized Tito's military and political achievements, including the "democratic federal regulation of our state community,"[17] thus introducing a peaceful transfer of power to the communist regime under construction. Tito's revolution was thereby "legalized."

Sovietization and the Break with Moscow 1945–1954

Harsh from the beginning, Tito's regime carried out swift executions of various opponents, including the retreating members of various hostile armed forces, their families, and other civilians who expected to be saved through surrender to the Western Allies in Austria. The exact or even approximate number of the executed is still elusive, although there is increasing agreement on several hundreds of thousands of victims, one of the worst records in Eastern Europe.[18] Nor was the KPJ mild toward various shades of opposition. The Yugoslavs were not only the first to abolish monarchy in Eastern Europe, they were also the first to adopt a Soviet-style constitution (January 1946), the first to institute legal procedures against church dignitaries of episcopal rank (the trial of Archbishop Alojzije Stepinac in October 1946) and the "opposition within the united front," the first to use rigged trials against their own wayward members (the Dachau trials of April and August of 1948 and July 1949), the first to introduce Soviet-style planning (First Five-Year Plan of April 1947 with the highest rate of state investment of 27 percent of GNP in Eastern Europe) and the first to establish collective farms (1,318 by the end of 1948).

---

16 Ivo Banac (ed.), *The Diary of Georgi Dimitrov 1933–1949* (New Haven: Yale University Press, 2003), 298.

17 "Sporazum Nacionalnog komiteta oslobođenja Jugoslavije i Kraljevske jugoslovenske vlade," in Branko Petranović and Momčilo Zečević (eds.), *Jugoslavija 1918–1984. Zbirka dokumenata* (Belgrade: Rad, 1985), 567.

18 Jera Vodušek Starič, *Prevzem oblasti 1944–1946* (Ljubljana: Cankarjeva založba, 1992), 230–50. See also Jera Vodušek Starič, *Kako su komunisti osvojili vlast 1944–1946* (Zagreb: Naklada PIP, 2006), 7, 258–82.

Their internal pursuit of revolution was matched by a radical regional foreign policy.

Yugoslav communists displayed overweening ambitions in their early contacts with Moscow. In negotiations with Stalin on 9 January 1945 Hebrang suggested that the Yugoslavs intended "to participate in the occupation of individual German regions." He also proposed numerous border "corrections" with the neighboring countries in favor of Yugoslavia and outlined Belgrade's thinking on a federation with Bulgaria in which the latter would have the status of one of the seven federal units (in other words, no dualism), but presumably would be deprived of Pirin Macedonia. Stalin cautioned against this as well as against possible clashes with Britain over Albania. He pointedly observed that the Yugoslavs were "preparing to wage war with the whole world" and expressed regret that they had not sought Soviet advice before making important decisions.[19]

It was Tito's radicalism rather than his supposed laxity that was the chief source of conflict with Stalin. The growing tensions over the unfair economic arrangements that the Soviets imposed on Yugoslavia after the war were secondary to Moscow's growing apprehension that Yugoslavia was seeing itself as a regional communist center and that it could stir up unwelcome conflicts with the West. The shooting down of an American military transport plane over Yugoslavia in August 1946 and the mining of Albanian waters off Corfu in October 1946, with the loss of forty-four sailors on two damaged British warships, were among the incidents that alarmed Moscow. To be sure, the Soviets credited Yugoslav zeal at the conference at Szklarska Poręba, Poland, in September 1947, where the Communist Information Bureau (Cominform) was established, moreover with headquarters in Belgrade. But it was the Yugoslav aid offered to Greek insurgents in the third round of the Greek Civil War (1946–49) and especially the projected stationing of two Yugoslav army divisions at Korçë, in southern Albania, opposite the Greek insurgent base at Grámmos, with the prospect of confrontation with the West in Greece, that prompted Stalin's swift reaction.[20] His message to both the Yugoslav and Bulgarian communists in February 1948 was that Greek insurgency ought to be "restricted." To insist on continuing insurgency was to court war.[21]

---

19 G. P. Murashko et al. (eds.), *Vostochnaia Evropa v dokumentakh rossiikii arkhivov 1944–1953* (Moscow and Novosibirsk: Sibirskii khronograf, 1997), vol. I, 118–33.
20 Ivo Banac, *With Stalin Against Tito: Cominformist Splits in Yugoslav Communism* (Ithaca: Cornell University Press, 1988), 28–40.
21 Banac (ed.), *The Diary of Georgi Dimitrov*, 441, 443.

Stalin determined that Tito's policies were systemically unacceptable and incorrigible. Having made up his mind, he sought to undermine Tito in three letters that spelled out the KPJ's errors. After disavowing the anti-Soviet statements of "dubious Marxists" in the Yugoslav leadership, and later those of Tito and his deputy Edvard Kardelj (1910–79), Stalin condemned the KPJ's "semi-legal" status, its excessive secrecy and lack of "internal party democracy," the oversight of the security apparatus and the primacy of the front organization over the party, avoidance of class struggle, particularly in the countryside, and boastfulness about the KPJ's supposed merits and achievements. Despite the weight of these criticisms, the Yugoslav leadership survived the challenge of Stalin's adherents (Andrija Hebrang and Sreten Žujović-Crni), who were expelled from the KPJ and then arrested,[22] and refused to attend the meeting of the Cominform, scheduled for 28 June 1948 at Bucharest, where the other member parties adopted the resolution that expelled the KPJ from the ranks of the communist family and called for the removal of the Tito leadership.[23]

For Tito, the confrontation with the Soviets was only secondarily over ideology. From the beginning, the Yugoslav leadership emphasized that the Soviet attack was an attack on the Yugoslav state, not just an ideological dispute among communists. He responded with a mass mobilization inaugurated at the Fifth Congress of the KPJ (Belgrade, 21–28 July 1948), but did not initially promote any alternative model of socialism. He was defending his homemade revolution against all challengers, if need be by brutal repression. In the course of confrontation with what was usually referred as the Cominform, but really the rest of the communist world, Tito's secret police registered 55,663 and arrested 16,288 alleged Cominformists. Depending on their party status and the dynamics of KPJ's recruitment during post-Cominform mobilization, this would constitute between a tenth and a fifth of total party membership, which is anything but an ephemeral phenomenon. Some 8,250 of them were interned in the concentration camp of Goli Otok (literally, Naked Island) in the northern Adriatic, where they were forced to "revise their stand."[24] Their mistreatment constitutes the essence of "Stalinist anti-Stalinism," by which Tito crushed the opposition and created his own version of Stalin's "revolution from above."[25]

---

22 Hebrang was prepared for a show trial, but died in prison under unexplained circumstances in June 1949.
23 Banac, *With Stalin*, 117–26.   24 Ibid., 148–51, 243–54.
25 Svetozar Stojanović, "Od postrevolucionarne diktature ka socijalističkoj demokratiji," *Praxis* 9, 3–4 (1972), 381.

Isolated from the West before the split and now boycotted by the communist world, the Yugoslav leadership had no choice, however, but to rethink its strategy. This led to moderation in foreign policy, an improvement in relations with the West and the acceptance of economic and military aid from the United States.[26] In addition, it led to a reappraisal of Soviet Marxism and to three years of heady ideological revisionism (1950–53) in an attempt not simply to find a Yugoslav alternative, but to devise ways of avoiding the repetition of Soviet degeneration and to develop a genuine socialist model. In Yugoslav practice, critiques of Soviet conceptions translated into a search for mechanisms that would control the state bureaucracy and promote governance by the producers via assemblies of voters, citizens' councils and – in industry – workers' councils. These were the building blocks of the uniquely Yugoslav model of self-management, which despite appearances depended on the invisible hand of the party. The process of de-Sovietization seemed irreversible at the Sixth Congress of the KPJ (1952), when the party renamed itself the League of Communists of Yugoslavia (Savez komunista Jugoslavije, SKJ) and proclaimed that it was no longer "the direct operational leader and taskmaster in economic, state and social life, but would act ... principally by persuasion, in all organizations, organs and institutions."[27]

The Sixth Congress, which undoubtedly marked the highest point of liberalization in the Tito period, is sometimes referred to as Djilas's congress. Formerly a prominent dogmatist, Milovan Djilas became the most liberal member of the Yugoslav Politburo and used the podium at the congress to proclaim that "without democracy there is no – and there can be no – socialism."[28] But Tito, too, according to Djilas's subsequent account, reached his highest "achievement not only in criticism of the Soviet leadership, but in criticism of the party of Leninist type and of autocratic power."[29] Most especially, Tito criticized Soviet imperialism and Russian chauvinism, leaving little doubt that he saw Yugoslav practice as the model for the development of international communism. Contrary to the Soviet example, Tito claimed, "we went down the true socialist road, the road of decentralization and democratic management in economy and, generally, by the road of withering

---

26 Tito reciprocated with concessions on Trieste and Austria and, most importantly, by closing the frontier with Greece and withdrawing all support from the Greek insurgents: Banac, *With Stalin*, 137–39.
27 *Borba komunista Jugoslavije za socijalističku demokratiju: Šesti kongres KPJ (Saveza komunista Jugoslavije)* (Belgrade: Kultura, 1952), 268.
28 Ibid., 231.   29 Milovan Djilas, *Vlast* (London: Naša reč, 1983), 229.

of state functions."[30] By February 1953 Yugoslavia joined the Balkan Pact with Greece and Turkey, thereby gaining backdoor access to NATO. In the spring of 1953, Tito even expressed hope that the SKJ would quickly join the Socialist International.

Despite these daring departures from the Soviet model, Yugoslav revisionism had its limits. After Stalin's death, with the curtailment of Soviet pressures, Tito quickly started backpedaling. At the Second Plenum of the SKJ CC (Central Committee; Brijuni, June 1953) he announced a halt in party reform, denouncing the view that the "development of democratism means that it is no longer necessary to struggle against the anti-socialist tendencies."[31] For his part, Djilas understood the plenum as a "decisive about-turn in putting the brakes on democratization, that is, in returning to Leninist ideology and the 'dictatorship of the proletariat.'"[32] Despite these reversals, starting with mid October, Djilas started a series of columns in *Borba* (Struggle), the central SKJ organ. In his eighteen articles (the last one in the series was banned by order of the SKJ Executive Committee), as well as in the short story "The Anatomy of a Moral,"[33] Djilas argued for more democracy and declared that the Leninist party and state were obsolete. These articles provoked admiration and support not only among many intellectuals but in parts of the SKJ apparatus, leading to Tito's decision, however hesitant, that Djilas must be condemned and deprived of his functions. The consequences were dire. Djilas's fall "was seen within and outside the party as the end of democratization."[34]

Nonbloc Socialism 1955–1961

The sacrifice of Djilas was Tito's investment in the revival of Soviet ties. Despite a decline in hostilities and some contacts and exchanges, nothing of significance was changed until the visit of N. S. Khrushchev and N. A. Bulganin to Yugoslavia from 26 May to 3 June 1955. Although all members of the Soviet delegation were pointedly titled "Mr." in the protocol, their party functions having received second billing, the Yugoslav negotiators were reminded in theses prepared by their leaders that "reconciliation with

30 *Šesti kongres*, 34.
31 HDA, Vladimir Bakarić papers (ROVB), box 22, no. 161, "Svim organizacijama Saveza komunista Jugoslavije," 3.
32 Djilas, *Vlast*, 251.
33 Milovan Đilas, "Anatomija jednog morala," *Nova misao* 2, 1 (1954), 3–20.
34 Djilas, *Vlast*, 274.

this type of [imperialist] Soviet policy not only in relation to us, but generally, is impossible."[35] However, the atmosphere improved swiftly with the first encounters. Khrushchev's comradely greetings were replicated by Tito ("we talk like communists with communists"), both principals being anti-Western in their tone. Khrushchev teased Tito about "dependence" on the West and especially on treaty ties with Turkey, stressing that "for us, as countries that stand on specific class positions, there can be no absolute confidence between us and the capitalist countries." Tito, for his part, admitted that various Western social democrats and "progressives" had tried to suggest establishment of a multiparty system, but that the West did not like Yugoslavia's ties with India, Burma and Egypt or its "interference in colonial questions." Tito was adamant that, no matter how the ties with Moscow developed, "even if we were not with you, we would have broken with them ... because it is very unpleasant to take bribes."[36]

The only area where the two sides disagreed concerned matters of history. To Khrushchev, Stalin was "boundlessly loyal to the cause of the working class, boundlessly. And he was nonetheless a man of genius." One Soviet delegate even offered that the Cominform resolution of 1948 "was not entirely incorrect."[37] Under the circumstances, the greatest achievement of the meeting was the Belgrade Declaration, which was written by Kardelj and Dmitrii T. Shepilov, after the latter convinced Khrushchev that the hatchet should be buried despite Tito's refusal to agree to Soviet leadership in the communist world.[38] The most important part of the declaration recognized the "adherence to the principle of mutual respect and noninterference in internal affairs for whatever reason – economic, political or ideological – since the questions of internal organization of different social systems and different forms of development of socialism are exclusively a matter for people of individual countries."[39] In all the subsequent conflicts with the Soviets, the Yugoslav communists stubbornly held fast to the letter of the declaration.

High-level Yugoslav contacts with the Soviet leadership continued in 1955, but it was the Twentieth Congress of the CPSU in February 1956 and

35 Arhiv Jugoslavije (AJ), Belgrade, Fund 837, Kabinet Predsednika republike (KPR), I-3-a SSSR, Poseta delegacije Vlade SSSR-a na čelu sa N. S. Hruščovom: 'Teze," 3.
36 Ibid., "Tok konferencije jugoslovenske i sovjetske delegacije," passim.
37 Ibid., 3, 58, 60.
38 Dmitrii Shepilov, *The Kremlin's Scholar: A Memoir of Soviet Politics Under Stalin and Khrushchev* (New Haven: Yale University Press, 2007), 392.
39 AJ, Fund 837, KPR, I-3-a SSSR, Poseta delegacije Vlade SSSR-a na čelu sa N. S. Hruščovom: "Deklaracija Vlada FNRJ i SSSR," 2.

Khrushchev's "Secret Speech" inaugurating de-Stalinization that brought Belgrade closer to Moscow. Still, during the long return visit of the Yugoslav leaders to the USSR (1–23 June 1956), Tito successfully warded off Khrushchev's enticements to join the "socialist camp." Moreover, Tito's distinction between the "socialist camp" and the broader nonbloc "socialist world" was irritating to the Soviets. Khrushchev insisted that unity required discipline and that, from the point of view of safeguarding the unity of the socialist camp, the Cominform, too, was progressive. Shepilov felt that countries such as India, which Tito saw as part of the socialist world, did not meet the test of power.[40] Anastas Mikoian noted that Yugoslavia shared the Soviet socialist system, which was directed to struggle against capitalism. This required unity of action, effectively rejection of pluralism, as neither the Soviets nor the Yugoslavs permitted opposition – "other parties."[41]

Tito would not budge from his position of avoiding all Soviet associations. He pledged that the Yugoslavs had "no intention of weakening in any way the international organizations and institutions of the socialist countries" or of "pry[ing] some countries away from the Eastern camp" but – on Khrushchev's insistence that the Yugoslavs seemed intent on "remaining outside the camp" – completed the discussion with the words: "We are not outside the socialist front, but we are outside the Eastern bloc."[42]

After the Poznań protests of June 1956 and the crisis they engendered in Poland and Hungary, Tito had occasion to scuffle with vacationing Khrushchev (19 September 1956) over the charge that the West was using Yugoslavia's example "to provoke the disintegration of the East." Tito felt that, after the Twentieth Congress of the CPSU, the Soviets and East Europeans had succumbed to stagnation and remained suspicious of Yugoslavia. Since the Yugoslavs agreed with the USSR in almost all questions of foreign policy, the remaining differences could be narrowed through additional discussions.[43] Moreover, at the height of the Hungarian crisis, the Yugoslavs were helpful to Khrushchev and Georgii M. Malenkov when they arrived for a secret meeting with Tito, Kardelj and Aleksandar Ranković (1909–83) at Brijuni on the evening of 1 November 1956.

In the meeting that lasted a whole night, Khrushchev stated the Soviet case for intervention in Hungary, where "they are killing, butchering and hanging communists." Initially, Tito expressed reservations about intervention ("it

40 Ibid., 31.   41 Ibid., 31–33.   42 Ibid., 39, 51.
43 Ibid., KPR I-3-a SSSR, 'Zabeleške o razgovorima na večeri kod druga Tita u čast Hruščova," 4–5, 14.

would bring more harm than good in Hungary, and it would compromise socialism") but, after the Yugoslavs were led to understand that it was inevitable, they suggested that a revolutionary government made up of Hungarians be assembled: "Tito underscored: here it is important how to begin and how to end. It was as if a heavy load fell from Khrushchev's heart. He lifts his arms high above his head and says: That's it, that's it! It is obvious that the Russians came for this." Tito suggested the name for the Hungarian puppet government (revolutionary worker–peasant government) and its leader – János Kádár ("since he was persecuted in a bestial fashion under Rákosi and tortured in prison") – and proposed that the new government "recognize workers' councils, introduce self-management, decentralization, etc."[44] But when the intervention took place on 4 November the Soviets were not about to introduce the Yugoslav model to Hungary. There ensued a period of "hot and cold treatment," which could accommodate Belgrade's occasional pro-Soviet balancing (recognition of East Germany in October 1957), but was most often highlighted by examples of Yugoslav independence: refusal to sign the Declaration of the Twelve Communist and Workers' Parties (November 1957), introduction of the SKJ's new program at the Seventh Congress (Ljubljana, 23–26 April 1958), which was boycotted by the pro-Moscow parties, cancellation of credits to Yugoslavia (May 1958) and outcry at the execution of Imre Nagy, Pál Maléter and others (June 1958), which, according to Tito, was meant to revive the conflict with Yugoslavia.[45]

Tito's answer to Yugoslavia's new isolation from the Soviet bloc and the Moscow-dominated communist movement was increasingly engaging with the newly independent countries of Asia and Africa. Though initially conceived as contrary to the "establishment of some third bloc,"[46] it progressed into a conference of nonaligned countries (Belgrade, September 1961) at which Tito stressed that the majority in the world consisted of countries "that are outside the blocs and that accept peaceful and active coexistence as the only solution that can prevent the catastrophe of war."[47] From the Soviet point of view, Tito's nonalignment was an affront to the Marxist class stand.

44 Ibid., KPR, I-3-a SSSR, "Zabilješka o razgovorima drugova Tita, Rankovića i Kardelja sa Hruščovom i Maljenkovom od 2/3 novembra 1956 godine i na Brionima," 1–15.
45 Veljko Mićunović, *Moscow Diary* (Garden City, NY: Doubleday, 1980), 171–394.
46 AJ, Fund 387, KPR, I-2/4-1, Put J. B. Tita u Indiju: "Govor u Parlamentu – 21.XII.1954 g.," 5.
47 Josip Broz Tito, *Jugoslavija u borbi za nezavisnost i nesvrstanost* (Sarajevo: Svjetlost, 1980), 186–87.

As Leonid Brezhnev put it to Tito in 1962, "When you talk about the [Eastern] bloc, whether you want it or not, you are looking at it a nonclass way, and we, as Marxists, cannot agree."[48] Still, the challenge to the Soviet bloc was resented by China more than by the Soviet Union. In the early stages of the Sino-Soviet split, in January 1959, Tito explained the reason for this seeming oddity in a conversation with the Burmese socialist leaders Ba Swe and Kyaw Nyein. He stressed that China "a priori rejects the policy of coexistence, and since Yugoslavia is in the front ranks of struggle for coexistence it thereby harms China." He noted that China could not criticize Soviet "talk of coexistence ... therefore the full weight of China's criticism of the other socialist countries falls onto the shoulders of Yugoslavia."[49]

China's proxy war with the Soviet Union via attacks on Yugoslavia proceeded apace in the early 1960s. In the process, the Yugoslavs drew closer to Khrushchev and by 1963, when Khrushchev visited Yugoslavia, the two sides were to all intents and purposes close allies against Chinese "dogmatism." Tito made fun of supposed differences between Yugoslavia and the Soviet Union and gave evidence of his orthodoxy by stating that the role of the party in Yugoslavia was "very significant. Although we carried out decentralization, we never decentralized the party."[50] For his part, Khrushchev gave Tito a clean bill of ideological health: "We still do not understand your workers' councils, but that is good seed. A decentralized economy would not suit us, but we would be helped by a centralized economy plus workers' councils."[51] As both sides made plans to stem the influence of Chinese factions throughout the world, it was easy to forget the dogmatist potential of the USSR. This partially explains Tito's shock at the overthrow of Khrushchev in November 1964.

The Return of the National Question 1961–1972

The 1960s brought back Yugoslavia's national question. Of course, it had never quite gone away, but the harshness of KPJ/SKJ centralism and the

---

48 AJ, Fund 837, KPR, I-3-a SSSR, Poseta predsednika Prezidijuma Vrhovnog sovjeta SSSR-a Leonida Brežnjeva: "Zabeleška o jugoslovensko-sovjetskim razgovorima, vodjenim 29. septembra 1962 godine na Vangi," 27.
49 Ibid., I-2/11-3, Put J. B. Tita u Burmu: "Zabeleške o razgovoru Pretsednika Republike sa 10 članova Izvršnog komiteta Burmanske socijalističke partije na čelu sa U Ba Šve-om i U Čo Njenom pre podne 9 januara 1959 u rezidenciji druga Pretsednika u Rangunu," 3–4.
50 Ibid., I-3-a SSSR, Poseta Nikite Sergejevića Hruščova: "Brioni, 26. VIII 1963," 16.
51 Ibid., 18.

permanent campaign against nationalism made it an unwelcome topic of political discussion. There were occasional early warnings, as in Kardelj's new introduction (1957) to his prewar book on the Slovenian national question, in which the SKJ's foremost ideologist warned against the threat of "old chauvinist 'integral Yugoslavism,'" which negated the existing Yugoslav peoples and promoted a single, new Yugoslav nation. He noted that, "The remnants of the old Great Serbian nationalism naturally band together with the mentioned bureaucratic-centralist tendencies."[52]

Kardelj's warnings went unheeded even after the strike of 4,000 miners in Trbovlje, Slovenia (January 1958), the first postwar strike in Yugoslavia, in which the issue of national exploitation was raised. At an expanded meeting of the SKJ CC in February 1958 Tito attacked attitudes in the republics that portrayed Belgrade as "some sort of a Great Serbian center" and called for "administrative measures" if necessary. This discussion took place in a period of high economic growth (13.3 percent annually) and resulted in a modicum of economic reform (March 1961), whereby the firms were given the authority of autonomous decisions on salaries and investments. Full decentralization and market reforms were not yet contemplated.

In 1961 and 1962 a highly public discussion took place between the Serbian novelist and SKJ functionary Dobrica Ćosić and the Slovenian literary historian and philosopher Dušan Pirjevec-Ahac. Whereas Ćosić promoted recentralization and the struggle against "revived nationalisms," Pirjevec argued against the idea that nations come to an end with the liquidation of capitalism and the bourgeoisie. He affirmed the recognition of separate nations as a mark of democracy and liberty. These ideas were fundamental to a conflict of two blocs, within the SKJ and in Yugoslavia generally that would come to a head in the mid 1960s. The centralists, led by the conservative faction that formed around the most senior Serbian leader Aleksandar Ranković, were skeptical of self-management, market forces, decentralization and the growing distance from Moscow, precisely what the federalists – among others, Kardelj and the senior Croatian leader Vladimir Bakarić – increasingly espoused. Their differences were papered over in the new constitution (April 1963), which elevated Yugoslavia to the standing of a socialist republic, and gained Ranković the position of Yugoslavia's vice-president, with the evident prospect of succession. Still,

---

52 Edvard Kardelj (Sperans), *Razvoj slovenačkog nacionalnog pitanja*, 3rd edn. (Belgrade: Komunist, 1973), xxxvii, xliv–xlv.

by the end of 1964, Tito, with his traditional preference for centralism, started leaning toward the federalists at the SKJ's Eighth Congress (Belgrade, 7–13 December 1964). He condemned those "who think that in our socialist social development nationalities are already out of date and that they must die off" and favor "a single united Yugoslav nation, which looks a bit like assimilation and bureaucratic centralization, like unitarism and hegemonism."[53]

The federalist affirmation of decentralized republic-based economies permitted the radical economic reform of 1965, which was an attempt to repulse the remnants of the command economy by financial means. The dinar was devalued and the prices adjusted to Western standards, marking the return of Yugoslavia to the international market. The consequences, however, were dire. Industrial productivity and agriculture stagnated, unemployment rose sharply, forcing the authorities to permit "temporary employment" of workers in the West European countries. Opposition to these trends was centered in Serbia, with Ranković as its factional chief. Moreover, the state security apparatus (Uprava državne bezbednosti, UDB-a), for which Ranković was responsible and which was least affected by various reforms, fell within his area of influence. The federalists and Tito therefore launched their confrontation with Ranković on the issue of UDB-a's abuse of power. At a meeting of the SKJ CC Executive Committee (16 June 1966), Tito accused Ranković of placing listening devices not only in his office and reception areas, but also in his private quarters. Despite Ranković's denials of any wrongdoing, a commission was established to investigate the affair. Some two weeks later it produced its findings to the Fourth Plenum of SKJ CC, which met at Brijuni islands on 1–2 July 1966. As a result, the plenum removed Ranković and the service's leading members from their positions and accepted a proposal for the reform of the security service, which was criticized for "deformations" and "chauvinist practices" toward the non-Serbs. The dimension of political repression was evident from revelations that in Croatia alone (with a population of 4.12 million in 1961) there were 1.3 million police dossiers. In the subsequent purge, some 671 of 1,473 employees of the federal Interior Ministry alone were dismissed, leading to the inescapable interpretation that the aim of the federalist bloc was to weaken the Serb cadres.

---

53 Josip Broz Tito, "Uloga Saveza komunista u daljoj [sic] izgradnji socijalističkih društvenih odnosa i aktualni problemi u međunarodnom radničkom pokretu i borbi za mir i socijalizam u svijetu," in *Osmi kongres SKJ* (Belgrade: Kultura, 1964), 32.

The fall of Ranković opened the floodgates for reform and national expression, especially in Croatia, Bosnia and Herzegovina, and Kosovo, where UDB-a's policies were highly repressive. The Catholic Church benefited from the renewal of diplomatic ties between the Vatican and Yugoslavia (1966). During that year the circulation of the Catholic press reached 8.5 million copies in Croatia, 60,000 copies of the Bible were printed in Zagreb in 1968, and building permits for the construction of new churches were increasingly granted. The old restrictions did not entirely disappear. In September 1966 Mihajlo Mihajlov, a lecturer at the University of Zadar, was sentenced to three and a half years in prison for his essay "Moscow Summer," published in a Belgrade literary journal, because he calumniated the USSR by pushing the history of the Soviet death camps back to the age of Lenin.[54] And in March 1967 an elite group of Croat institutions, writers and linguists, most of them prominent SKJ members, promulgated a declaration for a constitutional amendment that would guarantee greater Croatian-language rights.[55] The SKJ denounced the initiative as "unacceptable."[56] Tito called it a "stab in the back."[57] The signers received various party penalties, including expulsions.

Despite Tito's foot-dragging, the SKJ consensus was increasingly in favor of greater liberalization. Driven by the industrial northwest – Slovenia and Croatia – the republics were becoming responsible for cadre appointments, and the federal government was being transferred into the space for negotiation. This trend was not weakened by various challenges. Tito fended off the left-wing opposition, notably the Praxis group that showed its strength in the Belgrade student demonstrations in June 1968,[58] but drew lessons from the Soviet intervention in Czechoslovakia for a new wave of confrontation with the Soviet Union. At the Ninth Congress of the SKJ (Belgrade, 11–15 March 1968), Tito carefully registered Yugoslavia's opposition to the invasion, the "broad anti-Yugoslav campaign that ensued," and the "unacceptable doctrine on 'collective,' 'integrated' but in essence – limited sovereignty" that appeared

---

54 Mihajlo Mihajlov, *Moscow Summer* (New York: Farrar, Straus and Giroux, 1965), 69–70. Tito charged Mihajlov with advancing a "new form of Djilasism."
55 "Deklaracija o nazivu i položaju hrvatskog književnog jezika," *Telegram* (17 Mar. 1967), 1.
56 "Deklaracija nije prihvatljiva," *Telegram* (24 Mar. 1967), 3.
57 "Novosadski dogovor najbolje rješenje," *Telegram* (31 Mar. 1967), 1.
58 The Zagreb journal *Praxis* became the flagship of the left opposition and had an impact beyond Yugoslavia. See Gerson S. Sher, *Praxis: Marxist Criticism and Dissent in Socialist Yugoslavia* (Bloomington: Indiana University Press, 1977).

"in certain East European countries."[59] The decline in relations was characterized by a series of incidents and confrontations, in which the Soviets regularly accused the Yugoslav side of stirring up anti-Soviet sentiments,[60] while they simultaneously stirred up internal Yugoslav antagonisms.

The decentralizing trend was strengthened in 1967 and 1968 through constitutional amendments that gave greater autonomy to the autonomous provinces of Kosovo and Vojvodina. At the Ninth Congress, Tito admitted errors in Kosovo and the "neglect of interests of the Albanian nationality."[61] With Tito's blessing, the new – and generationally younger – Croatian leadership (Miko Tripalo and Savka Dabčević-Kučar) opened the processes of Croatia's national emancipation. For the first time after 1945, at least in Croatia, the communists legitimated their rule through reaffirmation of national sentiment and once again, as in the interwar period, tried to nationalize their history. In January 1970 they beat back the unitarist opposition within the Croatian party organization that insinuated that decentralization and liberalization promoted Croat nationalism. Savka Dabčević-Kučar, president of the Croatian party CC, provided a response to the unitarist–centralist theses by claiming that "unitarism is a mask – behind which [Serbian] hegemonism is hiding its face . . . For the unitarists there is no such thing as the national question and the national problem. They simply negate the national feeling of the people because it interferes with their bureaucratic preconception of society."[62]

The ensuing period of reform, subsequently labeled the Croatian Spring, opened the question of the position of Croatia in Yugoslavia, the Yugoslav economy and international representation, but inevitably moved into discussions of national culture and identity and of freedom of personality and conviction and, finally, into questions of pluralism and democracy – all of this under conditions of reduced censorship and the rise of alternative political centers.[63] As in the Prague Spring, this was a period of unprecedented cultural

59 "Referat predsednika SKJ Josipa Broza Tita," in *Deveti kongres Saveza komunista Jugoslavije* (Belgrade: Kultura, 1969), 132–33.
60 AJ, Fund 837, KPR, I-3-a/101-131, 3: "Sovjetske izjave o odnosima sa Jugoslavijom," 3.
61 "Referat," *Deveti kongres*, 87. The usage of the term "minority" was eliminated in favor of "nationality." The Yugoslav "nationalities" in addition obtained the right to use the flags of their home countries.
62 Milovan Baletić and Zdravko Židovec (eds.), *Deseta sjednica Centralnog komiteta Saveza komunista Hrvatske* (Zagreb: NIP Vjesnik, 1970), 8.
63 The principal leaders of the reform movement later produced their own accounts of this period. See Miko Tripalo, *Hrvatsko proljeće* (Zagreb: Globus, 1990); Savka Dabčević-Kučar, *'71: Hrvatski snovi i stvarnost* (Zagreb: Interpublic, 1997), vols. I–II.

and publishing activity. The stage was set for arbitration over the limit of republic autonomy, which also meant the limit of reform. Though Tito promoted the reform of the Yugoslav federation, which through a series of constitutional amendments in 1971 transferred sovereign rights to the republics, he still hedged his bets on the course of the Croat reformers. As for Moscow, there was no dilemma over its preferences in the case. After a serious row over a concocted case of contact between the Croatian leadership and a Croat émigré leader who was reputed to have ties with Moscow, which the SKJ CC covered up (April 1971), Brezhnev called Tito with offers of help.[64]

This threatening experience convinced Tito to curtail the influence of the Croat reformers. In early July 1971 he warned the Croatian leadership that their republic had "become the key problem in the country when it concerns the rampage of nationalism." Calling for a "determined class struggle," Tito commented on the worsening state of Croat–Serb relations and demanded to know whether the leadership was aware that the Soviets were "watching this. Can't you see that [they] will immediately present themselves should there be disorder? I will create order using our army before allowing others to do that." He added that in April they had "already decided to [attack] Yugoslavia, but had not decided when."[65]

After August 1971, when Richard Nixon announced his forthcoming visit to China, the diplomatic alignment was rapidly changed. The USSR was now on the defensive and Brezhnev ready to patch up relations with Tito. Brezhnev's visit to Yugoslavia in September 1971 marked the end of hostilities, though it is fair to say that Brezhnev's reaffirmation of Yugoslav "sovereignty" was paid for by ideological concessions on reform. During the fall of 1971, particularly in the meetings with Richard Nixon, Pierre Trudeau and Edward Heath, Tito painted a rosy picture of Soviet intentions. It is significant that he was now openly skeptical about the prospects of reform: "Dubček made many errors. They were hasty, and went too far, too quickly. They negated everything in the past. They allowed the press to attack the USSR fiercely . . . If the people in Czechoslovakia are ready to accept the situation that they have, that's their business. One must look at the situation realistically."[66] And in a meeting with Nicolae Ceauşescu on 23 November 1971, Tito explained to the Romanian leader that, "We certainly have more problems since we have

---

64 AJ, Fund 837, KPR, I-3-a-1, "Završna reč predsednika Tita na sednici Predsedništva SKJ," 104/1–2 MS.
65 Ibid., "Riječ druga Tita na sastanku sa Izvršnim komitetom," 1–2, 6.
66 Ibid., I-2/50-53, "Zabeleška," 10.

six republics." The reason was that based on Yugoslav federalism some people have concluded that the party, too, must be federalized. He was determined to change that: "Cohesive force, democratic centralism."[67]

With this background in mind, it is clear that Tito was ready for a confrontation with the Croatian reformers. The opportunity presented itself when the students at the University of Zagreb went on strike over a series of political demands on 25 November. Tito immediately summoned an emergency meeting with the Croatian and federal SKJ leaders at Karadordevo (Vojvodina) for 1 December 1971. Backed by the army and the conservatives, Tito forced a major party purge, which devastated Croatia's reformist leadership and, by the fall of 1972, was extended to the Serbian party leadership (Marko Nikezić and Latinka Perović) and individual reformists in the other republics. In Croatia itself, more than 2,000 people were arrested and several thousand SKJ members were expelled. Members of a select group of intellectual and student leaders were tried and sentenced. The Soviets were pleased at this development.[68] By June 1972, when Tito visited the USSR, the relations were so harmonious that Brezhnev stated that, "Comrade Tito knows all of our military secrets. We then [September 1971] agreed that we shall have no networks of agents [*agenture*], that we shall trust in one another."[69] As for the purge in Croatia, Tito claimed that the expelled leadership "conceded politics to the various anti-socialist elements," mainly nationalists, to which Brezhnev responded with a sour comment, "There the West, too, has the 'smell' of nationalism."[70]

Kardelj's "Perpetuum Mobile" and the Withering of the Center 1972–1990

Tito's purges of 1971–72 removed the ostensible causes for Soviet meddling. Political independence was defended by sacrificing the most offensive (to the Soviets and Tito) examples of ideological independence. The price was very high. Cut to the bone, shorn of the illusions of hope, reform and democratization, the Yugoslav system became more brittle. If the marginalization of

67 Ibid., I-2/51, "Stenografske beleške sa razgovora predsednika republike i Saveza komunista Jugoslavije Josipa Broza Tita i predsednika državnog saveta i generalnog sekretara Rumunske komunističke partije Nikolae Čaušeskua," 23, 25–26.
68 Ibid., I-3-a/101-133, "Beleška o razgovoru Predsednika Republike sa Bajbakovim," 3, 6.
69 Ibid., I-2/53, "Stenogradske beleške sa razgovora vodjenih izmedju predsednika SFRJ Josipa Broza Tita [i] generalnog sekretara CK KPSS Leonida Iljiča Brežnjeva, održanih 6. juna 1972. godine u 11,00 časova u Kremlju," 40.
70 Ibid., 22.

the SKJ was the source of all errors since the Sixth Congress, if liberalism had become the chief error, if the party once again had to be at the center of politics, could systemic retrogression be a solution? Only if the old dogma were reinterpreted innovatively. It was discovered that self-management was a form of the dictatorship of the proletariat. Under the circumstances, decentralization (withering away of the workers' state, deetatization) should not be seen as a means for the empowerment of bureaucracy (democratization). Instead, decentralization should promote an "association of free producers," the Yugoslav version of a classless society. With Kardelj's help, Tito tried to compensate for the loss of democratic illusions through a new bargain: decentralization instead of democratization. This became Titoism's last innovative half-solution.

The legislative basis of the new bargain was the constitution of 1974 and the Law of Associated Labor (Zakon o udruženom radu, ZUR, 1976). The first, the classic of Kardeljism, expounded "associated labor" in more than a hundred pages of turgid prose. The second created a system of indirect administration from the "basic organizations of associated labor" (Osnovne organizacije udruženog rada, OOUR), the basic cells of the system, to the more complex forms of organization and decision-making in enterprises, but also in the communes, republics and the federation, always under the watchful eye of the SKJ by way of indirect elections ("delegate system"), which was not the object of reform. Since the new system depended on "agreements on associated labor," it produced a separate branch of law (self-managerial law) and between 1.25 million and 1.5 million legal acts. It is claimed that each OOUR produced some 30 legal acts with between 500 to 1,000 pages of legal norms.[71] In fact, the ZUR fragmented and paralyzed society, leaving it exposed to the perils of Caesarism.

As the chief ideologist of high Titoism, Edvard Kardelj was responsible for two additional innovations. In an attempt to maintain the balance of power between otherwise unequal republics and provinces, and in anticipation of Tito's passing (in the constitution of 1974, Article 333, it was allowed that Tito could be the head of state "without the termination of mandate"), Kardelj created a system of rotating presidencies in the party and the state. This "perpetuum mobile," which allowed representatives of each republic and autonomous province to preside over the party and the state in a fixed order for a limited period (usually a year), was then duplicated in every statewide

---

71 Dušan Bilandžić, *Historija Socijalističke Federativne Republike Jugoslavije: glavni procesi, 1918–1985* (Zagreb: Školska knjiga, 1985), 446–47.

association or organization. In addition, in his last theoretical work *Directions of Development of the Political System of Socialist Self-Management* (1978), Kardelj allowed that the rejection of "political pluralism of bourgeois society" was not necessarily an endorsement of a "one-party system as a specific variant of that system." His intention, despite caveats about the advantages of one-party rule under the necessity of revolutionary circumstances, was to promote the idea that the SKJ was not a monopolistic party, but rather the "pillar of democracy of self-managerial interests."[72]

After the deaths of Kardelj (1979), Tito (1980) and Bakarić (1983), Yugoslav communism was increasingly shorn of authority and ideas. Moreover, committed to the proposition of "After Tito – Tito," the system was vulnerable to the assaults of those factions that recognized that Tito was no longer available as the chief arbitrator. The leading members of the Serbian party organization started a campaign against the constitution of 1974 even before Tito's death (the Blue Book on the autonomy of Kosovo, 1977). Now, they used the Albanian student demonstrations that commenced at the University of Priština in March 1981 as a battering ram against the Kosovo provincial leadership of Mahmut Bakalli and the autonomy of the two provinces within Serbia. The Belgrade press systematically exaggerated the violence that the Albanian majority in Kosovo had supposedly exercised against the Serb minority, the term "ethnic cleansing" being used for first time in Serb recriminations about the Kosovar Albanian intensions.

In an attempt to upset the federalist and decentralist norms of the Tito era, Tito's reputation was systematically blackened in various ways. The Serbian Academy of Arts and Sciences produced a memorandum (1986) in which Tito and Kardelj were accused of longstanding anti-Serb tendencies, inherited from the Comintern, specifically by promoting "new nations" (Montenegrins, Macedonians, Bosnian Muslims) out of the complex Serb identity. All of these developments ultimately produced the "anti-bureaucratic" movement of Slobodan Milošević, which ended the autonomy of Kosovo and Vojvodina by brutal street actions that were legalized in the new Serbian constitution of March 1989. Milošević, increasingly a transitional figure who preserved the party's power by discarding communism for collectivist nationalism, also annexed Montenegro and was on the way to extend his power westward, until the systemic collapse of

---

72 Edvard Kardelj, *Pravci razvoja političkog sistema socijalističkog samoupravljanja* (Belgrade: Komunist, 1978), 63–65.

communism in Eastern Europe in the fall of 1989 provided the opportunity for multiparty elections and political pluralism in Slovenia and Croatia. But before the SKJ was de-Titoized and transformed into *the* party of Serb nationalism (Serbia and Montenegro), or lost power in free elections in the northwestern republics, it fell apart at its last and extraordinary Fourteenth Congress (Belgrade, 20–22 January 1991). Curiously, as the various republic branches of the SKJ transformed themselves into social-democratic postcommunist parties, the last echo of Tito's SKJ survived in the party organization of the Yugoslav People's Army (Jugoslavenska narodna armija, JNA), which in November 1990 produced the "generals' party," the League of Communists–Movement for Yugoslavia (Savez komunista – Pokret za Jugoslaviju, SK–PJ), with its theory that in societies of authentic revolution, like Yugoslavia, capitalism could not be restored. The fanaticism of this group was weakened by the failure of the August coup of 1991 in the USSR, but certainly contributed to the violence of Milošević's war against Croatia and Bosnia (1991–95), where the rump JNA with its metamorphosed party provided the muscle for what was essentially a nationalist project.

The sad end of Titoism, which was the dominant tradition of Yugoslav communism, did not, however, preclude a modicum of revival. The latterday Titoists of the postwar period exist in all the post-Yugoslav states, though more as a nostalgic memory than as organized parties and movements. They thrive on the transitional failures, the end of the welfare state, and illusions of full employment and of a mighty and respected nonaligned state. The twenty-first-century Titonostalgics form a fellowship of resentment, and are in fact utterly at odds with the politics of survival and bipolarism, of complicated ideological innovations, always backed up by the monopoly of power, which were the mark of Titoism.

Bibliographical Essay

The scarcity of compelling literature for various phases of Yugoslav communist history stands in stark contrast to the excess of controversies engendered by the communist record both in scholarship and in popular debates. All official and unofficial party histories are now out of date, although the last official attempt is still a useful reference. See Stanislav Stojanović (ed.), *Istorija Saveza komunista Jugoslavije* (Belgrade: Kommunist, 1985). On the beginning of the communist movement in Yugoslavia, see Ivo Banac, "The Communist Party of Yugoslavia During the Period of Legality, 1919–1921," in Ivo Banac (ed.), *The Effects of World War I. The Class War After the Great War: The Rise of Communist Parties in East Central Europe, 1918–1921* (New York: Columbia University Press, 1983), 188–230, and Ivo Banac, *The National Question in Yugoslavia: Origins, History, Politics* (Ithaca: Cornell University Press, 1984), 328–39. For the KPJ's appraisal of the national question, see Dušan Lukač, *Radnički pokret u Jugoslaviji i nacionalno pitanje, 1918–1941* [The Workers' Movement in Yugoslavia and the National Question, 1918–1941] (Belgrade: Institut za savremenu istoriju, NIP Export-press, 1972); Latinka Perović, *Od centralizma do federalizma: KPJ u nacionalnom pitanju* [From Centralism to Federalism: The KPJ on the National Question] (Zagreb: Globus, 1984); and Paul Shoup, *Communism and the Yugoslav National Question* (New York: Columbia University Press, 1968). For a close examination of factionalism in the KPJ, which was almost without exception connected with stable and predictable responses to the national question, see Ivo Banac, *With Stalin Against Tito: Cominformist Splits in Yugoslav Communism* (Ithaca: Cornell University Press, 1988), 45–116. On the KPJ leadership before Tito, see Ivan Očak, *Vojnik revolucije: Život i rad Vladimira Ćopića* [Soldier of Revolution: The Life and Work of Vladimir Ćopić] (Zagreb: Spektar, 1980); Ivan Očak, *Braća Cvijići* [The Cvijić Brothers] (Zagreb: Spektar-Globus, 1982); and Ivan Očak, *Gorkić: Život, rad i pogibija* [Gorkić: His Life, Work and Death] (Zagreb: Globus, 1988).

None of Tito's numerous biographies are adequate or complete, meaning that much of his political career remains unresearched. For Tito's part in the conflicts over strategy immediately before the beginning of World War II and during the partisan insurgency, see Ivan Očak, *Krleža–Partija: Miroslav Krleža u radničkom i komunističkom pokretu 1917–1941* [Krleža–Party: Miroslav Krleža in the Workers' and Communist Movement 1917–1941] (Zagreb: Spektar, 1982), and Stanko Lasić, *Sukob na književnoj ljevici, 1928–1952* [The Conflict on the Literary Left] (Zagreb: Liber, 1970). On partisan diplomacy and Tito's wartime relations with the Moscow center, see Walter R. Roberts, *Tito, Mihailović and the Allies, 1941–1945* (New Brunswick, NJ: Rutgers University Press, 1973), and Paul Ivan Jukić, "Uncommon Cause: The Soviet Union and the Rise of Tito's Yugoslavia, 1941–1945," Ph.D. dissertation (Yale University, 1997). On conflict with the Chetniks and the overall KPJ strategy as manifested in the Bosnian cauldron, see two model monographs by Marko Attila Hoare, *Genocide and Resistance in Hitler's Bosnia: The Partisans and the Chetniks, 1941–1943* (Oxford: Oxford University Press, 2006), and Marko Attila Hoare,

The Bosnian Muslims in the Second World War: A History (Oxford: Oxford University Press, 2013). On the "left errors," see Branko Petranović, "O levim skretanjima KPJ krajem 1941. i u prvoj polovini 1942. godine," [On the KPJ's Left Deviations in 1941 and the First Half of 1942] *Matica srpska: Zbornik za istoriju* 4 (1971), 39–80, and Rasim Hurem, *Kriza narod-nooslobodilačkog pokreta u Bosni i Hercegovini krajem 1941. i početkom 1942. godine* [The Crisis of the National Liberation Movement in Bosnia and Herzegovina in Late 1941 and Early 1942] (Sarajevo: Svjetlost, 1972). On Hebrang's line in wartime Croatia, see Jill A. Irvine, *The Croat Question: Partisan Politics in the Formation of the Yugoslav Socialist State* (Boulder: Westwood Press, 1993), and Nada Kisić Kolanović, *Andrija Hebrang: Iluzije i otrežnjenja* [Andrija Hebrang: Illusions and Disillusionment] (Zagreb: Institut za suvremenu povijest, 1996).

For a detailed account of the communist takeover, see Jerca Vodušek Starič, *Prevzem oblasti 1944–1946* [Takeover 1944–1946] (Ljubljana: Cankarjeva založba, 1992), and Jerca Vodušek Starič, *Kako su komunisti osvojili vlast 1944–1946* [How the Communists Came to Power 1944–1946] (Zagreb: Naklada PIP, 2006). Of the memoir literature, Djilas's recollections are especially useful for the wartime period, the conflict with the USSR and the post-Cominform reconstruction. See Milovan Djilas, *Wartime* (New York: Harcourt Brace Jovanovich, 1977), and Milovan Djilas, *Rise and Fall* (San Diego: Harcourt Brace Jovanovich, 1985). On the Cominform split, see Banac, *With Stalin Against Tito.* For the most detailed and best-documented account of the Goli Otok concentration camp, see Martin Previšić, "Povijest informbirovskog logora na Golom otoku 1949–1956" [History of the Cominform Prison Camp on Goli Otok 1949–1956], Ph.D. dissertation (University of Zagreb, 2014). For a close reading of the de-Sovietization of Yugoslav communism, see A. Ross Johnson, *The Transformation of Communist Ideology: The Yugoslav Case, 1945–1953* (Cambridge, MA: MIT Press, 1972).

The period after the revival of Soviet ties (1955) has not been treated adequately in historical research. The principal lines of investigation, however, are suggested in political and memoir literature that become rather voluminous in various accounts of Yugoslavia's dissolution. Seven studies ought to be mentioned: Dennison Rusinow, *Yugoslav Experiment 1948–1974* (Berkeley: University of California Press, 1977); Veljko Mićunović, *Moscow Diary* (Garden City, NY: Doubleday, 1980), although some of the original sources in this diary have been significantly edited; Dušan Bilandžić, *Historija Socijalističke Federativne Republike Jugoslavije: glavni procesi,*

1918–1985 [History of the Socialist Federal Republic of Yugoslavia: The Main Processes, 1918–1985] (Zagreb: Školska knjiga, 1985); Miko Tripalo, *Hrvatsko proljeće* [Croatian Spring] (Zagreb: Globus, 1990); Latinka Perović, *Zatvaranje kruga: Ishod političkog rascepa u SKJ, 1971/1972* [Closing the Circle: The Outcome of the Political Split in the SKJ, 1971/1972] (Sarajevo: Svjetlost, 1991); Audrey Helfant Budding, "Serb Intellectuals and the National Question, 1961–1991," Ph.D. dissertation (Harvard University, 1998); and Sabrina P. Ramet, *Three Yugoslavias: State-Building and Legitimation, 1918–2005* (Bloomington: Indiana University Press, 2006).

24

Italian Communism

GIOVANNI GOZZINI

The history of the Italian Communist Party (Partito Comunista Italiano, PCI) has always been interpreted as the history of an exception. The PCI was generally considered by Western politicians and social scientists to be an exceptional party that was unfit to govern because it was part of the Soviet bloc. Being anti-systemic by nature, it provided the foundation for interpretations of Italian politics in terms of "imperfect bipartyism" and "polarized pluralism." It is a matter of fact that the dates of birth and death of the PCI and the USSR were almost contemporaneous. At the same time, the PCI was an exceptional communist party endowed with a long sequence of special authorizations from Moscow – the "Italian way to socialism" proclaimed in 1956, "polycentrism" as a new direction of the international communist movement affirmed by PCI secretary Palmiro Togliatti in his political testament, the so-called Yalta Memorandum written in August 1964, the condemnation of the Soviet invasion of Czechoslovakia in 1968 and Eurocommunism in the 1970s. On the basis of the existing ambiguity between national roots and international identity – "doppiezza" (literally "double-faced strategy") was the term most frequently used in the Italian political debate – the PCI was the only Western communist party capable of constantly winning electoral competitions with the Italian Socialist Party (Partito Socialista Italiano, PSI) and played a dominant role within the Italian left up to 1989.

The aim of this chapter is to get past this double – and exceptional – standard of analysis by considering the PCI to be a normal party, belonging to the family of communist parties and encumbered with the considerable task of surviving without political power in a hostile environment (under fascism at first, and then during the Cold War). Over the last two centuries, only a restricted minority of Western political parties (fewer than one-third) were able to achieve similar results.[1]

Gramsci and the Peculiarities of the PCI's Political Culture

Antonio Gramsci played a crucial role in making the PCI distinctive: He was the party's general secretary from 1924 to 1926, after which he was arrested by the fascist police and sent to jail, where he died in 1937. According to the popular image created by Togliatti after 1945, Gramsci was a victim of Mussolini's regime and the leading thinker whose *Prison Notebooks* (published in 1948–51) elaborated an original view of Italian history, rivaling Benedetto Croce and the conservative intellectual tradition, while representing a remarkable anomaly in the cultural desert of Stalinist communism. However, new archival evidence stresses Gramsci's opposition to Stalin's brutal methods of government and his detachment from the party in the last years of his life. It is likely that the ruling elite of the PCI, and particularly Togliatti, avoided doing whatever was necessary to free Gramsci in order to prevent a disruptive conflict within the Comintern and Gramsci's prosecution by Stalin in the first half of the 1930s. With the exception of Togliatti's refusal to lead the Cominform in 1951, he never really challenged Stalin's authority and remained silent regarding crimes and killings at the hands of the Soviet regime.

Nowadays, Gramsci enjoys longlasting world notoriety because he offered a nonviolent perspective on the communist revolution, one founded on the concept of "hegemony" as a peaceful struggle to win over the majority. In terms of the PCI's political culture, Gramsci was considered the symbol of a continuous national identity, originating from the theses approved at the Third Congress in Lyon (1926), which emphasized the weakness of the Italian bourgeoisie. In light of Togliatti's "Lectures on Fascism" held in Moscow (1935), it was apparent that he was aware of the broad popular base of support for the fascist regime; therefore, the struggle for hegemony was the consequence of such national analysis. Thus Gramsci's legacy supported a coherent historicist framework, by which the Italian mass parties were legitimized to rule in order to integrate a part of civil society (the urban and rural workers' movement, in the case of PCI) into Italian institutions. Their ability to solve

---

1 Richard Rose and Thomas T. Mackie, "Do Parties Persist or Fail? The Big Trade-off Facing Organizations," in Kay Lawson and Peter H. Merkl (eds.), *When Parties Fail: Emerging Alternative Organizations* (Princeton: Princeton University Press, 1988), 533–60.

problems and, consequently, their socioeconomic methods of analysis were considered of minor importance.

Gramsci and the Italian historicist identity formed only one component of the PCI's culture, which also included longstanding loyalty to Leninism and its idea of revolution, embodied by the USSR. For the old-guard cadres of the fascist era as well as the fresh recruits, the USSR was a living testament to the socialist dream that could become reality, and after 1947 a Manichean vision of the world was established with an imperialist United States in the role of the "Evil Empire." Ideologies universally work at two different levels: the teleological dimension, as political religions can require the sacrifice of human lives, and the societal one, in order to reduce complex realities to the simpler and reassuring level of fairytales, clearly separating the good guys from the bad.[2] For the communist militants, proletarian internationalism was not an "external constraint": It was a key factor in forming their identity and a living connection to a unified front whose material and spiritual center was in Moscow. The PCI was not a mere detachment of the Kremlin but its strategy was founded on the primacy of foreign policy that created the "iron linkage" with the USSR: a protective guarantee, an irreplaceable symbolic resource of mass consensus and a provider of additional funds whose inflow to Italy was stopped by general secretary Enrico Berlinguer only in the early 1980s.

Therefore, the Soviet myth played a surprisingly longlasting role. According to nearly one-third of the representatives at the Seventeenth PCI Congress (1986), the USSR was the country which best represented the model for a socialist society, and the percentage came close to three-fourths at the Congress if one included China and Yugoslavia alongside the USSR. Only at the following congress (1989) did the latter percentage fall to 26 percent.[3] The multifaceted image of the USSR spread by party propaganda (egalitarian and technological; frugal and futuristic; reliable and efficient) was able to evoke deeply rooted symbols of popular folklore such as the Land of Milk and Honey. At the same time, it aimed at capturing the traditional (and rural) values of the Catholics represented by the Christian Democracy party (Democrazia Cristiana, DC) whose members, like the communists, shared some doubts about the imagined consumerist and easy-divorce habits of

2 Stéphane Courtois and Marc Lazar, *Le communisme* (Paris: MA Éditions, 1987); Vladimir Tismaneanu, *The Devil in History: Communism, Fascism, and Some Lessons of the Twentieth Century* (Berkeley: University of California Press, 2012), ch. 5.
3 Aris Accornero and Nino Magna, "Il nuovo PCI: due congressi a confronto. Ricerca sui delegati al 18° Congresso nazionale," attached to *Politica ed economia* 6 (Jun. 1989).

American society. Until 1956, Stalin's myth consisted of three images: the priest of a political religion called Marxism-Leninism, the warrior who had defeated Hitler and the king-producer of modern Russia. They mirrored the three basic functions that Georges Dumézil identified in the Indo-European cultures.[4]

Even after 1956 the Soviet myth was saved by the dismissing of Stalin's crimes as personal deviations, whose violence was justified by the backwardness of the country – this unwillingness to condemn Stalin demonstrated the persistent yet diverse anti-capitalism of the PCI. The idea that socialism was better than capitalism (and a revolution could happen in the future), the state better than the market, and equality better than freedom formed the identity of every Italian communist militant. It also inhibited a complete adherence to democracy, at least as a permanent rule of the game, one that secures peaceful changes in government by reciprocally legitimizing political parties. In fact, especially after the crushing defeat in the 1948 elections, there was a clear correspondence between these subjective anti-democratic attitudes of the PCI members and voters and the objective international constraints imposed by the Cold War on Italy's domestic politics, which excluded the communists from government.

The Italian Republic and Togliatti's "New Party"

Within the political context of the Italian Republic, the PCI stood as a party that was far removed from the Leninist matrix (a vanguard formed of few revolutionaries) and the experience of conspiratorial networks that had operated under the fascist regime. Participation in armed resistance against the Nazi occupier allowed the PCI to exert a new influence on the masses and paved the way for its transformation into a mass "party of social integration," characterized by an abnormally large size (2 million members vs. the half-million of the French Socialist Party, the German Social-Democratic Party and the UK's Labour Party) that was more akin to the model of social-democratic parties than their communist counterparts.

The Italian historical context of the late 1940s presented a particular scenario: The communists were excluded from government in 1947; Togliatti suffered an attempt on his life in 1948; the labor movement previously unified by anti-fascism was split into different unions; and

---

4 Georges Dumézil, *Mythe et épopée. L'idéologie des trois fonctions dans les épopées des peuples indo-européens* (Paris: Gallimard, 1968).

productivity rose by 100 percent while wages rose by only 6 percent. Within the PCI a siege mentality took hold, and the option for an armed insurrection was kept open by an internal minority led by the vice-secretary Pietro Secchia, but its importance – notwithstanding the exaggerations of many reports compiled by Italian police and uncritically accepted by a few scholars – was dismissed by Mario Scelba himself, then minister of the interior.[5] In any case, in 1954 Secchia was obliged to resign, and the "military" wing of the party lost its influence.

Its large size not only guaranteed the continued existence of the PCI and protected Italy against a reactionary turn, but was also the result of a precise strategy – the "*partito nuovo*" – adopted by Togliatti already in 1944 on the basis of a twofold analysis. First, the PCI had to adapt a peculiar model of the "mother-party," which the Italian people had experienced under Mussolini: It had to be omnipresent and able to provide solutions for an entire range of social issues. Second, the PCI had to compete with the network of parishes established over the course of several centuries by the Catholic Church, which constituted the real grassroots of the DC party consensus. "A Communist Party Branch for Every Bell-Tower" was the motto of the PCI organization: The outcome was a party not restricted to just factories and workers, but that also included a higher social interclass composition and a significant number of women (25–30 percent) when compared to other European communist parties. Far from mirroring an external model (Leninist and workerist) embedded in a different environment, the PCI was able to recreate communitarian links as well as to interact with the social processes of urbanization and industrialization which were transforming Italy. Especially in central Italy, PCI local organizations supported the administrations ruled by left governments. Unlike the DC local administrators (who based their mandate on the ability to mediate with the national government in Rome), communist (and socialist) mayors and councils fought against the central state in order to gain resources and autonomy. In the long run, this position made the "red" administrative local system more popular and deeply rooted (perhaps more honest, too) than their "white" counterparts, which were concentrated in the northeast and in the south. It was a paradox, however, that the communist local administrators were always underrepresented in the central PCI's governing body, with a resulting deficit of any problem-solving attitude in the party's political culture.

5 Mario Scelba, "Ecco come difesi la libertà degli italiani," *Prospettive nel mondo* 12 (Jan.–Feb. 1988), 9.

As happened in many European countries, the "freezing proposition" was applied even to Republican Italy.[6] In the 1946 elections the total number of votes for the leftist parties (39 percent) was similar to that of the 1919 elections (35 percent), two decades of fascist dictatorship notwithstanding. Although the electorate increased from 11 million to 23 million (which included women for the first time), well-entrenched political traditions, which had been dormant during the fascist period, seemed to be still there. This can be interpreted in terms of longstanding cleavages (i.e., between church and state), which were divided along left/right partisanship lines and brought to light a consequent lack of a shared civic culture.[7] But equally important was the mass implantation of the political parties. According to a 1972 survey, about 75 percent of the respondents had "always voted for the same party" and "all or almost all of the members of their family had the same political preference." A comparative study of voter fluctuation between 1950 and 1980 showed that Italians rarely changed their minds in terms of party preference, and voting patterns almost mirrored those of the British and Swedes.[8]

Italian families, and particularly communist ones, were characterized by a high degree of political homogeneity and a strong "hereditary" vein, handing down political opinions from father to son, in spite of the increasing influence of national media, especially television. In 1979 almost 50 percent of the 16,000 delegates at the local congresses of the PCI had a father who had joined the same party, and 75 percent of them had come to their political choice without facing family conflict.[9]

This kind of "moral familism" can in turn be attributed to a traditional Italian exceptionalism defined by a lack of national identity; citizens are concerned only with their *particulare* rather than the *res publica*, and so civic culture is replaced by ideological subcultures. In fact, however, notwithstanding the internal cleavages, Italian politics up to the 1970s had managed to save the fundamental unity and cohesion of national civil society as well as its

---

6 Seymour Lipset and Stein Rokkan, "Cleavage Structures, Party Systems, and Voter Alignments: An Introduction," in Seymour Lipset and Stein Rokkan (eds.), *Party Systems and Voter Alignments: Cross-National Perspectives* (New York: Free Press, 1967), 1–64.

7 Gabriel Almond and Sidney Verba, *The Civic Culture: Political Attitudes and Democracy in Five Nations* (Boston: Little Brown, 1965).

8 Giacomo Sani, "Political Traditions as Contextual Variables: Partisanship in Italy," *American Journal of Political Science* 20 (1976), 375–405; Klaus von Beyme, *Political Parties in Western Democracies* (Aldershot: Gower, 1985), 303.

9 Aris Accornero, Renato Mannheimer and Chiara Sebastiani (eds.), *L'identità comunista. I militanti, le strutture, la cultura del PCI* (Rome: Editori Riuniti, 1983), 164.

increasingly productive economic structure. The Italian political parties were efficient tools for democratic participation, recruiting elites, producing culture and representing interests. In southern Italy, where political parties were weaker, criminal organizations were stronger. Far from being an exception inside another exception, the PCI contributed to the peculiar modernization of Italy, supporting the integration of the former peasants, sharecroppers and rural laborers in the urban networks and providing them with a smattering of constitutional culture.

Participating and having responsibility in the making of the democratic constitution (ratified in 1947) clearly distinguished the PCI from the French Communist Party, which, in contrast, assumed a much more negative attitude toward constitutional projects in its own country. The outcome of negotiations with the Catholic culture represented by DC was a peculiar "presbyopia" of the Italian constitution, embodying a set of ideals and establishing programs (rather than rules) aimed at orienting the future progress of the country more than at regulating the political game. Thus, the communists considered the constitution as a map for a "progressive democracy" (according Togliatti's definition) oriented toward socialism.

Paradoxically, besides the ideological opposition ignited by the Cold War, both the two leftist parties and the DC shared a view of democracy that seemed basically totalitarian and lacked the principle of alternating governments. The government was also supposed to incorporate the interests of the opposition through a process of permanent political mediation. Even that was a peculiarity of Italian history dating back to the prefascist era, to which historians applied the term of "*trasformismo*." In the eyes of the PCI in the early Republican period, that kind of national bloc (experimented with until 1947 and increasingly demanded thereafter) was very close to Eastern Europe's "people's democracies" whose institutional model the party strongly supported.

The Primacy of Foreign Policy

Historians have called into question the reductionist approach to Italian politics founded on the concept of "limited sovereignty," which reduced domestic political actors to their foreign loyalties. Increasingly, the Cold War bipolar system has been described as a dynamic network of interactions and compatibilities that connected political actors of different countries and established a two-track relationship between the center and the periphery of the two empires.

In fact, a creative interpretation of the international constraints imposed by the USSR shaped the strategy of the PCI. By undertaking the *"svolta di Salerno"* (1944), the PCI unified the country's domestic anti-fascist forces, supporting Stalin's strategy, which was concerned with the Allied military presence and, consequently, rejected the option of a violent takeover in Italy as excessively dangerous.[10] The PCI transformed what was for Stalin only a temporary expedient into a policy that encouraged active citizen involvement and established a loyal bloc of supporters in national politics. Italian communists considered their strong base of support as well as their large size a means of survival in the Atlantic world. In the Constituent Assembly the PCI, unlike the PSI, voted in favor of Article 7 of the constitution (enshrining the *"Concordato"* between Italy and the Vatican that had been signed by Mussolini in 1929), for it was in keeping with the preservation of political and religious peace. This decision was based on a tacit recognition of Italy's international position and, as a consequence, of the powerful impact of the alliance with the United States on domestic politics. Therefore, the Italian leftist parties were loyal to the constitution because they saw democracy as an instrument – it could provide the most favorable environment for the free expression of class struggle and could be used to establish another kind of society, one founded on socialist principles.

Only after Nikita Khrushchev accused Stalin of committing crimes, and especially after the violent Soviet repression of the Hungarian upheavals in 1956, was there an irreversible separation between the PSI and the PCI. The former severed ties with the Kremlin and opened lines of communication with the DC and the West, and found an outlet in the center–left coalition government of the 1960s. The latter, in contrast, reaffirmed the superiority of socialist *substantial* democracy (founded on economic equality) over bourgeois *formal* democracy (where a law that was theoretically equal for everyone was in fact discriminatory when economic and cultural conditions were taken into account). Togliatti openly criticized Stalinism in an interview in the literary periodical *Nuovi Argomenti* in 1956: He used the shocking (because Trotskyite) term of "bureaucratic degeneration" to define Soviet society. However, Togliatti abruptly ceased all criticism of the USSR after the Hungarian crisis, and he urged a still reluctant Kremlin to repress the

10 Francesca Gori and Silvio Pons (eds.), *Dagli archivi di Mosca. L'URSS, il Cominform e il PCI (1943–1951)* (Rome: Carocci, 1998), 83 and 289; Elena Aga Rossi and Victor Zaslavsky, *Stalin and Togliatti: Italy and the Origins of the Cold War* (Stanford: Stanford University Press, 2011), 271.

revolt; after all, the PCI identified its survival with a reaffirmation of Soviet leadership.[11]

The phrase "Italian way to socialism," coined at the Eighth Congress in 1956, meant a kind of tacit pact of nonbelligerence which was confirmed at the time of the Sino-Soviet split in the mid 1960s by the Yalta Memorandum and the formula of "polycentrism." The PCI gained partial autonomy for its domestic strategy but maintained its international loyalty to the USSR, rejecting the Chinese "heresy" as a threat to peaceful coexistence which could also hinder the PCI's room for maneuver. Still, Togliatti asked Moscow to postpone the International Conference of Communist Parties requested by the Soviets to condemn China (it was ultimately held in 1969) and disclosed the mentality of the Italian communists toward newly constituted postcolonial independent countries and the movement of non-aligned states. The PCI launched an autonomous foreign policy, consisting of bilateral relations whose main outcome was the rapprochement with Tito's Yugoslavia. The traditional anti-imperialist motif against the United States merged with the appreciation of different national paths toward socialist revolution. However, such a foreign policy was restricted to the socialist world; like the other European communist parties, the PCI firmly opposed the initial process of European integration and the Common Market, conceived as instruments of American imperialism in alliance with economic private monopolies. It was only during the 1960s that this radical attitude was partially amended, and in 1969 an official delegation of the PCI entered the European Parliament.

In 1968 the party (like the French Communist Party) explicitly disapproved of the Soviet invasion of Czechoslovakia. The Prague Spring represented a potential experiment for socialism with higher levels of freedom and pluralism, which the PCI interpreted as being very close to the "Italian way to socialism." Its violent repression by Moscow made it clear that the Soviet concept of international détente – aimed at stabilizing its area of influence – was not supportive of a transition to socialism in Western Europe and obliged the PCI to separate Soviet foreign policy from proletarian internationalism, and also from the party's domestic strategy.[12] From that moment on, the loosening and eventually the

11 Jonathan Haslam, "I dilemmi della destalinizzazione: Togliatti, il XX Congresso del PCUS e le sue conseguenze (1956)," in Roberto Gualtieri, Carlo Spagnolo and Ermanno Taviani (eds.), *Togliatti nel suo tempo* (Rome: Carocci, 2007), 236.
12 Maud A. Bracke, *Which Socialism, Whose Détente? West European Communism and the Czechoslovak Crisis of 1968* (Budapest: Central European University Press, 2007).

overcoming of blocs – including the process of European integration –
became the new political perspective of the PCI, whose emerging leader
Enrico Berlinguer refused to undersign the whole final declaration of the
Moscow conference of the communist parties in 1969. It is important to
underline that these turning points in the cultural and political identity of
the PCI were always closely related to international events: The creative
use of the constraints imposed by the bipolar equilibrium represented
the priority for the development of policy.

Italian communists came to the conclusion that the revolution was
impossible for internal reasons (the resilient power and consensus of the
DC) as well as external ones (Italy's adherence to NATO). Since Italy could
not change its Atlantic setting, a return to governmental collaboration
with the DC and the PSI (experimented with until 1947) was at this point
the foremost aim: Even if the PCI could potentially gain 51 percent of the
voters, the Cold War context would obstruct a government ruled solely by
the Italian left. That was the lesson Berlinguer drew from the experience of
the leftist Salvador Allende's government in Chile, boycotted by the
United States until the bloody military coup in 1973. Berlinguer's proposal
for a "historic compromise" with the DC and the PSI was the outcome of
both a political culture that excluded the democratic principle of alternating majorities and an international strategy that tried to depict Italy –
thanks to the presence of the Holy See – as a relatively free and "demilitarized" zone within the framework of superpower confrontation and
détente. Again, Italian democracy did not seem to exhibit the characteristics of a system of shared rule, but seemed to be in a condition of constant
risk, leaving Italy exposed to plots by unknown and unreliable interlocutors. Such was the permanent mood of Italian political life after the 1969
terror attack in Milan. While NATO protected military dictatorships in
Portugal, Spain, Greece and Turkey, Italy was the only surviving democracy in Southern Europe. The dramatic juxtaposition of fascism and anti-
fascism was still deeply influencing the PCI.

Apart from the motivation of crisis survival, Berlinguer's strategy had
a strong basis in Italian politics. Actually, Italy is included among the case
studies of segmented societies that manifest a model of informally negotiated
politics – "consociational democracy."[13] Notwithstanding moments of rhetorical opposition (e.g. Italy's accession to NATO in 1949 or electoral reform

13 Arend Lijphart, *Democracy in Plural Societies: A Comparative Exploration* (New Haven:
Yale University Press, 1977).

in 1953) the PCI's parliamentary behavior was quite cooperative. Since the first legislature, the favorable vote of the PCI and the PSI largely exceeded 50 percent in the discussion of drafts in the Assembly, and increased to 90 percent when the approval of the law took place at the parliamentary committee stages. The consequence was a steady divergence between government majority and legislative majority – a peculiarity that in the European area was matched only by Germany.[14] In order to defend the social interests they represented, both the PCI and the PSI ran after the DC asking for more public spending and creating an increasingly fragmented "particularistic welfare state." Thanks to such tacit and reciprocal exchange of favors between government and opposition, the Italian political system never cracked and instead evolved into a peculiar system of "centripetal pluralism."

The Watershed of 1968

In the PCI's political culture, the Soviet myth and revolutionary utopia were intertwined with the paradigm of the organic and permanent crisis of capitalism. However, when the post-Stalinist USSR embraced peaceful coexistence with its rival, the United States, by the mid 1950s, the prophecy of an imminent end to capitalism was implicitly dismissed. Accordingly, the struggle for peace enlarged the ranks of the PCI and was translated by Gramscian Marxism into a historicist version of Italian exceptionalism: The Italian bourgeoisie was considered exceptionally weak, unable to stage great revolutions (unlike Britain and France), prone to compromise with the landowning aristocracy and ready to take subversive anti-democratic shortcuts (such as fascism). Italian capitalism was consequently represented as precociously monopolistic, risk-averse, inimical to free competition and protected by the state: In the end, it would suffocate its productive forces and consequently collapse. Hence, the solution was to follow a different political direction in public spending and state investments. As in any communist party, the Keynesian arguments of internal demand and mass consumption remained remote from the PCI's political culture, which by contrast was founded on the principle of state planning. This was a striking contradiction in a period when the economic miracle of the early 1960s was improving Italian people's everyday life. In fact,

14 Massimo Morisi, *Le leggi del consenso. Partiti e interessi nei primi parlamenti della Repubblica* (Soveria Mannelli: Rubbettino, 1992); Wolfgang Kralewski, *Oppositionelles Verhalten im ersten Deutschen Bundestag 1949–1953* (Cologne: Westdeutscher Verlag, 1963).

consumerism, private entrepreneurship and social democracy remained enduring taboos for Italian communists.

After Togliatti's death in 1964, the exceptionalist view of the Italian economy was particularly advocated by Giorgio Amendola, a leading politician, on the basis of a typical interpretation of Gramsci: Since the backwardness of the south demonstrated the congenital weakness of Italian capitalism, the leftist parties were forced to play a "national" role and it was up to them to establish an alliance between the workers and the urban middle classes. Italy's weak capitalist system required extended state intervention in the economy, while the equally weak Italian state required help from the PCI. An ineffectual, even if more realistic, minority view was maintained by Pietro Ingrao, the leader of an internal informal left wing, who believed that the economic miracle was transforming Italian capitalism into a form of neocapitalism, marked by the dynamic presence of the state in industrial development. The struggle for structural reforms (land-ownership redistribution, progressive taxation, nationaliza-tion of the industrial and financial monopolies, the public health system) became the fundamental key for the party's strategy, based on a concep-tual framework not too far from the one adopted by European social democracies. In fact, the ancient dogma of dictatorship by the proletariat was replaced with a strategy of social and political alliances. But in Italy the center–left governments implemented reformist designs, and the PCI was allowed to use them only as propaganda. Both the PCI and the PSI overvalued central state power, which had to combat the "animal spirits" of capitalism supported by the DC, and Italy as a whole failed to take advantage of the opportunity of the favorable economic cycle of the 1960s to achieve a well-balanced plan for national growth and to solve the southern Italian question.

Until 1968 the stability of the Italian electorate mirrored a social division. The PCI's electorate was mainly composed of young men, characterized by wage employment and low levels of education. By contrast, the DC electorate was almost exactly the opposite (basically formed by women and older people), while the PSI's electorate covered the middle ground in between the two major parties.[15] A defensive political competition was aimed at reproducing separate areas of consensus, without exchanges and reciprocal legitimization. The year 1968 marked a turning point in the

---

15 Samuel H. Barnes, "Italy: Religion and Class in Electoral Behavior," in Richard Rose (ed.), *Electoral Behavior: A Comparative Handbook* (New York: Free Press, 1974), 171–225.

history of the PCI, when it once again made its foreign and domestic policies consistent.

The Soviet invasion of Czechoslovakia put a halt to and then reversed a period of relative liberalization and economic reforms in the Eastern bloc countries. The unintentional consequence was that the USSR and its satellite countries would be barred from the technological revolution, paving the way to the watershed mark of 1989.[16] The evolution of the PCI followed a similar path; it sought its own autonomous room for maneuver by launching the joint strategies of the historic compromise and Eurocommunism during the 1970s but suffered the crisis of détente and the military involution of the USSR in the early 1980s.

The student revolt in 1968 and the "hot autumn" of the working class in 1969 heralded the most important cycle of reforms in the entire experience of the Italian Republic: a new pension system, divorce legislation, a workers' charter, regional governments, a new tax system, universal national health service, new family laws with equal rights for women and men. From the benches of the opposition, the PCI was an effective agent for change and also used the wave of mobilization to gain new spaces within the sphere of influence, by sharing public offices in central and local state administrations, state television networks and other state-owned corporations that were subject to parliamentary supervision. Party propaganda highlighted the principle of "democratic participation," but those public offices were distributed according to standards of proportional representation, which actually left power in the hands of the government coalition. The PCI's role in those public offices was reduced to a subordinate one, which however left the opposition accountable for DC's choices. In a situation of mounting unemployment after the 1973 oil shock, the main countercyclical effect on the economy was the expansion of public employment at the cost of increasing the budget deficit and inflation.

The rapidly worsening economic situation compelled the PCI to transform the struggle for reforms into a tradeoff between economic offerings (i.e. moderate wage claims) and political compensation (access to government). In 1977 Berlinguer proclaimed "austerity" as a tool of equality against the excesses of private consumption. It was a different path from the one followed by European social democracies, which used the strategy of conflict resolution within the market in order to safeguard workers'

16 Mark Harrison, "Economic Information in the Life and Death of the Soviet Command System," in Silvio Pons and Federico Romero (eds.), *Reinterpreting the End of the Cold War: Issues, Interpretations, Periodizations* (London: Cass, 2005), 93–115.

interests, to support real wages and internal demand and thus to force employers to restore productivity through technological innovation alone. Meanwhile, in Italy the constant emphasis on the cost of labor without a coordinated income policy produced a general and irreversible loss of competitiveness, which was only temporarily masked by the expansion of the public debt.[17]

The Failure of the Historic Compromise

The radicalized social struggles of the early 1970s mobilized the Italian electorate and put an end to the long period of electoral stability that had characterized the postwar era. The result of the referendum in favor of divorce in 1974 showed Italy's increasing secularization, and the PCI obtained its best results in the 1975 regional and local elections and in the 1976 general election. For the first time, Italian communists were seen as an alternative vehicle for change in Italian politics by a large portion of public opinion, including women and feminist movements.[18] But that new appeal soon clashed with the moderate and consociational strategy of the historic compromise as well as with the steady decrease in economic resources. This apparent contradiction was further deepened by the threat of terrorism, which spread especially in Italy at that time. The murder of the DC leader Aldo Moro by the Red Brigades (1978) paved the way for a new government coalition of national solidarity supported by the PCI's abstention, in a negative and defensive atmosphere, which almost totally lacked the reformatory zeal of the early 1970s. Confined to the no-man's land of abstention, the PCI was forced to carry the burden of the sacrifices imposed by the economic crisis but did not have the power to substantially modify the DC's policies. In 1979 Berlinguer had to take the PCI out of the governing coalition, and the ensuing general elections marked a defeat for the party. It was no coincidence that the divisive issue within the government coalition was the PCI's request to delay Italy's entrance into the European Monetary System; the longstanding PCI criticism of the European Community and a new pessimistic attitude about the Italian economy converged toward that conservative request, which was rejected by the DC and the PSI.

17 Leonardo Paggi and Massimo D'Angelillo, *I comunisti italiani e il riformismo. Un confronto con le socialdemocrazie europee* (Turin: Einaudi, 1986).
18 Giacomo Sani, "Italy: The Changing Role of the PCI," in David E. Albright (ed.), *Communism and Political Systems in Western Europe* (Boulder: Westview, 1979), 43–94.

Nevertheless, the peak of domestic consensus in the mid 1970s was accompanied by a new international dynamism. The PCI intensified its contacts with the communist parties of France and Spain (the latter was returning to democracy after the death of Franco in 1975) – what came to be known as Eurocommunism – in order to outline a "third way" for political and economic development which was distant from both the Soviet and the social-democratic European models. It was a short-lived experiment that conflicted with the pronounced traditional orthodoxy of the other communist parties. The PCI was the only one to dissent from the strategy pursued by the Portuguese Communist Party conjointly with the Armed Forces Movement, which aimed at excluding Christian Democracy from the 1975 elections to the Constituent Assembly, as it canceled all ties between socialism and democracy.[19] Still, the most important legacy of the failed Eurocommunist experiment was that it changed the PCI's attitude toward European institutions and the European socialist and labor parties. The campaign for the first election of the European Parliament in 1979 managed to put aside the original distrust of the process of European integration. The practice of communication and exchange with other, non-communist parties (inaugurated with the German Social Democratic Party at the time of Willy Brandt's *Ostpolitik*) was extended. But the wishful thinking of a new European actor emerging against the bipolar equilibrium (and to be achieved through the unity of the European left) surpassed the awareness of the problems of integration between sovereign nation-states and European institutions.

Conversely, the struggle against the so-called Euromissiles in 1979 (conceived by NATO in response to the deployment of the Soviet SS-20 missiles) brought the PCI back to a traditional pro-Soviet alignment. It was still working on a double bias, which identified the USSR with socialism and peace and the USA with imperialism and war. Once again the primacy of foreign policy was shaping the PCI's evolution. The Soviet invasion of Afghanistan and the 1981 military coup in Poland enlarged its distance once more from the Eastern bloc. Berlinguer openly declared that the October Revolution had exhausted its driving force and that he felt safer being within the Atlantic Pact. The real dilemma he was facing, in any case, was that the USSR-led second Cold War had forcefully restricted any room for political maneuver for Italian international neutrality, which was so important for the historic compromise.

19 Silvio Pons, *Berlinguer e la fine del comunismo* (Turin: Einaudi, 2006), 53.

The international divide accompanied increasingly intricate domestic strategies. The new PSI leader, Bettino Craxi, led the party into a much more autonomous direction, toward competition with and imitation of the DC; its more important outcomes were the abolition of automatic wage indexation in 1984 and the doubling of the public debt during the 1980s. Hence in Italy Craxi embodied the negative side of Thatcherism – reducing the power of trade unions – without pursuing the positive side – the retreat of state intervention in the market economy.[20]

In 1981 Berlinguer denounced the corruption of the other Italian parties and proclaimed the ethical distinction of the PCI. Thus the "moral problem" became a political priority, and the historic compromise was replaced by the claim for a "democratic alternative" and a "government led by honest people." It was in striking contradiction to the moderate strategy that had been pursued during the Cold War, even if it stemmed from realistic criticism: The Italian paradox was that, unlike the rest of Europe, the competing DC and PSI had set off an explosion of public debt by patronizing various interest groups without an alternation in the government and with only weak opposition from the Bank of Italy. In the early 1990s an amazing sequence of financial scandals highlighted the shocking level of corruption in Italy and destroyed the credibility of the parties in government. Still, the abnormal expansion of the public sector in the Italian economy (often originating in the indiscriminate bailout of private-sector businesses) severely challenged the communist idea of state planning as regulated capitalism. However, the democratic alternative was hardly an immediately feasible prospect, and in fact it exposed the political isolation of the party. For the first time since Togliatti's era, the PCI abandoned the tried-and-tested political strategy of collaboration with the other Italian mass parties. In both the foreign and the domestic spheres, the PCI had to face the failure of the twofold strategy – Eurocommunism and historic compromise – that Berlinguer had elaborated. His sudden death in 1984 symbolically mirrored the political tragedy that had already played out.

It was also a tragedy because Berlinguer's heirs were inadequately prepared to face the rapidly changing national context. The new generation had joined the ranks during the 1968 mobilization and enjoyed the material benefits of political power in many local administrations. The moral

20 Federico Romero, "L'Italia nelle trasformazioni internazionali di fine Novecento," in Silvio Pons, Adriano Roccucci and Federico Romero (eds.), *L'Italia contemporanea dagli anni Ottanta ad oggi* (Rome: Carocci, 2014), vol. I, 15–34.

"difference" stressed by Berlinguer as a symbolic incentive, as opposed to material perks for party members, felt like a straitjacket to them, and it reduced the party's ability to represent and satisfy social interests or to strike alliances and establish programs with other political parties. Besides, they were a cross-section of the "baby-boom generation" which was transforming Italy as a whole, not just in terms of cultural secularization and electoral mobility. During the 1970s small and medium-sized enterprises clustered in the industrial districts of northeastern and central Italy and took the lead in technical innovation, productivity and job creation, while conversely the large enterprises in northern Italy began to reduce numbers of employees.[21] At the same time, self-employed individuals and freelancers increased, particularly in the services sector. A new "third Italy," different from the developed north and the underdeveloped south, was emerging: The political and collective mobilization of 1968 transformed itself into an entrepreneurial and individual dynamism. But the local and regional experience of many PCI administrators supporting the small-scale private enterprises (especially in central Italy) did not influence the central party's program.

The social emergence of the baby-boom generation corresponded to an increasing detachment from politics, which was documented by a constant downturn in voter turnout. Italian politics not only lost the reforming zeal of the early 1970s, but also continued to represent Italian society by employing old categories (social class, ideological adherence, income inequalities) which were no longer representative of the individualistic, consumerist and postmaterialist transformation that was occurring in Italy as in other Western countries.[22] Even before Berlinguer's death the PCI began to register a decrease in its membership; it was not only a quantitative problem but also a real issue as the younger and more dynamic part of civil society was moving away from politics. Thus the fall of the communist regimes in Eastern Europe in 1989 took the PCI by surprise in the middle of its own long and problematic transition. The majority of the ruling elite decided that it was time to change the party's name from "Communist" to "Leftist Democratic" (Partito Democratico della Sinistra), in order to avoid the slow decline in membership seen in other communist parties throughout Europe as well as the abrupt disappearance which had befallen its counterparts in

21 Frank Pyke, Giacomo Becattini and Werner Sengenberger (eds.), *Industrial Districts and Inter-Firm Cooperation in Italy* (Geneva: Ilo, 1990).
22 Ronald Inglehart, "Changing Values Among Western Publics from 1970 to 2006," *West European Politics* 31, 1–2 (Jan.–Mar. 2008), 130–46.

Italian politics. The very difficult task of survival without political power in a hostile environment was accomplished. However, the choice to change its name did present some important contradictions to be addressed. First, the leadership acknowledged that the PCI's history was not autonomous; on the contrary, they saw it as connected to and compromised by the history of the USSR to the extent that a solemn act of divorce was not only justified but also necessary. Second, the leadership wanted to underline that they were different from the rest of the social-democratic and labor parties by choosing a name ("Democratic") that did not belong to the European tradition of the working-class movements but came instead from the American experience. This furthermore stressed the distinction (and isolation) of the PCI party. Third, a significant minority founded a new party, the Rifondazione Comunista, which advocated saving both the party's national strength and its communist ideals in order to affirm that the Italian communists had broken away from the USSR. Their political culture retained many features (anti-Americanism, a state-centered approach, hostility to social democracy) from the PCI's experience.

Concluding Remarks

Unlike other European communist parties, the PCI played a decisive role in pushing for and implementing the structural reforms which were then enacted by the centrist and center–left governments, as well as defending Italian democracy in dramatic circumstances, particularly in the 1970s during the threat of terrorism. While this was not the deterministic effect of an endogenous diversity, it was the outcome of a successful process of institutionalization which concerned an original anti-system party. Nevertheless, the process was limited by the party's belonging to the Soviet bloc, which conditioned not only its foreign policy but also its theory and practice of democracy. The Gramscian concept of "hegemony" helped the PCI to take some significant steps forward on the road to political pluralism, but the Cold War inhibited the mere possibility of alternating majorities in government. At the same time, communist ideology, which nourished the dream of revolution, was translated into a framework of rights aimed at improving the life of the weaker part of Italian society.

This said, Italian communism failed to define the nexus between democracy and socialism. The latter term increasingly dissolved into the practice of a welfare state aimed at reducing social inequality, not so different from the expansion of public spending led by the DC and the PSI. The Marxist vision of ownership of the means of production was tacitly replaced by a generic and eventually abstract reference to "democratic planning": In practice, it was no more than a request for the state to play an even larger role in the economy, and unfortunately the Italian experience of state-owned enterprises failed with very few exceptions. Nothing resembling the German model of *Mitbestimmung* (workers' representation in the managing boards of companies) was claimed by the PCI; its ideological reasoning, shared by the trade unions, was to defend the autonomy of the working class. The humanistic rather than scientific framework of Gramscian Marxism provided an inadequate basis for the creation of the party's economic program and interpretation of the changes in Italian society. Furthermore, the positive experience of many PCI local administrators did not influence the reformist capabilities of the central leadership. The slogan of "struggle against monopolies" failed to actively support small entrepreneurs.

Ultimately, the PCI never renounced its position within the political family of communist parties and constantly refused any assimilation with European social democracies. Permanent confinement to the ranks of opposition limited its peculiar democratic development. First, the PCI's role was reduced to mere propaganda by the center–left governments during the economic expansion of the 1960s, and then the crisis of the subsequent decade obliged the party to follow a moderate line. The primacy of foreign policy and the consideration of the constraints exerted by the Cold War pushed the PCI to overvalue the reforming bent of the DC and the PSI and undervalue the resilience, desire for change and dynamism of civil society; "austerity" replaced social conflict and the Keynesian support for domestic demand. The final retreat into the moral "difference" stressed by Berlinguer in the early 1980s was a result of the PCI's unfinished evolution toward European social democracy; the defensive safeguard of its peculiar history and domestic consensus isolated the party politically. Far from being a liberation, the demise of the Soviet state brought about the dissolution of the PCI.

Bibliographical Essay

The thesis of the PCI's diversity is founded on the five-volume work by Paolo Spriano, *Storia del Partito comunista italiano* (Turin: Einaudi, 1967–75). The most important authors connected with this line of reasoning are Donald L. M. Blackmer, *Unity in Diversity: Italian Communism and the Communist World* (Cambridge, MA: MIT Press, 1968); Donald Sassoon,

The Strategy of the Italian Communist Party from the Resistance to the Historic Compromise (London: Pinter, 1981 [1st edn. Turin: Einaudi, 1980]); Joan B. Urban, *Moscow and the Italian Communist Party: From Togliatti to Berlinguer* (Ithaca: Cornell University Press, 1986); Chris Shore, *Italian Communism: The Escape from Leninism: An Anthropological Perspective* (London: Pluto, 1990); and Aldo Agosti, *Togliatti. Un uomo di frontiera* (Turin: UTET, 1996). A different approach, which stresses the international–domestic interaction, is followed by Giovanni Gozzini and Renzo Martinelli, *Storia del Partito comunista italiano,* vol. VII, *Dall'attentato a Togliatti all'VIII Congresso* (Turin: Einaudi, 1998), and the proceedings of two congresses organized in Rome by the Fondazione Istituto Gramsci: Roberto Gualtieri (ed.), *Il PCI nell'Italia repubblicana (1943–1991)* (Rome: Carocci, 2001); Roberto Gualtieri, Carlo Spagnolo and Ermanno Taviani (eds.), *Togliatti nel suo tempo* (Rome: Carocci, 2007).

Gramsci's relationship with the party is discussed in more detail in Chiara Daniele (ed.), *Gramsci a Roma, Togliatti a Mosca. Il carteggio del 1926* (Turin: Einaudi, 1999); Silvio Pons, "L''affare Gramsci–Togliatti' a Mosca 1938–1941," *Studi Storici* 45, 1 (Jan.–Mar. 2004), 83–117; Giuseppe Vacca, *Vita e pensieri di Antonio Gramsci. 1926–1937* (Turin: Einaudi, 2012); and Mauro Canali, *Il tradimento. Gramsci, Togliatti e la verità negata* (Venice: Marsilio, 2013). Among several studies on current Gramsci's influence are Mark McNally and John Schwarzmantel (eds.), *Gramsci and Global Politics: Hegemony and Resistance* (London: Routledge, 2009), and Neelam Srivastava and Baidik Bhattacharya (eds.), *The Postcolonial Gramsci* (New York: Routledge, 2012).

The evolution of the PCI has been investigated in Donald L. M. Blackmer and Sidney G. Tarrow (eds.), *Communism in Italy and France* (Princeton: Princeton University Press, 1975); and Massimo Ilardi and Aris Accornero (eds.), *Il Partito comunista italiano. Struttura e storia dell'organizzazione 1921–1979* (Milan: Fondazione Giangiacomo Feltrinelli, 1981). A conceptual location of the PCI in the long-run historical context of the European left can be found in Donald Sassoon, *One Hundred Years of Socialism: The West European Left in the Twentieth Century* (London: I. B. Tauris, 1996); Stefano Bartolini, *The Political Mobilization of the European Left 1860–1980: The Class Cleavage* (Cambridge: Cambridge University Press, 2000); and Geoff Eley, *Forging Democracy: The History of the Left in Europe 1850–2000* (Oxford: Oxford University Press, 2002).

For recent archival evidence on the *"svolta di Salerno,"* see Elena Aga Rossi and Victor Zaslavsky, *Stalin and Togliatti: Italy and the Origins of the Cold War*

(Stanford: Stanford University Press, 2011 [1st ed., Il Mulino: Bologna, 1997]); Silvio Pons, "Stalin, Togliatti and the Origins of the Cold War in Europe," *Journal of Cold War Studies* 3, 2 (Spring 2001), 3–27; and Roberta Alonzi, *Stalin e l'Italia 1943–1945. Diplomazia, sfere d'influenza, comunismi* (Soveria Mannelli: Rubbettino, 2013). On the Soviet financial aid to the PCI, see Gianni Cervetti, *L'oro di Mosca. La testimonianza di un Protagonista* (Milan: Baldini e Castoldi, 1993); and Valerio Riva, *Oro da Mosca. I finanziamenti fovietici al PCI dalla Rivoluzione d'ottobre al crollo dell'URSS* (Milan: Mondadori, 1999). A recent study on US policies and communist anti-Americanism in Western Europe is Alessandro Brogi, *Confronting America: The Cold War Between the United States and the Communists in France and Italy* (Chapel Hill: University of North Carolina Press, 2011).

The anthropological dimension of PCI militancy was studied by David I. Kertzer, *Politics and Symbols: The Italian Communist Party and the Fall of Communism* (New Haven: Yale University Press, 1996); Franco Andreucci, *Falce e martello. Identità e linguaggi dei comunisti italiani fra stalinismo e guerra fredda* (Bologna: Bononia University Press, 2005); and Maria Casalini, *Famiglie comuniste. Ideologie e vita quotidiana nell'Italia degli anni Cinquanta* (Bologna: Il Mulino, 2010). Local case studies can be found in Sidney G. Tarrow, *Peasant Communism in Southern Italy* (New Haven: Yale University Press, 1967); Grant Amyot, *The Italian Communist Party: The Crisis of the Popular Front Strategy* (London: Croom Helm, 1981); and Stephen Hellman, *Italian Communism in Transition: The Rise and Fall of the Historic Compromise in Turin, 1975–1980* (New York: Oxford University Press, 1988).

A large amount of literature explores the comparison between the French and Italian Communist Parties: Marc Lazar, *Maisons rouges. Les partis communistes français et italien de la Libération à nos jours* (Paris: Aubier, 1992), Elena Aga Rossi and Gaetano Quagliariello (eds.), *L'altra faccia della luna. I rapporti tra PCI, PCF e Unione Sovietica* (Bologna: Il Mulino, 1997); Cyrille Guiat, *The French and Italian Communist Parties: Comrades and Culture* (London: Cass, 2003); and W. Rand Smith, *Enemy Brothers: Socialists and Communists in France, Italy, and Spain* (New York: Rowman & Littlefield, 2012). On PCI foreign policy, see Onofrio Pappagallo, *Il PCI e la rivoluzione cubana. La "via latino-americana al socialismo" tra Mosca e Pechino 1959–1965* (Rome: Carocci, 2009); Paolo Borruso, *Il PCI e l'Africa indipendente. Apogeo e crisi di un'utopia socialista 1956–1989* (Florence: Le Monnier, 2009); Marco Galeazzi, *Il PCI e il movimento dei paesi non allineati 1955–1975* (Milan: FrancoAngeli, 2011); and Luca Riccardi, *L'internazionalismo difficile. La "diplomazia" del PCI e il Medio Oriente dalla crisi petrolifera alla caduta del muro di Berlino* (Soveria Mannelli: Rubbettino, 2013).

On Luigi Longo, see Alexander Höbel, *Il PCI di Luigi Longo (1964–1969)* (Naples: ESI, 2010). For a biography of Berlinguer, see Francesco Barbagallo, *Enrico Berlinguer* (Rome: Carocci, 2006). On the PCI and Eurocommunism, see Silvio Pons, *Berlinguer e la fine del comunismo* (Turin: Einaudi, 2006). Among the vast literature on Eurocommunism and the revision of the original opposition to unified Europe, see Frédéric Heurtebize, *Le péril rouge. Washington face à l'eurocommunisme* (Paris: Presses Universitaires de France, 2014); Mauro Maggiorani, *L'Europa degli altri. Comunisti italiani e integrazione europea (1957–1969)* (Rome: Carocci, 1998); and Paolo Ferrari, *In cammino verso Occidente. Berlinguer, il PCI e la Comunità europea negli anni settanta* (Bologna: Clueb, 2007). An overall discussion of the difficult relationship between PCI and reformism can be found in Luciano Cafagna, *C'era una volta ... Riflessioni sul comunismo italiano* (Venice: Marsilio, 1991). On the postcommunist evolution after 1989, see Piero Ignazi, *Dal PCI al PDS* (Bologna: Il Mulino, 1992); and Leonard Weinberg, *The Transformation of Italian Communism* (New Brunswick, NJ: Transaction, 1995).

25

The French Communist Party

MARC LAZAR

The French Communist Party (Parti communiste français, PCF) experienced a most striking evolution in the period spanning the 1940s to the late 1970s. On the momentum gained during the interwar period and owing to its active participation in the resistance, the PCF, along with its Italian counterpart, emerged after World War II and for years to come as one of the most powerful communist parties in Western Europe. Its power resided in its organization, its numbers, the prestige of its secretary-general, Maurice Thorez, its place in the international communist movement, its impact on the national political system, its firm grounding in French society and its influence among the intelligentsia and in the cultural sphere. Its importance also stemmed from its rooting in France, a major European power and member of the UN Security Council, boasting a vast colonial empire that soon faced aspirations for independence. These geostrategic factors were all fundamental in a world dominated by the confrontation between the Soviet bloc and the Atlantic alliance. Despite various vicissitudes, moments of waning strength, phases of isolation, internal crises and even the repression it suffered, for nearly three decades its power seemed virtually unshakeable and its position deeply entrenched. But at the end of this period, within the space of a few years, the PCF underwent a complete upheaval: serious electoral setbacks, a swift erosion of its support base, a severe decline in membership, a weakening of its apparatus, a fading of its influence and a loss of its aura. This political, social and cultural regression revealed a surprising vulnerability behind the imposing edifice it had constructed and the vigorous self-image it projected.

To understand such a reversal of fate, it is first necessary to recall the major stages in the history of the PCF, then examine the multiple strengths and shortcomings of what Annie Kriegel, the pioneer historian of communist studies, called "the communist countersociety," before scrutinizing how and why the PCF fell into such a state of collapse. Like communist parties the world over, the existence and the characteristics of the PCF are determined by the coexistence, at times harmonious, at times conflictual, of two ideal-typical dimensions: the teleological dimension, which stems from the revolutionary and universalist ambition rooted in the foundational experience of Bolshevik and Soviet communism; and the societal dimension supplied by the set of political, social and cultural elements that make up the entire society in which it operates. The first tends toward homogeneity, the second toward diversity. The resulting tension would appear with increasing salience during the three decades discussed in this chapter and would contribute to destabilizing a communist party that was tied at once to the Soviet camp and to France, two spheres that were themselves in constant evolution.

The Main Stages of Communist Strength
from the 1940s to the 1970s

Founded in December 1920 by a majority that split off from the French Section of the Workers' International (Section française de l'internationale ouvrière, SFIO), the PCF experienced a rough start due to serious internal rivalries and the vagaries of the policy orientations imposed by Moscow, themselves related to conflicts that were shaking the Soviet leadership. The Communist International (Comintern) and its representatives set out to purge, Bolshevize and Stalinize the fledgling organization. As of 1931, they favored the development of cadres and leaders from rural and worker backgrounds, such as Maurice Thorez, most of whom would remain in place for nearly three decades. This solid apparatus formed the backbone of a party that had somewhat the features of a sect with its 32,000 members in 1932 and capturing 8.4 percent of the vote in the legislative elections that same year. Nevertheless, the PCF gained a foothold in certain rural areas (around the Massif Central) and, via the Confédération Générale du Travail Unitaire (CGTU), in a few industrial areas (around Paris, in the north and in the east), and also attracted a variety of intellectuals. But a spectacular upheaval occurred. The economic crisis of the 1930s caused unemployment to sky-rocket, and trade union and communist activists were on the frontline to organize aid and relief as well as to protest. Furthermore, the events that took place in Paris on 6 February 1934, when far-right war veterans clashed violently with the police, provoked a unified reaction on the left against what they perceived as a fascist threat. Last, the USSR itself, as of May 1934, altered its strategic orientation in the name of anti-fascism and encouraged the formation of the Front Populaire. Thorez provided impetus for this policy by sealing a pact with the socialists and adding his own personal touch: He broadened the alliance to include the Parti Radical and, according to his famous expression, "reached out to the Catholics." Following the Front Populaire victory at the polls in 1936, the French leader had hoped to join Léon Blum's cabinet but Moscow forbade him to. This period considerably altered the physiognomy, culture and identity of the PCF. In 1936, it won 15.4 percent of the vote, and the following year its membership exceeded 292,000. Taking advantage of the trade union reunification of March 1936, it furthered its gains among a large swathe of the working class during the major strikes of May–June 1936. It also exerted considerable fascination over a segment of the intelligentsia such as authors Henri Barbusse (who died in 1935), Louis Aragon and Paul Nizan, and painters such as Jean Lurçat and Edouard Pignon. The combination of anti-fascism, its activism in support of the Spanish Republic (particularly through the International Brigades) and its defense of the interests of workers, the Soviet Union and henceforth the French nation turned out to be profitable. The disappointments and disillusions of the Front Populaire did not undermine the firm grounding that the PCF had achieved.

However, the German–Soviet Nonaggression Pact signed on 23 August 1939 took the party by surprise and destabilized it. It suffered a heavy anti-communist backlash when a ban was imposed on its press on 26 August. At first, the PCF attempted to justify the pact while continuing to denounce the warmongering aspect of Hitler's regime. On 2 September, the day after Germany invaded Poland, the communist bloc in the parliament voted for war appropriations. But in the ensuing days, the Comintern, at Stalin's behest, aligned itself on the Soviet position and the PCF followed suit. It thus qualified the war as imperialist, demanded an instant peace settlement and lambasted the British and French bourgeoisie. On 26 September, the government dissolved the PCF and its mass organizations. This repression, together with the confusion felt by activists and the disorganization upsetting their activities, resulted in a vertiginous drop in membership: From estimates of between 202,000 and 229,000 in August 1939, depending on calculation methods, it fell to around 5,000 during the phony war. Although defections increased among elected officials, most of the party cadres remained loyal. Following France's defeat in May–June 1940, the PCF called on Thorez – who had deserted in October 1939 on orders from Moscow and secretly escaped to the USSR – to take the reins of power. In Paris, communist leaders contacted the German authorities to resume publishing *L'Humanité*, as negotiations had been broken off in late August.[1] The PCF reorganized underground but was quashed by the Germans and the Vichy government, whose collaborationist policy the party condemned. Militants undertook actions against the occupying forces and, following the example of the Comintern, a more anti-German line was promoted as of spring 1941. Upon Germany's invasion of the USSR on 22 June 1941, the party truly joined the resistance. The PCF reactivated its anti-fascist and patriotic stance. Its presence in the country, its experience with underground action and armed struggle, and the discipline, dedication and courage of its activists enabled it to become the most dynamic and powerful component of the internal resistance. However, it failed to gain control of the movement and make it independent from de Gaulle. In January 1943, it sent an official representative to meet with the general; four months later it had a seat on the National Resistance Council, and in April 1944 it took part in the Provisional Government of the French Republic. Subsequently, it tried in vain to instigate a widespread national uprising and a dual-power strategy. Having returned to France in November 1944, Maurice Thorez clearly outlined another orientation set by Stalin in person, with a priority of defeating Germany. The PCF joined the government and started the "production battle." After Germany's surrender, it strove to increase its already considerable influence. It pushed de Gaulle to resign in January 1946, infiltrated the state and penetrated various sectors of society through the CGT labor union and the countless collateral organizations it controlled. It also dominated the intellectual and cultural spheres. The PCF enjoyed the prestige of its martyrs – it presented itself as "the party of the 75,000 firing-squad victims" – and of the USSR and Stalin. It became the largest party in France; in 1946, it probably counted more than 525,000 members and reached its peak in the November elections with 28.6 percent of the votes cast.[2]

However, at the same time and even more so early the following year, the situation grew tougher on both the international and national fronts. Incidents broke out within the national unity government. In March 1947, the communists refused to approve war appropriations for Indochina, in April they denounced the crackdown on the Malagasy independence movement and, after having tried to stop it, they backed a wide-scale strike

1 Sylvain Boulouque, *L'affaire de "l'Humanité"* (Paris: Larousse, 2010); Roger Bourderon, *La négociation, été 1940* (Paris: Syllepses, 2001).
2 Philippe Buton, *Les lendemains qui déchantent. Le Parti communiste français à la Libération* (Paris: Presses de la FNSP, 1993).

in the large Paris Renault automobile plant. On 4 May, the socialist president of the council (prime minister) Paul Ramadier dismissed his communist ministers. After months of claiming to wish to rejoin the government, in the fall the PCF altered its position. The policy shift came from Moscow and was outlined by Andrei Zhdanov during the founding meeting of the Communist Information Bureau (Cominform) in September 1947. In the course of the meeting, both the PCF and the Italian Communist Party (PCI) were forced to engage in a humiliating exercise of self-criticism of their past policies and adhere to the objectives set for the participants. These involved working to preserve the peace jeopardized by "American imperialism" and "lackeys" of its policy, particularly the socialists, and to defend and praise the USSR and the socialist countries. The PCF applied this new orientation with great zeal. Its shift into an intransigent opposition liberated the expression of discontent and social exasperation that had built up since the occupation in large segments of the working class that were suffering from price hikes, food and commodity shortages, and rationing. The party actively contributed, together with the CGT, to launching and leading the massive strikes in 1947 and 1948 that at times took an insurrectional turn.[3] It claimed to be the staunchest champion of national independence, threatened in its view by the United States and its allies within France. It was successful, moreover, in preventing the creation of the European Defence Community in 1954, through the explicit or objective convergence with a number of other opponents, including the Gaullists. Subsequently, it sought to reactivate bonds among participants in the resistance by opposing Germany's rearmament. It also instigated campaigns against the wars in Indochina and Korea, and more generally in favor of peace and defense of the USSR, one of its characteristic themes. Some of its actions were unifying in spirit, such as the Partisans of Peace movement and its "Stockholm Appeal" in 1950 for "an absolute ban on nuclear weapons," bringing together renowned intellectuals, representatives of the various religions and personalities from philosophical horizons other than Marxism. Others were more targeted, such as on the occasion of General Matthew Ridgway's visit to Paris in May 1952, during which it organized a violent demonstration, the last one in its history.[4]

3 Robert Mencherini, *Guerre froide, grèves rouges. Parti communiste, stalinisme et luttes sociales en France. Les grèves insurrectionnelles de 1947–1948* (Paris: Syllepse, 1998).
4 Yves Santamaria, *Le pacifisme, une passion française* (Paris: A. Colin, 2005); *Le Parti de l'ennemi? Le Parti communiste français dans la lutte pour la paix (1947–1958)* (Paris: A. Colin, 2006); Michel Pigenet, *Au cœur de l'activisme communiste des années de guerre froide. "La manifestation Ridgway"* (Paris: L'Harmattan, 1992).

The PCF's intolerance and intransigence led to a serious bloodletting of its membership. According to Roger Martelli's estimate, based on unpublished sources, in 1952 the party had only 220,000 members, or a loss of 60 percent with respect to December 1947.[5] Within its ranks, a second "Stalinist freeze-out" took place, to use the famous expression coined by Edgar Morin, who paid the price of exclusion from the party in 1949. Usually isolated, despite the support of prestigious communist intellectuals, artists and fellow travelers – such as the painters Picasso and Fernand Léger, the poet Paul Eluard, the singer Yves Montand and, for a short time, the philosopher Jean-Paul Sartre – facing fairly severe repression, especially between 1950 and 1952, although this was exploited in return by the PCF itself to claim victimhood,[6] activists closed ranks around the party, the USSR, Stalin and Thorez, the two men being surrounded by well-orchestrated personality cults, in 1949 for the seventieth birthday of the master of the Kremlin and the following year for Thorez's fiftieth.[7] Periodically within the party, often as a consequence of events in the USSR and the communist countries, "scandals" broke out that enabled Thorez and his closest associates to sideline leaders who from one day to the next were presented as opponents, but were actually potential rivals, having often played an active role during the Spanish Civil War and the resistance – unlike the secretary-general, who had remained in the USSR. In 1950, at the Twelfth Party Congress, fourteen members and fifteen alternates of the Central Committee were ousted, producing one of the highest renewal rates (34.5 percent) in the history of the party. In 1952, André Marty and Charles Tillon were both excluded from the Politburo, and Marty subsequently from the party. Two years later, Thorez, having returned a year before from the USSR where he had been receiving care since 1950, went after Auguste Lecoeur. Thorez accused Lecoeur of being responsible for the factionalist ways of the PCF during his absence and suspected him of wanting to instigate changes in the party leadership's working methods following recommendations handed down from Moscow that intended to break with practices of the Stalinist period. Despite its setbacks, the PCF remained the strongest party in France, garnering 26.9 percent of the vote in 1951 and 25.9 percent in 1956, and taking advantage of the proportional

5 Roger Martelli, *Prendre sa carte 1920–2009. Données nouvelles sur les effectifs du PCF* (Paris: Fondation Gabriel Péri, 2010).
6 Vanessa Codaccioni, *Punir les opposants. PCF et procès politiques 1947–1962* (Paris: CNRS Editions, 2013).
7 Jean-Marie Goulemot, *Pour l'amour de Staline. La face cachée du communisme français* (Paris: CNRS Editions, 2009).

representation system to put together a powerful opposition group in the parliament. It could rely on its activists and elected officials, in particular in city governments, the CGT and the various mass organizations. Stalin's death in 1953, the de-Stalinization policy that Thorez resisted, the events in East Germany in 1953, and in Poland and especially Hungary in 1956 caused strife, particularly among the intelligentsia: In 1957, nearly 15 percent of the party's members resigned. But such defections did not in the end affect the membership, which remained primarily working class.[8]

On the other hand, General de Gaulle's return to power during the crisis of May 1958 badly shook the party. The call it made, together with other political forces, for a "no" vote in the referendum on the constitution of the Fifth Republic was not followed (79 percent voted "yes"). In the November 1958 legislative elections, the PCF garnered only 19.2 percent of the vote, losing 1,600,000 voters compared to 1956, many of them from working-class backgrounds. With the new two-round majority system used for elections, it no longer had more than 10 representatives as opposed to 150 two years before. Nevertheless, it thereafter and for some fifteen years stabilized at a slightly higher level, and its electoral geography, although resized, remained unchanged. As for its membership numbers, they hardly evolved. The PCF was no longer France's largest party, but it remained the largest left-wing party, albeit destabilized and hesitant. It had considerable trouble characterizing Gaullism, grasping its originality and combating it, all the more as the USSR valued its foreign policy. The leadership, being opposed to the Khrushchev line, was at first inclined to move toward China's positions, but then rallied around Moscow when the Sino-Soviet conflict erupted. Changes deeply affecting French society put it on the defensive, prompting it for instance in 1955 to talk about the "relative and absolute pauperization" of workers, whereas in actuality their living conditions were improving. It disappointed a segment of the youth that was playing an increasing role as a social category not only in the cultural but also in the political sphere, particularly due to the party's attitudes toward Algeria.

At first, the PCF, eager not to offend its worker base and out of fear of being banned, was wary of Algeria's Front de libération nationale (FLN). Fairly quickly, however, through its youth organization, the UJRF (Union de la jeunesse républicaine de France), it reactivated its anti-colonial rhetoric and

---

8 Fondation Gabriel Péri, *Le Parti communiste français et l'année 1956* (Paris: Fondation G. Péri-Conseil Général Seine St-Denis, 2007).

undertook actions against the war, especially as of 1955, when the government began to mobilize recalled soldiers.[9] When on 12 March 1956 its members in the parliament voted to give Guy Mollet special powers, which resulted in an ever more repressive policy, something the communists had not bargained for, this sparked internal criticism and a decision by some activists to promote more radical action supporting the independence struggle, which embarrassed the party leadership. Starting that same year, the PCF worked more actively toward peace in Algeria, denouncing crackdowns and torture more explicitly, and gradually came around to the idea of independence, which once again earned it stern reprisals from the government. However, it was unable to dissipate a sense of cautiousness that would be criticized by intellectuals, university students (increasing in numbers at the same time) and young communists whose political socialization occurred through the fight for Algeria's independence, as well as by other parties (including the Italian Communist Party) and national liberation movements. In 1961, the secretary-general eliminated several leaders (Laurent Casanova, Marcel Servin, Maurice Kriegel-Valrimont), who were guilty of expounding analyses that were fairly innovative but at odds with his own.

In 1964, Maurice Thorez died and the new secretary-general, Waldeck Rochet, immediately engaged a process of *"aggiornamento."*[10] He pursued a strategy initiated by his predecessor in 1962 that involved resuming a dialogue with the socialists. This led the PCF to back François Mitterrand's candidacy in his first presidential bid in 1965 and striking an electoral agreement with the Fédération de la Gauche Démocratique et Socialiste (Federation of the Democratic and Socialist Left) for the 1967 legislative elections that resulted in overall gains for the left, the PCF winning thirty-two more seats than in 1962. The PCF remained faithful to the priority it gave the working class, which was experiencing a period of mass mobilization in which the CGT played a major role. The party nevertheless sought to attract other rising social strata (elementary and secondary school teachers, clerical workers and technical workers) with the age of what it labeled, along with other communist parties, state monopolistic capitalism. It still defined itself as revolutionary but foreswore the use of violence, except when necessary, backed the notion of peaceful coexistence advocated by the USSR and accepted the idea of political pluralism: In late 1968, it put forward the idea of an "advanced democracy" as the first step

---

9 Guillaume Quashie-Vauclin, *L'Union de la jeunesse républicaine de France 1945–1956* (Paris: L'Harmattan, 2009).
10 Jean Vigreux, *Waldeck Rochet. Une biographie politique* (Paris: La Dispute, 2000).

on the way to socialism. Furthermore, according to the terms of a Central Committee meeting in 1966, it worked out a compromise among the various versions of Marxism expounded by its philosophers (Louis Althusser, Roger Garaudy and Lucien Sève) and ensured its intellectuals a certain degree of freedom.[11] It persisted in its criticism of the Fifth Republic but de facto accepted its rules of the game, in particular the election of the president by universal suffrage. Attentive to Third World struggles, the PCF campaigned actively for peace in Vietnam, even envisaging, in 1967, as did other communist parties, sending volunteers to fight in the country. But, there again, it was challenged by leftist organizations, whose repertoires of action were more radical and spectacular, forcing the PCF to redouble its efforts to try to reestablish its hegemony over the "anti-imperialist" struggle.[12] At the same time, the PCF took part in international communist party meetings but jealously guarded its independence. It resumed contact with the PCI, with which it had fallen out in 1956. It henceforth recognized as a reality the European Common Market it had previously denounced and sought to adapt to it. For the first time, on 16 February 1966, *L'Humanité* published an article by the prestigious communist writer Louis Aragon, protesting against the condemnation of Soviet writers Yulii Daniel and Andrei Siniavskii to seven years in camp while praising the USSR.[13] In fact, the strategy for the Union of the Left pursued by Rochet ran counter to the interests of the Soviets, who preferred to see de Gaulle remain in power for as long as possible due to his policy of independence vis-à-vis Washington and NATO, rather than to see France venture on a risky course toward socialism, especially with Mitterrand, who was not to their liking. Therein lay a real nexus of tension.

These perceptible tensions came out in the open with the Prague Spring. In this incident, Waldeck Rochet tried to play the role of a highly ambiguous conciliator between the Czechoslovak leaders, whom he backed for the most part, and the Soviet officials, whose concerns he understood. He went to great lengths to try to prevent the use of force. The PCF criticized the invasion of Czechoslovakia by Warsaw Pact troops on 21 August 1968, splitting the PCF leadership between Roger Garaudy, who argued in favor of taking an even harsher stance, and Jeannette Vermeersch, Maurice Thorez's

11 "Aragon et le Comité central d'Argenteuil," *Annales de la Société des amis de Louis Aragon et Elsa Triolet* 2 (2000); and Frédérique Matonti, *Intellectuels communistes. Essai sur l'obéissance politique* (Paris: La Découverte, 2005).

12 Marc Lazar, "Le Parti communiste français et l'action de solidarité avec le Vietnam," in Christopher Gosha and Maurice Vaïsse (eds.), *La guerre du Vietnam et l'Europe. 1963–1973* (Brussels and Paris: Bruylant and LGDJ, 2003), 241–52.

13 Pierre Juquin, *Aragon. Un destin français*, vol. II (Paris: La Martinière, 2013).

widow, who was against it and resigned from the Politburo as well as the Central Committee. "Criticism" then dwindled to "disapproval," the PCF eventually accepting the disgraceful normalization of Czechoslovakia, which prompted the desertion of many intellectuals.[14]

During that same year, 1968, despite internal contestation, especially within its student organization, the PCF seemed to embody a new dynamic, its membership having exceeded 288,000 by the end of 1967. But in the major crisis of May–June, during which nearly 10 million workers were on strike, the PCF found itself rather isolated. The leftists, whom it resolutely combated, denounced its moderation. The moderate left was wary while the Gaullists and the right denounced a communist plot when the PCF put forward the slogan of a "people's government" in the month of May. Like the rest of the left, the PCF came out weakened by the June 1968 legislative elections, with 20 percent of the vote, 600,000 voters lost and a parliamentary group that had shrunk by 39 seats. On one hand, it continued to dominate the left and had proven that with the CGT it retained control over its traditional worker base. On the other hand, confirming a growing trend, it had lost touch with part of the educated youth, new workers and immigrants. It did not understand their aspirations, values and forms of action, which would become even more pronounced in the years to follow. This is, moreover, what communist notables and intellectual figures criticized their leaders for, but they were preaching in the wilderness. All the more so as the PCF seemed to be recovering rapidly. Its ranks swelled with new members, exceeding 300,000 at the start of the 1970s. Its candidate for the 1969 presidential election, the Comintern member and historical leader Jacques Duclos, gathered more than 4,800,000 voters and 21.5 percent of the vote. The same year, an ailing Waldeck Rochet could no longer assume the PCF leadership, which was then handed to Georges Marchais. Thus an era came to a close and with it the control of a generation born with the century (Rochet was born in 1905) that had been at the helm of the apparatus since the 1930s.

Strengths and Shortcomings of the Communist Countersociety

This changeover justifies a more detailed examination of French communism at one of the high points in its history. Indeed, beyond the changes in strategy

---

14 Maud A. Bracke, *Which Socialism, Whose Détente? West European Communism and the 1968 Czechoslovak Crisis* (Budapest: Central European University Press, 2007).

the PCF leadership made at different phases, since the 1930s, excluding the hiatus of its period underground between 1939 and 1945, it managed to forge a countersociety to some extent separate from the rest of society without ever being totally cut off from it, composed of a mosaic of many and varied entities into which it sought to instill uniform values, norms and rules that fluctuated over time. Communism was in fact at once characterized by its essential unity, especially in standing up to its enemies and opponents, and its multiple ways of viewing, experiencing and practicing this same communism. The PCF's firm foothold in the diverse aspects of French society is evidence that it was an emanation of it and in return influenced it deeply.

The primacy of its ties with the USSR is the foremost characteristic of the communist countersociety, the one that precisely differentiates the PCF from all the other French political parties. This is first because France represented an essential political, ideological and geostrategic symbol for Moscow. The land of the Great Revolution in the eighteenth century and the Paris Commune in 1871, both of which held great significance in the Bolshevik mythology, also constituted a major colonial power, first on a global scale and then in Europe after World War II. Furthermore, after Hitler destroyed the German Communist Party in 1933, the PCF was the largest communist party in the West. It was thus the object of particular attention from the USSR which during the interwar period – via Comintern envoys, especially the best known of them, Eugen Fried – built up and financed its apparatus; selected and trained its leaders and cadres, eliminating declared opponents and those who merely resisted party discipline; and defined its strategy according to Soviet interests, while occasionally leaving the French leadership a little bit of leeway.[15] Taking the USSR into account in its strategy was an abiding characteristic of the PCF leadership, even after it had gained greater independence in the mid 1950s, periodically creating tension as in the 1960s and throughout the following decade. During those years, the PCF expressed only two real differences of opinion with the Communist Party of the Soviet Union (CPSU), and these, moreover, created internal turmoil. The first was in 1956, when Thorez took a stand against the de-Stalinization initiated by the Khrushchev report with the Twentieth Congress of the CPSU, the second in 1968 over Czechoslovakia. The unfailing loyalty of PCF leaders and

---

15 Annie Kriegel and Stéphane Courtois, *Eugen Fried. Le grand secret du PCF* (Paris: Seuil, 1997).

cadres, the overwhelming majority of whom came from the working class or a rural milieu, was rooted in gratitude for what they owed the USSR – an education, a culture, a trade, a status, material and symbolic advantages within the world communist circles – and by what it represented for them. This is because in their eyes, as well as for many activists and sympathizers, the strength of the USSR derived from the imaginary power it conveyed. Throughout its history, the USSR cultivated a positive image through its propaganda, touting various features that could be substituted for one another or combined, but which in the end constituted a mythology in the true sense and that was effective until the mid 1950s, at which time de-Stalinization marked an irreversible turning point. The USSR first and foremost presented itself as the symbol of the revolution, the antithesis of capitalism, the land of the dictatorship of the proletariat, the embodiment of socialism, utopia on earth and the promise of its expansion worldwide. Starting in the 1930s, it prided itself as a model of democracy, the vanguard of the fight against fascism and Nazism, which it brilliantly illustrated with the Red Army's triumph at the Battle of Stalingrad. It also claimed to be an edifying example of rational organization of the economy through planning, capable of pulling off remarkable industrial and agricultural feats, of demonstrating scientific and technical expertise and of building a harmonious, egalitarian, healthy and educated society. Last, it considered itself a guarantor of peace and champion of struggles in favor of oppressed and colonized peoples.

The PCF and its organizations ("Les amis de l'Union soviétique," renamed "France–USSR" after 1945, for instance) continually relayed these themes to members, to voters and to French public opinion more generally speaking. But its methods were precisely targeted: While the communist propaganda directed at workers explained that the USSR was a sort of paradise for their fellow laborers, it carefully refrained from discussing land collectivization with farmers. Similarly, reception and assimilation of this propaganda varied considerably. The PCF leaders could adhere to it out of conviction, and even belief, but out of self-interest as well, believing that perhaps one day they, too, would have all the power in their hands, like their counterparts in communist countries. The wide variety of ideological reasons behind the enthusiasm communist intellectuals felt for the USSR are better known because they wrote extensively about it: a fascination with the regenerative virtue of violence, a yearning for radical change, a quest for humanism, beliefs of a religious variety, an appeal for fraternity, a rationalist and scientific spirit, and so on – not to mention the fact that the USSR and its allies spared little in terms of material benefits, symbolic rewards or flattery.[16] On the other hand, it is more difficult to document the appeal the USSR held for the communist working class. In most cases, their support for communism mainly came from their working conditions, their situations in the workplace or their place of residence and their participation in struggles. The USSR perhaps represented a hope for them, a dream, an argument as well to be used to scare the boss, against the socialists to differentiate themselves, in short one aspect of their identity among others, though maybe not the underlying motive for their commitment. However, on the whole, the communists' philo-Sovietism, especially among workers, set them apart with respect to the rest of the French population, as several opinion surveys conducted in the 1950s attest. Their sympathy toward the USSR nevertheless had already begun to wane at the end of the 1960s.

Communism, mainly a political and ideological phenomenon, meshed with various structural elements of French political culture. First and foremost this was because the PCF, having rejected the national question for more than a decade following the change in direction of the Comintern, eventually made the nation its own. It was in fact starting in the mid 1930s that the PCF attempted to reconcile national interest and internationalist solidarity, even though when an agonizing choice had to be made between the two, as in 1939 and in 1947, it chose the latter. The need to defend France's independence, which in the PCF could be done only through a close alliance with the USSR and then after 1945 with the entire communist bloc, became an abiding feature as of 1934–35. It was asserted even more forcefully as of 1941 during the resistance. It persisted throughout the Cold War, accompanied by virulent anti-Americanism and an abiding hostility toward Europe, accused of being a Christian democratic NATO-supported structure hostile to the USSR. Starting in 1940, this ambition to represent the nation fueled a constant and bitter rivalry with General de Gaulle that lasted nearly thirty years, structuring the political game and ending with de Gaulle winning out. The PCF and de Gaulle embodied two radically different conceptions of the nation. However, sharing certain sensibilities, they converged de facto in common struggles during the resistance, against Europe or again with regard to the United States. The communist embracing of the national issue virtually brought about a cult of nation-worship. As of 1935, the PCF systematically waved the red

16 Sophie Cœuré and Rachel Mazuy, *Cousu de fil rouge. Voyages des intellectuels français en Union soviétique* (Paris: CNRS Editions, 2012).

flag and the French flag, singing in unison "La Marseillaise" and "The Internationale" at every occasion. It laid claim to foundational events of France's glorious past, naturally starting with those of the French Revolution, the nineteenth-century revolutions and more broadly speaking the class struggles studied by Karl Marx. But it even further broadened its filiations. Thus in the aftermath of World War II and for several years, the PCF glorified Joan of Arc, wrestling her from the extreme right to hold her up as a symbol of national independence. It also poached on the grounds of other cultural legacies: It claimed kinship with the Enlightenment, major authors, famous painters, especially those in a realist vein, and also paid tribute to the cathedrals, gastronomic specialties, craftsmen's masterworks and achievements of French industry. It viewed itself at once as the heir of this centuries-old history and as the one that would carry it on. It used patriotic sentiment as a social lever. It thus strengthened its foothold in the working class, attached to France, but also among many immigrants eager to integrate who did so by participating in trade union and political activities.

The PCF, moreover, fell in line with firmly anchored political traditions in France that it attempted to monopolize, competing for them with other political forces. Laying claim to a revolutionary filiation begun with the French Revolution, it was part of that current that advocated a radical break as the only method for change and aspired to the regeneration of humanity, consequently denigrating reformism, especially the socialist variety, and compromise, viewed invariably as a compromise of principles. It extolled the virtues of political will in the Jacobin tradition, thereby justifying the party's avant-garde role. Considering in the aftermath of World War II and even more so in the 1960s that the state could serve as the essential instrument for political, economic and social change, it sought to take the reins of government and believed in the need for a strong state. Also with the 1930s, the PCF ceased denouncing the bourgeois republic as it had done in its early stages. It came around to supporting it and there again attempted to virtually monopolize it, recurrently citing the republic. During its phases of isolation and withdrawal, it embraced a revolutionary version of the republic but when it pursued a strategy of broad alliances (in the 1930s, during the resistance, at the liberation and during the 1960s and 1970s), it defended an almost ecumenical conception of republican government. Thus, while critical of the Fourth Republic, it launched mobilizations calling to defend it on several occasions, especially in 1958. The result was a PCF that was at once internationalist and nationalist, revolutionary and republican, a mixture that proved beneficial and that had strong resonance in many sectors of society.

The PCF, again as of the 1930s, styled itself as the greatest defender of democracy. Actually, its relationship to this form of government proved ambivalent: first, because during the entire period it fervently supported the communist regimes. Second, following World War II, it suggested building a "new popular democracy," the product of its own design with inspiration from similar trends at the time in Italy and in Eastern Europe. Last and above all, its organization, as was the case with all communist parties at the time, was an authoritarian, rigid, centralized structure that precluded any real internal debate, with a highly codified ideology based on opposition between "us" and "them," hoping to unify the body politic. The PCF displayed all the aspects of a totalitarian movement that failed at once due to the bulwark of the French republican regime and its own evolution, especially as of the 1960s, mainly owing to its elected officials and some of its active members and leaders; it gradually assimilated the principles of liberal, representative democracy while hoping to improve it.

The power of the communist countersociety stemmed from the depth of its entrenchment in France, particularly among the working class. The PCF benefited from CGT trade union actions, from countless other associations and networks and from the work of its elected officials, particularly at the municipal level.[17] It thus gained a following among well-organized and often skilled worker categories – such as metalworkers, steelworkers, miners and dockers, especially in the Paris area, the north of France, Lorraine and the environs of Lyon – and among farmers, mostly the small landholders and tenant farmers, particularly those in the Massif Central region. This working-class support is one of the most fundamental characteristics of the PCF and its countersociety. The PCF presented itself as the party of the working class, an overstatement, but one that contains an element of truth. It could count on solid electoral support from the wage-earning class: In 1956, according to the IFOP survey institute, 50 to 60 percent of workers voted communist. Workers on the whole made up between 40 and 45 percent of the PCF membership and delegates to its congresses between 1945 and the late 1960s. Its personnel, its leadership and its elected officials were overwhelmingly from a worker background,

---

17 Dominique Andolfatto and Dominique Labbé, *Histoire des syndicats (1906–2006)* (Paris: Seuil, 2006).

which set it apart from all the other French political parties.[18] The PCF also developed a veritable workerist mythology that rhapsodized and heroized the working class in a country where until then it had virtually no representation and was ignored, scorned and even stigmatized. This entrenchment reflected a threefold reality: the second and third wave of industrialization in France in the 1930s and then the 1950s, the concomitant development of a wage-earning class that reached its statistical peak in 1975, nourished among other things by rural exodus and immigration and, last, a new phase of urbanization, as from 1954 to 1975 the number of urban dwellers rose from 59 to 73 percent of the total population. Together with the CGT, it offered working-class groups protection and hope, structured their social horizons and supplied them with a territorial, social and political identity.[19] The PCF also appealed to women, creating the Union des Jeunes Filles de France in 1936, headed by Danièle Casanova who was deported and died at Auschwitz in 1943, and later the Union des Femmes Françaises in 1944, in which Jeannette Vermeersch would play an essential role along with Marie-Claude Vaillant-Couturier and Irène Joliot-Curie. Communist women, who took part in the resistance, strove to offset the influence of Catholic associations. They advocated equal rights for women, especially by campaigning for the right to vote (granted by General de Gaulle in 1944), encouraging them to take part in public life and mobilize in the fight for peace. The PCF primarily focused, however, on female manual workers, and as of the mid 1930s, at Moscow's behest, it developed a fairly traditional conception of the working woman and mother. While it played a major role in promoting painless childbirth methods, it ferociously combated birth-control policies in 1956. This stance put it out of step with the expansion of feminism in the 1960s and 1970s. It was only gradually and following serious internal tension that it integrated some of the women's movement's demands.[20] Moreover,

---

18 Jean-Paul Molinari, *Les ouvriers communistes* (Thonon-les-Bains: L'Albaron, 1991).
19 Julian Mischi, *Servir la classe ouvrière. Sociabilités militantes au PCF* (Rennes: Presses Universitaires de Rennes, 2010).
20 Christine Bard and Jean-Louis Robert, "The French Communist Party and Women 1920–1939," in Helmut Gruber and Pamela Graves (eds.), *Women and Socialism, Socialism and Women: Europe Between the Two World Wars* (New York and Oxford: Berghahn Books, 1998), 321–47; Sandra Fayolle, "Réagir aux premiers votes des femmes. Le cas du Parti communiste français," *Cahiers d'Histoire. Revue d'histoire critique* 94–95 (2005), 223–39; Sandra Fayolle, "Le débat sur le *birth contrôle*: une simple diversion?," in Fondation Gabriel Péri, *Le Parti communiste français et l'année 1956*, 105–13; Sandra Fayolle, "L'Union des femmes françaises et les sentiments supposés féminins," in Christophe Traïni (ed.), *Emotions . . . Mobilisation!* (Paris: Sciences Po-Les Presses, 2009), 169–92.

from 1945 to the early 1970s, the PCF attracted many renowned intellectuals, writers, scholars and artists and exercised strong cultural leadership over the teaching profession, which helped to disseminate its worldview.[21] Its many mass organizations and publishing houses long enabled it to consolidate its influence in these circles.[22]

The communist countersociety also has an anthropological aspect. The PCF did not engage in politics in the same manner as most other political parties. It treated politics as sacred, giving it almost a religious dimension, at least up until the 1950s. For the most active members, espousing communism implied self-sacrifice, sometimes even compromising their private life. The PCF promised happiness, the end of war and the reconciliation of humanity. It was at once open to the world via the USSR and withdrawn into a closed society, an agent of a form of modernization and hostile to change. However, disenchantment began to emerge in the 1970s.

Success and Then Decline

The momentum of the previous period continued into the early 1970s and even grew, the PCF having a very broad outreach. But the reversal of the trend in a very short time was equally spectacular.

Georges Marchais, having officially become secretary-general of the PCF in 1972, embarked on a "Union of the Left" strategy based on a common program, unique in Western Europe, signed with the new Parti Socialiste, restructured by François Mitterrand, and the Parti Radical de Gauche. This program largely took into account communist proposals except in matters of European and international policy. Internally, the PCF leadership harbored no illusions: It explained to its cadres that "unity is a struggle" and that the socialists had to be controlled. From the outset, however, it benefited from the pact. Its membership was on the upswing and rose from 305,540 to 540,565 in 1979. In 1973, it won 21.4 percent of the vote in the legislative elections; it remained the biggest left-wing party even though the Parti socialiste (PS) was not far behind. The following year, it backed Mitterrand's second candidacy

---

21 Sudhir Hazareesingh, *How the French Think: An Affectionate Portrait of an Intellectual People* (London: Penguin Books, 2015), ch. 3; Laurent Jalabert, *Le Grand Débat. Les universitaires français – historiens et géographes – et les pays communistes de 1945 à 1991* (Toulouse: GRHI, 2001).

22 Marie-Cécile Bouju, *Lire en communiste. Les Maisons d'édition du Parti communiste français 1920–1968* (Paris: Presses Universitaires de Rennes, 2010).

in the presidential election, which he lost narrowly to Valéry Giscard d'Estaing. The PCF was nevertheless disturbed by the liberties the candidate took with respect to the common program and the obvious progress the PS was making. In 1977, the PCF won a number of municipalities, and major ones at that. The year marked the peak of municipal communism, with the party controlling 1,465 town and city councils for a total population of more than 8.6 million inhabitants.[23] At the same time, it pursued its modernization. In 1976 it renounced the dictatorship of the proletariat in a sudden announcement made by Secretary-General Marchais that would be ratified by the Twenty-Second Congress of the PCF, despite the criticism of certain intellectuals, among them Louis Althusser. During this same congress, the PCF declared it would follow the path of "socialism under French colors." This was the period of Eurocommunism, embodied by the Italian, Spanish and French parties among which real divergences remained, however, as to the attitude to take toward the Soviet leaders, toward Europe (even if the PCF was slowly evolving, having accepted the election of the European Parliament by universal suffrage in 1977) as well as toward the situation in Portugal. The PCF, while continuing to defend the USSR's economic and social achievements, voiced sharp criticism regarding domestic policy in the USSR, particularly regarding human rights, in the name of a more democratic form of socialism, and also because abuses in communist countries jeopardized the PCF's success at the polls. But it remained silent about its foreign policy, for it believed that the USSR was an essential element in the progressive forces of the world that were gaining ground in Southeast Asia and in Africa, and with respect to the United States. However, Moscow implicitly disapproved of the Union of the Left strategy, as the Soviet regime maintained excellent relations with Giscard d'Estaing, as it had done with de Gaulle and Georges Pompidou before that, and remained distrustful of Mitterrand. In February 1976, contrary to tradition, no Soviet leader of significant stature attended the Twenty-Second Congress of the PCF and Georges Marchais was conspicuously absent from the Twenty-Fifth CPSU Congress. In October, Politburo member Pierre Juquin took part in a meeting in Paris together with the Soviet dissident Leonid Pliushch, with whom he shook hands; the PCF reproduced 6 million copies of the speech he gave on this occasion. By choosing the Union of the Left and accepting the insertion of

23 Emmanuel Bellanger and Julian Mischi (ed.), *Les territoires du communisme. Elus locaux, politiques publiques et sociabilités militantes* (Paris: A. Colin, 2013).

a European echelon between the two standard levels of communism, national and international, the PCF substantially altered its relationship with the USSR. As a result, relations between the Soviets and the French communist leaders grew extremely strained. On 18 March 1977, the CPSU sent a very harsh secret missive (it would be made public at a later date) to the PCF expressing outrage at its criticism of the USSR. The PCF refuted the accusations, while taking care not to slide into anti-Sovietism. A few weeks later, urged by a report by Jean Kanapa, the leader in charge of foreign policy, the PCF accepted France's nuclear defense program. The declaration was a complete turnaround from its usual opposition to the bomb. This time, the leadership of the PCF was subject to much harsher Soviet pressure than what had followed in the wake of its decision to condemn the invasion of Czechoslovakia by Warsaw Pact troops.[24] At the same time, party historians, intellectuals and experts were taking an interest in the USSR and publishing books about it, generally critical, and extensively discussed among the communists. It was in 1975 that for the first time the PCF mentioned the term "Stalinism," a notion that it had hitherto refused to employ. An entire generation, for the most part young, that had joined the PCF during the 1960s and 1970s was indifferent to the Soviet Union, or even openly distant.

But the PCF noted that the PS continued, to the communists' detriment, to progress more than ever while their own strategy came up against serious misgivings within PCF ranks. This situation prompted it to demand a revision of the Common Program of Government. Negotiating was intense, and just when a new accord seemed to be in the offing, Georges Marchais, for reasons that remain obscure still today, chose to break with the Union of the Left in September 1977. This almost automatically led to its defeat in the legislative elections the following year, an outcome that seems to have been what Marchais was seeking. The year 1978 represents a turning point for the left because, for the first time since 1945, the PCF, with 20.7 percent of the vote, fell behind the PS (21.4 percent). The PCF launched vicious attacks against its former ally. To better highlight its difference with the PS and reaffirm its revolutionary identity, it realigned with the USSR in 1979, declaring its record "globally positive" and approving its invasion of Afghanistan via a televised statement by Marchais from

24 Philippe Buton, "El Partido Comunista Francés frente al eurocomunismo: un partido en la encrucijada," *Historia del Presente* 18 (2011), 9–23; Valentine Lomellini, *Les relations dangereuses: French Socialists, Communists and the Human Rights Issue in the Soviet Bloc* (Brussels: Peter Lang, 2012).

Moscow. Vehement controversy drove a wedge in its ranks, and the leadership vilified its opponents. The PCF was battling alone against the world, but this splendid isolation came at a huge cost. Its membership began to shrink in 1980 and Marchais, despite a roaring campaign with rallies drawing huge crowds, was humiliated in the 1981 presidential election, won by Mitterrand, by taking only 15 percent of the vote in the first round. This defeat set off a rapid and steady decline, causing the PCF to fall below the 10 percent mark five years later. Forced to take part in a leftist government led by the socialist Pierre Mauroy in 1981, the PCF seemed like a rudderless ship. Its leadership had trouble positioning itself with respect to its four ministers who, left to their own devices, found themselves in an uneasy position. Its strategy became incomprehensible. In 1984, when Mitterrand embarked on an austerity policy and appointed a new prime minister, Laurent Fabius, the PCF refused to join the government. Internal dissent grew more common and was harshly reprimanded, leading to a series of departures that weakened a party already destabilized by Mikhail Gorbachev's Soviet reform policies, which the PCF had initially approved; it subsequently worried about the effects these policies might have on the communist movement.[25]

Yet, at the start of the 1970s, the PCF seemed robust, even flourishing. Its leader, Georges Marchais, achieved record viewership with each televised appearance. While not disowning the preeminence of the working class, the PCF sought more than ever to diversify its electorate to prevent the PS from gaining votes among the booming salaried and urban middle class. It started promoting officials chosen from these same categories, who were younger and better educated, through the echelons of its apparatus and elected representatives, especially in local governments.[26] It was modernizing its communication and self-image, symbolized for instance in its new headquarters, an ultra-modern building designed by Brazilian architect Oscar Niemeyer, who had laid out the city of Brasília.[27] Greater freedom of expression was allowed among its ranks, but still with certain red lines not to be crossed, as democratic centralism remained a guiding principle. Its various mass organizations continued to gain independence from the party,

25 Roger Martelli, *L'occasion manquée. Eté 1984, quand le PCF se referme* (Paris: Les éditions Arcane 17, 2014).
26 Julian Mischi, *Le communisme désarmé. Le PCF et les classes populaires depuis les années 70* (Marseille: Agone, 2014).
27 Vanessa Grossman, *Le PCF a changé! Niemeyer et le siège du Parti Communiste Français (1966–1981)* (Paris: Editions B2, 2013).

as Secours Populaire had done. The process proved to be far more complex, however, for the CGT.[28]

But in the second half of the 1970s, a complete turnaround occurred at dizzying speed. Mitterrand's tactical skill, as he continued to claim the Union of the Left, made the PCF out to be an uncompromising party, serving its own interests first and foremost at a time when the left was thriving in France both politically and culturally. The determination to beat the right after twenty-three years in power and a desire for radical change motivated a vote for the PS whose political platform blended traditional leftist demands (i.e. nationalizations, a break from capitalism and a shift toward socialism) and themes in vogue at the time (regionalism, self-management, cultural liberalism). But, in particular, the 1973–74 crisis brought considerable transformations in tow. The traditional labor movement crumbled in the space of a few years under the pressure of major industrial restructuring that affected the steel and metallurgy industries among others. The PCF lost its strongholds. Society on the whole was undergoing profound changes, in its relationship toward work, for instance, with the advance of the individualization process and an overall reshaping of value systems. The PCF leadership's return to basics, with its defense of the USSR, the party and the working class, ran completely counter to the trend. The image of the USSR deteriorated rapidly with the "era of stagnation" characterizing the Brezhnev years, the crisis of the Vietnamese and Cambodian boat people harmed the communist cause, and criticism of totalitarianism spread throughout intellectual circles including in the left. An increasing number of citizens questioned party politics and were appalled by the intransigence with which the PCF leadership fought off internal contestation, making the party look more like a sect. Last, workerism became a totally outdated ideology.

By falling back on its rural and working-class bastions of support, which themselves were crumbling, cracking and weakened, the PCF divorced itself from society. Thrashed by its adversaries, taunted by most of the media, undermined by internal divisions, its leadership was unable to rise to the challenges facing it despite the various proposals put forward by some of its members to stem the decline, alter the party's political course and invent new practices. But perhaps it was impossible in view of the wholesale failure of attempts to reform communism. The fall of the European communist

---

28 Axelle Brodiez, *Le Secours populaire français 1945–2000* (Paris: Sciences Po-Les Presses, 2006).

countries and then the disintegration of the USSR between 1989 and 1991 only hastened the political marginalization of the PCF. The party has nevertheless left behind a cultural legacy that continues to influence a large segment of the French left.

Bibliographical Essay

The only book that retraces the history of the French Communist Party from its inception to the late 1990s in a detailed and synthetic manner, drawing on a wealth of documentation and archival material, is the tome by Stéphane Courtois and Marc Lazar, *Histoire du Parti communiste français* (Paris: PUF, 2000). The authors hold that the PCF can be understood only by examining the teleological dimension together with the societal dimension of communism. Political scientists have contributed interesting perspectives. John Gaffney, in *The French Left and the Fifth Republic: The Discourses of Communism and Socialism in Contemporary France* (London: Macmillan Press, 1989), studies the discourses and attitudes of the socialists and communists regarding the institutional innovations of the Fifth Republic, which posed a real challenge to the entire French left. W. Rand Smith, in *Enemy Brothers: Socialists and Communists in France, Italy, and Spain* (Lanham, MD: Rowman & Littlefield, 2012), has undertaken a comparative analysis of the conflictual relations between socialists and communists in three south European countries. The aspects the French case shares with other situations as well as its distinct features are thus better brought to the fore. Stéphane Courtois, in *Le bolchévisme à la française* (Paris: Fayard, 2010), seeks to understand the scope and originality of the communist phenomenon with respect to other political parties from an ideological perspective and in line with an approach based on the concept of totalitarianism. An analysis combining history and sociology aiming to grasp the reasons for the PCF's strength in France without disregarding its close relationship with the USSR was penned by Annie Kriegel, the historian who founded scholarly studies of communism in France (with the participation of Guillaume Bourgeois), *Les communistes français dans leur premier demi-siècle, 1920–1970* (Paris: Seuil, 1985). Her book, first published in 1968, remains a particularly interesting and profound classic, especially due to the author's knowledge of the communist organization and its militants. Jacques Girault (ed.), in *Des communistes en France (années 1920–années 1960)* (Paris: Publications de la Sorbonne, 2002), favors an approach focusing on how communism became firmly established in the very heart of France, his idea being that communism is to some extent the expression of social and national realities. The decline of the PCF has been studied by Bernard Pudal, who pinpoints the start of this process in 1956, in *Un monde défait. Les communistes français de 1956 à nos jours* (Bellecombe-en-Bauges: Editions du Croquant, 2009). The influence of communism from the 1930s to the late 1970s and the cultural legacy it bequeathed to the French left even as the party became marginalized as of the early 1980s are analyzed by Marc Lazar in *Le communisme, une passion française* (Paris: Tempus, 2005) and by Roger Martelli in *L'empreinte communiste. PCF et société française, 1920–2010* (Paris: Éditions sociales, 2010). These two authors, whose approaches differ significantly, set out to analyze the factors that enabled communism to have such an important presence in France and examine what remains of the PCF's erstwhile strength.

26

American Communism

PHILLIP DEERY

The contribution of American communism to the political, social and cultural life of the United States from the 1930s to the 1960s was controversial, uneven and complicated. Like all Western communist parties in this period, the Communist Party of the United States of America (CPUSA) was in thrall to the Soviet Union. The party blindly followed its foreign-policy twists and turns, was convinced that it provided the only path to enlightenment and until 1956 was unquestioningly devoted to its deity, Joseph Stalin. But the CPUSA also had roots in a longer history of domestic radicalism and worked, tirelessly, for its working-class constituency. The struggles against social injustice, economic inequality and racism were as important to the rank and file as interpreting the latest Soviet position was to the leadership. This tension, between international imperatives and local commitments, lay at the heart of American communism and was never resolved. It is a tension reflected in the historiography of the CPUSA, polarized between the "traditionalists" – who argue that slavish adherence to Moscow's instructions, extensive involvement in Soviet espionage by an underground network, and manipulation of causes and organizations are the defining features – and the "revisionists," who emphasize that semi-autonomous, often spontaneous local activity by members on industrial and cultural fronts must be incorporated. This chapter straddles both positions and presupposes that the CPUSA comprised a blend of international communism and national experience.

The Great Depression and "Third Period" Communism

When the American stock market crashed on 29 October 1929, ushering in the Great Depression and condemning more than one-third of the workforce to unemployment, the CPUSA felt vindicated. Only five months before, Stalin had proclaimed "the moment is not far off when a revolutionary crisis will develop in America." The economic crisis in the citadel of capitalism confirmed, it seemed, not only Stalin's prescience but the veracity of Marxist theory. Among American communists a conviction quickly emerged that the jobless would be radicalized, militant class struggle would be inaugurated and revolutionary conditions would ripen. As occurred so often in the history of American communism, optimistic predictions were not grounded in objective appraisals. The unemployed hungered for work, not revolution. The strike wave in 1934 confronted significant, and effective, state repression. And many potential converts to the communist cause embraced New Deal reforms.

CPUSA policies and strategies were also self-defeating. The Great Depression coincided with the ultra-left "Third Period." In July–August 1928, the Sixth Congress of the Communist International (Comintern) promulgated a tough, inflexible line that permeated all Western communist parties. A central tenet of this new line, whose context was the anticipation of a new era of imperialist wars, economic depressions and proletarian revolutions, was that socialists and "reformists" in the labor movement would become the worst enemy, the biggest betrayer, of the working class and therefore must be denounced as "social-fascist."[1] The more left they were, the more dangerous. So the ultimate epithet became "left social-fascist." In Germany, this proved fatal: The induced hostility and widening gap between the communists and the socialists contributed to the Nazis' success in 1933. The German Communist Party, the largest outside the Soviet Union, was destroyed. In the United States, rival organizations were attacked, likely allies alienated, New Deal agencies accused of collaborating with monopoly capital, and Roosevelt condemned as a racist and a fascist comparable to Mussolini.[2] "Class against class," the defining slogan of the Third Period, proved a major hindrance to organizing the workers under communist party leadership. Indicative were the disheartening membership figures: By the first half of 1933, only 15,000 Americans had joined.

Two further Third Period casualties were language and leadership. Communist rhetoric was not only uncompromising and virulent; it also became, to those not steeped in Marxist ideology, esoteric and apocalyptic.

1 Earl Browder, "How We Must Fight Against the Demagogy of Fascists and Social Fascists," *Communist* 10 (Apr. 1931), 300–04.
2 William Z. Foster, *The Words and Deeds of Franklin D. Roosevelt* (New York: Workers Library, 1932), 9–10, 14.

It was not surprising the "toiling masses" did not respond or that William Z. Foster's *Towards a Soviet America* (1932) did not resonate. The leaders of the CPUSA were replaced after the Sixth Comintern Congress in a series of bitter, protracted factional fights against "deviationists." The general secretary, Jay Lovestone, was personally chastised by Stalin in the spring of 1929 for his belief in "American exceptionalism," which argued that the United States was immune to socialism and the American proletariat was indifferent toward revolution.[3] Under instructions from the Comintern, the heretics were expelled, and Bolshevization of the party proceeded. Democratic centralism became a euphemism for authoritarian top-down decision-making and the byword for unquestioning loyalty and compliance to a single, centralized leadership. This defining feature – of an undemocratic national leadership taking its cue from the Kremlin – dominated the subsequent history of American communism.

Despite this rigid hierarchical structure, the dogmatic application of Soviet doctrines to incompatible American political conditions and the disproportionate attacks on noncommunist leftists, CPUSA activists worked tenaciously and courageously among the victims of the economic catastrophe: the voiceless, the dispossessed and the marginalized. Thus we find idealistic rank-and-file communists leading anti-eviction struggles in the north, agitating against Jim Crow segregationism in the south and organizing itinerant agricultural laborers and immigrant camps in the west. They were also there, fighting for better working conditions, in the steel mills of Pittsburgh, in the coalmines of West Virginia, in the auto plants of Detroit, in the United Workers Cooperative Colony in the Bronx, among share croppers and tenant farmers in Alabama and on the waterfront of San Francisco. And when they were beaten up, shot at or arrested, were they "thinking of Stalin"?[4] While not autonomous, organizers in the field worked with a degree of flexibility, modifying and adapting official policy to local conditions of life on the shop floor. This may not have typified long-term communist behavior but it does suggest that the history of American communism is more complex than the simple domination / acquiescence dichotomy. As one former activist recalled,

3 See Theodore Draper, *American Communism and Soviet Russia* (New York: Vintage Books, 1986 [1st edn. 1960]), 414–15.
4 This phrase refers to an incident in Alabama in 1931. A New York lawyer investigating the Scottsboro case was pursued by a posse of southern whites; when hiding from their guns and their pitchforks, he recounted, he was not "thinking of Stalin." See Nora Sayre, *Previous Convictions: A Journey Through the 1950s* (New Brunswick, NJ: Rutgers University Press, 1995), 354.

in general, while directives coming down from headquarters to the CP members ... may have amounted to a great deal of paper – that's all they amounted to. In many cases there was very little time or energy spent by local [communist party] organizations, busy with their own problems and their own urgent agendas, in following directives through, unless they fitted in concretely with their own immediate concerns.[5]

In California, branches were especially independent, much to the chagrin of the national leadership in New York from which, remarked one Californian communist, "we were three thousand *lovely* miles away."[6]

The Popular Period 1935–1939

This apparent disjuncture, between a remote and rigid leadership and a more attuned rank and file, dissolved after 1935. At the Seventh Congress of the Comintern, held in Moscow in August 1935, a new "popular front" line emerged. The reasons are complex and need not concern us here, but the effects do, and they were profound. The CPUSA emphasized unity of action with the Socialist Party, led by the erstwhile social-fascist, Norman Thomas; embraced and endorsed both Franklin D. Roosevelt and his New Deal policies; supported Fiorello La Guardia as New York mayor; and sought to insert itself into mainstream politics as the left wing of a broad united front coalition. The popular front strategy also involved the creation of a plethora of "front" organizations with varying degrees of communist control. Their range, and reach, is suggested by their titles: American League Against War and Fascism, American Student Union, American Youth Congress, International Labor Defense, International Workers Order, National Lawyers Guild, National Negro Congress, North American Committee to Aid Spanish Democracy and the Screen Writers Guild. They became, in communist parlance, transmission belts to the masses, and attracted huge numbers of recruits and sympathizers to the party. The party also made significant inroads in intellectual and artistic circles through the League of American Writers and the Federal Theatre Project, a New Deal program. It became a major force within organized labor through its sway over the new industrial unions in the Congress of Industrial Organizations (CIO) and worked closely with the CIO's formidable president, John L. Lewis. It played

5 Annette T. Rubinstein, "The Cultural World of the Communist Party: An Historical Overview," in Michael E. Brown *et al* (eds.), *New Studies in the Politics and Culture of US Communism* (New York: Monthly Review Press, 1993), 241.
6 Dorothy Healey, cited in Sayre, *Previous Convictions*, 364 (emphasis in original).

a key role in mobilizing liberals' support for a range of causes, from the Spanish Republic to the Scottsboro boys. These, therefore, were heady, idealistic days for communist organizers. According to one cadre,

> I cannot recall a comparable period in terms of grass-roots participation, enthusiasm and optimistic perspective . . . The harsh intolerance of life in the party, the many limitations, the illusions, came to light much later; then we were inspired by a common purpose and a common goal, and distant as it was, it enhanced its appeal. Every act – a speech at a street corner meeting, a demonstration, a conference in a church – all seemed a vitally integral part of this mission.[7]

Third Period sectarianism was replaced by collaboration and the building of alliances. The CPUSA had secured a firm foothold in cultural, social and industrial institutions. Now, American communism was congruent with mainstream politics. Now, in Earl Browder's oft-quoted 1936 slogan, "Communism Is Twentieth-Century Americanism," it associated itself with the best traditions of Jeffersonian democracy. "The Star-Spangled Banner," not the "The Internationale," was sung at party meetings. By 1939, its membership had soared to more than 90,000, its zenith and, for the first time, native-born American communists outnumbered foreign-born. During the popular front, about 200,000 to 250,000 passed through the ranks of the party (although most left after a short period). Membership figures masked influence. As Browder stated, with only minimal hyperbole, "Millions of people consider and are influenced by our decision."[8]

Return of the Hard Line

It was "our decision" in the autumn of 1939, however, that reversed the party's fortunes. With the signing of the Nazi–Soviet Nonaggression Pact on 23 August 1939, the CPUSA parroted Soviet foreign policy and pledged opposition to the "imperialist" war. Being a loyal communist meant an unhesitating defense of the Soviet Union. It meant ideological myopia: being blinded by the Soviet myth. It meant an unquestioning adherence to the current party line, however sectarian or self-defeating or contradictory it may have seemed. And it meant discarding intellectual integrity and moral balance. The stricture to conform to orthodoxy was intense, as was the pressure to close eyes or mouths when challenged with doubts about the

---

7 George Charney, *A Long Journey* (Chicago: Quadrangle, 1968), 90, 103.
8 Earl Browder, *Unity for Peace and Democracy* (New York: Workers Library, 1939), 24.

Moscow purges in the late 1930s or confronted with evidence of Soviet anti-Semitism in the late 1940s.

So in 1939 American communists denied their popular front experience and returned to policies and rhetoric that revived the Third Period. Previous enthusiasm for Roosevelt was retracted, and he and his "war party" were designated as quasi-fascist. Alliances were splintered or broken. Progressives with whom the party had worked closely were now denounced as traitors to the working class. Intellectuals who deserted were lampooned as lily-livered weaklings who "fawn when their imperialist masters crack the whip."[9] Key supporters, such as the American Labor Party's Vito Marcantonio, were judged, and jettisoned, according to the litmus test of "proletarian internationalism": what one thought about the foreign policy of the Soviet Union. Consistent with Comintern communications, fervent isolationism became the order of the day: People wore "The Yanks are not coming" buttons and a "Keep America out of war" committee was quickly formed.

This *volte-face* astonished, confused, demoralized and angered CPUSA members. In the words of one, they were "knocked off balance by this abrupt turn."[10] A great many Jewish communists felt betrayed: Seeing photos of Viacheslav Molotov shaking hands with Joachim von Ribbentrop was too much. Resignations flooded in. Critics were expelled. Others quietly melted away. A few became committed anti-Stalinists; in the 1950s they had neither forgiven nor forgotten. Overall, the CPUSA lost approximately 40 percent of its membership. Less tangibly but more significantly, it also lost much of the goodwill and respectability that had steadily accumulated over the previous four years. Defections continued and isolation increased during the "winter war," when the USSR invaded Finland (1939–40): a naked act of aggression unquestioningly supported by the CPUSA leadership. In Harlem, the party lost its black base and its "betrayal" was attacked by former long-time radical allies, such as Adam Clayton Powell, Jr.[11] Even the charismatic communist leader, Harry Bridges, was repudiated by militant San Franciscan longshoremen when he condemned Roosevelt in October 1940.

9 Victor Jeremy Jerome, *Intellectuals and the War* (New York: Workers Library, 1940), 63.
10 Al Richmond, *A Long View from the Left: Memoirs of an American Revolutionary* (Boston: Houghton Mifflin, 1973), 283.
11 See Mark Naison, *Communists in Harlem During the Depression* (Urbana: University of Illinois Press, 1983), 291–93, for the breadth of hostility in Harlem to the party's position in 1939–40.

Besieged and on the defensive, communists became vulnerable to attack from state and federal authorities. In a foretaste of McCarthyism, the House Un-American Activities Committee (HUAC), chaired by Martin Dies since 1938, investigated front organizations, and the FBI raided CPUSA offices in several cities in February 1940 and arrested numerous party members on a variety of charges. "Little Dies" committees were established by state legislatures, and suspected communist sympathizers were purged from New Deal agencies. In New York, the Rapp–Courdert Committee purged teachers from city colleges. A battery of legislative responses to the threat of "subversion" was implemented in 1940, including the repressive Alien Registration (or Smith) Act and the Voorhis Registration Act. That year, Earl Browder was sentenced to four years in jail for violation of passport laws. Some local leaders were stripped of citizenship, and hundreds of rank-and-file members were indicted under archaic state electoral laws. The party itself teetered on the edge of illegality.

The "Great Patriotic War"

Yet the "red scare" dress rehearsal and the diminished status during the Nazi–Soviet pact period did not sound the CPUSA's death knell, for these two years proved a mere hiatus. On 22 June 1941, Germany invaded Russia, the imperialist war became the Great Patriotic War and the party, almost overnight, switched back to anti-fascism. Uniquely, defense of the Soviet Union coincided with the national interest of the United States. The USSR became "our gallant ally"; Stalin was named *Time* magazine's "Man of the Year" in 1942; the pro-Soviet film "Mission to Moscow" (based on the memoirs, recently serialized in the conservative *Reader's Digest*, of Joseph E. Davies, the former US ambassador to the Soviet Union) opened to enthusiastic audiences in 1943; and local communists, their respectability returned, basked in the reflected glory of the Red Army, especially after the Battle of Stalingrad.

American communism underwent a metamorphosis. Embracing a national road to socialism, the CPUSA worked with all other democratic forces to forge popular support for the war effort and Soviet–American cooperation. On some issues, such as universal military conscription, the party went further to the right than its liberal allies. Promotion of wartime national unity became paramount. Nowhere was this more evident than in labor relations. Reversing its customary industrial militancy, the CPUSA endorsed in December 1941 a no-strike pledge, to which it rigidly adhered throughout the war. John L. Lewis, who opposed the pledge, was denounced. The party abolished its fractions in the unions, campaigned against absenteeism, supported the resolution of industrial disputes without interruption of production and proposed an incentive-pay system to max-imize productivity. Workers in defense plants, termed "soldiers in overalls," were exhorted to make heavier sacrifices. If unwilling, they were being influenced by "defeatist groups." Industrial restlessness was not tolerated. By 1944 the party declared that strikes should be outlawed.

The issue of race illuminates the complicated position of American communism during World War II. Although the CPUSA, through its CIO connections, campaigned for equal employment opportunities for African-Americans and encouraged their elevation into positions of union leader-ship, it fell far short of full support for civil rights. It opposed both the "Double V" campaign (victory against fascism abroad and racism at home) and A. Philip Randolph's March on Washington movement as "disruptive" to wartime imperatives. Communists took an ambiguous position during the mass mobilization of black workers that culminated in the Detroit race riots in 1943; fifth-column "agents of Hitler," not Jim Crow, were blamed. Indeed, support for black rights was, generally, narrowly channeled only into those activities that benefited the war effort or over which the party had influence. Broader questions of discrimination were simply put on hold. The concept of black self-determination, championed in the 1930s, was dropped entirely.

The same ambivalence extended to women workers. Consistent with federal government propaganda, CPUSA members helped to open more doors to female employment and actively struggled for equal pay. But communist-led CIO unions remained resistant to the promotion of women organizers, and many male communists scorned discussions of the "woman question." Within the party, large numbers of women joined, and some became second-tier leaders (to replace male leaders serving overseas). However, they comprised only 25 percent of the national committee and 1 percent of the political committee. In the "good war," the CPUSA was only a perfunctory vehicle for feminism. There was no ambiguity about local Trotskyists. The party cheered on the prosecution of the Socialist Workers Party under the Smith Act of 1940 and endorsed tough punitive measures against the strike-prone, Trotskyist-led Teamsters' Union in Minneapolis. Nor was there ambi-guity about Japanese-Americans. When they were evacuated en masse from California and incarcerated in internment camps in desert states from 1942 until 1945, the CPUSA justified this as "a necessary war measure."

Browderism

In a gesture to national unity, President Roosevelt commuted Earl Browder's prison sentence. On resuming active party leadership in May 1942, Browder began the transformation of the American communist movement. His *Victory – and After*, published in September, assembled the various elements of communist praxis since June 1941 into a coherent framework. In addition to the no-strike pledge, productivity incentives, unwavering support for Roosevelt, alliance with liberals, downplaying of socialism and, in general, ultra-patriotism and all-out-for-unity, Browder went further. He envisaged – and it was he alone, since *Victory – and After* was not seen by the CPUSA political committee until after its publication – a prolonged era of social harmony and class collaboration. This would underpin peaceful American–Soviet relations in the postwar period. "Browderism," with its own full-blown cult of personality, was born.

The exigencies of war meant that links with the Soviet Union were severed. In May 1943, the Comintern was dissolved (in part to assuage Roosevelt) and, with it, the call for revolution in capitalist countries was formally shelved. In November 1943, the historic Tehran conference (when Churchill, Roosevelt and Stalin first met) seemed to justify Browder's optimistic hope for enduring "Grand Alliance" cooperation. These developments provided the context for Browder's restructuring of the CPUSA in 1944. The party was dissolved and renamed the Communist Political Association. It was a bold, iconoclastic move. The CPUSA ceased to be a separate political entity; it was now to be a pressure group, an advocacy organization, incorporated into the political mainstream. The increasingly autocratic Browder adopted the more "American" title of president, and even recommended that "Communist" be removed from Communist Political Association. The class struggle was dead. The way forward was cooperation with the Democratic Party and accommodation with capital. For the first time in the party's history, no shibboleths of Marxism-Leninism were invoked.

These were favorable conditions for recruitment. In 1945, the CPUSA had 63,000 members, 50 percent of whom were trade unionists and 10 percent African-American. Its educational schools, such as the Thomas Jefferson

School of Social Science in New York, enrolled tens of thousands eager to understand the principles of Marxism and the achievements of the Soviet Union. Many became "Red Army communists," later disparaged by party apparatchiks for being insufficiently proletarian. Indeed, it was easier being a communist when democratic centralism was weaker.

During the party's embrace of Browderism, the latitude taken by the rank and file reached its high-water mark. There is considerable evidence of discord on the shopfloor. A great many militant unionists, perceiving or experiencing an inequality of sacrifice, bristled against the no-strike pledge. The result was a wave of wildcat strikes that Roosevelt's punitive measures, endorsed by Browder, did little to quell. CIO communists often ignored the speed-up propaganda and kept the leadership at a distance. Black communists continued to criticize racism in labor organizations in the southern Black Belt when party policy emphasized unanimity. A pro-communist folk group, The Union Boys, added songs to its repertoire that supported the Double V campaign (opposed by the CPUSA) by exposing the hypocrisy of fighting for freedom while ignoring Jim Crow. In Harlem local, independent initiatives included agitation for racial integration in organized sport, especially baseball. To many party members it was repugnant that Browder should publicly offer, in September 1943, to shake hands with the industrial magnate J. P. Morgan as a symbol of home-front harmony. And when Browder announced the transition from Party to Association and the peaceful coexistence of capitalism with socialism to a packed Madison Square Garden rally in January 1944, the applause was muted, and many walked out.

World War II also provided the context, or cover, for another development – parallel but clandestine. The CPUSA significantly expanded its covert underground apparatus, with close links to the Soviet security services. Browder, codenamed "Helmsman," was a talent-spotter: He personally recommended some local contacts as potential sources for Soviet recruitment. He was certainly aware of and, it appears, was actively involved in the CPUSA's "nonlegal" networks that directly engaged in wartime espionage. "Traditionalist" historians, such as John Earl Haynes and Harvey Klehr, drawing on newly available Soviet archival documents and the Venona decrypts, now see such espionage as a central feature of CPUSA activity during World War II.[12] Nonetheless, spying and communist party

---

12 These include Harvey Klehr, John Earl Haynes and Fridrikh Igorevich Firsov, *The Secret World of American Communism* (New Haven: Yale University Press, 1995); Allen Weinstein and Alexander Vassiliev, *The Haunted Wood: Soviet Espionage in America – The Stalin Era* (New York: Random House, 1999); John Earl Haynes,

membership are not interchangeable categories. A clear historical delineation must be drawn between that small handful of communists who passed classified information to the Soviet Union, and the average rank-and-file communist who neither knew of it nor approved of it. Of the approximately 50,000 American communists in World War II, about 49,700 were not involved in espionage. But both groups have been tarred with the same brush of betrayal. The average communist was far more likely to be an auto worker or public school teacher than a policymaker in the Treasury Department with access to classified government secrets. And certainly the complicity of a small minority of American communists in Soviet espionage does not justify the broader forms of bureaucratic and institutionalized anti-communism that disfigured American political life. Regardless, communism, subversion and spying became synonymous in the public mind and would haunt the CPUSA throughout the McCarthy period.

The removal of Earl Browder in February 1946 was triggered by an article in *Les Cahiers du Communisme* by Jacques Duclos, a French communist leader, in April 1945. The article repudiated Browderism and its "Tehran line" as "rightist" and "revisionist." Significantly, it was sanctioned, if not inspired, by Moscow.[13] The second meeting of the "Big Three," at Yalta in February 1945, signaled the beginning of the end of the Grand Alliance. By Potsdam it was clear that the "spirit of Tehran" was a chimera. Soviet foreign policy was shifting and so was Moscow's imprimatur for Browder's position. In short, Duclos's article became the Soviets' message. This emboldened the previously marginalized but still unreconstructed William Z. Foster, but Browder – theoretically rigid if tactically flexible – remained defiant and intransigent. Eventually, after sustained internecine factional fighting throughout the fall of 1945, Foster and Eugene Dennis became the leaders, the CPA reverted to the CPUSA and Browder was expelled. The eulogizing of Stalin returned along with the spurning of old alliances, the elimination of internal dissent and a renewed commitment to the class struggle. Whatever Browder's flaws were, he embodied the chance to navigate a path toward a national form of communism within the established political system. He opened the door to a communist movement freed from the Soviet mindset,

Harvey Klehr and Alexander Vassiliev, *Spies: The Rise and Fall of the KGB in America* (New Haven: Yale University Press, 2009).

13 The head of the Soviet Central Committee's Department of International Information, Georgi Dimitrov, wrote on 8 March 1944 that he was "disturbed" by the CPUSA's new directions, and instructed Browder to "reconsider" and "report" back. Browder did not comply. See Ivo Banac (ed.), *The Diary of Georgi Dimitrov 1933–1949* (New Haven: Yale University Press, 2003), 307.

sensitive to American issues and conditions, and rooted in actual struggles in factories, on farms and in communities. With Foster's ascendancy converging with the onset of the Cold War, that door was shut.

Onset of Cold War Hostility

Until the establishment of the Communist Information Bureau (Cominform) in September 1947, the CPUSA pursued a militant rather than revolutionary road. It was fortified by, rather than seeking to politicize, the strike wave – a product of pent-up wage claims suppressed by wartime controls – that swept through industry in the immediate postwar period. Some sections within the party, such as those associated with the *Daily Worker* in New York, were still ready to cooperate with left liberals and labor leaders. But this changed when Andrei Zhdanov, a leading member of the Soviet Politburo, addressed the inaugural meeting of the Cominform in Szklarska Poręba, Poland. He postulated the division of the world into two opposing camps: the progressive, peace-loving camp led by the Soviet Union, and the reactionary, imperialist and warmongering camp led by the United States. There was no middle ground or third way. This new position was adopted by all Western communist parties. In the United States, the CPUSA slotted the Democratic Party and the administration of Harry S. Truman into the second camp, along with treacherous "reformist" officials in the labor movement. All must be exposed – a prerequisite to winning over the masses to the communist side.

The context for this new line was complex. It included the belief, then widely held, in the imminence of another capitalist depression; the perception of a drift toward fascism, manifested by the increasing assaults from the state; and the conviction that the class struggle was sharpening and, consequently, communists must be utterly irreconcilable toward the class enemy. Under Foster, the party had been edging toward these perspectives; with Zhdanov's pronouncement, they were confirmed and entrenched. Just as the rhetoric and strategies of the Third Period were revived during the forty-four months of the Nazi–Soviet pact, so – in essence – they reappeared from late 1947. So, at precisely the time the Truman administration was veering to the right, the CPUSA was veering to the left. It adopted policies and pursued strategies that were rigid, aggressive and doctrinaire. They were also self-deluding and, ultimately, self-defeating.

I will not discuss here the international environment in 1948–49 in which the CPUSA operated. Suffice it to say that it included the following: the consolidation of Soviet control in Eastern Europe; the communist-inspired *coup d'état* in Czechoslovakia in February 1948; the likelihood of a communist electoral victory (until covert CIA intervention) in Italy in April; the commencement of the Berlin blockade in June; the detonation of a Soviet atomic bomb in August 1949; and the communist victory in China in October 1949. These overseas events exacerbated the fears and anxieties that nurtured a virulent strain of American anti-communism.

But domestic developments also provided abundant fuel. Allegations of espionage began to dominate perceptions of communism. While the *Amerasia* case, in which stolen classified government documents surfaced in a published article, made few national headlines in 1945, Elizabeth Bentley's explosive revelations in 1947 did. Dubbed the "Red Spy Queen," Bentley informed HUAC that she had been the link between Soviet intelligence services and two rings of communist party spies inside the government. She named names, including that of a senior Treasury Department official, Harry Dexter White. Another former Soviet spy, Whittaker Chambers, alleged in 1948 that a Harvard-educated, highly credentialed State Department official who had accompanied Truman to Potsdam and helped found the United Nations, Alger Hiss, was both a communist and a Soviet agent. This sensational case wound its way before HUAC testimony, a grand jury indictment and a federal court conviction until Hiss was sentenced to imprisonment in January 1950. In 1949, a Justice Department employee and communist sympathizer, Judith Coplon, was arrested for passing files on FBI operations to the Soviets. All this occurred before the "trial of the century" of Ethel and Julius Rosenberg in 1951.

The "Red Scare" and Anti-Communist Repression

The Truman administration responded to these international and domestic developments in the late 1940s with a series of draconian measures that, in effect, launched the "second red scare." The dominant historiographical consensus is that, in order to ensure popular acceptance of his interventionist and combative Truman Doctrine (which pledged military and economic aid to Greece and Turkey in March 1947), the president accepted senator Arthur Vandenberg's advice to "scare the hell out of the American people."[14] Under Executive Order 9835, Truman initiated a vast loyalty–security program that

14 Robert A. Divine, *Foreign Policy and US Presidential Elections, 1940–1948* (New York: New Viewpoints, 1974), 170.

established "Loyalty Boards" that investigated 3 million government employees in order to unmask communist sympathizers. Mostly, they unmasked
nonconformists, homosexuals, dissenters and defenders of civil liberties.
Under suspicion, for example, were those who wrote letters to the Red
Cross opposing segregation of blood donations or women who dressed
unconventionally or employees whose homes contained paintings by communist artists: all litmus tests of the fellow traveler. Fewer than 3,000 employees were dismissed on security grounds, but tens of thousands of other
employees investigated experienced some form of workplace discrimination
and personal anxiety, even if subsequently cleared. The loyalty–security
program institutionalized anti-communism – it was now official government
ideology – and legitimized the alleged link between communism and
disloyalty.

More direct damage was inflicted on the CPUSA through the Smith
Act. First invoked, as we have seen, against Trotskyists in 1941, it made it
illegal to advocate the overthrow of the United States government.
The prosecution did not need to prove any overt acts of revolutionary
activity: only their advocacy. In July 1948 twelve leaders of the CPUSA's
highest body, the National Board, were indicted and arrested (Foster, the
party's chairman, was not tried due to ill health). The trial lasted nine
months, from January to October 1949. Instead of arguing that the Smith
Act was a violation of the First Amendment's protection of free speech
(acknowledged by the Supreme Court in 1957), the party's lawyers tried,
unsuccessfully, to defend communist doctrine, especially its support for
a nonviolent, constitutional path to socialism. The prosecution, assisted by
thirteen ex-communists and FBI undercover informants, easily convinced
the jury otherwise. The proceedings were turbulent and frequently combative, both inside and outside the Foley Square courtroom in New York.
Communist-organized protest demonstrations were met with formidable
cordons of police, day after day, month after month. An exasperated (and
exhausted) Judge Harold Medina sentenced not only the eleven CPUSA
leaders to five years' imprisonment but also their defense attorneys to two
years' imprisonment for contempt.

Worse was in store. After the Supreme Court upheld the convictions in the
Dennis decision of 1951, scores of "second-string" and "third-string" leaders
were prosecuted under the Smith Act over the next three years. These
prosecutions undoubtedly damaged the party. They diverted energies and
financial resources to time-consuming self-defense and, with the jailing of its
leaders, they decapitated the party. Why was there such silence from liberals

and the broader labor movement in the face of this flagrant trampling on the constitutional right to free speech? One reason was the CPUSA's squandering of political capital. Just as popular front gains were surrendered during the Nazi–Soviet Pact, so the goodwill generated by Browder's "Americanization" was dissipated by Foster's intransigence. In particular, the CPUSA's third party venture (its role in forming the Progressive Party and in openly supporting the ill-fated presidential bid of Henry Wallace under the Progressive Party banner) alienated its left supporters in the Democratic Party and its allies in the CIO, both intent on defeating the Republicans in 1948. Anti-communists in the CIO mobilized, ousting communists from affiliated unions and sometimes expelling the entire union. The purge meant the loss of communist influence in the CIO – which had given the Progressive Party organizational muscle and institutional backing – and the loss of CIO support for Wallace's campaign. Both losses were crippling. Neither, however, prompted the CPUSA to reevaluate its strategy.

In a fateful decision, the CPUSA leadership instructed its cadres to go underground in 1951. The context was twofold: the common belief that the United States was about to turn fascist, and the mass imprisonment of party leaders. To preserve an organizational structure capable of withstanding intensified state repression, and with prominent leaders being rounded up, the decision was taken to create a shadow leadership responsible for guiding the party. After reconstituting the party post-Browder, the Foster leadership, in effect, now dissolved it. In the realm of public opinion, it was a disastrous tactic. The clandestine leadership appeared to confirm what J. Edgar Hoover, his FBI and conservative crusaders had long alleged – that the communist party was a furtive, conspiratorial organization. It was not for another five years, from late 1955, that the party disbanded the underground network and ordered those underground, including the handful of fugitive leaders who had jumped bail, to surface from their hiding places.

And what of the "ordinary" communist during this "scoundrel time," as the playwright Lillian Hellman memorably called these years? The numerous memoirs of former communists testify to the range of emotions generated by harassment, persecution or imprisonment: a sense of isolation and disconnection (from families as well as neighborhoods) and a testing of resilience and commitment, as well as self-doubt, sustained fear and psychological depression. The impact of high-level FBI surveillance on the young daughter of low-level rank-and-file communist unionists was recalled in one memoir. The narrative is prosaic but the sense of anxiety evoked is palpable:

The FBI began to appear at our door every afternoon when I got home from school. This was in 1952 when I was fourteen. I'll never forget seeing them as they drove up in their black Ford Sedan ... And there was the car again as I left school in the afternoon following me home ... I felt frightened. It was scary dealing with them every day. I wished I could disappear ... I knew we were doing nothing wrong. They were the bad guys. Why did I feel like I was the one being punished?[15]

When one of her parent's friends was arrested under the "second string" Smith Act indictments in 1952, "I felt helpless and frightened. What if this was like the Rosenbergs? What if they arrested my mother and Irma too and wanted to execute them just because they were fighting for a better world?" And, when the Rosenbergs *were* executed, "It was the most unthinkable, horrifying moment ... there is no way to even come close to conveying our feelings of shock, sadness and great fear that rippled through everyone I knew."[16]

This profound psychological strain was hidden from public view. Fear was experienced privately and silently. Communists were political pariahs in a hostile world. FBI penetration of their ranks, and the transformation of trusted comrades into government witnesses, created mistrust and suspicion. Friendships were poisoned, marriages broken and, with widespread black-listing, careers abandoned or stymied. If subpoenaed, rank-and-file communists grappled with difficult political, even existential, choices: between acquiescence, informing and naming names; or defying inquisitorial committees, taking the First or Fifth Amendment leading to the blacklist, or risking a contempt citation leading to a federal penitentiary.

To gauge the human dimensions of the impact of McCarthyism on American communism, it is instructive to focus on the individual. Since 1931, Dr. Edward K. Barsky had been a highly respected New York surgeon. He joined the CPUSA during its popular front heyday, in 1935. Two years later he sailed to Spain along with sixteen other doctors to tend the wounded in the civil war. In 1942 he helped establish the Joint Anti-Fascist Refugee Committee (JAFRC), in response to the plight of the half-million Spanish

---

15 Maxine Louise Michel De Felice, *May the Spirit Be Unbroken: Search for the Mother Root* (Bloomington, IN: AuthorHouse, 2012), 199–200.
16 Ibid., 201, 203. Forty-six such "red diaper" recollections, many from Jewish and immigrant backgrounds, can be found in Judy Kaplan and Linn Shapiro (eds.), *Red Diapers: Growing Up in the Communist Left* (Urbana: University of Illinois Press, 1998). See also Kim Chernin, *In My Mother's House: A Daughter's Story* (New Haven: Ticknor & Fields, 1983); Carl Bernstein, *Loyalties: A Son's Memoir* (New York: Simon & Schuster, 1989); Griffin Fariello, *Red Scare: Memories of the American Inquisition: An Oral History* (New York: Norton, 1995), 47–73.

refugees who had supported the Republican side. The Roosevelt administration's War Relief Control Board licensed the JAFRC to provide aid and exempted it from taxation. But the Cold War began very early for the JAFRC. In 1945 HUAC designated it a "communist front." In December it pounced, and its chairman, Dr. Barsky, was subpoenaed. For refusing to hand over the financial records of the JAFRC to a committee whose legitimacy he repudiated, he was cited for contempt, sentenced to six months' jail and fined US$ 1,000. After a series of lengthy and unsuccessful legal appeals, Barsky entered a federal penitentiary in June 1950.

If Barsky thought deprivation of freedom would end when he was released from jail, he was wrong. Another round of persecution commenced. This time it concerned not his humanitarian activities for the JAFRC, but his right to practice medicine. And it did not end until 1955, a decade after it commenced. When in jail, his medical license, first issued in 1919, was revoked. Restoring it, it seemed, would be a mere formality, but this was 1951 and anti-communism was deeply gouging the political landscape. His various appeals were all rejected. In a blistering dissenting opinion of the Supreme Court in April 1954, Justice William O. Douglas wrote: "nothing in a man's political beliefs disables him from setting bones or removing appendices ... When a doctor cannot save lives in America because he is opposed to Franco in Spain, it is time to call a halt and look critically at the neurosis that has possessed us."[17]

Meanwhile, repression of the CPUSA intensified. The draconian and sweeping McCarran (Internal Security) Act was passed by Congress, over Truman's veto, in September 1950. It established the Subversive Activities Control Board, which was empowered to investigate persons suspected of "subversion" who might be arrested, deprived of citizenship or deported. The act required all communist front organizations (identified by the attorney general's List of Subversive Organizations) to register with the Justice Department and provide information about their membership and activities. Failure to comply was punishable. The act also provided for the apprehension and detention of communists in the event of an "internal security emergency," and internment camps for Japanese-Americans in wartime were converted for political prisoners in peacetime. The McCarran–Walter (Immigration and Nationality) Act of 1952 restructured immigration law to prevent infiltration from communists; again, Truman's attempt to veto it failed. From the CPUSA's perspective it did not seem overly apocalyptic to

---

17 *Barsky* v. *Board of Regents*, 347 U.S. 442 (1954), 69–Dissent (A), 4.

predict imminent fascism. All this threw American communism into a state of near-panic. It was during this period that large numbers of American communists relocated, without the need for a passport, to Cuernavaca, a resort town sixty-five miles south of Mexico City. When the Communist Control Act was passed in 1954, most feared returning home.

This act charged that the party's role "as the agency of a hostile foreign power" rendered its continued existence to be "a clear and continuing danger to the security of the United States." It went further than the Internal Security Act since it criminalized membership of the CPUSA, stipulated that all party members would be imprisoned for five years or fined US$ 10,000 or both, and deprived the party of "the rights, privileges, and immunities attendant upon a legal body." In effect, it outlawed the communist party. Paradoxically, the anti-communist assault was most intense when the communist threat was weakest. CPUSA membership had plummeted; its industrial base in the CIO had eroded; front organizations were investigated and circumscribed; its fellow-traveling supporters were fearful and intimidated; and its leadership was underground or imprisoned. It confronted the combined force of different arms of the state: the Federal Bureau of Investigation, the House and Senate Investigatory Committees, the Internal Revenue Service, the Immigration and Naturalization Service, the Treasury Department, the Subversive Activities Control Board, the US Justice Department, the US State Department, Congressional legislators and presidential executive orders. The bureaucracy of McCarthyism was formidable. These government agencies were not necessarily working in unison, nor were their different roles and activities coordinated. But they complemented one another through a consensual framework: the pursuit of a shared goal to eliminate all activity and influence deemed "un-American." They were also complemented by an array of private, quasi-vigilante organizations that exposed and anathematized communists in all walks of life with a relentless zeal. Against all this, the CPUSA was no match.

By 1954, Stalin was dead, the Korean War was over and McCarthy's star was about to fall. Neither global war nor fascism had materialized. For the next two years, until the lightning bolts of 1956, the CPUSA, already badly crippled, was subjected to further assault. In this context of enfeeblement and vulnerability, the party softened its line in order to "reach the masses." In three areas it was Browderism without Browder. First, it abandoned its third party gamble with the Progressive Party (which promptly collapsed) and revived its "united front" electoral tactic of supporting the liberal wing of the Democratic Party. Second, it switched its policy on trade unions. It was now more conciliatory and ready to work alongside "moderate" unions to achieve a united labor movement. Third, on matters of race, its policy shifted from the right to self-determination in the Black Belt to working within mass organizations such as the National Association for the Advancement of Colored People. Such softening was in vain: Political and industrial organizations refused to embrace their former detractors, and the black mainstream remained resistant to red infiltration. In January 1956, the party's general secretary, Eugene Dennis, acknowledged fundamental mistakes and called for a different approach from the "left-sectarianism" of the past.[18] At the same time, red-hunting lost its momentum, and anti-communist crusaders lost their *raison d'être*. But neither self-criticism nor McCarthyism's demise were bulwarks against the cataclysm of 1956.

The Earthquake of 1956

Close to midnight on 24 February 1956, the First Secretary of the Communist Party of the Soviet Union (CPSU), Nikita Khrushchev, began a four-hour report to a closed session of delegates at the Twentieth Party Congress. His focus was on Stalin, and the speech was eviscerating. Khrushchev exposed the mechanism of terror and the system of arbitrary rule that had dominated the country for thirty years. He used dozens of documents and a wealth of detail to document the criminality and brutality of Stalin's rule. Khrushchev punctured the mystical aura that surrounded Stalin. He revealed that, instead of the wise and beneficent object of their adulation, Stalin was a bloodthirsty criminal responsible for systematic physical and psychological terror. Within the Soviet Union, only a brief summary of the speech was published, but even the abbreviated version was a shock, "like the explosion of a neutron bomb."[19] Within East European "satellite" countries, the time seemed ripe to challenge the legitimacy of Soviet rule and Stalinist structures. In both Poland and Hungary, defiance was expressed openly although resolved differently: the first through compromise; the second through brutal repression. Within communist parties throughout the world the impact was profound and its effects convulsive. The United States was no exception.

18 See Eugene Dennis, *The Communists Take a New Look* (New York: New Century, 1956).
19 Zhores A. Medvedev and Roy A. Medvedev, *The Unknown Stalin* (London: I. B. Tauris, 2006), 98.

Vague rumors about a "special report" that referred to "errors" committed under Stalin and a "cult of personality" had been circulating within the CPUSA but were believed to be baseless. Then, on the evening of 30 April, at the Jefferson School of Social Science where the National Committee was meeting, rumor became reality. The party's political secretary, Leon Wofsy, began to read from a document obtained from a British comrade. Notes were forbidden and confidentiality was sought. For the next three hours, dumb-struck delegates sat in a deathly, stunned silence as a résumé of Khrushchev's report on the Stalin era was read aloud. To the chairman of the meeting, the veteran organizer and proletarian hero, Steve Nelson, the words of the speech were "like bullets"; furthermore, he said, "I felt betrayed. I said simply, 'This was not why I joined the Party.' The meeting ended in shock."[20] Within half an hour Dorothy Healey was "convulsed with tears" and could not stop crying.[21] George Charney was "too shocked, too unstrung," to say anything. The mood was "eerie," he recalled. "Thus it was on that night each of us went home to die."[22] Indeed, on that night, at home in West Harlem, Peggy Dennis did experience a kind of spiritual death: "I lay in the half darkness, and I wept . . . For Gene's years in prison . . . For the years of silence in which we had buried doubts and questions. For a thirty-year life's commitment that lay shattered. I lay sobbing low, hiccoughing whispers."[23] These traumatic private reactions were a foretaste of what would soon happen generally within the party: "With the Khrushchev report, all the accumulated frustra-tions, discontents, doubts, grievances in and around the Communist party erupted with an elemental force."[24] The eruptions continued and the divi-sions widened, with the Soviet suppression of the Hungarian Uprising in November 1956.

One who was at this landmark April meeting was John Gates, the recently appointed editor of the *Daily Worker*. In 1955 he had emerged from jail after a five-year sentence imposed under the Smith Act and was now jostling to displace Foster as leader. As a "reformist" opposed to the rigidly orthodox Foster faction, Gates opened the pages of the *Daily Worker* to critical com-ment; it became a key vehicle for genuine debate within the CPUSA.

20 Steve Nelson, James R. Barrett and Rob Ruck, *Steve Nelson: American Radical* (Pittsburgh: University of Pittsburgh Press, 1981), 387.
21 Dorothy Healey and Maurice Isserman, *Dorothy Healey Remembers: A Life in the American Communist Party* (New York: Oxford University Press, 1990), 152, 154.
22 Charney, *A Long Journey*, 270.
23 Peggy Dennis, *The Autobiography of an American Communist: A Personal View of a Political Life, 1925–1975* (Westport, CT, and Berkeley: Lawrence Hill & Co., 1977), 225.
24 Richmond, *Long View from the Left*, 369.

The staff was strongly aligned with the Gates faction. In comparable communist parties overseas – for example, in Australia, Canada and Britain – there were debates and ideological fractures but not the bloodletting or the overflow of grief. One of the reasons (and there are several) was that the *Daily Worker* was the only communist paper in the world that printed Khrushchev's "Secret Speech." In the face of opposition from much of the CPUSA leadership, it appeared on the same day, 5 June 1956, that it was published, famously, by the *New York Times*. It was accompanied by a long, teeth-gnashing editorial. Thereafter, in the words of Gates, "readers spoke out as never before, pouring out the anguish of many difficult years."[25] Institutional histories usually sidestep such moral anguish. Despair is difficult to document or retrieve. Thus, we know nothing of Samuel Sillen's near-emotional collapse. Sillen was the well-respected editor of the communist literary magazine, *Masses & Mainstream*; one day in late 1956 he walked out of his office and never returned. Nor do we know much more than a newspaper report about the plea in early 1957 of John Steuben, a communist union organizer, to live out his life "in agony and silence"; the reporter noted that his "spiritual pain" was "acute."[26]

Dénouement and Demise

By mid 1957, William Z. Foster was firmly in the saddle. He had beaten his centrist and "revisionist" factional opponents by default: Those who would have supported John Gates at the Sixteenth National Convention in February 1957 (and initially Gates had "the numbers") had simply walked away from the party. One who later left, but was there, at the February convention, was a party organizer, Junius Scales. He painted a vivid picture of the party's convulsions and of his own sense of "utter futility and pain":

> By this time, the division and hatred inside the Party was just so thick you could cut it with a knife . . . Foster was vicious as a snake, and he was much more contained than the others. I wish I hadn't gone to the convention. Our differences of opinion were so great, and we had such contempt for the people who wanted to stay in this ingrown infected bubble, that there was just no possibility of working with these people anymore.[27]

---

25 John Gates, *The Story of an American Communist* (New York: Nelson, 1958), 161.
26 *New York Times*, 19 Jan. 1957.
27 Mickey Friedman, *A Red Family: Junius, Gladys, and Barbara Scales* (Urbana: University of Illinois Press, 2009), 86–87.

Foster, now seventy-seven and in poor health, failed to see that his victory was pyrrhic. When challenged by Dorothy Healey about his indifference to the hemorrhaging of membership and the loss of valued comrades, he replied, "Let them go, who cares?"[28] These were people who had experienced the worst years of McCarthyism; many had experienced the abnormalities of life underground or in prison. They had once been animated by lofty ideals and burning desires to transform society. Now, they were dispirited, embittered or exhausted, their intimate bonds of camaraderie broken, their sense of loss palpable and painful, their lives emptied of meaning. The *Daily Worker* ceased publication, the exodus of members continued and Gates, a veteran of the Comintern and political commissar in the International Brigades in Spain, was denounced as "an enemy of the working class." Cleansed of reformers, the party shrank further.

The near-moribund remnant of the CPUSA remained loyal to the Soviet Union. The folksinger, Pete Seeger, was one. He had recently penned a song, "Big Joe Blues," that was more critical of Joe Stalin than it was of Joe McCarthy, but he never performed it publicly and remained outwardly unrepentant.[29] He did not subscribe to the "God that failed" narrative. Unsurprisingly, the party was not acknowledged nor its offices visited by the man who triggered the party's political death, Nikita Khrushchev, when he made a triumphant tour of the United States in September 1959. Just before his Secret Speech, a membership registration revealed 20,000 members. In April 1958 there were 3,000 members, its nadir – a membership loss of more than 85 percent in two years. So the CPUSA limped into the 1960s a skeletal husk of its former self. It resembled a sect, not a movement. It was also politically impotent and, with the rise of the "new left," increasingly irrelevant. Its aging membership and its unbending leader, Gus Hall, made it seem an anachronism. Its influence in the labor movement was negligible; the commanding heights it once occupied in CIO unions were a distant memory. After 1958 its survival was reliant on increasing sums of money from the Soviet Union.[30] Although some communists took a leading role in various anti-Vietnam war organizations, for the first time in its history, the CPUSA was not the dominant force on the left.

28 Healey and Isserman, *Dorothy Healey Remembers*, 164.
29 Ronald Radosh, "The Communist Party's Role in the Folk Revival: From Woody Guthrie to Bob Dylan," *American Communist History* 14, 1 (2015), 17, www.nysun.com /arts/seeger-speaks-and-sings-against-stalin/61666/.
30 Andrew Campbell, "Moscow's Gold: Soviet Financing of Global Subversion," *National Observer* 40 (1999), 19. The amount rose from US$ 75,000 in 1958 to US$ 1,516,808.90 in 1969, and totaled just under US$ 7 million in this eleven-year period.

And yet many rank-and-file communists continued their activism in specific day-to-day struggles, as they always had, independent of instructions from party headquarters. In 1960, for example, the maverick Californian communist, Jessica Mitford, and her lawyer husband, Robert Treuhaft, subverted homeowner-enforced residential segregation by fronting for African-American couples attempting to purchase homes in an all-white neighborhood in Oakland.[31] Even the apostates remained active. From 1959 to 1963, George Charney, a former fulltime cadre, formed a Marxist discussion group; an occasional participant was Earl Browder.[32] Aging veterans of the communist-organized Abraham Lincoln Brigade, which had fought in Spain in the 1930s, maintained their political activism until the 1990s. And, in face of claims that it was "a vanishing species,"[33] the CPUSA itself continues, today, to host a website, publish a paper, engage in various political campaigns and hold conventions for the faithful. But it barely resembles the party that has been the subject of this chapter. That party inspired hope, encouraged sacrifice and sought to transform society for the better. But – and here lies the tragedy of American communism – it was beholden to a foreign power and it imitated Stalinist doctrinal and organizational praxis. While that connection gave the party discipline and direction, it also invited some of the repression that crippled it, undermined the ground-level successes that nourished it and invalidated much of the idealism that underpinned it.

Bibliographical Essay

American communism has attracted a large and diverse range of scholars to write its history, from the "traditionalists," such as Theodore Draper in the 1950s; to the "revisionists" in the 1980s–1990s, exemplified by the Michael E. Brown collection; to the "post-traditionalists," especially John Haynes and Harvey Klehr, in the post-Cold War period. This is a sample, listed in reverse chronological order: Jacob Zumoff, *The Communist International and US Communism, 1919–1929* (Leiden: Brill, 2014); Harvey Klehr, *The Communist Experience in America: A Political and Social History* (New Brunswick, NJ:

---

31 Peter Y. Sussman (ed.), *Decca: The Letters of Jessica Mitford* (London: Weidenfeld & Nicholson, 2006), 238, n. 88.
32 Charney, *A Long Journey*, 313–18. When Browder died in 1973, the communist press carried no obituary.
33 Harvey Klehr and John Earl Haynes, *The American Communist Movement: Storming Heaven Itself* (New York: Twayne, 1992), 176.

Transaction Publishers, 2010); Michael E. Brown et al., *New Studies in the Politics and Culture of US Communism* (New York: Monthly Review Press, 1993); Harvey Klehr and John Earl Haynes, *The American Communist Movement: Storming Heaven Itself* (New York: Twayne, 1992); Fraser M. Ottanelli, *The Communist Party of the United States: From the Depression to World War II* (New Brunswick, NJ: Rutgers University Press, 1991); Maurice Isserman, *Which Side Were You On? The American Communist Party During the Second World War* (Middletown, CT: Wesleyan University Press, 1982); Joseph Starobin, *American Communism in Crisis, 1943–1957* (Cambridge, MA: Harvard University Press, 1972); Theodore Draper, *American Communism and Soviet Russia: The Formative Period* (New York: Viking, 1960); David A. Shannon, *The Decline of American Communism: A History of the Communist Party of the United States Since 1945* (New York: Harcourt, Brace & Company, 1959); Irving Howe and Louis Coser, *The American Communist Party: A Critical History (1919–1957)* (Boston: Beacon, 1957); and Theodore Draper, *The Roots of American Communism* (New York: Viking, 1957).

There are two sets of documentary histories: Alfred Fried (ed.), *Communism in America: A History in Documents* (New York: Columbia University Press, 1997), and Bernard K. Johnpoll (ed.), *A Documentary History of the Communist Party of the United States*, vols. I–VIII (Westport, CT: Greenwood, 1994). A useful resource is Michael Brown, *The Historiography of Communism* (Philadelphia: Temple University Press, 2008).

American communism was active in specific areas and with specific groups. See Kate Weigand, *Red Feminism: American Communism and the Making of Women's Liberation* (Baltimore: Johns Hopkins University Press, 2001); Robbie Lieberman, *The Strangest Dream: Communism, Anticommunism, and the US Peace Movement, 1945–1963* (Syracuse, NY: Syracuse University Press, 2000); Paul C. Mischler, *Raising Reds: The Young Pioneers, Radical Summer Camps, and Communist Political Culture in the United States* (New York: Columbia University Press, 1999); Robbie Lieberman, *"My Song Is My Weapon": People's Songs, American Communism and the Politics of Culture 1930–1950* (Urbana: University of Illinois Press, 1989); Gerald Horne, *Communist Front? The Civil Rights Congress, 1946–1956* (Rutherford, NJ: Fairleigh Dickinson University Press, 1988); Mark Naison, *Communists in Harlem During the Depression* (Urbana: University of Illinois Press, 1983); and Lowell K. Dyson, *Red Harvest: The Communist Party and American Farmers* (Lincoln: University of Nebraska Press, 1982).

665

Biographies of communist leaders include Gary Murrell, *"The Most Dangerous Communist in the United States": A Biography of Herbert Aptheker* (Amherst: University of Massachusetts Press, 2015); James R. Barrett, *William Z. Foster and the Tragedy of American Radicalism* (Urbana: University of Illinois Press, 1999); James G. Ryan, *Earl Browder: The Failure of an American Communist* (Tuscaloosa: University of Alabama Press, 1997); and Gerald Horne, *Black Liberation/Red Scare: Ben Davis and the Communist Party* (Newark: University of Delaware Press, 1994).

Illuminating insights into party life at the "ground level" can be found in literally dozens of memoirs of former communists. Among the more useful are Sally Belfrage, *Un-American Activities: A Memoir of the Fifties* (New York: HarperCollins, 1994); John J. Abt with Michael Myerson, *Advocate and Activist: Memoirs of an American Communist Lawyer* (Urbana: University of Illinois Press, 1993); Dorothy Healey and Maurice Isserman, *Dorothy Healey Remembers: A Life in the American Communist Party* (New York: Oxford University Press, 1990); Junius Irving Scales and Richard Nickson, *Cause at Heart: A Former Communist Remembers* (Athens: University of Georgia Press, 1987); Steve Nelson, James Barrett and Rob Ruck, *Steve Nelson: American Radical* (Pittsburgh: University of Pittsburgh Press, 1981); Peggy Dennis, *The Autobiography of an American Communist : A Personal View of a Political Life, 1925–1975* (Westport, CT, and Berkeley, CA: Lawrence Hill & Co. and Creative Arts Book Co., 1977); Jessica Mitford, *A Fine Old Conflict* (New York: Knopf, 1977); Al Richmond, *A Long View from the Left: Memoirs of an American Revolutionary* (Boston: Houghton Mifflin, 1973); and George Charney, *A Long Journey* (Chicago: Quadrangle Press, 1972).

Index